The SELF
in Growth,
Teaching,
and Learning

PRENTICE-HALL PSYCHOLOGY SERIES
Arthur T. Jersild, *Editor*

PRENTICE-HALL INTERNATIONAL, INC., *London*
PRENTICE-HALL OF AUSTRALIA, PTY., LTD., *Sydney*
PRENTICE-HALL OF CANADA, LTD., *Toronto*
PRENTICE-HALL OF INDIA (PRIVATE) LTD., *New Delhi*
PRENTICE-HALL OF JAPAN, INC., *Tokyo*

The SELF in Growth, Teaching, and Learning

Selected Readings

Edited by

DON E. HAMACHEK
Michigan State University

PRENTICE-HALL, INC. *Englewood Cliffs, N. J.*

Second printing.....November, 1965

Library of Congress Catalog Card No.: 65-14943

PRINTED IN THE UNITED STATES OF AMERICA
80312-C

Preface

"All the world's a stage," and psychologists are discovering that at least one way of arriving at a descriptive account of each person's world is through an analysis of the central character, the principal actor; namely, the self. It is with an eye toward a closer examination of this principal actor that this collection of readings is offered.

As a theoretical construct, the self has ebbed and flowed with the currents of philosophical and psychological pondering since the seventeenth century when Descartes first discussed the "cogito," or self, as a thinking substance. With Descartes pointing the way, the self was subjected to the vigorous philosophical examinations of such thinkers as Leibnitz, Locke, Hume, and Berkeley. As psychology evolved from philosophy as a separate entity, the self, as a related construct, moved along with it. At the turn of the twentieth century, the self occupied a prominent place in psychological writings. However, as the tides of behaviorism swept the shores of psychological thinking during the first forty years of the century, the self all but disappeared as a theoretical construct of any stature. It has been only recently that the self has emerged anew and has been revitalized in psychological thought. Indeed, it would not be incorrect to observe that as a psychological construct of legitimate standing, the self is enjoying a belated, but enthusiastic, curtain call.

Today one cannot pick up a textbook in psychology, educational psychology, psychiatry, mental hygiene, counseling, or child development which does not deal, at least in part, with the idea of the self and the implications of this construct for understanding and predicting human behavior.

This book represents an effort to bring together a collection of readings which focus specifically on the self as it is influenced by growth, teaching, learning, and perception. Also included are selections which reflect both the theoretical and philosophical undercurrents beneath its growth as a psychological frame of reference. The readings represent a wide variety of sources and emphases. Some are empirical studies; others are purely speculative discussions; and still others are interpretative analyses of trends and issues relevant to the theme of this volume.

It is hoped that this collection of readings can be a useful tool in courses concerned with the training of teachers, mental hygienists, counselors, social workers, and psychologists. Wherever the volume is used, the editor is hopeful that it will be conducive to raising questions and provoking discussions. Indeed, if the selections are more successful in raising questions than they are in giving easy answers, then this book will have accomplished its purpose.

In each article, acknowledgment is made to the authors and publishers of the selections used. The editor would like to underscore his appreciation for the privilege of reprinting these significant papers. If there is merit to any volume of this nature, it must ultimately be due to the scholarly and creative efforts of the authors who graciously consented to having their previously published and unpublished work reproduced.

Finally, the editor would like to extend a sincere "thank you" to Arthur T. Jersild for his generous advice and wise counsel throughout all stages of this book.

D. E. H.

Table of contents

Part III
perceptual processes and the self

Part IV
how the self is formed

Part VII
teaching and the self

Part VIII
learning and the self

The SELF in Growth, Teaching, and Learning

Part I

the self as a frame of reference

1. The self-image: a theory of the dynamics of behavior[1]

CAMILLA M. ANDERSON

Reprinted from *Mental Hygiene,* Vol. 36 (1952), 227-244, by permission of the National Association for Mental Health.

Prior to understanding and predicting behavior, we must first have a conceptual framework for interpreting behavior. The author presents a conceptual framework of the dynamics of behavior organized around the theme that each individual has both a physical self-image and a psychological self-image. Interesting speculations are raised about how each individual strives toward safety and survival as he endeavors to live in harmony with his self-image.

It is increasingly accepted that the final word has not been said in psychiatry in regard either to the dynamics of behavior or to the technique of achieving therapeutic results in any given case. In an effort to contribute somewhat to the thinking in psychiatric fields, I wish to present a concept of the dynamics of behavior that seems to me to be the simplest, the most comprehensive, as well as the most practical that has been evolved to date. It is one that experience has shown to be useful to the medical practitioner.

While no attempt has been made either to include or to exclude the ideas or theories characteristic of any psychiatric frame of reference, the formulation, as might be expected, contains words and ideas that are present

---

[1] Sponsored by the Veterans Administration and published with the approval of the chief medical director. The statements and conclusions published by the author are the results of her own study and do not necessarily reflect the opinion or policy of the Veterans Administration.

in various schools of thought, outstanding among which are those of Sullivan, Adler, Freud, and Schilder. It is reasonable to expect that any theory worthy of being taken seriously will have concepts that are valid and that will, therefore, be an integral part of any progressively more accurate or more precise theory.

No attempt will be made to clarify the source or background of the concepts or to give credit to anyone who has held the same ideas previously. However, it is freely acknowledged that there is really nothing new under the sun. The primary aim here is to present a useful tool for understanding and for treating individuals—and perhaps cultural groups—rather than to make acknowledgments or to pay tribute to any authority. As far as I have been able to determine, the concepts as set forth here have not previously been organized in this particular manner by psychiatry.

Everyone has an image or a concept of himself as a unique person or self, different from every other self. This concept pertains to one's self both as a physical person and as a psychological person—*i.e.,* each one has a physical self-image and a psychological self-image.

Neither of these images is complete and neither is more than roughly accurate. The development of highly reflecting surfaces of scientific tools for investigation and of language has made possible increasingly accurate physical self-images, though even these aids do not eliminate obfuscations arising from the attitudes and feelings of significant people. For example, it is not uncommon to find adults who regard themselves as ugly or unattractive or excessively fat or thin or weak because their parents imbued them with these beliefs in regard to themselves while they were young, and no amount of contrary evidence can disabuse them.

The development of techniques for the clarification of psychological self-images is still far from complete, but Freud would seem to stand in approximately the same relationship to the psyche as Vesalius does to the soma.

The self-concept or image is composed of many parts, and each part is conceived of as having both structure and function or as having both anatomy and physiology. Every organ or member that is conceived of as doing a specific job is included in the individual's physical self-image. Organs are also given different values, depending on the conceived functional value of each one. The heart, for example, is ordinarily more highly valued than is the hand.

It is likewise true that every character trait that carries with it the implication of a result to be obtained through its use is a part of the psychological self-image. Every portion of the psychological self-image thus also has both anatomy and physiology, structure and function. As in a physical area, so in the psychological, there is a hierarchy of traits, some having great value in the individual's conceptual thinking and others having less.

Whereas we have been thinking and talking for years in terms of the division of the self-structure into id, ego, superego, and ego ideal, these concepts are, in my opinion, far too broad and general, if not actually erroneous, for application to any specific individual, with any hope of understanding or treating him. We need to think with more precision than these terms imply.

The structure-function concept is, however, as essential in dealing with the psyche as with the soma, since this is the only concept that can lead to logical thinking and prediction. Just as the thinking in somatic medicine has become increasingly precise and refined, so the thinking in psychological medicine needs to move toward more precise definition and understanding of the detailed structure of the psyche, together with the function of each structure.

The characteristics of the psychic structures are as general and also as specific or individual as are those of the somatic structure. Everything that pertains or relates to "I," "me," "my" conceptual thinking is included here. These structures have to do exclusively with interpersonal relations and effects and are morally oriented—*i.e.,* they are accounted as good or bad. This moral orientation is due to the moral pressures under which the traits were structuralized, wherein "good" or "right" is what significant people demand and "bad" or "wrong" is what they reject. We might clarify further by saying that whatever made the significant people feel more comfortable is accounted right and whatever made them feel more uncomfortable is accounted wrong.

For every "bad" portion of the self-concept, there are other "good" portions which are emphasized and enhanced: "I may not be pretty, but at least I am honest." To the extent that a baby finds himself inadequate to cope with life or is unacceptable to the people on whom he depends—*e.g.,* is not pretty—he will feel the threat of danger or he must structuralize such traits—*e.g.,* honesty—within himself as will restore the balance toward safety and survival. We thus have character traits actually becoming defense mechanisms in the interest of physical survival.

We are dealing in each individual, therefore, not with the basic self, which is all too often overlooked entirely, but with the conceptual value of the self as determined by the attitudes of significant people toward the child (the parental price tag) and with his efforts to counteract this appraisal, the composite of which is the character structure or psyche with which we deal in psychiatry.

Because this whole process takes place before language and higher thought processes are well established, we have the roots of character structure in the unconscious or the unlabeled. Were children born with language facility and the conceptual thinking that goes along with labeling, the domain of the unconscious would be far smaller than it is. It thus becomes clear why psychotherapy must render the unconscious conscious.

Just as structure and function are a conceptual unit in the soma—*e.g.,* eyes-vision, ears-hearing—so will any structuralized trait in the psyche and the response it has characteristically engendered become a conceptual unit or assumption in the psychological image—*e.g.,* obedience-acceptance.

For every trait structuralized, there is an assumed function to be obtained through the use of it, and this function is interpersonal—that is, the function is supplied by another person. The fact of the assumed function of a trait is usually overlooked, but is of vast importance in understanding any person's behavior. Every character trait put into action is designed to bring about some specific response (functional result) from some person outside the self. This response may be in fact or in fantasy, as when one feels that one has some person's approval even though that person may be dead.

The function of any trait is not arbitrarily assumed, but is established only after experience has led to the conclusion that it is useful. A certain trait or behavior will have been found to bring a certain result from significant people. Let us say that "I am obedient" has been structuralized because this has brought maximum security and freedom from the threat of annihilation. Henceforth, the structural trait of obedience will have a certain functional value associated with it, depending on early experience, which might be something like this: (1) "People will accept me," (2) "People will not punish me," or (3) "People will give me a certain coveted reward." The specificity of the assumed function is coexistent with the individual's psychic structure.

Those traits which have not had a recognized interpersonal function are not included in the self-image, just as those physical structures which have not had a recognized function are not included in the individual's physical self-image. It is function that determines not only structuralization but the inclusion or exclusion of the trait in the psychological self-image.

Common traits in the psychic structure are such as, "I am honest," "I am dependable," "I am helpless," "I am acquiescent," "I figure things out for myself," "I keep out of the way," "I make no demands." The structures or traits are unique to the individual because they arise out of his own particular relationships.

The anticipated functional result of any trait may be found in the specific feelings of entitlement which are present in each individual. No two people have duplicate traits and entitlements. One may feel entitled to acceptance because he is meek, while another will feel so because he is aggressive. Common examples of these entitlements are entitlement to cooperation, to assistance, to freedom from criticism, to being left alone, to special consideration, or to endless varieties of special privilege or protection.

The feeling of entitlement is seldom recognized by the individual or causes any difficulty unless or until it fails to be gratified. This fact makes many of us believe that we are not neurotic! The bases of the entitlements are often very subtle. Everybody behaves with symbolic patterns, and everybody is supposed to understand the symbolism, is what we, in effect, say throughout our lives.

Whereas the over-all function of the components of the psychological self-image was the maintenance of life through obtaining "love" or the gratified dependency of an otherwise helpless individual, and, therefore, freedom from fear of annihilation (perhaps "anxiety" would be a better term here because the fear was nonlabeled and, therefore, unconscious), the individual parts come to have specific functions as varied as do those of the physical self. A comparable situation exists in the physical area in which all parts of one's physical self in combination are oriented toward contributing to the maintenance of life, yet the individual component parts have functions that in themselves are over and beyond this goal.

The reason the psychological traits were structuralized was to secure the life of the child during the period of absolute or relative helplessness, when he was dependent on the people of his environment to prevent his annihilation through neglect or rejection. The psychic structure may, therefore, be thought of as a particular combination of behavioral elaborations developed for the purpose of maintaining life—*i.e.,* for their survival value. Without these traits, the child would have been at the mercy of the hostile elements in his specific interpersonal environment and, therefore, unable to withstand the physical dangers of his situation by reason of his inadequacy. The reason humans have an elaborate character structure is the exceedingly long early period of helplessness as compared with that of all other animals.

The psychological self-image is thus formed early in life as a result of the succession of experiences of the child with significant people in his environment. It is built out of interpersonal experiences for survival. It is no wonder that people cling so desperately to the character traits (defense mechanisms) that they have structuralized.

No consideration of the development of character can afford to disregard the basic protoplasm out of which the child is made. There are those who are weak and those who are strong, those who are anatomically and physiologically sound and those who are not, those whose physiochemical make-up is such as to make them "reactors" or "nonreactors." The intellectual equipment is also vastly important, and both the physical and the intellectual factors are important not only in and of themselves, but in relation to the endowments and attitudes of the significant people. The character structure will be determined by the resultant of the interplay between the child, with his physical and intellectual capacities, and the total personalities, physical and psychological, of those people who are significant to the child.

By significant people is meant those persons who are important or who have significance to the child by reason of his sensing their ability to allay insecurity or to intensify it—to increase or to decrease his sense of helplessness, to promote or to diminish his sense of well-being.

The sex of the significant person or persons is important chiefly in so far as identification is affected. If the significant person's values are not in harmony with the cultural norm, there may be confusion later because of the discrepancy between the structuralized traits and the cultural demands. It is not the "strength" or "weakness" of the particular significant person that is so important, or even his sex, but the security-insecurity resultant that evolves. Whereas mother-son, father-daughter attachments may develop into the proverbial Oedipus complex, this is not a normal or an inevitable result, but is engendered out of the neurotic libidinal needs of the parent. This is in accordance with the earlier statement that the child develops those traits which satisfy the needs of his significant people.

Factors that will be reflected in the traits structuralized are the capacity or incapacity of the child to meet specifications, either innately or through the use of effort; the basic acceptance or rejection by the significant people; the self-images of the significant people; whether the significant people are capable of giving love or only of promising it. Neurotic (nonself-accepting) parents bring insatiable pressures to bear on their children, since they are dependent on their children to make up their own deficiencies. Structuralization of traits may take place out of such feelings as love or gratified dependency, out of fear, out of hope, out of a sense of futility, out of simple fear of being overlooked, or out of rebellion.

The most rigid (nonadaptable) structures are built out of the greatest insecurities. Those who have to become something in order to merit acceptance will have to build elaborate structures, and these tend to be more precarious. There is much potential energy stored within these traits; the greater the cost to build and to maintain, the more energy is stored and the greater the danger of breaking. The energy set free if they are disrupted in either structure or function may be compared with the energy set free with the disruption of the atom.

When love or acceptance at any price is sensed to be futile, the child can fall back upon his nuisance value to be sure of not being neglected, and he may incorporate such nuisance traits into his structure. It is commonly regarded as more threatening to be overlooked than to be punished.

If the demands and assumptions of the significant people are in harmony with those of the cultural norm, and within the capacity of the individual to achieve with relative ease, and if the rewards given by these significant people are satisfactory, the individual may be expected to have a relatively stable and contented life experience. We ordinarily speak of such people as normal, but the fact is that they are normal or without symptomatology only because they are suited or adjusted to their specific cultural assumptions. Change any of these, and the "normal" label will no longer apply.

Whatever traits are structuralized, it will be found not only that they are logical—given the particular circumstances—but that to have failed to structuralize these particular traits would have been to court disaster. To the extent that the significant people give satisfactory rewards (sense of security), the child will tend to structuralize acquiescence (identification). If the rewards are not satisfactory or the demands tax his limited capacity, he will tend to structuralize rebellion or acquiescence with resentment.

In the development of the self-image, the first year of life is the most important, each succeeding year becoming of lesser importance, until the image is essentially completed before adolescence. This is not due to the fact that the earliest period of life is the most plastic or the most impressionable, but rather to the fact that the helplessness and dependency of the child are maximum in the earliest period and, therefore, his necessity is so much greater. The greater the sense of helplessness, the more surely will structuralization take place in order to insure survival. Structuralization may take place in later years, but primarily out of a sense of helplessness. To the extent that a person feels inadequate, he can be taught.

Whereas people outside the family, such as contemporaries or teachers, may become the significant ones, their influence and their impact tend to be less because of the more advanced and, therefore, less helpless age at which they usually enter the picture. The process of structuralization is then less buried in the unconscious and is more amenable to scrutiny by the higher intellectual faculties and easier of modification. The less language and labeling enter the picture, the more difficult of access it is for appraisal or evaluation.

The assumptions and standards of the significant people tend to be accepted without critical judgment (Mother knows best!). If there is any discrepancy between these values and those of the culture in which they live, it will be the standards of the significant people the child will structuralize, provided he derives a sense of security from these significant people. Behavior that is contrary to these patterns will be accounted as morally reprehensible rather than practically unsuitable.

The basis of or the reason for the particular traits in the self-image is almost invariably not registered clearly, since language has been minimally developed. In addition, the significant people who inculcate the patterns have usually received their own standards in the same way in which they are passing them on to their children—*i.e.,* with moral judgment—and to that extent are incapable of transmitting them with anything but feeling. The details both of the structure and of the function of the component parts of the image are the individual's fixed convictions and are removed from the realm of the questionable or the debatable. They are the specific and unique beliefs in regard to one's self and other people that every person lives by. This is equivalent to each person having his own private religion.

Once the psychological self-image has been formed, behavior loses its free or experimental nature (in search of security) and becomes compulsive, because it has become in effect structuralized. Once having structuralized any specific trait (assumption), each individual proceeds through life behaving according to his structure and expecting the succession of people in his subsequent environment to treat him in the same manner as the original significant people treated or regarded him. This automatic maneuvering of people into reactions and responses toward him that are familiar is the essence of the transference phenomenon of Freud or the parataxic phenomenon of Sullivan. Considering the variety of experiences and situations to which each individual is exposed, it is really remarkable that there are as few changes in the course of the years as there are. A large portion of therapy has to do with discovering and clarifying these maneuverings, since they arise out of assumptions that are not valid.

To alter one's patterns of behavior is to court the anxiety which common idiom has described in the phrase, "As uncomfortable as a fish out of water." One might expect that a person who has structuralized the assumption that he is incompetent would be eager to change. This is not according to fact, for it is the familiar rather than the hypothetically desirable that is the comfortable role. Likewise, everybody behaves symbolically at all times, and each one succeeds in making whatever he does into a virtue or something that is morally correct, and this effectively precludes change. We see that freedom of choice is largely a myth.

The fact of structuralization and the fact of the need to maintain structure (one's moral standards) intact, produces the consistency of behavior with which we are familiar in all people. The pattern of life of every individual is a living out of his self-image; it is his road map for living. People can be counted on to behave according to their own patterns. This consistency is not voluntary or deliberate, but compulsive, and generally is outside of awareness.

People compulsively (unawaredly) maneuver themselves into situations, behavior, and feelings that are habitual and natural, and thus avoid the anxiety that would otherwise be their lot. It is failure to do this that causes misery. It is well known by therapists that whatever anxiety an individual may be experiencing, it is less than he would experience if he behaved in any other manner. The only way to alter behavior—that is, the symbolic value of it—is to alter the assumptions that lie back of it, since assumptions determine behavior.

The pattern of behavior may be a simple living out of the basic image provided by the attitudes of the significant people (the price tag), and be associated with smug feelings of being actually better than the surface appearances (the need to be "discovered"), or it may be the persistent attempt to deny the validity of this basic image by some form of overcompensation through the defense mechanism of the self-image, but the need to deny it is sufficient evidence of the acceptance of its validity. Otherwise the individual would not be concerned with it. Every defense mechanism (sensed virtue) implies an assumed inadequacy or self-devaluation (nonself-acceptance). Associated with every neurotic trait is a felt need that is insatiable, for the individual never ceases to try to gratify this need, and the discovery of these insatiable needs is the discovery of the defense mechanisms.

The structure of the self-image (neurotic defense mechanisms) determines the day-by-day and the moment-by-moment behavior. Decisions, choices, activities, and reactions are all determined in such a fashion as will best retain the image intact (satisfy the needs), rather than as reality calls for. This need to maintain the image (the defense structure or moral standards) intact is the true neurosis. We might say that the compulsive need to keep one's skirts clean is the true neurosis.

If "I am compliant" has been structuralized, every detail of every interpersonal relation will be lived in such a way as to enable the individual to continue to regard himself in these terms, and the slightest variation from this pattern will provoke anxiety. If "I am competent" has been structuralized, the individual's life patterns will be such as to harmonize with this image, for he will "need" to keep his defenses intact.

Without significant people, or without their pressures and assumptions and attitudes to cause the self-image to be formed and have content (a hypothetical situation), the growing child and, later, the adult would have nothing to measure up to, to rebel against, or to stop him. He would have no compass and no landmarks to help him chart his course, and life would become chaotic. In the course of therapy, one of the real difficulties of patients is the sense of helplessness they feel in moving into a pattern of life that will be their own or that they choose for themselves, and that does not have as its basis the old compulsive defense mechanisms.

As long as a person can maintain his self-image intact and function according to anticipation, he will be free from anxiety. But whenever a person feels that there is a threat to the integrity of the whole or to any portion of his self-structure (physical or psychological), or whenever a part of his structure does not function in the anticipated manner, he will experience psychic pain, which is anxiety. Anxiety, thus, is the feeling produced whenever there is a sensed threat to survival, physical or psychological. When the sensed threat is recognized and labeled, we call it fear; when it is not labeled, we call it anxiety.

There is still another source of anxiety, one in which the structure is not broken nor is the function disturbed, but rather there is a sense of being overwhelmed or of being incapable of dealing with the danger with the resources at one's command. The primary feeling here is one of helplessness. This sense of helplessness is at first attached only to the physical resources, but as the psychological self becomes increasingly structuralized, it may be applied to the psyche exclusively.

In the physical area, we are familiar with anxiety produced through threat to the integrity of the structure, as witness the feelings generated by war, accident, mutilations, or diseases such as cancer. Also, anxiety is the usual result when any organ or part of the physical structure does not function in the accumstomed or anticipated manner, as in heart irregularities, paralyses, pains, impotence, or other physical symptoms. The physician who deals with organic medical problems deals with these anxieties every day and in the majority of his patients.

This concept of anxiety produced by threat to the integrity of the structure and disturbance in the anticipated function of any part of the structure is as valid for the psychological image as it is for the somatic. It is a concept of the origin of anxiety so simple and so reasonable that it is intelligible to anybody. It is likewise valid as one analyzes individual people, both those with a psychiatric label and those without. The important thing to bear in mind is the uniqueness of individual character structure, and the symbolic nature of each detail of behavior. Two people may be doing what appears to be exactly the same thing, yet the symbolic value of what they are doing may be entirely different in the two people. We cannot take it for granted that anything anyone does means any particular thing until we know the individual's own particular symbolic language.

Anxiety is minimal in obsessive-compulsive patients because they have been able to this point to maintain both their structure and the anticipated function intact. They tend to be oriented toward a fixed, incorporated set of values and are, therefore, less dependent on the external world for gratification. The hysteroid character structures are oriented toward no such fixed values, but more toward immediate, external gratification of their dependency, and are thus more subject to disturbances and to transient anxieties. The development of these particular types of character structure, with the evolution of symptomatology with decompensation of their usual defense mechanisms, will provide material for a subsequent paper.

Analytic psychotherapy itself will inevitably produce anxiety in all patients because the process of treatment must necessarily produce a sense of helplessness, destroy assumptions, and thus produce disruption of both structure and anticipated function in any individual who seriously undertakes treatment.

As frequently happens, structure has been built at vast cost to the individual. He may have done that which almost exceeded his capacity, either because the functional result was satisfactory or because it seemed as if it would be satisfactory if only he exerted himself a little more. Any discrepancy between the energy required to build and maintain the structure, and the product or functional result that it delivers, will be interpreted as psychic pain.

A child who has obtained deep satisfaction out of acting like a burden-bearing adult—being "mother's big girl"—may eventually find such rewards increasingly unsatisfactory, but being structuralized as a person who undertakes much, she will find herself in a dilemma: if she continues according to her structure, she gets anxiety from disturbed function, and if she ceases living out her pattern and takes it easy or is obviously self-seeking, she gets anxiety from broken structure.

This inability to move in either direction—toward living out one's image or departing from it—is the essence of conflict. With conflict we have a sense of helplessness, and helplessness is the mother of anxiety.

It is as important to every individual that he maintain his psychological self-image intact as it is that he maintain his physical self-image intact. Everyone is familiar with the concept that maintaining one's honor is more important than maintaining one's life or physical integrity. The problem as to which self should be sacrificed—the physical or the psychological—is ever present among G.I.'s. It is worthy of note that no one but the person himself can destroy the psychological self-structure, so in psychological medicine we deal not with psychological homicide, but with psychological suicide. No person's standards can be destroyed without his sanction.

In the beginning of life we have character structure developing in order to insure physical survival. Then, as the character traits become "set," these defense mechanisms in and of themselves take over dominance, so that maintenance of the psyche becomes the dissociated goal. The anxiety experienced when the psyche is endangered in any way is felt as comparable to the anxiety produced by threat of physical disintegration or non-survival, like the terror of a child on being lost or left alone.

Whenever the structure of the psychological self-image is broken or threatened, the anxiety felt is known as guilt. Since the structure is composed of the many traits demanded by the significant people, there is attached a value to each one which is that of "good" or "right." The nature of the trait is of little consequence, but only the acceptability of the trait to the significant people. It may be inadequacy, dependency, sexual infantilism, or some hostility that is structuralized (and these traits are, indeed, often structuralized), but it took place out of necessity (having these traits made the significant person feel more comfortable), and the trait is highly regarded morally. To break one's structure, therefore, implies breaking one's moral code, and the result will be a feeling of guilt.

To the extent that changes can be made in behavior with little or no difficulty or guilt, we are dealing either with superficial changes and no change in the symbolic value, or with traits that are not a part of the defense structure and are merely habits, with no moral implications attached to them. These have often been the traits that did not come under the moral judgment of the significant people during the growth process. It was not necessary to structuralize them in order to insure survival.

Whenever the anticipated function of the psychological self-image is disturbed, the anxiety feeling aroused thereby is felt as frustrated entitlement or outraged virtue. Since the use of any character trait implies some conceived virtue in action, it is clear that if it does not bring about the anticipated response from the other person or get the "correct" functional results, the disturbed feeling that is generated in the individual will be that he is the innocent victim of a malignant assault. Since no two people necessarily have the same assumptions, it is easy to see why there is so much outraged virtue in any interpersonal relation. Perhaps more occurs in marriage than in any other relation.

If one has structuralized "I do right by others" and the assumed function is "Others will do right by me," and if the actual functional result in a given circumstance is that the other person fails to give the anticipated response, and, instead, takes one for a sucker, the anxiety produced is felt as outraged virtue. To some extent such disturbed functioning is equated with a psychologic homicidal attack.

This whole area is commonly very difficult both to spot and to grasp because the very culture in which we live has structuralized the assumption that virtues merit rewards. Our culture is, in effect, in a childhood state wherein cause-and-effect relationships are scarcely grasped, but life is lived on the basis of moral judgments wherein "being a good boy" results in an extra piece of pie. The whole fabric of our culture is morally, rather than practically, oriented. Many people behave with the utmost practicality, but they have confused morality with practicality and so proceed on their way with unrealistic and unnecessary feelings of virtue. This whole cultural coloring with moral assumptions explains why few people can successfully practice psychotherapy, for to the extent that the moral judgment cannot be relinquished, one cannot be objective.

Whenever one becomes aware that such feelings as guilt or resentment or outraged virtue or helplessness are present, one may be led directly to important information about the self-image, and, therefore, to the defense mechanisms and the true neurosis that one harbors. The assumptions thereby uncovered are actually portions of the self-image. The entitlements will disclose both the structure and the implicit function of the image. These strong feelings are evidences of minute decompensations. The discovery of the "needs" will show how the individual attempts to maintain himself so as to be in no danger of decompensation.

Whenever anxiety has been aroused, it may be experienced as pure anxiety, varying in degree from mild discomfort to stark terror. But generally one of, or a combination of, three reactions occurs: (1) there may be reaction against or attack upon the anxiety-provoking situation or agent, with some degree of rage or resentment (hyperkinetic activity); (2) there may be withdrawal from the anxiety-provoking situation or paralysis of attack responses (hypokinetic activity); (3) there may be a conversion of the forces for attack into some type of physical symptom. In fact, physical symtomatology may represent merely a partial rather than a total response. Muscles and glands may be expressing the overall psychic response with hyperkinetic or hypokinetic activity. . . .

To conclude, the concept of the dynamics of behavior presented here, as it works practically, has several advantages over current theories: The concepts and the terminology are simple. It unites the psyche and the soma in a common language and conceptual thinking, so that it is teachable and meaningful to medical students, to physicians, to beginners in psychotherapy, as well as to thoughtful people in unrelated fields. It makes survival basic, rather than sex, and in this respect adheres to established concepts. It is applicable to all people—those regarded as normal as well as those who are labeled with a psychiatric diagnosis. Its applicability is not local or restricted to any one particular culture, but is general and timeless. It clarifies the common meeting ground of Psychiatry and Religion. It is practical as a map or chart in the conduct of psychotherapy, and seems to be a definite factor in cutting down the time required for successful therapeutic results.

I suspect also that the theory is applicable on a wider scale than the individual and may apply to groups within a culture and to international relations, an area in which current theories of behavior have been sorely lacking.

2. The psychological self, the ego, and personality

PETER A. BERTOCCI

Reprinted from *Psychological Review*, Vol. 52 (1945), 91-99, by permission of the author and the American Psychological Association.

The concepts "ego," "self," and "personality" are frequently used interchangeably in psychological literature, and it has been difficult to know whether each concept means the same thing or different things. Does, for example, ego-involvement mean the same thing as self-involvement? The author examines these concepts in relation to each other.

In a recent article in this Journal, Professor Gordon W. Allport,[1] called attention to the pervasive, unifying, and motivating function which the ego plays in the organization of human activity. He called attention also to the growing status accorded to the ego by contemporary psychologists. Readers of that exploratory paper will recall his recognition of, and concern with, the confusion among contemporary conceptions of the ego. In this paper we shall attempt to reduce the confusion and at the same time solve problems implicit in the discussion of the ego. Let us restate the problem.

---

[1] With the deepest pleasure I gratefully acknowledge the encouragement, acute criticism, and numerous suggestions made by Professor Gordon W. Allport in the development of this theme for which I alone must take the responsibility. The writings of Professor Edgar S. Brightman have exerted the strongest influence on the central concept here entertained.

I. The Ego-Problem and the Function of the Self

As the concept was presented by Allport, there seemed to be a perpetual squinting on the part of the ego. By our author it is used at one moment in the substantive sense as a subject producing changes in behavior. For example: "The patient's ego takes command." "It senses the threats, . . . meets the world head-on" (3, p. 473). ". . . one other property of the ego . . . is its customary preoccupation with the future" (3, p. 474). But while the ego in these instances is itself the agent producing effects, it is also the object (and objective) of an implied subject. The ego has its own possessions and is itself possessed. This sense may be called the objective sense. It is now the object of knowledge, of striving, on the part of a knower, striver, feeler, and purposer. It is the development by something and "in" something.

The ego, then, functions in both substantive and objective senses. The article leaves no doubt that the ego itself is a development (3, p. 473), that it is not always involved in behavior, that it changes. When it is involved, it is an integrating and purposive magnet, but it is itself not a continuous function. The question, therefore, arises inevitably: What develops it, involves it, participates in it, and explains whatever continuity it does have? This question, "What or who involves the ego?" may remind one of the futile infinite regress, but before declaring this verdict, let us see if an answer can be given which accounts for what we do know about the ego and personality.

What seems to be called for is a psychological agent whose activities endure throughout changes in egos, personalities, and, for that matter, all other experiences which are identified as "my" or "his" experiences. My ego and personality may change, but it is clear to me that they are my readjustments, and that I am never completely exhausted or absorbed in any one adjustment. What, then, is the referent for the *I* or *he, my* or *his* to whom egos, personalities, or experiences are attributed?

The hypothesis here suggested is that *I* refers to a complex, unitary activity of sensing, remembering, imagining, perceiving, wanting, feeling, and thinking. These *activities are the dynamic unity* referred to by the word *self* (6). This hypothesis presupposes that there is no acceptable reason for postulating an inactive or unchanging substantive self or soul beyond or underlying these activities in the manner of many scholastic and modern philosophers. The activities are distinguishable aspects, not distinct parts, of the total unitary activity of what I am calling the psychological self.[2]

From birth onward these functions of the self mature and change through learning as the self interacts with the social and physical environment. While much influenced by the kind of environment it has, this psychological self discriminates and selects, within hereditary limits and environmental opportunities, its living adjustments to other selves and things. As a vital part of this adjustment process, it develops a personality and an ego. The exact meaning of these terms will be discussed in a moment. What needs emphasis here is that the self's thinking, remembering, feeling, wanting, *etc.,* are not identical with the ego and personality (or any developed "subsystems"), for these change as the self evaluates its adjustments in a different way.

The activities which constitute this self, such as sensing, remembering, perceiving, imagining, thinking, feeling, and emoting, constitute the "acts" of man discussed in chapter after chapter of texts in general psychology. There may be debate as to the exact relation between these activities, as to whether these are all the irreducible aspects, or as to whether they are completely dependent on bodily activities. There have been fascinating arguments as to what man's essential wants are, and what the sources of his knowledge are, but there has been no denying of knowing and wanting (we telescope the other activities into these two). What we are suggesting is that these processes are phases of one ongoing process which is itself not an abstraction from them but which is they. They are, in Stern's term, a *unitas multiplex* (36) and constitute, in Bergson's sense, *durée réele!*

The psychological self, then, is a knower and a fighter for ends. And here we find the clue for the unification of the eight different conceptions of egos listed by Allport. As he says (3, p. 459), "The ego has been conceived, *viz.* (1) as knower, (2) as object of knowledge, (3) as primordial

---

[2] I am using the term psychological self, first, because this conception is here being advanced to clarify certain psychological problems, and, second, because the philosophical conceptions of the self have invariably considered it to be nonphysiological. My discussion here skirts the mind-body problem and defines the self in terms of certain psychological activities, leaving the problem of whether they are "mental" or "physiological," both, or neither, to further analysis.

Perhaps I should add, however, that for psychological and philosphical reasons I am more sympathetic with interactionistic views like that of James (21, p. 414), Calkins (13), Brightman (7, 8, 9), Pratt (30), and McDougall (28) which restrict the term "self" to the purely mental, rather than with the psychophysically neutral views like that of Stern (33), the isomorphic contentions of the Gestaltists, the "organismic neutralism" with attendant parallelism of J. B. Brown (12), or double-aspect views like H. Murray's (31) or Moore's (29, 30).

However, let our individual theoretical solutions of the mind-body problem differ as they may, the empirical data for the psychologist and philosopher seem to be interrelated knowing-wanting for which mind-body theories must account. These interrelated activities, whatever the final conclusion be as to their "mental" or "physiological" components (32), I am calling the psychological self.

selfishness, (4) as dominator, (5) as a passive organizer and rationalizer, (6) as a fighter for ends, (7) as one segregated behaviorial system among others, (8) as a subjective patterning of cultural values." But if we unify the functions of knower and fighter for ends as activities of the psychological self, then the other egos may be seen as possible modes of adjustment by this conative and cognitive self in interaction with the world. They become not egos but properties of the ego which, as we shall see, is the variable region of the personality which the self evaluates. It is a knowing and striving self (I, individual, organism, or person) which knows and preserves itself, be it through selfishness, domination, rationalization, as a particular behavioral system or as a pattern of cultural values. All of these egos presuppose some form of knowing and wanting in their development, alteration, and preservation.[3]

One word should be added perhaps about the self and ego as "object of knowledge" (2 above). Among the things which the self can know as existing is itself,[4] and in this sense the self is an object of knowledge. The self knows, in reflective self-consciousness especially, that it is knowing, feeling, as well as what it is knowing. If the self is an object of knowledge, it may be asked, how does it differ from the ego? Haven't we got the squinting substantive and objective ego back again, and if we have, why not leave the matter there instead of multiplying entities needlessly?

The answer is twofold. First, the self in knowing itself is itself the knower. The ego in the sense being discussed here is known but is never a knower. It is an object of the knowing-fighting self, but itself is not a knower or fighter. Such expressions as "My ego is hurt" or "My ego won't stand that" suggest that the ego is a knower and a fighter, but they really mean: "I (the self) don't like, and disagree with, the evaluation you are putting on my activities, and what is more I'll fight to prevent your doing that again." In other words, the self can know itself and its relation to the world, and the ego symbolizes for the self a particular evaluation of that self's predicament. The self knows its ego, as a phase in its adjustment, and fights to maintain it. The adolescent, who knows that his "place" in the gang's esteem depends in large part upon his ability to "swat" the ball, or to "strike 'em out," will carefully protect that arm and seek to develop

[3] As Paul Schilder has said (34): "The individual has to compare again and again, and must not only know that he perceives but must also be aware of his effort in the construction of perception." For the ambiguous word "individual" I would substitute psychological self, and agree that it brings experiences into an ego context.

[4] Professor Helge Lundholm (26) gives a description of the conditions under which the self expands and contracts. The self as he describes it is an object of knowledge. This expansion and contraction of the self's boundaries is, I should say, a function of the cognitive-conative activities of self which finds itself thus contracting and expanding.

that system of abilities on which his "ego" depends. If conditions change substantially, he may strive to change his ego to the extent desired, as, for example, when the problem becomes that of getting into college with most of "the crowd."

Thus, the second difference between the self and the ego becomes explicit. The ego is the self's evaluation of its activities in the life situation. The self knows and fights, and can know that it knows and fights, as the ego cannot. But the ego represents the evaluation of the self's activities, influenced of course by the evaluations placed on the self's activities by others. What has been said about the ego will be developed and made clearer after we discuss the relation between the psychological self and the personality, but an analysis of Wallen's experiment, cited by Allport, may here clarify further the need for and function of the self.

Wallen in his experiment (38), "Ego-Involvement and Selective Forgetting," discovered that subjects, in recalling ratings of their personality traits after a period of time, tend to alter them "in such a way as to make them more compatible with subjects' opinion of themselves." The explanation offered for the alteration of these ratings or "trace-systems" is "interaction between the ego-field and the trace-system of our material." In sum, "the similarity between a particular structure in the ego-field and the trace-system of the material (or ratings) must have partially accounted for the substitution of function" (38, pp. 37, 38, 39).

Now, the desirable traits, similar to the ego-system, certainly did not realize their own similarity or "ego-relatedness" and relate themselves to the ego-system. Nor can the ego-system to which they are assimilated relate them, or see the similarity, for the ego is the subjective standard to which they are related. What, then, noting the similarity, relates them? The hypothesis offered to explain such communication is the cognitive-conative psychological self which has certain evaluations of itself (ego), relates other ratings to them, and alters the ratings ego-ward to avoid conflict. Similar considerations would apply to other investigations of this sort (14, 15, 16, 22).

Should we, perhaps, substitute the term self-involvement for ego-involvement in such experiments? The answer is negative, for the purpose of such experiments is to discover what factors influence the self—in the instance cited remembering is influenced by the factor of ego-formations, *et cetera.* The self, as Brightman has said, is involved as the presupposition of every experiment (10), and there is no point in referring to self-involvement especially when the psychologist is trying to study the particular course self-activities take. As James said (21, p. 3) about the faculty of memory, so we can say about the self: it "does not exist absolutely but works under conditions and the quest of the conditions becomes the psychologist's most interesting task." Note he did not say the only task! Intellectual clarity and avoidance of confusion is also a scientific objective. When we overlook the unobtrusive but inescapable self, we tend not only to bring back "the squint," but also to create the artificial problem of how "communication" and "interaction" between aspects of experiences can take place. When we forget the self, we tend to reify its "systems" or aspects, and misplace concreteness by attributing activities to them which belong only to the self.

II. The Self and Its Personality

"Personality is the dynamic organization within the individual of those psychophysical systems that determine his unique adjustments to his environment" (2, p. 48). In this definition the personality is clearly a function of the undefined "individual." Let "the individual" mean the complex unity of cognitive-conative activities. This is our definition of the self. The definition would therefore read: "A self's personality is its dynamic organization of its own unique psychophysical wants and abilities which renders adjustments to its environment unique." The personality is indeed a self's mode of survival, unique because no two selves have the same basic inherited constitution. These adjustments or maladjustments are what they are, in large part, because the acting self is reacting to the world as it perceives, imagines, or conceives that world and as it compares or evaluates the power of its activities and wants in a given socio-geographical situation. The personality a self develops is probably the most important by-product of the self's encounters with the world, for the personality is the particular adjustment the self has learned to make to the conceived world.

We need not stress here the importance of self-consciousness in the development of personality. But, as Allport says, "the advent of self-consciousness is gradual" (2, p. 165). There is consciousness before there is self-consciousness. Whatever the exact nature of the experience whereby the infant becomes aware of himself as a being distinct from the natural and social environment, consciousness of self presupposes a knowing-wanting self to begin with which as yet was not aware of itself. Nor can there be "successive moments of consciousness with their imbrication of temporal reference and content" (2, p. 157), unless there is an enduring knowing-wanting self. For a succession of experiences to be known as a succession, consistent or inconsistent, similar or dissimilar, involves an embracing unity persistent through change. If the organization of personality, in particular, must be regarded as constantly evolving and changing, as motivational and "self-regulating" (2, p. 48), then, unless we are going to have separate and disparate globs of organization following each other, we must have a knowing-wanting self, an associative functioning, to whose destiny these organizations are related, for whom they exist, and by whom they are altered.

The personality, we have seen, represents the accessible organization of the self's functioning in a given world, which endures as long as that self and its environment allow it. But we must not even suggest that the personality is a mere mask which the self can put on or take off at will. For the self in "determining" one mode of adjustment, in "selecting" within limits, as it were, its battering ram and its defense, is restricting its activities to certain channels, and may indeed find itself "stuck" with its own evolved personality. Personality is anchored in a self, but a self's further actions are modified by or anchored to the personality developed.

This conception of a self-personality throws light on the nature of multiple personalities. Dr. Jekyll can switch to Mr. Hyde only because Dr. Jekyll represents one functional system of the knowing-wanting self which cannot at the moment control all of the self's activities, including the system represented by Mr. Hyde. But the self's activity is the mediating activity which may curb the development of Dr. Jekyll or Mr. Hyde, or relinquish itself completely to the one adjustment-system.

III. The Self, the Personality, and the Ego

In his article, Professor Allport suggested that the ego and the personality are not coextensive or identical. The ego "is only one portion, one region . . . of the personality." Again, "Many skills, habits, memories are components of personality but seldom, if ever, become ego-involved" (3, p. 473). The ego, furthermore, "varies greatly from time to time" and "its content keeps changing, for at certain moments the ego seems preoccupied with one activity and soon thereafter with a wholly different activity" (3, p. 474). (This last clause illustrates the ego's squint, for it is now reified into a knowing agent.)

It is clear from the above that the ego, like the personality, is acquired, and that it is not an entity separate from the personality, but a distinguishable functional unity within the system of personality. However, there seems to be no answer to the question: Why changes in the ego? Perhaps the functioning of the psychological self can clarify this situation also.

We have seen that the knowing-wanting self, in its interaction with the socio-geographical environment, is forced to extend its functioning in concrete ways (develop abilities, habits, sentiments, attitudes, traits, secondary personalities), which eventually become the self's more or less organized mode of adjustment, or personality. The personality does not have independent thinking-wanting functions, but represents the unique adjustment-system in which a given self has used and is using its inherent energies. The complexity and degree of unity within a given personality, or, in general, the kind of personality developed, indicates the degree of "success" a given self has had in meeting the demands of the socio-geographical environment with its own intrinsic potentialities. For example, a self may so develop its inherent needs and activities through the years that a genial, trustworthy, industrious, social, and theoretical personality results. However, careful analysis often reveals a growing religious interest also. In other words, the self's investments in life have taken a fairly definite form, but not a final form. At the moment, let us say, this person is an appealing public speaker, but he takes special pride in his capacity for theoretical analysis which experts have praised. If he were asked what he prized most in his personality from the point of view of the public speaking, whereby he earned a good living, he would stand by his geniality and golden voice, but if asked what he prized most in his achievements, he would immediately refer to his analytical ability which experts have admired. It is the analytical ability which constitutes the ego at one point, while the geniality and golden voice, other aspects of his personality, comprise his ego at others. Challenge either, and there will be a persistent attempt to show you how incorrect your evaluation is. In each instance he (the self) has identified his long struggle for achievement with the traits (parts of the personality) now questioned. His ego, the self's ego, is involved. Strike at the ego and you indeed strike at the self.

The ego, accordingly, is that portion of the personality with which the self has identified its greatest value or adjustment-segment at the time (24, pp. 73ff.). The rest of the personality the self may be aware of and evaluate in different ways at different times, depending on where the stress or theatening conflict happens to fall in the total life-situation. For the ego represents a roughly determinable portion of his mode of survival which he evaluates as "central" and essential to his welfare at the time. Generally speaking, then, the ego will be the core or cluster of values (perhaps actually embodied in traits) with which the self identifies its "security" or success at the time. When its ego is involved, the self's value-citadel is in question, its investment in life is at stake. That is why what is relevant to the ego produces tensions in the self, for the conflict with or threat to the ego is really conflict with or threat to the self's prized achievement (ego). To say, as Allport says, that there are "two forms of motivation, one ego-involved and one not" (3, p. 469), is to say that in some instances the greatest values conceived by the self are involved, and in other instances less critical needs, segmentally conceived, are involved. "Ego-involved tasks often demand changing goals and new responses" (3, p. 468). When this is true, it is because the self has put a premium on growth. Again, "many cultural frames having to do with language, etiquette, or dress, determine our perceptions, our memory, our conduct, but their influence is not felt as personally relevant!" (3, p. 464). The reason is not that the self does not value them at all, but because at the moment they can be taken for granted. But if the situation changes and the connection between them and the security of the self's acknowledged values is clarified, they change their psychological status and become "personally relevant."

It will be seen, then, that the ego, though it may be a fairly stable focus of activity and of further organization in any personality, is not a separable organization in personality. The ego could not be understood unless the personality pattern were understood, though an understanding of the personality pattern at a given time would not be complete without understanding the ego, or the critical-value-complex.

IV. The Self as Unifier of Subsystems

Lack of complete understanding, and not of respect, has made me hesitant to relate the psychological self with the concept of the ego as developed by Koffka and Lewin. But what I do comprehend leads me to suspect an underlying squint and lurking disunity in their ego-concept. Professor Koffka stresses the importance of the ego as a unifying, enduring system which maintains "its identity in the stream of varying conditions" and develops "in accordance with the disturbances to which it is exposed and the kind of Ego it is" (23, p. 332). This passage would describe the psychological self admirably if that were all there were to it. But the subjective-objective squint appears as soon as it becomes clear that the ego is itself one type of experience among others: "discomfort may be experienced without an Ego" (23, p. 327). At one moment we are told that the ego is segregated and in the next we read: "No Ego could exist, as a special system, unless it *segregated itself* [italics mine] from other systems" (23, p. 328). Can it be that something like the psychological self might fill in the gap which Koffka admits when he says that "we have, at the moment, no real knowledge of the forces which keep the Ego unified and segregated from the rest"? Koffka simply rested at this point with the assumption that the ego is "a particular field part in constant interaction with the rest of the field."

Another resemblance to the psychological self appears when Koffka finds that the ego is a complex of subsystems with a "permanent subsystem" which he calls "the Self." This "Self" is the core of enveloping subsystems interacting with each other and with it, comparable to different layers in surface-depth organization. But is this inner self simply the deepest and permanent layer? Are the other systems ultimately unified by its activities, or do they have their own? Are the tensions which originate in the self related to the tensions in the subsystems?

Lewin, as if to reply, tells us not only that "a dominant system 'uses' a subordinate system as its tool" (25, p. 101), but that a tension from the "inner-personal region" may spread throughout the personality. The exact interrelation is not clarified, and we are not told that these subsystems are nourished by the inner-personal (as I should contend). It may be that the topographical methodology gets in the way of clarity at this point. Yet, when the inner-personal system is itself said to be differentiated into "central and peripheral inner-personal systems," we begin to wonder what the differentiating agent is. To speak of "a central need" setting up "a peripheral 'quasi-need' as a tool for its fulfillment" (25, p. 105) is meaningless unless it is a linguistic short cut for something like: "The concrete cognitive-conative self, in order to fulfill one of its most intense or highly valued needs, is forced in a given situation to find a different or devious route for its satisfaction." Better, with Stern, to say *"Keine Gestalt, ohne Gestalter"* (2, p. 553), and to emphasize that the self, as Stern said of the Person, "is a living whole, individual, unique, striving toward goals, self-contained and yet open to the world around" it (36). We shall then more readily realize that the self, its personality, and ego are not like layers of an onion, but one interpenetrating psychological organization.

In closing, one other theoretical consequence emerges which we would here reemphasize (5, 27). Most recent discussion (2, 11, 14, 17, 18, 19, 20, 35) of the formation of personality has belabored the enormous part played by the cultural situation in which the individual finds himself. Now, it certainly is impossible to account for the self's development without preponderant attention, perhaps, to the cultural environment. If the self, for example, identifies its well-being with social norms and social objectives, like democracy, then in action this social norm becomes the self's highest ego-value, by which the self judges and controls the future course of its activities. But should these major considerations for the course of development not be more closely connected with the cogenerator and codirector of specific human changes in a personality, namely, the functioning self? After all, it is the activities of this self which create demands for the environment and society to challenge, fulfill, or frustrate (1, 5). The self challenges the culture in which it is born even as it responds to its moulding norms. Thus, the ego and the personality are never merely the "subjective side of culture." They are always, in varying degree, the means a self has taken in developing itself among the possibilities suggested to it by the surrounding world. The great abstraction or artifact, psychologically speaking, is the world "environment" or "society" in the singular. Every self senses, feels, needs, perceives, and thinks about the stimuli which impinge upon it; it relates them in various ways, but always with some uniqueness, to its own developing conception of itself. For the self stands as the unique active unity, ready to be influenced and sometimes forced by demands outside itself, but always eking out its own style and mode of adjustment. Indeed, "society" represents what selves have more or less agreed upon as valuable aims for self-development.

Summary

The concept of the psychological self, as an enduring, unique, complex unity of knowing-wanting activities, serves not only to unify diverse descriptions of the ego, but to clarify the function of the ego in personality organization. The adoption of this self, as the agent ever organizing its activities in relatively stable personality patterns and evaluating its adjustments in the light of environmental demands, helps us (1) to understand the close functional relationship between ego, personality, and self, and (2) to explain the possibility of continuity, succession, and interaction within the personality-ego systems.

The self does not, of course, explain the existence of any one system, or any specific development within personality; it has no specific experimental value. But if we experiment in order to improve our understanding and interpretation of human experience, then this interpretative concept may be found useful, even as it may have to be modified or expanded as empirical data pile up.

References

1. Alexander, F., *Our Age of Unreason* (Philadelphia: Lippincott, 1942), p. 371.
2. Allport, G. W., *Personality: A Psychological Interpretation* (New York: Holt, Rinehart & Winston, 1937), pp. xiv, 588.
3. ———, "The Ego in Contemporary Psychology," *Psychological Review*, Vol. 50 (1943), pp. 451-476.
4. ———, "The Productive Paradoxes of William James," *Psychological Review*, Vol. 50 (1943), pp. 95-120.

5. Bertocci, P. A., "A Critique of Professor Cantril's Theory of Motivation," *Psychological Review,* Vol. 49 (1942), pp. 365-385.
6. Brentano, F., *Psychologie Von Empirischen Standpunkt* (Leipzig: Felix Meiner, 1924). His view of the self analyzed in 9, by Brightman.
7. Brightman, E. S., *Introduction to Philosophy* (New York: Holt, Rinehart & Winston, 1925), Chapter VI.
8. ———, *A Philosophy of Ideals* (New York: Holt, Rinehart & Winston, 1928), Chapter I.
9. ———, "The Finite Self," in *Contemporary Idealism in America,* C. Barrett, ed. (New York: Macmillan, 1932), pp. 172-195.
10. ———, "The Presuppositions of Experiment," *The Personalist,* Vol. 20 (1938), pp. 136-143.
11. Brown, J. B., *Social Psychology* (New York: McGraw, 1934), Chapter XII.
12. ———, *Psychodynamics of Abnormal Behavior* (New York: McGraw, 1940), Chapter III.
13. Calkins, M. W., *Introduction to Psychology* (New York: Macmillan, 1905), Chapters I, XII.
14. Cantril, H., *The Psychology of Social Movements* (New York: Wiley, 1941).
15. Edwards, A. L., "Political Frames of Reference as a Factor Influencing Recognition," *Journal of Abnormal Social Psychology,* Vol. 36 (1941), pp. 34-50.
16. ———, "Rationalization in Recognition as a Result of a Political Frame of Reference," *Journal of Abnormal Social Psychology,* Vol. 36 (1941), pp. 224-235.
17. Freeman, E., *Social Psychology* (New York: Holt, Rinehart & Winston, 1936), pp. xii, 491.
18. Fromm, E., *Escape from Freedom* (New York: Holt, Rinehart & Winston, 1941), pp. ix, 305.
19. Horney, K., *The Neurotic Personality of Our Time* (New York: Norton, 1937), pp. xii, 299.
20. ———, *New Ways in Psychoanalysis* (New York: Norton, 1939), p. 313.
21. James, W., *The Principles of Psychology* (New York: Holt, Rinehart & Winston, 1918), pp. xii, 689.
22. Klein, G. S., and N. Schoenfeld, "The Influence of Ego-Involvement on Confidence," *Journal of Abnormal Social Psychology,* Vol. 36 (1941), pp. 249-258.
23. Koffka, K., *Principles of Gestalt Psychology* (New York, Harcourt, 1935), pp. xi, 720.
24. Kunkel, F., *In Search of Maturity* (New York: Scribner, 1943), pp. xii, 292.
25. Lewin, K., "The Conceptual Representation and the Measurement of Psychological Forces," *Contributions to Psychological Theory,* No. 4 (1938).
26. Lundholm, H., "Reflections Upon the Nature of the Psychological Self," *Psychological Review,* Vol. 47 (1940), pp. 110-126.
27. McCurdy, H. G., "Some Remarks on the Place of the Individual in Social Psychology," *Psychological Review,* Vol. 50 (1943), pp. 408-414.
28. McDougall, W., *Body and Mind: A History and a Defense of Animism* (London: Methuen, 1911), Chapter XXVI.

29. Moore, J. S., and H. Gurnee, *The Foundations of Psychology,* rev. ed. (Princeton: Princeton, 1933), pp. xix, 287.
30. ———, "The Problem of the Self," *Philosophical Review,* Vol. 42 (1933), pp. 487-499.
31. Murray, H. A., *Explorations in Personality* (New York: Oxford U. P., 1938), pp. 46ff.
32. Myers, C. S., *In the Realm of Mind* (Cambridge, Eng.: Cambridge, 1937), Chapters VIII, IX.
33. Pratt, J. B., *Personal Realism* (New York: Macmillan, 1937), Chapters XVI-XX.
34. Schilder, P., *Mind: Perception and Thought in Their Constructive Aspects* (New York: Columbia, 1942), pp. 389-390.
35. Sherif, M., *The Psychology of Social Norms* (New York: Harper, 1936), pp. xii, 209.
36. Stern, W., *General Psychology from a Personalistic Standpoint,* trans. H. W. Spoerl (New York: Macmillan, 1938), p. 70.
37. Tennant, F. R., *Philosophical Theology* (Cambridge, Eng.: Cambridge, 1928), Vol. I, Chapters I-VI.
38. Wallen, R., "Ego-Involvement as a Determinant of Selective Forgetting," *Journal of Abnormal Social Psychology,* Vol. 37 (1942), pp. 20-39.
39. Watson, G., "Morale During Unemployment," *Civilian Morale,* G. Watson, ed. (Boston: Houghton, 1942), Chapter XVI.

3. The dynamics of the conscious and the unconscious

BARTLETT H. STOODLEY

One can hardly consider the dynamics of behavior without at the same time examining relationships between the conscious, preconscious, and unconscious dimensions of the psyche. In contrast to the article by Anderson in this section, who assigns more credit to the conscious in determining behavior, the author of this chapter skillfully documents why Freud, in particular, thought that the unconscious was the dominant force in mental events. Note particularly the symbolic expressions of the unconscious. Stoodley indicates how potent the unconscious might be in influencing one's self-image.

The Unconscious as an Independent Region

Dream analysis introduced phenomena of such a varied type that Freud's theory, in the form we have examined it, was subject to great strain. We now will see new, ingenious threads in the fabric of Freud's thought. Yet behind the new we find the hard core of the old, zealously maintained. One root idea is that libido-quantum introduces energic impulses into the psychic life at some point. In Freud's mind, no matter how much complexity is introduced into mental events, this fundamental insight must not be lost. And connected with this insight is the twin conviction that organically derived sexual impulses influence the mind mainly through unconscious channels. These basic ideas focused Freud's attention on the Unconscious as the dominant factor in mental events. Our examination therefore properly starts with a close look at Freud's developing views of the Unconscious.

"Everything," said Freud, "points to the . . . conclusion . . . that we need not assume that any special symbolizing activity of the psyche is operative in dream-formation; that, on the contrary, the dream makes use of such symbolizations as are to be found ready-made in unconscious thinking, since these, by reason of their ease of representation, and for the most part by reason of their being exempt from censorship, satisfy more effectively the requirements of dream-formation" (1, p. 368). Symbolism, then, has an origin beyond the individual. ". . . it should be noted that symbolism does not appertain especially to dreams, but rather to the unconscious imagination, and particularly to that of the people, and it is to be found in a more developed condition in folklore, myths, legends, idiomatic phrases, proverbs, and the current witticisms of a people than in dreams" (1, p. 369). Freud indicated what some of those symbols were. "The Emperor and the Empress (king and queen) in most cases really represent the dreamer's parents; the dreamer himself or herself is the prince or princess. . . . All elongated objects, sticks, tree trunks, umbrellas (on account of the opening, which might be likened to an erection), all sharp and elongated weapons, knives, daggers, and pikes represent the male member. . . . Small boxes, chests, cupboards, and ovens correspond to the female organ; also cavities, ships, and all kinds of vessels. . . . A room in a dream generally represents a woman; the description of its various entrances and exits is scarcely calculated to make us doubt this interpretation. The interest as to whether the room is 'open' or 'locked' will be readily understood in this connection. . . . The dream of walking through a suite of rooms signifies a brothel or a harem. . . . Steep inclines, ladders, and stairs, and going up or down them, are symbolic representations of the sexual act. Smooth walls over which one climbs, facades of houses, across which one lets oneself—often with a sense of great anxiety—correspond to erect human bodies, and probably repeat in our dreams childish memories of climbing up parents or nurses. 'Smooth' walls are men; in anxiety dreams one often holds firmly to 'projections' on houses. Tables, whether bare or covered, and boards, are women, perhaps by virtue of contrast, since they have no protruding contours. . . . Of articles of dress, a woman's hat may very often be interpreted with certainty as the male genitals. In the dreams of men one often finds the necktie as a symbol for the penis. . . . All complicated machines and appliances are very probably the genitals. . ." (1, pp. 371-373).

These symbols are not learned. They may well characterize the dreams of a child of four, and therefore we may conclude that the ". . . dreamer has command of symbolism from the very first" (1, p. 381). This symbolism is at a lower level than the Preconscious and therefore is in the

Unconscious and is subject to the control of the "censor." The dreams of normal persons are simple and transparent, displaying the purest symbolism. In the case of neurotics, however, ". . . owing to the greater strictness of the censorship and the more extensive dream-distortion resulting therefrom" (1, p. 382), the dreams are obscured and more difficult to translate, or interpret.

Freud made a three-way association between symbols, sex, and the Unconscious. These were seen as the major characteristics of the mind. As a result of his dream analysis Freud concluded that the Unconscious had other characteristics. He said that an act of judgment in a dream was ". . . merely the repetition of an original act of judgment in the dream-thoughts" (1, p. 433). The dream-thoughts are latent and unconscious and originate below the censor. Freud assigned critical faculties to these dream-thoughts. "Everything in dreams which occurs as the apparent functioning of the critical faculty is to be regarded, not as the intellectual performance of the dream-work, but as belonging to the substance of the dream-thoughts, and it has found its way from there, as a completed structure, into the manifest dream-content. I may even go farther than this! I may even say that the judgments which are passed upon the dream as it is remembered after waking, and the feelings which are aroused by the reproduction of the dream, belong largely to the latent dream-content, and must be fitted into place in the interpretation of the dream" (1, p. 423). We see then that this region in which the unconscious, the sexual, and the symbolic are conjoined has functions with reference to judgments. The Unconscious is blossoming forth with a variety of potentialities not dreamed of in the system of libido-quantum and resistance.

But the Unconscious is an even richer system than we have yet disclosed. In it there are also native fantasies. Freud said that the dream process ". . . threads its way progressively from the unconscious scenes or fantasies to the preconscious" (1, p. 515). This region also is the source of affect, or emotion. "The mortification suffered thirty years as though it were a recent experience" (1, p. 518). Here is the indication of the connection between the Unconscious region and the sexual somatic base. This "affect" is the libido-quantum translated into the mental area, and it lingers in this area, electrifying the material that it touches. We can visualize this area now. It is at the bottom of the mental topology, under the censor, and at the border of the somatic terrain. A thin wall, perhaps, exists between the Unconscious and the somatic. Through this wall somatic sexual energy gets changed into mental energy. An osmosis takes place that locates libido-quantum in the Unconscious. In this same area is the dream-wish. "We have built up the theory of dreams," Freud said, "on the assumption that the actuating dream-wish invariably originates in the unconscious; which, as we ourselves admitted, cannot be universally demonstrated, even though it cannot be refuted" (1, p. 532).

What is this dream-wish? A "wish" is a concept derived from the behavior of the organism in relation to pleasure and pain. Freud explained it this way: "We . . . discussed the psychic results of experiences of gratification, and were able at this point to introduce a second assumption, namely, that the accumulation of excitation—by processes that do not concern us here—is felt as pain, and sets the apparatus in operation in order to bring about again a state of gratification, in which the diminution of excitation is perceived as pleasure. Such a current, in the apparatus, issuing from pain and striving for pleasure, we call a wish" (1, p. 533). A wish is the basic initiator of action, and the "pleasure principle" is fundamental. ". . . nothing but a wish is capable of setting the apparatus in motion and . . . the course of any excitation in the apparatus is regulated automatically by the perception of pleasure and pain" (1, p. 533).

This term "wish" indicates the somatic impulse after it has passed through the wall between the psychic and the somatic. It can been that a "wish" is very similar to an "instinct" as Freud used the term and also very similar to "libido-quantum." This search for more and more adequate representations of mental activity resulted in new concepts that trod upon the toes of old ones.

Another characteristic of the Unconscious is that the wish which exists in this region is capable of "cathexis." "The first occurrence of wishing," said Freud, "may well have taken the form of a hallucinatory cathexis of the memory of gratification" (1, p. 533). We can see more clearly now how the concept, "wish," includes something more in it than the concepts, "libido-quantum" or "instinct." We could say it has a cognitive aspect. It seeks things out that are related to its pleasure.

To summarize, the Unconscious area has the following characteristics: (a) material is in an unconscious state; (b) the source of power is sexual, somatic energy; (c) it contains "primal" symbolism and native fantasies; (d) there is a faculty for making judgments; (e) there is strong affect (libido-quantum) derived from sexual, somatic excitation; (f) the "wish" is the basic impulse to action, a current "issuing from pain and striving for pleasure"; (g) this wish is capable of "hallucinatory cathexis" (1, p. 223).

There is not much left of the simple somatic view of the Unconscious now. You cannot reduce judgments, cognitions, fantasies to somatic excitation. The Unconscious has independent faculties that are used by the libido-quantum. And, as we have seen, all is not well with the Meynert overlay. Perhaps we can say of this rich and confusing region that all that is not sexual is "primal" and all that is not primal is infantile, but all that counts is sexual.

This is not a very good way of putting theory together. But it is the way that Freud proposes to think until he can get his theory in better order. In the meantime he has accepted the operational philosophy of the sentiment—"full speed ahead and damn the torpedoes!"

The Resistance as a Conscious Region

This "region" we are now discussing is concerned with that vexatious opposition in individuals to purely sexual reactions. Freud found it necessary to examine this opposition more and more carefully since, like the Unconscious, it was more complex than seemed to be the case at first.

The Conscious area (including the Preconscious), or secondary ego in Meynert's view, has the function of censorship. The psychic force resulting in this censorship is conceived to be different from the psychic force which forms the wish expressed by the dream. The secondary ego also has the power of "secondary elaboration" of the dream, and a single wish-impulse, the wish to sleep. About secondary elaboration Freud states, "It is indisputable that the censoring agency, whose influence we have so far recognized only in the restrictions of and emissions in the dream-content, is likewise responsible for interpolations in and amplifications of this content. . . . Only in the most extreme cases does the psychic function in dream-formation which we are now considering rise to original creation. . . . I do not wish to deny to this . . . factor the faculty of creatively making new contributions to our dreams. But its influence is certainly exerted . . . mainly in the preference and selection of psychic material already formed in the dream-thoughts" (1, pp. 455-457). The dream-thoughts, as Freud has pointed out, originate below the censor in the Unconscious.

The secondary ego has other, if precarious, functions. It contains the day residues (memory traces of the day's experiences) which ". . . may be either wishes, or psychic impulses of any other kind, or simply recent impressions" (1, p. 508). We must assume, by this use of the word "wish," that Freud is referring to an ordinary feeling of preference, not to the Unconscious wish. These day residues offer to the Unconscious something of great importance to it, ". . . the points of attachment necessary for transference" (1, p. 508). The Unconscious may use these day residues to express the Unconscious wish if they can in any way be put to their use. While the day residues or the day thoughts may be pressed into service by the Unconscious they may also find the motive power to express a wish of their own. Freud admits that, "It might even prove possible to explain, on the basis of our train of thought, those extreme cases in which the dream, continuing the work of the day, brings to a happy issue an unsolved problem of waking life" (1, p. 508).

Freud came close to making the admission that the secondary ego may form its own dream. But he hastily retreated and tried to take a permanent position upon a razor's edge. In taking this position he first made a needed distinction between a wish and an "incitement." An "incitement" belonged in the secondary ego. It is a simple preference. When the secondary ego feels this preference it is in a state of "incitement." Freud said, "I will admit that there is a whole class of dreams in which the incitement originates mainly or even exclusively from the residues of the day . . ." but ". . . the motive-power needed by the dream had to be contributed by a wish . . ." (1, pp. 505-506). The day residues, then, may contain incitements, and these incitements may in fact find expression in dreams and appear therefore to have caused the dream. In fact, however, these incitements were picked up and employed by the Unconscious wish which really furnished the power to form the dream. However, there is evidence that the secondary ego may, upon occasion, express "incitements" in dreams that appear unrelated to any dependency on the unconscious wish. Thus, in dreams that are painful to the secondary ego, the ego sometimes ". . . reacts with violent resentment to the accomplished satisfaction of the repressed wish, and even goes so far as to make an end of the dream by means of anxiety. It is thus not difficult to recognize that dreams of pain and anxiety are, in accordance with our theory, just as much wish fulfillments as are the straightforward dreams of gratification" (1, p. 503). Punishment-dreams are even more important in this connection. ". . . it would be the essential characteristic of punishment-dreams that in them it is not the unconscious wish from the repressed material (from the system Ucs) that is responsible for dream-formation, but the punitive wish reacting against it, a wish pertaining to the ego, even though it is unconscious (*i.e.,* preconscious)" (1, p. 504).

Freud has stated that a dream ". . . must be furnished by a wish belonging to the unconscious" (1, p. 503). We know that the "unconscious" to which he referred is not the state of unconsciousness. He referred to the Unconscious area where "wishes" lurked along with fantasies and libido-quantum. The "wish" or "incitement" in punishment-dreams comes from the Preconscious area of the Conscious and is thus powered by a different force than the Unconscious wish. The fact that this wish is also in an unconscious state does not qualify or alter the important exception that Freud has made here. If "painful" dreams and "punishment"-dreams are to be reconciled with the rule requiring an Unconscious wish to form a dream, then a more expert method of reconciliation must be devised. (The dialectic we find here is a characteristic "stage" in Freud's encounters with theoretical problems.)

The power of the secondary ego in dream formation may extend even further. ". . . there are persons in whom the retention at night of the knowledge that they are sleeping and dreaming, becomes quite manifest, and who are thus apparently endowed with the conscious faculty of guiding their dream-life. Such a dreamer . . . is dissatisfied . . . he breaks off the dream . . . and begins it afresh, in order to continue it along different lines, just like the . . . author who . . . gives a happier ending to his play. Or on another occasion, when the dream places him in a sexually exciting situation, he thinks in his sleep: 'I don't want to continue this dream and exhaust myself by an emission; I would rather save it for a real situation.' The Marquis Hervey (Vaschide) declared that he had gained such power over his dreams that he could accelerate their course at will, and turn them in any direction he wished. It seems that in him the wish to sleep had accorded a place to another, a preconscious wish, the wish to observe his dreams and to derive pleasure from them. Sleep is just as compatible with such a wish-resolve as it is with some proviso as a condition of waking up (wet-nurse's sleep)" (1, pp. 513-514).

It appears that a dreamer can direct a dream. This is more than the "wish to observe" a dream or "derive pleasure" from it. Freud's comment assumed that the secondary ego had a ringside seat at the spectacle and enjoyed the performance. The evidence in the cited passage shows that the dreamer may continue a dream along different lines, accelerate it, turn it in any direction; in other words, assume an ascendant position over the wish in the Unconscious.

Freud encountered a similar problem earlier with relation to the concept "resistance." He avoided coming to grips with it at first but finally reduced it to the somatic by means of the ephemeral insight in the thirteen cases of hysteria. Like a compass needle he comes to rest only when aligned with his magnetic pole—somatic excitation. Other forces set him awhirl.

Clearly, if you assume the predominant power in the Unconscious you are confronted with a most difficult assignment in explaining the secondary ego's role in some dreams. Freud suggested a solution to this problem in *The Interpretation of Dreams*. It aligned him anew with his somatic "pole." The concept employed was "ideal masochism." And again we get back to that illusive term, "sexual constitution." "In the sexual constitution of many persons," Freud suggested, ". . . there is a masochistic component, which has arisen through the conversion of the aggressive, sadistic component into its opposite. Such people are called 'ideal' masochists if they seek pleasure not in the bodily pain which may be inflicted upon them, but in humiliation and psychic chastisement. It is obvious that such persons may have counter-wish-dreams and disagreeable dreams, yet these are for them nothing more than wish-fulfillments, which satisfy their masochistic inclinations" (1, p. 234). (Here is an idea that will develop into the "death-instinct.")

Freud touched on the question of masochism again and again. He wondered, ". . . how is it possible for a dream to place itself at the service of self-criticism in its conflict with parvenu pride, and to take as its content a rational warning instead of a prohibited wish-fulfillment?" (1, p. 446). By way of explanation he said, "We may conclude that the foundation of the dream consisted at first of an arrogant fantasy of ambition; but that in its stead only its suppression and abasement has reached the dream-content. One must remember that there are masochistic tendencies in mental life to which such an inversion might be attributed. I see no objection to regarding such dreams as punishment-dreams, as distinguished from wish-fulfilling dreams. I should not see in this any limitation of the theory of dreams, hitherto as presented, but merely a verbal concession to the point of view to which the convergence of contraries seems strange" (1, p. 446).

This "convergence of contraries" does seem strange to the writer. Time and again Freud tried to pass off this kind of convergence as nothing new. Yet he returned to a logical attack on it again and again. It is, of course, a threat to the very heart of his theory. "Ideal masochism" has a stop-gap function like "sub-cortical conduction" and pre-pubescent "seduction." Perhaps the most apposite prior view is in the "reversal of the relative efficacy." This latter phrase developed from a consideration of repression. The "convergence of contraries" emerges not so much to meet the problem of repression as to explain the power of the Conscious system. Obviously both problems are closely related.

The sails of theory were fluttering aimlessly. To catch the wind again Freud needed a new hypothesis and he came up with one.

The Ego and the Repressed—A New Hypothesis

As we have seen, Freud's views were threatened by the discovery that various ego "wishes" or "incitements" were fulfilled in dreams. Fears and punishments were the two main types. These fears and punishments had nothing to do with the stream of libido-quantum in the Unconscious which searched for gratification. They ran counter to that search, and were strong enough to prevail. If we were to take a position that accorded with our data, we would either consider our Conscious system as stronger and more creative than we had imagined, or we would somehow transfer these strong and creative elements into the Unconscious system. Freud suggested a solution. "The mechanism of dream-formation," he said, "becomes indeed in every way more transparent if in place of the antithesis 'conscious' and 'unconscious' we put the antithesis: 'ego' and 'repressed.' This however cannot be done without taking into account what happens in the psychoneuroses, and for this reason it has not been done in this book. Here I need only remark that the occurrence of punishment-dreams is not generally subject to the presence of painful day residues. They originate indeed most readily if the contrary is true, if the thoughts which are day residues are of a gratifying nature, but express illicit gratifications. Of these thoughts nothing then finds its way into the manifest dream except their contrary . . ." (1, pp. 503-504).

In the above manner Freud tried to accommodate the punishment-wish in the Unconscious even at the expense of getting the rest of the Unconscious into the Conscious system. Without "painful day residues" the Conscious system had no motive for acting: the distorting influence must come from a lower level.

Freud was sending up a trial balloon. He was facing the knotty problem of explaining punishment-dreams without equivocation and without robbing the Unconscious area of its dominant energy. Both the Preconscious and the Unconscious were seen as existing under repression and struggling against the Conscious system which was now called the "ego." The fear at the base of punishment-dreams was a part of the ego but was repressed. It was repressed into the Preconscious. At the same time it was proper to refer to it as an "ego-fear" or an "ego punishment-wish." But these wishes were also unconscious. So the ego-wish and the purely libidinous-wish had these common characteristics: they were both repressed and they were both in an unconscious state. But the ego-wish was in the Preconscious functional system, while the libidinous-wish was in the Unconscious.

Instead of two mental regions we now have three. The punishment-wish did not gain access into the Unconscious, only into the unconscious state. The Preconscious system belonged with the "ego" since its wishes were in the ego and came from the ego. Freud's compromise was an admission that the Conscious-Preconscious system can form dreams of its own. But the evidence in the psychoneuroses prevented him from making an explicit admission, and he had no explanation of the wish for punishment.

Freud's tentative categories, ego and repressed, do not at first examination appear to be very helpful. They are artfully devised for the moment but quickly become part of that array of irreconcilable generalizations that make Freud so hard to pin down. But these generalizations must be dovetailed sooner or later if we are to get a fuller understanding of mental events. It does not do to have one generalization (out of an entire stock) ready at hand for whatever happens.

It seems to me, however, that there is a strong and valid intuition in Freud's suggestion of the antithesis: ego and repressed. It pointed toward mutually exclusive categories that would sort out mental events into distinct classes. Freud's suggestion could lead us to this: It is not so important whether a mental event is conscious or unconscious. It may not be so important whether a wish is sexual or nonsexual. What may be of great importance is whether a mental event is repressed or not. It suggests that the major axis of analysis is repression and nonrepression and that other axes are subsidiary. Following Freud's cue we could call the totality of nonrepressed events the ego, and the totality of repressed events the repressed. If we take it that the major axis is this distinction, then Freud's assimilation of all wishes to repression was a definite advance in his thinking. It puts like with like. It concentrates attention on the dynamics of the relations between repressed material and the ego. Since repression is an act performed by the ego, this view would assume that the characteristics of repressed material would be determined by the preferences of the ego which performs the repression.

Freud did not totally commit himself to this line of thought, possibly because the corollaries attached to it did not point to a dominant Unconscious energy. Instead, he harnessed part of the repressed with the secondary ego and maintained the Unconscious as a separate area. The view of the Preconscious as partly repressed came in handy also in analyzing the Unconscious.

The Relations Between the Conscious and the Unconscious

Freud suggested the idea of the "censor" as an expression of the restraints that the Conscious imposed upon the Unconscious. (We have used Conscious to apply to the Conscious-Preconscious functional system. Now Freud is dividing them. When we divide the main system, we will refer to the Preconscious and the Conscious subsystem.) Therefore, he placed the censor in that part of the Conscious system that he termed the Preconscious. But we shall see that he had just as much difficulty trying to express the dynamics of the "resistance" in terms of his Conscious-Preconscious categories as he had in "reducing" the resistance to sexual excitation. The Preconscious was considered to ally itself with the objectives of the Conscious. It was on the side of the "resistance." But material in the

Preconscious was in the unconscious state. Freud referred to the Preconscious as the "criticizing system." Exciting processes in this system could reach consciousness—when not under repressions, as we shall see later—if they attained a definite degree of intensity and a certain ". . . apportionment of the function which we must call attention" (1, p. 491). Most things which are not "in our minds" but which can be remembered, in time, if we "think hard enough" are, in Freud's view, in the Preconscious. These things may "pop into our minds" without particular concern of our own. We assume then that they come to consciousness through some "intensity" of their own. Or we may search for something in the Preconscious, perhaps an old telephone number or the chemical formula that will help us in an examination, and finally it may come to us "like a flash." Here we have "apportioned" our attention, and it has finally ferreted the information out of the Preconscious. The Preconscious is innocuous. It is full of the furniture and trappings of our minds that are not being used at the time. When we want any of these things, we can get them although it may take us time and give us trouble. This, of course, is not at all like the situation in the Unconscious. We cannot get at things in the Unconscious. They have their own meanings and their own vitalities.

Freud put the censor in the Preconscious. He assumed that the Unconscious wish, proceeding toward Consciousness, entered the Preconscious and somewhere along the way was confronted by the censorship to whose influence "it soon succumbs." Under this view the Unconscious wish could become Preconscious at least for a period of time. This made the Preconscious an unsatisfactory "region" since a part of it, the part that admitted the Unconscious wishes, appeared to resemble the Unconscious system. Uncertainty about the nature of this region is indicated by Freud's description of thinking in the Preconscious. He said, "We call such a train of thought [one in the Preconscious] a preconscious train, and we believe it to be perfectly correct, and that it may equally well be a merely neglected train or one that has been interrupted and suppressed" (1, p. 529). It does not add much to our understanding to assume that material in the suppressing system is itself suppressed.

Developing his ideas about a train of thought, Freud said that it might die out in the Preconscious system. But there was another possibility. ". . . other directing ideas are lurking in the preconscious, which have their source in our unconscious and ever-active wishes." These "lurking" ideas may establish a connection with the train of thought, thus bestowing on it the energy of the wishes. "We may say, then," Freud reported, "that the hitherto preconscious train of thought has been drawn into the unconscious" (1, p. 530).

This question of what goes on in the Preconscious turns into an analysis of passageways and routes because Freud is visualizing a sort of geographical area. His topological thinking has become dominant. We shall look at these routes now, but we should keep in mind that more is involved than topological ingenuity. The essential problem concerns the fundamental forces in personality and their relations. Freud was trying to draw up a model depicting the balance of power as between the Conscious and the Unconscious.

He suggested that two kinds of trains of thought may exist in the Preconscious, (a) a neglected train, and (b) a suppressed train. Both of these trains may die out where they are unless they establish some kind of connection with the Unconscious. It appeared then that some trains of thought may be repressed before they have any contact with the Unconscious. Freud described a dynamic process here and not a maturation process, and therefore the Meynert overlay cannot be used to explain it. It also appears that the repression must have taken place not because the train of thought was allied with the Unconscious but because it was unacceptable to the Conscious. We would conclude that the Conscious subsystem represses what it does not like, at least so far as material in its own subsystem is concerned.

A further point to be noticed is that the Preconscious is emphatically catholic in its tastes. Neglected and repressed trains of thought may be there; also "other directing ideas" lurk there which are based on wishes from the Unconscious. These ideas may connect with the trains of thought, thus gaining additional energy. These ideas are not the Unconscious "wishes." They "have their source" in these wishes. But these ideas have some energy. They attach to the trains of thought—those that are pertinent—and thus revitalize them. So we are presented with a perplexing problem about the censor. The Unconscious "wish" could not get into the Preconscious. There must be a censor there. But ideas with sources in the Unconscious wishes could get by that censor. They could attach themselves to "thoughts" in the Preconscious, some of which might already have been suppressed. When such a connection was made, Freud imagined a rather curious event. He said that the "hitherto preconscious train of thought has been drawn into the unconscious." We remember that the normal direction of Unconscious wishes is toward Consciousness. In this situation the Unconscious establishes a beachhead in the Preconscious and then voluntarily retreats into the Unconscious. This course is suggested by Freud in order to get the formation under repression where it can behave as Unconscious formations are supposed to behave. If Freud did not avail himself of this little conceit, he would have the Unconscious formations becoming part of the Conscious and so upsetting his convictions about them. There was an alternative, which consisted of imagining two censors, one at the border between the Unconscious and the Preconscious, and another between the Preconscious and the Conscious subsystems. This hypothesis would make more complex the whole question of "resistance." But it would help us to see how Unconscious "ideas" could attach to Preconscious trains of thought and still be under repression. Furthermore, it would help us to make a distinction between the "lower part" of the Preconscious and the Unconscious. A censor was needed between these two areas. And the fact that repressed trains of thought could be higher up in the Preconscious lent color to the idea that there might be another censor somewhere between the upper Preconscious and the Conscious subsystems. Freud cautiously suggested the double censor. He said, of the Preconscious, that its excitations may be capable of reaching consciousness but ". . . perhaps not before they have again undergone censorship" (1, p. 544). This hypothesis appeared satisfactory, and he put it forth frankly in a later passage. "It is only on a dissection of hysterial mental processes that the manifold nature of the problem of consciousness becomes apparent. One then receives the impression that the transition from the preconscious to the conscious cathexis is associated with a censorship similar to that between the Ucs (Unconscious) and the Pcs (Preconscious)" (1, p. 546).

The actions, relations, and locations of these censors are impossible to determine. Freud has not been able to construct an "ego" system that can be kept theoretically separate from the Unconscious and whose relations with the Unconscious are determinate. But he has tried to implement the insight that the major mental axis runs along the line: ego-repressed.

Reference

1. Freud, Sigmund, "The Interpretation of Dreams," *The Basic Writings of Sigmund Freud* (New York: Modern Lib., 1938).

4. True experience and the self

CLARK E. MOUSTAKAS

In contrast to the preceding three readings, Moustakas views the self as a more global, personal, and existential construct. He maintains that terms such as "self-concept," "negative-self," "ideal-self," and so forth, only serve to obstruct and obscure what the self really is in the person whom we seek to understand. How, then, do *we understand another's "self"? Moustakas suggests some ways.*

Experience is true to the person when he is himself alone. In such experience perception is unique and undifferentiated. The individual is free to discover and express his potentialities. In true experience every expression is creative, the creation of the person one is and is becoming. There is only the exploring, spontaneously expressing self, finding satisfaction in personal being.

There are no goals to pursue, directions to follow, or techniques to use. There is the growing, experiencing self, significance and meaning in personal experience, and exploration and discovery. True experience may be understood through empathy in communal living or in self-expression or utterance. But it cannot be communicated. To communicate the self is to abstract from it, speak of its aspects or parts and thus do violence to it. Communication represents or symbolizes the self. It distinguishes, compares, and characterizes. Communication is used to influence and often to change. Communication requires explanation, analysis, description, and clarification. It must make what is known by one person common to be understood. The self is not its symbol or external behavior. The self is itself alone existing as a totality and constantly emerging. It can be understood only as unique personal experience. Self-expression is not persuasive and is without special purpose or function. The self is undifferentiated in time and space. It is being, becoming, moving, undivided from the world of nature or the social world.

True being is self and other, individual and universal, personal and cultural. It cannot be understood by comparison, evaluation, diagnosis, or analysis. Such an approach breaks up an experience and violates its nature.

From the beginning the human person wants to feel that his who-ness is respected and his individuality is treasured. Too often the person is respected for what he represents in intelligence, achievement, or social status. This distorts the real nature of the person and interferes with human understandingness. It blocks the potential forces that exist within the person for creativity, for unique, peculiar, and idiosyncratic expression.

True growth, actualization of one's potential, occurs in a setting where the person is felt and experienced as sheer personal being. In such an atmosphere the person is free to explore his capacities and to discover for himself meanings and values of life consistent with the self.

In spite of all the advances in tests and measurements and in analyzing human behavior, understanding the person from his own point of view, in the light of his own unique experience, is the most real way of knowing him. More and more we are realizing that the self-expression of the individual in true experience is complete in itself. To see the person as he sees himself is the deepest way to know him and respect him.

Even the growing evidence, however, has not helped us to feel more trust in individual self-expression. The tendency remains to rely heavily on external measures. Recently Allport (2) reported a series of studies in which the great need for food among men on a starvation diet failed to be uncovered on tests given these men. The number of food associations actually declined with longer periods of fasting. No one would question the importance of strong hunger in motivating behavior, yet it could not be determined without approaching the men directly and asking them to tell about this important need.

Adler (1) once wrote that the only people who really know human nature are those who have experienced the worth and value of others through their own empathy. Correspondence of perceptual experience is perhaps the best basis for understanding what an experience means to another individual, but without such similarity of perception we can still know the meanings that experiences have for others through listening with objectivity and warmth, through attempting to understand the essence of the experience through the perceptions of the other person. Objectivity as used here refers to seeing what an experience is for another person, not how it fits or relates to other experiences, not what causes it, why it exists, or for what purpose. It is an attempt to see attitudes and concepts, beliefs and values of an individual as they are to him, not what they were or will become. The experience of the other person as he perceives it is sufficient unto itself, true and of value as itself, understood in terms of itself.

Knowing the content of individual experience does not explain the unique meaning or totality any more than knowing that a tree has a trunk and branches tells how it will be perceived by the different people who see it. The "facts" regarding human behavior have little meanings in themselves. It is the manner in which they are perceived and known that tells how they will be expressed in behavior. Experiments at the Hanover Institute have shown that we do not get our perceptions from the things around us, but that our perceptions come from us (7). There is no reality except individual reality, and that is based on a background of unique experience.

It sometimes requires complex and thorough examination to diagnose tuberculosis, cancer, or a heart ailment in an individual, but knowing the presence of such a serious illness does not tell what it will mean in the life of an individual or his family. A group of physicians may find it easy to communicate with each other regarding the nature of an illness, but difficult to talk to patients when they have not taken into account the perceptions the patient has of his illness. To the extent that physicians fail to consider the personal experiences and meanings of the individual, they do not understand the full nature of the illness and often talk in authoritative terms disclosing their lack of real knowledge. These physicians show complete faith in the object or the part which has medical significance but little recognition of the person as a unique, special individual who in some ways is unlike any other person who has had a painful disease. When the physician doubts the impact of the individual's self-perception on his illness, he distrusts the potential curative powers within the person and his striving for health. This threatens the strength of being and self-confidence of the individual.

Facts regarding human living gain their full value when examined in the context of unique individual experience. Most experts are expert in pointing out facts, in making evaluations and diagnoses, but when they fail to recognize that facts gain their meaning in a personal context and these meanings differ for different individuals, then they fail to understand fully the true nature of the fact. When experts discard the individual's discrete experiences as insignificant, they often make generalizations about human growth and development which contradict the true nature of the person. Or they give recommendations which are inconsistent with the individual's purposes and values and interfere with his growth. These recommendations based on "facts" cannot be accepted and utilized and sometimes frighten and disturb the person.

In the final analysis the individual must know for himself the totality that he is. He alone has had touch with all his experiences. He alone knows his feelings and thoughts and what his experiences mean to him. The meaning depends on the values involved in the situation, event, or experience, and these values come from the person's personal background. The individual alone can tell the true meaning of his experience.

There is a tendency among analytic people to see an individual in terms of someone else—his father, mother, or siblings. This approach distorts the real nature of the person and interferes with valid understanding of him. One does not recognize the otherness of a person as a reality by projecting into him someone else or by abstracting out of him transferred feelings and attitudes. And when one sees in a person his father or mother or anyone else, one ignores the person as he really is. Angyal (3) regards this as a fundamental disregard for and destructive attitude toward the other person. He points out that real understanding of the other person is not some sort of shrewd analysis which has a keen eye for the weaknesses of people but a deep perception of the core, of the essential nature of the other person as he is.

All psychological phenomena can be understood as illustrative of the single principle of unity or self-consistency (8). When the individual is free to be himself his acts are always consistent with his values. No matter what we are told, our own perceptions of ourselves will always seem substantial and solid to us (11). Resistance is a way for the individual to maintain consistency of self in the light of external pressure. It is a healthy response, a sign that the will of the individual is still intact. It is an effort by the individual to sustain the integrity of the self. When the individual submits without wanting to submit, he is weakened and unable to function effectively. Conformity blocks creativity while freedom and spontaneity foster growth.

Rank (10) stressed the importance of positive will expression. He believed that the denial of will expression is the essence of neurosis. His aim was to strengthen will, not weaken it. In the light of external pressures (attempts to frighten and even terrify the person, to force him to submit to symbols, standards, and values outside himself) which, yielded to, may mean disintegration of self and destruction of will, the individual must often call upon the forces within himself, follow his internal cues, awareness, and direction, maintain his position and assert himself in order not to seriously distort his essence, his being. When the individual submits while the very core of his existence cries out against submission, the health and stability of the person is seriously impaired and he is often unable to think, decide, or act. Sometimes he becomes the expectations, convictions, and values of others.

It is within the nature of the individual to actualize himself and become whatever he is meant to be, to explore his individual potential as fully as possible (5, 6). He will resist all attempts to change him that threaten his perception of self, and will respond favorably to situations which permit him to express and explore his potentials. The individual will not respond to stimuli which are inadequate to him. Such stimuli can be effective only if they are very strong and force themselves upon him. Then the person is driven into a catastrophic situation not only because he is unable to react adequately, but also because he is shocked and disturbed, sometimes so severely he is unable to react at all (5). Thus when we force an individual to behave according to external values, when we impose our convictions on the other person, we impair his creativity and his will to explore and actualize.

Maintenance of the real self is of primary significance for the individual. It is the most stable consistent value in his life. The real self is the central core within each individual which is the deep source of growth (6). To operate in terms of the persons we are is natural, comforting, and satisfying. It permits us to be creative, to utilize our capacities.

It is not possible to accept the other person and at the same time openly reject his values and ideas. Such a concept is antithetical to the consistency of self. We cannot separate the individual from his behavior and say that we accept him but do not accept his behavior. This type of distinction is possible when the self is viewed in terms of categories instead of holism or unity. Individuals do not see themselves in categories. Behavior is self.

Sometimes people are forced to reject the behavior of another person and, therefore, to reject the person. This rejection may be less severe if one focuses on the behavior itself. However, by rejecting the behavior of the person, one cannot escape a rejection of the person himself. Even though this is so, if the rejection occurs only occasionally in a relationship and it is limited to the behavioral act while at the same time the feelings are recognized and accepted, a general attitude of acceptance can still exist and be conveyed.

In the face of drastic action that will markedly affect the behavior of the person, can the individual continue to be silent and objective or must he express his own convictions? Must he live by whoever he is? Integrity of the self is the main source of strength in the individual. To be untrue to oneself, dishonest, or insincere may result in self-impairment. When the self is threatened and endangered, continued attempts completely to accept the other might eventuate in a disorganization of oneself. Two teachers may be able to listen and accept one another's opposing approaches within the same school system as long as administrative changes which will affect their work are not contemplated. Two teachers with varying philosophies and ideas may be able to work effectively in adjacent rooms, but if they had to work with the same group of children at the same time, it would be difficult for them to accept one another's methods and work harmoniously.

The following principles summarize the basic approach and recognition of the self in true experience and the creation of human understandingness.

1. The individual knows himself better than anyone else.

2. Only the individual himself can develop his potentialities.

3. The individual's perception of his own feelings, attitudes, and ideas is more valid than any outside diagnosis can be.

4. Behavior can best be understood from the individual's own point of view.

5. The individual responds in such ways as to be consistent with himself

6. The individual's perception of himself determines how he will behave.

7. Objects have no meaning in themselves. Individuals give meanings and reality to them. These meanings reflect the individual's background.

8. Every individual is logical in the context of his own personal experience. His point of view may seem illogical to others when he is not understood.

9. As long as the individual accepts himself, he will continue to grow and develop his potentialities. When he does not accept himself, much of his energies will be used to defend rather than explore and to actualize himself.

10. Every individual wants to grow toward self-fulfillment. These growth strivings are present at all times.

11. An individual learns significantly only those things which *are* involved in the maintenance or enhancement of *self*. No one can force the individual to permanent or creative learning. He will learn only if he wills to. Any other type of learning is temporary and inconsistent with the self and will disappear as soon as threat is removed.

12. Concepts, ideas, symbols, and events can be denied or distorted, but experience is experienced in the unique reality of the individual person and cannot be untrue to itself. If it threatens the maintenance or enhancement of self, the experience will be of little relevance or consequence to the individual though it may temporarily stifle further growth.

13. We cannot teach another person directly, and we cannot facilitate real learning in the sense of making it easier. We can make learning for another person possible by providing information, the setting, atmosphere,

materials, resources, and *by being* there. The learning process itself is a unique individualistic experience. It may be a difficult experience for the individual person even if it has significance for the enhancement of self.

14. Under threat the self is less open to spontaneous expression; that is, is more passive and controlled. When free from threat, the self is more open, that is, free to be and to strive for actualization.

The educational situation which most effectively promotes significant learning is one in which (a) the threat to the self of the learner is at a minimum while at the same time the uniqueness of the individual is regarded as worthwhile and is deeply respected, and (b) the person is free to explore the materials and resources which are available to him in the light of his own interests and potentiality.

Most research studies on the self have been highly structured and intellectualized. An increasingly narrow definition is emerging. Descriptions imply and sometimes clearly state that a definition of self is self. Statements an individual can make about himself or that someone else makes about him are tabulated, and the score an individual receives is interpreted as an expression of the individual's self. These reports abstract the self into such parts as "self-concept," "negative-self," "inferred-self," and "ideal-self." The self finally becomes limited to verbal statements and categories. Viewing the self as categories, characteristics, and in other abstractive ways makes such studies possible, but they do not enrich our understanding of the experience of self. Thus conceptions of self are shared, communicated, and conveyed in words, but the natural, spontaneous immanence of self is somehow lost.

The self is not its definition or description but rather the central being of the individual person. The self is not definable in words. Any verbal analysis tends to categorize or segment the self into communicable aspects or parts. The self can only be experienced. Any attempt to convey its meaning verbally must be based on function or structure and on language which can be partially understood. Therefore, comparison, relatedness, and association to situations and events are required in a communicable definition of self. When the self is understood only in words, the experience of the self is lost. The self as experienced involves the totality of the individual. It is a natural, automatic, and complete expression, only partially available to verbal communication. Understanding of self is possible through unqualified perception and empathy, that is, human presence and being.

When the focus is placed on words of the self rather than on the self itself, the unique perception of the individual person as expressed in the totality of his behavior is not really understood. In such a setting the opportunity for fuller expression of uniqueness and individuality is threatened.

When we attempt to abstract from our experience facts, knowledge, and information, we tend to focus on limited aspects of experience which will have relevance to another person, which can be conveyed in precise words. In that way, we tend to close the possibility for fuller impact, meaning, and significance of experience as it influences us naturally and automatically in the pursuit and exploration of our potentialities.

Fromm (4) has emphasized that the duty to be alive is the same as the duty to become oneself. Somehow we do not have faith that if we simply permit a person to explore his interests in his own way he will become a truly human person. We fear that the individual will develop antisocial tendencies, emerge as inadequate, or become socially destructive. Autonomy is regarded with suspicion or distrust or simply interpreted and categorized as resistant behavior. We feel we have to condition the person, teach him directly, keep after him to socialize him and make him behave like others. We do not trust ourselves or have enough confidence that our own personal experiences with children will provide a healthy basis for social growth. We do not accept our own being, we do not own the self, when we act on external standards, judgments, and expectations. We seem satisfied when the child is like others and troubled when he turns out to be different.

Individuality must be encouraged, not stifled. Only what is true and therefore of value to society can emerge from individual interests, that is, expressions of one's true nature. All children may need love, safety, belongingness, acceptance, and respect as basic conditions to their growth, and when these conditions are provided by the human environment, growth will occur naturally through the person's potential. Adults may offer resources, make available opportunities, and give information and help when it is meaningful to the child, but to force standards, social values, and concepts on the child is to stifle his potential creativity and difference.

Relations must be such that the person is free to affirm, express, actualize, and experience his own uniqueness. Adults help to make this possible when they show they deeply care for him, respect his individuality, and accept the child's being without qualification. To permit the person to be and become is not to promote selfishness, but to affirm the person's truly human self.

Somehow we must remove the beliefs that make men mistrust themselves and each other. Being given the opportunity to grow and to actualize one's self provides the best basis for interacting with others, and within the framework of groups and society. When individuals are free to operate in terms of their real selves, they do not violate the trust that is conveyed to them. Under such an atmosphere, individual integrity is maintained and fostered and society is enriched. We must not accept as intrinsic an antagonism between individual interests and social interests. Maslow (9) has strongly emphasized that this kind of antagonism exists only in a sick society. But it need not be true. Individual and social interests are synergetic, *not* antagonistic. Creative individual expression, that is, expression of one's own intrinsic nature, results in social creativity and growth which in turn encourage and free the individual to further self-expression and discovery.

References

1. Adler, Alfred, *Understanding Human Nature* (New York: Greenberg, 1927).
2. Allport, Gordon W., "The Trend in Motivational Theory," *American Journal of Orthopsychiatry,* Vol. 23 (1953), pp. 107-119.
3. Angyal, Andras, "A Theoretical Model for Personality Studies," *Journal of Personality,* Vol. 20 (1951), pp. 131-141.
4. Fromm, Erich, *Man for Himself: An Inquiry Into the Psychology of Ethics* (New York: Holt, Rinehart & Winston, 1947).
5. Goldstein, Kurt, *Human Nature: In the Light of Psychotherapy* (Cambridge, Mass.: Harvard, 1940).
6. Horney, Karen, *Neurosis and Human Growth* (New York: Norton, 1950).
7. Kelley, Earl C., *Education for What Is Real* (New York: Harper, 1947).
8. Lecky, Prescott, *Self-Consistency: A Theory of Personality,* Frederick C. Thorne, ed. (Fort Myers Beach, Fla.: Island, 1951).
9. Maslow, A. H., "The Instinctoid Nature of Basic Needs," *Journal of Personality,* Vol. 22 (March, 1954), pp. 326-347.
10. Rank, Otto, *Will Therapy* (New York: Knopf, 1936).
11. Rogers, Carl R., *Client-Centered Therapy* (Boston: Houghton, 1951).

QUESTIONS FOR DISCUSSION

Anderson Article

1. It is an accepted fact that a "significant" person can influence, for better or worse, the self-image of another individual. But what makes one "significant" to another person anyway? Would, for example, a teacher be a "significant" person to his students? Why or why not?
2. The author states, "For every bad portion of the self-concept, there are other good portions which are emphasized. . . ." Suppose a student says to you, "I may not be smart, but I'm a good basketball player." Do you think it is psychologically healthy to substitute a strength for a weakness the way this student does? Why or why not?
3. Why should the most rigid self-concepts be built out of the greatest insecurities? What is the relationship between anxiety and rigidity?
4. Why is survival, rather than sex, basic in Anderson's concept of behavioral dynamics?

Bertocci Article

1. How does "self" differ from "ego"?
2. What does the author mean when he suggests that "the personality is the particular adjustment the self has learned to make. . . ."?
3 What role do social norms and social objectives play in the development of self?
4. The author suggests that the self is a "unique active unity," but that it stands ". . . ready to be influenced and sometimes forced by demands outside itself." How can the self be unique while at the same time be so amenable to outside influences?

Stoodley Article

1. Why do you suppose the unconscious expresses itself in so many symbolic representations rather than in a more straightforward manner?
2. Why are our unconscious sentiments sometimes expressed via dreams? What roles do the self and ego play in the nature and expression of our dreams?
3. What are the relationships between the unconscious, preconscious, and conscious? Do you think behavior is influenced more by the unconscious or conscious? Why do you feel as you do?

Moustakas Article

1. What does the author mean when he says, "The self is not definable in words"? Would you agree?
2. Autonomy, empathy, trust, and acceptance are terms the author frequently refers to. How are they related to his ideas about self-enhancement and self-maintenance?

Part II

theoretical issues and the self

1. The need for a phenomenological system of psychology

DONALD SNYGG

Reprinted from *Psychological Review*, Vol. 48 (1941), 404-424, by permission of the author and the American Psychological Association.

Although this article was published some time ago, its first paragraph is as true today as it was when originally written. The author compares the "objective" approach to understanding behavior to the "phenomenological" approach. The contrast is striking. Implications for teachers, psychiatrists, and applied psychologists are noted. For the other side of the coin, read the next article in this part.

No visitor to a meeting of any psychological society in the last few years can fail to be impressed by the wide diversity of opinion there expressed. After fifty years of apparent progress American psychology has reached a point where two psychologists wishing to carry on a professional discussion must spend most of the time defining the terms they are using. As Hull has said, "One of the most striking things about the theory of learning and of psychological theory in general is the wide disagreement among individual psychologists" (8). The confusion is so great that already leading psychologists have predicted the impending dismemberment of psychology.

Controversy over clear-cut and well-defined points of view is a necessary prelude to progress in the development of any science. It does not appear, however, that the "wide disagreement" cited by Hull above holds the promise of an impending step forward in the history of psychology. It is more likely that the confusion is a symptom of defeat and of the present inability of the science to live up to its early promise, a failure that is implicit in Pratt's statement that "For a long time to come psychology should remain in the laboratory and the library" (13).

Some writers have sought to gloss over this chaotic situation by insisting that the disagreements concern theory only and that there is little difference over questions of fact. This evasion can be of little consolation to the vast number of parents, teachers, physicians, and other workers in the applied fields who must depend upon theory for guidance in their attempts to predict and control human behavior.

Prediction of new phenomena is necessarily based upon theory, not directly upon the results of previous observations. Knowledge of the results of a large number of discrete experiments, without theoretical interpretation, offers no way of predicting results when the experimental situation is different in the least degree. It may be anticipated that the differing conditions may lead to different behavior, but the kind and degree of differences are unpredictable without some theory of causation. Such circumstances are universal in any field of applied psychology where the teacher, the clinician, or the psychiatrist is always endeavoring to predict and control behavior in situations which are in some degree new and unique. Applied psychology is in vital need of principles of prediction that are simple, accurate, and unambiguous, that can function as principles for prediction rather than as myths for explanation, and that can be applied with precision in situations never before investigated.

It is precisely at these points that the current body of psychological theory is defective. It is complex, cumbersome, and contradictory, and each of the conflicting systems is itself a welter of contradictory principles of causation and description. Catching phenomena coming and going, these systems serve nicely as explanatory concepts after the event but, because of their antagonistic character, are relatively useless for prediction. Ego-id, primacy-recency, similarity-contrast, differentiation-integration, facilitation-inhibition, learning-forgetting, self-preservation-death wish are only a few examples. In the effort to explain all known facts every current system has been forced into the use of conflicting principles such as these. Each system has a large number of principles because it must account for a large number of facts; and in each system some of the principles are conflicting because the facts which they attempt to explain are conflicting. It is the thesis of this paper that this apparent conflict is an artifact. The facts are conflicting because they are derived from two mutually exclusive frames of reference.

Two Frames of Reference for the Observation of Behavior

It has become a common-place in physics that the obtained figures for the mass, velocity, and path of any object are dependent upon the point from which they are observed. It is less widely recognized that the same principles apply to the collection of psychological data. For whatever purpose behavior is to be studied, it must be observed from one of two distinct points of view. It may be studied objectively, as by an outside observer; or it may be studied phenomenologically, from the point of view of the behaving organism itself (17). The facts derived from these two points of view are non-identical and are often completely contradictory. As seen by an outside observer, for instance, learning is a process of progressive change in the learner's response to a static situation. During this process the situation or task remains unchanged while the behavior becomes more relevant and efficient. Since the situation remains unchanged, improvement is ascribed to hypothetical changes within the learner. Thus the objective approach inevitably includes among its derived facts random molar behavior and improvement with repetition, usually by association or integration. Educational procedures based upon objective facts customarily stress frequency, drill, reward, and punishment.

From the phenomenological point of view, that is to say, from the point of view of the learner, the facts are quite different. The learner remains unchanged. It is his experience of the situation or task which changes. From his point of view his behavior is always insightful, that is to say, it is always relevant to the situation as he interprets it at the moment. Improvement is concurrent with changes in the observed nature of the task, usually described as differentiation, individuation, or increase in detail. These data are in direct contradiction to the data derived from the objective approach; the observed facts of one frame of reference completely contradict the observed facts of the other. Educational procedures based upon phenomenological facts also differ from those based upon objective facts since they stress understanding of the individual child, pacing, and clear presentation of material.

Twenty years ago the point of view in American psychology was predominantly objective. An attempt was being made by one school, the behaviorists, to construct a methodologically pure theory of learning from that point of view. Since then, largely due to the influence of the Gestalt movement, the trend has been toward increasing acceptance of facts derived from the phenomenological point of view. Unfortunately the trend has, in most cases, manifested itself in the attempted assimilation of phenomenological facts into a basically objective theory.

An analogous situation might have arisen during the shift of astronomers from the Ptolemaic to the Copernican frame of reference. If we take our place of residence as the fixed unmoving point of observation, it follows as a necessary and undeniable fact that the sun revolves around the earth. It is a fact that can be verified by independent observation on any clear day. On the other hand, if the sun is taken as the fixed point of reference, it is an equally observable fact that the earth revolves around the sun. Both facts not only are verifiable by observation but can be used in the prediction of phenomena, for example eclipses. They are not, however, coexistent facts since they are derived from two mutually exclusive points of view. It is not likely that during the long controversy over the "truth" of the two systems any eclectic ever had the hardihood to predict an eclipse from a synthesis of Ptolemaic and Copernican facts, with the earth going around the sun while the sun went around the earth and both stood still.

Precisely such a synthesis, however, is continually attempted in psychological discussions of learning. A glance at any current text will show how *error, reflexes, stimuli, frequency,* and other data derived from the objective point of view are complemented with such phenomenological concepts as *trial, insight,* and *belonging*. The statement found in a widely used outline for students, that we learn usually by trial and error but sometimes by insight, is only an extreme example of this generous and uncritical point of view. Nor should it be supposed that the indiscriminant amalgamation of objective and phenomenological data is confined to the works of avowed eclectics. "Effect" and "consequences" have long done duty in both camps, referring on the same page to changes in the structure of the organism and to changes in the way the learner experiences the task. Even Gestalt psychologists have failed to recognize the non-simultaneity of the derived data. Koffka's invocation of the "geographic" environment (9), necessitated by his desire to assimilate data derived from an objective approach, is a case in point. By its introduction into an essentially phenomenological system it is possible for him to take cognizance of items which exist in the phenomenal field of the experimenter but not in that of the behaving organism.

Given a theory of learning based upon one of the two points of view, an assimilation of facts derived from the other can be achieved only by introducing additional and necessarily conflicting laws and principles. This was done by Thorndike (effect-belonging, 21) and, more recently, by Maier (learning-reasoning, 11) in adding phenomenological data to objective systems. Koffka and Freud, in adding objective data to phenomenological systems, attempted to avoid the uncertainty involved in a multiplicity of independent processes but found it necessary to postulate new loci of action (geographic environment, unconscious) not open to direct observation by either the observer or the participant. Uncertainty in prediction arises, on the one hand, from the multiplicity of independent laws and, on the other, from the circumstance that the postulated law is held to be operating in a field inaccessible to observation. In either case the increased possibility of a plausible explanation for any specific act is more than counterbalanced by the decrease of certainty in prediction. Mixed systems are therefore better suited for explanation in retrospect than as principles for prediction in advance. Data derived from the two frames of reference are not coexistent, and a genuinely predictive psychology will be impossible of attainment until we stop treating them as if they were. Such a psychology must be either completely objective or completely phenomenological. It is the purpose of this paper to examine the value of data derived from each type of approach for their comparative value in prediction.

Inadequacy of the Objective Approach for Prediction of Human Behavior

Of the two possible points of view it is probable that most psychologists would prefer to use the objective approach because of its record of success in the physical sciences. It does not appear, however, that any observational approach is adequate at the present time to furnish the required principles for prediction. Whatever their possibilities for the future, attempted objective systems have up to now shared the defects of mixed systems by leaning heavily upon hypothetical loci of action or by requiring an unwieldy number of independent causal principles.

As viewed by outside observers, the behavior of living organisms varies even when the environment remains unchanged. This variability has been explained in the past by postulating mind as an unseen determiner of behavior. It is more frequently explained at present by assigning the same determining function to hypothetical changes in the organism, usually in the nervous system. If instruments can be invented which will make organic states more accessible to observation, the latter concept may prove to be a very fruitful one; but up to the present time both concepts have functioned almost exclusively as explanatory concepts, being relatively useless for prediction. Accurate prediction is possible only when the causal entities are open to inspection.

A tempting alternative to the use of unexplored causal fields is that adopted by the early behaviorists who attempted to refrain completely from causal inferences and to restrict themselves to data which could be objectively observed. Because of the notorious variability of animal behavior under objectively identical conditions, such attempts to discover purely descriptive laws have not, however, been very successful. A common and necessary assumption of the objective way of search has been that the apparent irresponsibility of living organisms to physical causation is due to the gross character of the units studied. Further analysis, it is hoped, will show the parts of the organism functioning in ways predictable by an adequate physics. By withdrawing from the study of organismic behavior into the study of part behavior, of reflexes, or of S-R bonds, it is possible to maintain the concept of lawful causation of events and at the same time maintain the objective approach. This procedure, however, involves an indefinite multiplication of causal processes, with attendant confusion in prediction. Since it is possible to investigate the relation between an animal's behavior and any feature of a situation which can be experienced by the experimenter, present-day objectivists are embarrassed by a plethora of causal factors. Buel (4) reviewed eighty-three factors which have been found to affect the pathway chosen by a white rat approaching a point of bifurcation in a maze. He points out that the list is not exhaustive and the eighty-third factor is "chance." The hopelessness of using such a large number of independent principles as bases for accurate prediction is obvious.

The situation, then, is this: From the objective point of view, behavior which is not pertinent to the situation as viewed by the experimenter is random, indeterminate, fortuitous. To accept this indeterminism, however, as final would involve the abandonment of all hope for accurate prediction. Any science which hopes to predict must postulate lawfulness. Lawfulness in an objective system, however, can be maintained only by postulating additional causal agents unseen by the experimenter, as mind, past experience, instincts, or organic change. As long as these entities remain inaccessible to the experimenter they can be endowed with any necessary characteristics and are ideally suited to function as explanatory concepts. But, conversely, as long as these agents remain inaccessible the systems of which they are parts will have vital gaps in their causal fields with consequent inaccuracy in prediction. Since the unseen agents are usually invoked to explain individual variations in behavior, objective systems are apt to restrict themselves in practice to the prediction of normative behavior, concerning themselves chiefly with the establishment of norms and coefficients of correlation. This knowledge of what "most people," "the average individual," or "the typical three-year-old" is most likely to do in a given situation "other things being equal" is of little value, however, to the applied worker, the clinical psychologist, or the classroom teacher who must predict and control the specific behavior of particular individuals, If the analysis of this paper is correct, the accurate prediction of such specific individual behavior, from an objective point of view, will have to wait until one of the explanatory agents, most probably the physical organism, is laid open to observation by methods and instruments not yet devised.

Pending the perfection of these devices, it appears desirable that an attempt be made to explore the possibilities of the alternatvie point of view, that of the behaving organism. The remainder of this paper is devoted to a discussion of a phenomenological system that has been used with some success in predicting previously unobserved behavior (18, 19, 20). The discussion is restricted roughly to the field of learning, which is the most crucial to the problem of prediction.

The reader will bear in mind that the "facts" of such a system will necessarily conflict with those derived from the objective point of view and that the validity of any frame of reference must be judged, not by the degree to which its facts correspond to the facts derived from other approaches, but by its usefulness in prediction.

The Characteristics of a Phenomenological System

1. The basic postulates

Assuming that the task of psychology is the prediction and control of behavior, a phenomenological system must rest upon three basic assumptions [1] and three principles.

A. All behavior is lawful. This is a necessary assumption of any system since chance behavior would be unpredictable.

B. Behavior is completely determined by and pertinent to the phenomenological field of the behaving organism. By phenomenological field, hereafter abbreviated to p.f., is meant the universe, including himself, as experienced by the behaver at the moment.

C. There is some relationship between the phenomenological fields of different individuals. This is a necessary assumption, since control is impossible if one individual is unable to affect another's field. The locus of the relationship, usually presumed to be an underlying reality, is not open to observation.

D. Greater precision of behavior (learning) is concomitant with greater differentiation of the phenomenological field. Another characteristic of p.f.'s is that they are fluid and shifting; their phenomena are continually reshaped and given new meanings by the character of the total configuration. Memories, for example, are strongly affected in this way (1). Maier (11) found that the crucial act of solutions was forgotten as soon as the solution was made; and Wees and Line (23) found that school children, in the act of reading a story, distorted its details in ways that made it more meaningful

[1] The first assumption is common to all scientific systems, the second and third are matters of direct observation but impossible of proof.

and pertinent to their own experiences. Since behavior is part of the field, taking part in the field's interaction, principle *E* is in some ways a restatement of the second postulate *B*.

E. The characteristics of the parts of the phenomenological field are determined by the character of the field itself. More specifically, the direction and degree of differentiation are determined by the phenomenological needs of the behaver.[2] The reader may find, for example, that in reading this paper he has been particularly aware of the points which substantiate his own views. The fundamental need in a phenomenological system appears to be the preservation of the organization and integrity of the p.f. and especially of that part of the field which is the phenomenal self, whence our tendency to remain unaware of, or to reject with emotion, data inconsistent with our own beliefs.[3]

F. Differentiation takes time. It follows from this principle that the way to accelerate learning is to arrange the situation so that the required differentiations are either more obvious or are unnecessary. For instance, in a black Warden multiple-U maze of LRRRLLRLLR pattern which had been learned by a group of white rats in a median of 29 trials, the application of white paint to the critical 2, 5, 7, 8, and 10 sections, where changes in procedure were necessary, enabled an experimental group to learn the maze in a median of 12 trials (19). When the differentiation of individual sections from one another was made completely unnecessary by painting the blind alleys white and the correct pathway black, or vice-versa, the median number of trials required for learning was lowered to 7 (18).

2. The problem of prediction

By postulate *B* the determining locus of action is the behaver's p.f. This is not open to direct observation by any outside observer. The process of prediction therefore involves two steps: (1) the securing of an understanding of the subject's field by inference or reconstruction, (2) the projection of the future field.

---

[2] Both *D* and *E* invalidate introspection by the learner as a means of reconstructing his own field. Much of the field is too vague and undifferentiated (*D*) to be verbalized; and the need to observe and report may considerably alter the character of the field (*E*) and the nature of the problem.

[3] This recognition that the self we are trying to preserve is the phenomenal self, that is to say, is our own picture of ourselves, explains the need which various schools have described as drives for self-esteem, self-respect, security, status, superiority, power, or complacency. When self-preservation is thus referred to the phenomenal self, it is adequate for the explanation of suicide and martyrdom. These two forms of behavior have always been a source of difficulty from a systematic point of view. Objective systems have been forced to ignore them, along with other un-normal behavior, and mixed systems can include them only by postulation of independent motives conflicting with self-preservation, such as Menninger's death wish (12).

The first operation is of the common "Now why did he do that?" or "Under what circumstances would I have done that?" character. Much of the topological work of Lewin is of this type, and essentially the same procedure was used by Shepard (15) when from the behavior of his rats he inferred the existence of floor cues which he himself was unable to experience. The teacher who hears his pupil report that 3 × 0 is 3 and infers that his reasoning is "Zero is nothing so it does nothing to the three" has taken this step. The operation acquires its validity in this system by the postulate (*B*) that behavior is completely determined by the p.f., whence it follows that variations in behavior are always indicative of concurrent variations in the field. The complete operation of prediction imposes two important conditions. To reconstruct an individual's field from his behavior, it is necessary to have some idea what fields are like, and to project the future field, it is necessary to understand how fields change.

3. The nature of the field

The p.f. is simply the world of naive, immediate experience in which each individual lives, the everyday situation of self and surroundings which the unsophisticated person takes to be real. Studies on the nature of this field indicate that all parts of the field are not equally distinct. The field consists of figure and ground, or focus and margin; there are not two definite, static levels, but one level may shade the other so that the figure may be large and relatively indistinct or small and highly differentiated. Experience in any sense field can be figure. Pain, fatigue, or the disturbed organic states involved in emotion may emerge so sharply as the focus of the field, with all the rest of the field fading into the homogeneity of ground, that the individual will lose touch with his surroundings and become unconscious. Since by postulate *B* behavior is completely determined by the p.f., a highly detailed and differentiated field will include definite and precise behavior, while, as anyone who has tried to find a snap switch in a strange room in the dark will agree, behavior in a vague and undifferentiated field is vague and confused. This leads to principle *D*.

4. How fields change

Principle *D* of our system identified differentiation with learning; principle *E* made the determinants of differentiation somewhat explicit. Differentiation may be defined as knowing a difference, the basic act of knowledge. It is the manifestation of the continuous process by which the integrity and organization of the field are maintained. "When an individual, rat or human, is confronted with a task . . . the general procedure is determined by his initial perception of the nature of the problem; it is a gross response to a relatively undifferentiated situation. Should the first procedure, the response to the gross situation, prove inadequate, the task is differentiated perceptually into segments each of which is solved by simple procedures" (19).

Although he is aware that his own field may be affected (*E*) by his desire to maintain the predictive advantages of having only one process in the system, the writer feels that differentiation may be safely assumed to be the only process of change in the p.f. The emergence of a new entity or character into figure implies the lapse of other characters into ground. Both are necessary for the existence of a difference and are not two independent processes, but complementary aspects of the same process, which might be called "change." Since, however, it is the newly emerged figure, the focus of the behaver's field, which is the most directly potent in determining behavior, it seems more practical to emphasize the more effective aspect of the process and call it "differentiation" or "individuation" rather than the nonvaluative "change."

The basic assumptions and principles are now complete. There remains to be discussed principle *F*, which is subsidiary and based on experimental evidence (3, 16).

5. Use of the system in prediction

Several examples of the use of this system for the prediction of previously unreported animal behavior have been published (2, 18, 19, 20), the last of which may serve as an example. The purpose of the study was to test the comparative usefulness of phenomenological and objective principles in the prediction of maze behavior. Since DeCamp's experiment (5), reported in 1920, it had been almost axiomatic that rats tend to adopt the shorter of two alternative paths to food. Now suppose that the structure of a rat's field is such that a path which is objectively the longer of two alternative paths to food appears to the rat to be the shorter. If, as we have postulated (*B*), the animal's behavior is completely determined by his p.f. he will choose this phenomenological shorter path in spite of the fact that it appears to the experimenter to be the longer. According to objective principles, on the other hand, the effective determinant would be the physical lengths of the two paths "other things being equal," irrespective of how the situation was experienced by the rat.

Such a situation was arranged in a ten-section Warden U LLLLLLL-LLL maze, in which an alternative food-box was attached to the right-hand alley of the third section. Thus it was possible for the rats to take either a short three-section LLR path or a long ten-section LLLLLLL-

LL path to the food. If the behavior were governed by the objective situation, it would be predicted that they would choose the shorter LLR path. However, previous experiments from a phenomenological point of view had led to the inference that "maze learning is a process of increasing differentiation in the total situation, during which the maze is first perceived as a general path to the food-box and is then differentiated into submazes. . ." (19). It was therefore predicted that in this maze the animals would at the end of the first trial experience the path to either food-box as a general leftward path. As a consequence they would take the longer LLLLLLLLL path on later trials. The experiment was made by running a group of rats in this maze once a day for 100 days. During the first 75 days the animals verified the prediction by taking the longer path on 74 per cent of the runs. During the last ten days the longer path was taken on 89 per cent of the runs. This behavior conformed to the inferred p.f.'s of the rats, thus demonstrating the usefulness of the postulates used in prediction.

In the same way, it was predicted that animals in a similar maze where the alternative food-box was on the right-hand alley of the second section, which is directly in front of the maze entrance, would experience this LR path as something like "ahead" or "around the corner." This would not lead them to take the long leftward path. This prediction, also, was verified. The rats in this maze took the shorter path on 64 per cent of the runs during the first 75 days, and on 66 per cent of the runs during the last ten days.

6. The conditioned response

The only real and valid test of any system in science is its effectiveness in predicting previously undiscovered phenomena, as in the case just cited. Ability to explain phenomena already known is, of course, no criterion of usefulness in prediction. It is true, nevertheless, that inability to explain known phenomena is presumptive evidence of inadequacy in prediction as well. For this reason it is interesting to test the adequacy of the proposed system to explain some of the phenomena of the conditioned response, upon which objective systems commonly base their description of learning. A phenomenological explanation would be something like the following, the capital letters referring to the principles involved:

(1) Conditioning

a. Objective description: Given an animal with a need (*e.g.,* for food) and a means of affecting that need (*e.g.,* food). Present a signal (*e.g.,* a tone) of a kind that in sufficient volume and under favorable circumstances is capable of eliciting a response from the animal; then, in fairly close temporal and spatial contiguity, present the means of affecting the need (the "unconditioned stimulus"). After one or more presentations the signal will elicit the same response as the unconditioned stimulus or a response similar to it.

b. Explanation: Given time (*F*) and a need to be satisfied (*E*), the signal and the unconditioned stimulus will be differentiated as a unit from a relatively homogeneous field. Since the degree of differentiation required is determined by the precision of response required (*D*), signals for diffuse bodily and postural activity may be effective at a very low level of awareness. The closer the signal and unconditioned stimulus in the experimenter's time and space, the more apt they are to be differentiated as a unit from the rest of the learner's field (*C*). It would not be expected (*B*) that the response to the signal-stimulus unit would be exactly the same as to the stimulus alone. In a class demonstration with a human subject, using a strong buzzer tone one second before a strong shock to the right forefinger from a curved finger rest, the unconditioned response was an extension of the finger. The conditioned response, however, was flexion together with a lifting of the finger, the whole action taking it off the grill. Phenomenologically the subject was bracing himself for the expected shock.

(2) *Irradiation*

a. Objective description: If the signal is altered within a varying range, the established response will still be made.

b. Explanation: If the signal is incompletely differentiated, it may be confused with other signals. If it is experienced as a vague feeling of discomfort or expectancy, a large number of signals in different sense fields might elicit the response. If it is more clearly individuated, there will be less opportunity for confusion with other signals.

On the basis of this inference that "irradiation" and "generalization" are incomplete differentiation, it would be predicted that continued presentations of the signal-stimulus unit will, by giving more opportunity for precise differentiation (*F*) of the signal, lessen the number of signals with which it might be confused and diminish the probability of "irradiation" responses. This prediction corresponds to the results reported by Razran (14, see pages 7 and 8), although it does not agree with his interpretation.

(3) *Differentiation*

a. Objective description: Both signal A and signal A′ elicit the response. If signal A is given with the unconditioned stimulus and signal A′ without it, the latter signal will cease to elicit the response.

b. Explanation: Presentation of signal A′ without food makes it necessary (*E*) and possible (*F*) for the subject to differentiate it from signal A.

(*4*) *Unconditioning*

a. Objective description: If the signal is given without the unconditioned stimulus or some time after it, it will, after a varying number of presentations, cease to elicit the unit response.

b. Explanation: Separate presentation provides the subject with an opportunity for differentiating them from one another (*C*) (*F*). The signal from a signal-food unit should have no effect even the first time it is given food if the need for food has been completely satisfied (*E*). The signal from signal-punishment units, however, would be effective for several presentations when given after the punishment, since the need to escape punishment is not satiable. Repeated presentations, however, will give an opportunity for differentiation and the signal will eventually emerge as a cue that punishment has ceased and will then evoke a different response.

(*5*) *Pseudoconditioning*

a. Objective description: "In some cases a response is elicited by a formerly inadequate stimulus (signal) which has been preceded by an unconditioned stimulus" (7).

b. Explanation: In cases where the unconditioned stimulus is one, like punishment, that leads to a continuing state of need and tension, the animal will differentiate out and respond to features of the field previously ignored. The signal is effective because it is unfamiliar, that is to say, it is incompletely differentiated from the shock situation. "The animals gave the impression of responding *as if* a shock were expected and *as if* they knew no appropriate response to make" (7, p. 372). In cases where the unconditioned stimulus satisfies the subject's need pseudoconditioning will not occur.

7. Other concepts of learning

One of the greatest advantages of the phenomenological method is that it is able to bring the experimenter within the scope of its system and to apply its laws to the observer himself. When examined in this manner, most of the conventional concepts of learning prove to be products of the relationship between the p.f.'s of the observer and the learner. For example: If the observer's field is more highly differentiated than the learner's, the latter's less precise behavior (*D*), since it does not conform to the situation as experienced by the observer, is said to be *error*. Phenomenologically errors are recognized only in retrospect, that is to say, when an individual compares his past behavior with his present more highly differentiated field.

If the learner's field closely approximates the field of the observer, so that the learner does what the observer would do, the behavior is said to be *correct* or *insightful.*

If the observer's field is less differentiated than the learner's, there are two possibilities: (1) The learner's more precise and efficient behavior may lead the observer to discover features of the situation of which he had previously been unaware; in which case a third party might infer the observer had learned by *imitation.* (2) The learner's mysteriously precise behavior in what to the observer is a relatively undifferentiated field may lead to the assumption that the behavior is determined by *instinct.* The farther removed an animal is from the human in sensory and behavioral possibilities, and the more difficult the reconstruction of its field, the greater the chances that instinct will be invoked as an explanation for its behavior.

8. Association or differentiation

If an observer in a highly differentiated field, which he naively takes to be real, watches the behavior of a learner, he is certain to interpret the process as one in which the highly individuated items in his own field are *combined, organized, associated,* or *integrated* by the learner. Because he believes his own field to be real, he postulates that the learner's field is made up of the same items, but in an inferior state of organization. Objective theories of learning, therefore, begin with an unorganized field and attempt to show how it becomes organized.

Cross-section studies of the learner's p.f. at different stages of learning, however, show that the field is always organized. The change lies in increasing detail rather than organization. Entities are thus "associated" when they are incompletely differentiated, having emerged together out of a common ground to satisfy a need. They are experienced as contiguous when they are incompletely differentiated in space or time and as like or opposite when they emerge in some mutual relationship. The so-called laws of association—*contiguity, similarity,* and *contrast*—thus become descriptive of incomplete differentiation in the phenomenological field.

9. Frequency

Frequency is the basic but unreliable causal factor of most objective systems. From the phenomenological point of view it may afford an opportunity for learning (F) but cannot cause or guarantee it. What is learned depends upon the phenomenological needs of the learner (*E*). This accounts for the success of Dunlap's method of breaking habits by practicing them (6, 22).

10. Relationship to the physical sciences

One of the most interesting implications of the phenomenological approach is the status it assigns to the physical sciences. Physicists secure regularity and lawfulness by restricting themselves to a common and rigorously limited phenomenological field. They share this common p.f. (sometimes called the physical universe) by the process of taking all measurements from a standard position in front of their instruments and confining their observations to the pointer-readings thus derived. This process gives to physical scientists the unique advantage of a common field; but it is a field where all the characteristics of phenomena are eliminated except those reducible to length; where light, color, temperature, taste, and odor exist, if at all, only as readings on a scale; and where song, oratory, poetry, and propaganda are alternating areas of condensation and rarefaction. As long as the physicists can remain in this common field their behavior is identical. They make the same calculations and predictions because they are living in identical fields.

This use of mediate observation in the physical sciences has led to spectacular agreement in some fields. It is, however, essentially a search for agreement by elimination of phenomena and is therefore limited in its possibilities. Since the phenomena that must be excluded are essentially those necessary for the prediction and control of human behavior, it is becoming apparent that the methods of the physical sciences cannot be taken over bodily by the psychologists.

11. Advantages of the phenomenological approach

Philosophically a phenomenological system has a number of advantages, several of which have been enumerated or implied. From the point of view of practical use for the prediction and control of behavior, however, four are outstanding:

1. A phenomenological system in anthropomorphic. Its data are stated in terms of immediate experience and require no translation to make them meaningful.

2. It is concerned with the prediction and control of individual behavior, a field closed to objective systems because of their necessary assumption of variability in individual behavior. For this reason, psychiatrists, applied psychologists, and teachers when dealing with individuals commonly adopt

a phenomenological view. This accounts for the great use by these groups of psychoanalysis, Gestalt, and private nonacademic systems which have large phenomenological components. The use of a general field can result in the prediction of general, normative behavior only.

3. As compared with the objective approach, the phenomenological approach is more inclusive. Individual behavior cannot be predicted from normative behavior. On the other hand, accuracy in predicting individual behavior makes possible the prediction of normative behavior as well.

4. The particular system outlined in this paper has the predictive advantage of postulating only one process, which is descriptive rather than causal or explanatory.

12. Relation to other systems

It is impossible to say whether this system is the only possible phenomenological system. The first three principles are certainly basic and the next three appear to follow. Gestalt psychologists and their pupils have made the major recent contributions in this field and have failed to achieve a purely phenomenological system only because of their failure to appreciate its necessity. As soon as nonphenomenological data are eliminated from Gestalt psychology, it becomes the system that has been described.

Psychoanalysis, the other semiphenomenological system, differs basically in its interpretation of the nature of the field. Freud recognized the figure-ground character of the field and the importance of the ground in behavior but, lacking experimental evidence, distorted the figure-ground relations into an antagonistic dichotomy in which the ground (unconscious) had all the characteristics of figure (conscious) including a self (id). Since these characteristics are not experienced by the individual, the system ceased to be purely phenomenological. The methods of analysis are directed toward securing an understanding of the patient's field and have resulted in the accumulation of important data, especially in the area of motivation. Since the conscious-unconscious dichotomy is the cornerstone of the system, it is impossible tc see, however, how psychoanalysis can evolve into the purely phenomenological system that is needed.

Summary

The current confusion in psychology is largely due to the uncritical combination of data from two different frames of reference. Facts derived from a phenomenological point of view are non-identical with and often completely contradictory to facts derived from an objective point of view.

Systems attempting to combine facts derived from both frames of reference are forced into a multiplicity of conflicting laws and concepts or into the postulation of loci of action inaccessible to observation. In either case accurate prediction of behavior is impossible. Objective systems, although philosophically more satisfactory than mixed systems, have been forced in practice to confine themselves to the prediction of normative behavior. For this reason, psychiatrists, applied psychologists, and teachers when dealing with individuals commonly adopt a phenomenological view. This accounts for the great use by these groups of psychoanalysis, Gestalt, and private nonacademic systems having large phenomenological components. The best immediate prospects for a psychology able to accurately predict individual behavior lie in the development of Gestalt psychology along purely phenomenological lines.

References

1. Bartlett, F. C., *Remembering* (New York: Macmillan, 1932).
2. Bernhardt, K., and D. Snygg, "The Effect of Cues Upon the Choice of the Shorter Path," *Journal of Comparative Psychology,* Vol. 24 (1937), pp. 269-276.
3. Brigden, R. L., "A Tachistoscopic Study of the Differentiation of Perception," *Psychological Monograph,* Vol. 44 (1933), pp. 153-166.
4. Buel, J., "Differential Errors in Animal Mazes," *Psychological Bulletin,* Vol. 32 (1935), pp. 67-99.
5. DeCamp, J. E., "Relative Distance as a Factor in the White Rat's Selection of a Path," *Psycho-biology,* Vol. 2 (1920), pp. 245-253.
6. Dunlap, K., *Habits: Their Making and Unmaking* (New York: Liveright, 1932).
7. Harlow, H. F., and F. Toltzien, "Formation of Pseudo-Conditioned Responses in the Cat," *Journal of General Psychology,* Vol. 23 (1940), pp. 367-375.
8. Hull, C. L., "The Conflicting Psychologies of Learning—A Way Out," *Psychological Review,* Vol. 42 (1935), pp. 491-516.
9. Koffka, K., *The Principles of Gestalt Psychology* (New York: Harcourt, 1935).
10. Maier, N. R. F., "Reasoning in Humans, II," *Journal of Comparative Psychology,* Vol. 12 (1931), pp. 181-194.
11. ———, 'The Behavior Mechanisms Concerned with Problem Solving," *Psychological Review,* Vol. 47 (1940), pp. 43-58.
12. Menninger, K., *Man Against Himself* (New York: Harcourt, 1938).
13. Pratt, C. C., *The Logic of Modern Psychology* (New York: Macmillan, 1939).
14. Razran, G. H. S., "Studies in Configural Conditioning: V. Generalization and Transposition," *Journal of Genetic Psychology,* Vol. 56 (1940), pp. 3-11.
15. Shepard, J. F., "More About the Floor Cue," *Psychological Bulletin,* Vol. 32 (1935), p. 696.

16. Snygg, D., *Configurational Aspects of Tachistoscopic Observation.* Unpublished thesis, State University of Iowa, 1931.
17. ———, "The Relative Difficulty of Mechanically Equivalent Tasks: I. Human Learning," *Journal of Genetic Psychology,* Vol. 47 (1935), pp. 299-320.
18. ———, "The Relative Difficulty of Mechanically Equivalent Tasks: II. Animal Learning," *Journal of Genetic Psychology,* Vol. 47 (1935), pp. 321-336.
19. ———, "Maze Learning as Perception," *Journal of Genetic Psychology,* Vol. 49 (1936), pp. 231-239.
20. ———, "Mazes in Which Rats Take the Longer Path to Food," *Journal of Psychology,* Vol. 1 (1936), pp. 153-166.
21. Thorndike, E. L., *Human Learning* (New York: Appleton, 1931).
22. Wakeham, G. A., "A Quantitative Experiment on Dunlap's Revision of the Law of Habit Formation," *Journal of Comparative Psychology,* Vol. 10 (1930), pp. 235-236.
23. Wees, W. R., and W. Line, "The Influence of the Form of a Presentation Upon Reproduction: The Principle of Determination," *British Journal of Psychology* (Gen. Section), Vol. 28 (1937), pp. 167-189.

2. The phenomenological approach in personality theory: some critical remarks

M. Brewster Smith

Reprinted from the *Journal of Abnormal and Social Psychology,* Vol. 45 (1950), 516-522, by permission of the author and the American Psychological Association.

In the preceding article, Snygg suggested that phenomenology is the answer to accurately predicting individual behavior. Smith, in effect, maintains that this approach can only describe *rather than* explain *behavior, and he presents a substantial case to support his view. Snygg and Combs defend their position in reading three of this section.*

The "phenomenological approach" has recently come to be something of a rallying cry to a number of psychologists who share the "tender-minded" bias that psychology must, after all, come to terms with human experience, and who go so far as to believe that careful attention to this experience will leave the science of psychology not merely more satisfying to like-minded people, but also better science. Sharing this point of view and agreeing heartily with the program recommended by MacLeod (7) in his article on "The Phenomenological Approach to Social Psychology," the present writer has been dismayed by some recent publications which, it seems to him, misconstrue the appropriate role of a phenomenological approach in a way that invites the critical to reject humanized psychology lock, stock, and barrel. Since the writer would regard such an outcome as highly unfortunate, he feels that a clarification of the issues is badly needed, and herewith makes an attempt in this direction.

The position with which he would take particular issue is that of Snygg and Combs (3, 11) whose point of view has also been espoused by Rogers (9). These authors contrast the objective or external frame of reference in psychology with the phenomenological, or internal frame of reference, and, declaring their stand firmly with phenomenology, proceed to muster on their side the names of Lewis, Lecky, Allport, Murphy, and Angyal, among others, even including the seemingly less tractable father-figure of Freud. In essence, their contention is that the locus of psychological causation lies entirely within the phenomenal field of conscious experience, and that it therefore behooves the psychological theorist—and therapist—to formulate his problems and concepts accordingly. Snygg and Combs give much attention to the individual's perceptual-cognitive field, particularly to the *self,* as its most salient feature. Written from this standpoint, psychology comes close to a rapprochement with common sense.

While applauding their emphasis on perception and the self, the present writer proposes that they are confusing phenomenology with what may be termed the subjective frame of reference. Sharply maintained, this distinction further helps to clarify certain persistent ambiguities in the theory of ego and self.

Phenomenology and Common Sense

One of the genuine merits of the phenomenological approach is that it brings psychology somewhat closer to the world of common sense. There is always the danger that psychology, in its concern for rigor and neatness, may divorce itself too completely from this source of problems and partial insights. Focusing scientific attention on the phenomenal world as it is presented to us, the world from which common sense also takes its start, the phenomenological approach can bring into the ken of the psychologist data and problems too often left to common sense by default. Like common sense, and unlike some current varieties of psychological theory, it does deal with experience, and thus presents itself as an attractive alternative to those who find a behavioristic psychology uncongenial.

But phenomenology is not common sense, nor can it rightly be called upon to justify a common-sense psychology. In MacLeod's phrase, the phenomenological approach "involves the adoption of what might be called an attitude of disciplined naivete" (7, p. 194). In many respects, its results may run exactly counter to common-sense conclusions. Common sense, with its preconceived categories and stock explanations, neither disciplined nor naive, is full of pseudoscientific theory, while phenomenology limits

its concern to the unprejudiced *description* of the world of phenomena. To take the phenomenal world presented in conscious experience as completely explanatory of behavior is closer to common sense than to phenomenology or adequate science.

Yet this is essentially what Snygg and Combs have done in their attempt to rewrite psychology in a "phenomenological frame of reference." *"All behavior, without exception,"* they say, *"is completely determined by and pertinent to the phenomenal field of the behaving organism"* (11, p. 15, italics theirs). And they go on to explain that

> by the phenomenal field we mean the entire universe, including himself, as it is experienced by the individual at the instant of action. . . . Unlike the "objective" physical field, the phenomenal field is not an abstraction or an artificial construction. It is simply the universe of naive experience in which each individual lives, the everyday situation of self and surroundings which each person takes to be reality (11, p. 15).

While they bow unnecessarily to current prejudice in avoiding the word *consciousness,* their meaning is clear, and their index spells it out: "Consciousness, *see* Phenomenal field."

It is one variant of common sense that consciousness completely explains behavior, but at this juncture it is hard to see how such a view can be regarded as an acceptable scientific postulate. Quite apart from the metaphysical controversy about the status of consciousness as "real" or respectable, we have behind us Würzburg and we have behind us Freud, to mention but two major sources of evidence that a psychology of experience or consciousness has distinct explanatory limits. Where is the determining tendency represented in the phenomenal field? What of the inacceptable strivings that warp our behavior, what of our defensive techniques of adjustment that so often prove most effective precisely when we are least aware of them? It is no satisfactory solution to speak, as Snygg and Combs do, of a "unified field of figure-ground phenomena of which the individual is more or less conscious . . . [in which] the vague and fuzzy aspects of behavior correspond to and are parts of the vague and incompletely differentiated aspects of the field" (11, p. 17). The clinical literature abounds with instances of unconsciously determined behavior which, far from being "vague and fuzzy," is on the contrary highly differentiated.

One suspects that such a psychology of consciousness has an element of common-sense appeal not unlike the attraction of allied forms of psychotherapy. It does make sense to the layman: it accords with what he is ready and able to recognize in himself. And it has distinct value within limits that it refuses to recognize. Because it overstates its claims, however, it may tend to promote the state of affairs away from which we have been striving—every man his own psychologist.

But MacLeod has already made the relevant point succinctly: "The phenomenological method, in social psychology as in the psychology of perception (and we would add, psychology generally) can never be more than an approach to a scientific inquiry" (7, p. 207). It provides certain kinds of data, not *all* the data. It furnishes the basis for certain valuable theoretical constructs; it does not give birth to them in full concreteness. It sets some problems and provides some clues; the psychologist, theorist, or clinician must *infer* the answers.

Subjective Constructs and the Observer's Frame of Reference

Here we reach the crux of the matter. If a psychology of consciousness is necessarily incomplete yet we do not abandon our hope for a psychology that comes to terms with human experience, what is the solution? A discussion of two lesser questions may indicate the nature of the answer. In the first place, does the decision to frame our psychological concepts and theories in terms appropriate to the "private world" of the behaving person commit us to the exclusive use of phenomenal concepts? Secondly, what is the appropriate role of the phenomenological approach in the service of this kind of theory-building?

Lewin, whose psychological life space Snygg and Combs equate to their phenomenal field (11, p. 15), was entirely clear in maintaining a sharp distinction between the two concepts. He said:

> It is likewise doubtful whether one can use consciousness as the sole criterion of what belongs to the psychological life space at a given moment in regard to social facts and relationships. The mother, the father, the brothers and sisters are not to be included as real facts in the psychological situation of the child only when they are immediately present. For example, the little child playing in the garden behaves differently when he knows his mother is at home than when he knows she is out. One cannot assume that this fact is continually in the child's consciousness. Also a prohibition or a goal can play an essential role in the psychological situation without being clearly present in consciousness. . . . Here, as in many other cases, it is clear that one must distinguish between "appearance" and the "underlying reality" in a dynamic sense. In other words, the phenomenal properties are to be distinguished from the conditional-genetic characteristics of objects and events, that is, from the prop-

> erties which determine their causal relationships. . . . As far as the conceptual derivation is concerned, one may use effectiveness as the criterion for existence: *"What is real is what has effects"* (6, p. 19).

Lewin's life space, then, is *not* merely the phenomenal field. And he adds to our previous considerations cogent reasons for thinking that a psychology of the phenomenal field cannot be adequately explanatory. His life space is not immediately given in the concreteness of experience; it is an abstract, hypothetical construct, inferred by the psychologist-observer to account for the individual's behavior.

It is, however, a construct of a type that differs from constructs of behavioristic psychology. It is formulated in terms of what is behaviorally real to the acting individual, not primarily in terms of what is physically observable to the scientist. Hence it is legitimate to speak of theories like Lewin's as anchored in a *subjective* (not phenomenological) *frame of reference*. Lewin's concepts and many of Freud's are in this sense *subjective constructs,* not because they are built of the stuff of conscious experience, but because they attempt to deal with what is effectively real to the individual, even when it is real to the scientific observer only in this secondary, indirect way.

The subjective frame of reference in theory construction is to be contrasted with the *objective frame of reference,* wherein concepts are chosen so as to be rooted as closely as possible in effective realities shared by any qualified observer. This is the distinction which Snygg and Combs seek, which makes them see both Freud and Lewin as precursors. There is no absolute difference between the two frames of reference; it is rather a question of which criteria are weighted most strongly in the selection of constructs.

Both the subjective and objective frames of reference pertain to the choice of constructs and the theoretical context in which they are embedded. They in no sense conflict with what has been called the *observer's frame of reference,* which, indeed, lies at the foundation of all science. The problem establishing a bridge between the point of view of the observer and *either* subjective or objective inferential constructs is the familiar one of operational definition. It cannot, in the last analysis, be avoided unless one chooses the alternative of claiming *direct* access to the point of view of the observed. This is the point of view of intuitionism, which asserts that the observer's and subject's points of view can be merged. But is this science? Not in the sense of a systematic search for understanding that can withstand the equally systematic doubt of the man from Missouri.

Subjective constructs framed in terms of the "private world" of the behaving individual remain constructs, and as such must ultimately be rooted in data accessible to the observer's frame of reference. There is no reason at all why their source should be restricted to the data of communicated conscious experience, in answer to our first question. But the phenomenological approach, or, more generally, any means of access to the experience of the subject, is of course crucial to the formulation of subjective constructs and the investigation of their relationships. Perhaps the point has been labored, but it is an essential one: the phenomenological approach, the clinical interview, the projective protocol, the behavioral observation—none of these yield direct knowledge of psychological constructs, subjective or objective, while all of them can provide the basis for inferring explanatory constructs and their relationships. If the canons of inference can be made sufficiently explicit, they provide the operational definitions that secure the constructs in the scientific home base of the observer's frame of reference.

Methods that get the subject to reveal his private world as he sees it need to be supplemented by others which permit the observer to infer effective factors that are distorted or disguised in the subject's awareness. But the broadly phenomenological methods remain a signally important source of data. Certain important subjective constructs such as the *self,* moreover, are anchored fairly directly in the data of phenomenological report.

Ego, Self, and Phenomenology

Although there is still considerable confusion in usage, a degree of consensus seems to be emerging to employ the term *self* for the phenomenal content of the experience of personal identity. A salient feature of the phenomenal field that has figured largely in personality theory, the self in this sense has the conceptual properties of a phenomenal object. Murphy (8) and Chein (2) use it with this meaning. Snygg and Combs agree, writing with somewhat franker circularity:

> Of particular importance in the motivation of behavior will be those parts of the phenomenal field perceived by him to be part or characteristic of himself. To refer to this important aspect of the total field we have used the term *phenomenal self* (11, p. 111).

Within the phenomenal self, they distinguish as a stable core the *self concept:* "Those parts of the phenomenal field which the individual has differentiated as definite and fairly stable characteristics of himself" (11, p. 112).

Sharing with Murphy a strong emphasis on responses to the self as fundamental to motivational theory, Snygg and Combs go so far as to state that the basic human need is "the preservation and enhancement of the phenomenal self" (11, p. 58). Changes in the perception of the self play a major role in the theory of the therapeutic process that they share with Rogers (9).

Let us look more closely, however, at how these writers actually use the term. Passages like the following can readily be found:

> . . . when the self is free from any threat of attack or likelihood of attack, then it is possible for the self to consider these hitherto rejected perceptions, to make new differentiations, and to reintegrate the self in such a way as to include them (9, p. 365).
>
> A self threatened by its perceptions may deny the perception by simply refusing to enter the situation where such a perception is forced upon him (11, p. 148).

Can a phenomenal self consider perceptions and reintegrate itself; can a threatened phenomenal self deny perceptions; or is this rather double-talk resulting from the attempt to make one good concept do the work of two? If, as this writer suspects, the latter is the case, what is the nature of the hidden second concept, which evidently is not merely a percept or phenomenal entity? To give it a name he would suggest the conventional term *ego,* realizing that usage in this respect is even more ambiguous than with the term *self*. The important point is that the concept, implicit in the writings of Rogers and of Snygg and Combs, is a subjective construct but does not refer to a phenomenal entity, whereas the self, on the other hand, is a coordinate subjective construct that does. The relation between the two will bear closer examination.

It is not necessary, at this juncture, to propose a definitive theory of the ego, nor to enter into an involved discussion of alternative views about its nature. What is relevant is that starting from an attempt to write a psychology in phenomenal terms, our authors in spite of themselves give implicit recognition to organizing, selective processes in the personality which are somehow guided by the nature and status of the self (among other things) and somehow, in turn, have an influence in its nature and status. So conceived, the relation of ego and self is highly interdependent [1] but by no means an identity. The distinction is that between a dynamic configuration of on-going processes, inferred from many facts of biography and behavior, and a phenomenal entity resulting from these processes and affecting them in turn, inferred primarily (but not exclusively) from phenomenological report.

---

[1] The writer doubts that it is advisable to construct the ego as narrowly around the self as do Chein (2) and Murphy (8).

Approaching the problem on a slightly different tack, we may find it rewarding to consider three of the eight conceptions of the ego listed by Allport (1, p. 459) in the light of the distinction just made: the ego "as one segregated behavioral system among others," "as knower," and "as object of knowledge." The fundamental conception advanced here is not unlike the first of these senses, if one reads into it a dynamic quality not expressed in Allport's formulation. As an on-going system or organizing and selective processes mediating the individual's intercourse with reality, it includes a variety of processes without being coterminous with the total personality.[2] Among these processes or functions is that of the ego as "knower," which the writer would take in a less metaphysical sense than Allport's to embrace the cognitive-perceptual functions of personality. These have been described with reason in psychoanalytic theory (5, pp. 105-106) as an integral aspect of the ego system. Among the phenomena that the ego "knows" is the *self,* Allport's "ego as object of knowledge." Like any cognitive-perceptual object, the self only imperfectly mirrors the physical, psychological, and social facts that underlie the perception. And also like similar phenomenal objects it serves as a guide to appropriate behavior. But the relation of self to ego-processes is no more and no less obscure than the relation of cognitive structures to behavior generally.

"Ego-Involvements" and "Ego-Defense"

We have sought to reinstate the ego as a subjective but non-phenomenal construct mainly through an examination of the pitfalls encountered by the attempt to avoid such a concept. If the ego-self distinction as outlined above is worth making, however, it should make a difference in the formulation of other knotty problems. Does it? Two such problems—the nature of "ego-involvements" and of the "mechanisms of defense" will be examined briefly as test cases.

As it emerges in the work of Sherif and Cantril (10), the concept of ego-involvement lacks clarity and focus. Widely divergent sorts of psychological facts turn out to be embraced by the term, which like so many in popular psychological currency rather identifies a disparate group of problems than clarifies them. More often than not, ego-involvement means the involvement of a person's pride and self-esteem in a task; he feels put to the test and ready to be ashamed of a poor performance. In other

[2] How to distinguish within the personality between *ego* and *non-ego* is, of course, an important problem, though it will not be attempted here. The distinction, however, is not the same as the phenomenal one between the *self* and *not-self* (often described, confusingly, as *ego-alien*).

instances, the term is invoked to cover immersion in a cause, or falling in love—cases in which the person, to be sure, cares as deeply about outcomes as in the first type, but may be engrossed to the point of losing self-awareness.

Now the present self-ego distinction makes excellent sense when applied here. Since the distinctive character of the first sort of examples lies in the fact that the individual's conception of his self and its worth is at stake, these can aptly be described as *self-involvement*. The second type of case can often still be called ego-involvement without inconsistency. The situation in the latter instances touches on the person's central system of on-going psychological processes so closely that he may lose himself in it. Similar engrossment can, to be sure, result from the involvement of equally imperative non-ego processes: who is to say, without intimate acquaintance with the principals, whether being in love should be called ego-involvement or "id-involvement"! However that may be, note that self-involvement and ego-involvement thus conceived may vary independently. A person may care about a task both because of its intrinsic meaning for him and with afterthought for its bearing on his prestige and self-esteem. Or either or neither may be the case. The behavioral conditions and consequences of ego- and self-involvement should furthermore be quite distinct.

The situation is somewhat different in regard to the theoretical status of the mechanisms of defense. Here the classical formulation by Anna Freud (4) regards the defense mechanisms as employed by the ego (the term is used essentially in our sense) to protect itself, primarily from disruption by strong unassimilated urges, but also from threats from the external world. As a more or less precariously balanced system mediating between inner strivings and outer reality, the ego, in this view, has recourse to these sometimes drastic techniques in order to preserve its balance and maintain the course of behavior at a lower level of adjustment if need be rather than run the risk of its catastrophic disruption. Murphy (8), and later Snygg and Combs (11), on the other hand, say in effect that it is rather the self that is defended. Under conditions of threat, enhancement and preservation of the self may be achieved by the classical defense mechanisms. Is it necessary to choose between these divergent formulations, or can the conflict be resolved?

The present writer would maintain that the mechanisms of defense can ultimately all be conceived as defenses of the ego, since they serve to bolster up the ego's adjustive compromise. As contributors to this compromise, they can also best be regarded as a part of the activity included in the ego system. But in a more immediate sense, any particular one of an individual's defenses may or may *not* be a *self*-defense mechanism. Since the maintenance of a favorable self-image is important to sound ego functioning, though not its only requisite, the end of ego defense can often be served most efficiently by self-defense mechanisms. Certain mechanisms, like identification, may, indeed, always take effect through the defense of the self. There are, however, instances of ego-defense mechanisms which involve the self only indirectly, if at all. In regression, for example, one can hardly suppose that the self is enhanced in any way. What is more likely is that by retreating to an earlier, more deeply established, or simpler level of ego organization, the person seeks, perhaps ineptly, to cope with disturbing experiences that, by reason of circumstance, constitution, or previous learning, he has not the strength to meet maturely. In most cases, the relative significance of the self in the defensive process probably cannot be assessed in any simple way, since changes in the self for better or worse may be the *consequence* of the fortunes of the ego and its defenses, as well as the focus of defensive techniques.

A formulation of this sort, which seems to agree with present clinical experience, again suggests the usefulness of a distinction between phenomenal and nonphenomenal (shall we say *functional*?) subjective constructs, with both employed in proper coordination. A purely phenomenological psychology, on the other hand, cannot adequately describe *all* the defensive processes, since neither all the effective threats to the ego nor all the defenses against them are registered accurately in conscious awareness. Indeed, it is largely the consequence of "silent" defensive processes that phenomenological reports must be viewed with so much circumspection in personality research.

Conclusions

Starting from a discussion of Snygg and Combs' proposal of a phenomenological frame of reference for psychology (11), the writer has sought to establish the following major points:

1. While common sense may favor an explanatory psychology framed entirely in terms of conscious experience, such a psychological system does violence to currently available knowledge.

2. Phenomenology, as distinct from common sense, is descriptive, not explanatory. It is an approach or method ancillary to the formulation of problems and derivation of constructs, and does not give birth to these constructs full blown.

3. The subjective and objective frames of reference, which denote relatively different alternative contexts within which constructs may be selected, are both entirely compatible with the observer's frame of reference. Subjective constructs to be scientifically admissible must ultimately be anchored in the data of observation.

4. The phenomenological approach provides one method of deriving subjective constructs. But not all subjective constructs need represent phenomenal entities. They may, thus, denote functional entities that are either absent from the phenomenal field or inaccurately presented in it.

5. The coordinate use of phenomenal and nonphenomenal subjective constructs, maintained in clear distinction from one another, serves to clarify the theory of the ego and the self. It is proposed that an adequate theory of personality must distinguish, among other constructs: (a) the *ego,* a *nonphenomenal* subjective construct representing a configuration of on-going processes, among which is the cognitive-perceptual function. Through exercise of this function, the ego "knows," among other things, (b) the *self,* a *phenomenal* subjective construct.

6. When carried into current problems concerning the nature of "ego-involvement" and of the "mechanisms of defense," the above distinction seems productive.

References

1. Allport, G. W., "The Ego in Contemporary Psychology," *Psychological Review,* Vol. 50 (1943), pp. 451-478.
2. Chein, I., "The Awareness of Self and the Structure of the Ego," *Psychological Review,* Vol. 51 (1944), pp. 304-314.
3. Combs, A. W., "A Phenomenological Approach to Adjustment Theory," *Journal of Abnormal Social Psychology,* Vol. 44 (1949), pp. 29-35.
4. Freud, A., *The Ego and the Mechanisms of Defense* (New York: Int. Univ., 1946).
5. Freud, S., *New Introductory Lectures on Psychoanalysis* (New York: Norton, 1933).
6. Lewin, K., *Principles of Topological Psychology* (New York: McGraw, 1936).
7. MacLeod, R. B., "The Phenomenological Approach to Social Psychology," *Psychological Review,* Vol. 54 (1947), pp. 193-210.
8. Murphy, G., *Personality: A Biosocial Approach to Origins and Structure* (New York: Harper, 1947).
9. Rogers, C. R., "Some Observations on the Organization of Personality," *American Psychologist,* Vol. 2 (1947), pp. 358-368.
10. Sherif, M., and H. Cantril, *The Psychology of Ego-Involvement* (New York: Wiley, 1947).
11. Snygg, D., and A. W. Combs, *Individual Behavior* (New York: Harper, 1949).

3. The phenomenological approach and the problem of "unconscious" behavior: a reply to Dr. Smith

Donald Snygg
and Arthur W. Combs

Reprinted from the *Journal of Abnormal and Social Psychology,* Vol. 45 (1950), 523-528, by permission of the authors and the American Psychological Association.

The authors adroitly lock horns with Smith as they come back with a fine tactical argument to support their contention that it is one's "conscious" rather than his "unconscious" motives which determine behavior. The reader will want to reread Stoodley's article in Part I for a complete discussion of the relationships between the conscious and unconscious.

We are grateful for this opportunity to comment on Dr. Smith's paper (4) and to clarify some aspects of our own position which we do not seem to have made completely clear in *Individual Behavior* (5). As we see it, Dr. Smith's major criticisms are based on the contention that many factors in behavior are unconscious and are never part of the behaver's phenomenal field. Since we seem to have skipped over this extremely important question rather rapidly in our earlier publications, we are glad to have this chance to explain why we do not accept this assumption, which is so widely held that it has almost come to be "common sense."

Is Behavior Ever "Unconscious"?

It seems to us that two somewhat different types of behavior have been generally ascribed to "unconscious" motives. One is the kind we described in the passage Dr. Smith has quoted (4): "the vague and fuzzy aspects of behavior (which) correspond to and are parts of the vague and incompletely differentiated aspects of the field" (5). This kind of behavior includes the postural shifts of which we are only very vaguely aware and the expressive behavior which Maslow (3) has described as being without a definite goal, "unconscious or at least not fully conscious," and correlated with "deep-lying character structure," *i.e.* (our phraseology) with the total field rather than its differentiated parts. Dr. Smith does not seem to challenge our explanation of this type of behavior.

He does point out, however, that behavior which is much more precise and conscious is also ascribed to unconscious factors. "The clinical literature abounds with instances of unconsciously determined behavior which far from being 'vague and fuzzy,' is, on the contrary, highly differentiated" (4). It is our contention that the assumption that such behavior is determined by unconscious factors is not an inevitable one and that it results from the selection of an inadequate causal field.

Does an individual ever behave with precision toward a goal he does not perceive? Or does he ever show highly differentiated behavior for reasons of which he is not aware?

It seems to us that the answers that a psychologist makes to these questions will depend on how far back in time he goes in his search for the alleged cause of the behavior. If he traces the causal chain back to a point where it is outside the behaver's present perceptual field and then designates one of these forgotten events as *the* cause, then this cause has to be called unconscious. Freudian psychology, in taking the whole life span as a single causal field, has to come to this conclusion. This is a perfectly reasonable and valid observation, provided only that one understands that this observation is made from the frame of reference of the observer and *not the behaver*.

But there is no reason why the psychologist, in looking for the immediate causes of behavior, needs to go back to find an historical cause outside of the present perceptual field. If he is attempting to predict behavior with precision, it is better if he does not.

Certainly, the events of an individual's life affect his behavior. But it is important for us to recognize that it is the perceptions of these events and not the physical events themselves which are the *immediate* causes of behavior. Thus an individual's behavior today may be highly precise and direct because his perceptions are precise, although the reason for having that perception in the first place may no longer exist in his perceptual field at all. A psychologist, knowing of the earlier event, and perceiving that event as *the* cause of the individual's present behavior, concludes that the person is behaving for a reason of which he is not aware, *i.e.,* of which he is unconscious. But this is only the inference of an external observer; and it is made only when the subject's behavior seems out of harmony with the situation as the observer sees it. The subject himself does not see his behavior in this way at all.

For example, a young man had a severe phobia for flying birds. A sparrow alighting on his window sill would throw him into such a panic that he would attempt to retreat by any available means. In his perceptual field a bird was an extraordinarily threatening object. What is more, his perceptions were highly differentiated and his behavior extremely precise. Now his objective psychologist, knowing that he had been most insecure as a child and knowing that his nurse had been accustomed to control him by threats of feeding to "the wild geese in the attic" sees these events as the causes of his present behavior. Indeed, the young man himself may, at other times, ascribe his present behavior to those events because in describing his behavior he is making an external observation, just as the psychologist does. *At the instant of his panic,* however, he is not behaving in terms of unconscious causes but in terms of sharply differentiated present perceptions that birds are vicious, dangerous, and immediate threats to himself. Thus it appears that behavior described from an external point of view as unconscious, from a phenomenological point of view is not unconscious at all but, on the contrary, may be very highly "conscious."

We believe that this explains the inadequacy of mere explanations as a means of therapy. Clients say, "I can see the reasons why I feel this way, but it doesn't seem to help. I still feel this way." It is the present feelings that determine the behavior. If forgotten attitudes and events have an effect on behavior, it is through the transformation they have brought about in the genesis of the present field and the effects they have thus had on its organization. The explanation of maladjustment as a function of trauma in the genetic history of the individual is so well established in psychology as to be unquestioned. It is necessary for us to remind ourselves, however, that this understanding is the psychologist's, *not* the behaver's. This principle, it seems to us, is extraordinarily important for applied psychology. It is conceivable that the applied psychologist acting in terms of his externally conceived analysis of an individual's problem may completely misfire or, even worse, complicate his client's problem by the intrusion of irrelevant data.[1] We wish to reiterate our postulate that "All

[1] This seems to us a most important principle, particularly with respect to its application in psychotherapy. If present perceptions govern behavior, psychotherapy must concern itself with present perceptions rather than genetic understandings. It is the understanding and implementation of this point which probably represents the most important single difference between client-centered therapy and traditional psychoanalysis.

behavior is determined by (and pertinent to) the phenomenological field at the moment of action" (5, p. 45).

It seems to us that Professor Smith's basic objection may be due to our failure to underline the important words in the definition of the phenomenal field which he has quoted. These words are "at the instant of action." This is important because it is only at this instant that all of the convergent lines of causation come together.[2] And they come together in the perceptual field, of which the perceived behavior is a part. At that instant the behaver cannot behave in a way inappropriate to the field, because at that instant the field in a way seems to him to be reality, and acts which are inappropriate to it would be self-sabotage.

The arguments against our postulate are based upon a field with a longer time span than the one we have used. We have postulated a one-to-one relationship between the field and the behavior which is part of it, *i.e.*, between the field and behavior at time *x*. If we tried to relate the field at an earlier time, *x-y,* with the behavior at time *x,* we would, of course, expect to find no such one-to-one relation. As of that moment some of the causal factors which will play a part in determining the nature of the phenomenal field at time *x* have not yet impinged upon the field, so the phenomenal field at time *x-y* is not, by itself, adequate for the prediction of behavior at time *x* and, since all predictions of behavior have to be made before the event, *i.e.,* at time *x-y,* this may lead to the erroneous conclusion that causes may operate without ever entering the perceptual field.

An observer at 11:53 watching a tavern loafer give a dozing customer the hot foot may assume that when the practical joker lights the match he is seeing a cause of behavior which is not part of the behaver's perceptual field. In this regard we should like to make two points: (a) The joker and his match are not acting as a cause of the customer's behavior at 11:53. (b) Whether they will affect his behavior at a future time is still uncertain. The match will not affect the potential victim's behavior unless he perceives it or its effects. If he is dead drunk or wearing an artificial foot, it will burn down to his shoe and go out without having any effect on his behavior.

We are making so much of this point because if our analysis is correct, the psychologist has an important new technique for the prediction of behavior. No one has ever had any trouble explaining behavior after it has occurred, because in any situation there is an almost infinite number of

[2] As Lewin points out (2) "the behaver's field at any given instant contains also the views of that individual about his future and past. . . . The psychological past and the psychological future are simultaneous parts of the psychological field existing at a given time. . . ."

factors which *might* have an effect on behavior. It is easy to look back *after* the behavior has occurred and construct a plausible theory about which of these might have been operating. There are so many possibilities that there can be a great many different theories, all plausible. But the prediction of behavior in advance is much more risky because predictions can be checked. And the large number of potential causal factors which make explanation after the event so easy make prediction very difficult. There are too many possibilities. The psychologist, if he is to predict with any accuracy at all, must have some principle by which he can select, from the countless potential factors physically present [3] those which will actually become determinants of the subject's behavior. If we are right in postulating that such "physical" factors can only become operative by way of the behaver's phenomenal field, we have a principle capable of narrowing the behavioral possibilities to a marked degree. When we can follow this up with a reconstruction of the behaver's field at time *x-y* and a knowledge of the field dynamics which will enable us to predict how the factors which are at that time "external" will effect that field and be transformed in it, we shall have the basis for a genuinely predictive science of psychology. In our opinion that time has already arrived.

Step by step the process of prediction from this point of view is as follows:

1. Inference of the behaver's present field from his behavior.
2. Projection of the future field, taking into consideration the factors perceived by the observer which, on the basis of the behaver's present inferred field, will affect his future field.[4]
3. From the inferred future field the future behavior is predicted.
4. Since the approach assumes a one-to-one relation between the phenomenal field and the concurrent behavior, the accuracy of the inferences can be checked. This gives the psychologist using the approach a method of successive approximation by which each reconstruction of the subject's field becomes more accurate, leading to equally accurate predictions of his behavior.

We do not feel that this approach, particularly as used in step 2, is just "common sense." It is certainly subjective and, because the inferences are made in terms of the behaver's perceptual field, we have called it phenomenological.

---

[3] Or, more accurately, from the factors in the situation which he is able to observe.

[4] Most of the theoretical constructs and principles presented in *Individual Behavior* describe the processes by which these potential causes of behavior are rejected or admitted and modified.

The Perceiver in a Phenomenological System

This brings us to the perceiving ego which Dr. Smith has, somewhat to our surprise, found hidden in at least one of our remarks. We have used the term self to mean something else, at times, than the phenomenal self; and we will try to be more careful in the future. But we still have some reservations about Dr. Smith's formalization of the concept which we carelessly introduced.

It is quite logical to infer that if there is organization there may be an organizer and that if there are perceptions there must be a perceiver. We have at times made such an inference, as Dr. Smith points out. But we do not need to make it. It is not a necessary or even helpful part of our system. But it is a necessary part of Dr. Smith's, which is why he has to be insistent about it. As a construct it has the grave (but not fatal) defect that inferences about it are very difficult to check, and the fact that he has to resort to such a concept serves to illustrate the difficulties we can get into when we fail to define the time limits of our causal field. When events which were part of the field at time *x* are lumped together with events which were part of the field at times *x-y* and *x-z,* the organization of the field is lost. Objects and events in the phenomenal field derive their meaning from the field at that instant. Out of that context they will have different meanings, like food before and after a heavy dinner. An incident which would be traumatic in one phenomenal situation can be highly gratifying in another and be barely perceived in a third. If events and objects from different phases of the same developing field are treated as if they were independent, stable entities operating in a single field, an accurate reconstruction of their true field relations becomes impossible. The task of a psychologist attempting to predict behavior from such data is as difficult as would be the task of a person who was given a thousand words cut individually from a book and scrambled and then asked to predict what would happen in the next chapter.

The common-sense way of explaining organized behavior which seems to emerge from such an unorganized field is to endow the unorganized field with a hidden organizer. The six-year-old daughter of one of the writers did it the other day.

"Why did you do that, Frances?" she was asked.

"Oh, my brain told me to do it."

"Well, why did your brain tell you to do it?"

"Oh, (with a giggle) I guess its brain told it to do it."

Such explanatory constructs are fairly common in psychology, but they have never been very fruitful. Dr. Smith's ego is a much more sophisticated construct than the "brain's brain," but they are both second-order constructs set up to explain the first-order constructs which are set up to explain the observed behavior. In effect they are attempts to explain a mystery by a greater mystery.

In our own approach this assumption of a hidden organizer is, as we have said, neither necessary nor helpful. When organization is found, it does not need to be explained in order to be used in prediction. It only needs to be described. The essential characteristic of any organized field is its tendency to maintain its organization in the face of intruding forces. Since the phenomenal field, at any given instant, is organized, the behavior of its parts can be predicted from knowledge of the field itself, without knowing why the field is organized. Our procedure is analogous to that of a meteorologist predicting the weather over a given area. Considering his map as the representation of a dynamic field, he predicts the future states of the field, taking into account the probable transformation and effect of forces coming up over the edge of the map from the outside. It is not necessary to postulate a nonobservable selective agency to determine the effect of these forces on the meteorological field. The meteorologist's analysis of the field itself, at the time of their entrance, provides all the information that is necessary.

It is quite reasonable for Dr. Smith to explain the individual organization of a behavioral field by postulating an hypothetical construct to do the organizing. But since our causal field is already organized, we do not need to use such a concept. At the present time it seems much safer to make as few constructs as possible and base our predictions on the dynamics of the phenomenal field itself.

In these terms our definition of the basic human need as "the maintenance and enhancement of the phenomenal self" (5) is a little too limited and we may have to return to the earlier position that "the fundamental need . . . [is] the preservation of the organization and integrity of the [phenomenal] field and especially of that part of the field which is the phenomenal self" [5] (6, p. 412). This is wordier and harder to apply at once but somewhat more accurate.

---

[5] Our reasons for believing that, in a phenomenal field which includes a phenomenal future, maintenance of the self also requires its enhancement are given in *Individual Behavior*. We wish we could find a better term than self-enhancement. It does not carry the full weight of meaning since to many people it carries the connotation of purely selfish behavior. It can also imply a growing extension of the self into the rest of the phenomenal field and a decrease in the feeling of conflict with it. Consequently, the greater the self-enhancement the less will be the chances that another person will interpret the individual's behavior as selfish. The maximum degree of self-enhancement, as we see it, would be achieved by the individual who feels at one with the universe, so completely a part of the universe that he does not need to defend himself against any other part.

In returning to the earlier formulation, which states more explicitly the function of the whole phenomenal field, we are accepting Dr. Smith's point that regression cannot, without forcing, be considered a mechanism for defense of the phenomenal self. Some of the devices that are sometimes called regression can, for example the bed-wetting of the three-year-old in a home where there is a new baby. But others cannot. As we see it, "regression," like all of the Freudian devices, is a manifestation of the organized nature of the phenomenal field. Since it is not a closed field, its organization is always in a state of fluidity, moving toward adjustment. In some cases the attack from the outside is so violent that organization can be maintained only by consolidation at a lower (but not necessarily earlier) level, *i.e.,* by "regression," or by abandoning part of the field, *i.e.,* by "dissociation." The so-called "self"-protective mechanisms like rationalization and identification may occur where the attack on the field is less severe. In these cases the reorganization required is less and can take place without much effect on the phenomenal self, which acts as a point of reference for the rest of the field and is consequently very resistant to change.

As a matter of fact, all objects and events in the phenomenal field have such a high degree of relation to the self that the statement that the basic need is for the maintenance and enhancement of the phenomenal self is a very close approximation of the actual situation and conveys much more to the reader than the longer and more careful statement. Certainly, if we are to see the behaver's field as he does himself, we must stress the central position and active behavior of the phenomenal self.

Taking up some of the minor points made by Professor Smith, we used "phenomenal field" and "perceptual field" instead of "consciousness" not as a "bow to current prejudice," (4) but in an attempt to make clear the fact that our concept took cognizance of the organized nature of the field and of the ground characteristics which have to be derived by inference rather than by direct report.

We have never been under the illusion that a subject could give an accurate report of his phenomenal field. Our reasons are to be found on pages 35-36 of *Individual Behavior* and in a symposium paper (1).

In general we think that Dr. Smith's position is well thought out and very similar to the one we would have to take if we started from the same premises. He will be neither disappointed nor surprised at our failure to agree with him at all points. Whether we look at it in terms of his need for ego-enhancement or in terms of our general concept of persisting organization of the perceptual field or our specific concept of maintenance of the phenomenal self, it would have been predicted by all of us that our point of view would change just enough to maintain our concepts of ourselves as responsible scientists, and no more. We shall accordingly not hold it against Dr. Smith if, after reading this, he still fails to agree with us. We are grateful for the stimulation to our own thinking his presentation has afforded us.

References

1. Coombs, A. W., and D. Snygg, "Implications of the Phenomenological Approach for the Evaluation of Psychotherapy," *Psychological Services Center Journal,* Vol. 2 (1950), pp. 96-103.
2. Lewin, K., "Defining the Field at a Given Time," *Psychological Review,* Vol. 50 (1943), pp. 292-310.
3. Maslow, A. H., "The Expressive Component of Behavior," *Psychological Review,* Vol. 56 (1949), pp. 261-272.
4. Smith, M. B., "The Phenomenological Approach in Personality Theory: Some Critical Remarks," *Journal of Abnormal Social Psychology,* Vol. 45 (1950), pp. 516-522.
5. Snygg, D., and A. W. Combs, *Individual Behavior* (New York: Harper, 1949).
6. Snygg, D., "The Need for a Phenomenological System of Psychology," *Psychological Review,* Vol. 48 (1941), pp. 404-424.

4. Existential psychology —what's in it for us?

A. H. Maslow

Self-psychology has more than a passing relationship to existential ideas and movements. European existentialists notwithstanding, Maslow carefully details how self-psychology can be bolstered with the underlying existential philosophy that it now lacks.

I am not an existentialist, nor am I even a careful and thorough student of this movement. There is much in the existentialist writings that I find extremely difficult, or even impossible, to understand and that I have not made much effort to struggle with.

I must confess also that I have studied existentialism not so much for its own sake as in the spirit of, "What's in it for me as a psychologist?" trying all the time to translate it into terms I could use. Perhaps this is why I have found it to be not so much a totally new revelation as a stressing, confirming, sharpening, and rediscovering of trends already existing in American psychology (the various self psychologies, growth psychologies, self-actualization psychologies, organismic psychologies, certain neo-Freudian psychologies, the Jungian psychology, not to mention some of the psychoanalytic ego psychologists, the Gestalt therapists, and I don't know how many more).

For this and other reasons, reading the existentialists has been for me a very interesting, gratifying, and instructive experience. And I think this will also be true for many other psychologists, especially those who are interested in personality theory and in clinical psychology. It has enriched, enlarged, corrected, and strengthened my thinking about the human personality, even though it has not necessitated any fundamental reconstruction.

First of all, permit me to define existentialism in a personal way, in terms of "what's in it for me." To me it means essentially a radical stress on the concept of identity and the experience of identity as a *sine qua non* of human nature and of any philosophy or science of human nature. I choose this concept as *the* basic one partly because I understand it better than terms like essence, existence, and ontology and partly because I also feel that it can be worked with empirically, if not now, then soon.

But then a paradox results, for the Americans have *also* been impressed with the quest for identity (Allport, Rogers, Goldstein, Fromm, Wheelis, Erikson, Horney, May, *et al.*). And I must say that these writers are a lot clearer and a lot closer to raw fact, that is, more empirical than are, *e.g.,* the Germans, Heidegger and Jaspers.

(1) Conclusion number one is, then, that the Europeans and Americans are not so far apart as appears at first. We Americans have been "talking prose all the time and didn't know it." Partly, of course, this simultaneous development in different countries is itself an indication that the people who have independently been coming to the same conclusions are all responding to something real outside themselves.

(2) This something real is, I believe, the total collapse of all sources of values outside the individual. Many European existentialists are largely reacting to Nietzsche's conclusion that God is dead and perhaps to the fact that Marx also is dead. The Americans have learned that political democracy and economic prosperity do not in themselves solve any of the basic value problems. There is no place else to turn but inward, to the self, as the locus of values. Paradoxically, even some of the religious existentialists will go along with this conclusion part of the way.

(3) It is extremely important for psychologists that the existentialists may supply psychology with the underlying philosophy that it now lacks. Logical positivism has been a failure, especially for clinical and personality psychologists. At any rate, the basic philosophical problems will surely be opened up for discussion again, and perhaps psychologists will stop relying on pseudosolutions or on unconscious, unexamined philosophies that they picked up as children.

(4) An alternative phrasing of the core (for us Americans) of European existentialism is that it deals radically with that human predicament presented by the gap between human aspirations and human limitations

(between what the human being *is,* what he would *like* to be, and what he *could* be). This is not so far off from the identity problem as it might at first sound. A person is both actuality *and* potentiality.

That serious concern with this discrepancy could revolutionize psychology, there is no doubt in my mind. Various literatures already support such a conclusion, *e.g.,* projective testing, self-actualization, the various peak experiences (in which this gap is bridged), the Jungian psychologies, various theological thinkers.

Not only this, but they raise also the problems and techniques of integration of this twofold nature of man, his lower and his higher, his creatureliness and his Godlikeness. On the whole, most philosophies and religions, Eastern as well as Western, have dichotomized them, teaching that the way to become "higher" is to renounce and master "the lower." The existentialists, however, teach that *both* are simultaneously defining characteristics of human nature. Neither can be repudiated; they can only be integrated. But we already know something of these integration techniques —of insight, of intellect in the broader sense, of love, of creativeness, of humor and tragedy, of play, of art. I suspect we will focus our studies on these integrative techniques more than we have in the past. Another consequence for my thinking of this stress on the twofold nature of man is the realization that some problems must remain eternally insoluble.

(5) From this flows naturally a concern with the ideal, authentic, or perfect, or Godlike human being, a study of human potentialities as *now* existing in a certain sense, as *current* knowable reality. This, too, may sound merely literary, but it is not. I remind you that this is just a fancy way of asking the old, unanswered questions, "What are the goals of therapy, of education, of bringing up children?"

It also implies another truth and another problem that calls urgently for attention. Practically every serious description of the "authentic person" extant implies that such a person, by virtue of what he has become, assumes a new relation to his society and, indeed, to society in general. He not only transcends himself in various ways; he also transcends his culture. He resists enculturation. He becomes more detached from his culture and from his society. He becomes a little more a member of his species and a little less a member of his local group. My feeling is that most sociologists and anthropologists will take this hard. I therefore confidently expect controversy in this area.

(6) From the European writers, we can and should pick up their greater emphasis on what they call "philosophical anthropology," that is, the attempt to define man, and the differences between man and any other species, between man and objects, and between man and robots. What are his unique and defining characteristics? What is as essential to man that without it he would no longer be defined as a man?

On the whole, this is a task from which American psychology has abdicated. The various behaviorisms do not generate any such definition, at least none that can be taken seriously. (What would an S-R man be like?) Freud's picture of man was clearly unsuitable, leaving out as it did his aspirations, his realizable hopes, his Godlike qualities. The fact that he supplied us with our most comprehensive systems of psychopathology and psychotherapy is beside the point, as the contemporary ego psychologists are finding out.

(7) The Europeans are stressing the self-making of the self, in a way that the Americans do not. Both the Freudians and the self-actualization and growth theorists in this country talk more about discovering the *self* (as if it were there waiting to be found) and of *uncovering* therapy (shovel away the top layers and you will see what has been always lying there, hidden). To say, however, that the self is a project and is *altogether* created by the continual choices of the person himself is almost surely an overstatement in view of what we know of, *e.g.,* the constitutional and genetic determinants of personality. This clash of opinion is a problem that can be settled empirically.

(8) A problem we psychologists have been ducking is the problem of responsibility and, necessarily tied in with it, the concepts of courage and of will in the personality. Perhaps this is close to what the psychoanalysts are now calling "ego strength."

(9) American psychologists have listened to Allport's call for an idiographic psychology but have not done much about it. Not even the clinical psychologists have. We now have an added push from the phenomenologists and existentialists in this direction, one that will be *very* hard to resist, indeed, I think, theoretically *impossible* to resist. If the study of the uniqueness of the individual does not fit into what we know of science, then so much the worse for the conception of science. It, too, will have to endure re-creation.

(10) Phenomenology has a history in American psychological thinking, but on the whole I think it has languished. The European phenomenologists, with their excruciatingly careful and laborious demonstrations, can reteach us that the best way of understanding another human being, or at least *a* way necessary for some purposes, is to get into *his Weltanschauung* and to be able to see *his* world through *his* eyes. Of course such a conclusion is rough on any positivistic philosophy of science.

(11) The existentialist stress on the ultimate aloneness of the individual is a useful reminder for us not only to work out further the concepts of decision, of responsibility, of choice, of self-creation, of autonomy, of identity itself. It also makes more problematic and more fascinating the mystery of communication between alonenesses via, *e.g.,* intuition and empathy, love and altruism, identification with others, and homonomy in

general. We take these for granted. It would be better if we regarded them as miracles to be explained.

(12) Another preoccupation of existentialist writers can be phrased very simply, I think. It is the dimension of seriousness and profundity of living (or perhaps the "tragic sense of life") contrasted with the shallow and superficial life, which is a kind of diminished living, a defense against the ultimate problems of life. This is not just a literary concept. It has real operational meaning, for instance, in psychotherapy. I (and others) have been increasingly impressed with the fact that tragedy can sometimes be therapeutic and that therapy often seems to work best when people are *driven* into it by pain. It is when the shallow life does not work that it is questioned and that there occurs a call to fundamentals. Shallowness in psychology does not work either, as the existentialists are demonstrating very clearly.

(13) The existentialists, along with many other groups, are helping to teach us about the limits of verbal, analytic, conceptual rationality. They are part of the current call back to raw experience as prior to any concepts or abstractions. This amounts to what I believe to be a justified critique of the whole way of thinking of the Western world in the twentieth century, including orthodox positivistic science and philosophy, both of which badly need re-examination.

(14) Possibly most important of all the changes to be wrought by phenomenologists and existentialists is an overdue revolution in the theory of science. I should not say "wrought by," but rather "helped along by," because there are many other forces helping to destroy the official philosophy of science or "scientism." It is not only the Cartesian split between subject and object that needs to be overcome. There are other radical changes made necessary by the inclusion of the psyche and of raw experience in reality, and such a change will affect not only the science of psychology but all other sciences as well. For example, parsimony, simplicity, precision, orderliness, logic, elegance, definition are all of the realm of abstraction.

(15) I close with the stimulus that has most powerfully affected me in the existentialist literature, namely, the problem of future time in psychology. Not that this, like all the other problems or pushes I have mentioned up to this point, was totally unfamiliar to me, nor, I imagine, to *any* serious student of the theory of personality. The writings of Charlotte Buhler, of Gordon Allport, and of Kurt Goldstein should also have sensitized us to the necessity of grappling with and systematizing the dynamic role of the future in the presently existing personality, *e.g.*, growth and becoming and possibility necessarily point toward the future, as do the concepts of potentiality and hoping and of wishing and imagining; reduction to the concrete is a loss of future; threat and apprehension point to the future (no future = no neurosis); self-actualization is meaningless without reference to a currently active future; life can be a gestalt in time, *etc., etc.*

And yet the *basic and central* importance of this problem for the existentialists has something to teach us, *e.g.,* Erwin Strauss's paper in *Existence* (1). I think it fair to say that no theory of psychology will ever be complete that does not centrally incorporate the concept that man has his future within him, dynamically active at this present moment. In this sense, the future can be treated as ahistorical in Kurt Lewin's sense. Also we must realize that *only* the future is *in principle* unknown and unknowable, which means that all habits, defenses, and coping mechanisms are doubtful and ambiguous because they are based on past experience. Only the flexibly creative person can really manage future, *only* the one who can face novelty with confidence and without fear. I am convinced that much of what we now call psychology is the study of the tricks we use to avoid the anxiety of absolute novelty by making believe the future will be like the past.

I have tried to say that every European stress has its American equivalent. I do not think that this has been clear enough. I have recommended to Rollo May a companion American volume to the one he has already turned out. And of course most of all this represents my hope that we are witnessing an expansion of psychology, not a new "ism" that could turn into an antipsychology or into an antiscience.

It is possible that existentialism will not only enrich psychology. It may also be an additional push toward the establishment of another *branch* of psychology, the psychology of the fully evolved and authentic self and its ways of being. Sutich has suggested calling this ontopsychology.

Certainly it seems more and more clear that what we call "normal" in psychology is really a psychopathology of the average, so undramatic and so widely spread that we do not even notice it ordinarily. The existentialist's study of the authentic person and of authentic living helps to throw this general phoniness, this living by illusions and by fear, into a harsh, clear light which reveals it clearly as sickness, even though widely shared.

I do not think we need take too seriously the European existentialists' harping on dread, on anguish, on despair, and the like, for which their only remedy seems to be to keep a stiff upper lip. This high-I.Q. whimpering on a cosmic scale occurs whenever an external source of values fails to work. They should have learned from the psychotherapists that the loss of illusions and the discovery of identity, though painful at first, can be ultimately exhilarating and strengthening.

Reference

1. May, R., E. Angel, and H. F. Ellenberger, eds., *Existence: A New Dimension in Psychiatry and Psychology* (New York: Basic Books, 1953).

5. Some issues concerning the control of human behavior

Carl R. Rogers
and B. F. Skinner

Reprinted from *Science,* Vol. 124 (30 November 1956), 1057-1066, by permission of the authors and the American Association for the Advancement of Science.

There are powerful psychological and *philosophical overtones in this article. Rogers and Skinner are in agreement that science holds tremendous potential power for the prediction and control of behavior, but they are at odds about who the controlled will be and who will do the controlling. Both see their own position as enhancing the lot, the welfare, indeed, the "self" of man. What is your stand?*

I [Skinner]

Science is readily increasing our power to influence, change, mold—in a word, control—human behavior. It has extended our "understanding" (whatever that may be) so that we deal more successfully with people in nonscientific ways, but it has also identified conditions or variables which can be used to predict and control behavior in a new, and increasingly rigorous, technology. The broad disciplines of government and economics offer examples of this, but there is special cogency in those contributions of anthropology, sociology, and psychology which deal with individual behavior. Carl Rogers has listed some of the achievements to date in a recent paper (14). Those of his examples which show or imply the control of the single organism are primarily due, as we should expect, to psychology. It is the experimental study of behavior which carries us beyond awkward or inaccessible "principles," "factors," and so on, to variables which are able to be directly manipulated.

It is also, and for more or less the same reasons, the conception of human behavior emerging from an experimental analysis which most directly challenges traditional views. Psychologists themselves often do not seem to be aware of how far they have moved in this direction. But the change is not passing unnoticed by others. Until only recently it was customary to deny the possibility of a rigorous science of human behavior by arguing, either that a lawful science was impossible because man was a free agent, or that merely statistical predictions would always leave room for personal freedom. But those who used to take this line have become most vociferous in expressing their alarm at the way these obstacles are being surmounted.

Now, the control of human behavior has always been unpopular. Any undisguised effort to control usually arouses emotional reactions. We hesitate to admit, even to ourselves, that we are engaged in control, and we may refuse to control, even when this would be helpful, for fear of criticism. Those who have explicitly avowed an interest in control have been roughly treated by history. Machiavelli is the great prototype. As Macaulay said of him, "Out of his surname they coined an epithet for a knave and out of his Christian name a synonym for the devil." There were obvious reasons. The control that Machiavelli analyzed and recommended, like most political control, used techniques that were aversive to the controllee. The threats and punishments of the bully, like those of the government operating on the same plan, are not designed—whatever their success—to endear themselves to those who are controlled. Even when the techniques themselves are not aversive, control is usually exercised for the selfish purposes of the controller and, hence, has indirectly punishing effects upon others.

Man's natural inclination to revolt against selfish control has been exploited to good purpose in what we call the philosophy and literature of democracy. The doctrine of the rights of man has been effective in arousing individuals to concerted action against governmental and religious tyranny. The literature which has had this effect has greatly extended the number of terms in our language which express reactions to the control of men. But the ubiquity and ease of expression of this attitude spells trouble for any science which may give birth to a powerful technology of behavior. Intelligent men and women, dominated by the humanistic philosophy of the past two centuries, cannot view with equanimity what Andrew Hacker has called "the specter of predictable man" (3). Even the statistical or actuarial prediction of human events, such as the number of fatalities to be expected on a holiday weekend, strikes many people as uncanny and evil, while the prediction and control of individual behavior is regarded as little less than the work of the devil. I am not so much concerned here with the political or economic consequences for psychology, although research following certain channels may well suffer harmful effects. We ourselves, as intelligent men and women, and as exponents of Western thought, share these attitudes. They have already interfered with the free exercise of a scientific analysis, and their influence threatens to assume more serious proportions.

Three broad areas of human behavior supply good examples. The first of these—*personal control*—may be taken to include person-to-person relationships in the family, among friends, in social and work groups, and in counseling and psychotherapy. Other fields are *education* and *government*. A few examples from each will show how nonscientific preconceptions are affecting our current thinking about human behavior.

Personal control

People living together in groups come to control one another with a technique which is not inappropriately called "ethical." When an individual behaves in a fashion acceptable to the group, he receives admiration, approval, affection, and many other reinforcements which increase the likelihood that he will continue to behave in that fashion. When his behavior is not acceptable, he is criticized, censured, blamed, or otherwise punished. In the first case the group calls him "good"; in the second, "bad." This practice is so thoroughly ingrained in our culture that we often fail to see that it is a technique of control. Yet we are almost always engaged in such control, even though the reinforcements and punishments are often subtle.

The practice of admiration is an important part of a culture, because behavior which is otherwise inclined to be weak can be set up and maintained with its help. The individual is especially likely to be praised, admired, or loved when he acts for the group in the face of great danger, for example, or sacrifices himself or his possessions, or submits to prolonged hardship, or suffers martyrdom. These actions are not admirable in any absolute sense, but they require admiration if they are to be strong. Similarly, we admire people who behave in original or exceptional ways, not because such behavior is itself admirable, but because we do not know how to encourage original or exceptional behavior in any other way. The group acclaims independent, unaided behavior in part because it is easier to reinforce than to help.

As long as this technique of control is misunderstood, we cannot judge correctly an environment in which there is less need for heroism, hardship, or independent action. We are likely to argue that such an environment is itself less admirable or produces less admirable people. In the old days, for example, young scholars often lived in undesirable quarters, ate unappetizing or inadequate food, performed unprofitable tasks for a living or to pay for necessary books and materials or publication. Older scholars and other members of the group offered compensating reinforcement in the form of approval and admiration for these sacrifices. When the modern graduate student receives a generous scholarship, enjoys good living conditions, and has his research and publication subsidized, the grounds for evaluation seem to be pulled from under us. Such a student no longer *needs* admiration to carry him over a series of obstacles (no matter how much he may need it for other reasons), and, in missing certain familiar objects of admiration, we are likely to conclude that such *conditions* are less admirable. Obstacles to scholarly work may serve as a useful measure of motivation—and we may go wrong unless some substitute is found—but we can scarcely defend a deliberate harassment of the student for this purpose. The productivity of any set of conditions can be evaluated only when we have freed ourselves of the attitudes which have been generated in us as members of an ethical group.

A similar difficulty arises from our use of punishment in the form of censure or blame. The concept of responsibility and the related concepts of foreknowledge and choice are used to justify techniques of control using punishment. Was So-and-So aware of the probable consequences of his action, and was the action deliberate? If so, we are justified in punishing him. But what does this mean? It appears to be a question concerning the efficacy of the contingent relations between behavior and punishing consequences. We punish behavior because it is objectionable to us or the group, but in a minor refinement of rather recent origin we have come to withhold punishment when it cannot be expected to have any effect. If the objectionable consequences of an act were accidental and not likely to occur again, there is no point in punishing. We say that the individual was not "aware of the consequences of his action" or that the consequences were not "intentional." If the action could not have been avoided—if the individual "had no choice"—punishment is also withheld, as it is if the individual is incapable of being changed by punishment because he is of "unsound mind." In all these cases—different as they are—the individual is held "not responsible" and goes unpunished.

Just as we say that it is "not fair" to punish a man for something he could not help doing, so we call it "unfair" when one is rewarded beyond his due or for something he could not help doing. In other words, we also object to wasting *reinforcers* where they are not needed or will do no good. We make the same point with the words *just* and *right*. Thus we have no right to punish the irresponsible, and a man has no right to reinforcers he does not earn or deserve. But concepts of choice, responsibility, justice, and so on, provide a most inadequate analysis of efficient reinforcing and punishing contingencies because they carry a heavy semantic cargo of a quite different sort, which obscures any attempt to clarify controlling practices or to improve techniques. In particular, they fail to prepare us for techniques based on other than aversive techniques of control. Most people would object to forcing prisoners to serve as subjects of dangerous medical experiments, but few object when they are induced to serve by the offer of return privileges—even when the reinforcing effect of these privileges has been created by forcible deprivation. In the traditional scheme the right to refuse guarantees the individual against coercion or an unfair bargain. But to what extent *can* a prisoner refuse under such circumstances?

We need not go so far afield to make the point. We can observe our own attitude toward personal freedom in the way we resent any interference with what we want to do. Suppose we want to buy a car of a particular sort. Then we may object, for example, if our wife urges us to buy a less expensive model and to put the difference into a new refrigerator. Or we may resent it if our neighbor questions our need for such a car or our ability to pay for it. We would certainly resent it if it were illegal to buy such a car (remember Prohibition); and if we find we cannot actually afford it, we may resent governmental control of the price through tariffs and taxes. We resent it if we discover that we cannot get the car because the manufacturer is holding the model in deliberately short supply in order to push a model we do not want. In all this we assert our democratic right to buy the car of our choice. We are well prepared to do so and to resent any restriction on our freedom.

But why do we not ask *why* it is the car of our choice and resent the forces which made it so? Perhaps our favorite toy as a child was a car, of a very different model, but nevertheless bearing the name of the car we now want. Perhaps our favorite TV program is sponsored by the manufacturer of that car. Perhaps we have seen pictures of many beautiful or prestigeful persons driving it—in pleasant or glamorous places. Perhaps the car has been designed with respect to our motivational patterns: the device on the hood is a phallic symbol; or the horsepower has been stepped up to please our competitive spirit in enabling us to pass other cars swiftly (or, as the advertisements say, "safely"). The concept of freedom that has emerged as part of the cultural practice of our group makes little or no provision for recognizing or dealing with these kinds of control. Concepts like "responsibility" and "rights" are scarcely applicable. We are prepared to deal with coercive measures, but we have no traditional recourse with respect to other measures which in the long run (and especially with the help of science) may be much more powerful and dangerous.

EDUCATION

The techniques of education were once frankly aversive. The teacher was usually older and stronger than his pupils and was able to "make them learn." This meant that they were not actually taught but were surrounded by a threatening world from which they could escape only by learning. Usually they were left to their own resources in discovering how to do so. Claude Coleman has published a grimly amusing reminder of these older practices (1). He tells of a schoolteacher who published a careful account of his services during 51 years of teaching, during which he administered: ". . . 911,527 blows with a cane; 124,010 with a rod; 20,989 with a ruler; 136,715 with the hand; 10,295 over the mouth; 7,905 boxes on the ear; [and] 1,115,800 slaps on the head. . . ."

Progressive education was a humanitarian effort to substitute positive reinforcement for such aversive measures, but in the search for useful human values in the classroom it has never fully replaced the variables it abandoned. Viewed as a branch of behavioral technology, education remains relatively inefficient. We supplement it, and rationalize it, by admiring the pupil who learns *for himself*; and we often attribute the learning process, or knowledge itself, to something *inside* the individual. We admire behavior which seems to have inner sources. Thus we admire one who *recites* a poem more than one who simply *reads* it. We admire one who *knows* the answer more than one who *knows where to look it up*. We admire the *writer* rather than the *reader*. We admire the arithmetician who can do a problem in his head rather than with a slide rule or calculating machine, or in "original" ways rather than by a strict application of rules. In general we feel that any aid or "crutch"—except those aids to which we are now thoroughly accustomed—reduces the credit due. In Plato's *Phaedus,* Thamus, the king, attacks the invention of the alphabet on similar grounds! He is afraid "it will produce forgetfulness in the minds of those who learn to use it, because they will not practice their memories. . . ." In other words, he holds it more admirable to remember than to use a memorandum. He also objects that pupils "will read many things without instruction . . . [and] will therefore seem to know many things when they are for the most part ignorant." In the same vein we are today sometimes contemptuous of book learning, but, as educators, we can scarcely afford to adopt this view without reservation.

By admiring the student for knowledge and blaming him for ignorance, we escape some of the responsibility of teaching him. We resist any analysis of the educational process which threatens the notion of inner wisdom or questions the contention that the fault of ignorance lies with the student.

More powerful techniques which bring about the same changes in behavior by manipulating *external* variables are decried as brain-washing or thought control. We are quite unprepared to judge *effective* educational measures. As long as only a few pupils learn much of what is taught, we do not worry about uniformity or regimentation. We do not fear the feeble technique; but we should view with dismay a system under which every student learned everything listed in a syllabus—although such a condition is far from unthinkable. Similarly, we do not fear a system which is so defective that the student must *work* for an education; but we are loath to give credit for anything learned without effort—although this could well be taken as an ideal result—and we flatly refuse to give credit if the student already knows what a school teaches.

A world in which people are wise and good without trying, without "having to be," without "choosing to be," could conceivably be a far better world for everyone. In such a world we should not have to "give anyone credit"—we should not need to admire anyone—for being wise and good. From our present point of view we cannot believe that such a world would be admirable. We do not even permit ourselves to imagine what it would be like.

GOVERNMENT

Government has always been the special field of aversive control. The state is frequently defined in terms of the power to punish, and jurisprudence leans heavily upon the associated notion of personal responsibility. Yet it is becoming increasingly difficult to reconcile current practice and theory with these earlier views. In criminology, for example, there is a strong tendency to drop the notion of responsibility in favor of some such alternative as capacity or controllability. But no matter how strongly the facts, or even practical expedience, support such a change, it is difficult to make the change in a legal system designed on a different plan. When governments resort to other techniques (for example, positive reinforcement), the concept of responsibility is no longer relevant and the theory of government is no longer applicable.

The conflict is illustrated by two decisions of the Supreme Court in the 1930's which dealt with, and disagreed on, the definition of control or coercion (2, p. 233). The Agricultural Adjustment Act proposed that the Secretary of Agriculture make "rental or benefit payments" to those farmers who agreed to reduce production. The government agreed that the Act would be unconstitutional if the farmer had been *compelled* to reduce production but was not, since he was merely *invited* to do so. Justice Roberts (2) expressed the contrary majority view of the court that "The power to confer or withhold unlimited benefits is the power to coerce or destroy." This recognition of positive reinforcement was withdrawn a few years later in another case in which Justice Cardozo (2, p. 244) wrote "To hold that motive or temptation is equivalent to coercion is to plunge the law in endless difficulties." We may agree with him, without implying that the proposition is therefore wrong. Sooner or later the law must be prepared to deal with all possible techniques of governmental control.

The uneasiness with which we view government (in the broadest possible sense) when it does not use punishment is shown by the reception of my utopian novel, *Walden Two* (20). This was essentially a proposal to apply a behavioral technology to the construction of a workable, effective, and productive pattern of government. It was greeted with wrathful violence. *Life* magazine called it "a travesty on the good life," and "a menace . . . a triumph of mortmain or the dead hand not envisaged since the days of Sparta . . . a slur upon a name, a corruption of an impulse." Joseph Wood Krutch devoted a substantial part of his book, *The Measure of Man* (5), to attacking my views and those of the protagonist, Frazier, in the same vein, and Morris Viteles has recently criticized the book is a similar manner in *Science* (22). Perhaps the reaction is best expressed in a quotation from *The Quest for Utopia* by Negley and Patrick (7):

"Halfway through this contemporary utopia, the reader may feel sure, as we did, that this is a beautifully ironic satire on what has been called 'behavioral engineering.' The longer one stays in this better world of the psychologist, however, the plainer it becomes that the inspiration is not satiric, but messianic. This is indeed the behaviorally engineered society, and while it was to be expected that sooner or later the principle of psychological conditioning would be made the basis of a serious construction of utopia—Brown anticipated it in *Limanora*—yet not even the effective satire of Huxley is adequate preparation for the shocking horror of the idea when positively presented. Of all the dictatorships espoused by utopists, this is the most profound, and incipient dictators might well find in this utopia a guidebook of political practice."

One would scarcely guess that the authors are talking about a world in which there is food, clothing, and shelter for all, where everyone chooses his own work and works on the average only 4 hours a day, where music and the arts flourish, where personal relationships develop under the most favorable circumstances, where education prepares every child for the social and intellectual life which lies before him, where—in short—people are truly happy, secure, productive, creative, and forward-looking. What is wrong with it? Only one thing: someone "planned it that way." If these critics had come upon a society in some remote corner of the world which boasted similar advantages, they would undoubtedly have hailed it as providing a pattern we all might well follow—provided that it was clearly the result of a natural process of cultural evolution. Any evidence that intelligence had been used in arriving at this version of the good life would, in their eyes, be a serious flaw. No matter if the planner of *Walden Two* diverts none of the proceeds of the community to his own use, no matter if he has no current control or is, indeed, unknown to most of the other members of the community (he planned that, too), somewhere back of it all he occupies the position of prime mover. And this, to the child of the democratic tradition, spoils it all.

The dangers inherent in the control of human behavior are very real. The possibility of the misuse of scientific knowledge must always be faced. We cannot escape by denying the power of a science of behavior or arresting its development. It is no help to cling to familiar philosophies of human behavior simply because they are more reassuring. As I have pointed out elsewhere (19), the new techniques emerging from a science of behavior must be subject to the explicit countercontrol which has already been applied to earlier and cruder forms. Brute force and deception, for example, are now fairly generally suppressed by ethical practices and by explicit governmental and religious agencies. A similar countercontrol of scientific knowledge in the interests of the group is a feasible and promising possibility. Although we cannot say how devious the course of its evolution may be, a cultural pattern of control and countercontrol will presumably emerge which will be most widely supported because it is most widely reinforcing.

If we cannot foresee all the details of this (as we obviously cannot), it is important to remember that this is true of the critics of science as well. The dire consequences of new techniques of control, the hidden menace in original cultural designs—these need some proof. It is only another example of ~~my~~ present point that the need for proof is so often overlooked. Man has got himself into some pretty fixes, and it is easy to believe that he will do so again. But there is a more optimistic possibility. The slow growth of the methods of science, now for the first time being applied to human affairs, *may* mean a new and exciting phase of human life to which historical analogies will not apply and in which earlier political slogans will not be appropriate. If we are to use the knowledge that a science of behavior is now making available with any hope of success, we must look at human nature as it is brought into focus through the methods of science rather than as it has been presented to us in a series of historical accidents.

If the advent of a powerful science of behavior causes trouble, it will not be because science itself is inimical to human welfare but because older conceptions have not yielded easily or gracefully. We expect resistance to new techniques of control from those who have heavy investments in the old, but we have no reason to help them preserve a series of principles that are not ends in themselves but rather outmoded means to an end. What is needed is a new conception of human behavior which is compatible with the implications of a scientific analysis. All men control and are controlled. The question of government in the broadest possible sense is not how freedom is to be preserved but what kinds of control are to be used and to what ends. Control must be analyzed and considered in its proper proportions. No one, I am sure, wishes to develop new master-slave relationships or bend the will of the people to despotic rulers in new ways. These are patterns of control appropriate to a world without science. They may well be the first to go when the experimental analysis of behavior comes into its own in the design of cultural practices.

II [Rogers]

There are, I believe, a number of matters in connection with this important topic on which the authors of this article, and probably a large majority of psychologists, are in agreement. These matters then are not issues as far as we are concerned, and I should like to mention them briefly in order to put them to one side.

Points of agreement

I am sure we agree that men—as individuals and as societies—have always endeavored to understand, predict, influence, and control human behavior—their own behavior and that of others.

I believe we agree that the behavioral sciences are making and will continue to make increasingly rapid progress in the understanding of behavior, and that as a consequence the capacity to predict and to control behavior is developing with equal rapidity.

I believe we agree that to deny these advances, or to claim that man's behavior cannot be a field of science, is unrealistic. Even though this is not an issue for us, we should recognize that many intelligent men still hold strongly to the view that the actions of men are free in some sense such that scientific knowledge of man's behavior is impossible. Thus Reinhold Niebuhr, the noted theologian, heaps scorn on the concept of psychology as a science of man's behavior and even says, "In any event, no scientific investigation of past behavior can become the basis of predictions of future behavior" (8). So, while this is not an issue for psychologists, we should at least notice in passing that it is an issue for many people.

I believe we are in agreement that the tremendous potential power of a science which permits the prediction and control of behavior may be misused, and that the possibility of such misuse constitutes a serious threat.

Consequently, Skinner and I are in agreement that the whole question of the scientific control of human behavior is a matter with which psychologists and the general public should concern themselves. As Robert Oppenheimer told the American Psychological Association in 1955 (9) the problems that psychologists will pose for society by their growing ability to control behavior will be much more grave than the problems posed by the ability of physicists to control the reactions of matter. I am not sure whether psychologists generally recognize this. My impression is that by and large they hold a *laissez-faire* attitude. Obviously Skinner and I do not hold this *laissez-faire* view, or we would not have written this article.

Points at issue

With these several points of basic and important agreement, are there then any issues that remain on which there are differences? I believe there are. They can be stated very briefly: Who will be controlled? Who will exercise control? What type of control will be exercised? Most important of all, toward what end or what purpose, or in the pursuit of what value, will control be exercised?

It is on questions of this sort that there exist ambiguities, misunderstandings, and probably deep differences. These differences exist among psychologists, among members of the general public in this country, and among various world cultures. Without any hope of achieving a final resolution of these questions, we can, I believe, put these issues in clearer form.

Some meanings

To avoid ambiguity and faulty communication, I would like to clarify the meanings of some of the terms we are using.

Behavioral science is a term that might be defined from several angles but in the context of this discussion it refers primarily to knowledge that the existence of certain describable conditions in the human being and/or in his environment is followed by certain describable consequences in his actions.

Prediction means the prior identification of behaviors which then occur. Because it is important in some things I wish to say later, I would point out that one may predict a highly specific behavior, such as an eye blink, or one may predict a class of behaviors. One might correctly predict "avoidant behavior," for example, without being able to specify whether the individual will run away or simply close his eyes.

The word *control* is a very slippery one, which can be used with any one of several meanings. I would like to specify three that seem most important for our present purposes. *Control* may mean: (i) The setting of conditions by *B* for *A*, *A* having no voice in the matter, such that certain predictable behaviors then occur in *A*. I refer to this as external control. (ii) The setting of conditions by *B* for *A*, *A* giving some degree of consent to these conditions, such that certain predictable behaviors then occur in *A*. I refer to this as the influence of *B* on *A*. (iii) The setting of conditions by *A* such that certain predictable behaviors then occur in himself. I refer to this as internal control. It will be noted that Skinner lumps together the first two meanings, external control and influence, under the concept of control. I find this confusing.

Usual concept of control of human behavior

With the underbrush thus cleared away (I hope), let us review very briefly the various elements that are involved in the usual concept of the control of human behavior as mediated by the behavorial sciences. I am drawing here on the previous writings of Skinner, on his present statements, on the writings of others who have considered in either friendly or antagonistic fashion the meanings that would be involved in such control. I have not excluded the science fiction writers, as reported recently by Vandenberg (21), since they often show an awareness of the issues involved, even though the methods described are as yet fictional. These then are the elements that seem common to these different concepts of the application of science to human behavior.

1) There must first be some sort of decision about goals. Usually desirable goals are assumed, but sometimes, as in George Orwell's book *1984,* the goal that is selected is an aggrandizement of individual power with which most of us would disagree. In a recent paper Skinner suggests that one possible set of goals to be assigned to the behavioral technology is this: "Let men be happy, informed, skillful, well-behaved and productive" (17). In the first draft of his part of this article, which he was kind enough to show me, he did not mention such definite goals as these, but desired "improved" educational practices, "wiser" use of knowledge in government, and the like. In the final version of his article he avoids even these value-laden terms, and his implicit goal is the very general one that scientific control of behavior is desirable, because it would perhaps bring "a far better world for everyone."

Thus the first step in thinking about the control of human behavior is the choice of goals, whether specific or general. It is necessary to come to terms in some way with the issue, "For what purpose?"

2) A second element is that, whether the end selected is highly specific or is a very general one, such as wanting "a better world," we proceed by the methods of science to discover the means to these ends. We continue through further experimentation and investigation to discover more effective means. The method of science is self-correcting in thus arriving at increasingly effective ways of achieving the purpose we have in mind.

3) The third aspect of such control is that as the conditions or methods are discovered by which to reach the goal, some person or some group establishes these conditions and uses these methods, having in one way or another obtained the power to do so.

4) The fourth element is the exposure of individuals to the prescribed conditions, and this leads, with a high degree of probability, to behavior which is in line with the goals desired. Individuals are now happy, if that has been the goal, or well-behaved, or submissive, or whatever it has been decided to make them.

5) The fifth element is that if the process I have described is put in motion then there is a continuing social organization which will continue to produce the types of behavior that have been valued.

Some flaws

Are there any flaws in this way of viewing the control of human behavior? I believe there are. In fact the only element in this description with which I find myself in agreement is the second. It seems to me quite incontrovertibly true that the scientific method is an excellent way to discover the means by which to achieve our goals. Beyond that, I feel many sharp differences, which I will try to spell out.

I believe that in Skinner's presentation here and in his previous writings, there is a serious underestimation of the problem of power. To hope that the power which is being made available by the behavioral sciences will be exercised by the scientists, or by a benevolent group, seems to me a hope little supported by either recent or distant history. It seems far more likely that behavioral scientists, holding their present attitudes, will be in the position of the German rocket scientists specializing in guided missiles. First they worked devotedly for Hitler to destroy the U.S.S.R. and the United States. Now, depending on who captured them, they work devotedly for the U.S.S.R. in the interest of destroying the United States, or devotedly for the United States in the interest of destroying the U.S.S.R. If behavioral scientists are concerned solely with advancing their science, it seems most probable that they will serve the purposes of whatever individual or group has the power.

But the major flaw I see in this review of what is involved in the scientific control of human behavior is the denial, misunderstanding, or gross underestimation of the place of ends, goals or values in their relationship to science. This error (as it seems to me) has so many implications that I would like to devote some space to it.

ENDS AND VALUES IN RELATION TO SCIENCE

In sharp contradiction to some views that have been advanced, I would like to propose a two-pronged thesis: (i) In any scientific endeavor—whether "pure" or applied science—there is a prior subjective choice of the purpose or value which that scientific work is perceived as serving. (ii) This subjective value choice which brings the scientific endeavor into being must always lie outside of that endeavor and can never become a part of the science involved in that endeavor.

Let me illustrate the first point from Skinner himself. It is clear that in his earlier writing (17) it is recognized that a prior value choice is necessary, and it is specified as the goal that men are to become happy, well-behaved, productive, and so on. I am pleased that Skinner has retreated from the goals he then chose, because to me they seem to be stultifying values. I can only feel that he was choosing these goals for others, not for himself. I would hate to see Skinner become "well-behaved," as that term would be defined for him by behavioral scientists. His recent article in the *American Psychologist* (16) shows that he certainly does not want to be "productive" as that value is defined by most psychologists. And the most awful fate I can imagine for him would be to have him constantly "happy." It is the fact that he is very unhappy about many things which makes me prize him.

In the first draft of his part of this article, he also included such prior value choices, saying for example, "We must decide how we are to use the knowledge which a science of human behavior is now making available." Now he has dropped all mention of such choices, and if I understand him correctly, he believes that science can proceed without them. He has suggested this view in another recent paper, stating that "We must continue to experiment in cultural design . . . testing the consequences as we go. Eventually the practices which make for the greatest biological and psychological strength of the group will presumably survive" (19, p. 549).

I would point out, however, that to choose to experiment is a value choice. Even to move in the direction of perfectly random experimentation is a value choice. To test the consequences of an experiment is possible only if we have first made a subjective choice of a criterion value. And implicit in his statement is a valuing of biological and psychological strength. So even when trying to avoid such choice, it seems inescapable that a prior subjective value choice is necessary for any scientific endeavor, or for any application of scientific knowledge.

I wish to make it clear that I am not saying that values cannot be included as a subject of science. It is not true that science deals only with certain classes of "facts" and that these classes do not include values. It is a bit more complex than that, as a simple illustration or two may make clear.

If I value knowledge of the "three R's" as a goal of education, the methods of science can give me increasingly accurate information on how this goal may be achieved. If I value problem-solving ability as a goal of education, the scientific method can give me the same kind of help.

Now, if I wish to determine whether problem-solving ability is "better" than knowledge of the three R's, then scientific method can also study those two values but *only*—and this is very important—in terms of some other value which I have subjectively chosen. I may value college success. Then I can determine whether problem-solving ability or knowledge of the three R's is most closely associated with that value. I may value personal integration or vocational success or responsible citizenship. I can determine whether problem-solving ability or knowledge of the three R's is "better" for achieving any one of these values. But the value or purpose that gives meaning to a particular scientific endeavor must always lie outside of that endeavor.

Although our concern in this symposium is largely with applied science, what I have been saying seems equally true of so-called "pure" science. In pure science the usual prior subjective value choice is the discovery of truth. But this is a subjective choice, and science can never say whether it is the best choice, save in the light of some other value. Geneticists in the U.S.S.R., for example, had to make a subjective choice of whether it was better to pursue truth or to discover facts which upheld a governmental dogma. Which choice is "better"? We could make a scientific investigation of those alternatives but only in the light of some other subjectively chosen value. If, for example, we value the survival of a culture, then we could begin to investigate with the methods of science the question of whether pursuit of truth or support of governmental dogma is more closely associated with cultural survival.

My point then is that any endeavor in science, pure or applied, is carried on in the pursuit of a purpose or value that is subjectively chosen by persons. It is important that this choice be made explicit, since the particular value which is being sought can never be tested or evaluated, confirmed or denied, by the scientific endeavor to which it gives birth. The initial purpose or value always and necessarily lies outside the scope of the scientific effort which it sets in motion.

Among other things this means that if we choose some particular goal or series of goals for human beings and then set out on a large scale to control human behavior to the end of achieving those goals, we are locked in the rigidity of our initial choice, because such a scientific endeavor can never transcend itself to select new goals. Only subjective human persons can do that. Thus if we chose as our goal the state of happiness for human beings (a goal deservedly ridiculed by Aldous Huxley in *Brave New World*), and if we involved all of society in a successful scientific program by which people became happy, we would be locked in a colossal rigidity in which no one would be free to question this goal, because our scientific operations could not transcend themselves to question their guiding purposes. And without laboring this point, I would remark that colossal rigidity, whether in dinosaurs or dictatorships, has a very poor record of evolutionary survival.

If, however, a part of our scheme is to set free some "planners" who do not have to be happy, who are not controlled, and who are therefore free to choose other values, this has several meanings. It means that the purpose we have chosen as our goal is not a sufficient and a satisfying one for human beings but must be supplemented. It also means that if it is necessary to set up an elite group which is free, then this shows all too clearly that the great majority are only the slaves—no matter by what high-sounding name we call them—of those who select the goals.

Perhaps, however, the thought is that a continuing scientific endeavor will evolve its own goals; that the initial findings will alter the directions, and subsequent findings will alter them still further, and that science somehow develops its own purpose. Although he does not clearly say so, this appears to be the pattern Skinner has in mind. It is surely a reasonable description, but it overlooks one element in this continuing development, which is that subjective personal choice enters in at every point at which the direction changes. The findings of a science, the results of an experiment, do not and never can tell us what next scientific purpose to pursue. Even in the purest of science, the scientist must decide what the findings mean and must subjectively choose what next step will be most profitable in the pursuit of his purpose. And if we are speaking of the application of scientific knowledge, then it is distressingly clear that the increasing scientific knowledge of the structure of the atom carries with it no necessary choice as to the purpose to which this knowledge will be put. This is a subjective personal choice which must be made by many individuals.

Thus I return to the proposition with which I began this section of my remarks—and which I now repeat in different words. Science has its meaning as the objective pursuit of a purpose which has been subjectively chosen by a person or persons. This purpose or value can never be investigated by the particular scientific experiment or investigation to which it has given birth and meaning. Consequently, any discussion of the control of human beings by the behavioral sciences must first and most deeply concern itself with the subjectively chosen purposes which such an application of science is intended to implement.

Is the situation hopeless?

The thoughtful reader may recognize that, although my remarks up to this point have introduced some modifications in the conception of the processes by which human behavior will be controlled, these remarks may have made such control seem, if anything, even more inevitable. We might sum it up this way: Behavioral science is clearly moving forward; the increasing power for control which it gives will be held by someone or some group; such an individual or group will surely choose the values of goals to be achieved; and most of us will then be increasingly controlled by means so subtle that we will not even be aware of them as controls. Thus, whether a council of wise psychologists (if this is not a contradiction in terms), or a Stalin, or a Big Brother has the power, and whether the goal is happiness, or productivity, or resolution of the Oedipus complex, or submission, or love of Big Brother, we will inevitably find ourselves moving toward the chosen goal and probably thinking that we ourselves desire it. Thus, if this line of reasoning is correct, it appears that some form of *Walden Two* or of *1984* (and at a deep philosophic level they seem indistinguishable) is coming. The fact that it would surely arrive piecemeal rather than all at once does not greatly change the fundamental issues. In any event, as Skinner has indicated in his writings, we would then look back upon the concepts of human freedom, the capacity for choice, the responsibility for choice, and the worth of the human individual as historical curiosities which once existed by cultural accident as values in a prescientific civilization.

I believe that any person observant of trends must regard something like the foregoing sequence as a real possibility. It is not simply a fantasy. Something of that sort may even be the most likely future. But is it an inevitable future? I want to devote the remainder of my remarks to an alternative possibility.

Alternative set of values

Suppose we start with a set of ends, values, purposes, quite different from the type of goals we have been considering. Suppose we do this quite openly, setting them forth as a possible value choice to be accepted or rejected. Suppose we select a set of values that focuses on fluid elements of process rather than static attributes. We might then value: man as a process of becoming, as a process of achieving worth and dignity through the development of his potentialities; the individual human being as a self-actualizing process, moving on to more challenging and enriching experiences; the process by which the individual creatively adapts to an ever-new and changing world; the process by which knowledge transcends itself, as, for example, the theory of relativity transcended Newtonian physics, itself to be transcended in some future day by a new perception.

If we select values such as these we turn to our science and technology of behavior with a very different set of questions. We will want to know such things as these: Can science aid in the discovery of new modes of richly rewarding living? more meaningful and satisfying modes of interpersonal relationships? Can science inform us on how the human race can become a more intelligent participant in its own evolution—its physical, psychological, and social evolution? Can science inform us on ways of releasing the creative capacity of individuals, which seem so necessary if we are to survive in this fantastically expanding atomic age? Oppenheimer has pointed out (10) that knowledge, which used to double in millennia or centuries, now doubles in a generation or a decade. It appears that we must discover the utmost in release of creativity if we are to be able to adapt effectively. In short, can science discover the methods by which man can most readily become a continually developing and self-transcending process, in his behavior, his thinking, his knowledge? Can science predict and release an essentially "unpredictable" freedom?

It is one of the virtues of science as a method that it is as able to advance and implement goals and purposes of this sort as it is to serve static values, such as states of being well-informed, happy, obedient. Indeed, we have some evidence of this.

Small example

I will perhaps be forgiven if I document some of the possibilities along this line by turning to psychotherapy, the field I know best.

Psychotherapy, as Meerloo (6) and others have pointed out, can be one of the most subtle tools for the control of *A* by *B*. The therapist can subtly mold individuals in imitation of himself. He can cause an individual to become a submissive and conforming being. When certain therapeutic principles are used in extreme fashion, we call it brainwashing, an instance of the disintegration of the personality and a reformulation of the person along lines desired by the controlling individual. So the principles of therapy can be used as an effective means of external control of human personality and behavior. Can psychotherapy be anything else?

Here I find the developments going on in client-centered psychotherapy

(13) an exciting hint of what a behavioral science can do in achieving the kinds of values I have stated. Quite aside from being a somewhat new orientation in psychotherapy, this development has important implications regarding the relation of a behavioral science to the control of human behavior. Let me describe our experience as it relates to the issues of this discussion.

In client-centered therapy, we are deeply engaged in the prediction and influencing of behavior, or even the control of behavior. As therapists, we institute certain attitudinal conditions, and the client has relatively little voice in the establishment of these conditions. We predict that if these conditions are instituted, certain behavioral consequences will ensue in the client. Up to this point this is largely external control, no different from what Skinner has described, and no different from what I have discussed in the preceding sections of this article. But here any similarity ceases.

The conditions we have chosen to establish predict such behavioral consequences as these: that the client will become self-directing, less rigid, more open to the evidence of his senses, better organized and integrated, more similar to the ideal which he has chosen for himself. In other words, we have established by external control conditions which we predict will be followed by internal control by the individual, in pursuit of internally chosen goals. We have set the conditions which predict various classes of behaviors—self-directing behaviors, sensitivity to realities within and without, flexible adaptiveness—which are by their very nature unpredictable in their specifics. Our recent research (15) indicates that our predictions are to a significant degree corroborated, and our commitment to the scientific method causes us to believe that more effective means of achieving these goals may be realized.

Research exists in other fields—industry, education, group dynamics—which seems to support our own findings. I believe it may be conservatively stated that scientific progress has been made in identifying those conditions in an interpersonal relationship which, if they exist in *B*, are followed in *A* by greater maturity in behavior, less dependence on others, an increase in expressiveness as a person, an increase in variability, flexibility and effectiveness of adaptation, an increase in self-responsibility and self-direction. And, quite in contrast to the concern expressed by some, we do not find that the creatively adaptive behavior which results from such self-directed variability of expression is a "happy accident" which occurs in "chaos." Rather, the individual who is open to his experience, and self-directing, is harmonious not chaotic, ingenious rather than random, as he orders his responses imaginatively toward the achievement of his own purposes. His creative actions are no more a "happy accident" than was Einstein's development of the theory of relativity.

Thus we find ourselves in fundamental agreement with John Dewey's statement: "Science has made its way by releasing, not by suppressing, the elements of variation, of invention and innovation, of novel creation in individuals" (12). Progress in personal life and in group living is, we believe, made in the same way.

Possible Concept of the Control of Human Behavior

It is quite clear that the point of view I am expressing is in sharp contrast to the usual conception of the relationship of the behavioral sciences to the control of human behavior. In order to make this contrast even more blunt, I will state this possibility in paragraphs parallel to those used before.

1) It is possible for us to choose to value man as a self-actualizing process of becoming; to value creativity and the process by which knowledge becomes self-transcending.

2) We can proceed, by the methods of science, to discover the conditions which necessarily precede these processes and, through continuing experimentation, to discover better means of achieving these purposes.

3) It is possible for individuals or groups to set these conditions, with a minimum of power of control. According to present knowledge, the only authority necessary is the authority to establish certain qualities of interpersonal relationship.

4) Exposed to these conditions, present knowledge suggests that individuals become more self-responsible, make progress in self-actualization, become more flexible, and become more creatively adaptive.

5) Thus such an initial choice would inaugurate the beginnings of a social system or subsystem in which values, knowledge, adaptive skills, and even the concept of science would be continually changing and self-transcending. The emphasis would be upon man as a process of becoming.

I believe it is clear that such a view as I have been describing does not lead to any definable utopia. It would be impossible to predict its final outcome. It involves a step-by-step development, based on a continuing subjective choice of purposes, which are implemented by the behavioral sciences. It is in the direction of the "open society," as that term has been defined by Popper (11), where individuals carry responsibility for personal decisions. It is at the opposite pole from his concept of the closed society, of which *Walden Two* would be an example.

I trust it is also evident that the whole emphasis is on process, not on end-states of being. I am suggesting that it is by choosing to value certain qualitative elements of the process of becoming that we can find a pathway toward the open society.

THE CHOICE

It is my hope that we have helped to clarify the range of choice which will lie before us and our children in regard to the behavioral sciences. We can choose to use our growing knowledge to enslave people in ways never dreamed of before, depersonalizing them, controlling them by means so carefully selected that they will perhaps never be aware of their loss of personhood. We can choose to utilize our scientific knowledge to make men happy, well-behaved, and productive, as Skinner earlier suggested. Or we can insure that each person learns all the syllabus which we select and set before him, as Skinner now suggests. Or at the other end of the spectrum of choice we can choose to use the behavioral sciences in ways which will free, not control; which will bring about constructive variability, not conformity; which will develop creativity, not contentment; which will facilitate each person in his self-directed process of becoming; which will aid individuals, groups, and even the concept of science to become self-transcending in freshly adaptive ways of meeting life and its problems. The choice is up to us, and, the human race being what it is, we are likely to stumble about, making at times some nearly disastrous value choices and at other times highly constructive ones.

I am aware that to some, this setting forth of a choice is unrealistic, because a choice of values is regarded as not possible. Skinner has stated: "Man's vaunted creative powers . . . his capacity to choose and our right to hold him responsible for his choice—none of these is conspicuous in this new self-portrait (provided by science). Man, we once believed, was free to express himself in art, music, and literature, to inquire into nature, to seek salvation in his own way. He could initiate action and make spontaneous and capricious changes of course. . . . But science insists that action is initiated by forces impinging upon the individual, and that caprice is only another name for behavior for which we have not yet found a cause" (17, pp. 52-53).

I can understand this point of view, but I believe that it avoids looking at the great paradox of behavioral science. Behavior, when it is examined scientifically, is surely best understood as determined by prior causation. This is one great fact of science. But responsible personal choice, which is the most essential element in being a person, which is the core experience in psychotherapy, which exists prior to any scientific endeavor, is an equally prominent fact in our lives. To deny the experience of responsible choice is, to me, as restricted a view as to deny the possibility of a behavioral science. That these two important elements of our experience appear to be in contradiction has perhaps the same significance as the contradiction between the wave theory and the corpuscular theory of light, both of which can be shown to be true, even though incompatible. We cannot profitably deny our subjective life, any more than we can deny the objective description of that life.

In conclusion, then, it is my contention that science cannot come into being without a personal choice of the values we wish to achieve. And these values we choose to implement will forever lie outside of the science which implements them; the goals we select, the purposes we wish to follow, must always be outside of the science which achieves them. To me, this has the encouraging meaning that the human person, with his capacity of subjective choice, can and will always exist, separate from and prior to any of his scientific undertakings. Unless as individuals and groups we choose to relinquish our capacity of subjective choice, we will always remain persons, not simply pawns of a self-created science.

III [Skinner]

I cannot quite agree that the practice of science *requires* a prior decision about goals or a prior choice of values. The metallurgist can study the properties of steel and the engineer can design a bridge without raising the question of whether a bridge is to be built. But such questions are certainly frequently raised and tentatively answered. Rogers wants to call the answers "subjective choices of values." To me, such an expression suggests that we have had to abandon more rigorous scientific practices in order to talk about our own behavior. In the experimental analysis of other organisms I would use other terms, and I shall try to do so here. Any list of values is a list of reinforcers—conditioned or otherwise. We are so constituted that under certain circumstances food, water, sexual contact, and so on, will make any behavior which produces them more likely to occur again. Other things may acquire this power. We do not need to say that an organism chooses to eat rather than to starve. If you answer that it is a very different thing when a man chooses to starve, I am only too happy to agree. If it were not so, we should have cleared up the question of choice long ago. An organism can be reinforced by—can be made to "choose"—almost any given state of affairs.

Rogers is concerned with choices that involve multiple and usually conflicting consequences. I have dealt with some of these elsewhere (18) in an analysis of self-control. Shall I eat these delicious strawberries today if I will then suffer an annoying rash tomorrow? The decision I am to make used to be assigned to the province of ethics. But we are now studying similar combinations of positive and negative consequences, as well as collateral conditions which affect the results in the laboratory. Even a pigeon can be taught some measure of self-control! And this work helps us to understand the operation of certain formulas—among them value judgments—which folk-wisdom, religion, and psychotherapy have advanced in the interests of self-discipline. The observable effect of any statement of value is to alter the relative effectiveness of reinforcers. We may no longer enjoy the strawberries for thinking about the rash. If rashes are made sufficiently shameful, illegal, sinful, maladjusted, or unwise, we may glow with satisfaction as we push the strawberries aside in a grandiose avoidance response which would bring a smile to the lips of Murray Sidman.

People behave in ways which, as we say, conform to ethical, governmental, or religious patterns because they are reinforced for doing so. The resulting behavior may have far-reaching consequences for the survival of the pattern to which it conforms. And whether we like it or not, survival is the ultimate criterion. This is where, it seems to me, science can help—not in choosing a goal, but in enabling us to predict the survival value of cultural practices. Man has too long tried to get the kind of world he wants by glorifying some brand of immediate reinforcement. As science points up more and more of the remoter consequences, he may begin to work to strengthen behavior, not in a slavish devotion to a chosen value, but with respect to the ultimate survival of mankind. Do not ask me why I want mankind to survive. I can tell you why only in the sense in which the physiologist can tell you why I want to breathe. Once the relation between a given step and the survival of my group has been pointed out, I will take that step. And it is the business of science to point out just such relations.

The values I have occasionally recommended (and Rogers has not led me to recant) are transitional. Other things being equal, I am betting on the group whose practices make for healthy, happy, secure, productive, and creative people. And I insist that the values recommended by Rogers are transitional, too, for I can ask him the same kind of question. Man as a process of becoming—*what?* Self-actualization—for what? Inner control is no more a goal than external.

What Rogers seems to me to be proposing, both here and elsewhere (14), is this: Let us use our increasing power of control to create individuals who will not need and perhaps will no longer respond to control. Let us solve the problem of our power by renouncing it. At first blush this seems as implausible as a benevolent despot. Yet power has occasionally been foresworn. A nation has burned its Reichstag, rich men have given away their wealth, beautiful women have become ugly hermits in the desert, and psychotherapists have become nondirective. When this happens, I look to other possible reinforcements for a plausible explanation. A people relinquish democratic power when a tyrant promises them the earth. Rich men give away wealth to escape the accusing finger of their fellowmen. A woman destroys her beauty in the hope of salvation. And a psychotherapist relinquishes control because he can thus help his client more effectively.

The solution that Rogers is suggesting is thus understandable. But is he correctly interpreting the result? What evidence is there that a client ever becomes truly *self*-directing? What evidence is there that he ever makes a truly *inner* choice of ideal or goal? Even though the therapist does not do the choosing, even though he encourages "self-actualization"—he is not out of control as long as he holds himself ready to step in when occasion demands—when, for example, the client chooses the goal of becoming a more accomplished liar or murdering his boss. But supposing the therapist does withdraw completely or is no longer necessary—what about all the other forces acting upon the client? Is the self-chosen goal independent of his early ethical and religious training? of the folk-wisdom of his group? of the opinions and attitudes of others who are important to him? Surely not. The therapeutic situation is only a small part of the world of the client. From the therapist's point of view it may appear to be possible to relinquish control. But the control passes, not to a "self," but to forces in other parts of the client's world. The solution of the therapist's problem of power cannot be *our* solution, for we must consider *all* the forces acting upon the individual.

The child who must be prodded and nagged is something less than a fully developed human being. We want to see him hurrying to his appointment, not because each step is taken in response to verbal reminders from his mother, but because certain temporal contingencies, in which dawdling has been punished and hurrying reinforced, have worked a change in his behavior. Call this a state of better organization, a greater sensitivity to reality, or what you will. The plain fact is that the child passes from a temporary verbal control exercised by his parents to control by certain inexorable features of the environment. I should suppose that something of the same sort happens in successful psychotherapy. Rogers seems to me to be saying this: Let us put an end, as quickly as possible, to any pattern of master-and-slave, to any direct obedience to command, to the submissive following of suggestions. Let the individual be free to adjust himself to more rewarding features of the world about him. In the end, let his teachers and counselors "wither away," like the Marxist state. I not only agree with this as a useful ideal, I have constructed a fanciful world to demonstrate its advantages. It saddens me to hear Rogers say that "at a deep philosophic level" *Walden Two* and George Orwell's *1984* "seem indistinguishable." They could scarcely be more unlike—at any level. The book *1984* is a picture of immediate aversive control for vicious selfish purposes. The founder of *Walden Two,* on the other hand, has built a community in which neither he nor any other person exerts any *current* control. His achievement lay in his original *plan,* and when he boasts of this ("It is enough to satisfy the thirstiest tyrant") we do not fear him but only pity him for his weakness.

Another critic of *Walden Two,* Andrew Hacker (4), has discussed this point in considering the bearing of mass conditioning upon the liberal notion of autonomous man. In drawing certain parallels between the Grand Inquisition passage in Dostoevsky's *Brothers Karamazov,* Huxley's *Brave New World,* and *Walden Two,* he attempts to set up a distinction to be drawn in any society between conditioners and conditioned. He assumes that "the conditioner can be said to be autonomous in the traditional liberal sense." But then he notes: "Of course the conditioner has been conditioned. But he has not been conditioned by the conscious manipulation of another *person.*" But how does this affect the resulting behavior? Can we not soon forget the origins of the "artificial" diamond which is identical with the real thing? Whether it is an "accidental" cultural pattern, such as is said to have produced the founder of *Walden Two,* or the engineered environment which is about to produce his successors, we are dealing with sets of conditions generating human behavior which will ultimately be measured by their contribution to the strength of the group. We look to the future, not the past, for the test of "goodness" or acceptability.

If we are worthy of our democratic heritage, we shall, of course, be ready to resist any tyrannical use of science for immediate or selfish purposes. But if we value the achievements and goals of democracy, we must not refuse to apply science to the design and construction of cultural patterns, even though we may then find ourselves in some sense in the position of controllers. Fear of control, generalized beyond any warrant, has led to a misinterpretation of valid practices and the blind rejection of intelligent planning for a better way of life. In terms which I trust Rogers will approve, in conquering this fear we shall become more mature and better organized and shall, thus, more fully actualize ourselves as human beings.

References

1. Coleman, C., *Bulletin of the American Association of University Professors,* Vol. 39 (1953), p. 457.
2. Freund, P. A., *et al., Constitutional Law: Cases and Other Problems,* Vol. 1 (Boston: Little, 1954).
3. Hacker, A., *Antioch Review,* Vol. 14 (1954), p. 195.
4. ———, *Journal of Politics,* Vol. 17 (1955), p. 590.
5. Krutch, J. W., *The Measure of Man* (Indianapolis: Bobbs, 1953).
6. Meerloo, J. A. M., *Journal of Nervous Mental Disease,* Vol. 122 (1955), p. 353.

7. Negley, G., and J. M. Patrick, *The Quest for Utopia* (New York: Abelard, 1952).
8. Niebuhr, R., *The Self and the Dramas of History* (New York: Scribner, 1955), p. 47.
9. Oppenheimer, R., *American Psychologist,* Vol. 11 (1956), p. 127.
10. ———, Roosevelt University Occasional Papers 2 (1956).
11. Popper, K. R., *The Open Society and Its Enemies* (London: Routledge, 1945).
12. Ratner, J., ed., *Intelligence in the Modern World: John Dewey's Philosophy* (New York: Modern Lib., 1939), p. 359.
13. Rogers, C. R., *Client-Centered Therapy* (Boston: Houghton, 1951).
14. ———, *Teachers College Record,* Vol. 57 (1956), p. 316.
15. ———, and R. Dymonds, eds., *Psychotherapy and Personality Change* (Chicago: Chicago, 1954).
16. Skinner, B. F., *American Psychologist,* Vol. 11 (1956), p. 221.
17. ———, *American Scholar,* Vol. 25 (1955-1956), p. 47.
18. ———, *Science and Human Behavior* (New York: Macmillan, 1953).
19. ———, *Transactions of the New York Academy of Sciences,* Vol. 17 (1955), p. 547.
20. ———, *Walden Two* (New York: Macmillan, 1948).
21. Vandenberg, S. G., *American Psychologist,* Vol. 11 (1956), p. 339.
22. Viteles, M., *Science,* Vol. 122 (1955), p. 1167.

QUESTIONS FOR DISCUSSION

Snygg Article

1. Explain the differences between the "objective" and the "phenomenological" frames of reference.
2. Which frame of reference would be more appropriate for understanding "self"? Explain your choice and reasoning.
3. What does it mean to say, "Objective systems have been forced to confine themselves to the prediction of normative behavior"?
4. What is the role of the unconscious in the phenomenological system?

Smith Article

1. What theoretical issues divide Snygg and Smith?
2. What arguments does the author advance in suggesting that a psychology of consciousness is a "common-sense" psychology? Do you agree? Why or why not?

Snygg and Combs Article

1. Smith maintains that Snygg and Combs overlook the unconscious determinants of behavior. What reasons do Snygg and Combs advance which support their contention that it is the conscious and not the unconscious which plays a stronger role in determining behavior? What are your views on this?

Maslow Article

1. Maslow voices concern about existentialist writers' tragic sense of life and their harping on dread, anguish, and despair. In light of the theme of his article, *why* is he concerned?
2. What is there in existentialism which Maslow identifies as beneficial to psychology? Would you agree?

Rogers and Skinner Article

1. The readings to this point have stressed the "uniqueness" of the self. In your opinion, under which system, Rogers' or Skinner's, is the "self" more apt to *remain* unique? Explain your position.
2. Explain the concept "reinforcement" as it is used in Skinner's system.
3. Rogers asserts that there must be some decision about goals prior to any effort to control human behavior. Skinner diagrees with this. What philosophical overtones are inherent in this disagreement?
4. Would you prefer to teach school in a Rogerian word or a Skinnerian world? Why?

Part III

perceptual processes and the self

1. Social psychology and perception

Jerome S. Bruner

From *Readings in Social Psychology,* 3rd Edition, edited by E. E. Maccoby, T. M. Newcomb, and E. L. Hartley (New York: Holt, Rinehart & Winston, Inc., 1958), pp. 85-94. Reprinted by permission of the author and the publisher.

The concept "perception" is growing to increased stature in psychological circles. What we perceive is one thing, but how we interpret *what we perceive is quite another. Bruner presents fascinating evidence to indicate possible variables which influence perceptual processes and, ultimately, behavior.*

Contemporary social psychology, one finds in looking through the contents of its professional journals, is much concerned, indeed even preoccupied, with problems of perception. There is constant reference to the manner in which subjects in experiments "perceive the situation." The term "social perception" has come widely into use to describe the manner in which one person perceives or infers the traits and intentions of another, and there is a steady flow of experimental studies on the manner in which social factors induce types of selectivity in what a person perceives and how he interprets it. Social attitudes are defined as a readiness to experience events in certain consistent and selective ways, and the most recent writings on the psychology of language, inspired by Benjamin Lee Whorf, urge that the structure of a language and its lexical units determine or at least influence what one habitually notices in the world about one. Without appropriate attitudes and an appropriate linguistic structure, one does not readily register upon certain events in the environment that another person, appropriately armed with attitudes and a language, would notice as salient.

While this point of view about the central importance of perception has always to some measure been a feature of social psychology—McDougall in his classic textbook of 1912, for example, was sharply aware of the role of social sentiments in biasing the selectivity of attention, and Thomas and Znaniecki made "the definition of the situation" a key concept in their pioneering acculturation study of *The Polish Peasant*—it is only within the last 10 or 15 years that the role of perception and "selective registration" has come to be dominant in social psychological theory. In the pages that follow, we shall examine the backgrounds of this emphasis, some of the reasons why perceptual concepts are indispensable to the social psychologist, and the nature of these concepts as they have emerged in the last decade or so.

To the uninitiated, one with a background neither in psychology nor in classical philosophy, perceiving may pose no problems. The simple view, sometimes called naive realism, would hold that there are objects and events in the external world and that somehow representations of these, called *Eidola* by the pre-Socratic philosophers, emanate from the things in the world and find their way into the nervous system and eventually into consciousness. Such, however, is not the case save in the most metaphoric sense; rather, the problem is how we integrate into a unitary percept the myriads of sensory stimuli that come from our specialized sense organs. In most instances, there are more things to be noticed than one can possibly register upon simultaneously—as when one walks into a room full of people with several conversations going on at once—and even when the stimulus input is fairly simple, there are various ways in which it can be "looked at" or organized. A tree can be perceived from the point of view of the soundness of its wood, the seasonal status of its foliage, its species, its shade-giving quality, and so on. Perhaps we can notice four or five or six of these features at once, but rarely do we register on more of them. For the abiding fact about the process of knowing, of which perceiving is one aspect, is that organisms have a highly limited span of attention and a highly limited span of immediate memory. Selectivity is forced upon us by the nature of these limitations, and indeed, even if we should operate at maximum capacity (estimated to be an ability to notice and keep in mind about seven independent things simultaneously), the cost in cognitive strain would be considerable.

In the interests of economizing effort we do three things. On the one hand, we narrow the selectivity of attention more or less to those things that are somehow essential to the enterprises in which we are engaged. In social situations, we register on the color of people's skins, but not on the texture. Moreover, we simplify even here and may register solely on whether they are white or colored. Secondly, we "recode" into simpler form the diversity of events that we encounter so that our limited attention and memory span can be protected. Instead of trying to remember how far falling bodies fall, we simply commit to memory the formula $S = \frac{gt^2}{2}$ which preserves the necessary information and allows us to recreate any specific information about distance we want. Sometimes these recodings of information serve their economical function but lead to a serious loss of information, as when we recode information in terms of what Walter Lippmann long ago called a "stereotype." We see a Negro sitting on a park bench, a Jew or Texan changing a check at a bank window, a German dressing down a taxicab driver, and allocate each experience to an established and well-memorized stereotype: lazy Negro, mercenary Jew, rich Texan, bullying German. The behavior is perceived according to the formula, the person saved from having to do much perceptual work aside from picking up a few cues. Not only is information lost, but misinformation is added; the person "sees" the stereotyped individuals he has created—"Why, I saw a big healthy Negro sitting there idle in the park doing nothing the other day," and the behavior is perceived as lazy rather than, perhaps, that the Negro worked the swing shift and was enjoying his hours off in the park. Finally, we deal with the overload of information provided by the environment, the overload relative to our limited capacities for noticing and registering and remembering, by the use of technological aids, aids that are designed to lengthen the noticing process. A simple example of such an aid is pencil and paper: trying to list all that is before us from every point of view. Or we use a camera in the hope of being able to go back over the picture and extract the last ounce of meaning from an event. All of these methods help. None of them can succeed fully, for, as Robert Oppenheimer has noted about the cognitive processes, in order to know anything we must somehow give up the aspiration of knowing everything about a particular situation.

All of the ways in which we deal with environmental complexity at the perceptual level are deeply tinged with the hues of the society in which we live. That we notice skin color and not skin texture results from the nature of social customs. Yet, it is curious that closely below the level of habitual awareness there is also a kind of "noticing" of socially less relevant things. Morphologists tell us, for example, that human skin texture can be divided roughly and metaphorically into three types: apple skins, onion skins, and orange skins, the first associated with round pyknic physiques, the second with thin or "scrawny" types, the last with athletic builds. The moment this is mentioned, you have what Herman Melville once called a "shock of recognition"—you somehow knew these types but did not quite recognize them explicitly. So it is, too, with recoding information: new methods of organizing experience, once one can break through the old methods, are "obvious." A mother has been seeing her obstreperous child as "naughty" or "rebellious." A psychologist explains to her that it is five o'clock and that the child is principally tired. If this new way of organizing the welter of movements and expressions that constitute a child's behavior can be accepted by the mother, likely as not she will say, "Of course, but I should have thought of that." The alternative ways of organizing a percept seem somehow to be there in nascent form. So, too, with technological aids like languages and cameras and lists. A photographic plate is immensely limited: the noises that make a Roman street so memorable do not register, no matter how fine-grained the film. But, as in the other two modes of dealing with stimulation overload, technological aids also produce a surplus beyond what is immediately "used" consciously.

I have mentioned the "nascent surplus" of information one obtains in encounters with the environment even though one has been highly selective in noticing things, because it is important from the point of view of creativity and social change and innovation. If it is true that people are selective, must be selective to match their limited cognitive capacities to the complexities of the social and physical environment, it is also true that they are not completely trapped in this selectivity, that the conditions for producing a change in perceiving and thinking about events are there.

The reader will properly ask at this point, "But *is* selectivity forced on a person by the nature of his cognitive apparatus? Can he not take his time and perceive more carefully and comprehensively and get a better sense of what things really mean around him?" The question is a good one, indeed a deep one, and can be answered in several ways. First, there are great individual differences between people in the degree to which they "gamble" in their selectivity, some seemingly content with noticing only a few relevant-to-them things about events they encounter, others being much more deliberate and aware about alternatives and subtleties. Elsewhere in this volume, for example, the reader will find discussions of the authoritarian personality, one of whose notable characteristics is a proneness to seeing things very selectively, in black and white unrelieved by gray. It is also worth remembering that a constant regimen of close inspection of events, a devotion to the alternative ways in which events can be perceived, may conflict with requirements for action. We are forced to decide whether a man is honest or not, whether a group is friendly toward us. If we are to adjust to problems of segregation and desegregation, we must notice whether skins are white or colored. We cannot, like Hamlet, remain long in the state of being "sicklied o'er with the pale cast of thought"—not if we are to act. Finally, there are times when the world is too much like one of Rorschach's ink blots, with ambiguity prevailing. The cues we are forced to use are highly random and probabilistic. We must often decide whether a man is friendly or not on the basis of a cue no more trustworthy than whether or not he is smiling, and are thus forced to fall back on what may be a groundless stereotype. In such situations, perceptual interference may reflect little more than the social conventions or the particular strategy a person uses for coping with his difficulties. It is characteristic, for example, that people are inaccurate, indeed only a bit better than chance, in being able to recognize those members of a group who dislike them—far less good at it than in telling whether others like them. The masking of cues by politesse—we are subtle about showing dislike—plus the protective need of avoiding the sense of being disliked lead perception into all sorts of traps. We end up by seeing those people as disliking us whom we ourselves dislike.

The "New Look" in Perception

Perhaps the immediate impetus to contemporary concern with the role of perceptual processes in social behavior came from a series of experiments on determinants of perceptual organization—determinants that could be called "behavioral" which relate to such influences as need, social values, attitudes, stress, cultural background, *etc.*, in contrast to "autochthonous" which refers to stimulus factors. These experiments, taken as a sequence, came, rather waggishly, to be called the "New Look" in perception. A sampling of some of the principal studies carried out will serve to highlight some of the critical problems that have faced the theorist concerned with formulating a model of the perceptual process that has some relevance to the understanding of social behavior. In the final section we shall return to the nature of such a theoretical model.[1]

The early studies were principally concerned with showing the nature of "distortion" in perception and the sources of perceptual inaccuracy and were, in the main, influenced by thinking imported from clinical psychiatry where such doctrines as "autistic thinking," "defense," "primary process" (hypothesized infantile wishful hallucination) had become dominant as a result of Freud's pioneering work. The studies of Gardner Murphy and his colleagues are a case in point. Levine, Chein, and Murphy (11)

---

[1] Since there have appeared several hundred experimental investigations of motivational and social determinants of perception, it is indeed difficult and certainly arbitrary to select a few for special mention. The choice of the experiments is based partly on their importance, partly upon the degree to which they illustrate basic theoretical issues, and partly on expository convenience—in about that order.

showed their subjects a set of food pictures behind a ground-glass screen that obscured them to the point of ambiguity. The subjects were then asked to give the first association that the obscured pictures brought to mind. They found that associations connected with food and eating increased as the hours of food deprivation of the subjects increased, reaching a maximum around 10 to 12 hours of starvation. After this, the number of food associations declined. The authors attempted to explain the finding in terms of the pleasure principle operating under conditions of mild drive, being supplanted by the reality principle when hunger became severe. Like many pioneering experiments, there was much wrong with the design of this study—the kind of associational response employed, the fact that the subjects knew they would be fed after the requisite number of hours of being without food, *etc.* But it stimulated many follow-up studies. We now know that the results of Levine, Chein, and Murphy are a special case of a more general one whose nature is not yet clear.

McClelland and Atkinson (12), for example, worked with subjects who were unaware of the relation between their hunger and the perceptual test they were being given. The subjects, sailors at a submarine base, were asked to "recognize" "barely perceptible" objects on a screen. Actually the screen was blank. The men showed an increase in instrumental food response—seeing eating utensils and the like—but no increase with hours of deprivation in the number of consummatory food objects seen.

Yet, in another study, under conditions of prolonged and chronic semi-starvation, conscientious objectors showed no increase at all in the number or quality of food associations or readiness to perceive food objects (see the wartime work of Brozek and his colleagues [2]). Here the question may well have been one of pride: these dedicated young men were doing their service by serving as subjects in an experiment. Giving in to hunger may have been something to avoid as almost a matter of honor. With respect to chronically food-deprived prisoners of war and concentration camp victims that I have interviewed shortly after release, one finds that there is repeated mention of two extreme types: those preoccupied with food and those who avoid the topic as much as possible. One can cite other studies that add further subtleties to the complex pattern that seems to emerge, but there is now enough evidence before us to suggest that not the *amount* of need but the way in which a person learns to *handle* his needs determines the manner in which motivation and cognitive selectivity will interact. Autism or wishful thinking are scarcely universal modes of coping with one's needs. It is conceivable that in a culture or in a family setting where emphasis is placed upon asceticism and denial of needs, autism would be the exception. On the whole, then, selectivity reflects the nature of the person's mode of striving for goals rather than the amount of need which he seems to be undergoing.

Closely related to this line of investigation are studies on the role of interest, value, and attitude, and this work brings up several additional subtleties. The experimental work of Postman, Bruner, and McGinnies (13) indicated that the speed and ease with which words were recognized when briefly presented in a fast-exposure apparatus (tachistoscope) was a function of the value areas these words represented and of the interest the subjects in the experiment evinced in these various value areas as measured by the Allport-Vernon Study of Values, which tests for the relative dominance of religious, esthetic, political, social, theoretical, and economic interests. The general finding was that the greater the dominance of a value in the person, the more rapidly he would recognize words representing that area. The authors found that the hypotheses offered by subjects prior to correct recognition were particularly revealing, suggesting that in the presence of low-value words there was some form of defensive avoidance—the perceiving of blanks, scrambled letters, or even derogatory words which the authors called "contravaluant hypotheses." With high-value words, on the contrary, subjects tended in excess of chance to propose guesses that were in the value area of the stimulus word prior to correct recognition, in keeping with a subsequent finding of Bricker and Chapanis (1) that subjects can obtain partial information from words when they are presented below threshold. Later studies by Bruner and Postman (6) on blocks in perceiving personally threatening words and by McGinnies (14) on the raising of identification thresholds for taboo words led to the development of the concept of "perceptual defense," a kind of blocking of recognition for classes of materials that were personally and/or culturally unacceptable to the perceiver, a "proscribed list" at the entry port so to speak.

It was argued by Solomon and Howes (18) that the findings on the effect of values could be accounted for by a factor of frequency—that the person interested in religion was more likely to have selective exposure to religious words and symbols. Howes (10) then went on to show that the amount of time required to recognize a word in the English language could be expressed rather precisely as a function of the logarithm of the frequency with which the word appeared in printed English as recorded in the useful Thorndike-Lorge frequency count (20). But since economic words are likely to be more frequently encountered in printed English than theoretical words, the general frequency of words in English would not be sufficient grounds to explain why some individuals, high in theoretical interests, recognize theoretical words more quickly than economic words such as "money" or "price." We must invoke a notion of "idiosyncratic frequency," an individual's frequency of encounter without regard to frequency in English. Indeed, Postman and Schneider (16) showed that for very common words drawn from the six value areas of the Allport-Vernon test, the relative position of the values for the subject made little difference. With rarer words it did, with the more valued ones being recognized more easily.

The upshot of this debate, it would appear, is twofold and of considerable significance. Perceptual readiness, the ease with which items are recognized under less than optimal viewing conditions, seems to not only reflect the needs and modes of striving of an organism but also to reflect the requirement that surprise be minimized—that perceptual readiness be predictive in the sense of being tuned to what is likely to be present in the environment as well as what is needed for the pursuit of our enterprises. The predictive nature of perceptual readiness, however, reflects more than the frequency with which things occur. Rather, it is best thought of as the matching of perceptual readiness to the probable sequences of events in the environment. We come to learn what goes with what. We *hear* the approaching whistle of a train and are readied to *see* the train. We learn, if you will, the probabilistic texture of the world, conserve this learning, use it as a guide to tuning our perceptual readiness to what is most likely next. It is this that permits us to "go beyond the information given." That there is danger in using such a guide is illustrated in a study by Bruner and Postman on the perception of incongruity (6). If playing cards with suit and color reversed—a red four of clubs, say—are presented to subjects for brief intervals of a few milliseconds, what occurs is perceptual completion according to high probability linkages we have already learned; the subject "sees" a red four of hearts or a black four of clubs. Thresholds of identification increase grossly: when subjects are presented with these incongruous stimuli, it takes them an inordinately long exposure time to "see" what is actually there. But human organisms unlearn and learn quickly: having seen the incongruity finally, later instances are much more rapidly identified correctly.

It is characteristic of perceptual identification of things that the larger the number of alternatives the person is expecting, the more difficult it is to recognize any single one of the alternatives that does occur. In an experiment by Bruner, Miller, and Zimmerman (5) it was found that it is much easier to recognize a word when it is one of four that may occur than when it is one of 8 or 16 or 32 that may occur. This suggests that where speed is required in perception—as under stress conditions or under conditions of exigent motivation—the likelihood of erroneous perception increases. That is to say, to gain speed, we limit the alternative hypotheses that we are willing to entertain. In the event of ambiguous stimulation, as in social perception generally, such speed-producing monopolistic hypotheses are likely to be confirmed. We expect, for example, a hostile action from a disliked person; he does something equivocal; we "see" it as a hostile act and thus confirm our expectation. It is the case, moreover, that under conditions where alternative expectancies must be limited, we will be more likely to adopt socially conventional expectancies or ones that reflect our more basic needs. It is in this sense that stress and social pressure serve to reduce the subtlety of the registration process.

One final matter must be mentioned before turning briefly to theory. It has to do with the perception of magnitude, a subject which does not at first seem closely related to social psychology. An early study by Bruner and Goodman (4) opened the issue. The study was simply conceived—in both a good and a bad sense. Children, ages 10 to 11, divided into those from fairly prosperous homes and those from a slum settlement house, were given the task of adjusting a variable patch of light to the sizes of pennies, nickles, dimes, quarters, and half dollars. Half the subjects worked with coins in hand, half from memory. Control groups adjusted the light patch to cardboard discs of the same sizes. The findings, in general, were that the sizes of the more valuable coins were overestimated, of less valuable coins underestimated. The effects were greater for the memory condition than for the condition with coin present. No significant effect was found for paper discs. In general, the economically well-to-do children showed less of the value-distortion effect than the poor children.

The study has been repeated several times, and as McCurdy (13) and Tajfel (19) point out, the same effect found more often than not under a variety of conditions. One experiment by Carter and Schooler (9) found somewhat contrary results. The same trends were observed, but they fell short of statistical significance save for the condition where size was estimated from memory, where significant results were observed. A later study by Bruner and Rodrigues (8) pointed up one faulty assumption of the earlier studies mentioned. Overestimation and underestimation of size is always stated with respect to the measured sizes of the coins, the "physically accurate" size. This is a psychologically naive way of describing what goes on in judgment of magnitude. Rather, one should ask about the *relative* subjective sizes of coins of different value. The study by Bruner and Rodrigues had as its principal object to show that there was a *greater* separation in subjective size between a nickel and a quarter than there was for comparable-sized white metal discs. Tajfel (19) has developed this point in an interesting theoretical paper, pointing out that it is one of the functions of perceptual judgment to accentuate the apparent difference in magnitudes between objects that differ in value, provided that the difference in magnitude is associated with the difference in value—as if, so to speak, the two attributes, value and magnitude, are confounded in a way to point up and accentuate value difference. In short, even in the estimation of magnitude, judgmental processes reflect the social conventions that establish values for various elements of the environment.[2]

On Theoretical Models of Perception

Given the operation of behavioral factors in perceiving and cognizing generally, including the operation of social factors, what can be said about a theoretical model of perception that would be of relevance to the social psychologist? It is quite clear at the outset that the psychologist principally concerned with perception cannot work with one kind of theory and the social psychologist, interested in the effects of perceptual selectivity on social behavior and in the cultural patterning of perception as well, work with yet another theory of perception. Let me briefly outline, in conclusion, some of the features that I believe a theory of perception must have in order to do justice to the concerns of both kinds of psychologists. For a fuller account of the points to be made, the reader is referred to Bruner (3).

The first, and perhaps most self-evident point upon reflection, is that perceiving or registering on an object or an event in the environment involves an act of categorization. We "place" things in categories. That is a "man" and he is "honest" and he is now "walking" in a manner that is "leisurely" with the "intention" of "getting some relaxation." Each of the words in quotation marks involves a sorting or placement of stimulus input on the basis of certain cues that we learn how to use. Now it is of great importance to bear in mind that most of the categories into which we sort for identification are learned on the basis of experience, by virtue of our membership in a culture and a linguistic community, and by the nature of the needs we must fulfill in order to exist beyond some degraded level. Not only are the categories learned, but we learn to estimate the likelihood that placement of an event into a category on the basis of a few cues will be "accurate"—by which we mean, *predictive* in the sense that a closer look will bear it out or that it will be consensually validated when other perceivers come on the scene or it will be confirmed by technological inspection.

We may take it as self-evident that some categories we employ are more amenable to check by prediction. The cues we use for judging an object

[2] So brief a summary of a field of research as complicated as magnitude estimation and the role of value factors in it is bound to be oversimplified. For a fuller account, the reader is referred to the excellent papers of Tajfel, *op. cit.*, and McCurdy, *op. cit.*

"distant" or a surface "impenetrable" are checked a thousand times a day in getting about: walking, driving, reaching. Others are less readily checked. Whether, on the basis of a few signs, we can judge whether a man is "honorable," given the difficulty of establishing a quick and adequate criterion, is questionable. The category, established by a culture in response to its social needs, resists validation. It is perhaps the case that modes of categorizing that are amenable to firm and immediate validation with respect to predictiveness are the ones that are more universal to the human race, more easily diffused and learned. The less readily a form of categorizing is able to be predictively validated, the more will it reflect the idiosyncrasies of a culture. It is not surprising that the famous Cambridge expedition to the Torres Straits (17) at the opening of this century found so few differences in the perception of distance, size, *etc.*, in comparing primitive Pacific Islanders and English undergraduates.

It is also apparent that the categories of events with which we become accustomed to dealing are organized into systems or structures, bound together in various ways: by virtue of the fact that one class of events is likely to follow another or because classes of events are closely bound by some other principle than mere association as, for example, that several are required in order for certain objectives to be reached. Thus, displacement of a dot from one position to another is categorized as "a dot moving" and not as "first a dot at position *A*, then another dot at position *B*." As we have noted before, recoding into systems serves to keep mental life from becoming burdened with a diversity of unrelated particulars. Highly practiced perception is a case in point. A practiced baseball spectator joins and meshes a highly complex set of categorized events into a structure called a "double play."

In addition to the problem of categories and category systems and how they are formed, there is also a question of the accessibility of such categories for use by a perceiver. It is often the case that we fail to identify an event properly although we are knowledgeable about the class of events which it exemplifies; fail to do so even though the cues are clear. And as the work cited earlier in this paper has shown, certain categories manifest their accessibility by permitting rapid identification of relevant objects under conditions of very brief or very "fuzzy" exposure. What makes certain kinds of categorizing responses sometimes available and sometimes not? What can be said in general is that category accessibility reflects two sets of factors. Need and interest states, as we have implied, increase accessibility of those categories of objects that relate to their fulfillment or furthering—not necessarily in a wish-fulfilling or autistic way, as noted before, but in a manner consonant with achieving realistically a desired goal. The second set of factors governing category accessibility has to do with the predictive requirements of perception and the need to avoid disruptive mistakes. These requirements tune the readiness of the perceiver to match the likelihood of events in the environment. When we are hungry, we tend to be alerted to signs of restaurants, if we usually assuage hunger in restaurants. We notice ones we have never noticed before. Our "restaurant" category has become highly "available." But we look for and expect restaurants at the street level and not in the sky or atop trees. It is this balancing of need-induced alertness and event-matching expectancy that makes it possible for perception to act in the service of needs and interests and, at the same time, with due regard for reality.

In conclusion, perceptual readiness reflects the dual requirements of coping with an environment—directedness with respect to goals and efficiency with respect to the means by which the goals can be attained. It is no matter of idle interest that a religious man picks up perceptually things that are relevant to his interest more easily and more quickly than other things, and at the same time, this efficiency continues to reflect what is likely to occur in his surroundings. What it suggests is that once a society has patterned a man's interests and trained him to expect what is likely in that society, it has gained a great measure of control not only on his thought processes, but also on the very material on which thought works—the experienced data of perception. It is not surprising, then, that the social psychologist has shown a renewed interest in the process of perceiving. To understand the manner in which man responds to and copes with his social environment we must know what that environment is *to him*. The physicist provides a description of the nature of stimulation in such terms as wave lengths, radiant energy, chemical compounds. Nobody confuses these descriptions with what we experience—colors, brightness, tastes. The student of society, like the physicist, provides descriptions of the "external environment" in terms of stratification, totemic clans, moities. The question is how people perceive or register upon these features of the social environment. That is what is crucial in determining how we respond.

References

1. Bricker, P. D., and A. Chapanis, "Do Incorrectly Perceived Tachistoscopic Stimuli Convey Some Information?" *Psychological Review,* Vol. 60 (1953), pp. 181-188.
2. Brozek, J., H. Guetzkow, and M. G. Baldwin, "A Quantitative Study of Perception and Association in Experimental Semi-Starvation," *Journal of Personality,* Vol. 19 (1951), pp. 245-264.
3. Bruner, J. S., "On Perceptual Readiness," *Psychological Review,* Vol. 64 (1957), pp. 123-152.

4. ———, and C. C. Goodman, "Value and Need as Organizing Factors in Perception," *Journal of Abnormal and Social Psychology,* Vol. 42 (1947), pp. 33-44.
5. ———, G. A. Miller, and C. Zimmerman, "Discriminative Skill and Discriminative Matching in Perceptual Recognition," *Journal of Experimental Psychology,* Vol. 44 (1955), pp. 187-192.
6. ———, and L. Postman, "Emotional Selectivity in Perception and Reaction," *Journal of Personality,* Vol. 16 (1947), pp. 69-77.
7. ———, and L. Postman, "On the Perception of Incongruity: A Paradigm," *Journal of Personality,* Vol. 18 (1949), pp. 206-223.
8. ———, and J. S. Rodrigues, "Some Determinants of Apparent Size," *Journal of Abnormal and Social Psychology,* Vol. 48 (1953), pp. 17-24.
9. Carter, L. F., and K. Schooler, "Value, Need, and Other Factors in Perception," *Psychological Review,* Vol. 56 (1949), pp. 200-207.
10. Howes, D., "On the Interpretation of Word Frequency as a Variable Affecting Speed of Recognition," *Journal of Experimental Psychology,* Vol. 48 (1954), pp. 106-122.
11. Levine, R., I. Chein, and G. Murphy, "The Relation of the Intensity of a Need to the Amount of Perceptual Distortion, a Preliminary Report," *Journal of Psychology,* Vol. 13 (1942), pp. 283-293.
12. McClelland, D. C., and J. W. Atkinson, "The Projective Expression of Needs: I. The Effect of Different Intensities of the Hunger Drive on Perception," *Journal of Psychology,* Vol. 25 (1948), pp. 205-222.
13. McCurdy, H. G., "Coin Perception Studies and the Concept of Schemata," *Psychological Review,* Vol. 63 (1956), pp. 160-168.
14. McGinnies, E., "Emotionality and Perceptual Defense," *Psychological Review,* Vol. 56 (1949), pp. 244-251.
15. Postman, L., J. S. Bruner, and E. McGinnies, "Personal Values as Selective Factors in Perception," *Journal of Abnormal and Social Psychology,* Vol. 83 (1948), pp. 148-153.
16. ———, and B. Schneider, "Personal Values, Visual Recognition, and Recall," *Psychological Review,* Vol. 58 (1951), pp. 271-284.
17. Rivers, W. H. R., "Vision," *Reports of the Cambridge Anthropological Expedition to Torres Straits,* Vol. 2 (1901), pp. 1-132.
18. Solomon, R. L., and D. W. Howes, "Word Frequency, Personal Values, and Visual Deviation Thresholds," *Psychological Review,* Vol. 58 (1951), pp. 256-270.
19. Tajfel, H., "Value and the Perceptual Judgment of Magnitude," *Psychological Review,* Vol. 64 (1957), pp. 197-204.
20. Thorndike, E. L., and I. Lorge, *The Teacher's Word Book of 30,000 Words* (New York: Teachers College, Columbia University, 1944).

2. Intelligence from a perceptual point of view

Arthur W. Combs

Reprinted from the *Journal of Abnormal and Social Psychology,* Vol. 47 (1952), 662-673, by permission of the author and the American Psychological Association.

Are one's perceptions so important that they could even affect his level of intelligence? Combs suggests that this may be true and speculates further that what one learns may be related to what he perceives himself capable of learning. Factors which influence perceptions and implications for schools are discussed.

Has the time-honored static conception of intelligence and human capacity proved more restrictive than constructive in educational practice? Dr. Combs suggests that it has and explores the idea of intelligence as a function of an individual's perceptions. If this view is tenable, it follows that the school, having the opportunity to influence appreciably some of the factors that affect perception, can thereby better educate most students, even those formerly believed to be operating near "capacity."

There is a growing trend in psychology toward viewing behavior as a function of perception. More and more we have come to understand that the individual's behavior is not so much a function of the physical stimulus as it is a function of his perceptions of the events to which he is exposed. It is the meaning of events to the individual rather than the externally observed nature of events which seems crucial in behavior. As a result, psychologists in increasing numbers are turning their attention to the problems of human perception and are attempting to observe behavior, not from an external point of view, but from the point of view of the individual who is behaving. This paper is an attempt to relate this method of observation to the problem of intelligence. The question we wish to explore in this paper is: "What is the nature of intelligence viewed from a perceptual or phenomenological frame of reference?"

INTELLIGENCE AS A PROBLEM OF PERCEPTION

By the term *intelligence* we ordinarily refer to the effectiveness of the individual's behavior. In a personal frame of reference the individual's behavior is described in terms of the perceptions that he can make his own unique perceptive field. This perceptive field has been called by Snygg and Combs *The Phenomenal Field* and has been defined by them as "the universe of experience open to the individual at the moment of his behavior." In other words, the behavior of the individual will be dependent upon the perceptions that the individual makes in his phenomenal field at the moment of action. The effectiveness of his behavior will necessarily be a function of the adequacy of those perceptions.

If an entity in the perceptive field is vague and ill defined, the behavior of the individual will be correspondingly vague and lacking in precision. Until the child has clearly differentiated that 2 plus 2 equals 4, this function is comparatively meaningless and his behavior in arithmetic is correspondingly inaccurate and ineffective. Thus, the precision and effectiveness of the individual's behavior will be dependent upon the scope and clarity of his personal field of awareness. Intelligence, then, from a perceptual point of view becomes a function of the factors which limit the scope and clarity of an individual's phenomenal field.

The perceptions that could be made of any given situation, such as looking at a stone wall, for example, are, theoretically, practically infinite in number and quality. As a matter of fact, however, we are strictly limited in our perceptions of a stone wall to those which we, as human beings, can make. The perceptions possible to us are only those that people can make. We cannot, for instance, perceive the wall as it would appear to a man from Mars, or from the interior of an atom, or as it would appear to a centipede. What is more, we cannot even perceive it as it would appear to all people. Different people will perceive different aspects of the wall differently, even at the same instant. I can only perceive the wall, and hence behave toward it, in terms of the perceptions that I, as an individual, can make regarding it. I may, for instance, perceive it as a fine, sturdy fence enclosing my property, while a stone mason friend might perceive it as having been poorly designed or as having been built with too little cement in the mortar mixture. The perceptions open to my mason friend are the result of his unique experience. I, not having such experience, am incapable of those perceptions at this moment.

Potential and functional perceptions

Before proceeding further with our discussion of the limiting factors in perception, it is necessary for us to pause for a moment to distinguish between potential and functional perceptions. By potential perceptions I mean those perceptions that exist in the individual's unique field of awareness and that, given the right circumstances at any particular moment, *could* occur. The fact that a perception is potentially possible to any individual, by no means, however, means that it will occur at the moment of action. Even those perceptions that I can make potentially may not be active for me at any given moment. Potentially, I might be able, for instance, to perceive the wall that we have just been using as an example as a barrier to be gotten over, as an eyesore to be beautified, as composed of 687 bricks costing me $80.27, or as providing pleasant shade on a hot day. These are all potential perceptions I am capable of making about the wall. They will affect my behavior, however, only when they are active or functioning in my field of perceptions. When I am beating a hasty retreat pursued by a neighbor's angry dog, perceptions about the shade, beauty, or cost of the wall, though potential, are not functional in affecting my behavior. I behave only in terms of my functioning perception of the wall as something to get over—and quickly. The fact that particular perceptions may exist potentially in the phenomenal field of an individual is by no means a guarantee that they may exist functionally at the moment of action.

While the potential intelligence of the individual is of interest in judging his capacities, it is practically always a matter impossible to measure with any degree of accuracy. We can only sample those parts of a phenomenal field that *we* happen to feel are important. Obviously the measurement of a person's potential perceptions in these terms is open to extremely grave sampling error and improves in accuracy only as the individuals tested have common experience in the materials chosen for testing. It seems probable that an intelligence test cannot accurately measure the potential differentiations that the individual can make in his phenomenal field. Rather, what we usually measure are the subject's functional perceptions. That is, we measure what differentiations he can make when confronted with the necessity to do so for one reason or another. We may define these functional perceptions as: those perceptions in the field experienced by the individual at the moment of behaving.

From a perceptual viewpoint, if intelligence is the capacity for effective behavior, *the intelligence of an individual will be dependent upon the richness and variety of perceptions possible to him at a given moment.* To understand and effectively to foster intelligent behavior, it will be necessary for us to be concerned with the limiting factors upon the perceptions of an individual. We need to know not only what the individual *could* perceive, but what he *would* perceive at a given moment of behaving.

Some Limiting Factors Upon Perception

PHYSIOLOGIC LIMITATIONS UPON PERCEPTION

Certainly the physical limitations upon the organism affect the differentiations possible in the phenomenal field. Some forms of prenatal anomalies, like mongolism, microcephalia, and similar disorders, indubitably reduce the level of operation at which the individual can function and seriously impair the ability of the organism to make adequate perceptions. Similarly, there seems good reason to believe that some types of mechanical or disease injury to the central nervous system may result in impaired functioning, such as occurs in cerebral palsy, birth injuries, prefrontal lobotomy, the aftermath of such diseases as encephalitis or, even, in common childhood diseases accompanied by prolonged high fever. Various forms of endocrinopathies, particularly cretinism, also appear to have limiting effects upon differentiational capacity for some individuals. Such physical or biological limitations upon the organism have been widely studied but account for only a small proportion of those persons operating at impaired intelligence levels.

Other less dramatic forms of physical handicaps may also have important effects upon the perceptions possible to the individual, however. This is particularly true of individuals suffering impairment of various sense modalities which may inhibit the clarity or even the existence of some perceptions. We need to remind ourselves, however, that such persons may have as rich and varied a perceptive field within their own limitations as we have within ours. Testing persons living in one frame of reference with tests based on those of another can easily lead us astray, a fact well known to the makers of some tests for the handicapped. The limitations imposed upon perception by such physical handicaps as the loss or impairment of locomotion or the use of arms or hands are also important in limiting certain kinds of perceptions. These people experience different, but not necessarily fewer or poorer, perceptions of events than so-called "normals."

Perhaps less well recognized in their effects upon perception are such factors as malnutrition, focal infections, and chronic fatigue, which may reduce both the need for and the ability to make adequate perceptions. It is well known in industrial psychology, for example, that fatigued workers are more likely to have accidents, perhaps because of failure to make the right differentiations at the right time. It is conceivable that persons suffering from chronic fatigue over long periods similarly fail to make differentiations useful to them on later occasions.

Certainly such physical factors as these have important effects upon the ability of the individual to make adequate differentiations in his perceptive field. The more dramatic of these have often been recognized and studied. Others, such as the effects of malnutrition, fatigue, and the like, have been less adequately explored. In spite of the lack of research in respect to some of the physical limitations upon intelligence, far more work has been done in this area, however, than in some of those to be discussed below.

ENVIRONMENT AND OPPORTUNITY AS A LIMITATION UPON PERCEPTION

The differentiations in the phenomenal field that an individual can make will, of course, be affected by the opportunities for perception to which he has been exposed. To appear in the perceptive field an event must have been, in some manner, experienced by the person who perceives it. Environmental effects upon perception appear to be of two types, actual or concrete and symbolic or vicarious.

Exposure to Actual Environmental Events

In the first place the perceptions possible to any individual will be limited, in part, by the actual environmental factors to which he has been exposed. Eskimos ordinarily do not comprehend bananas, nor African Bushmen, snow, since neither has had the opportunity to experience these events in their respective environments. It is not necessary to go so far afield for illustration, however. In our own country our experience with the testing of children in various parts of the nation has shown that perceptions are highly limited by the environmental conditions surrounding the individual. Mountain children, for example, often give bizarre responses on intelligence tests. Sherman and Henry found intelligence test results on such children arranged themselves in order of the opportunities provided by their environment.

There are differences also between the perceptions of rural and urban children, children from the North and children from the South, mountain and valley, seaboard and plains. Nor are such differences confined only to children. Adults, too, are limited in their perceptions by environmental factors. During the war I worked for a time in an induction station receiving men from the mountains of Kentucky, West Virginia, and southern Ohio. An intelligence test in use at this station was composed of a series of five pictures with instructions to the subject to cross out that one of each series of five objects that did not belong with the others. One set of five pictures showed four stringed instruments, a guitar, harp, violin, bass fiddle, and a trumpet. Large numbers of these back country men crossed out the harp because they had never seen one or because "all the others are things in our band." We cannot assume that these men were less able to make differentiations or had perceptive fields less rich than their examiner on the basis of these tests. We can only suggest that their perceptions are different from those who made the test. Presumably, had they made the test and administered it to the psychologist, the psychologist would have appeared rather dull!

Exposure to Symbolic or Vicarious Events

Differentiations may occur in the perceptive field upon a symbolic basis as well as from exposure to an actual event. That is, perceptions may occur in the individual's field through indirect exposure to experience as in reading, conversation, movies, and other means of communication. Although I cannot directly perceive that it is dangerous to expose myself to rays from an atomic pile, for example, I can differentiate this notion through what others whom I respect have told me. Ideas and concepts are largely differentiations of this sort, and it is probable that many of our perceptions are acquired through a symbolic rather than an actual exposure. Certainly most of our formal schooling falls in this category which may explain, in part, why so little of it is effective in our behavior.

It will be recognized at once that exposure to events in no sense completely determines the perceptions that the individual will make. Exposure to events is only one of the factors involved in determining whether or not an event will be differentiated. Even with equivalent exposure, the perceptions we make are not alike. Perception is not an all or none proposition but a selective process. The same person in the same situation at different times may perceive quite different aspects of the situation and behave accordingly. The provisions of opportunity to perceive is by no means a guarantee that a particular perception will occur, a phenomenon of which teachers are only too aware. The personal field of the individual is always organized and meaningful and, even with exposure to events, only those aspects that have meaning for the individual in his own unique economy will be differentiated with permanence.

The individual in a particular culture perceives those aspects of his environment that, from his point of view, he needs to perceive to maintain and enhance his self in the world in which he lives. This does not mean he makes fewer perceptions than an individual in another culture; he makes only *different* perceptions. Thus, intelligence tests made in one culture and applied in another do not measure the ability to differentiate, nor do they measure the richness of the individual's field. Perhaps what they really measure is no more than the difference between cultures. American-made intelligence tests applied to other cultures generally show the following arrangement of nationality groups in decreasing order: British Isles, Germany, France, Italy, the Balkans, Asiatic countries. It will be noted that these nationality groups are also roughly arranged in order of the degree of commonality with our own culture.

TIME AS A LIMITATION UPON PERCEPTION

Differentiation requires time. The richness of perception, therefore, will be in part a function of how long the individual has been in touch with experiences. While it is true that a perception is possible only when confronted by an experience, it is also true that this exposure must be long enough to make differentiation possible. This principle is familiar to anyone who has looked at a painting for a period of time. The perceptions which can be made are almost limitless if one looks long enough.

In thinking of the effect of time upon differentiation, it is necessary for us to keep in mind that we are speaking of the duration of the individual's experience with an event and not of the observer's experience. Thus, while it may appear to an outside observer that an individual is confronted by an experience, from the individual's own point of view, he may have no contact with it whatever. A child may sit in school all day, apparently exposed to the curriculum, but may actually be experiencing and perceiving quite different aspects of the situation. Perception is an internal, individual phenomenon and may be quite different from that of another person, even in the same situation.

Most perceptions that the individual makes are functions of previous differentiations he has made in his phenomenal field. For example, before one can perceive the mechanics of multiplication, he must have perceived addition. In the same way, before he can perceive the function of a sand dome on top of the locomotive, he must differentiate the fact that locomotive wheels sometimes slip. Clearly this process of differentiation takes time. It seems axiomatic that to make differentiations an individual must have lived long enough to do so, a fact we recognize in the construction of intelligence tests calibrated for various age levels, and which teachers recognize in the concept of readiness.

Differentiations in the phenomenal field seem to be occurring continuously as the organism seeks to satisfy its needs in the myriad situations of life. In this sense, intelligence never ceases to develop but is continuously increasing so long as the individual remains alive and operating. That intelligence seems to level off at age sixteen or later is probably a mere artifact of our method of observation. So long as the individual remains in school we have at least a modicum of comparable experience which can be tested in different persons. After the school years, when individuals are free to go their separate ways, this modicum of comparable experience rapidly disappears. The older one gets, the more diverse is his experience. Intelligence tests based upon comparability of experience may thus fail to evaluate properly the effectiveness of adults.

THE INDIVIDUAL'S GOALS AND VALUES AS A LIMITING FACTOR UPON PERCEPTION

Up to this point in our discussion we have been dealing with factors affecting perception that are widely discussed in the literature and for the most part are well understood. In the remainder of this paper let us turn our attention to several factors less well explored as they appear in a phenomenological setting. The first of these has to do with the effects of the individual's own goals and values as a limiting factor on perception.

From a phenomenological view the individual is forever engaged in a ceaseless attempt to achieve satisfaction of his need through the goals and values he has differentiated as leading to that end. These goals and values may be explicit or implicit, simple or complex, but they are always unique to the personality itself. The goals of an individual will vary in another respect as well. The individual's goals and values may be either positive or negative. That is, in the course of his experience, the person may differentiate some things as matters to be sought, while other things may be differentiated as matters to be avoided. What is more, although there is a considerable degree of stability in the major goals and values of a particular individual, there may be great fluctuations in how some goals are perceived from time to time, depending upon the total organization of the perceptual field at any moment.

The goals and values an individual seeks have a most important effect upon the perceptions he can make. Once goals have been established by the individual they continue to affect his every experience. Thus, the person who has differentiated good music as a goal to be sought perceives music more frequently. His entire experience with music is likely to be affected. Certainly his experience will differ markedly from the person who has formulated a goal to avoid music at all costs. In the same way the experiences of children who perceive schooling as something to be sought are vastly different from those of children who try to avoid all aspects of schooling. If the fundamental thesis of this paper is accurate, that intelligence is a function of the variety and richness of the perceptive field, then the individual's goals must have a most important effect upon intelligence. A considerable body of research has been accumulating over the past several years, demonstrating this controlling effect of goals and values on the individual's perceptive experience. Such studies as those of J. M. Levine, R. Levine, Postman, and Bruner are fascinating cases in point.

This effect of goals on perception is by no means limited to the subject whose intelligence we wish to measure. It is equally true of the intelligence test constructor. It leads to the very confusing situation wherein the test constructor with one organization of goals perceives certain experiences to be marks of intelligence for another person who may or may not have similar goals. Indeed, the likelihood is that he, almost certainly, does not have similar goals. Intelligence tests thus become highly selected samplings of perception in terms of what the testers consider important. Low scores do not necessarily mean less rich and varied fields of perception; they may mean only fields of perception more widely divergent from those of the examiner. A young man whom the writer tested at an induction center during the war illustrates the point very well. This young man was a newsboy on the streets of a West Virginia city. Although he had failed repeatedly in grammar school and was generally regarded as "not bright," he appeared on a national radio hook-up as "The Human Adding Machine." He was a wizard at figures. He could multiply correctly such figures as 6235941 × 397 almost as fast as the problem could be written down. He astounded our induction center for half a day with his numerical feats. Yet, on the Binet Test given by the writer he achieved an IQ of less than 60! People in his home town, who bought his papers, amused themselves by giving him problems to figure constantly. When not so occupied this young man entertained himself by adding up the license numbers of cars that passed his corner. He was a specialist in numbers. Apparently as a result of some early success in this field, he had been led to practice numbers constantly, eventually to the exclusion of all else. This was one area in which a poor colored boy could succeed and he made the most of it. His number perceptions were certainly rich and varied but other things were not. Although he was capable of arithmetic feats not achieved by one in millions, he was classified as dull! I do not mean to argue that variety of perception is unimportant in effective behavior. I do mean to suggest the importance of goals in determining perception.

Cultural effects on goals and perceptions

We have stated here that the richness of the individual's perceptive field is in part a function of the goals he has differentiated as important or threatening to him. But, clearly these goals are themselves the results of the individual's experience. The culture one grows up in deeply affects the goals one holds. Cultures both restrict and encourage, approve and disapprove the formulation of goals in the individual. This selective effect of the culture in large measure determines the goals sought and avoided by the individual. These goals in turn must exert important effects upon the perceptions that become part of the individual's perceptive field.

I remember the Kentucky moonshiner to whom I once administered the Wechsler-Bellevue. This man could not tell me "how many pints in a quart" although he had certainly been taught this fact in his early schooling. Knowing that my client did a considerable business in bootleg liquor, I framed the question differently and asked "Well, how do you sell your liquor?" He smiled tolerantly and replied, "Oh Boss, I just sell it by the jug full!" In his community to have done otherwise would have been to risk bankruptcy. In a culture where a jug is standard container for spirits, what need to know about quarts?

It is conceivable that low intelligence may be, at least in part, no more than a function of the goals an individual is striving to reach in achieving his need satisfaction. The well-known phenomenon in which intelligence tests give best results in the school years, when experience and goals have a degree of commonality, and break down badly following those years would seem to corroborate this point. Perhaps by concerning ourselves with human goals we can affect perception, and thus intelligence, much more than we believed possible. Can it be that the child of low apparent intelligence is not so much a problem of an unfortunate heredity as an unfortunate constellation of goals or values? We could do a great deal about intelligence if that were true.

The self-concept as a factor limiting perception

We are just beginning to understand the tremendous effects of the individual's concept of self upon his perceptions and behavior. Lecky, for instance, reports the effect of a change in self-concept in improving the ability of children to spell. Other researches have reported similar effects of the self-concept upon the perceptions which the individual may make. Clinical experience would tend to bear out such observations. Any clinician is familiar with numerous instances in which a child's conception of his abilities severely limited his achievement, even though his real abilities may have been superior to his perception of them. One needs but to go shopping with one's spouse to discover again how one's conception of himself as a male or female affects the things he sees and the things he hears.

Perception is a selective process, and the conception one holds of himself is a vital factor in determining the richness and the variety of perception selected. It makes a great deal of difference, for example, how one perceives the president of our country if one conceives of himself as a Democrat, a Republican, or a Communist. One needs but to observe a group of children to become aware that little boys perceive things quite differently from little girls. Professors do not perceive like truck drivers, although when I have had to ride with professor automobile-drivers, I have often wished they did. Thousands of people in our society avoid perceptions having to do with mathematical functions by their firm concept of themselves as people who "cannot do mathematics." The self-concepts we hold have a very vital effect in selecting the perceptions which become part of our perceptive fields. If the effectiveness of behavior is dependent on our perceptive fields, it follows that the self-concepts we hold must affect the "intelligence" of our behavior.

There is another factor in the effect of the self-concept upon perception that makes it even more important as a selector of experience. That factor is the circular effect of a given concept of self. Let us take, as an example, the child who has developed a concept of himself as "unable to read." Such a child is likely to avoid reading, and thus the very experience which might change his concept of self is bypassed. Worse still, the child who believes himself unable to read, confronted with the necessity for reading, is more likely than not to do badly. The external evaluation of his teachers and fellow pupils, as well as his own observations of his performance, all provide proof to the child of how right he was in the first place! The possession of a particular concept of self tends to produce behavior that corroborates the self-concept with which the behavior originated.

Every clinician has had experience with children of ability who conceive of themselves as unable, unliked, unwanted, or unacceptable and perceive and behave in accordance with their perceptions. And this effect is not limited to children alone. It seems to me one of the great tragedies of our society that millions of people in our society perceiving themselves as able to produce only *X* amount, behave in these terms. Society, in turn, evaluates them in terms of this behavior and so lends proof to what is already conceived by the individual. Compared to this waste of human potential in our society, our losses in automobile accidents seem like a mere drop in the bucket. It is even conceivable in these terms that we create losses in intelligence. If, in our schools, we teach a child that he is unable and if he believes us and behaves in these terms, we need not be surprised when we test his intelligence to discover that he produces at the level at which we taught him!

It is conceivable that psychology has unwittingly contributed to this situation by the widespread publication of a static conception of intelligence and human capacities. The concept of severe limits upon the capacities of the organism simply corroborates the self-concept of the man in the street and decreases the likelihood of change in his concept of self. Even more important must be the effect upon our educational system. Teachers who believe in an unchanging character of child capacities provide the attitudes and experiences that produce and maintain a child's conception of self and his abilities. It is notorious that children's grades vary very little from year to year through the course of schooling. This continuous and little-changing evaluation must have important effects on the self-concept of the child. If the school system in which the child lives is thoroughly imbued with the notion that a child's capacities are comparatively fixed, it is even conceivable that the system may in large measure produce a child's intelligence level by the circular effect we have mentioned above.

THREAT AS A FACTOR IN PERCEPTION

The last of the factors I should like to discuss as a possible factor in intelligence is the effect of threat upon the perceptive field. If our fundamental assumption that intelligence is a function of the richness and breadth of the phenomenal field is correct, the effect of threat on this field becomes a most important consideration. Although these effects have been so widely understood by the layman that they have been made a part of his everyday speech, it is interesting that until very recently the phenomenon has been given little attention by psychologists. The perception by the individual of threat to himself seems to have at least two major effects upon the perceptive field.

Restriction of the Perceptive Field Under Threat

The first of these effects is the restrictive effect that the perception of threat to self seems to have on the individual's perception. When he feels himself threatened, there appears to be a narrowing of the perceptive field to the object of threat. This has often been described in the psychology of vision as "tunnel vision." The phenomenon is extremely common, and almost everyone has experienced it at some moment of crisis in his lifetime. One hears it described in such comments as "All I could see was the truck coming at us," or, "I was so scared I couldn't think of a thing." There seems reason to believe that this effect is not limited to traumatic experiences alone, but exists in lesser degree in response to milder threats as well. Combs and Taylor, for example, have demonstrated the effect under extremely mild forms of threat.

Such limiting effects on perception must certainly have a bearing upon perceptions available to the individual in his phenomenal field. Subjects who have participated in food deprivation experiments report uniformly that when threatened by hunger, food becomes an obsession. Recently, at the dinner table, I asked my young daughter what she had learned at school that day. "Oh nothing," said she with much feeling, "but was our teacher mad! Wow!" It would appear from her remarks that, feeling threatened by an angry teacher, it was difficult for her to perceive much else. Her perceptions of the day were apparently entirely concerned with the nature of anger. No doubt these are valuable perceptions to possess, but I know of no intelligence test which measures them.

I recall, too, the behavior of two little girls whose mother was taken to a mental hospital at the beginning of the summer. The matter was kept a deep secret from these two children for fear they "would not understand." The children spent most of the summer with the writer's daughter in an incessant game of "hospital." From morning to night this game went on outside our living-room window. Apparently, this preoccupation was the direct outcome of the threat they felt in the loss of their mother, for with the mother's return the game ceased as suddenly as it had begun. To the best of my knowledge it has not occurred since. Under threat there seem to be severe limits imposed upon the breadth and character of perception.

Defense of the Perceptive Field Under Threat

There is a second effect of threat upon the individual's perceptions. This effect has to do with the defense reactions induced in the individual on perceiving himself to be threatened. The perception of threat not only narrows the field and reduces the possibility of wide perceptions, but causes the individual to protect and cling to the perceptions he already holds. Thus, the possibility of perceptual changes is reduced, and the opportunities for new perceptions or learning are decreased. Under threat, behavior becomes rigid. The fluidity and adaptation which we generally associate with intelligent behavior is vastly decreased. A number of interesting experiments in the past few years have demonstrated this phenomenon. Cowen, for example, illustrated this effect in problem solving.

Our own experiment previously mentioned also demonstrated this effect with even very mild forms of threat. This rigidity or resistance of perception to change under threat is well known to the layman and is well illustrated in some of the sayings of our culture. Such aphorisms as "Nobody ever wins an argument" or "You can lead a horse to water but you cannot make him drink" seem to be illustrations of a vague understanding of the phenomenon in the public mind. It is surprising that this principle has been so long overlooked.

I think it will be generally agreed that intelligent behavior is quite the antithesis of rigidity. In the terms we have used in this article, intelligent behavior is a function of the variety and richness of perception in the phenomenal field. Whatever produces narrowness and rigidity of perception becomes an important factor in limiting intelligence. If this reasoning is accurate, or even partly so, one is led to wonder about the effects of long-continued threat upon the development of intelligence. What of the child who has suffered serious threats to himself for long periods of his life, as in the case of the delinquent, for example? Or what of the child who has been seriously deprived of affection and warmth from those who surround him over a period of years? Is it possible that we have created low intelligence in such children? Axline has reported a number of cases in which intelligence scores improved considerably under therapy. We have observed similar changes in our own clinical practice.

It may be argued that, although threat seems to reduce perception, some people under threat apparently produce more effectively. I think, however, it is necessary for us to distinguish between "threat" and "challenge." In threat, the individual perceives himself in jeopardy and feels, in addition, a degree of inadequacy to deal effectively with the threat perceived. In challenge, the individual perceives himself threatened but feels at the same time a degree of adequacy to deal with the threat. It would appear that whether an event is perceived as threatening or challenging is a function of the individual's feeling of competence to deal with it. If this analysis is correct, it would explain why a situation that appears threatening to a person, from the viewpoint of an outside observer, might one time produce rigidity and another highly effective behavior. This description of events seems characteristic of the history of civilization as well as of individuals, if Toynbee's explanation can be given credence. He points out that the most productive (more intelligent?) societies are those in which the society faces some crisis within its capacities to cope with the situation (challenge), while societies without crisis or in which the crisis is overwhelming produce very little or collapse entirely.

Some Implications of This Conception of Intelligent Behavior

If the conception of intelligence we have been discussing in this paper should prove accurate, it seems to me to raise serious questions about some of our common assumptions with respect to intelligence and, at the same time, opens some exciting new possibilities for the treatment or education of persons we have often assumed to be beyond help. It implies that our conception of the limiting factors of intelligence may have been too narrow. It would suggest perhaps that our very point of view with respect to intelligence may have resulted in our own tunnel vision, such that we have not been able to perceive other factors given little attention to this point. Perhaps we have been too impressed with the limitations upon growth and development which we observe in physical maturation. We may, for instance, have jumped too quickly to the assumption that intelligent behavior was limited as severely as physical growth and that we have explored to exhaustion other factors that may limit intelligence.

I am not suggesting that physiologic limits do not exist in respect to intelligence. I am suggesting that we may have conceded too early that we had approached those limits. There is no doubt that we can demonstrate in some cases, such as mongolism, cretinism, and the like, that physical factors severely limit intelligence. But these cases are comparatively few compared to the so-called "familial" cases of low intelligence that we often assume are hereditary in origin. What evidence do we really possess that would lead us to the position that an individual of "normal" physical condition and vigor may be limited in his capacity for effective behavior by some physical condition? We assume there must be such factors operating because we cannot explain his handicap otherwise. That biological science has not yet been able to demonstrate such physical bases has not deterred us in this. On the contrary, we have simply deplored the lack of sufficient advance in that discipline to demonstrate our conclusion! I should like to suggest that this may not be their failure but ours. Until it can be definitely established that limitations exist as biological functions, our task as psychologists is to assume that they may just as well be social or psychological in character and to work just as hard exploring the matter in our discipline as we expect the biologist to work in his.

Let us, for example, explore to the very fullest the possibility that in those cases where we cannot demonstrate biologic impairment, the limitations upon intelligence may be psychological. If it turns out not to be true, we shall find out in time. I do not believe we can afford to limit the places where we look by the preperceptions we have about the matter. Our responsibility here is too great. Education, to name but the most obvious of our social institutions, has in large measure predicated its goals and methods on a concept of humanity with certain static limitations on intelligence. If these limitations are not static, it is up to us as psychologists to find out. The task of the scientist is to question, not to be content with answers. We cannot afford to accept an undemonstrated point of view that prevents us from asking questions.

SOME IMPLICATIONS FOR INTELLIGENCE TESTING

If the concepts of intelligence we have been discussing prove accurate, another area of psychological thought toward which we must cast a quizzical eye is the area of intelligence testing. This is particularly important at a time when our culture has come to accept these instruments as trustingly as the family doctor's prescription. If our approach to intelligent behavior as a function of the variety and richness of the perceptual field is a valid consideration, we need to ask regarding these tests at least the following questions:

1. Is our sampling of the perceptive field truly adequate? If I lived for years in a prison cell, I presume I should become expert in perceptions about that cell. Unfortunately, they would be of little value outside the prison walls, but can it truthfully be said that my perceptions are less rich or varied, or only that they are less rich and varied about things I have not had opportunity to experience? Is the delinquent, with rich and varied perceptions on how to elude the police, less intelligent or has he simply not perceived things society wishes he had?

2. Since perceptions are always closely affected by need, by whose need shall we sample perceptions—yours, mine, society's, the subject's own? I suspect that in terms of his own needs and perceptions the subject might be deemed quite brilliant, though he might or might not appear so from the point of view of society. For the most part our tests are based on the assumption that academic, upper middle-class, intellectual perceptions are important. But are they? Can we assume that the expert machinist, who can perceive things "out of this world" for most of the rest of us about a piece of stock on his lathe, is less intelligent than a diplomat who perceives many things about foreign affairs? Can we be so sure of our values as to call one bright and the other dull? Can we blame the machinist for his lack of perception about foreign affairs without asking the diplomat to be equally skilled in the machinist's field of perceptions?

3. Finally, if perceptions are affected by the factors we have discussed in this paper, is it fair to sample intelligence irrespective of the control of such factors? Shall we, for example, examine the child who has lacked opportunity to perceive, has possessed a concept of self or been so threatened over a long period of time so as to have been unable to perceive what we wish to sample without consideration of those factors? Shall we overlook such factors and be satisfied that the perceptions important to us are not there, or shall we seek for ways to make it possible for the child to have them? Shall we assume that our failure to discover a particular perception present in the field is, *ipso facto,* evidence of lack of capacity; or seek to discover why it is not? On the positive side of the picture, if the concepts we have here been discussing are sound, there is reason to believe that intelligence may be far less immutable than we have thought. It may be that we can do far more than we have dreamed we could. Perhaps we may even be able to create intelligence!

Implications for constructive action

Who can say, for example, what results we might be able to achieve by a systematic effort to remove or decrease the effectiveness of the limitations on perception discussed in this paper? It is fascinating to speculate on the possibilities one might try in constructing a situation for a child, or adult, consciously designed to minimize the limitations imposed on perception by physical condition, environment, goals, the individual's self-concept, and the effects of perceived personal threat.

If the position we have taken is accurate, it would suggest that there is much we can do (*a*) to free individuals from the restraints upon perception and (*b*) to provide the opportunities for perception to occur.

1. First and most obviously, we should be able to discover and make available to far more people the means to achieve better physical condition. We have already done a good deal in this area but much needs yet to be done. Who can say, for instance, what completely adequate medical care for all our people might mean a generation hence?

2. If this discussion has merit, there lies the possibility of providing experiences for people that will make adequate perceptions possible. We have tried to do this in our schools, but have not always accomplished it. We have succeeded very well in gathering information and in making it available to students. We have not succeeded too well in making such information meaningful. Can it be that the decreases in school success with advance through the school years is more a function of lack of meaning for students than lack of intelligence? Is it enough to assume that

experience provided by us to the student is truly provided when he is free to experience it? Has the child in school, who is so worried about his relationship with his peers that he cannot perceive what his book is saying, truly been provided opportunity to perceive?

In our training of children of "low intelligence," we often provide situations wherein they are carefully taught to perform repeatedly a simple act. Is it possible that in so doing we may be further narrowing their fields of perception and building self-concepts that produce even narrower perceptive fields?

What kinds of environments could we construct that might more effectively result in increased perception? Such experiments as Lippitt and White have carried on with democratic and autocratic environments suggest some possibilities, but we need to know much more. Perhaps we could learn to build such environments from observing with greater care and understanding the methods of good teachers.

3. Who can say what possible effects might occur from a systematic release of the individual's perceptions by the satisfaction of his most pressing needs or goals? We college professors insist we can produce more, which is another way of saying perceive more, when we have the leisure time to do so, when we are freed from the necessity of spending our time satisfying our needs for sheer existence. Can this be less true of others? It is possible that the child with needs of love, affection, status, prestige, or a girl friend might also be freed to perceive more widely and richly, if we could but find ways of helping him satisfy his needs. Ordinarily, we pay a good deal of attention to the physical needs of a child, understanding that with these needs unfulfilled, he makes a poor student. Is there any good reason to suppose his psychological needs are less pressing or less important in freeing him to perceive widely and accurately? We spend much time and energy trying to find ways of "motivating" people or blaming them for not being motivated to do what we need them to do. We assume that if permitted to seek their own needs, people will not satisfy ours. Perhaps we should get further by helping them satisfy their needs; they might then be free to satisfy ours.

4. Most of our educational methods are directed at the provision of perceptions for the student. He is lectured, required, shown, exhorted, and coerced to perceive what someone thinks he should. It seems possible that with equal energy devoted to the matter of creating needs, goals, and values in students, rich and varied perceptions might be more efficiently produced.

What effects might we be able to produce by providing experiences that build adequate concepts of self in children and adults? What differences in the richness and variety of perception might result from a generation of people with "I can" rather than "I can't" conceptions of themselves? What possibilities of increased perceptions and hence of increased intelligence might accrue to such a program? Clinical experience has demonstrated frequently how a changed perception of self as a more adequate personality can free children for improved school performance, for example.

What would happen if we were consciously and carefully to set about the task of providing experiences that would lead people to conceptions of themselves as adequate, worthy, self-respecting people? If freedom to perceive is a function of adequate perceptions of self, it should not surprise us that the child who perceives himself as unwanted, unacceptable, unable, or unliked behaves in rigid fashion. It should be possible, too, to reverse this process and produce more adequate perceptions by systematic efforts at producing more adequate definitions of self. The possibilities seem tremendous but we have scarcely scratched the surface of this problem.

Finally, if threat to the individual has as important effects as seem indicated in this discussion, the removal of threat would seem a most important factor to consider in the release of the individual to perceive more adequately. The work of Rogers and his students in client-centered therapy has already illustrated to some degree what possibilities freeing the individual to perceive more adequately may accomplish through the provision of a permissive nonthreatening relationship between counselor and client. We have already mentioned the effects Axline has reported following a permissive, nonthreatening form of play therapy.

Such effects do not seem limited to the therapeutic situation, however. A number of workers have applied this principle of permissiveness to the classroom situation with equally gratifying results. Experiments in student-centered teaching at Syracuse have led many of us to believe in the tremendous educational possibilities in the removal of threat.

This paper has asked many questions. Indeed, it has asked far more questions than it has presumed to answer. That, it seems to me, is the function of theory. The picture of intelligence presented here as it seems from a phenomenological viewpoint may be accurate or false or, more likely, partly true and partly false. Only time and the industry of many observers can check its adequacy or inadequacy. It seems to me to pose problems that are both exciting and challenging. If it proves as stimulating to the reader as it has to the author, I shall rest content that a theory has achieved its purpose.

3. Social perceptions and attitudes of children

Marian Radke-Yarrow,
Helen G. Trager,
and Hadassah Davis

Abridged from *Genetic Psychology Monographs,* Vol. 40 (1949), 327-447, by permission of the senior author and The Journal Press.

Using 250 early elementary school youngsters, the authors report a study concerned with children's perceptions of their social environment in terms of racial and religious groups and the development of group membership aspects in their individual concepts of self. A child's perceptions of his social environment do not occur independently of the development of his self-concept. This study presents evidence to show why this is so.

I. Introduction

The child entering school already has a long past of social learning. He brings with him perceptions of the self and differentiations of his social environment. Both may be unstable and, in some respects, indefinite; nevertheless, to many parts of self and environment there may be affixed strong affects.

The social learning in these early years has taken place mainly within the family and play groups of children. Through these agents the child becomes aware of and reacts to social forces which constitute culture; through them content, structuring, and attitudes concerning his social-psychological environment are conveyed to him; and cultural standards and mores begin to have consequences for his personality and behavior.

In this process of socialization, one of the important components of the culture which the child takes over, one of the important determinants of his needs and his social and self-perceptions, is the factor of social groups in society (3, 9, 11). Even while the child's experience is within the bounds of his family, values of class and group enter into his world as they are part of the family life and customs and as they affect the goals and anxieties of his parents. As the child's experience extends to neighborhood and school, there is greater opportunity for cultural values with respect to groups to affect his outlook on life.

When the child arrives at school, he is not just "Bill," the individual personality. His concept of himself and his place among his peers and teachers are influenced by a great many variables such as his family's socio-economic status, his father's occupation, the street on which he lives, the language of his parents, his national background, his race and religion. In many ways and in repeated situations, differences among people, such as these, which are group-derived differences, are reinforced. "Bill" knows that how his family lives is different from the families down the street; and that his parents want to move because there are too many colored or foreign or Catholics in the neighborhood. He learns that his family goes to one place of religious worship, his playmate's to another, a second playmate's to none at all. His mother's advice and admonitions help him to sense the meaning of group differences; one day as he is playing on the corner lot, his mother calls him in and warns him never again to play with those children with some group designation because they are "bad," "tough," "dirty," and so on. His response is uncertain when some boys call his brother a derogatory group name, but he quickly senses all the anger, fear, or shame of it from the way his brother reacts to the situation.

Not all children participate in the same culture patterns or are exposed to the same sanctions and taboos; but even in a rare, "isolated" environment a child cannot become socialized without becoming aware of group differentiations which exist beyond his own "isolated" group.

This research is concerned with the child's differentiation of his social environment in terms of racial and religious groups, his attitudes toward these groups, and the development of group membership aspects in his concept of himself.

Despite observations and research data to the contrary (1, 2, 7, 8), it has been assumed (5) that the development of values attached to race and religion and the awareness of social group conflicts do not occur until some vaguely designated time in "late" childhood.

For the study of social perceptions and social attitudes in their early stages of development, this investigation is concerned with "early" rather than "late" childhood, the child's first years in school (kindergarten, first and second grades). The social groups studied are Negro and white, and Catholic, Protestant, and Jewish.

The basic theories which have contributed to the formulation of this research are: (*a*) theories of learning of social attitudes, particularly the development of attitudes and prejudices relating to social groups, and (*b*) theories of the development of the self-concept, those perceptions of self concerned with group membership.

In the process of socialization (4, 12) the child is confronted with culture's many ready-made social habits and social valuations. These patterns are experienced variously by the child, depending upon the constellation of forces to which he is exposed and upon his needs and personality. In the host of new situations which confront him, the child is likely to accept uncritically the attitudes and modes of behavior which the culture (or adult) supplies.

Since differentiations and valuations of social groups are a part of this learning, just as other aspects of the culture are accepted uncritically, it is to be expected that the child's perceptions and attitudes about groups conform to cultural patterns which convey group chauvinisms, harmonies, prejudices, and hostilities. Thus conformity to environmental standards and expectations rather than individual securities or insecurities would appear to be the root of the child's earliest content and valences for social groups. Conformity to culture which may be seen as an "induced" need may, in the course of time, change in character in the direction of "own" needs (9). That is, the individual not only follows the dictates of his environment concerning attitudes toward Negroes, Catholics, *etc.*, but he comes to "accept" these attitudes as his own, he uses them conveniently, and, perhaps, he finds them an accepted source of security or outlet for aggression (6, p. 21).

Structuring of the child's social environment does not proceed independently of the development of his self-concept. With increased differentiation of the self, group membership factors become increasingly important. Belonging or not belonging to certain groups is crucial in the child's feelings of security or insecurity (9). When group-belonging is experienced as a barrier, as a source of punishment or ridicule, there is a tendency for the individual to develop negative valences for his group and to develop both negative and positive valences for the groups imposing the discrimination. Such dominant groups are the source of frustration and, at the same time, they possess coveted and inaccessible advantages. This theory of "self-hate" has been discussed most extensively by Lewin (10). In the same way, when group-belonging is experienced as an advantage, positive valences develop toward that group and, by comparison, negative valences may develop toward other groups.

For both minority and other children group membership may be the source of values and goals, of exaggerated chauvinism, of deep satisfactions and securities. Whatever their form or origins, the group membership aspects of the self-concept are related (in our present culture) to the child's basic need for acceptance of himself by others.

The specific hypotheses which grow out of the preceding theories and which are the primary concern of this research are presented below:

A. Cultural content and attitudes with respect to racial and religious groups are learned early in childhood, in the process of differentiating the social environment.

1. The learning reflects the particular context (subcultures) in which the child lives.
2. The child accepts adults' attitudes toward groups. These attitudes are learned through direct teaching and "unconscious" teaching of the adults.
3. The extent of learning about groups and the degree of crystalization of attitudes increase with the age of the child.
4. When allowed to discuss the topic, the child shows considerable interest in and concern for cultural differences. Combined with this interest is an awareness of the "verboten" nature of the topic.

B. Group membership is one aspect of the self-concept of children.

1. It is related to the child's basic need for acceptance.
2. Negative self-feelings and personal conflicts concerning group-belonging arise frequently in the minority child.
3. The role of group membership in the concept of self varies with the role of each group in society, which may be to increase or decrease its importance for the individual.

II. Sample

Data were obtained on 250 children, five to eight years of age, in kindergarten, first, and second grades. The children were from six public schools in one school district of Philadelphia in which various religious, ethnic, and racial groups are represented. The selection of the schools was made by school administrators.[1]

The children were chosen by taking every third name from the class lists of kindergarten, first, and second grades. In several of the schools one or another of these grades was not available. The only exception to this procedure of selection was the elimination of children with pronounced speech defects or with prolonged absence from school due to illness.

The following racial and religious groups are represented in the sample:

---

[1] This research is part of the larger study in the Philadelphia public schools referred to in the statement on the title page. A district superintendent and school principals selected the schools.

TABLE 1

RACIAL AND RELIGIOUS GROUPINGS OF SAMPLE
(Number of children)

Group	*School 1*	*School 2*	*School 3*	*School 4*	*School 5*	*School 6*	*Total*
Negro children							
Protestant	51	0	6	9	0	29	95
White children							
Jewish	0	0	10	2	23	0	35
Catholic	0	20	0	16	22	0	58
Protestant	0	25	5	22	5	4	61
Unspecified	0	0	0	1	0	0	1
Total	51	45	21	50	50	33	250

There are 155 white children, 35 of whom are Jewish, 58 Catholic, and 61 Protestant, and one whose religion could not be determined; and 95 Negro children, all of whom are Protestant (Table 1).

The 250 families represented in the study are mainly of the lower-middle income levels, though some of them are in the low-income groups. The father's occupation in 49 per cent of the cases falls into the two categories of skilled trades and factory work. The next most numerous are workers in the service trades (cab drivers, truckers, milkmen) (16 per cent) and in civil service (policemen, post-office clerks) (8 per cent). Owners of small businesses and office and sales workers account for 6 per cent and 4 per cent of the group, respectively. Only 2 per cent of the families are in the professional group. Five per cent of the fathers are unemployed (see Table 2).

Investigation of family conditions revealed 14 homes broken by divorce or death of one of the parents. Both mother and father were employed in 42 families, while in five the mother alone was employed.

The religious, racial, and ethnic distribution and socioeconomic factors differ from one school to another. Since each school area is unique in these respects and since these variables have been considered in the analysis of the data, each school area is described below.

School 1 is a large, modern school which is staffed by a Negro principal and Negro teachers (with the exception of one white teacher) and is attended exclusively by Negro children. It is located near a highly industrialized section of the city. The area was once an exclusive residential district, but has become a poor area in which there is a large proportion of substandard housing. The population of the district is predominantly Negro. The children of the few white families living in the neighborhood attend schools outside the school boundaries. The only break in the pattern of "all

TABLE 2

OCCUPATIONS OF FATHERS OF CHILDREN IN SAMPLE
(Percentage of children)

Occupation	*School 1* N=51	*School 2* N=45	*School 3* N=21	*School 4* N=50	*School 5* N=50	*School 6* N=33	*Total* N=250
Professional	2	2	19	0	2	0	2
Small business	0	2	24	4	12	0	6
Office & sales	0	2	5	4	14	0	4
Civil service (such as policemen, postmen)	8	9	19	8	8	3	8
Skilled trades	23	38	14	44	38	31	33
U. S. military service	0	0	0	4	0	0	1
Service trades	25	16	0	8	14	24	16
Factory	20	18	5	28	2	21	16
Unemployed	8	4	0	0	0	18	5
No information or can't classify	14	9	14	0	10	3	4

Negro neighborhood" is along the central commercial street, which is lined with small shops operated by non-Negro owners, many of whom are Jewish. All the children in our sample from this school are Protestant. The parents of the children from this school are engaged in service trades, some in skilled trades or factory work. The number of unemployed is high as compared to the other schools participating in the study.

School 2 is an old school located in a neighborhood of two- and three-story brick, attached row houses, and large houses converted to small apartments. The population is predominantly Anglo-white Protestant. There are some Polish and Irish Catholic families, and a few Jewish families. Strong feelings on the part of the dominant white Protestant group against outsiders and the tendency for children to take to the trade of their parents and to remain in the neighborhood tighten the dividing line between those who "belong" and those who do not. The main industry consists of knitting mills, manned by weavers whose forebears in the British Isles, four or five generations back, were also weavers. No Negro families live within the school area, but some live on the border of the community. Feelings of hostility are high. For instance: a Negro family moved into an old converted store. A police guard was placed on 24-hour duty. So much pressure was brought to bear on the family that they soon moved out.

School 3 is located in an industrial area. It was, until about 1940, a training school for teachers, and as such has retained some of its prestige. Children of all grades are admitted from a waiting list. The nearby residential district consists mostly of rooming houses. Only about one tenth of the school population comes from the immediate neighborhood; these children are mostly Negro and white children from low-income families. The other children who come from outside the school boundaries, many of them traveling a distance of several miles to school, come primarily from families of professional workers, owners of small businesses, and civil service workers.

School 4 is located in a thickly populated area of small factories, stores, and houses. Originally, the population was of German-American and Pennsylvania-Dutch extraction. Later, Irish, Italian, Polish, and other nationality groups settled in this area, with the result of hostile feelings between the old and new groups. At present, the school population represents at least 26 nationality groups. Negroes constitute 10 per cent of the population in this area. The majority of the families are Catholic and Protestant, in about equal proportions; there are a few Jewish families. Most of the fathers are skilled workers or factory workers.

School 5 is located in an old section of the city. The homes are two-story brick, attached row houses; some of them have small lawns. The general atmosphere is that of a residential area. The extreme southern section of the district is used as a city dump and is a slum area. The Negro population is only about 2 per cent of the school population. The Italian-American group contributes a little more than one third the school population. The Jewish group represents about 40 per cent of the school population. Although most of the fathers are skilled workers, this school differs from the other schools in the greater number of fathers who are in office or sales work or owners of small businesses.

School 6 was built in 1897. Like the population of the area, the school population shows great fluctuation. (In an average enrollment of 649 for the year 1946-47, there were 585 withdrawals and admissions, representing a turnover of 90 per cent for the year.) Although once a fashionable residential district, the area has become run-down. The residents are predominantly low-income Negro families. The school population is 94 per cent Negro. Of the white children, some are Catholic, a few Jewish, the others Protestant. The teaching staff is made up of 9 white teachers and 11 Negro teachers. Fathers of children in this school are engaged in service trades, factory work, or skilled trades. Six of the families were numbered among the unemployed.

III. Summary and Theoretical Considerations

This study of young children is an investigation of the early stages of social awareness and attitude development concerning social group phenomena. The results can be viewed, first, as they contribute to an understanding of the nature of social concepts held by young children and the sensitivity of young children to value and status differences and conflicts among social groups in our culture. The results can be considered, also, in terms of their contribution to theories on attitude development and on the role of group membership in the development of the individual. An examination of the educational and social implications of the data is also important.

A. Summary of Procedure

Perceptions and attitudes concerning racial and religious groups were obtained from 250 children of kindergarten, first, and second grades. The data were obtained in two sessions with each child. Interviews were carried out with the aid of a series of pictures (Social Episodes Test) which permit the projections of content and attitudes regarding racial and religious groups and which permit the examiner to probe particular aspects of attitudes. The pictures are of simple social situations involving children on a playground, in a schoolroom, and on a city street. The situations are sufficiently ambiguous to elicit a variety of interpretations. After initial interpretations by the child, racial and religious identifications are introduced by the examiner. Questions, nondirective at the beginning and progressing to specific probing questions, are asked by the tester.

The Social Episodes Test as a technique for studying social attitudes was evaluated. As a means of eliciting such data the test is highly effective. The pictures bring responses of considerable variety, proof of their providing a sufficiently interesting and ambiguous field to permit the children, after the introduction of group labels, to ignore the group factors in their story themes or to incorporate them in themes of neutral, friendly, or hostile interactions.

It might be supposed that the tester's introduction of the words "colored," "white," "Protestant," "Catholic," "Jewish"—which are generally verboten topics in the schools—has a loading effect upon the responses. It is loading the responses only in attempting to create a situation in which it is permissible for the child to express his associations and feelings about groups. This is necessary to an investigation of his attitudes. It is not loading (with one exception) with respect to its influence upon the kind of reactions to group factors. This point rests on the data, which show (*a*) that content and feelings vary from one group to another, and (*b*) that content and affect are drawn from experiences beyond the immediate suggestions of the pictures. The special influences of the Barrier Picture, which exerts some directional bias, have been analyzed in detail.

B. SUMMARY OF FINDINGS RELATED TO THE HYPOTHESES OF THE RESEARCH

1. *Hypothesis A: Cultural Content and Attitudes with Respect to Racial and Religious Groups Are Learned Early in Childhood*

The social environment of almost all the children studied is differentiated in some degree into social groups. This differentiation at its minimum involves an association of group identifications with some fragment of personal experence ("Catholic is St. Ann's school") or with hearsay ("Colored is bad"). It reaches a high point of differentiation in some children, in which characteristics and customs of groups are described in detail, in which status positions and group conflicts are enumerated, in which the child expresses his own feelings, and in which he sees social relations among persons modified by such considerations as:

> "White don't like colored, but maybe they know the boy (and will let him play)."
>
> "They (children in picture) are saying, 'I don't like these people. I hate them and they are too fresh.' I don't say that to hurt other people's feelings. I play with them."

The groups studied are not equally familiar to the children. While none of the subjects fails to recognize Negro and white differences, many are unable to supply content for one or more of the religious groups. "Catholic" is unknown to 19 per cent of the white children and 53 per cent of the Negro children; "Protestant" is unknown to 61 per cent of the white children and 87 per cent of the Negro children; and "Jewish" is unknown to 21 per cent of the white children and 59 per cent of the Negro children.

Group differentiations are recognized at various levels of understanding: (*a*) The label is only a thing, something to do, an institution, but without clear reference to people (Catholic is "beads"; Jewish is "pickles"; Protestant is "sing songs"). (*b*) Group labels represent classifications of people along clearly or vaguely defined dimensions ("Jewish is people" or "Catholic, Jew, any kind of people, Protestants"). (*c*) Group labels stand for transitory conditions or behavior which make one into a certain kind of person or give one a certain kind of experience ("When he gets dirty, he turns into a colored boy," "You are Catholic when you go to Catholic school"). (*d*) Group labels represent classifications of people about whom evaluations are made ("They are saying the Catholic people are no good. Some people just hate Catholic people").

Not only are races and religious groups differentiated in content, but varying shades of hostility and friendliness are expressed about each. Group differences are recognized as signals for various kinds of "appropriate" social behavior.

The group receiving the greatest amount of hostility and rejection is Negro. Responses toward Negro correspond to adult culture patterns: (*a*) segregation of white and Negro ("White and colored can't play together"); (*b*) racial hostility ("I don't like nigger kids"); and (*c*) stereotypes of Negro character ("tough," "dirty," "kill whites").

Aggression is seen by the white children as coming from both races; when it is aggression in the sense of exclusion and rejection, it is more frequently seen as expressed by whites; when it is physical aggression, it is frequently attributed to Negroes.

The Negro children have learned the same culture patterns of rejection by the white group and hostility between the races. The effects of awareness upon self-feelings are discussed below (Hypothesis B-2).

Among the religious groups, there is a higher frequency of expressions of aggression against Jewish than against Catholic and Protestant. The nature of the aggressions against each religious group again follows cultural prescriptions and, more evidently than in the case of Negro and white, follows the peculiar patterns of the immediate neighborhoods (see Hypothesis A-1 below).

Based on responses to questions, "Is this little boy glad he is ——— (Negro, white, Catholic, Protestant, Jewish)?" and "Why?" the relative acceptance of each group compared with every other group is obtained. The results are, in general, in line with the status positions of these groups in American culture. The groups, in ascending order of acceptance, are Negro least accepted, Jewish next, and Catholic and Protestant next, about equal. (It is hazardous to interpret too literally the results on "Protestant," since it is an unfamiliar term to many children.) The order of acceptance is the same when responses of children who do not belong to the group in question and responses of children who are members of the group in question are considered separately.

2. *Hypothesis A-1: The Learning, with Respect to Racial and Religious Factors, Reflects the Particular Content (Subcultures) in Which the Child Lives*

To the extent that customs and values are identical in the individual environments of the children, the nature of group differentiations and attitudes toward them will be similar for all children, allowing, of course, for the individual differences in experience and personality needs. The data present this picture, one of considerable uniformity in content and attitudes, which is attributable to cultural uniformities in group status and group conflicts.

The dissimilarity in the responses, however, is evidence of the fact that quite different cultural forces impinge upon the children. Local neighborhood patterns and family group memberships are among the important subcultural differences which influence the responses. In the neighborhood in which tensions exist between Italian Catholic and Jewish groups (in School 5), the children show a heightened awareness of these groups; classify people with reference to these groups (thus, if told "These children are Jewish," a probable continuation by the child is "These others are Italian"); assume a competitive and hostile attitude toward one or the other group. Attitudes and concepts of Catholic and Protestant assume the characteristics of another neighborhood (School 4), where Protestant and Catholic religions are an issue. Here the children are more aware of Protestant and Catholic. "Jewish" is a more remote out-group, often classified as "not American." Similar, though less striking, local variations appear in the other neighborhoods. There is much less neighborhood variation with respect to responses on Negro than on religious groups.

Within the neighborhoods in the study, the local patterns modify the particular content of group differentiations and increase or decrease the salience of group identifications and conflicts, but they do not erase the basic similarity in group hierarchy and prejudices in all neighborhoods studied.

The group membership of the family is another important context to consider in analyzing the social attitudes of the child. The data show the following influences of family group membership. Children who belong to a given group tend to have more information (no data on Negro and white) about it and tend to express more favorable attitudes toward it than children who do not belong to the group. The data do not indicate that children belonging to any one group show reliably more group prejudice than children of other groups. Children of minority groups (Negro and Jewish) tend to show greater sensitivity, anxious concern, and personal involvement about group distinctions which include their own group than other children (see Hypotheses B-2 and B-3).

3. *Hypothesis A-2: The Child Accepts Adult Attitudes Toward Groups*

These attitudes may be learned from direct teaching or from the "unconscious" teaching of the adult. The importance of this hypothesis is immediately evident to anyone who confronts himself with one or both of the following questions: How, in the family, neighborhood, school, community, are group standards and prejudices communicated to the child? How are the child's misconceptions and hostilities involving groups to be unlearned?

This research provides mainly indirect data bearing on the hypothesis. Many clues are to be found by culling from the responses the children's references to sources of attitudes and by examining the form in which expressions of attitudes are given. Adult values and interpretations of the social world play a considerably more prominent role than do interpersonal experiences of the child with members of any one of the groups. The role of the adult as intermediary can be inferred from the children's references to parents' admonitions ("Sometimes other people's mothers don't like Protestants to play with Catholics"); to adult accounts of experience ("A colored man gave my father [taxi-driver] a dollar tip"); to religious teachings which "justify" attitudes ("They put God on the cross and that's why they [children in the picture] don't like them," "I learned about colored and white in Sunday School"); and to generalizations which are probably formulated by adults ("If you're kind, you play with everybody").

Many of the statements which express the child's own reactions to a group are of the kind, "It is bad to play with ———" or "I don't like ———." They are rarely of the kind in which personal experience alone leads to a negative reaction, such as the hypothetical response, "I played with a Negro boy; he was mean to me, and therefore, I don't like Negroes." There are numerous responses which show that prohibitions or expectations set up by adults either prevent personal experience which is available in the child's environment and by which the child could form his own opinions ("If she's white, she's allowed to play in people's yards") or which predispose him to negatively affected perceptions of his experience ("Well, my mother said that sometimes colored people beat up white children").

4. *Hypothesis A-3: The Extent of Learning About Groups and the Degree of Crystallization of Attitudes Increases with the Age of the Child*

Increases in social learning correlated with age are in the direction of greater *awareness* of group conflicts, patterns of exclusion, and forms of stereotyping and derogation; and in the direction of greater *acceptance* of prejudiced attitudes. There is no age trend (between kindergarten and second grade) in the accuracy of information about group differences. There are as many misconceptions and distortions of facts among the older children as among the younger.

The following are indications of increasing crystallization of attitudes. Each of these factors increases slightly from kindergarten to second grade children, but is not solely a function of age: (*a*) picture interpretations include rationalizations for the behavior projected concerning groups; (*b*) there is a consistent attitude expressed on each appearance of a given group; (*c*) a philosophy of behavior toward persons or groups is expressed; (*d*) the meanings of group identifications are attached to people rather than to symbols or institutions or behavior; (*e*) there is personal involvement, either through identification of self or in emotional reactions to groups other than the child's own.

It is to be stressed that none of the phenomena studied (awareness of group differentiations, group concepts, group attitudes) develops by stages which can be related strictly to age or maturity. It is not possible to ignore a context of cultural influences and personality factors, and to ascribe to certain ages (5, pp. 338, 356-8) a given kind of response to group factors.

5. *Hypothesis A-4: When Allowed to Discuss the Topic, the Child Shows Considerable Interest in and Concern for Cultural Differences and Combined with This Interest Is an Awareness of the "Verboten" Nature of the Topic*

The data support this hypothesis. Initial reactions to the interview topic invariably portray a reserve, an uneasiness, or an effort to avoid the topic of race and religion. This is most evident in reactions to Negro and white. An effort to avoid discussion occurs most frequently among Negro children.

With the establishment of a permissive situation, the responses demonstrate that the children possess many ideas, curiosities, and also some preoccupations about racial and religious differences, and that these topics are discussed among children themselves.

6. *Hypothesis B: Group Membership Is One Aspect of the Self-Concept of Children*

Many of the children interviewed indicate a sense of own group membership. This is seen most strongly in regard to racial belonging. The child places himself in his own race and often attaches an affective meaning to it; in many cases, there is a competitive aspect in the affect (of glad to belong to this group rather than that group).

Self-awareness of religious group-belonging is not apparent in all children. Jewish children show greater awareness than either Catholic or Protestant children. Negro children least of all identify themselves in religious group terms. There is confusion, too, for some children who are uncertain as to whether they are Protestant or Catholic. A very few children who say, outright, that they are either Catholic or Protestant identify themselves incorrectly.

It should be noted that nonmembership in a group may be sensed by the child with as much import for his self-picture as membership in a group ("I'm glad I'm not Catholic"; Negro girl referring to Negro child in picture, "She wishes she was white").

7. *Hypothesis B-1: Group Membership Is Related to the Child's Basic Need for Acceptance*

Recognition of the social meanings of group differences and identification with their own racial and/or religious groups which appear in many of the subjects have been discussed above. From these findings, certain effects of group factors upon the child's feelings of acceptance and rejection are inferred: (*a*) Group-belonging is seen as one determinant of acceptance in the play groups of children; the most marked influence is with racial membership. (*b*) Group-belonging is linked with conflicts in which the child anticipates he will become engaged. (*c*) Some children find security in belonging to a group which is seen as most desired ("I am glad I am a white boy. Some colored people say, 'I wish I was a white boy and [the children] would like to play with me.' " "They wishes they was American like us"). (*d*) Concepts of groups which give an inherent "badness" or "goodness" to members of these groups contribute an abasing or enhancing quality to the child's self-image.

8. *Hypothesis B-2: Negative Self-Feelings and Personal Conflict Concerning Group-Belonging Arise Frequently in Minority Children*

Many children experience serious ego-threats as a result of group prejudices. Negro children reveal most vividly and often the feelings of insecurity resulting from anticipated rejection or insult from the white children. The same phenomenon appears among the Jewish children. On occasion, Catholic and Protestant children show an anxious concern over an anti-Catholic or anti-Protestant remark which has been the topic of competitive discussion among their playmates. Experience of cultural conflict in some of the children belonging to minority groups has given rise to ambivalent feelings toward their own group, documentation for the theory of self-hatred at an early age in childhood.

9. *Hypothesis B-3: The Role of Group Membership in the Concept of the Self Varies with the Role of Each Group in Society, Which May Be to Increase or to Decrease Its Importance for the Individual*

The frequency with which children identify themselves by group membership and the function of the identification varies with the group and neighborhood to which the children belong. The importance it assumes is appreciably greater (as evidenced in the kind and amount of content offered in the projections) for children of minority groups and for children belonging to groups involved in local community conflicts. Where a group is not greatly involved in cultural tensions, where there is no attack upon it to increase its "group consciousness," there is relatively little personal involvement by the children (as with the Protestant group, except in School 2; and with the Christian group, except in School 5). The role of group variables for the individual child cannot be predicted solely on the basis of cultural forces, but factors of intrafamily relations and personality, illustrated in the case studies, modify attitudes, intensify or diminish cultural conflicts experienced by the child.

C. Some implications of findings

The findings of this study challenge a number of familiar assumptions and practices concerned with the development of children. It has been assumed that social prejudices and group consciousness do not arise until late childhood or the teens, and therefore education of younger children has proceeded as if needs or interests concerning group differentiations in the social environment did not exist at these ages.

The data demonstrate the falsity and danger in this assumption. If the personal-social needs of children in our culture are to be met, their awarenesses, interests, fears, and securities related to group factors must be dealt with. This cannot be postponed until adolescence, but must be begun in preschool and early school years.

Research on children's concepts of the world has explored with great thoroughness children's abilities to comprehend time, space, physical phenomena, *etc.* Research on methods of teaching these facts is extensive. But children's concepts of anthropology and sociology have not had the benefit of the same amount of research effort. For the most part, the concepts are allowed to "just grow" without the benefit of planned teaching. Surely they are no more difficult or no less important in personal development than the concepts in arithmetic, geography, physiology, *etc.*

The data from this study on concepts of race and religion show the high level of understanding of young children. At the same time they show the many misconceptions and distortions of fact which they accept. Since attitudes and feelings about race and religion are involved, as well as cognition, special methodological problems arise. Several theories concerned with such problems are examined in the light of the findings.

One theory is that the public school is a democratizing institution per se. Some corollaries are: (*a*) Children of various groups as they work together in the same classroom develop attitudes of acceptance and friendliness toward their classmates. It is tacitly assumed that this acceptance and friendliness are carried over to relations with people outside of school. (*b*) In a homogeneous school, good relations also develop automatically and problems of intergroup relations do not even exist. (*c*) Differences represented in the classroom or neighborhood must not be mentioned, for by so doing, problems of differences are created.

The findings do not support these beliefs. Friendly and cooperative classroom behavior in School 5 between Jewish and Catholic children did not prevent the growth of many group stereotypes and group prejudices in these children. Similarly, in the school where there were few or no Negro children, there was at least as much prejudice toward Negroes as in the school where there were more Negro children. Stereotypes and prejudices do not arise primarily from interpersonal contacts. Contact cannot then be used as the only means for prevention or changing of prejudices. Children very often simply regard their happy contacts with persons of rejected groups as exceptions which in no way alter the generalizations which they make about the groups as a whole. (For example: "I hate to be near them [colored people], but our cleaning lady is nice, she helps me." "My boy friend is Jewish, but I like him.")

The theory which advocates ignoring cultural diversities can be challenged on several points. Since children *are* aware of differences and have questions about them, an atmosphere in which these differences cannot be recognized and discussed puts cultural questions in the realm of tabooed subjects and may create suspicions and fears about them.

To proceed as if group differences do not exist is to ignore the cultural context in which children live, for society does not ignore differences; family customs and values and names and languages all reflect group-derived variations. A rule of silence about differences not only fails the child in not helping him to achieve a better understanding than he has of group factors, but the silence may also be perceived by the child as tacit agreement with societal prejudices. (For is it not part of "polite" prejudice to endure while the rejected group is present or to accept the person present as an exception?)

Another theory considers group prejudices and conflict over group-belonging as by-products of unhappy, insecure personal situations. Personally secure and happy children, it is held, will not develop prejudices or insecurities about groups. This theory seems untenable in view of the extremely high proportion of the children whose responses show awareness or acceptance of group prejudices. The case material also suggests that personal security or insecurity is not the sole determinant of group attitude. And perhaps most important of all is the evidence that children's perceptions of groups develop out of adult values and the status quo; that is to say, that many of the children have opportunity for only the kind of learning about groups which involves stereotypes and rejection, especially of groups not present in the child's environment. This learning cannot be interpreted as a form of aggression consequent on personal insecurities and frustrations.

The data of this study are relevant to another assumption about the teaching of good human relations. Teaching general democratic principles or the "Golden Rule" is inadequate unless the teaching is specific in its applications. Such specific teaching is reflected in the response of the child who gives a friendly response in the Negro Barrier Picture and adds, "It's not nice to make fun of colored people." The specific training needed is the kind which faces cultural diversities in the form and in the situations in which the child experiences them (as the child differs from his playmates, as he observes ritual, customs, characteristics for which he knows no explanation) and which provides him with information and attitudes and social techniques to meet these situations.

This investigation gives rise to many unanswered problems which require further research. Experimentation with methods of retraining attitudes and developing social concepts is necessary if the present theories and methods which appear to be inadequate are to be followed by more effective approaches to intercultural education.

Some of the problems which are raised in this research but which are not answered by it are:

1. What is the relation between the perceptions and attitudes obtained in the test situation and the children's behavior with members of the groups involved?

2. How does the home perform its "educative" function with respect to social concepts and attitudes? How strong are the forces of the home in comparison with other influences upon children's attitudes? [2]

3. What are the determinants of the reactions of minority children to social discrimination? In this problem analysis of the home influences would be especially important.

---

[2] Data on these problems were gathered in a later phase of the Philadelphia Early Childhood Project.

4. What are the awarenesses and attitudes of children of different ages with other environmental backgrounds? How do personality factors relate to the acquisition of attitudes and their change?

References

1. Clark, K., and M. Clark, "The Development of Consciousness of Self and the Emergence of Racial Identification in Negro Preschool Children," *Journal of Social Psychology,* Vol. 10 (1939), pp. 591-599.
2. ———, "Skin Color as a Factor in Racial Identification of Negro Preschool Children," *Journal of Social Psychology,* Vol. 11 (1940), pp. 159-169.
3. Davis, A., "American Status Systems and the Socialization of the Child," in C. Kluckhohn and H. Murray, eds., *Personality in Nature, Society, and Culture* (New York: Knopf, 1948), pp. 459-468.
4. Dollard, J., *et al., Frustration and Aggression* (New Haven: Yale, 1939).
5. Gesell, A., and F. Ilg *The Child from Five to Ten,* 4th ed. (New York: Harper, 1946).
6. Horowitz, E. L., "The Development of Attitude Towards the Negro," *Archives of Psychology,* No. 194 (1936).
7. Kluckhohn, C., and H. Murray, eds., *Personality in Nature, Society, and Culture* (New York: Knopf, 1948).
8. Lasker, B., *Race Attitudes in Children* (New York: Holt, Rinehart & Winston, 1929).
9. Lewin, K., "Behavior and Development as a Function of the Total Situation," in L. Carmichael, ed., *Manual of Psychology* (New York: Wiley, 1946), Chapter 16.
10. ———, *Resolving Social Conflicts* (New York: Harper, 1948).
11. Murphy, G., *Personality* (New York: Harper, 1947).
12. Murphy, L., "Childhood Experience in Relation to Personality Development," in J. McV. Hunt, ed., *Personality and Behavior Disorders,* Vol. II (New York: Ronald, 1944), Chapter 21.

4. Cognition of being in the peak experiences[1]

A. H. MASLOW

Reprinted from the *Journal of Genetic Psychology,* Vol. 94 (1957), 44-66, by permission of the author and The Journal Press.

Maslow asserts that the average human being in his highest moments—in his "peak" experiences—is more able to perceive the world in its own Being rather than something to be reacted to, or to be afraid of, or to be used. Perception, in peak experiences, can be ego-transcending and egoless. In a lucid analysis the author explains how perceptions of unsuspected skill, confidence, and creativeness in oneself can become increasingly possible.

A. Introduction

Self-actualizing people, those who have come to a high level of maturation, health, and self-fulfillment, have so much to teach us that sometimes they seem almost like a different breed of human beings. But, because it is so new, the study of the exploration of the highest reaches of human nature and of its ultimate possibilities and aspirations is a difficult and tortuous task. It has involved for me the continuous destruction of cherished axioms, the perpetual coping with seeming paradoxes, contradictions, and vaguenesses and the occasional collapse around my ears of long-established, firmly believed in, and seemingly unassailable laws of psychology. Often these have turned out to be no laws at all but only rules for living in a state of mild and chronic psycho-

[1] *Presidential Address, Division 8, A.P.A., Chicago, Sept. 1, 1956.*

I wish to thank James Klee, Frances Wilson Schwartz, and Harry Rand for helping me with this paper.—THE AUTHOR

pathology, and fearfulness, of stunting and crippling, and immaturity which we don't notice because most others have this same disease that we have.

Most frequently, as is typical in the history of scientific theorizing, this probing into the unknown first takes the form of a felt dissatisfaction, an uneasiness with what is missing, long before any scientific solution becomes available. For instance, one of the first problems presented to me in my studies of self-actualizing people was the vague perception that their motivational life was in some important way different from all that I had learned. I first described it as being expressive rather than coping, but this wasn't *quite* right as a total statement. Then I pointed out that it was unmotivated rather than motivated, but this statement rests so heavily on which theory of motivation you accept, that it made as much trouble as help. In a more recent paper, I have contrasted growth-motivation with deficiency-need motivations which helps, I think, but isn't definitive enough yet, because it doesn't differentiate Becoming from Being. In this address, I shall propose a new tack (into a psychology of Being) which should include and generalize the three attempts already made to put into words somehow the observed differences between the motivational and cognitive life of fully developed people and of most others.

This analysis of states of Being (temporary, nonstriving, purposeless, self-validating, end experiences and states) emerged first from a study of the love relations and sexual experiences of self-actualizing people, and then of other people as well, and finally from dipping into the theological and philosophical literatures. It became necessary to differentiate two types of love. The one is love that comes from ordinary love-need, what Fenichel calls love as the need for narcissistic supplies, for gratification of a deficiency of love. It can therefore be conveniently called deficiency-love (D-love). It is typically and normally found in children and adolescents (of whatever age) in our culture.

But this creates a paradox. Self-actualizing people, by definition gratified in their basic needs, including the love-need, should cease loving and wanting love, if the only determinant of love were the basic love-need. But the finding is that they are *more* loving people than the average, rather than *less* loving, especially from the point of view of being able to give love as well as to receive it. The attempt to understand this led to the formulation of another form or type of love, closely akin to what the theologians have called Agapean love, or Godly love, and which the psychoanalysts have named object-love and never described further. It is a love for the essence of or the Being of the other person, in the style that Scheler has described, quite apart from what he can give the lover, a love for the person in himself rather than for what we can get from him, detached, altruistic, admiring, unneeded, unselfish. It is love for another person because he is what he is, rather than because he is a need-gratifier.

In this state of love for the Being of the other person or object, I found a particular kind of cognition for which my knowledge of psychology had not prepared me but which I have since seen well described by certain writers on aesthetics, religion, and philosophy. This I shall call Cognition of Being, or for short, B-Cognition. This is in contrast to cognition organized by the deficiency needs of the individual, which I shall call D-Cognition. The B-lover is able to perceive realities in the beloved to which others are blind, *i.e.,* he is more acutely and penetratingly perceptive.

This paper is an attempt to generalize in a single description some of these basic cognitive happenings in the B-love experience, the parental experience, the mystic or oceanic, or nature experience, the aesthetic perception, the creative moment, the therapeutic or intellectual insight, the orgasmic experience, certain forms of athletic fulfillment. These and other moments of highest happiness and fulfillment I shall call the peak experiences.

This is then a chapter in the Positive or Ortho-Psychology of the future in that it deals with fully functioning and healthy human beings, and not alone with normally sick ones. It is therefore not in contradiction to Psychology as a Psychopathology of the Average; it transcends it and can in theory incorporate all its findings in a more inclusive and comprehensive structure which includes both the sick and the healthy, both deficiency, Becoming and Being.

B. B-Cognition in Peak Experiences

I shall present one by one now in a condensed summary, each of the characteristics of the cognition found in the generalized peak experience, using the term cognition in an extremely broad sense.

1. *In B-Cognition the experience or the object tends to be seen as a whole, as a complete unit, detached from relations, from possible usefulness, from expediency, and from purpose.* It is seen as if it were all there was in the universe, as if it were all of Being, synonymous with the universe.

This contrasts with D-Cognition, which includes most human cognitive experiences. These experiences are partial and incomplete in ways that will be described below.

We are reminded here of the absolute idealism of the nineteenth century in which all of the universe was conceived to be a unit. Since this unity could never be encompassed or perceived or cognized in any other fashion by a limited human being, all actual human cognitions were perceived as necessarily part of Being, and never conceivably the whole of it.

2. *When there is a B-Cognition, the percept is exclusively and fully attended to.* This may be called "total attention," or as Schachtel has called it, "focal attention." What I am trying to describe here is very akin to fascination or complete absorption. In such attention the figure becomes *all* figure and the ground, in effect, disappears, or at least is not importantly perceived. It is as if the figure were isolated for the time being from all else, as if the world were forgotten, as if the percept had bcome for the moment the whole of Being.

Since the whole of Being is being perceived, then all those laws obtain which would obtain if the whole of the cosmos could be encompassed at once. I shall discuss this further below.

This kind of perception is in sharp contrast to normal perception. Here the object is attended to simultaneously with attention to all else that is relevant. It is seen imbedded in its relationships with everything else in the world, and as *part* of the world. Normal figure ground relationships hold, *i.e.,* both the ground and the figure are attended to, although in different ways. Furthermore in ordinary cognition, the object is seen not so much per se but as a member of a class, as an instance in a larger category. This kind of perception I have described as "rubricizing," and again would point out that this is not so much a full perception of all aspects of the objects or person being perceived, as it is a kind of taxonomy, a classifying, a ticketing off into one file cabinet or another.

To a far greater degree than we ordinarily realize, cognition involves also placing on a continuum. It involves a kind of automatic comparing or judging or evaluating. It implies higher than, less than, better than, taller than, *etc.*

B-Cognition is quite different. It may be called noncomparing cognition or nonevaluating or judging cognition. I mean this in the sense in which Dorothy Lee has described the way in which certain primitive peoples differ from us in their perceptions.

A person can be seen per se, in himself and by himself. He can be seen uniquely and idiosyncratically, as if he were the sole member of his class. This is what we mean by perception of the unique individual, and this is, of course, what all clinicians try to achieve. But it is a very difficult task, far more difficult than we are ordinarily willing to admit. However, it can happen, if only transiently, and it does happen characteristically in the peak experience. The healthy mother, perceiving her infant in love, approaches to this kind of perception of the uniqueness of the person. Her baby is not quite like anybody else in the world. It is marvelous, perfect, and fascinating (at least to the extent that she is able to detach herself from Gesell's norms and comparisons with neighbors' children).

Concrete perceiving of the whole of the object implies, also, that it is seen with "care." Contrariwise, "caring" for the object will produce the sustained attention, the repeated examination that is so necessary for perception of all aspects of the object. The caring minuteness with which a mother will gaze upon her infant again and again, or the lover at his beloved, or the connoisseur at his painting will surely produce a more complete perception than the usual casual rubricizing which passes illegitimately for perception. We may expect richness of detail and a many-sided awareness of the object from this kind of absorbed, fascinated, fully attending cognition. This contrasts with the product of casual observation which gives only the bare bones of the experience, an object which is seen in only some of its aspects in a selective way and from a point of view.

3. While it is true that all human perception is a product of the human being and is his creation to an extent, still we can make some differentiation between the perception of *external objects as relevant to human concerns and as irrelevant to human concerns*. Self-actualizing people are more able to perceive the world as if it were independent not only of them but also of human beings in general. This also tends to be true of the average human being in his highest moments, *i.e.,* in his peak experiences. He can then more readily look upon nature as if it were there in itself and for itself, and not simply as if it were a human playground put there for human purposes. He can more easily refrain from projecting human purposes upon it. In a word, he can see it in its own Being rather than as something to be used, or something to be afraid of, or to be reacted to in some other human way.

As one example, let us take the microscope which can reveal to us as we look at histological slides either a world of per se beauty or else a world of threat, danger, and pathology. A section of cancer seen through a microscope, if only we can forget that it is a cancer, can be seen as a beautiful and intricate and awe-inspiring organization. A mosquito is a wondrous object. Viruses under the electron microscope are fascinating objects (or, at least, they *can* be if we can only forget their human relevance).

B-Cognition, because it makes human irrelevance more possible, enables us thereby to see more truly the nature of the object in itself.

4. One difference between B-Cognition and average cognition which is now emerging in my studies, but of which I am as yet uncertain, is that repeated *B-cognizing seems to make the perception richer*. The repeated experiencing of a face that we love or a painting that we admire makes us like it more, and permits us to see more and more of it in various senses. This we may call intra-object richness.

But this so far contrasts rather sharply with the more usual effects of repeated experiencing, *i.e.,* boredom, familiarization effects, loss of attention, and the like. I have found to my own satisfaction—although I cannot prove it to anyone else—that repeated exposures to what I consider a good painting will make the painting look more beautiful to people preselected as perceptive and sensitive, while repeated exposures to what I consider a bad painting will make it look less beautiful.

In this more usual kind of perception, where so frequently the initial perception is simply a classification into useful or not useful, dangerous or not dangerous, repeated looking makes it become more and more empty. The task of normal perception which is so frequently anxiety-based or motivation-determined, is fulfilled in the first viewing and thereafter the object or person, now that it has been catalogued, is simply no longer perceived. Poverty shows up in repeated experiencing; so, also, does richness. Furthermore, not only does poverty of the percept show up in repeated looking, but also the poverty of the beholder.

I am becoming more convinced that one of the main mechanisms by which love produces a profounder perception of the intrinsic qualities of the love-object than does nonlove, is that love involves fascination with the love-object, and therefore repeated and intent and searching looking, seeing with "care." Lovers can see potentialities in each other that other people are blind to. Customarily we snicker and say "Love is blind," but we must now make room for the possibility that love may be under certain circumstances more perceptive than nonlove. Of course, this implies that it is possible in some sense to perceive potentialities which are not yet actual. I do not think that this is as difficult a research problem as it sounds. The Rorschach test in the hands of an expert is also a perception of potentialities which are not yet actualized. I think this is a testable hypothesis in principle.

5. American psychology, or, more broadly, Western psychology, in what I consider to be an ethnocentric way, assumes that human needs, fears, and interests must always be determinants of perception. The "New Look" in perception is based upon the assumption that cognition must always be motivated. The further assumption is implied that cognition is a coping, instrumental mechanism, and that it must to some extent be egocentric. It assumes that the world can be seen *only* from the vantage point of the interests of the perceiver and that the experience must be organized around the ego as a centering and determining point.

I consider this point of view ethnocentric not only because it arises so clearly as an unconscious expression of the Western world outlook, but also because it involves a persistent and assiduous neglect of the writings of philosophers, theologians, and psychologists of the Eastern world, particularly of the Chinese, Japanese, and Hindus, not to mention Western writers like Goldstein and Angyal.

My findings indicate that in the normal perceptions of self-actualizing people and in the more occasional peak experiences of average people, *perception can be relatively ego-transcending, self-forgetful, egoless.* It can be unmotivated, impersonal, desireless, unselfish, not needed, detached. It can be object-centered rather than ego-centered. That is to say, that the perceptual experience can be organized around the object as a centering point rather than being based upon the ego. It is as if they were perceiving something that had independent reality of its own and was not dependent upon the beholder. It is possible in the aesthetic experience or the love experience to become so absorbed and "poured into" the object that the self, in a very real sense, disappears. Some writers on aesthetics, on mysticism, on motherhood, and on love have gone so far as to say that in the peak experience we may even speak of identification of the perceiver and the perceived, a fusion of what was two into a new and larger whole, a superordinate unit. This could remind us of some of the definitions of empathy and of identification, and, of course, at once opens up the possibilities of research in this direction.

6. *The peak experience is felt as a self-validating, self-justifying moment which carries its own intrinsic value with it.* That is to say, it is an end in itself, what we may call an end experience rather than a means experience. It is felt to be so valuable an experience, so great a revelation, that even to attempt to justify it takes away from its dignity and worth. This is universally attested to by my subjects as they report their love experiences, their mystic experiences, their aesthetic experiences, their creative experiences, and their bursts of insight. Particularly with the moment of insight in the therapeutic situation does this become obvious. By virtue of the very fact that the person defends himself against the insight, it is therefore by definition painful to accept. Its breaking through into consciousness is customarily crushing to the person. And yet, in spite of this fact, it is universally reported to be worthwhile, desirable, and wanted. Seeing is better than being blind, even when seeing hurts. It is a case in which the intrinsic self-justifying, self-validating worth of the experience makes the pain worthwhile. Not only do my subjects attest to this finding but so, also, do the numerous writers on aesthetics, religion, creativeness, and love. Uniformly they describe these experiences not only as valuable intrinsically, but as *so* valuable that they make life worthwhile by their occasional occurrence. The mystics have always affirmed this great value of the great mystic experience which may come only two or three times in a lifetime.

The contrast is very sharp with the ordinary experiences of life, especially in the West, and, most especially, for American psychologists. Behavicr is so identified with means to ends that by many writers the words "behavior" and "instrumental behavior" are taken as synonymous.

Everything is done for the sake of some further goal, *in order to* achieve something else. The apotheosis of this attitude is reached by John Dewey in his theory of value, in which he finds no ends at all but only means to ends. Even this statement is not quite accurate because it implies the existence of ends. Rather, to be quite accurate, he implies that means are means to other means, which in turn are means, and so on ad infinitum.

The peak experiences are for my subjects ultimate goals of living and the ultimate validations and justifications for it. That the psychologist should bypass them or even be officially unaware of their existence, or, what is even worse, in the objectivistic psychologies, deny a priori the possibility of their existence as objects for scientific study, is incomprehensible.

7. *In all the common peak experiences, or at least in those which I have studied, there is a very characteristic disorientation in time and space.* This goes so far that it would be more accurate to say that in these moments the person is outside of time and space subjectively. For instance, in the creative furor, the poet or artist becomes oblivious of his surroundings and of the passage of time. It is impossible for him when he wakes up to judge how much time has passed. Frequently he has to shake his head as if emerging from a daze to rediscover where he is.

But more than this is the frequent report especially by lovers of the complete loss of extension in time. Not only does time pass in their ecstasies with a frightening rapidity so that a day may pass as if it were a minute but also a minute so intensely lived may feel like a day or a year. It is as if they had, in a way, some place in another world in which time simultaneously stood still and moved with great rapidity. For our ordinary categories, this is of course a paradox and a contradiction. And yet this is what is reported, and it is, therefore, a fact that we must take account of. I see no reason why this kind of experiencing of time should not be amenable to experimental research. The judgment of the passing of time in peak experience must be very inaccurate; so, also, for consciousness of surroundings. This, too, must be much less accurate than in normal living and, therefore, can be researched with.

8. I have been much impressed with the implications of my findings for a psychology of values. I find them very puzzling and yet so uniform that it is necessary not only to report them but also to try somehow to understand them. To start at the end first, *the peak experience is only good and desirable, and is never evil or painful or undesirable.* The experience is intrinsically valid, and the experience is perfect, complete, and needs nothing else. It is sufficient to itself. It is felt as being intrinsically necessary and inevitable. It is just as good as it *should* be. It is reacted to with awe, wonder, amazement, humility, and even reverence, exaltation,

and piety. The word "sacred" is occasionally used to describe the person's reaction to it.

The philosophical implications here are tremendous. If, for the sake of argument, we accept the thesis that in the peak experience the nature of reality *may* be seen more clearly and its essence penetrated more profoundly, then this is almost the same as saying what so many philosophers and theologians have affirmed, that the whole of Being is only neutral or good, and that evil or pain or threat is only a partial phenomenon, a product of not seeing the world whole and unified.

Another way of saying this is to compare it with one aspect of the concept of God which is very widespread in many religions. Those gods who can contemplate and encompass the whole of Being, and who therefore understand it, must see it as good, just, inevitable, and must see "evil" as a product of limited vision and understanding. If we could be godlike in this sense then we, too, out of universal understanding would never blame or condemn or be disappointed or shocked. Our only possible emotions would be pity, charity, kindliness, and perhaps sadness for the shortcomings of the other. But this is precisely the way in which self-actualizing people react to the world, and in which *all* of us react in our peak moments. I remind you that this is precisely the way in which all psychotherapists *try* to react to their patients. We must grant, of course, that this godlike, universally tolerant, and accepting attitude is extremely difficult to attain, probably even impossible in a pure form, and yet we know that this is a relative matter. We can approximate it more closely or less closely and it would be foolish to deny the phenomenon simply because it comes rarely and impurely. Though we can never be gods in this sense, we can be more godlike or less godlike.

In any case the contrast with our ordinary cognitions and reactions is very sharp. Ordinarily we proceed under the aegis of means-values, *i.e.,* of usefulness, desirability, badness or goodness, of suitability for a purpose. We evaluate, judge, condemn, or approve. We react to the experience in personal terms and perceive the world in reference to ourselves and our ends, thereby making the world no more than means to our ends. This is the opposite of being detached from the world, which means in turn that we are not really perceiving *it,* but perceiving ourselves in it. We perceive then in a deficiency-motivated way and can therefore perceive only D-values. This is different from perceiving the whole world, or that portion of it which in the peak experience we take as surrogate for the world. Then and only then can we perceive *its* values rather than our own. These I call the values of Being, or for short, the B-values. These are the same as Robert Hartman's "intrinsic values."

These B-values are, so far as I can make out at this point, (*a*) wholeness, integration, unity, and interconnectedness; (*b*) necessity, perfection, completeness, and inevitability; (*c*) aliveness, good functioning, spontaneity, and process; (*d*) richness, intricacy, and complexity; (*e*) beauty, awefulness; (*f*) goodness, rightness, desirability; (*g*) uniqueness, idiosyncrasy, and expressiveness; (*h*) effortlessness, ease of achievement, lack of strain or striving; and finally (*i*) occasionally, but not always, an element of humor or playfulness.

Not only is this, then, a demonstration of fusion and unity of the old trinity of the true, the good, and the beautiful, but it is more than that. I have elsewhere reported my finding that truth, goodness, and beauty are in the normal person only fairly well correlated with each other, and in the neurotic even less so. It is only in the healthy and mature human being, in the self-actualizing, fully functioning person that they are so highly correlated that for all practical purposes they may be said to fuse into a unity. I would now add that this is also true for other people in their highest moments, *i.e.,* in their peak experiences of love, of sex, of creativity, of aesthetic perception, of religious or mystic experience, and of insight and understanding.

This finding, if it turns out to be correct, is in direct and flat contradiction to one of the basic axioms that guides all scientific thought, namely, that the more objective and impersonal perception becomes, the more detached it becomes from value. Fact and value have almost always (by intellectuals) been considered to be antonyms and mutually exclusive. But perhaps the opposite is true, for when we examine the most ego-detached, objective, motivationless, passive cognition, we find that it claims to perceive values directly, that values cannot be shorn away from reality and that the most profound perceptions of "facts" are tinged with wonder, admiration, awe and approval, *i.e.,* with value.

9. Normal experience is imbedded in history and in culture as well as in the shifting and relative needs of man. It is organized in time and in space. That is to say it is part of larger wholes and therefore is relative to these larger wholes and frames of reference. Since it is felt to depend upon man for whatever reality it has, then if man were to disappear, *it,* also, would disappear. Its organizing frames of reference shift from the interests of the person to the demands of the situation, from the immediate in time to the past and the future and from the here to the there. In these senses experience and behavior are relative.

Peak experiences are from this point of view more absolute and less relative. Not only are they timeless and spaceless in the senses which I have indicated above, not only are they detached from the ground and perceived more in themselves, not only are they relatively unmotivated and detached from the interests of man, but they are also perceived and reacted to as if they were in themselves "out there," as if they were perceptions of a reality independent of man and persisting beyond his life. It is certainly very difficult and also very dangerous scientifically to speak of relative and absolute, and I am quite aware that I am walking into a semantic swamp. And yet I am compelled by the many introspective reports of my subjects to report this differentiation as a finding with which we psychologists will ultimately have to make our peace. These are the words that the subjects themselves use in trying to describe experiences which are essentially ineffable. *They* speak of "absolute," *they* speak of "relative," and it is my duty to report it.

Again and again we ourselves are tempted to this kind of vocabulary, for instance, in the realm of art. A Chinese vase may be perfect in itself, may be simultaneously 2000 years old and yet fresh in this moment, universal rather than Chinese. In these senses at least it is absolute, even though also simultaneously relative to time, to the culture of its origin, and to the aesthetic standards of the beholder. Is it not meaningful also that the mystic experience has been described in almost identical words by people in every religion, in every era, and in every culture? No wonder Aldous Huxley has called it "The Perennial Philosophy." The great creators, let us say as anthologized by Brewster Ghiselin, have described their creative moments in almost identical terms, even though they were variously poets, chemists, sculptors, philosophers, and mathematicians.

The concept of absolute has been made difficult partly because it has almost always been permeated with a static taint. It is now clear from the experience of my subjects that this is not necessary or inevitable. Perception of an aesthetic object or a beloved face or a beautiful theory is a fluctuating, shifting process, but this fluctuation of attention is strictly *within* the perception. Its richness can be infinite, and the continued gaze can go from one aspect of the perfection to another, now concentrating on one side of it, now on another. A fine painting has many organizations, not just one, so that the aesthetic experience can be a continuous though fluctuating delight as it is seen, in itself, now in one way, now in another. Also it can be seen relatively in one moment, absolutely in the next. We needn't struggle over whether it is *either* relative *or* absolute. It can be both.

10. Ordinary cognition is a very active process. It is characteristically a kind of shaping and selection by the beholder. *He* chooses what to perceive and what not to perceive, he relates it to his needs and fears and interests, he gives it organization, arranging and rearranging it. In a word, he works at it. Cognition is an energy-consuming process. It involves alertness, vigilance, and tension and is, therefore, fatiguing.

B-Cognition is much more passive and receptive than active although, of course, it never can be completely so. The best descriptions that I have found of this "passive" kind of cognizing come from Eastern philosophers, especially from Lao-Tse and the Taoistic philosophers. Krishnamurti has an excellent phrase to describe my data. He calls it "choiceless awareness." We could also name it "desireless awareness." The Taoistic conception of "let be" also says what I am trying to say, namely, that perception may be undemanding rather than demanding, contemplative rather than forceful. It can be humble before the experience, noninterfering, receiving rather than taking, it can let the percept be itself. I am reminded here, also, of Freud's description of "free floating attention." This, too, is passive rather than active, selfless rather than egocentric, dreamy rather than vigilant, patient rather than impatient. It is gazing rather than looking, surrendering and submitting to the experience.

I have also found useful a recent memorandum by John Shlien on the difference between passive listening and active, forceful listening. The good therapist must be able to listen in the receiving rather than the taking sense in order to be able to hear what is actually said rather than what he expects to hear or demands to hear. He must not impose himself but rather let the words flow in upon him. Only so can their own shape and pattern be assimilated. Otherwise one hears only one's own theories and expectations.

As a matter of fact we may say that it is this criterion, of being able to be receiving and passive, that marks off the good therapist from the poor one of whatever school. The good therapist is able to perceive each person in his own right, freshly and without the urge to taxonomize, to rubricize, to classify and pigeonhole. The poor therapist through a hundred years of clinical experience may find only repeated corroborations of the theories which he learned at the beginning of his career. It is in this sense that it has been pointed out that a therapist can repeat the same mistakes for 40 years and then call it "rich clinical experience."

An entirely different, though equally unfashionable, way of communicating the feeling of this characteristic of B-Cognition, is to call it, with D. H. Lawrence and other Romantics, nonvoluntary rather than volitional. Ordinary cognition is highly volitional and therefore demanding, prearranged, and preconceived. In the cognition of the peak experience, the will does not interfere. It is held in abeyance. It receives and doesn't demand. We cannot command the peak experience. It happens *to* us.

11. *The emotional reaction in the peak experience has a special flavor of wonder, of awe, of humility before the experience.* This sometimes has a touch of fear (although pleasant fear) of being overwhelmed. My subjects report this in such phrases as "This is too much for me." "It is more than I can bear." "It is too wonderful." The experience may have a certain poignancy and piercing quality which may bring either tears or

laughter and which may be paradoxically akin to pain, although this is a desirable pain which is often described as "sweet." This may go so far as to involve thoughts of death in a peculiar way. Not only my subjects but many writers on the various peak experiences have made the parallel with the experience of dying, that is, an eager dying. A typical phrase might be: "This is too wonderful. I don't know how I can bear it. I could die now and it would be all right." Perhaps this is in part a hanging on to the experience and a reluctance to go down from this peak into the valley of ordinary existence. Perhaps it is in part, also, an aspect of the profound sense of humility, smallness, unworthiness before the enormity of the experience.

12. Another paradox with which we must deal, difficult though it is, is found in the conflicting reports of perception of the world. *In some reports, particularly of the mystic experience or the religious experience or philosophical experience, the whole of the world is seen as a unity, as a single rich entity. In other of the peak experiences, most particularly the love experience and the aesthetic experience, one small part of the world is perceived as if it were for the moment all of the world.* In both cases the perception is of unity. Probably the fact that the B-Cognition of a painting or a person or a theory retains all the attributes of the whole of Being, *i.e.,* the B-values, derives from this fact of perceiving it as if it were all that existed at the moment.

13. In another paper I have tried to demonstrate the substantial difference between the cognition that abstracts and categorizes (rubricizing) and the fresh cognition of the concrete, the raw, and the particular. This is the sense in which I shall use the terms abstract and concrete. They are not very different from Goldstein's terms. There I pointed out also that most of our cognitions (attendings, perceivings, rememberings, thinkings, and learnings) were abstract rather than concrete. That is, we mostly categorize, schematize, classify, and abstract in our cognitive life. We do not so much cognize the nature of the world as it actually is, as we cognize the organization of our own inner world outlook. Most of experience is filtered through our system of categories and rubrics, as Schachtel has also pointed out in his classical paper, "On Childhood Amnesia and the Problem of Memory." I was led to this differentiation by my studies of self-actualizing people, *finding in them simultaneously the ability to abstract without giving up concreteness and the ability to be concrete without giving up abstractness.* This adds a little to Goldstein's description because I found not only a reduction to the concrete but also what we might call a reduction to the abstract, *i.e.,* a loss of ability to cognize the concrete. Since then I have found this same exceptional ability to perceive the concrete in good artists as well, even though not self-actualizing. More recently

I find this same ability in ordinary people in their peak moments. They are then more able to grasp the percept in its own concrete idiosyncratic nature.

Since this kind of idiographic perceiving has customarily been described as the core of aesthetic perceiving, as for instance by Northrop, they have almost been made synonymous. For most philosophers and artists, to perceive a person concretely, in his intrinsic uniqueness, is to perceive him aesthetically. I prefer the broader usage and think that I have already demonstrated that this kind of perception of the unique nature of the object is characteristic of *all* peak experiences, not only the aesthetic one.

I find it useful to understand the concrete perceiving which takes place in B-Cognition as a perception of all aspects and attributes of the object simultaneously or in quick succession. Abstracting is in essence a selection out of certain aspects only of the object, those which are of use to us, those which threaten us, those with which we are familiar, or those which fit our language categories. Both Whitehead and Bergson have made this sufficiently clear, as have many other philosophers since. Vivanti has phrased it well when he pointed out that abstractions to the extent that they are useful are also false. In a word, to perceive an object abstractly means *not* to perceive some aspects of it. It clearly implies selection of some attributes, rejection of other attributes, creation or distortion of still others. We make of it what we wish. We create it. We manufacture it. Furthermore, extremely important is the strong tendency in abstracting to relate the aspects of the object to our linguistic system. This makes special troubles because language is a secondary rather than a primary process in the Freudian sense, because it deals with external reality rather than psychic reality, with the conscious rather than the unconscious. It is true that this lack can be corrected to some extent by poetic language, but in the last analysis much of experience is ineffable and can be put into no language at all.

Let us take for example the perception of a painting or of a person. In order to perceive them fully we must fight our tendency to classify, to compare, to evaluate, to need, to use. The moment that we say this man is, *e.g.,* a foreigner, in that moment we have classified him, performed an abstracting act and, to some extent, cut ourselves off from the possibility of seeing him as a unique and whole human being, different from any other one in the whole world. In the moment that we approach the painting on the wall to read the name of the artist, we have cut ourselves off from the possibility of seeing it with complete freshness in its own uniqueness. To a certain extent, then, what we call *knowing, i.e.,* the placing of an experience in a system of concepts or words or relations, cuts off the possibility of full cognizing. Herbert Read has pointed out that the child has the "innocent eye," the ability to see something as if he were seeing it for the first time (frequently he *is* seeing it for the first time). He can then stare at it in wonder, examining all aspects of it, taking in all its attributes, since for the child in this situation, no attribute of a strange object is any more important than any other attribute. He does not organize it; he simply stares at it. In the similar situation for the adult, to the extent that we can prevent ourselves from only abstracting, naming, placing, comparing, relating, to that extent will we be able to see more and more aspects of the many-sidedness of the person or of the painting. Particularly I must underline the ability to perceive the ineffable, that which cannot be put into words. Trying to force it into words changes it, and makes it something other than it is, something else *like* it, something similar, and yet something different than *it* itself.

It is this ability to perceive the whole and to rise above parts which characterizes cognition in the various peak experiences. Since only thus can one know a person in the fullest sense of the word, it is not surprising that self-actualizing people are so much more astute in their perception of people, in their penetration to the core or essense of another person. This is also why I feel convinced that the ideal therapist, who presumably should be able as a professional necessity to understand another person in his uniqueness and in his wholeness, without presupposition, ought to be at least a fairly healthy human being. I maintain this even though willing to grant unexplained individual differences in this kind of perceptiveness, and that also therapeutic experience can itself be a kind of training in the cognition of the Being of another human being. This also explains why I feel that a training in aesthetic perceiving and creating could be a very desirable aspect of clinical training.

14. *At the higher levels of human maturation, many dichotomies, polarities, and conflicts are fused and resolved.* Self-actualizing people are simultaneously selfish and unselfish, Dionysian and Apollonian, individual and social, rational and irrational, fused with others and detached from others, and so on. What I had thought to be straight-line continua, whose extremes were polar to each other and as far apart as possible, turned out to be rather like circles or spirals, in which the polar extremes came together into a fused unity. So also do I find this as a strong tendency in the full cognition of the object. The more we understand the whole of Being, the more we can tolerate the simultaneous existence and perception of inconsistencies, of oppositions, and of flat contradictions. These seem to be products of partial cognition, and made away with cognition of the whole. The neurotic person, seen from a godlike vantage point, can then be seen as a wonderful, intricate even beautiful unity of process. What we normally see as conflict and contradiction and dissociation can then be perceived as inevitable, necessary, even fated. That is to say, if he can be fully under-

stood, then everything falls into its necessary place and he can be aesthetically perceived and appreciated. All his conflicts and splits turn out to have a kind of sense or wisdom. Even the concepts of sickness and of health may fuse and blur when we see the symptom as a pressure toward health, or see the neurosis as the healthiest possible solution at the moment to the problems of the individual.

15. *The person at the peak is godlike not only in senses that I have touched upon already but in certain other ways as well, particularly in the complete and loving and uncondemning acceptance of the world and of the person,* however bad he may look at more normal moments. The theologians have long struggled with the terrible task of reconciling sin and evil and pain in the world with the concept of an all-powerful, all-loving, all-knowing God. A subsidiary difficulty has been presented by the task of reconciling the necessity of rewards and punishments for good and evil with this concept of all-loving, all-forgiving God. He must somehow both punish and not punish, both forgive and condemn.

I think we can learn something about the resolution of this dilemma from the study of self-actualizing people and from the comparison of the two broadly different types of perception discussed so far, *i.e.,* B-perception and D-perception. B-perception is a momentary thing ordinarily. It is a peak, a high spot, an occasional achievement. It looks as if all human beings perceive most of the time in a deficiency way. That is, they compare, they judge, they approve, they relate, they use. This means that it is possible for us to perceive another human being alternately in two different ways, sometimes in his Being, as if he were the whole of the universe for the time being. Much more often, however, we perceive him as a part of the universe and related to the rest of it in many complex ways. When we B-perceive him, *then* we can be all-loving, all-forgiving, all-accepting, all-admiring, all-understanding. But these are precisely the attributes assigned to most conceptions of God. In such moments we can then be godlike in these attributes. For instance, in the therapeutic situation we can relate ourselves in this loving, understanding, accepting, forgiving way to all sorts of people whom we normally fear and condemn and even hate—murderers, pederasts, rapists, exploiters, cowards.

It is extremely interesting to me that all people behave at times as if they wanted to be B-cognized. They resent being classified, categorized, rubricized. Ticketing off a person as a waiter or a policeman or a dame instead of as an individual often offends. We all want to be recognized and accepted for what we are in our fullness, richness, and complexity. If such an acceptor cannot be found among human beings, then the very strong tendency appears to project and create a godlike figure.

Another kind of answer to the "problem of evil" is suggested by the way in which our subjects "accept reality" as being-in-itself, in its own right. It is neither *for* man nor is it *against* him. It just is impersonally what it is. An earthquake which kills poses a problem of reconciliation only for the man who needs a personal God who is simultaneously all-loving and omnipotent and who created the world. For the man who can perceive and accept it impersonally and uncreated, it presents no ethical or axiological problem, since it wasn't done "on purpose," to annoy him. He shrugs his shoulders, and if evil is defined anthropocentrically, he simply accepts evil as he does the seasons and the storms. Of course, it is much harder to achieve this attitude with human actions which are hurtful to him, but it is occasionally possible, and the more matured the man is, the more possible it is.

16. *Perception in the peak moment tends very strongly to be idiographic.* The percept, whether a person or the world or a tree or work of art, tends to be seen as a unique instance, and as the only member of its class. This is in contrast to our normal nomothetic way of handling the world which rests essentially on generalization and on an Aristotelian division of the world into classes of various sorts, of which the object is an example. The whole concept of classification rests upon general classes. If there were no classes the concepts of resemblance, of equality, of similarity and of difference would become totally useless. One cannot compare two objects which have nothing in common. Furthermore for two objects to have something in common means necessarily abstraction, *e.g.*, such qualities as redness, roundness, heaviness, *etc.* But if we perceive a person without abstracting, if we insist upon perceiving all his attributes simultaneously and as necessary to each other, then we no longer can classify. Every whole person from this point of view or every painting or every bird or flower becomes the sole member of a class and must therefore be perceived idiographically.

17. *One aspect of the peak experience is a complete, though momentary, loss of fear, anxiety, inhibition, defense, and control, a giving up of renunciation, delay, and restraint.* The fear of disintegration and dissolution, the fear of being overwhelmed by the "instincts," the fear of death and of insanity, the fear of giving in to unbridled pleasure and emotion, all tend to disappear or go into abeyance for the time being.

It may be thought of as pure gratification, pure expression, pure elation. But since it is "in the world," it represents a kind of fusion of the Freudian "pleasure principle" and "reality principle." It is therefore still another instance of the resolution of normally dichotomous concepts at higher levels of psychological functioning.

We may, therefore, expect to find a certain "permeability" in people who have such experiences commonly, a closeness and openness to the unconscious, and a relative lack of fear of it.

C. Other Changes in the Person

In addition to all these changes in the cognition of the world (including attitudes toward it), all sorts of other changes occur in the person in the peak experience and afterward.

For one thing, not only the world but also he himself becomes more a unity, more integrated, and self-consistent. This is another way of saying that he becomes more completely himself, idiosyncratic, unique. And since he is so, he can be more easily expressive and spontaneous without effort. All his powers then come together in their most efficient integration and coordination, organized and coordinated much more perfectly than usual. Everything then can be done with unusual ease and lack of effort. Inhibition, doubt, control, self-criticism, diminish toward a zero point, and he becomes the spontaneous, coordinated, efficient organism, functioning like an animal without conflict or split, without hesitation or doubt, in a great flow of power that is so peculiarly effortless, that it may become like play, masterful, virtuosolike. In such a moment, his powers are at their height, and he may be startled (afterwards) by his unsuspected skill, confidence, creativeness, perceptiveness, and virtuosity of performance. It is all so easy that it can be enjoyed and laughed with. Things can be dared that would be impossible at other times.

To put it simply, he becomes more whole and unified, more unique and idiosyncratic, more alive and spontaneous, more perfectly expressive and uninhibited, more effortless and powerful, more daring and courageous (leaving fears and doubts behind), more ego-transcending and self-forgetful.

But these are almost the same as the list of B-values already described above. Which is to say that as the essential Being of the world is felt by the perceiver to be cognized, so also does he concurrently come closer to his own Being, or to being himself, or to self-actualization, or to perfection in his own kind, *etc.* As the experience becomes more unified, so does he also become more unified; as it becomes richer, so does he; as it becomes more itself, so does he as well; and so on. He and the world become more like each other as they both move toward perfection. Perhaps this is what is meant by the well-known fusion of lovers, the becoming one with the world in the mystic experience, the feeling of absorbed fusion and unity with the work of art in the aesthetic experience, the feeling so often reported by our great creators that their words take hold of them and practically write themselves as if they were being dictated, the great philosophical insights in which one becomes *part* of the unity one experiences and merged into it. This is what Angyal is talking about in part, when he speaks of the trend to homonomy. Also relevant here is my conclusion that just those qualities which describe a good painting (Wilson's criteria) also describe the good human being, *i.e.,* the B-values of wholeness, uniqueness, aliveness, richness, *etc.*

May I now attempt briefly to put all of this in another frame of reference which is more familiar to you, the psychoanalytic. Secondary processes deal with the real world outside the unconscious. Logic, science, common sense, good adjustment, enculturation, responsibility, planning, rationalism are all secondary process techniques. The primary processes were first discovered in neurotics and psychotics and then in children, and only recently in healthy people. The rules by which the unconscious works can be seen most clearly in dreams. Wishes and fears are the primary movers, the Freudian mechanisms, the primary techniques. The well-adjusted, responsible, common-sense man who gets along well in the real world must usually do this in part by turning his back on his unconscious and denying and repressing it.

For me, this realization came most keenly when I had to face the fact about 15 years ago that my self-actualizing subjects, picked because they were very mature, were, at the same time, also childish. I called it "healthy childishness," a "second naiveté." It has since been recognized by Kris and the ego-psychologists as "regression in the service of the ego," not only found in healthy people, but finally conceded to be a *sine qua non* of psychological health. Balint has recognized love to be a regression (*i.e.,* the person who can't regress can't love.) And, finally, the analysts agree that inspiration and great (primary) creativeness comes partly out of the unconsciousness, *i.e.,* is a healthy regression, a temporary turning away from the real world.

Now what I have been describing here may be seen as a fusion of ego, id, super-ego, and ego-ideal, of conscious and unconscious, of primary and secondary processes, a synthesizing of pleasure principle with reality principle, a regression without fear in the service of the greatest maturity, a true integration of the person at *all* levels.

D. Redefinition of Self-Actualization

In other words, any person in any of the peak experiences takes on temporarily many of the characteristics which I found in self-actualizing individuals. That is, for the time they become self-actualizers. We may think of it as a passing characterological change if we wish, and not just as an emotional-cognitive-expressive state. Not only are these his happiest and most thrilling moments, but they are also moments of greatest maturity, individuation, fulfillment—in a word his healthiest moments.

This makes it possible for us to redefine self-actualization in such a way as to purge it of all its static and typological shortcomings, and to make it less a kind of all-or-none pantheon into which some rare people enter at the age of 60. We may define it as an episode, or a spurt in which the powers of the organism come together in a particularly efficient and intensely enjoyable way, and in which he is more integrated and less split, more open for experience, more idiosyncratic, more perfectly expressive or spontaneous, or fully functioning, more creative, more humorous, more ego-transcending, more independent of his lower needs, *etc.* He becomes in these episodes more truly himself, more perfectly actualizing his potentialities, closer to the core of his Being.

Such states or episodes can, in theory, come at any time in life to any person. What seems to distinguish those individuals I have called self-actualizing people is that in them these episodes seem to come far more frequently, and intensely and perfectly than in average people. This makes self-actualization a matter of degree and of frequency rather than an all-or-none affair, and thereby makes it more amenable to available research procedures. We need no longer be limited to searching for those rare subjects who may be said to be fulfilling themselves most of the time. In theory at least we may also search *any* life history for episodes of self-actualization, especially those of artists, intellectuals, and other especially creative people, of profoundly religious people, and of people experiencing great insights in psychotherapy, or in other important growth experiences.

E. The Question of External Validity

So far I have described a subjective experience in a phenomenological fashion. Its relationship to the external world is another matter altogether. Just because the perceiver *believes* that he perceives more truly and more wholly is no proof that he actually does so. The criteria for judging the validity of this belief ordinarily lie in the objects or persons perceived or in the products created. They are therefore, in principle, simple problems for correlational research.

But in what sense can art be said to be knowledge? The aesthetic perception certainly has its intrinsic self-validation. It is felt as a valuable and wonderful experience. But so also are some illusions and hallucinations. And furthermore you may be aroused to an aesthetic experience by a painting which leaves me untouched. If we are to go at all beyond the private, the problem of external criteria of validity remains, just as it does with all other perceptions.

The same can be said for loving perception, for the mystic experience, for the creative moment, and for the flash of insight.

The lover perceives in the beloved what no one else can, and again, there is no question about the intrinsic value of his inner experience and of the many good consequences for him, for his beloved, and for the world. If we take as an example the mother loving her baby, the case is even more obvious. Not only does love perceive potentialities but it also actualizes them. The absence of love certainly stifles potentialities and even kills them. Personal growth demands courage, self-confidence, even daring, and nonlove from the parent or the mate produces the opposite, self-doubt, anxiety, feelings of worthlessness, and expectations of ridicule, all inhibitors of growth and of self-actualization.

All personological and psychotherapeutic experience is testimonial to this fact that love actualizes and nonlove stultifies, whether deserved or not.

The complex and circular question then arises here "To what extent is this phenomenon a self-fulfilling prophecy?" as Merton has called it. A husband's conviction that his wife is beautiful, or a wife's firm belief that her husband is courageous, to some extent *creates* the beauty or the courage. This is not so much a perception of something that already exists as a bringing into existence by belief. Shall we perhaps consider this an example of perception of a potentiality, since *every* person has the possibility of being beautiful and courageous? If so, then this is different from perceiving the real possibility that someone may become a great violinist, which is *not* a universal possibility.

And yet, even beyond all this complexity, the lurking doubts remain to those who hope ultimately to drag all these problems into the domain of public science. Frequently enough, love for another brings illusions, the perceptions of qualities and potentialities that don't exist, that are not therefore truly perceived but created in the mind of the beholder and which then rest on a system of needs, repressions, denials, projections, and rationalizations. If love can be more perceptive than nonlove, it can also be blinder. And the research problem remains to nag us, When is which? How can we select out those instances in which perception of the real world is more acute? I have already reported my observations at the personological level, that one answer to this question lies in the variable of the psychological health of the perceiver, in or out of the love relationship. The greater the health, the more acute and penetrating the perception of the world, all other things being equal. Since this conclusion was the product of uncontrolled observation, it must be presented only as a hypothesis awaiting controlled research.

In general, similar problems confront us in aesthetic and intellectual bursts of creativeness, and also in the insight experiences. In both instances, the external validation of the experience is not perfectly correlated with phenomenological self-validation. It is possible for the great insight to be mistaken, the great love to disappear. The poem that creates itself in a peak experience may have to be thrown away later as unsatisfactory. Creation of a product that will stand up feels subjectively the same as the creation of a product that folds up later under cold, objective critical scrutiny. The habitually creative person knows this well, expecting half of his great moments of insight not to work out. All peak experiences feel like Being-experience but not all are truly so. And yet, we dare not neglect the clear hints that, sometimes at least, greater perspicuity and greater efficiency of cognition can be found in healthier people and in healthier moments, *i.e.,* some peak experiences *are* B-experiences. I once suggested the principle that if self-actualizing people can and do perceive reality more efficiently, fully, and with less motivational contamination than we others do, then we may possibly use them as biological assays. Through *their* greater sensitivity and perception, we may get a better report of what reality is like, than through our own eyes, just as canaries can be used to detect gas in mines before less sensitive creatures can.

As a second string to this same bow, we may use ourselves in our most perceptive moments, in our peak experiences, when, for the moment, *we* are self-actualizing, to give us a report of the nature of reality that is truer than we can ordinarily manage.

F. The Aftereffects of Peak Experiences

Completely separable from the question of the external validity of cognition in the various peak experiences is that of the aftereffects upon the person of these experiences which, in still another sense, may be said to validate the experience. I have no controlled research data to present to you. I have only the unanimous agreement of my subjects that there *were* such effects, my own conviction that there were, and the complete agreement of all the writers on creativeness, love, insight, mystic experience, and aesthetic experience. On these grounds I feel justified in making at least the following affirmations or propositions, all of which are testable:

1. Peak experiences have some therapeutic effects, in the strict sense of removing symptoms. I have at least two reports—one from a psychologist, one from an anthropologist—of mystic or oceanic experiences so profound as to remove neurotic symptoms forever after. Such conversion experiences are, of course, plentifully recorded in human history, but so far as I know have never received the attention of psychologists or psychiatrists.

2. They change the person's view of himself in a healthy direction.

3. They change his view of other people and his relations to them in many ways.

4. They change more or less permanently his view of the world, or of aspects or parts of it.

5. They release him for greater creativity, spontaneity, expressiveness, idiosyncrasy.

6. He remembers the experience as a very important and desirable happening and seeks to repeat it.

7. The person is more apt to feel that life in general is worthwhile, even if it is usually drab, pedestrian, painful, or ungratifying, since beauty and goodness and excitement and honesty and truth and meaningfulness have been demonstrated to him to exist.

Many other effects could be reported that are ad hoc and idiosyncratic, depending on the particular person, and his particular problems which he considers to be solved or seen in a new light as the result of his experience.

I think that these aftereffects can *all* be generalized and a feeling for them communicated if the peak experience could be likened to a visit to a personally defined Heaven from which the person then returns to earth. Desirable aftereffects of such an experience, some universal and some individual, are then seen to be practically inevitable.

And may I also emphasize, that such aftereffects of aesthetic experience, creative experience, love experience, mystic experience, insight experience, and other peak experiences are taken for granted and commonly expected by artists and art educators, by creative teachers, by religious and philosophical theorists, by loving husbands, mothers, and therapists. As a matter of fact, they are a commonplace to all but psychologists.

References

Allport, G., *Becoming* (New Haven: Yale, 1955).

Balint, M., *Primary Love and Psychoanalytic Technique* (New York: Liveright, 1953).

Bucke, R., *Cosmic Consciousness* (New York: Dutton, 1923).

Buhler, C., "Maturation and Motivation," *Dialectica,* Vol. 5 (1951), pp. 312-361.

Dewey, J., "Theory of Valuation," *International Encyclopedia of Unified Science* (Chicago: Chicago, 1939).

Ghiselin, B., ed., *The Creative Process* (Berkeley: California, 1952).

Goldstein, K., *The Organism* (New York: Am. Bk. Co., 1939).

Hartman, R. (Forthcoming book).

Huxley, A., *The Perennial Philosophy* (New York: Harper, 1944).

———, *Heaven and Hell* (New York: Harper, 1955).

Klee, J., "The Absolute and the Relative" (Unpublished).

Kris, E., *Psychoanalytic Explorations in Art* (New York: International, 1952).
Lee, D., in C. Moustakas, ed., *The Self* (New York: Harper, 1956).
Maslow, A. H., *Motivation and Personality* (New York: Harper, 1954).
———, "Deficiency Motivation and Growth Motivation," in R. M. Jones, ed., *Nebraska Symposium on Motivation 1955* (Lincoln, Neb.: Nebraska, 1955).
Northrop, F., *The Meeting of East and West* (New York: Macmillan, 1946).
Perls, F., R. Hefferline, and P. Goodman, *Gestalt Therapy* (New York: Julian, 1951).
Rogers, C., in C. Moustakas, ed., *The Self* (New York: Harper, 1956).
Schachtel, E., "On Memory and Childhood Amnesia," *Psychiatry,* Vol. 10 (1947), pp. 1-26.
Scheler, M., *The Nature of Sympathy* (London: Routledge, 1954).
Schwartz, F. (Forthcoming book).
Shlien, J. (Unpublished memoranda).
Sorokin, P., *The Ways and Power of Love* (Boston: Beacon, 1954).
Tillich, P., *The Courage To Be* (New Haven: Yale, 1952).
Vivanti, L., *A Philosophy of Potentiality* (London: Routledge, 1955).
Werner, H., *Comparative Psychology of Mental Development* (New York: Harper, 1940).

QUESTIONS FOR DISCUSSION

Bruner Article

1. What does the experimental evidence offered by Bruner suggest about the relationship between "needs" and perception?
2. What does it mean to say that perception of an object or event in the environment involves, first of all, an act of categorization? Explain and give examples.
3. What is meant by "perceptual readiness"?

Combs Article

1. What does the author mean when he states that intelligence is dependent on the richness and variety of perceptions possible to an individual?
2. If the self-concept is a factor which can limit perception and, hence, intelligence, what implications are here for teachers?
3. Is the author suggesting that if people had the same opportunities, time, environment, and high self-concept, all people would be equally as "intelligent"? What limitations are there to a generalization like this? Why isn't it valid? What haven't we considered?

Radke-Yarrow, Trager, and Davis Article

1. In what ways can adults unconsciously influence young children's perceptions of themselves and other groups? What implications are here for teachers and parents?

2. What does this research suggest about the theory which holds that personally secure and happy children will not develop prejudices or insecurities about groups?
3. What familiar assumptions about young children's perceptions and group differentiations does this study challenge? What are the implications of these findings for elementary schools which enroll an intermixture of races and religions?

Maslow Article

1. What is meant by "self-actualization"?
2. Does one have to be an extraordinary, above-average person to experience self-actualization? Why or why not?
3. How would you explain the phenomenon reported by Maslow that his most self-actualized subjects were at the same time very childish? Does this seem inconsistent to you? If not, why?

Part IV

how the self is formed

1. Social and individual origins of the self

ARTHUR T. JERSILD

Reprinted from *Child Psychology,* 5th ed. (Englewood Cliffs, N. J.: Prentice-Hall, Inc., 1960), pp. 116-126, by permission of the author and the publisher.

The self develops and grows through a long and complex process of individual and group interactions. When does a child become aware of "self"? What influence do others have on self-development? How are the self and ideal-self related? Jersild explores these and related questions about the growing self.

The Structure of the Self

That which we call the *self* comes into being as the child, with all that is inherent in his make-up, comes to grips with the experiences of life. The self, as it finally evolves, is made up of all that goes into a person's experiences of his individual existence. It is a person's "inner world." It is a composite of a person's thoughts and feelings, strivings and hopes, fears and fantasies, his view of what he is, what he has been, what he might become, and his attitudes pertaining to his worth. As James (12) puts it, a person's self is the "sum-total of all that he can call his."

The self includes, among other things, a *perceptual* component: the way a person perceives himself—the image he has of the appearance of his body, the picture he has of the impressions he makes on others. It also includes a *conceptual* component: his conception of his distinctive characteristics, his abilities, resources, assets, lacks, and limitations, his conception of his background and origins, and of his future. There is also an *attitudinal* component of the self, including the feelings a person has about himself, his attitudes concerning his present status and future prospects, his tendency to view himself with pride or shame, his convictions concerning his worthiness or unworthiness and his attitudes (which may be mixed) of self-esteem and self-reproach. As a person reaches maturity, these attitudes relating to self include also the beliefs, convictions, ideals, values, aspirations, and commitments that comprise what we speak of as a person's philosophy of life.

Although the self is a subjective phenomenon, it is possible for a person to regard aspects of himself both as a subject and as an object. When a person says, "This is what I think and how I feel," he expresses a state which only he directly experiences. But he can also view himself objectively. He can (to a degree) examine his feelings and ask why he feels as he feels. He can also view his thoughts and examine his beliefs as though they were objects: he can review and question them. So when a person says, "This is me," he speaks both as a knower and something known, a perceiver and something perceived.

Development of the Self

When we try to assess the process through which a child becomes aware of himself, we do so largely by inference: we cannot directly assess the nature of his awareness. From his behavior we can reasonably infer that soon after he is born a flood of sensations pours in upon him; sensations from within his own body that probably are there when he cries in hunger; sensations from the surface of his body, such as occur when he withdraws his foot or hand from contact with a cold cloth while being bathed; sensations that reach him through his eyes and ears and probably also sensations of taste and smell. Judging from the diffuse nature of his earliest reactions, he is not at first able to make a clear distinction between these sensory experiences and the stimuli which give rise to them. The dawn of self-awareness probably occurs when a child begins to make a distinction between his sensations and the conditions which produce them.

The development of the self involves, among other things, a process of differentiation. The child begins life as though he were part of his mother's body. For some time after birth he continues to be helpless and dependent. Very soon, however, he is active in trying out his capacities. He cries and people come. He turns and gets another view. In time, he explores the boundaries of his person and his environment. He tests the limits of his reach.

In the development of a child's emerging view of himself as he grows older all of his capacities are mobilized; his senses; his ability to perceive and to think; his ability to learn; his ability to imagine and to embroider the happenings of his life with the glamour or the menace of a dream; his bodily appetites; his desires, which often conflict; his striving; his capacity for joy; his capacity for fear and rage which at first is freely expressed and then driven underground; his capacity for loving and need for affection; his ability to choose; and, in time, his experience of being free to make choices.

Beginnings of Self-Awareness

When does the child become aware of himself as a distinct individual? Many conjectures have been made about this, and one estimate is that it is sometime during the first year that the infant "discovers himself" and "finds a place in, yet apartness from, the outside world" (1).

The development of self-awareness does not occur in an all-or-none fashion which would enable us to assume that up to this point the child does not possess it but beyond this point he does. It is more likely that a child perceives different aspects of what he eventually calls himself with varying degrees of clarity at different times (16). His awareness of his distinctness from others seems to take place while he still has not gone very far in his perception and conception of many of the characteristics that eventually comprise what he calls himself. Moreover, the process of self-discovery is actively going on at least as long as the child is developing or discovering new potentialities, and in a healthy person the discovery of self continues as long as he lives.

Discovery of self as a performer

Among the early signs of self-awareness are those appearing when a child begins actively to control things in his environment. In his explorations, the child notices and manipulates things that are apart from him. At first he seems almost to proceed by accident, but later he does so by design. At first when objects are placed in his hand he is able to grasp them but not able, at will, to release them or throw or move them about. Soon, however, he is able to grasp and to release, to reach for things and place them in a certain spot. When he uses this ability he probably has a dim awareness of himself as one who can produce effects by his own actions. An account of a five-months-old child illustrates this point. The youngster seemed to discover, while tearing a page from a journal, that it was he who produced the sound and the severing. He then patiently proceeded to tear page after page as though gaining satisfaction from being a cause of change and from seeing "that the remarkable alteration of an entire journal into little scraps [was] due to his own activity" (15).

Awareness of the Body

An important feature of a child's eventual view of himself is his "body-image," the picture he has of the physical properties of his body, his appearance, including (as he perceives the situation) the figure he cuts in the eyes of others. This body image is not just a photographic impression; in common with all other aspects of the way in which a person views himself, it is likely to be colored by feelings and attitudes.

When we ask how a child at first perceives his body, we can answer only by conjecture. There is good reason to believe, as we have noted, that sensations play an important role in defining the boundaries of a child's image of his body. It also appears, however, that the child does not at first have anything approaching a clear perception of his body as a whole, or even a clearly defined awareness of the parts of his body. This can be seen, for example, when he fingers his hand in play or inspects his hand, gazing upon it as he might gaze upon another object. Some babies at first seem to treat their bodily parts almost as though they were separate objects. This appears, for example, when a baby bites his fingers and cries without seeming to realize that he is biting himself.

Response to mirror image

One approach to the study of self-awareness is to note the way infants respond to a mirror image of themselves. It has been observed that children recognize others (such as the mother) in the mirror and in pictures before they recognize themselves.

Five children who took part in a study of the development of "self-recognition" showed distinct changes with age in response to the mirror and the order of these changes was remarkably similar in all five infants (5). At first the infants regarded their reflections "briefly and soberly" but showed no sustained interest, even though, at this stage, they readily recognized their mothers' reflection in the mirror (also 19). At a later phase the children became more sociable with their images, smiling, talking, and trying to make contact with the image in the mirror. Dixon calls this the "playmate stage"—the child reacts to the mirror image in much the same way as he reacts when placed before another infant. Then came what Dixon calls the "Who dat? Who do dat when I do dat?" stage in which the child seems to be connecting the mirror image with himself—keeping his eye fixed on the changing image, the child repeats certain acts (such as opening and closing his mouth, raising his arm and moving his fingers) as though he were trying to "master and work his new-found puzzling discovery."

At this stage "an apparent attempt at conversation-testing, as though expecting an echo," was observed a few times but soon died out, as did pointing at the image while asking a portentous question such as "Dah?". Sometime between the age of twelve and eighteen months the children entered what Dixon calls the "coy" stage. When confronted with his mirror image, the child now "instead of basking in reflected vanity" might turn his head away, or cry, or smile coyly, or kiss the image after refusing for some time to approach it. Such coyness also has been noted by others.

EMOTIONAL UNDERTONES OF THE PROCESS OF SELF-DISCOVERY

As noted above, a child's growing awareness of himself has emotional overtones. When he first recognizes himself in a mirror, it is not as though he were merely eyeing a portrait. Some children show a great deal of animation in connection with this discovery. One investigator was especially impressed by the emotional coloring of this development, noting the "jubilant interest" shown by an infant at the sight of his own image in a mirror, and of the child's ecstasy when he saw that the movements in the mirror corresponded to his own movements. There appeared to be a real affective value in having a vision of the whole body as distinguished from knowing it in bits and pieces (13).

Emotional experiences such as those connected with a child's recognition of his body can also be noted in connection with other forms of self-discovery. A child lets forth a jubilant cry, for example, when he discovers how to ring a bell or how to take the lid off a box. A detailed record of joyful episodes in the life of a young child would probably show that a large proportion of these are connected with experiences in which he tries himself out and realizes, in a new way, the reaches of his own strength and ability. If we grant this, we still have the question, why, then, do some babies not only show an eager interest but also coyness, as though they were embarrassed when the first seem to realize that the image in the mirror is their own? And why should a child cry? Perhaps the child who cries is somewhat apprehensive, as though this new-found creature were both a stranger and a familiar figure.

Another approach to the study of early self-identification has been to note how children think of themselves with reference to their bodies. In one study (10) two-, three-, and four-year-olds and students in psychology were asked to "localize" themselves (*e.g.*, the experimenter would ask, while pointing to a leg, head, and so forth: "Is this Joan?"). One child located herself in the abdomen and lower thorax; another localized herself in her lower right jaw; another in the mouth region of the face. The students mentioned a variety of localization points, including the head, brain, eyes, face, heart, and genitals.

An important step in children's self-awareness occurs when they recognize the bodily differences between boys and girls and clearly identify the sex to which they belong. Many youngsters show a keen interest in the anatomical differences between the sexes in connction with this aspect of self-discovery. According to some writers, this discovery may be quite disturbing. One theory is that girls are especially likely to have feelings of inferiority or envy when they realize the difference between themselves and boys. However, the discovery of differences between the genital organs of the two sexes does not produce an emotional shock in the typical, healthy child (4), although children usually are greatly interested.

Other Evidences of Increasing Self-Awareness

After a child has learned to talk, signs of self-awareness become increasingly apparent, as when, for example, he correctly distinguishes between "I" and "you" and "mine" and "yours"; or is able to distinguish between dreams and actual happenings; or he is able to acknowledge feelings as his own, saying (as one four-year-old did) "Don't bother me, I'm in a bad mood"; or when he takes pains to conceal his feelings, saying, "I'm not scared," in spite of signs to the contrary.

Self-assertion and comparison of self with others

A notable phase in the development of the self occurs when a child begins to assert himself in opposition to others. As will be noted more particularly in a later chapter, many children go through a phase when they are especially obstinate or "negativistic," beginning at about the age of two. During this phase a youngster seems to be testing his powers of self-assertion in his relationship with others.

Another important phase in the development of a child's view of himself occurs when he is able to compare himself with his peers and to test his powers in competition with them. When a child knowingly competes, he is using others as a standard against which to measure himself. Still another significant sign of self-scrutiny occurs when a child is openly critical of his own work.

Awareness of Self as Belonging to a Particular Ethnic or Social Group

Sometime during childhood a youngster is likely to form a more or less clear conception of his family's socioeconomic status or social class. He also becomes aware, in time, of his religious affiliation, the nationality of his parents, and the ethnic stock from which he came. Children's awareness of social class differences does not usually appear to be well established until they are well along in the elementary school years (17).[1]

The age at which children realize the ethnic group to which they belong (whether Negro or white, for example) depends in part on circumstances in the environment in which they live. A child who associates only with his own ethnic group during early years of life does not particularly have reason to notice his ethnic identity. On the other hand, a youngster in a community which includes a mixture of ethnic groups or nationalities is likely to be reminded of his background at an earlier age. This will especially hold true if there are distinct cleavages within the community or if he is a member of a minority group against which there is a prejudice. Among the most moving accounts of childhood are those given by older children and adults of their first remembered encounter with prejudice. A child who is abused because of his ethnic origins bears an extra burden in the process of forming ideas and attitudes pertaining to himself, especially if he is made to feel ashamed of his background.

In a study in which Negro children aged three to five were asked to identify themselves by pointing to pictures they regarded as most nearly like themselves (3), it was found that light-skinned Negro children chose a white child as being most like themselves more often than did Negro children with darker skins, suggesting that children identify themselves in terms of skin color, which is to them a "concrete reality," before they identify themselves in terms of "race," which apparently is a more sophisticated concept. Pictures were also used in a study by Horowitz (11)[2] who noted that a child who seemed to be aware of being a member of a minority group

---

[1] See also W. E. Martin and C. B. Stendler, *Readings in Child Development* (New York: Harcourt, 1954).

[2] See also L. B. Murphy, *Social Behavior and Child Personality* (New York: Columbia, 1937).

might still choose a picture of a majority group member as being most like himself.

Influence of Others on a Child's View of Himself

Among the earliest experiences which influence the development of the child's view of himself are those with other people. The position that the child's attitudes pertaining to himself are influenced by "significant" people, notably at first by his mother or mother substitute, has been expressed most strongly by Sullivan.

According to Sullivan the "self-system" has its origins in interpersonal relationships and it is influenced by "reflected appraisals." If a child is accepted, approved, respected, and liked for what he is, he will be helped to acquire an attitude of self-acceptance and respect for himself. But if the significant people in his life—at first his parents and later his teachers, peers, and other persons who wield an influence—belittle him, blame him and reject him, the growing child's attitudes toward himself are likely to become unfavorable. As he is judged by others, he will tend to judge himself. Further, according to this position, the attitudes concerning himself which he has thus acquired will, in turn, color the attitudes he has toward other persons. He judges himself as he has been judged and then, in turn, judges others as he judges himself.

In assessing the influence of interpersonal relationships in the development of a child's view of himself it is essential, however, not to lost sight of the fact that the relationship is *inter*personal. It includes the child as well as others, and the child's own qualities play an important role in the relationship. As noted in other sections of this book, children differ from the time of birth in temperament and disposition, in their demands and in their response to the treatment they receive from others, and in the response they evoke from others. Infants, for example, differ in the extent to which they are active or passive, irrespective of the social environment in which they are reared (2). Similarly, parents who have reared two or more children report, for example, that almost from the day of birth one child was more sensitive than another and that as the youngsters grew older, one would show "hurt feelings" when mildly scolded while the other would take the scolding in stride or even strike back. Unfortunately, in the research literature there is no systematic account of the way in which the natural bent of children and the treatment they receive from others interact in the development of children's ideas and attitudes pertaining to themselves.

Self as Is Compared with the "Ideal Self"

When older children and adults are asked to describe themselves, most of them are able to make a distinction between what they think they are and what they would like to be or think they ought to be. A person's view of what he aspires to be or believes he ought to be is sometimes referred to as the "ideal self." In most persons there is some discrepancy between self-as-is and the ideal self. Such a discrepancy occurs, for example, when a child says he *never* studies hard, but *should always* study hard, or when he says he *often* loses his temper but he *ought never* to lose his temper. In some persons, the difference between what they say they *are* and what they *should be* is very marked.

When a child's view of what he is corresponds quite closely to what he believes he ideally ought to be, he expresses what seems to be a rather comfortable view of himself. When there is a marked difference between the self-picture and the ideal picture, it appears that the child, in his own eyes, is failing to live up to the mark and he is, in that sense, a self-rejecting person. However, there are several reasons why it is necessary to be very cautious in labeling a person as self-accepting or self-rejecting on the basis of what he tells about himself as-is and as he thinks he ought to be. What a person reports about himself depends upon: (1) what he is consciously *able to recognize* as qualities belonging to his make-up, (2) what he not only recognizes but also is *willing to admit,* (3) what he feels impelled to *deny,* and (4) what he feels impelied to *claim* about himself.

There is a low discrepancy between an item pertaining to self-as-perceived and the "ideal self" if, for example, a child claims that he studies hard (whether or not he really does) and also claims that ideally he should study hard. Again, there is a low discrepancy between these two measures if he freely admits that he doesn't study hard and then (in describing the ideal) sets a low "aspiration level" for himself, claiming that he doesn't think he should work any harder than he does. Due to the fact that it is possible thus to manipulate the answers, it is necessary to know more about a child than can be gained from a self-rating inventory if we are to be reasonably sure of what might be his conception of himself.

In describing themselves, children differ greatly in the extent to which they are able to recognize or are willing to admit even minor childhood foibles. In one study (18) children were asked to respond to a list of statements which were regarded as "probably true" of all children (*e.g.,* "I sometimes disobey my parents"; "I sometimes say mad words or swear"). The youngsters who had been rated as least well-adjusted according to an earlier measure (a test of personality) less frequently admitted common faults than those rated as well-adjusted. Such results raise a question as to the reliance that can be placed on self-rating inventories. Information supplied by such measures is interesting as far as it goes, but it is likely that a child will give a far more genuinely revealing account when talking about himself over a period of time to someone in whom he is willing to confide than when he responds to a quick paper and pencil check-list. It is also likely that children will reveal many facets of themselves when they tell about their fantasies and dreams or respond to projective techniques which they will not disclose when asked point-blank to describe themselves.

Maintenance of the self-image

While still in the process of making new discoveries concerning his properties as an individual, the growing child has a strong tendency to preserve ideas and attitudes he already has formed. He strives in the presence of others and in his own eyes to be himself (as he sees himself) and to live in accordance with his concepts or attitudes regarding himself, whether these be true or false. He tries to be consistent with himself (14). He is likely to resist anything that is inconsistent with his own view of himself. It may even be difficult for him to see or hear or grasp the meaning of anything, favorable or unfavorable, that goes counter to his picture of himself. His perception of new events in his life will be colored by views he already has established.

Conscious and unconscious processes underlying attitudes pertaining to self

The foregoing sections have dealt with various aspects of *self-awareness* and with the characteristics which a person is clearly able to *recognize* as part of his make-up. These constitute a person's *phenomenal self* (the self which, as a *phenomenon*, appears, shows, is perceptible). There also are facets of a person's make-up which influence his ideas and attitudes pertaining to himself but which are *unconscious* in the sense that he does not consciously recognize them.

The term *unconscious* has a vast variety of meanings and interpretations which we do not here need to explore. But it is necessary to take account of some of the meanings of the concept of the unconscious when we seek to understand children. There are many currents in a child's life concerning which he is not consciously aware. A child does not comprehend the roots of his experience, when, for example, he has fears springing from happenings which he has forgotten or has a phobia arising from conflicts which he does not grasp. Likewise, a child is not conscious of what is occurring when, for example, he warms up to a teacher without realizing that he does so because the teacher touches off sentiments he has for his mother, or if he is deeply wounded by a mild criticism without realizing that the criticism triggers off feelings of self-reproach springing from earlier experiences in his life.

What has frequently been referred to as "the unconscious" is also at work if a child who has learned to suppress his anger gamely grins and feels no rage when someone abuses him but then later, for no apparent reason, feels a pain in his gut and throws up his dinner. In later sections, notably those dealing with emotion and the devices a child uses to defend his pride, there will be other illustrations of the way in which motives which a youngster does not recognize influence his actions and his endeavor to maintain a cherished view of himself.

A condition which a person is not consciously aware of occurs when he has an "idealized image" of himself that is not in keeping with the realities of his life. An idealized image of self containing elements which a person does not knowingly perceive occurs when he adopts a pose or facade and than somehow loses sight of the fact that he is posing. Such a condition occurs, for example, if an adult sees himself as a cold-hearted cynic when actually his cynicism is only a veneer, covering warm-hearted impulses. It occurs if an older child, with a powerful, competitive drive, views himself as a disinterested scholar, eager to learn for the sake of learning, without recognizing that he is using his scholarly efforts as a vehicle for competing with others.

> The "idealized self" is discussed again in later sections of this book dealing with anxiety and personality problems. For a more complete discussion of the concept of the idealized image the reader is referred to the writings of Horney (6, 7, 8, and 9).[3] Horney describes the idealized self as a kind of pseudo-identity. The "idealized self," containing elements which a person is not consciously aware of, has a different meaning than the "ideal self" which a person describes when he knowingly tells about his aspirations. The idealized self is not, from a person's own point of view, an ideal toward which he is striving but something he actually has attained—it is is "real self" as he sees it.

[3] See also K. Goldstein, P. Hock, R. May, K. Horney, F. A. Weiss, and H. Gershman, "Neurotic Anxiety—A Panel Discussion," *American Journal of Psychoanalysis* Vol. 12 (1952), pp. 89-95.

When we use an inventory to measure a person's ideas about himself as he thinks he really is, or to measure his ideas concerning his ideal self—the kind of person he thinks he ought to be—we cannot be sure to what extent one or the other account reflects unrecognized elements of an idealized image of self. Moreover, as pointed out earlier in this chapter, neither can we know, without deeper inquiry, to what extent a person is revealing aspects of his inner life which he consciously recognizes but is unwilling to disclose.

In view of all this we might ask: Is it not futile for parents or teachers or any of us, with our ordinary minds, to apply the concept of the self in trying to understand children? The answer is no. Inquiry into the self is a complicated business, but it is far from futile for several reasons. One reason is that regardless of what might be hidden the typical child consciously harbors many thoughts and feelings about himself which he usually keeps secret but would willingly confide to someone whom he trusts. He is most likely to reveal himself to a person who does not view him solely in terms of his overt behavior. He is also more likely to reveal himself to a person who desires to understand him and who does not immediately pronounce a moral judgment on him. Further, even though a child may be impelled by motives which he cannot consciously perceive it is often possible for a sympathetic observer to look beneath the surface. We are inquiring into "unconscious" reaches of the child's life when, for example, we begin to look for clues in an effort to understand what might be the nature of a child's ideas and attitudes regarding himself when he plunges happily into things, or is shy, or shows off, or is withdrawn, or is extremely "good," or becomes angry on slight provocation, or is extremely competitive or afraid to compete.

References

1. Ames, L. B., "The Sense of Self of Nursery School Children as Manifested by Their Verbal Behavior," *Journal of Genetic Psychology,* Vol. 81 (1952), pp. 193-232.
2. Buhler, C., "The Social Behavior of Children," *A Handbook of Child Psychology,* 2d rev. ed., C. Murcheson, ed. (Worcester, Mass.: Clark U., 1933), pp. 374-416.
3. Clark, K. B., and M. K. Clark, "Skin Color as a Factor in Racial Identification of Negro Preschool Children," *Journal of Social Psychology,* Vol. 11 (1940), pp. 159-169.
4. Conn, J. H., "Children's Reactions to the Discovery of Genital Differences," *American Journal of Orthopsychiatry,* Vol. 10 (1940), pp. 747-755.

5. Dixon, J. C., "Development of Self Recognition," *Journal of Genetic Psychology,* Vol. 91 (1957), pp. 251-256.
6. Horney, K., *The Neurotic Personality of Our Time* (New York: Norton, 1937.)
7. ———, *New Ways in Psychoanalysis* (New York: Norton, 1939).
8. ———, *Our Inner Conflicts* (New York: Norton, 1945).
9. ———, *Neurosis and Human Growth* (New York: Norton, 1950).
10. Horowitz, E., "Spacial Localization of the Self," *Journal of Social Psychology,* Vol. 6 (1935), pp. 379-387.
11. Horowitz, R., "Racial Aspects of Self-Identification," *Journal of Psychology,* Vol. 7 (1939), pp. 91-99.
12. James, W., *Principles of Psychology,* 2 vols. (New York: Holt, Rinehart & Winston, 1890).
13. Lacan, J., "Some Reflections on the Ego," *International Journal of Psychoanalysis,* Vol. 34 (1953), pp. 11-17.
14. Lecky, P., *Self-Consistency: A Theory of Personality* (Fort Myers Beach, Fla.: Island, 1945).
15. Preyer, W., *The Mind of the Child* (New York: Appleton, 1888).
16. Sarbin, T. R., "A Preface to a Psychological Analysis of the Self," *Psychological Review,* Vol. 59 (1952), pp. 11-22.
17. Stendler, C. B., *Children of Brasstown* (Urbana: U. of Ill., 1949).
18. Taylor, C., and A. W. Combs, "Self-Acceptance and Adjustment," *Journal of Consulting Psychology,* Vol. 16 (1952), pp. 89-91.
19. Zazzo, R., "Images du Corps et Conscience de Soi Materiaux pour L'Étude Experimentale de la Conscience," *Enfance,* Vol. 1 (1948), pp. 29-43.

2. Criminals are made, not born

MORRIS L. HAIMOWITZ

From *Human Development, Selected Readings* (1960), pp. 359-375, edited by M. L. Haimowitz and N. R. Haimowitz (New York: Thomas Y. Crowell, Co.). Reprinted by permission.

This article is included here not only for its excellence in explaining the possible genesis of criminality, but for its sensitive portrayal of how social interaction patterns can influence the growing self. The author speculates that one's behavior can be influenced, for better or for worse, by his perceptions of how he thinks others expect him to behave. Can this happen even to the point of encouraging delinquent behavior? Are criminals "made"?

I. Introduction

There are a number of theories about how people come to be professional criminals. There is the widespread notion that poverty causes crime; or the theory that "bad" neighborhoods cause crime; or that movies, TV, comic books, or radio crime stories cause crime; or that criminal associates cause crime; or that broken homes cause crime; or that race, nationality, neuroses, or crowded housing cause crime. These theories do not explain why most poor people never become professional criminals. Nor do most people from bad neighborhoods, nor most children of broken homes, nor most members of any race or nationality, nor most neurotics become criminals. If crowded housing caused crime, all Eskimos would be criminals; actually, very few are.

Some studies show these factors to be associated with criminality. But science aims at generalizations which account for *all* cases, and not one of these theories accounts for even a majority of cases. These important studies indicate some *associated* factors, not the *causes* of crime. Let us illustrate the difference. Suppose we didn't know how a child is conceived and were seeking an explanation. We might make a survey and find the following factors associated with having children: poverty, illiteracy, race, religion, marriage, wedding rings, rural dwellings. Could we therefore state that poverty, illiteracy, and so on, were the causes of conception? Such a conclusion would completely overlook the crucial role of the sperm and ovary. Marriage is an associated factor, but it is not the cause of conception. The theory that poverty or the factors listed above cause crime is as untrue as the one that poverty, or a wedding ring, are the causes of conception.

II. Hypothesis

This paper seeks to develop the hypothesis that the only way a person can become a professional cirminal is by getting the idea that he is expected to be an outlaw by those whom he takes seriously: his parents, friends, neighbors, teachers, clergymen, police, social workers, and judges. He must form a mental picture of himself as different from others, different in a way requiring a different vocational career and requiring that he associate with persons ostracized as he is.

This hypothesis refers to professional criminals, not to occasional lawbreakers or alcoholics, or persons who murder or steal in a passionate outbreak. It applies to those persons who belong to professional criminal societies and whose trade or occupation is criminal, with "professional" standards or skills. It is not always easy to tell which criminal is the professional and which is the amateur because many criminals have conflicting self-conceptions.

We like to think that there are two classes of occupations, the legal and the illegal, but the actual situation is not so simple. There are many gradations between the strictly honest and the strictly criminal. Many activities of business or professional men, repairmen, or governmental workers fall into criminal categories. In addition, there are other activities, not definitely criminal, nor yet definitely honest, in the shady or unethical category. Moreover, there are perfectly legal activities which are of controversial value, such as manufacturing, advertising, or selling white flour, candy, alcohol, tobacco, patent medicines, or firearms, which may be declared illegal in the future. Finally, there are ideas which may be considered dangerous or illegal because they are new or different.

Some children are taught methods of stealing by their parents. But the usual delinquent cannot be explained so easily. Usually, his parents are frightened and embarrassed by his notoriety, even though they also may be secretly proud of their little rascal.

It is popular to explain socially disapproved behavior by labeling the person as neurotic. Neurosis is abnormal; so is criminality. For example, suppose a man steals or damages property and finds himself waiting, terrified and yet wanting to be caught. He may experience an anxiety, like the child playing hide-and-seek, with excitement reaching a climax when he is discovered. Such a person would be a neurotic criminal. However, one cannot say all criminals are neurotic, especially the one who performs his acts because he, his family, and his associates consider them proper and desirable. Furthermore, criminal law changes from time to time and is differently enforced from place to place. Betting is illegal in Chicago; legal in the suburbs. George Washington was a hero in America; a criminal in England.

III. The Setting: Some Factors Associated with Crime

When we study criminals we find certain factors statistically associated with crime.

Most delinquents are found in the slums, yet most slum children never become delinquents. Most delinquents come from broken homes, yet most children from broken homes never become delinquents. Most delinquents are of a different racial or ethnic stock than the natives, yet race or ethnic affiliation is no guarantee of law-abiding or criminal behavior. Most delinquents are probably neurotic, but most neurotics are not criminal. Most delinquents, finally, come from low-income families, but most persons with low incomes are law-abiding. A recent study of 2,000 white teenagers by Nye and Short showed that delinquency was not as closely related to income, religion, or to broken homes, as to the feeling, "My parents hate me." We may conclude that living in the slum or in a broken home, belonging to a different racial or ethnic group, and being neurotic and poor are factors associated with crime, but they are not the causes.

Most people who steal are not professional criminals. The act of stealing something probably involves a conscious decision. But the act of becoming a professional criminal appears to involve a long list of experiences in which a pattern of behavior occurs, a drifting into a habit of life, into life with a group of friends which no one ever planned but which could have only one ending. The criminal may never have made a conscious decision to enter on a career of crime.

The people living in the slums and rooming house areas of the city are different from others not only in being on the average less well educated and earning less money, having higher mortality and morbidity rates, in appearing to have a higher rate of criminality, but also in being of different ethnic, racial, or national stocks. They are the newcomers. The immigrants usually settle in the slums; they bring with them not only poverty but also opinions as to what's right and what's wrong which were appropriate in the environment from which they came. It is a crime for the newcomer in Chicago to throw his garbage out the window; but it was perfectly proper to do so home in the South—for the chickens and hogs to eat. Prohibition was incomprehensible to Europeans accustomed to wine with dinner.

The rapid growth of the factories, and of the slums housing the factory workers, the high rate of immigration, and the rapid technological developments have made this country, as well as most countries of our time, an area of cultural ferment, with rapidly changing ideas of what is criminal and what is proper. What is legal today may be criminal tomorrow.

All children get into mischief. Technically, you could say they violate the law. A little boy two years old pulls down the curtains in the living room. When they fall, they knock over a lamp, dust flies all over the room, and his mother, hearing the commotion, runs in from the kitchen and helps him out of difficulty. He has behaved in utter disregard for life and property and is thus a lawbreaker, but no one calls him a criminal. His mother is caring for him all the time, getting him out of the refrigerator, turning off the gas which he has turned on, rescuing his toy rabbit from the toilet bowl. Like adults, all little children err, but few become gangsters.

Not all children have a mother at home caring for them. Especially not slum children. They live in the "zones of transition," called such because they are changing areas, changing from big homes to rooming houses, from residential to business, from native citizens to immigrants, from white to colored to Mexican and Puerto Rican. But in one way such a zone is not changing. It always has had the highest crime rate of any area in the city. The reasons many children do not have a mother supervising them are that their father is sick, or is dead, or is in jail, or cannot support his family. So the mother has to work, and cannot be home supervising the children; or she is sick or doesn't like caring for children.

A very high proportion of professional criminals come from the slums. Occasionally they come from nicer neighborhoods, but here too we find the unsupervised child. The child who steals and is caught and arrested is delinquent; if he steals and is not caught or not arrested, he is not delinquent. Of course, in nicer neighborhoods, police act more courteously to accused children.

There are many ways a child may react to the fears and loneliness resulting from parental neglect. He can become a dreamer; he can become sick or develop an inferiority complex; or he can become a fighter, and demand attention, stating in effect, "Love me or fear me." The self-conception he forms is determined by the way he perceives some crucial experiences.

IV. The Crucial Experiences

WITH PARENTS

Let's see what happens. A boy is involved in an incident during which someone is hurt or property is damaged or stolen. The injured party usually talks to the boy or his parents, and they make an amicable settlement. But sometimes the injured party feels frightened, angry with himself and his neighbors, and unable to deal with the situation alone, and so he calls the police. The boys see the police, and they all run away. One who did not run away, or was too slow, or had nothing to do with it, or has a bad reputation is caught. The parents are called in, and they protect or spank the boy and everyone is satisfied. Or for some reason parents and sons are brought in for questioning. What concerns us is how the child learns that people expect him to be untrustworthy.

There are many ways parents may tell their children they are not to be trusted. They may be direct and say, "You are becoming a little hoodlum." Or they may be subtle and say, "My boy is good," and the boy knows they mean, "He is bad."

Here is an example of this. A juvenile officer was told that a fifteen-year-old boy had been committing delinquencies with a girl of his age. The girl had admitted relations with him. So the boy, accompanied by his mother, was brought in for questioning.

POLICE OFFICER. "Did you see Miss X on December 15?"
MOTHER. "No, he didn't."
POLICE OFFICER. "Did you meet Miss X after school that day?"
MOTHER. "No, why don't you leave him alone?"
POLICE OFFICER. "Did you have relations with her?"
MOTHER. "Why do you keep picking on him. He's a good boy; he would never do such a thing!"
POLICE OFFICER. "Why don't you let him talk for himself? I've been asking him questions for thirty minutes and you haven't let him answer once."

Was this mother so convinced of her son's innocence? It is natural for a mother to defend her son. Her words said, "He is a good boy," but her manner said, "He can't be trusted to speak; he is either too stupid to say the right thing, or he is terribly guilty." Thus she became an accessory to the crime.

And how would the boy feel in a spot like this? "To die, to sink through the floor, where can I hide? It's even harder when she lies. Why don't the police mind their own business?"

When persons important to the child don't trust him, he may come to distrust himself. The conception of oneself as a law-violator, or just a hateful, worthless, public nuisance does not usually develop full-blown in a few minutes. We don't know exactly how it happens. Little children interact thousands of times with others, thereby learning what is expected of them. Little children of two, three, or four years like to help their mothers in the kitchen, wash the dishes, peel the potatoes, string the beans, crack the nuts, mop the floor. They like to help their father repair the clock, fix the furnace, paint the chairs, drive the car. Some mothers and fathers find this "help" more than they can bear. They tell the child, "Go away! You can't wash the dishes, you'll break them; you can't paint the furniture; you can't mop the floor; scram!"

We have observed eleven-year-old children who could not clear the table or wash a dish ("She might break them," the mother would say); and we have observed other children, five years old, who could clear the table, wash, and dry the dishes. One mother expects the child to break the dishes; the other mother expects the child to do a good job. Both children do what is expected of them, and by doing so, each is developing a self-conception.

Parents are very worried when their children are destructive. One mother who asked us for help could not understand her child: "Come see for yourself; that little boy was impossible." We went to her home, and she was right. He was impossible. But he wasn't learning how to be impossible all by himself; he was getting lots of help from his mother, and from his older brothers. During the hour of the visit we heard them tell him forty times, "Don't break the wall down; don't tear up your clothes; don't scream so loud; don't sweep the floor; don't be a bad boy; don't run; don't carry the tray. For God's sake, don't be impossible!" The boy told us, "I just wanted to help, and every time I try to help they make me do it wrong." His family wanted him to be good; but they told him they expected him to be bad. It appears that some children are more likely to act as people *expect* them to act than as they want to act. How many times a day may a parent tell the child, "I expect you to be bad." One hundred? And how many times by the child's sixth birthday? One hundred thousand? Some parents are more patient and can even enjoy the child's attempts to be useful. When the child strings one bean, they say, "Thank you," because they consider the child's age when judging his craftsmanship.

What is important is not so much just what words the parents say to the child as the way they act and the way their acts are interpreted by the child. The parents may say, "You are bad," but act as though the child were the most precious object in the world. Both the words and the other feelings are communicated. So the child may feel, "I am capable, but my parents are sometimes impatient."

Now let's see how the child may come to feel, "I am no good and can do nothing that is good." If by neglect, cruelty, or constant discouragement the actions of the parents are such that they indicate to the child he is the *least* precious object in the world, this self-conception may develop. It may happen because the child is often neglected, left uncared for, unfed. Or they just don't take time for the child. Every time the child wants to help wash dishes, they say, "Go away, dishes are not for you, you just make a mess." This may happen thousands of times between his second and sixth year. And one day his mother decides he is now old enough to help, and she calls him in—but now he has learned "Dishes are not for me." He refuses to help wash the dishes, or gets a headache, or has to go to the bathroom. More extreme situations, such as the parent's leaving the child alone for days at a time, or constant beatings, convey to him a sense of his worthlessness or undesirability.

WITH POLICE

Sometimes the boy is unsupervised, out on the streets. His parents prefer earning money to staying home and taking care of him. Something happens. He borrows a friend's bicycle, rides to the grocery store, goes inside, and buys an ice cream bar. As he comes out some bigger boys, wanting to share the ice cream, are waiting for him; he runs away from them, leaving the bicycle.

Meanwhile, the owner of the bicycle starts screaming, "Someone stole my bike." Fred says, "Tommy took it. I saw him." They find Tommy. He says he left it at the grocery store, but it is no longer there. The police are called. They try to locate Tommy's parents, but they are not at home. Now it is up to the police.

Usually the policeman is friendly but firm; he has children of his own who might have done the same thing, and he wouldn't want anyone roughing them up. He tells the boy, "You're a good boy. I know it was an accident. Be more careful next time," and lets him go. If he has the time and the desire, if he is well trained, if he has been assigned to that neighborhood long enough to know it well, if he is patient, the policeman will talk to the natural leaders of the boys to convert the leaders from delinquent to productive activities. The policeman knows that most leaders of boys' gangs will cooperate if they are given a chance to participate in the planning and that these leaders can influence their followers better than anyone else. Or the policeman may recognize the need for community aid for these boys and will talk to local adult leaders—the clergyman, teacher, school principal, businessman, his alderman, or police captain—for the purpose of getting more supervised activities underway. A number of studies have shown that participation in supervised activities deters juvenile delinquency. Even when such facilities are available, however, some supervisors refuse to permit delinquents to participate.

Often the policeman can't do these things. He just doesn't have the time or the training. Perhaps he is under strain because it has happened several times before, or the citizen wronged is very angry or influential, or the policeman was recently reprimanded for being lax, or another child hit him in the ear with a snowball ten minutes earlier. Or, most important of all, the lad is impertinent. Then our young citizen—five, ten, fifteen years old—may be taken in and detained. The policeman may feel less likely to get into trouble by such action. Or he may feel, "Today I am starting a boy off on the wrong road, but I can't help it."

Until this time the boy is like all the other kids; full of energy, going through many different kinds of activities all day long, singing, jumping, screaming, playing cops and robbers, tearing clothes, crying, fighting—just like everyone else. But once arrested he becomes different. He is asked questions which imply a difference—name, father's name, religion, age, father's occupation, nationality, race. Ordinary things become extraordinary. He never thought about such things before. He was just like everyone else until now. He wonders about himself. He is frightened but also may be very impressed with the whole procedure and perhaps with his own importance. He wants his mother. He is taken to a social worker. She is expected to ask questions. Tell me about your home, your father and mother, the implication being something is wrong with them. She might even go home and find out for herself. He is taken to a psychologist or sociologist. His intelligence is measured—I.Q.: 105. His emotions are wondered at. He is taken to a judge: he hears lawyers talking about him. He is getting an education that his brothers and sisters and neighbors never dreamed about. Being in a detention home or jail can terrify a child. Everyone is saying, "Something's wrong with you."

He may be interrogated. Did you ever hear a policeman interrogating a teenager alleged to be guilty of a crime? The policeman acts and speaks as though the prisoner is guilty. It's his duty to clear up the crime. He is usually courteous, but sometimes he is filthy with insults, especially if the boy is a member of an ethnic group the policeman doesn't trust:

POLICE. "What were you doing at that house?"

BOY. "I went there to collect $5.00 a man owed me."

POLICE. "Don't you know they're a pack of thieves?"

BOY. "I didn't know that."

POLICE. "If you sleep in a stable, you will smell like—."

BOY. "I just went to collect my $5.00."

POLICE. "Who did you lend it to?"

BOY. "Fred Johnson."

POLICE. "Fred Johnson! He's an old-timer. Been in jail a dozen times. Why did you lend him $5.00?"

BOY. "He asked me for it. He lent me money when we were in school together."

SECOND POLICE. "Oh boy! what a tale! [*Sarcastically*] They were planning another A&P job."

BOY. "I never had anything to do with any A&P. I go to Brundy School."

POLICE. "Who went through the transom, you or Fred?"

BOY. "I never robbed any store in my life!"

POLICE. [*All laugh*] "You're a damned liar!"

[*Boy cries.*] [1]

Some policemen treat him like a son. Others, like a step-son. The policeman has a tough job. It sounds easy, "Just enforce law and order." But what to do when John Doe, age eight, is caught for the third time stealing a bike? Scold him, let him go, arrest him? There must be an answer.

Why should a poorly paid, often semitrained policeman be permitted to bear the burden of such a major decision? Many people are involved; many should help decide—maybe a community council, including teenagers as well as adults. One thing police could do which would give the boy some idea of the problems of policemen would be to invite delinquents to patrol the city a few hours a week in a police squad car. Most cities have enough squad cars to keep every delinquent occupied several hours a week. It might work, properly supervised so that the officers are instructed to try to be friendly, courteous, to explain their jobs, to listen to the problems of the boys as a sort of get-acquainted, how-do-you-do gesture, or as a long-term intensive activity.

---

[1] This dialogue is quoted verbatim. Only names and obscenity are changed. The writer is grateful to many policemen in Chicago and prison officials in New York whose cooperation helped to formulate the ideas here.

In court

The boy may be taken to court. What happens in the court room? The state's attorney may appear if enough publicity is involved, and he makes a speech, such as: "(Crime) by teen-agers must be stopped. The energetic measures taken by police to deal with *these future hoodlums* will be backed to the limit by the state's attorney's office." (In this particular case, the judge in Boys' Court ordered bond increases from $100 to $4,000 for each of the six young men arrested.) The state's attorney continued his speech. "Either those boys will have a chance to reflect in jail while they are waiting trial, or their parents, through the expense of getting them out on bond, will realize that *parental irresponsibility doesn't pay.*"[2] His speech was longer. The boys might remember part of it, but we are sure they would like to forget that such a prominent man considered them "future hoodlums" and publicly proclaimed that not only they, but their parents as well, are tainted. Could the boys think: "He's important; he says we'll be criminals. He ought to know. I never thought I'd be a criminal; but he's a very important man." The public doesn't expect the state's attorney to furnish adequate homes, parents, playgrounds, and psychologists for these boys, so he doesn't bother with such details. But the public doesn't expect him to make these boys into permanent public enemies either.

The judge at the Boys' Court has many problems. Among some boys who had been arrested for participating in a riot, two were dismissed. Here's what the newspapers said about these two: "John ——, 21, of Chicago, a laborer, and his brother, 19, of Chicago, unemployed, were dismissed. They said they merely stopped nearby to see what the trouble was and were arrested. Judge —— told the defendants: 'We're going to give you a break. We operate on the theory that every dog is entitled to one bite.'"[3] Here were two bystanders arrested, taken to jail, and then instead of getting an apology for being inconvenienced, the judge says he will invoke a canine justice. But this is no dogs' court. These boys, like the judge, are human. What can the judge do? The police say, "They are guilty—we saw them rioting." The boys say, "We broke no law." Citizens, relatives, and neighbors testify, orate, hiss, and applaud both sides. The judge doesn't know who is right or what to do. The boys are our concern here. They may get the impression: "We are not like other human beings. We are bad."

What can the judge do? The voters are angry because there was a riot; the police are angry because the boys were not convicted; the boys, be-

[2] Chicago Sunday *Tribune,* August 23, 1953, part 1, p. 25.
[3] Chicago *Daily News,* August 17, 1953, p. 3.

cause they were arrested and scolded; the judge, because he too is on public trial in a difficult situation. Because of this many judges try to protect themselves and the public by utilizing medical, sociological, psychological, or other professional advice. Sometimes, though, they lose their tempers.

The writer has no quarrel with these officials. Thousands of such items appear in the papers every year. The point is that the police, state's attorney, and judges may not lead the defendants to expect honest, law-abiding behavior of themselves. If this were the end of it, probably the defendants would go back home and be upright citizens. The suggestions from the officials that they are disreputable might not be taken seriously. But this may not be the end.

Why should a solitary judge with fifty to one hundred cases in one day be permitted to make such vital decisions? Crime hurts everyone. These decisions are too important for any one person to make.

Back home

The boy goes back home. Whether or not he was found guilty, he is not quite like his friends any more. An object of curiosity: "What did they do to you?" "My lawyers defended me," he says. "I saw the judge." An object of adoration: his picture was in the paper; he has had his I.Q. measured; he has talked to lots of policemen. An object of scorn—he was arrested, put in jail with crooks—he is vicious. For some of his friends he is a hero; for others he must never be played with again. If he should see them, they turn away: "My mother says not to play with you. The state's attorney says you're a hoodlum."

Little boys soon forget. They play together as usual, except for those whose mothers are constantly reminding them, protecting them from the "criminal," the bad apple in the neighborhood. Then something happens again. The newspapers have a heyday. Who did it? The citizens are upset and impatient. They put pressure on the police. The police have to do something. Well, everyone knows who did it. Didn't someone just leave the detention home? Wasn't his name in the paper? It makes no difference that he was at school or visiting in another city when it happened. He is apprehended because he is convenient. He is found not guilty, but everyone suspects him just the same. He is getting a reputation, and a self-conception.

Lots of boys find their home life uncomfortable. Pick a child up off the street some night—say, at midnight. Take him home and you will see why he doesn't want to be home. His home may be physically repulsive; or it may be a lovely house but a miserable home. To say that it's the parents' fault misses the point. Most parents of delinquents are helpless, sorely in need of psychological, medical, religious or economic aid. Responsibility lies not with irresponsible parents but with the community.

We assume that parents mean well but many just do not have the energy and skills necessary to win the confidence of their children and to make plans together. Parents expect their children to mature gradually and become independent. That this can be done gracefully is proved by many happy parents who help their children settle on their own. Even in the better neighborhoods a barrier often develops between the parents and children. Most children on the street go home after a while and play inside, but some can't go home. In many instances help for the parents would prevent a child from going to the street.

On the street

Our young citizens may find friends on the street where things are more pleasant, where he can be a hero. We assume everyone wants to be liked, everyone wants a word of praise, and if it is not available at home and is available on the street, then one goes to the street. A little boy knows where he is afraid to breathe and where he is a regular guy like all the rest.

The boys he plays with on the street may like to play volleyball. They have a volleyball and play all the time. They don't get into trouble. Or they may not have a volleyball. Slum children have less equipment than other children. What can you do on the street?

Everyone needs someone to idealize, someone to be like, someone to dream he is like. These street children could idealize their parents, but it is not likely since they don't enjoy their parents. Their hero could be a policeman who saves a man's life; but not if the policeman hurts them or depreciates them. We don't know enough about whom the street boys idealize. Maybe it's a famous boxer who can beat anyone in the whole world; or a cowboy movie star. These boys can't be cowboys; but they can fight, they can be brave, not afraid of their parents, not afraid of the police. They can learn to be tough.

If the street boy could get along with his mother, he might be home with her, learning to keep his room straight: "Freddie, hang up your clothes. Freddie wash your hands. Freddie shine your shoes this minute. Freddie, here's some new crayons. That's a sweet boy." His mother cannot be at ease until she knows he is responding to her attempts at socialization.

The boys on the street are learning a different moral code: Who can throw the stone the straightest. Who can run faster. Who is a sissy. Who can do things and not get caught. Hundreds of times a day a boy is learning the code of the street: Be loyal to friends—never betray a comrade. Find out who you can trust. Avoid the police.

Street boys go to school. The teacher knows they have been in trouble and if anything out of the ordinary occurs in the classroom, she knows who is to blame. Even if they are not really to blame, she can guess who were the agitators. Because the street boys have more than average trouble at home, they may be more restless than the average pupils and not perform well in school. You can't want to please a teacher if this makes you a sissy, especially if this teacher is always picking on you or your friends. The teacher is not going to be his ideal or model. She could if she had a class of fifteen children instead of thirty to sixty and if her salary made it unnecessary to hold down an extra job or two, and if teachers had high morale, and if she had time to consult with parents, social workers, religious workers, a physician, a psychologist, a reading specialist, to discuss the boy's problems, and if she had professional training and attitudes. Sometimes she can do it without all these. But aren't we foolish to expect miracles of semi-trained, overworked teachers?

It takes most people years to settle down to one ego ideal. Little boys play at being policemen or cowboys or gangsters. When they are growing up they decide to be truck drivers or ambulance drivers or doctors. In school they want to be teachers or janitors or a principal or the coach. In college they want to be lawyers or scientists or philosophers or businessmen. After they leave college, they are deciding one day this, one day that. Who do I want to be like? What am I going to do? It takes years for the average citizen to decide.

Lots of people are helping the street boy to decide on his career. His mother and father and his home life are unbearable to him, so he joins the street boys. His friends on the street give him fellowship and praise for doing a good job. His teacher tells him he is too jumpy. The police suggest that he is a liar. The social worker suggests his family is tainted. The psychologist tells him he is not like other boys. The judge says, "Every dog deserves one bite." The state's attorney says, "You are the future hoodlums." Can one's career be that of a hoodlum?

Reform school

One day he is arrested, found guilty, and goes to reform school. He is frightened and angry. He wishes he were home. He wants to find out: "Who are my friends and who are enemies?" He learns that some of the inmates are regular guys; others snitch on you. The guards, the hired hands around the place, can't be trusted; they are against you. "What are you here for?" a friend asks. "I grabbed a pocketbook and ran." "Is that all? Boy! I robbed five filling stations! You know that kid with the glasses, the tall blond one? He killed a policeman! When he says something, you'd better jump."

How do you rob a filling station? What do you do with the tires? Which lawyers will help you if you get caught? Which is the easiest way to rob the A&P? How do you steal a car? Where can you sell it? Who buys the parts? How can you be successful? This sounds like an exciting career. He never realized so many people are in this business. The reform school teaches much about crime, but little about reform.

The guards are afraid the boys will run away, hurt each other or hurt the guards. The superintendent has his job to do. He has to keep the boys clean, working, in school, has to buy the groceries, get a new psychologist to replace the one leaving for a better job, get three new attendants, make out dozens of reports, read what the wardens at other schools are doing, go to meetings, see visitors from the Rotary Club, decide what to do about a boy who is always fighting. If he is strict, the boys hate him more. If he is less strict, the place gets dirty and citizens complain; newspapers take pictures. There is never enough money. The superintendent does what he can. The boys are learning a career. They can't help it, and he can't help it. And the respectable citizens back home are not aware of the fact that they are paying $500 to $5,000 per year to train each child to become a more professional criminal. There is not one reform school which reforms. Foster homes are a much better risk, especially if foster parents get special training in ways to handle these children. It's hard to find parents who would take disturbed children, but anything seems better than the typical reform school.

AFTER REFORM SCHOOL

When the boy leaves the reform school, he goes home. He has been a disgrace to the family, and his welcome is thin: "Your mother is ashamed to walk down the street!" "We hope they reformed you." He is now perhaps nine, twelve, or fifteen years old. His sister says, "You have ruined my life." He wonders who his friends are. Maybe a brother is friendly to him. Maybe his mother. She gives him a new necktie. But can she give him what will save him from the electric chair or from a life sentence? If she can give him the trust and patience every boy needs so much, and if his other relatives and friends are able to help, they can save him. Usually they cannot, any more than they could before reform school. If he is to be helped, it will be by foster parents or officials of the institutional kingdoms—school, church, scouts, PTA, settlement house, neighborhood center—working as an integrated unit. Today these kingdoms often work in competition and at odds with one another.

It is easy in the neighborhood to tell who can be trusted. Plenty of guys make nasty remarks. They go to school; they go to Sunday school; they brush their teeth and say, "Good afternoon," to the corner policeman. When their mothers see the returned "criminal" in the drug store, they say: "Look who's out! If I see my boy playing with you, I'll call the police. Stay away." You can understand that such mothers are trying to protect their own boys. But they are helping another boy to become a criminal. If good boys won't play with him, who will? Underworld characters?

Other mothers don't know much about him. They are working or sick or preoccupied. Their sons are the street boys. The boys want to know about reform school. Did they beat you? Let me show you what I learned. Let's pull a job tonight. I'll show you how to do it. I can chin with one hand.

He has to go to school. That's the law. The principal talks to him, the teacher talks to him, some kids talk to him, and what they say adds up to one thing: They are not his friends. They expect him to start something. It doesn't have to be that way. They could invite him to join the Scouts, or write on the school paper, or sing in the choir. If they did, it might save him.

His mother wants him to go to church. She has talked to the clergyman, who says he needs religion. He may not be as clean, as well dressed as the next boy—or he may be cleaner. The boy out of reform school wonders how his new clothes look. They feel strange. The people in Sunday school may not feel hostile towards him, but they are strangers. One looks at him in a friendly way; another says, "He just got out of reform school."

There is still a chance he won't go back to reform school, or graduate into prison, but the chance is slim. Let a window be broken, a store burglarized, a car stolen, and the neighbors will know who to blame. A nice neighborhood finds it easy to blame someone for its troubles, not only because he may be guilty, but because he is the one expected to perform such acts in this community. If he does not expect of himself what they expect of him, he will go straight, perhaps leaving the community, perhaps even changing the community, but that is unlikely.

Even after he comes to expect vicious or criminal behavior of himself, he may still act like a good citizen most of the time. But it appears that the self-concept, the picture of himself inside, is more powerful than anything else in determining his behavior. Here is part of an interview between a prisoner and a prison counselor to illustrate this:

PRISONER. Why do I keep getting in trouble? I want to go straight, but I'll go out and before you know it I'm with the same crowd. I know it's wrong and yet there I am.

COUNSELOR. Maybe you are forced back to the old crowd. Have you ever been treated like an ex-con?

PRISONER. I was going with a girl and couldn't get the nerve to tell her I'd been in the pen. I knew she'd find out sooner or later. I kept wanting to give her up, I finally did in a way. I took to drinking.

COUNSELOR. You had to. It's too much to bear. You knew she wouldn't understand.

PRISONER. I began to hate her. She kept asking what was wrong and all that. In fact I don't think I minded it too much when I had to leave her, knowing what she would think of me.

COUNSELOR. It's hard to love a person when you expect her to hate you.

PRISONER. You know, she still comes to see me, so I was wrong about how she would feel.

The prisoner could not bring himself to tell his girl friend that he had been in jail for fear that she would hate him. Since it was not true that she hated him, we must conclude that the hatred was in himself, that he hated himself because he felt he was a criminal or because he expected her to hate him because he was a criminal. Of course, it is difficult for one who has been arrested many times to feel, "I'm an honest and respected man." He wanted to go straight but felt he was not honest. In not telling the girl, he was in fact dishonest. If he had felt he was an honest man, it would have been much easier for him to say, "I was convicted of a crime and spent some time in jail, but now I am honest." But his self-conception must have been: "I'm a criminal. She would hate criminals like everyone else hates them, perhaps even as I myself do. So I can't tell her." With such a self-conception, he could not be comfortable around law-abiding citizens.

Gradually, over the years, if he comes to expect of himself what his neighbors expect of him, he becomes a professional criminal. But if along the way he can find satisfactions and social approval from legitimate activities, he will obey the law. When he has learned over and over again that he can find no satisfaction this way, he welcomes the greetings of his professional associates in the underworld. As a professional criminal, he has standards of performance to live up to, friends who will help him when in trouble, visit him in prison, send him presents at Christmas, give him a home when he is sick, tell him where the police are lax and where strict—hideouts, fences, and lawyers. At twelve, fourteen, sixteen, or eighteen he has come to a conclusion about his career that ordinary boys may not make until they are twenty or even forty. And he could not have drifted into this career without the help of his family and neighbors who sought a scapegoat and unwittingly suggested to him that he become an outlaw.

V. Implications

When a crime is committed in a community, it is, in a sense, caused by everyone. No one grows up and lives alone; the criminal grows up with people. He is molded by his social experiences. If he wants to murder, people have made him want to murder; if he wants to break school windows, his environment has taught him how and given him a reason. And if he is punished by the community, it is because the community feels guilty for his crime, for failing to provide positive experiences in schools, for not protecting him from severe cruelty, neglect, starvation, and rejection. Those in the community who most demand his punishment are usually those who feel most guilty for their own failures, real or imaginary. They punish the criminal as they have been punished themselves. If they could forgive themselves, accept themselves, they could forgive the delinquent, accept him, and, in accepting him, convert him before he becomes a hardened inconvertible criminal. This conversion process is usually too big a job for any one school, teacher, policeman, judge, psychologist, or social worker. It takes many people to make an ordinary little boy into a hardened criminal. It will take a lot of people to make a disturbed little boy into a good citizen. Every little boy or girl in trouble should be examined by a physician, a psychologist, a reading specialist, a social worker, and his home and neighborhood should be studied. Intelligent steps can then be taken by this team of people working with the community council, with the cooperation of the boy and taking into consideration his preferences, to give this boy what everybody needs: security, affection, adventure, a chance to get recognition, to learn and to give to others the best that he has to give.

Every city and hamlet has some special programs for handling delinquents. Every program in every city is different from the next. Naturally, some are better than others. Study and systematic evaluation of these programs is required so that we can find out what works and what does not. At present we do not know.

3. The development of the ideal self in childhood and adolescence

Robert J. Havighurst,
Myra Z. Robinson,
and Mildred Dorr

Reprinted from the *Journal of Educational Research,* Vol. 40 (1946), 241-257, by permission of the senior author and Dembar Publications, Inc.

The concept of the ideal self is frequently used to describe one's optimal level of personal aspiration, but there has been little research to demonstrate the influences on ideal self-development. What sorts of individuals in the child's environment influence his ideal self? This study will assist in answering that question.

The purpose of this article is to describe the development of the ideal self, or the ego-ideal, as this is revealed by self-reports during childhood and adolescence. The data were obtained by asking boys and girls to write a brief essay on the subject "The Person I Would Like To Be Like."

The concept of an ego-ideal or an ideal self has been found useful by the Freudian psychologists and by the social psychologists in studying the development of personality and character. But there is very little factual information on which to base an extensive use of this concept.

The Freudians explain the origin of the ego-ideal as due to *identification* with people whom the child loves or admires or fears. Through the process of identification the child comes to imitate the values and attitudes of other people. The parents are the first and most important objects of identification. It is not stated clearly by the Freudians how important the later objects of identification are—such as teachers, youth group leaders, heroes of adventure and romance, and attractive age-mates. However, these writers generally attribute some importance to the people who follow the parents as objects of identification, believing that the ego-ideal of the adult is a composite of all the identifications the individual has made, with the figures of the parents still holding the most prominent place.

The social psychologists think of the ideal self as a name for the integrated set of *roles* and *aspirations* which direct the individual's life. These roles and attitudes they believe are taken on by the individual from parents, and from a variety of others, such as siblings, playmates, teachers, preachers, and others with prestige, and historical and fictional heroes, and worked over into his own thought and action.

While it is generally agreed that the ideal self or ego-ideal is important in the development of character and personality, and much attention has been given to the problem of its origin in the early years of life, very little work has been done on its development during childhood and adolescence.

Procedure

The procedure in this study was to ask children to write a brief essay on the topic "The Person I Would Like To Be Like" . . . .

We have used the following directions with boys and girls in the age-range 8 to 18:

> Describe in a page or less the person you would most like to be like when you grow up. This may be a real person, or an imaginary person. He or she may be a combination of several people. Tell something about this person's age, character, appearance, occupation, and recreations. If he is a real person, say so. You need not give his real name if you do not want to.

These directions give some very definite leads to the subject. This seems desirable, for many children would not know how to begin unless they were given some suggestion. Furthermore, this insures a degree of comparability in the essays, which makes it possible to rate them for the quality of the ideals expressed, something that has proved useful, though it is not reported in this paper.

It will be noted that the directions prevent the child from telling about his own age-mates as sources of his ideals, for he is asked to tell about the person he would like to be like *when he grows up*. This is an important limitation on the procedure, and prevents us from getting data on the relative importance of age-mates and of adults in the formation of the ego-ideal. Yet some children ignore the directions and describe an age-mate. This happens most often with children aged about fourteen. . . .

Results

Analysis of the responses in several sets of papers led to the use of the following categories.

I P Parents and other relatives of the parental or grandparental generation.

II S Parent-surrogates: teachers, neighbors of the parental generation.

III G Glamorous adults: people with a romantic or ephemeral fame, due to the more superficial qualities of appearance and behavior—*e.g.,* movie stars, military figures, athletes. *Note:* characters in comic strips or radio dramas are included here, though they may be imaginary—*e.g.,* Superman, Dick Tracy.

IV H Heroes, people with a substantial claim to fame, usually tested by time—*e.g.,* Florence Nightingale and Abraham Lincoln. However, certain living persons are placed in this category—*e.g.,* Madame Chiang Kai-shek, the President, General MacArthur.

V A Attractive and successful young adults within the individual's range of observation: these are usually young people who live in the community, or go to a local college, or lead a scout group, or are related to the subject—elder siblings, cousins, young uncles and aunts. They can be observed by the subject in three dimensions, as it were—going about their daily work, making moral decisions, getting along with family and friends, preparing for an occupation.

VI C Composite or imaginary characters: these are abstractions of a number of people. Sometimes they appear to be wholly imaginary; other times they are clearly a coalescence of qualities of two or three real persons.

VII M Age-mates or youths, only two or three years older than the subject. While the directions sought to prevent the naming of these people, some were named.

VIII NC Miscellaneous responses, not classifiable among those mentioned above. A fairly frequent response in this category is "myself."

Essays from several groups of subjects have been classified, with results shown in Table 1. The age of the group increases from left to right in the table. Groups *A* and *I* came from the same community, as did groups *C* and *E*. Changes with age should show most clearly in a study of these two pairs of groups. From inspection of the table it is at once evident that there is much apparently random variation from group to group, which is not explainable as due to change with age. This kind of variability from group to group may be explained as due to any or all of the following possible causes: (1) unreliability of the instrument, either in the responses of the subjects or in the categorization of the responses; (2) accidents of sampling, since the numbers in several of the groups are small; (3) differences in the social environments of the various groups. No doubt some of the variability is due to the sampling factor, but a considerable part is due to the other two factors, as will be shown later.

Several general conclusions may be drawn from Table 1. One conclusion is that the responses fall mainly into four categories, those of parents, glamorous adults, attractive and visible young adults, and composite, imaginary characters. Parent-surrogates such as teachers and older adults are seldom named, and heroes are very seldom named.

TABLE 1

CLASSIFICATION OF PERSONS DESCRIBED AS THE IDEAL SELF
(Percentage distribution)

BOYS

*Group**	*A*	*B*	*C*	*D*	*E*	*F*	*G*	*H*	*I*
No. of papers	*60*	*26*	*89*		*94*	*85*	*106*	*31*	*48*
Category									
I P	7	23	11		16	7	16	3	6
II S	0	0	0		0	2	2	0	11
III G	12	32	47		23	37	40	22	6
IV H	3	6	11		10	5	3	13	2
V A	53	30	23		21	15	24	9	25
VI C	25	6	8		28	28	15	19	48
VII M	0	0	0		2	1	0	13	2
VIII NC	0	3	0		0	5	0	19	0

GIRLS

*Group**	*A*	*B*	*C*	*D*	*E*	*F*	*G*	*H*	*I*
No. of papers	*100*	*36*	*105*	*17*	*114*	*70*	*80*		*86*
Category									
I P	6	32	14	6	11	7	20		3
II S	2	0	2	0	4	12	9		1
III G	16	17	27	23	21	37	21		1
IV H	2	3	3	6	1	7	7		4
V A	36	13	25	18	25	18	23		28
VI C	33	22	23	29	35	18	15		61
VII M	3	8	6	12	3	1	5		2
VIII NC	0	5	0	6	0	0	0		0

* Description of groups:
A. Ten-, eleven-, and twelve-year-olds in a typical small midwestern community.
B. Sixth-graders (age 11-12) in an industrial section of Chicago.
C. Fifth- and sixth-graders (age 11-12) in a war industry community.
D. Girls at a Chicago Settlement House (age 11-14), mostly Italian.
E. Seventh- and eighth-graders (age 13-14) in a war industry community.
F. Middle-class Negro children (age 12-14) in Baltimore.
G. Ninth-graders (age 14-15) in a lower-middle-class suburb of Chicago.
H. Boys (age 16-17) in a Vocational High School in Chicago.
I. Sixteen- and seventeen-year-olds in a typical small midwestern community.

A second conclusion is that an age sequence exists, moving outward from the family circle, becoming more abstract, and culminating in the composite, imaginary person. This is by no means a rigid sequence. Some steps are omitted by some children. Yet a comparison of groups *A* and *I* and *C* and *E* gives evidence of the reality of the age sequence when the subjects of different ages are drawn from the same social environment.

The following hypothesis appears to account for the observed age trends. The child from the age of six to about eight generally chooses a parent or some other family member. Most children then move on to a choice either of a glamorous person or an attractive, visible young adult. The age for choosing a glamorous person is about eight to sixteen. The choice of an attractive, visible young adult may start at eight or ten and continue all through adolescence, or it may give way to a more abstract ego-ideal in the form of a composite imaginary person. The final and mature stage of the ego-ideal is the composite of desirable characteristics, drawn from all of the persons with whom the individual has identified himself during his childhood and adolescence.

A third conclusion is that social environment affects the choice of the ideal self. This is to be expected, since different social environments expose children to different kinds of people who may serve as objects of identification, and teach different values and aspirations. The effect of social environment is seen by comparing the frequencies of response in the glamorous person and composite person categories for various groups. Children from families of lower socioeconomic status name a higher proportion of glamorous persons. This is seen by comparing groups *A, B,* and *C,* in Table 1, the members of which are all about the same age. The average socioeconomic status of the members of group *A* is higher than that of the members of groups *B* and *C*. Carroll (1) compared a Negro middle-class with a Negro lower-class group (ages 12-14) and found that three-quarters of the lower-class responses fell into the category of glamorous adults, while only about half as many of the middle-class responses fell into this category.

A further influence of the social setting is to be found in the occasional presence of one or more unusually attractive adults in the environment of the group that is being tested. For example, one fifth-grade group happened to have a very attractive teacher, and the children mentioned this teacher frequently in their essays, although teachers generally are not mentioned very often.

The school program also has an influence on the responses of children in their essays. Sister Mary Phelan (4) reports that for children in Catholic parochial schools the frequency of mention of religious persons increased after several months of teaching about ideals. Even such an event as a Washington's Birthday celebration will stimulate more mention than usual of George Washington.

Table 2 shows the ages of the persons mentioned in the essays.

TABLE 2

AGES OF PERSONS DESCRIBED AS THE IDEAL SELF
(Percentage distribution)

*Age of persons mentioned**	*Group*					
	A	*B*	*C and E*	*F*	*G*	*I*
Under 20	16	18	23	14	13	6
20-29	72	33	35	49	36	65
30-39	9	29	29	27	51	16
40-49	3	16	10	4	(30 and	9
Over 50	0	4	3	6	over)	4

* Ten to forty per cent of the papers did not give ages. The age was often omitted when parents were mentioned. For description of groups, see Table 1.

While there is again a good deal of variation among the groups, this variation does not appear to be related to the ages of the children. Most of them think of their ideal selves as being in the twenties or thirties.

Reliability of the Categories and Consistency of Response

Before we can proceed with any assurance to draw conclusions from the data in Tables 1 and 2 we must find out, first, whether our analysis of the papers is reliable, and second, whether the children give consistent responses—whether they give the same type of response upon repeating the essay.

The reliability of the analysis was tested by computing the percentage of agreement among two or more judges who assigned the papers to the categories. In comparing the work of several people we found that the percentage of agreement between two judges is 85 to 90 per cent. Occasionally the agreement is less, with a new judge or an unusual set of papers. Seldom is the agreement greater than 90 per cent, unless the judges work out some conventions together beforehand. The differences between judges usually are due to the following uncertainties:

Whether to place a paper in the "attractive, visible adult" category or in the "composite, imaginary character" category when the paper seems to be describing a real person but does not say so explicitly.

Whether to place a paper in the "composite" category when it names two or three definite people, such as the father and a military person, without much attempt at integration of their characteristics into a new, composite character.

Whether to place a paper in the "parent-surrogate" category or the "attractive, visible adult" category when the person mentioned is neither clearly a young adult nor definitely of the parental generation.

To get an answer to the question of the consistency of children's responses, we used the test-retest method, comparing the responses of a group with another set of responses from the same group after a ten-week interval. This experiment was carried out by one of us (M. Z. R.) on group *G* of Table 1. This was a ninth-grade group, aged 14-15, in the high school of a lower-middle-class suburb of Chicago. This group was 3 per cent Mexican, 5 per cent Polish, 8 per cent Italian, 17 per cent Negro, and 67 per cent old American largely of German and Scandinavian origin. Family incomes ranged from $100 to $400 per month (in 1943), with most of them about $200 per month.

Ten weeks after the first assignment, it was repeated with the following additional instructions:

> Write on the subject "The Person I Would Like to Be Like." You will probably remember that you were asked to write on this same subject some time ago. Just write anything you like, and do the best you can.

A few pupils inquired whether it was all right to repeat what they had said; and some asked whether they might change. Whichever question arose, pupils were told it was "all right," and both possibilities were stressed equally.

The pupil's choice of an ideal self may be said to be stable or consistent if it remains unchanged with respect to the following:

1. The person or the type of person described.
2. The traits of character and personality ascribed to this person.
3. The age ascribed to this person.

The essays were analyzed to find out the degree of consistency of response according to these three criteria.

Stability in the type of person mentioned was measured in two ways. The first way, called the "group method," consisted in counting the number of persons in a given category—for example, "parents"—on the first administration of the essay, and comparing this number with the number of responses in the same category on the second administration. Thus, as is shown in Table 3, the girls made seven mentions of parents on the first administration, and nine on the second. As a group, then, they gave seven consistent choices. The extra choices of two parents on the second adminis-

TABLE 3

KINDS OF PEOPLE CHOSEN

Kind of people	*Number, first essay*	*Number, second essay*	*Number of consistent choices (Treated as a group)*	*Number of inconsistent choices (Treated as a group)*	*Number of consistent choices (Individual treatment)*	*Number of inconsistent choices (Individual treatment)*	*Average per cent in each category*
Boys							
Parents	11	6	6	5	5	6	16
Parent-surrogates	1	1	1	0	1	0	2
Glamorous adults	22	20	20	2	18	4	40
Heroes	3	0	0	3	0	3	3
Attractive young adults	11	15	11	0	10	1	24
Composite, abstract characters	7	9	7	0	6	1	15
Age-mates	0	0	0	0	0	0	0
Totals	55	51	45	10	40	15	—
Girls							
Parents	7	9	7	0	6	1	20
Parent-surrogates	3	4	3	0	3	0	9
Glamorous adults	9	8	8	1	7	2	21
Heroes	4	2	2	2	2	2	7
Attractive young adults	8	10	8	0	7	1	23
Composite, abstract characters	6	6	6	0	5	1	15
Age-mates	2	2	2	0	2	0	5
Totals	39	41	36	3	32	7	—

TABLE 4

CHARACTER AND PERSONALITY TRAITS MENTIONED

Character and personality trait	*Number, first essay*	*Number, second essay*	*Number of consistent choices (Treated as a group)*	*Number of inconsistent choices (Treated as a group)*	*Number of consistent choices (Individual treatment)*	*Number of inconsistent choices (Individual treatment)*	*Average per cent in each category*
Boys							
Material values—money, clothes, property	15	19	15	0	15	0	21
Good looks, good appearance, neat, clean	9	12	9	0	8	1	13
Good personality, stereotypes, popular	11	10	10	1	7	4	13
Friendly, lots of friends, courteous, polite, can take a joke	16	15	15	1	10	6	20
Honest, responsible, industrious, church-goer, kind	23	19	19	4	17	6	27
Cooperative, helpful, patient	3	2	2	1	1	2	3
Self-sacrificing, working for social justice, human brotherhood, altruism	3	1	1	2	1	2	3
Totals	80	78	71	9	59	21	—
Girls							
Material values—money, clothes, property	1	2	1	0	1	0	2
Good looks, good appearance, neat, clean	24	27	24	0	22	2	30
Good personality, stereotypes, popular	10	10	10	0	9	1	12
Friendly, lots of friends, courteous, polite, can take a joke	11	11	11	0	8	3	13
Honest, responsible, industrious, church-goer, kind	26	25	25	1	24	2	30
Cooperative, helpful, patient	10	8	8	2	8	2	11
Self-sacrificing, working for social justice, human brotherhood, altruism	2	1	1	1	1	1	2
Totals	84	84	80	4	73	11	—

tration are not counted as inconsistent because they mean two less choices in some other categories, and will be counted at these points.

The second way of measuring stability of choice, called the "individual method," consisted in finding out how many individuals made choices in the same category both times. For example, although seven girls chose parents the first time and nine the second time, only six individuals chose parents both times. Therefore, by the individual method, there were six consistent choices and one inconsistent choice (the seventh girl, who changed from a parent to a person in another category). The individual method gives a more rigorous test of stability than does the group method.

Stability of traits of character and personality mentioned was also measured by the group and individual methods. Here the amount of stability observed will depend partly upon the number and breadth of the categories used. If many highly specialized categories are used, the observed stability will tend to be lower than when a few broad categories are used. The number of categories chosen was seven, which allows for a considerable degree of differentiation of characteristics mentioned, and makes the test fairly rigorous. The items within a category were put together for two reasons: first, they tend to belong together psychologically (*e.g.*, "honest, responsible, industrious"); and second, they tend to appear together in the essays (*e.g.*, "friendly, courteous, polite, can take a joke").

Stability in the age ascribed to a person was measured by the same two methods, with ages thrown into three categories.

The results of this analysis are summarized in Tables 3, 4, and 5. They indicate that the degree of consistency is about 90 per cent when measured by the group method and 80 per cent when measured by the individual method. The girls were slightly more consistent than the boys.

We conclude that the reliability of the analysis and the consistency of responses are high enough to permit comparisons of groups of different ages and social backgrounds and to allow generalizations about the influence of these factors on the development of the ideal self.

TABLE 5

CONSISTENCY OF RESPONSE IN PERCENTAGES

	Boys		*Girls*	
Criteria	*Treated as a group*	*Treated as individuals*	*Treated as a group*	*Treated as individuals*
Choices of people	83	73	92	82
Choices of character and personality traits	89	74	95	88
Choices in respect to age	96	84	95	84

The earlier studies made with a somewhat similar assignment are not strictly comparable with this one for two reasons. First, the directions were different. The assignment given in an earlier study by Darrah (2) was,

> What person of whom you have heard or read would you most like to resemble? Why?

Hill (3) gave a similar direction.

> Of all persons whom you have heard, or read about, or seen, whom would you most care to be like or resemble? Why?

Sister Mary Phelan (4) gave the pupil more latitude by asking,

> Who is your ideal? Why have you chosen this ideal?

The directions given by Darrah and by Hill asked the child to name a person, whereas our direction explicitly told the child he could name a real person or an imaginary person. Sister Mary Phelan's direction falls between in the strength of its suggestion that a real person be mentioned.

In view of these differences in the assignment, we should expect that our study would get more frequent mentions of composite and imaginary characters; and this did happen. However, in the studies by Hill and Sister Mary Phelan a number of boys and girls insisted in spite of the directions, on describing abstract or composite characters, and their papers were thrown into a "Miscellaneous" category.

The second reason that our study is not strictly comparable with the earlier studies is that we have used a different scheme of analysis of the persons mentioned. We used this new scheme because it served to test our hypothesis concerning the development of the ideal self.

The earlier studies divided the persons mentioned on the essays into two broad groups, one belonging to the immediate environment and the other to the remote environment. The persons in the immediate environment were further divided into the categories of parents, teachers, and other acquaintances; those from the remote environment were separated into the categories of historical and contemporary, literary, and religious characters.

No single one of our categories is identical with one of those used in the earlier studies. The one which is most similar, our category *I P*, consists not only of parents but also of other relatives of the parental or grandparental generation. Consequently we shall not attempt to make detailed comparisons.

There is one difference between our results and those of earlier studies, however, which stands out quite clearly. We found very few mentions of "heroes" or great people of history or literature, while in the earlier studies the frequency of such characters was high. Sister Mary Phelan found over sixty per cent of the responses at ages from 11 to 18 to be either religious or historical or contemporary public figures. Hill got about the same over-all results from public school children, although the number of religious characters was much less than in the parochial school papers.

These figures are to be contrasted with our own finding of less than ten per cent of the responses in the category of "heroes." However, to make our data more nearly comparable with those of Hill and Phelan, we should add the "glamorous adults" to the "heroes"; for a movie star or a prize-fighter, if mentioned in one of Hill's or Phelan's papers, was counted in the category of "historical and contemporary characters." The examples given by these writers show that the counterparts of present-day "glamorous adults" were mentioned in the earlier studies, including: Clara Bow, Billie Dove, Babe Ruth, Douglas Fairbanks, Mary Pickford, Dizzy Dean, Jack Oakie, Eddie Cantor, The Arkansas Woodchopper, Shirley Temple, and Jackie Coogan.

It appears, however, that the "glamorous adult" was mentioned somewhat less frequently and the "hero" somewhat more frequently in the studies made ten, twenty, and fifty years ago.

Conclusions

This study shows a developmental trend in the ideal self of the following nature. The ideal self commences in childhood as an identification with a parental figure, moves during middle childhood and early adolescence through a stage of romanticism and glamour, and culminates in late adolescence as a composite of desirable characteristics which may be symbolized by an attractive, visible young adult, or may be simply an imaginary figure.

Parents or members of the parental generation play a declining role in the ideal self as it is described by children after the age of eight or ten. "Glamorous" adults have their day in the child's ego-ideal between the ages of ten and fifteen. Anyone older than fifteen who reports a "glamorous" person as his ego-ideal is probably immature, by standards of development as found in most young people. It is not certain whether the stage of greatest maturity is that represented by our category of the attractive, visible adult or that represented by our category of the composite, imaginary character. Evidence from adults might settle this point.

The environment of the child has a great effect on his ideal self. Children and young people from families of lower socioeconomic status as a group lag behind those of middle socioeconomic status in progressing through the stage of selection of a glamorous adult as the ideal. Individuals in the child's environment influence his ideal self, especially if they are young adults. Thus an especially attractive teacher or youth group leader may symbolize the ego-ideal during the age period usually dominated by the glamorous person. Furthermore, the teaching of the school, especially if it is aimed at inculcating ideals through teaching about the lives of great people, certainly influences the child's report concerning his ideal self.

The high susceptibility of the child's response about his ideal self to rather short-term and superficial teaching influences raises some doubts about the validity of our method of securing information. It seems probable that the individual's core values and attitudes do not change as rapidly and easily as might be suggested by his changing, for example, from a movie star to a solid, successful young man in the local community for the symbol of his ideal self. Probably very few children or adolescents have enough insight into their own personalities to give a full report on their ego-ideals. Some individuals may even have a good deal of unconscious resistance to recognizing the nature of the ideal self. This may be the case with a number of boys and a few girls who insist, in a defensive tone, that they want to be like themselves and no one else.

Nevertheless, we may be sure that an individual will not report an ideal which is repugnant to him, nor will he report a set of ideals which he has not thought about at all. There is nothing for the individual to gain in the essay-writing situation by giving false witness about himself. If there has been no coaching of the child to name certain kinds of people when asked questions about his ideal self, the results represent something genuine and deep down in his personality.

The set of categories we have used to classify the persons mentioned seems to us to be useful in testing hypotheses about *development* of the ideal self. However, it leaves something to be desired as a measure of increasing maturity of personality. We were forced to choose between categories of persons and categories of qualities of persons. Categories based upon qualities might serve as a better indicator of maturity. . . .

There is a great deal of evidence that the ideal self is deeply influenced by association with people who are in positions of prestige because they are older, more powerful, and better able to get the desirable things of life than the child or adolescent who observes them. Our study adds to this evidence. A boy or girl combines qualities of parents with qualities of attractive, successful young adults into a composite ego-ideal. The inference is clear that schools, churches, and youth-serving agencies influence the ideals of youth as much or more through the presence and behavior of teachers, clergy, and youth group leaders as through their verbal teachings.

References

1. Carroll, R. E., "Relation of Social Environment to the Moral Ideology and the Personal Aspirations of Negro Boys and Girls," *School Review,* Vol. 53 (1945), pp. 30-38.
2. Darrah, E. M., "A Study of Children's Ideals," *Popular Science Monthly,* Vol. 53 (1898), pp. 88-98.
3. Hill, D. S., "Personification of Ideals by Urban Children," *Journal of Social Psychology,* Vol. 1 (1930), pp. 379-393.
4. Phelan, M. I., *An Empirical Study of the Ideals of Adolescent Boys and Girls* (Washington, D.C.: Catholic U. of Am., 1936).

4. Excerpts from a diary of a teenage girl

LESTER D. CROW

Reprinted from *The Journal of Educational Sociology,* Vol. 36 (1962), 26-29, by permission of the author and the American Sociological Association.

Fear of parents or snoopy brothers or sisters deters most teenagers from keeping a diary account of the daily events and emotions in their lives, but those that are kept are rich with candid recordings. Let us look through the eyes of one teenage girl for a glimpse at the people and experiences which, ultimately, influence the growing self.

The struggle of growing up is expressed in numerous diary entries as this teenage girl records those feelings and emotions that she experiences in connection with various life issues, especially those associated with her relations with members of the opposite sex. Some of those highlights are presented here. Since this girl named her diary "Jane," it can be assumed by the reader that as each entry is made it is addressed to "Jane." Her diary was started on January 1, 1953. The following entries are representative of the problems experienced by girls of this age.

Dear Diary:

Happy New Year. Since you will have a lot to hear from me this year I'll give you a name. It is 'Jane.'

Well Jane, I just don't know what I'm going to do. All I have in common with my parents is fights. I wish we could be pals. I say "boo" and I'm being fresh. I fool around with them and I get smacked, and if I walk out of the room I am running away from everything. I stayed with Phyllis and Sharon to-day. Only 14 more days till my birthday. Good night.

1/3—I am going to stick to my resolution 'Don't talk about anyone.' Today I read Sharon's first love letters. It was mushy. 12 more days to go.

1/15—Happy Birthday to me! Tonight I am 13 years old. I was very surprised to see the gum corsage, and a piece of gum to each girl friend. I received a lovely handbag from my mother and father and ten dollars from my grandma. This afternoon I went for shoes with Sharon and met Phyllis and Irene in the shoestore. They were so loud and noisy that it was disgusting.

2/5—Today my mother went to the hospital for her operation. I went to visit her at night with my father. She was looking forward to it. I ate out with my Pop.

6/9—I have had many arguments with Sharon. She must think that without her I'm lost. But she should think again. Of course, I'll continue to be friends but I'm sure she senses the wall between us. I did not tell you that I quit the "Shadows SC" and after four months I am starting to be friendly with the girls.

7/11—Every time I see Howie I simply swoon. He's so handsome. Mm, boy! He's so snobby. Ever since he became 8th year vice president he forgot his old friends. I think Sharon is cold hearted. She insults everybody. If I wanted to, I could insult her real good.

8/21—I guess you must think I am lazy. Well, you're right. I am. I just forget to write.

12/18—I have two million and one things to say to you. As you know, I ran for president. I lost, but Jerry won. I am glad I didn't win because I am in a better club now—Senior Publications. We plan Senior activities. I don't dislike Jerry any more. He's not so bad when you get to know him. When you are a senior, you have a lot of freedom.

12/31—It is sad to say that 1953 is dead, that it only lives in memories. Lots of things have happened. I went on my first blind date. I had my first necking session with ——— whom I will probably forget in years to come. Right now I don't think I will ever forget it.

1/1/54—Well a new year starts. I hope I won't forget to keep in touch with you as much as last year. I baby-sat last night and made $3.50.

1/2—I am in a dreamy mood this morning. I feel very stupid but I can't forget that time with ———. I don't really like him. It happened almost three months ago, and I can forget it.

1/3—Janice kept me company tonight. We had a lot of fun. I read her my 1953 Diary. It's funny to laugh at now. But I was quite serious when I wrote it. I saw Arnie today. He's very handsome. I wonder if I like him. Sometimes I like a lot of boys at once.

1/5—Jerry and I acted the same as usual toward each other, like friendly enemies.

1/6—I saw Jerry today and ignored him. Sharon walked home at lunch time with Jerry. He told her that the last time he walked home with me I acted cold toward him (I didn't let him kiss me). I think he still likes me, but his pride won't let him admit it. I could like him—if only he was in the ninth grade.

1/20—After school Sharon and I went to the school dance. We wore the crazy shirts (all colors of the rainbow). At the dance Jerry made a fool of himself.

2/4—My parents don't try to understand me. They think it is a crime if they would laugh at something Gary (her younger brother) and I say. They would rather scold.

3/11—I WISH I COULD DIE! Two weeks ago my parents and I had a long talk. My parents said that they did not want me to see boys so much (much, ha!) and I should not stay with Sharon because she was a bad influence. Little do they know Sharon and I have different ideas on lots of things and she does things that are queer. My parents say that when I get older I will think of them. They look at it different from my point of view, and my stubborn self won't do what they want.

5/21—I won a contest in my school. I won for "The girl who did most for the school." I know I have done a lot but I still think Harriet has done more. During mid-terms, Howie came around to our school. We became friends and he has come over to the house a few times. Tomorrow is social dancing for my Gym class. I'm praying I'll get Jerry but I'll probably wind up with a drip.

9/3—I was on the T program "Dance Time." I was on it with Jerry. (He still likes me.)

9/20—Crazy me—I want you to know I still feel the same about Jerry. I still like him although there are boys whom I like just as much or even more.

10/12—Tonight I went out until 8.30. I was wearing my "Shadow Club" sweater. Keny was wearing his club jacket and he wanted to change with me. So I have his jacket and he has my sweater.

12/31—I go to . . . High School and I like it. I am moody lately. I think what I need is a boy friend. But who would like me?—short, fat and ugly. Oh well, maybe 1955 will be different.

1/1/55—Happy New Year! and I really hope it's a happy year. Peace on earth and good will to me is my wish. I am going to try and make this a really progressive year for myself.

5/24—Another summer is coming and I'm afraid it will be very boring.

I have a mad crush on a boy named Jay. I doubt that he will ever ask me out.

6/2—I haven't gone out since November. Of course, I have gone to parties but what is that. I have a very good baby-sitting job so whenever I baby-sit I tell the boys I have a date.

7/27—Jay is in the country. Before he left we had become very good friends. I think he has a little crush on Joan though. I am very friendly with his father. He told me that Jay is having a very nice time in camp. He promised to write but he hasn't yet.

8/20—As I predicted, the summer has been dull. I went out on a blind date. He was awful.

8/26—The boys that Joan and I were supposed to go out with came a little late. They got lost. Then, because we didn't want to go in the car, they left. So we didn't go out. Then Joan and I met Harvey and Jerry at the park.

8/27—I know that if I had a boy friend I would have much better peace of mind. I even think my studies would improve.

10/31—Harvey found out about my liking Jay. He gave me some advice but even now, going on November, I still like him. I think he knows. Harvey told him a few weeks ago that I used to have a crush on him. I constantly dream and think of him. I am constantly talking about him.

1/3/56—I realize now that I act pretty childish at times. I think I'm afraid to grow up. I kid around too much. A good example is, I like to play with my brother. He beats me up and I beat him up.

1/4—I am afraid there won't be enough boys at my party. I wish the whole thing were over. I must go on a diet.

1/13—Tomorrow is P-Day (Party Day). I hope it is a success. I know it has the ingredients for a success, but you can never tell if it will click. I don't care if I don't have a good time (I'm lying) but I really hope my guests enjoy themselves.

1/15—Well, I'm 16 at last. The party was a big success! Everyone had a great time, even me. Only four more years and I will be 20.

2/16—We have just started our new term. I like my teachers very much. I am chairman of the Props Committee for this year's Varsity Show. I have a great desire to go to the prom this June.

2/17—I realize now why a lot of girls want to go steady. Going steady means no worries about boys. I don't want to go steady right now, with anyone. I just want to go *steadily*.

4/30—I think I'm a big disappointment to my parents. I have to invite a boy to sweet 16. I might ask Harvey. But I'm afraid he will say no. Then he'll have something to tell his friends.

7/4—Sometimes I feel that my mother likes Gary better than me. Lately, I've been asking for money quite often. I always receive it without any arguments. My Mom and Dad are wonderful to me. They give Gary and me all they possibly can both material and spiritual. When I keep asking for money and they give it to me, I feel guilty. I really don't understand why I'm writing all this. Maybe because it's the 4th of July.

8/2—(The last entry) Today I helped Mom clean my room. This afternoon I went to work. I work one-half block away from my house. I work three days a week for three hours."

Teenagers are sensitive to their associates' attitudes toward themselves and want to be liked; any lack of popularity may be blamed on others, but more often it becomes the source of worry about a supposed personal failing. School study usually is important, but is secondary to peer-group relations. A parent once said that his adolescent son and daughter would not be happy unless they could find something to worry about. This statement may be somewhat strong, but adult maturity cannot be achieved without some relatively serious conflict during adolescnce.

QUESTIONS FOR DISCUSSION

Jersild Article

1. Why is the process of differentiation important to self-development? When does it begin? How could a parent, indeed, a teacher, inhibit this process?
2. What part does "body-image" play in self-development? What evidence can you cite to suggest that body-image is important even in adult life?
3. This article, along with the Anderson article in Part I and Haimowitz's paper in this section, emphasizes the crucialness of "significant" people in influencing the growing self. How dependent *is* one's self-concept on the appraisals and evaluations of other people? Is one ever free of this dependency?

Haimowitz Article

1. Do you agree or disagree with this speculative analysis of how people become criminals? If you agree, how would you explain the fact that not all youngsters who have negative experiences such as those described in this article become professional criminals?
2. A strong implication of this article is that one's environment not only can teach him *how* to be a criminal, by reinforcing the "criminal" self-image, but can also give him a reason *for being* a criminal. React to this. Is one *ever* responsible for his own "self," for his own behavior? Where is the dividing line?

Havighurst, Robinson, and Dorr Article

1. How does the "self" differ from the "ideal" self?
2. What role does identification play in ideal-self development?
3. Would there be advantages for a teacher to be the ego-ideal of his/her students? Why or why not?
4. Why should the choice of "glamorous" adults as ego-ideals decline after about age fifteen?

Crow Article

1. What would you say is the dominant theme which runs through this girl's diary account of "self"?
2. On the basis of the information you have, how would you describe this girl's concept of self? To what environmental influences is she most sensitive? Why?

Part V

personality development and the self

1. A theory of human motivation

A. H. MASLOW

Reprinted from *Psychological Review,* Vol. 50 (1943), 370-396, by permission of the author and the American Psychological Association.

Maslow presents a "general-dynamic" theory of human motivation and classifies what he considers to be the basic needs of man in a hierarchy of prepotency. If one is to give his personality maximum self-expression, he must satisfy his need for self-actualization. What does self-actualization mean? How can one become "self-actualized"?

I. Introduction

In a previous paper (13), various propositions were presented which would have to be included in any theory of human motivation that could lay claim to being definitive. These conclusions may be briefly summarized as follows:

1. The integrated wholeness of the organism must be one of the foundation stones of motivation theory.
2. The hunger drive (or any other physiological drive) was rejected as a centering point or model for a definitive theory of motivation. Any drive that is somatically based and localized was shown to be atypical rather than typical in human motivation.
3. Such a theory should stress and center itself upon ultimate or basic goals rather than partial or superficial ones, upon ends rather than means to these ends. Such a stress would imply a more central place for unconscious than for conscious motivations.

4. There are usually available various cultural paths to the same goal. Therefore, conscious, specific, local-cultural desires are not as fundamental in motivation theory as the more basic, unconscious goals.

5. Any motivated behavior, either preparatory or consummatory, must be understood to be a channel through which many basic needs may be simultaneously expressed or satisfied. Typically an act has *more* than one motivation.

6. Practically all organismic states are to be understood as motivated and as motivating.

7. Human needs arrange themselves in hierarchies of prepotency. That is to say, the appearance of one need usually rests on the prior satisfaction of another, more prepotent need. Man is a perpetually wanting animal. Also no need or drive can be treated as if it were isolated or discrete; every drive is related to the state of satisfaction or dissatisfaction of other drives.

8. *Lists* of drives will get us nowhere for various theoretical and practical reasons. Furthermore any classification of motivations must deal with the problem of levels of specificity or generalization of the motives to be classified.

9. Classifications of motivations must be based upon goals rather than upon instigating drives or motivated behavior.

10. Motivation theory should be human-centered rather than animal-centered.

11. The situation or the field in which the organism reacts must be taken into account but the field alone can rarely serve as an exclusive explanation for behavior. Furthermore the field itself must be interpreted in terms of the organism. Field theory cannot be a substitute for motivation theory.

12. Not only the integration of the organism must be taken into account, but also the possibility of isolated, specific, partial, or segmental reactions.

It has since become necessary to add to these another affirmation.

13. Motivation theory is not synonymous with behavior theory. The motivations are only one class of determinants of behavior. While behavior is almost always motivated, it is also almost always biologically, culturally, and situationally determined as well.

The present paper is an attempt to formulate a positive theory of motivation which will satisfy these theoretical demands and at the same time conform to the known facts, clinical and observational as well as experimental. It derives most directly, however, from clinical experience. This theory is, I think, in the functionalist tradition of James and Dewey, and is fused with the holism of Wertheimer (19), Goldstein (6), and Gestalt Psychology, and with the dynamicism of Freud (4) and Adler (1). This fusion or synthesis may arbitrarily be called a "general-dynamic" theory.

It is far easier to perceive and to criticize the aspects in motivation theory than to remedy them. Mostly this is because of the very serious lack of sound data in this area. I conceive this lack of sound facts to be due primarily to the absence of a valid theory of motivation. The present theory then must be considered to be a suggested program or framework for future research and must stand or fall, not so much on facts available or evidence presented, as upon researches yet to be done, researches suggested, perhaps, by the questions raised in this paper.

II. The Basic Needs

THE "PHYSIOLOGICAL" NEEDS

The needs that are usually taken as the starting point for motivation theory are the so-called physiological drives. Two recent lines of research make it necessary to revise our customary notions about these needs; first, the development of the concept of homeostasis, and second, the finding that appetites (preferential choices among foods) are a fairly efficient indication of actual needs or lacks in the body.

Homeostasis refers to the body's automatic efforts to maintain a constant, normal state of the blood stream. Cannon (2) has described this process for (1) the water content of the blood, (2) salt content, (3) sugar content, (4) protein content, (5) fat content, (6) calcium content, (7) oxygen content, (8) constant hydrogen-ion level (acid-base balance), and (9) constant temperature of the blood. Obviously this list can be extended to include other minerals, the hormones, vitamins, *etc.*

Young in a recent article (21) has summarized the work on appetite in its relation to body needs. If the body lacks some chemical, the individual will tend to develop a specific appetite or partial hunger for that food element.

Thus it seems impossible as well as useless to make any list of fundamental physiological needs for they can come to almost any number one might wish, depending on the degree of specificity of description. We cannot identify all physiological needs as homeostatic. That sexual desire, sleepiness, sheer activity, and maternal behavior in animals are homeostatic has not yet been demonstrated. Furthermore, this list would not include the various sensory pleasures (tastes, smells, tickling, stroking) which are probably physiological and which may become the goals of motivated behavior.

In a previous paper (13) it has been pointed out that these physiological drives or needs are to be considered unusual rather than typical because they are isolable, and because thy are localizable somatically. That is to say, they are relatively independent of each other, of other motivations, and of the organism as a whole, and secondly, in many cases, it is possible to demonstrate a localized, underlying somatic base for the drive. This is true less generally than has been thought (exceptions are fatigue, sleepiness, maternal responses), but it is still true in the classic instances of hunger, sex, and thirst.

It should be pointed out again that any of the physiological needs and the consummatory behavior involved with them serve as channels for all sorts of other needs as well. That is to say, the person who thinks he is hungry may actually be seeking more for comfort, or dependence, than for vitamins or proteins. Conversely, it is possible to satisfy the hunger needs in part by other activities, such as drinking water or smoking cigarettes. In other words, relatively isolable as these physiological needs are, they are not completely so.

Undoubtedly these physiological needs are the most prepotent of all needs. What this means specifically is that in the human being who is missing everything in life in an extreme fashion, it is most likely that the major motivation would be the physiological needs rather than any others. A person who is lacking food, safety, love, and esteem would most probably hunger for food more strongly than for anything else.

If all the needs are unsatisfied, and the organism is then dominated by the physiological needs, all other needs may become simply nonexistent or be pushed into the background. It is then fair to characterize the whole organism by saying simply that it is hungry, for consciousness is almost completely preempted by hunger. All capacities are put into the service of hunger-satisfaction, and the organization of these capacities is almost entirely determined by the one purpose of satisfying hunger. The receptors and effectors, the intelligence, memory, habits, all may now be defined simply as hunger-gratifying tools. Capacities that are not useful for this purpose lie dormant, or are pushed into the background. The urge to write poetry, the desire to acquire an automobile, the interest in American history, the desire for a new pair of shoes are, in the extreme case, forgotten or become of secondary importance. For the man who is extremely and dangerously hungry, no other interests exist but food. He dreams food, he remembers food, he thinks about food, he emotes only about food, he perceives only food, and he wants only food. The more subtle determinants that ordinarily fuse with the physiological drives in organizing even feeding, drinking, or sexual behavior may now be so completely overwhelmed as to allow us to speak at this time (but *only* at this time) of pure hunger drive and behavior, with the one unqualified aim of relief.

Another peculiar characteristic of the human organism when it is dominated by a certain need is that the whole philosophy of the future tends also to change. For our chronically and extremely hungry man, Utopia can be defined very simply as a place where there is plenty of food. He tends to think that if only he is guaranteed food for the rest of his life, he will be perfectly happy and will never want anything more. Life itself tends to be defined in terms of eating. Anything else will be defined as unimportant. Freedom, love, community feeling, respect, philosophy, may all be waved aside as fripperies which are useless since they fail to fill the stomach. Such a man may fairly be said to live by bread alone.

It cannot possibly be denied that such things are true but their *generality* can be denied. Emergency conditions are, almost by definition, rare in the normally functioning peaceful society. That this truism can be forgotten is due mainly to two reasons. First, rats have few motivations other than physiological ones, and since so much of the research upon motivation has been made with these animals, it is easy to carry the rat-picture over to the human being. Secondly, it is too often not realized that culture itself is an adaptive tool, one of whose main functions is to make the physiological emergencies come less and less often. In most of the known societies, chronic extreme hunger of the emergency type is rare, rather than common. In any case, this is still true in the United States. The average American citizen is experiencing appetite rather than hunger when he says "I am hungry." He is apt to experience sheer life-and-death hunger only by accident and then only a few times through his entire life.

Obviously a good way to obscure the "higher" motivations, and to get a lopsided view of human capacities and human nature, is to make the organism extremely and chronically hungry or thirsty. Anyone who attempts to make an emergency picture into a typical one, and who will measure all of man's goals and desires by his behavior during extreme physiological deprivation is certainly being blind to many things. It is quite true that man lives by bread alone—when there is no bread. But what happens to man's desires when there *is* plenty of bread and when his belly is chronically filled?

At once other (and "higher") needs emerge and these, rather than physiological hungers, dominate the organism. And when these in turn are satisfied, again new (and still "higher") needs emerge and so on. This is what we mean by saying that the basic human needs are organized into a hierarchy of relative prepotency.

One main implication of this phrasing is that gratification becomes as important a concept as deprivation in motivation theory, for it releases the organism from the domination of a relatively more physiological need, permitting thereby the emergence of other more social goals. The physiological needs, along with their partial goals, when chronically gratified cease to exist as active determinants or organizers of behavior. They now exist only in a potential fashion in the sense that they may emerge again to dominate the organism if they are thwarted. But a want that is satisfied is no longer a want. The organism is dominated and its behavior organized only by unsatisfied needs. If hunger is satisfied, it becomes unimportant in the current dynamics of the individual.

This statement is somewhat qualified by a hypothesis to be discussed more fully later, namely that it is precisely those individuals in whom a certain need has always been satisfied who are best equipped to tolerate deprivation of that need in the future, and that furthermore, those who have been deprived in the past will react differently to current satisfactions than the one who has never been deprived.

The safety needs

If the physiological needs are relatively well gratified, there then emerges a new set of needs, which we may categorize roughly as the safety needs. All that has been said of the physiological needs is equally true, although in lesser degree, of these desires. The organism may equally well be wholly dominated by them. They may serve as the almost exclusive organizers of behavior, recruiting all the capacities of the organism in their service, and we may then fairly describe the whole organism as a safety-seeking mechanism. Again we may say of the receptors, the effectors, the intellect, and the other capacities that they are primarily safety-seeking tools. Again, as in the hungry man, we find that the dominating goal is a strong determinant not only of his current world outlook and philosophy but also of his philosophy of the future. Practically everything looks less important than safety (even sometimes the physiological needs which being satisfied are now underestimated). A man in this state, if it is extreme enough and chronic enough, may be characterized as living almost for safety alone.

Although in this paper we are interested primarily in the needs of the adult, we can approach an understanding of his safety needs perhaps more efficiently by observation of infants and children, in whom these needs are much more simple and obvious. One reason for the clearer appearance of the threat or danger reaction in infants is that they do not inhibit this reaction at all, whereas adults in our society have been taught to inhibit it at all costs. Thus even when adults do feel their safety to be threatened, we may not be able to see this on the surface. Infants will react in a total fashion and as if they were endangered, if they are disturbed or dropped suddenly, startled by loud noises, flashing light, or other unusual sensory stimulation, by rough handling, by general loss of support in the mother's arms, or by inadequate support.[1]

In infants we can also see a much more direct reaction to bodily illnesses of various kinds. Sometimes these illnesses seem to be immediately and *per se* threatening and seem to make the child feel unsafe. For instance, vomiting, colic, or other sharp pains seem to make the child look at the whole world in a different way. At such a moment of pain, it may be postulated that, for the child, the appearance of the whole world suddenly changes from sunniness to darkness, so to speak, and becomes a place in which anything at all might happen, in which previously stable things have suddenly become unstable. Thus a child who because of some bad food is taken ill may, for a day or two, develop fear, nightmares, and a need for protection and reassurance never seen in him before his illness.

Another indication of the child's need for safety is his preference for some kind of undisrupted routine or rhythm. He seems to want a predictable, orderly world. For instance, injustice, unfairness, or inconsistency in the parents seems to make a child feel anxious and unsafe. This attitude may be not so much because of the injustice *per se* or any particular pains involved, but rather because this treatment threatens to make the world look unreliable, or unsafe, or unpredictable. Young children seem to thrive better under a system which has at least a skeletal outline of rigidity, in which there is a schedule of a kind, some sort of routine, something that can be counted upon, not only for the present but also far into the future. Perhaps one could express this more accurately by saying that the child needs an organized world rather than an unorganized or unstructured one.

The central role of the parents and the normal family setup are indisputable. Quarreling, physical assault, separation, divorce, or death within the family may be particularly terrifying. Also parental outbursts of rage or threats of punishment directed to the child, calling him names, speaking to him harshly, shaking him, handling him roughly, or actual physical punishment sometimes elicit such total panic and terror in the child that we must assume more is involved than the physical pain alone. While it is true that in some children this terror may represent also a fear of loss of parental love, it can also occur in completely rejected children, who seem to cling to the hating parents more for sheer safety and protection than because of hope of love.

---

[1] As the child grows up, sheer knowledge and familiarity as well as better motor development make these "dangers" less and less dangerous and more and more manageable. Throughout life it may be said that one of the main conative functions of education is this neutralizing of apparent dangers through knowledge, *e.g.*, I am not afraid of thunder because I know something about it.

Confronting the average child with new, unfamiliar, strange, unmanageable stimuli or situations will too frequently elicit the danger or terror reaction, as for example, getting lost or even being separated from the parents for a short time, being confronted with new faces, new situations or new tasks, the sight of strange, unfamiliar or uncontrollable objects, illness or death. Particularly at such times, the child's frantic clinging to his parents is eloquent testimony to their role as protectors (quite apart from their roles as food-givers and love-givers).

From these and similar observations, we may generalize and say that the average child in our society generally prefers a safe, orderly, predictable, organized world, which he can count on, and in which unexpected, unmanageable, or other dangerous things do not happen, and in which, in any case, he has all-powerful parents who protect and shield him from harm.

That these reactions may so easily be observed in children is in a way a proof of the fact that children in our society feel too unsafe (or, in a word, are badly brought up). Children who are reared in an unthreatening, loving family do *not* ordinarily react as we have described above (17). In such children the danger reactions are apt to come mostly to objects or situations that adults too would consider dangerous.[2]

The healthy, normal, fortunate adult in our culture is largely satisfied in his safety needs. The peaceful, smoothly running, "good" society ordinarily makes its members feel safe enough from wild animals, extremes of temperature, criminals, assault and murder, tyranny, *etc.* Therefore, in a very real sense, he no longer has any safety needs as active motivators. Just as a sated man no longer feels hungry, a safe man no longer feels endangered. If we wish to see these needs directly and clearly, we must turn to neurotic or near-neurotic individuals, and to the economic and social underdogs. In between these extremes, we can perceive the expressions of safety needs only in such phenomena as, for instance, the common preference for a job with tenure and protection, the desire for a savings account, and for insurance of various kinds (medical, dental, unemployment, disability, old age).

Other broader aspects of the attempt to seek safety and stability in the world are seen in the very common preference for familiar rather than

---

[2] A "test battery" for safety might be confronting the child with a small exploding firecracker, or with a bewhiskered face, having the mother leave the room, putting him upon a high ladder, a hypodermic injection, having a mouse crawl up to him, *etc.* Of course I cannot seriously recommend the deliberate use of such "tests" for they might very well harm the child being tested. But these and similar situations come up by the score in the child's ordinary day-to-day living and may be observed. There is no reason why these stimuli should not be used with, for example, young chimpanzees.

unfamiliar things, or for the known rather than the unknown. The tendency to have some religion or world philosophy that organizes the universe and the men in it into some sort of satisfactorily coherent, meaningful whole is also in part motivated by safety-seeking. Here too we may list science and philosophy in general as partially motivated by the safety needs (we shall see later that there are also other motivations to scientific, philosophical, or religious endeavor).

Otherwise the need for safety is seen as an active and dominant mobilizer of the organism's resources only in emergencies, *e.g.*, war, disease, natural catastrophes, crime waves, societal disorganization, neurosis, brain injury, chronically bad situation.

Some neurotic adults in our society are, in many ways, like the unsafe child in their desire for safety, although in the former it takes on a somewhat special appearance. Their reaction is often to unknown, psychological dangers in a world that is perceived to be hostile, overwhelming, and threatening. Such a person behaves as if a great catastrophe were almost always impending, *i.e.*, he is usually responding as if to an emergency. His safety needs often find specific expression in a search for a protector, or a stronger person on whom he may depend, or perhaps, a Fuehrer.

The neurotic individual may be described in a slightly different way with some usefulness as a grown-up person who retains his childish attitudes toward the world. That is to say, a neurotic adult may be said to behave "as if" he were actually afraid of a spanking, or of his mother's disapproval, or of being abandoned by his parents, or having his food taken away from him. It is as if his childish attitudes of fear and threat reaction to a dangerous world had gone underground and, untouched by the growing up and learning processes, were now ready to be called out by any stimulus that would make a child feel endangered and threatened.[3]

The neurosis in which the search for safety takes its clearest form is in the compulsive-obsessive neurosis. Compulsive-obsessives try frantically to order and stabilize the world so that no unmanageable, unexpected, or unfamiliar dangers will ever appear (14). They hedge themselves about with all sorts of ceremonials, rules, and formulas so that every possible contingency may be provided for and so that no new contingencies may appear. They are much like the brain injured cases, described by Goldstein (6), who manage to maintain their equilibrium by avoiding everything unfamiliar and strange and by ordering their restricted world in such a neat, disciplined, orderly fashion that everything in the world can be counted upon. They try to arrange the world so that anything unexpected

[3] Not all neurotic individuals feel unsafe. Neurosis may have at its core a thwarting of the affection and esteem needs in a person who is generally safe.

(dangers) cannot possibly occur. If, through no fault of their own, something unexpected does occur, they go into a panic reaction as if this unexpected occurrence constituted a grave danger. What we can see only as a none-too-strong preference in the healthy person, *e.g.*, preference for the familiar, becomes a life-and-death necessity in abnormal cases.

The love needs

If both the physiological and the safety needs are fairly well gratified, then there will emerge the love and affection and belongingness needs, and the whole cycle already described will repeat itself with this new center. Now the person will feel keenly, as never before, the absence of friends, or a sweetheart, or a wife, or children. He will hunger for affectionate relations with people in general, namely, for a place in his group, and he will strive with great intensity to achieve this goal. He will want to attain such a place more than anything else in the world and may even forget that once, when he was hungry, he sneered at love.

In our society the thwarting of these needs is the most commonly found core in cases of maladjustment and more severe psychopathology. Love and affection, as well as their possible expression in sexuality, are generally looked upon with ambivalence and are customarily hedged about with many restrictions and inhibitions. Practically all theorists of psychopathology have stressed thwarting of the love needs as basic in the picture of maladjustment. Many clinical studies have therefore been made of this need, and we know more about it perhaps than any of the other needs except the physiological ones (14).

One thing that must be stressed at this point is that love is not synonymous with sex. Sex may be studied as a purely physiological need. Ordinarily sexual behavior is multidetermined, that is to say, determined not only by sexual but also by other needs, chief among which are the love and affection needs. Also not to be overlooked is the fact that the love needs involve both giving and receiving love.[4]

The esteem needs

All people in our society (with a few pathological exceptions) have a need or desire for a stable, firmly based (usually) high evaluation of themselves, for self-respect, or self-esteem, and for the esteem of others. By firmly based self-esteem, we mean that which is soundly based upon real capacity, achievement, and respect from others. These needs may be clas-

[4] For further details see (12) and (16, Chap. 5).

sified into two subsidiary sets. These are, first, the desire for strength, for achievement, for adequacy, for confidence in the face of the world, and for independence and freedom.[5] Secondly, we have what we may call the desire for reputation or prestige (defining it as respect or esteem from other people), recognition, attention, importance, or appreciation.[6] These needs have been relatively stressed by Alfred Adler and his followers, and have been relatively neglected by Freud and the psychoanalysts. More and more today, however, there is appearing widespread appreciation of their central importance.

Satisfaction of the self-esteem need leads to feelings of self-confidence, worth, strength, capability, and adequacy of being useful and necessary in the world. But thwarting of these needs produces feelings of inferiority, of weakness, and of helplessness. These feelings in turn give rise to either basic discouragement or else compensatory or neurotic trends. An appreciation of the necessity of basic self-confidence and an understanding of how helpless people are without it can be easily gained from a study of severe traumatic neurosis (8).[7]

THE NEED FOR SELF-ACTUALIZATION

Even if all these needs are satisfied, we may still often (if not always) expect that a new discontent and restlessness will soon develop, unless the individual is doing what he is fitted for. A musician must make music, an artist must paint, a poet must write, if he is to be ultimately happy. What a man *can* be, he *must* be. This need we may call self-actualization.

This term, first coined by Kurt Goldstein, is being used in this paper in a much more specific and limited fashion. It refers to the desire for self-fulfillment, namely, to the tendency for one to become actualized in what he is potentially. This tendency might be phrased as the desire to become more and more what one is, to become everything that one is capable of becoming.

---

[5] Whether or not this particular desire is universal we do not know. The crucial question, especially important today, is "Will men who are enslaved and dominated inevitably feel dissatisfied and rebellious?" We may assume on the basis of commonly known clinical data that a man who has known true freedom (not paid for by giving up safety and security but rather built on the basis of adequate safety and security) will not willingly or easily allow his freedom to be taken away from him. But we do not know that this is true for the person born into slavery. The events of the next decade should give us our answer. See discussion of this problem in (5).

[6] Perhaps the desire for prestige and respect from others is subsidiary to the desire for self-esteem or confidence in oneself. Observation of children seems to indicate that this is so, but clinical data give no clear support for such a conclusion.

[7] For more extensive discussion of normal self-esteem, as well as for reports of various researches, see (11).

The specific form that these needs will take will of course vary greatly from person to person. In one individual it may take the form of the desire to be an ideal mother, in another it may be expressed athletically, and in still another it may be expressed in painting pictures or in inventions. It is not necessarily a creative urge although in people who have any capacities for creation it will take this form.

The clear emergence of these needs rests upon prior satisfaction of the physiological, safety, love, and esteem needs. We shall call people who are satisfied in these needs basically satisfied people, and it is from these that we may expect the fullest (and healthiest) creativeness.[8] Since, in our society, basically satisfied people are the exception, we do not know much about self-actualization, either experimentally or clinically. It remains a challenging problem for research.

THE PRECONDITIONS FOR THE BASIC NEED SATISFACTIONS

There are certain conditions which are immediate prerequisites for the basic need satisfactions. Danger to these is reacted to almost as if it were a direct danger to the basic needs themselves. Such conditions as freedom to speak, freedom to do what one wishes so long as no harm is done to others, freedom to express one's self, freedom to investigate and seek for information, freedom to defend one's self, justice, fairness, honesty, orderliness in the group are examples of such preconditions for basic need satisfactions. Thwarting in these freedoms will be reacted to with a threat or emergency response. These conditions are not ends in themselves, but they are *almost* so since they are so closely related to the basic needs, which are apparently the only ends in themselves. These conditions are defended because without them the basic satisfactions are quite impossible, or at least very severely endangered.

If we remember that the cognitive capacities (perceptual, intellectual, learning) are a set of adjustive tools, which have, among other functions, that of satisfaction of our basic needs, then it is clear that any danger to them, any deprivation or blocking of their free use, must also be indirectly threatening to the basic needs themselves. Such a statement is a partial solution of the general problems of curiosity, the search for

[8] Clearly creative behavior, like painting, is like any other behavior in having multiple determinants. It may be seen in "innately creative" people whether they are satisfied or not, happy or unhappy, hungry or sated. Also it is clear that creative activity may be compensatory, ameliorative, or purely economic. It is my impression (as yet unconfirmed) that it is possible to distinguish the artistic and intellectual products of basically satisfied people from those of basically unsatisfied people by inspection alone. In any case, here too we must distinguish, in a dynamic fashion, the overt behavior itself from its various motivations or purposes.

knowledge, truth and wisdom, and the ever-persistent urge to solve the cosmic mysteries.

We must therefore introduce another hypothesis and speak of degrees of closeness to the basic needs, for we have already pointed out that *any* conscious desires (partial goals) are more or less important as they are more or less close to the basic needs. The same statement may be made for various behavior acts. An act is psychologically important if it contributes directly to satisfaction of basic needs. The less directly it so contributes, or the weaker this contribution is, the less important this act must be conceived to be from the point of view of dynamic psychology. A similar statement may be made for the various defense or coping mechanisms. Some are very directly related to the protection or attainment of the basic needs, others are only weakly and distantly related. Indeed if we wished, we could speak of more basic and less basic defense mechanisms, and then affirm that danger to the more basic defenses is more threatening than danger to less basic defenses (always remembering that this is so only because of their relationship to the basic needs).

THE DESIRES TO KNOW AND TO UNDERSTAND

So far, we have mentioned the cognitive needs only in passing. Acquiring knowledge and systematizing the universe have been considered as, in part, techniques for the achievement of basic safety in the world, or, for the intelligent man, expressions of self-actualization. Also freedom of inquiry and expression have been discussed as pre-conditions of satisfactions of the basic needs. True though these formulations may be, they do not constitute definitive answers to the question as to the motivation role of curiosity, learning, philosophizing, experimenting, *etc.* They are, at best, no more than partial answers.

This question is especially difficult because we know so little about the facts. Curiosity, exploration, desire for the facts, desire to know may certainly be observed easily enough. The fact that they often are pursued even at great cost to the individual's safety is an [important indication] of the partial character of our previous discussion. In addition, the writer must admit that, though he has sufficient clinical evidence to postulate the desire to know as a very strong drive in intelligent people, no data are available for unintelligent people. It may then be largely a function of relatively high intelligence. Rather tentatively, then, and largely in the hope of stimulating discussion and research, we shall postulate a basic desire to know, to be aware of reality, to get the facts, to satisfy curiosity, or as Wertheimer phrases it, to see rather than to be blind.

This postulation, however, is not enough. Even after we know, we are impelled to know more and more minutely and microscopically on the one hand, and on the other, more and more extensively in the direction of a world philosophy, religion, *etc.* The facts that we acquire, if they are isolated or atomistic, inevitably get theorized about, and either analyzed or organized or both. This process has been phrased by some as the search for "meaning." We shall then postulate a desire to understand, to systematize, to organize, to analyze, to look for relations and meanings.

Once these desires are accepted for discussion, we see that they too form themselves into a small hierarchy in which the desire to know is prepotent over the desire to understand. All the characteristics of a hierarchy of prepotency that we have described above seem to hold for this one as well.

We must guard ourselves against the too easy tendency to separate these desires from the basic needs we have discussed above, *i.e.,* to make a sharp dichotomy between "cognitive" and "conative" needs. The desires to know and to understand are themselves conative, *i.e.,* have a striving character, and are as much personality needs as the "basic needs" we have already discussed (19).

III. Further Characteristics of the Basic Needs

THE DEGREE OF FIXITY OF THE HIERARCHY OF BASIC NEEDS

We have spoken so far as if this hierarchy were a fixed order, but actually it is not nearly as rigid as we may have implied. It is true that most of the people with whom we have worked have seemed to have these basic needs in about the order that has been indicated. However, there have been a number of exceptions.

1. There are some people in whom, for instance, self-esteem seems to be more important than love. This most common reversal in the hierarchy is usually due to the development of the notion that the person who is most likely to be loved is a strong or powerful person, one who inspires respect or fear, and who is self-confident or aggressive. Therefore, such people who lack love and seek it may try hard to put on a front of aggressive, confident behavior. But essentially they seek high self-esteem and its behavior expressions more as a means to an end than for its own sake; they seek self-assertion for the sake of love rather than for self-esteem itself.

2. There are other, apparently innately creative people in whom the drive to creativeness seems to be more important than any other counter-

determinant. Their creativeness might appear not as self-actualization released by basic satisfaction, but in spite of lack of basic satisfaction.

3. In certain people the level of aspiration may be permanently deadened or lowered. That is to say, the less prepotent goals may simply be lost, and may disappear forever, so that the person who has experienced life at a very low level, *i.e.,* chronic unemployment, may continue to be satisfied for the rest of his life if only he can get enough food.

4. The so-called "psychopathic personality" is another example of permanent loss of the love needs. These are people who, according to the best data available (9), have been starved for love in the earliest months of their lives and have simply lost forever the desire and the ability to give and to receive affection (as animals lose sucking or pecking reflexes that are not exercised soon enough after birth).

5. Another cause of reversal of the hierarchy is that when a need has been satisfied for a long time, this need may be underevaluated. People who have never experienced chronic hunger are apt to underestimate its effects and to look upon food as a rather unimportant thing. If they are dominated by a higher need, this higher need will seem to be the most important of all. It then becomes possible, and indeed does actually happen, that they may, for the sake of this higher need, put themselves into the position of being deprived in a more basic need. We may expect that after a long-time deprivation of the more basic need there will be a tendency to reevaluate both needs so that the more prepotent need will actually become consciously prepotent for the individual who may have given it up very lightly. Thus, a man who has given up his job rather than lose his self-respect, and who then starves for six months or so, may be willing to take his job back even at the price of losing his self-respect.

6. Another partial explanation of apparent reversals is seen in the fact that we have been talking about the hierarchy of prepotency in terms of consciously felt wants or desires rather than of behavior. Looking at behavior itself may give us the wrong impression. What we have claimed is that the person will want the more basic of two needs when deprived in both. There is no necessary implication here that he will act upon his desires. Let us say again that there are many determinants of behavior other than the needs and desires.

7. Perhaps more important than all these exceptions are the ones that involve ideals, high social standards, high values, and the like. With such values people become martyrs; they will give up everything for the sake of a particular ideal, or value. These people may be understood, at least in part, by reference to one basic concept (or hypothesis) which may be called "increased frustration tolerance through early gratification." People who have been satisfied in their basic needs throughout their lives, par-

ticularly in their earlier years, seem to develop exceptional power to withstand present or future thwarting of these needs simply because they have strong, healthy character structure as a result of basic satisfaction. They are the "strong" people who can easily weather disagreement or opposition, who can swim against the stream of public opinion, and who can stand up for the truth at great personal cost. It is just the ones who have loved and been well loved and who have had many deep friendships who can hold out against hatred, rejection, or persecution.

I say all this in spite of the fact that there is a certain amount of sheer habituation which is also involved in any full discussion of frustration tolerance. For instance, it is likely that those persons who have been accustomed to relative starvation for a long time are partially enabled thereby to withstand food deprivation. What sort of balance must be made between these two tendencies, of habituation on the one hand, and of past satisfaction breeding present frustration tolerance on the other hand, remains to be worked out by further research. Meanwhile we may assume that they are both operative, side by side, since they do not contradict each other. In respect to this phenomenon of increased frustration tolerance, it seems probable that the most important gratifications come in the first two years of life. That is to say, people who have been made secure and strong in the earliest years tend to remain secure and strong thereafter in the face of whatever threatens.

DEGREES OF RELATIVE SATISFACTION

So far, our theoretical discussion may have given the impression that these five sets of needs are somehow in a step-wise, all-or-none relationship to each other. We have spoken in such terms as the following: "If one need is satisfied, then another emerges." This statement might give the false impression that a need must be satisfied 100 per cent before the next need emerges. In actual fact, most members of our society who are normal are partially satisfied in all their basic needs and partially unsatisfied in all their basic needs at the same time. A more realistic description of the hierarchy would be in terms of decreasing percentages of satisfaction as we go up the hierarchy of prepotency. For instance, if I may assign arbitrary figures for the sake of illustration, it is as if the average citizen is satisfied perhaps 85 per cent in his physiological needs, 70 per cent in his safety needs, 50 per cent in his love needs, 40 per cent in his self-esteem needs, and 10 per cent in his self-actualization needs.

As for the concept of emergence of a new need after satisfaction of the prepotent need, this emergence is not a sudden, saltatory phenomenon but rather a gradual emergence by slow degrees from nothingness. For instance, if prepotent need A is satisfied only 10 per cent then need B may not be visible at all. However, as this need A becomes satisfied 25 per cent, need B may emerge 5 per cent, as need A becomes satisfied 75 per cent, need B may emerge 90 per cent, and so on.

Unconscious character of needs

These needs are neither necessarily conscious nor unconscious. On the whole, however, in the average person, they are more often unconscious rather than conscious. It is not necessary at this point to overhaul the tremendous mass of evidence which indicates the crucial importance of unconscious motivation. It would by now be expected, on *a priori* grounds alone, that unconscious motivations would on the whole be rather more important than the conscious motivations. What we have called the basic needs are very often largely unconscious although they may, with suitable techniques, and with sophisticated people, become conscious.

Cultural specificity and generality of needs

This classification of basic needs makes some attempt to take account of the relative unity behind the superficial differences in specific desires from one culture to another. Certainly in any particular culture an individual's conscious motivational content will usually be extremely different from the conscious motivational content of an individual in another society. However, it is the common experience of anthropologists that people, even in different societies, are much more alike than we would think from our first contact with them, and that as we know them better we seem to find more and more of this commonness. We then recognize the most startling differences to be superficial rather than basic, *e.g.,* differences in style of hairdress, clothes, tastes in food, *etc.* Our classification of basic needs is in part an attempt to account for this unity behind the apparent diversity from culture to culture. No claim is made that it is ultimate or universal for all cultures. The claim is made only that it is relatively more ultimate, more universal, more basic, than the superficial, conscious desires from culture to culture and makes a somewhat closer approach to common-human characteristics. Basic needs are *more* common-human than superficial desires or behaviors.

Multiple motivations of behavior

These needs must be understood *not* to be *exclusive* or single determiners of certain kinds of behavior. An example may be found in any behavior that seems to be physiologically motivated, such as eating, or sexual play, or the like. The clinical psychologists have long since found that any behavior may be a channel through which flow various determinants. Or to say it in another way, most behavior is multimotivated. Within the sphere of motivational determinants any behavior tends to be determined by several or *all* of the basic needs simultaneously rather than by only one of them. The latter would be more an exception than the former. Eating may be partially for the sake of filling the stomach and partially for the sake of comfort and amelioration of other needs. One may make love not only for pure sexual release, but also to convince one's self of one's masculinity, or to make a conquest, to feel powerful, or to win more basic affection. As an illustration, I may point out that it would be possible (theoretically if not practically) to analyze a single act of an individual and see in it the expression of his physiological needs, his safety needs, his love needs, his esteem needs, and self-actualization. This contrasts sharply with the more naive brand of trait psychology in which one trait or one motive accounts for a certain kind of act, *i.e.*, an aggressive act is traced solely to a trait of aggressiveness.

MULTIPLE DETERMINANTS OF BEHAVIOR

Not all behavior is determined by the basic needs. We might even say that not all behavior is motivated. There are many determinants of behavior other than motives.[9] For instance, one other important class of determinants is the so-called "field" determinants. Theoretically, at least, behavior may be determined completely by the field, or even by specific isolated external stimuli, as in association of ideas, or certain conditioned reflexes. If in response to the stimulus word "table," I immediately perceive a memory image of a table, this response certainly has nothing to do with my basic needs.

Secondly, we may call attention again to the concept of "degree of closeness to the basic needs" or "degree of motivation." Some behavior is highly motivated, other behavior is only weakly motivated. Some is not motivated at all (but all behavior is determined).

Another important point [10] is that there is a basic difference between expressive behavior and coping behavior (functional striving, purposive

---

[9] I am aware that many psychologists and psychoanalysts use the term "motivated" and "determined" synonymously, *e.g.*, Freud. But I consider this an obfuscating usage. Sharp distinctions are necessary for clarity of thought and precision in experimentation.

[10] To be discussed fully in a subsequent publication.

goal seeking). An expressive behavior does not try to do anything; it is simply a reflection of the personality. A stupid man behaves stupidly, not because he wants to, or tries to, or is motivated to, but simply because he *is* what he is. The same is true when I speak in a bass voice rather than tenor or soprano. The random movements of a healthy child, the smile on the face of a happy man even when he is alone, the springiness of the healthy man's walk, and the erectness of his carriage are other examples of expressive, nonfunctional behavior. Also the *style* in which a man carries out almost all his behavior, motivated as well as unmotivated, is often expressive.

We may then ask, is *all* behavior expressive or reflective of the character structure? The answer is "No." Rote, habitual, automatized, or conventional behavior may or may not be expressive. The same is true for most "stimulus-bound" behaviors.

It is finally necessary to stress that expressiveness of behavior and goal-directedness of behavior are not mutually exclusive categories. Average behavior is usually both.

Goals as centering principle in motivation theory

It will be observed that the basic principle in our classification has been neither the instigation nor the motivated behavior but rather the functions, effects, purposes, or goals of the behavior. It has been proven sufficiently by various people that this is the most suitable point for centering in any motivation theory.[11]

Animal- and human-centering

This theory starts with the human being rather than any lower and presumably "simpler" animal. Too many of the findings that have been made in animals have been proven to be true for animals but not for the human being. There is no reason whatsoever why we should start with animals in order to study human motivation. The logic or rather illogic behind this general fallacy of "pseudo-simplicity" has been exposed often enough by philosophers and logicians as well as by scientists in each of the various fields. It is no more necessary to study animals before one can study man than it is to study mathematics before one can study geology or psychology or biology.

[11] The interested reader is referred to the very excellent discussion of this point in Murray's *Explorations in Personality* (15).

We may also reject the old, naive behaviorism which assumed that it was somehow necessary, or at least more "scientific," to judge human beings by animal standards. One consequence of this belief was that the whole notion of purpose and goal was excluded from motivational psychology simply because one could not ask a white rat about his purposes. Tolman (18) has long since proven in animal studies themselves that this exclusion was not necessary.

MOTIVATION AND THE THEORY OF PSYCHOPATHOGENESIS

The conscious motivational content of everyday life has, according to the foregoing, been conceived to be relatively important or unimportant accordingly as it is more or less closely related to the basic goals. A desire for an ice cream cone might actually be an indirect expression of a desire for love. If it is, then this desire for the ice cream cone becomes extremely important motivation. If, however, the ice cream is simply something to cool the mouth with, or a casual appetitive reaction, then the desire is relatively unimportant. Everyday conscious desires are to be regarded as symptoms, as *surface indicators of more basic needs.* If we were to take these superficial desires at their face value we would find ourselves in a state of complete confusion which could never be resolved, since we would be dealing seriously with symptoms rather than with what lay behind the symptoms.

Thwarting of unimportant desires produces no psychopathological results; thwarting of a basically important need does produce such results. Any theory of psychopathogenesis must then be based on a sound theory of motivation. A conflict or a frustration is not necessarily pathogenic. It becomes so only when it threatens or thwarts the basic needs, or partial needs that are closely related to the basic needs (10).

THE ROLE OF GRATIFIED NEEDS

It has been pointed out above several times that our needs usually emerge only when more prepotent needs have been gratified. Thus gratification has an important role in motivation theory. Apart from this, however, needs cease to play an active determining or organizing role as soon as they are gratified.

What this means is that, *e.g.,* a basically satisfied person no longer has the needs for esteem, love, safety, *etc.* The only sense in which he might be said to have them is in the almost metaphysical sense that a sated man has hunger, or a filled bottle has emptiness. If we are interested in what *actually* motivates us, and not in what has, will, or might motivate us, then a satisfied need is not a motivator. It must be considered for all practical purposes simply not to exist, to have disappeared. This point should be emphasized because it has been either overlooked or contradicted in every theory of motivation I know.[12] The perfectly healthy, normal, fortunate man has no sex needs nor hunger needs, nor needs for safety, nor for love, nor for prestige, nor self-esteem, except in stray moments of quickly passing threat. If we were to say otherwise, we should also have to aver that every man had all the pathological reflexes, *e.g.,* Babinski, *etc.,* because if his nervous system were damaged, these would appear.

It is such considerations as these that suggest the bold postulation that a man who is thwarted in any of his basic needs may fairly be envisaged simply as a sick man. This is a fair parallel to our designation as "sick" of the man who lacks vitamins or minerals. Who is to say that a lack of love is less important than a lack of vitamins? Since we know the pathogenic effects of love starvation, who is to say that we are invoking value questions in an unscientific or illegitimate way, any more than the physician does who diagnoses and treats pellagra or scurvy? If I were permitted this usage, I should then say simply that a healthy man is primarily motivated by his needs to develop and actualize his fullest potentialities and capacities. If a man has any other basic needs in any active, chronic sense, then he is simply an unhealthy man. He is as surely sick as if he had suddenly developed a strong salt hunger or calcium hunger.[13]

If this statement seems unusual or paradoxical, the reader may be assured that this is only one among many such paradoxes that will appear as we revise our ways of looking at man's deeper motivations. When we ask what man wants of life, we deal with his very essence.

IV. Summary

1. There are at least five sets of goals, which we may call basic needs. These are briefly physiological, safety, love, esteem, and self-actualization. In addition, we are motivated by the desire to achieve or maintain the

[12] Note that acceptance of this theory necessitates basic revision of the Freudian theory.

[13] If we were to use the word "sick" in this way, we should then also have to face squarely the relations of man to his society. One clear implication of our definition would be that (a) since a man is to be called sick who is basically thwarted, and (b) since such basic thwarting is made possible ultimately only by forces outside the individual, then (c) sickness in the individual must come ultimately from a sickness in the society. The "good" or healthy society would then be defined as one that permitted man's highest purpose to emerge by satisfying all his prepotent basic needs.

various conditions upon which these basic satisfactions rest and by certain more intellectual desires.

2. These basic goals are related to each other, being arranged in a hierarchy of prepotency. This means that the most prepotent goal will monopolize consciousness and will tend of itself to organize the recruitment of the various capacities of the organism. The less prepotent needs are minimized, even forgotten or denied. But when a need is fairly well satisfied, the next prepotent ("higher") need emerges, in turn to dominate the conscious life and to serve as the center of organization of behavior, since gratified needs are not active motivators.

Thus, man is a perpetually wanting animal. Ordinarily the satisfaction of these wants is not altogether mutually exclusive, but only tends to be. The average member of our society is most often partially satisfied and partially unsatisfied in all of his wants. The hierarchy principle is usually empirically observed in terms of increasing percentages of nonsatisfaction as we go up the hierarchy. Reversals of the average order of the hierarchy are sometimes observed. Also it has been observed that an individual may permanently lose the higher wants in the hierarchy under social conditions. There are not only ordinarily multiple motivations for usual behavior, but in addition many determinants other than motives.

3. Any thwarting or possibility of thwarting of these basic human goals, or danger to the defenses which protect them, or to the conditions upon which they rest, is considered to be a psychological threat. With a few exceptions, all psychopathology may be partially traced to such threats. A basically thwarted man may actually be defined as a "sick" man, if we wish.

4. It is such basic threats which bring about the general emergency reactions.

5. Certain other basic problems have not been dealt with because of limitations of space. Among these are (a) the problem of values in any definitive motivation theory, (b) the relation between appetites, desires, needs, and what is "good" for the organism, (c) the etiology of the basic needs and their possible derivation in early childhood, (d) redefinition of motivational concepts, *i.e.,* drive, desire, wish, need, goal, (e) implication of our theory for hedonistic theory, (f) the nature of the uncompleted act, of success and failure, and of aspiration level, (g) the role of association, habit, and conditioning, (h) relation to the theory of interpersonal relations, (i) implications for psychotherapy, (j) implication for theory of society, (k) the theory of selfishness, (l) the relation between needs and cultural patterns, (m) the relation between this theory and Allport's theory of functional autonomy. These as well as certain other less important questions must be considered as motivation theory attempts to become definitive.

References

1. Adler, A., *Social Interest* (London: Faber, 1938).
2. Cannon, W. B., *Wisdom of the Body* (New York: Norton, 1932).
3. Freud, A., *The Ego and the Mechanisms of Defense* (London: Hogarth, 1937).
4. Freud, S., *New Introductory Lectures on Psychoanalysis* (New York: Norton, 1933).
5. Fromm, E., *Escape from Freedom* (New York: Holt, Rinehart & Winston, 1941).
6. Goldstein, K., *The Organism* (New York: Am. Bk. Co., 1939).
7. Horney, K., *The Neurotic Personality of Our Time* (New York: Norton, 1937).
8. Kardiner, A., *The Traumatic Neuroses of War* (New York: Hoeber, 1941).
9. Levy, D. M., "Primary Affect Hunger," *American Journal of Psychiatry,* Vol. 94 (1937), pp. 643-652.
10. Maslow, A. H., "Conflict, Frustration and the Theory of Threat," *Journal of Abnormal Social Psychology,* Vol. 38 (1943), pp. 81-86.
11. ———, "Dominance, Personality and Social Behavior in Women," *Journal of Social Psychology,* Vol. 10 (1939), pp. 3-39.
12. ———, "The Dynamics of Psychological Security-Insecurity," *Character and Personality,* Vol. 10 (1942), pp. 331-344.
13. ———, "A Preface to Motivation Theory," *Psychosomatic Medicine,* Vol. 5 (1943), pp. 85-92.
14. ———, and B. Mittelmann, *Principles of Abnormal Psychology* (New York: Harper, 1941).
15. Murray, H. A., *et al., Explorations in Personality* (New York: Oxford U. P., 1938).
16. Plant, J., *Personality and the Cultural Pattern* (New York: The Commonwealth Fund, 1937).
17. Shirley, M., "Children's Adjustments to a Strange Situation," *Journal of Abnormal Social Psychology,* Vol. 37 (1942), pp. 201-217.
18. Tolman, E., *Purposive Behavior in Animals and Men* (New York: Appleton, 1832).
19. Wertheimer, M., Unpublished lectures at the New School for Social Research.
20. Young, P. T., *Motivation of Behavior* (New York: Wiley, 1936).
21. ———, "The Experimental Analysis of Appetite," *Psychology Bulletin,* Vol. 38 (1941), p. 129-164.

2. Stability of the self-concept as a dimension of personality [1]

JOHN J. BROWNFAIN

Reprinted from the *Journal of Abnormal and Social Psychology,* Vol. 47 (1952), 597-606, by permission of the author and the American Psychological Association.

Is stability of self-concept or lack of its useful in understanding and predicting behavior? What are the relationships of stability or instability of self-concept to adjustment? In this well done study, the author suggests possible answers to these questions.

When an individual is assigned the task of evaluating himself, whatever the method of this evaluation, he inevitably makes reference to a system of central meanings that he has about himself and his relations to the world about him which we call the self-concept. Every evaluative statement a person makes about himself may be thought of as a sample of his self-concept, from which may be inferred certain properties of that self-concept. This study is concerned with one property of the self-concept—its stability.

The individual, as James (7) pointed out many years ago, has many selves. The individual might, for example, conceive of the self that he really be-

---

[1] This report is based upon a dissertation submitted to the University of Michigan in partial fulfillment of the requirements for the degree of Doctor of Philosophy. The writer is indebted to Dr. E. Lowell Kelly, who directed the dissertation, for his generous advice and criticism, and to the men of Michigan House and Owen House at the University of Michigan for fulfilling with such zeal the role of subjects.

lieves he is, the self he realistically aspires to be, the self which he believes is perceived by others, the self he hopes he is now, and the self he fears he is now. The self-concept is a configuration of these and of other possible self-definitions and the stability of the self-concept derives from interrelations among these various ways of defining the self. In this study, stability of the self-concept is measured in terms of the discrepancy between two definitions of the self: the self as it is "positively" conceived and the self as it is "negatively" conceived.

The relation between stability of the self-concept and adjustment has been spoken of in a variety of ways. While the two quotations which follow do not contain the word stability or the term self-concept, what they generally convey is highly relevant to the concept of stability which will be explored in this study.

Cameron remarks: "The basis of much frustration and many conflicts is in this universal circumstance, that no man ever fuses all his self-reactions together into a single, unambiguous, coherent whole" (4, p. 102).

Rogers states: "It would appear that when all of the ways in which the individual perceives himself—all perceptions of the qualities, abilities, impulses, and attitudes of the person, and all perceptions of himself in relation to others—are accepted into the organized conscious concept of the self, then this achievement is accompanied by feelings of comfort and freedom from tension which are experienced as psychological adjustment" (9, p. 364).

One need not go far afield in the literature of psychology, psychiatry, or psychoanalysis to find concepts that would be relevant to our concept of stability and its relation to adjustment. Terms such as "integration," "consistency," "differentiation," "style of life," "wholeness of personality" are all suggestive of the same underlying variable which we call stability of the self-concept.

Method and Design

SUBJECTS

The subjects (*S*s) of this research were 62 members of two men's cooperative houses at the University of Michigan. This group, compared to the student population at the University of Michigan, might be characterized as of lower than average socioeconomic background, of liberal, democratic outlook, of diverse ethnic origin, and of above average academic achievement. The *S*s ranged in age from 19 to 31, with a mean age of 23, and in academic level from sophomore to graduate. All *S*s had a minimum of five months' membership in the cooperative and were, therefore, considered to be sufficiently acquainted for purposes of mutual evaluation.

MEASURING THE SELF-CONCEPT

The instrument which was devised as the measure of the self-concept in this study will be referred to as the Self-Rating Inventory. This inventory consists of the following 25 items, each of which is defined at the high and low end by a brief paragraph on the printed form:

1. Intelligence
2. Emotional Maturity
3. General Culture
4. Social Poise
5. Physical Attractiveness
6. Neatness
7. Sociability
8. Generosity
9. Manners
10. Cheerfulness
11. Consistency
12. Sincerity
13. Initiative
14. Trustfulness
15. Flexibility
16. Sportsmanship
17. Individuality
18. Interest in Opposite Sex
19. Self-Understanding
20. Dependability
21. Understanding of Others
22. Self-Acceptance
23. Popularity
24. Prestige
25. Over-all Adjustment

In developing an instrument which was to serve as a measure of the self-concept an effort was made to sample as widely as possible the significant attributes of self-regard. Many of the items of the Self-Rating Inventory were adapted from the scale developed by E. Lowell Kelly and his associates (8) in their research on the selection of clinical psychologists—a scale, which, in turn, was partly based upon the factors of personality developed by Cattell (5). In addition, a number of variables were added to the Self-Rating Inventory because, according to pretest, they seemed pertinent to the requirements of this study.

Using the cooperative house membership as a reference group, each *S* rated himself four successive times on this inventory, in four different frames of judgment, each one designed to yield a different type of self-concept as follows:

1. The "private self": The most accurate estimate of himself as he really believed it to be.

2. The "positive self": A rating of himself slanted positively. Here the subject gave himself the benefit of every reasonable doubt while still conceiving of this as a believable self-picture. This is the self as he really hoped it was.

3. The "negative self": A rating of himself slanted negatively.

Here the subject denied himself the benefit of every reasonable doubt while still conceiving of this as a believable picture of himself. This is the self as he feared it really was.

4. The "social self": The most accurate estimate of himself as he believed other people in the group saw him.

Ratings were made on a scale of from 1 to 8 in the private and social frames of judgment. The high end of the scale was expanded to 9 for the positively slanted ratings and the low end to 0 for the negatively slanted ratings to encourage shift in those individuals who had already given themselves extreme ratings in the private self-ratings.

The *S*s made each set of ratings independently of the others. As a function of the unreliability of the scale, an individual could rate himself on a particular item higher in the negative and lower in the positive than in the private frame of judgment. On the few occasions that such errors occurred (the frequency being 4.6 per cent of the possible opportunities), the negative or positive rating was corrected to equal the private self-rating.

The odd-even reliability of the inventory, using ratings in the private frame of judgment, is .90 (estimated by the Spearman-Brown formula) for the sample of 62. An individual who sees himself unfavorably on some of the items is very likely to see himself unfavorably on the others. Rating behavior on this inventory appears to be essentially a reflection of the general level of self-esteem, the degree to which the individual accepts and values himslf.

THE MEASURE OF STABILITY

Stability of the self-concept is operationally defined as the differences between positive and negative self-ratings on each item summed over all the items on the inventory without regard to sign. This difference score will be referred to as the "stability index." The larger this discrepancy score the more unstable the self-concept is assumed to be. The *S*s with the largest discrepancies between ratings on the positive and negative self-ratings will be referred to as "the unstables"; those with the lowest discrepancy scores will be referred to as "the stables."

Theoretical considerations led us to derive a second discrepancy score from self-ratings in two different frames of judgment. It is operationally defined as the difference between private and social self-ratings on each item summed over all the inventory items without regard to sign. The greater this difference, the more discrepant is the individual's private concept of himself from the concept he believes others to have of him. We assume that when this difference is extreme, the individual cannot "be himself" in social situations, but only a facade of himself. It seems reasonable to assume that whether he believes the group overvalues him (which means that he privately undervalues himself) or undervalues him, his interpersonal relations will be fraught with possibilities of conflict and maladjustment. This discrepancy score is accordingly called the "social conflict" index.

Hypothesis

According to our general hypothesis, we expect to find that subjects whose self-concept is comparatively stable (*i.e.,* whose negative and positive self-ratings are minimally discrepant) are individuals who, according to several criteria evaluative of adjustment, are the happier, more adequate members of the group. We expect to find, on the other hand, that individuals with an unstable self-concept will be the more poorly adjusted, unhappier members of the group.

Stability, unfortunately, cannot be examined without due regard to its pathological kinsman, rigidity. May not, after all, stability be rigidity disguised? Our hypothesis assumes that stability of the self-concept reflects an integrative function rather than rigidity of personality. To justify this assumption it was necessary to identify and then to eliminate rigid *S*s whose stability was actually a pseudostability reflecting their intolerance of ambiguity about the self. The instrument which seemed appropriate for this purpose was the F (Predisposition for Fascism) Scale developed by Frenkel-Brunswik and her associates (2) in their researches on the authoritarian personality. According to Frenkel-Brunswik, high F people, those with marked authoritarian trends in personality, are also people intolerant of ambiguity about themselves and by that criterion people who might be described as rigid.

The Pearson correlation between F Scale scores and the stability index for the sample of 62 is —.25 ($p<.05$). In accordance with theory, the lower (the more stable) the stability index, the higher the F Scale score. The 15 cases constituting the top quarter of the F Scale distribution were considered to be sufficiently rigid, or more accurately, sufficiently under the suspicion of rigidity, to qualify for elimination prior to testing the hypothesis. Of the 15 *S*s thus characterized, 12 fell into the stable half of the stability index distribution, and three fell into the unstable half.

TABLE 1

Properties of Distributions of Stability Index and F Scale Scores for the Stable and Unstable Groups and for the Total Sample

Group	N	*Mean of stability index dist.*	*Range of stability index dist.*	*SD of stability index dist.*	*Mean of F scale scores*	*Range of F scale scores*
Stable	15	37	17 to 48	8	72	37 to 102
Unstable	15	86	71 to 124	14	69	46 to 96
Total	62	58	14 to 124	22	85	37 to 147

SELECTION AND COMPOSITION OF STABLE AND UNSTABLE GROUPS

Following the elimination of the 15 cases identified as rigid from the sample of 62, the remaining 47 cases were ordered according to the size of the stability index. The upper and lower approximate thirds of these 47 cases (*i.e.,* the 15 cases with the lowest and the 15 with the highest stability scores) were then selected. It is in terms of the differences between these two groups on various criteria of adjustment that the hypothesis will be tested. The characteristics of the stable, unstable, and total groups according to the stability index and the F Scale are presented in Table 1.

Since the stable and unstable groups were selected from extremes of the stability index distribution, there is naturally no overlap between these groups on the stability index. The F Scale scores for the stable and unstable groups are virtually equivalent; presumably these two groups are equally free of rigidity as defined by the F Scale.

Demographic data collected on these groups show that there is essentially no difference between the stable and unstable groups in the following respects: age (mean for both groups, 23 years), number of veterans (10 in each group), and number of *S*s referring to the coop as a group of importance to them (9 in each group). The mean period of membership in the cooperative is also identical for both groups (14 months), with a range for the stables of 5 to 40 months and for the unstables of 5 to 50. Thus, both groups had equal opportunity to know other members of the cooperative and in turn to be known by them.

CRITERIA OF ADJUSTMENT

There are four sources of data which provide measures relating to adjustment. These are:

1. Self-ratings in the four different frames of judgment;
2. Subject's scores on the Guilford-Martin Inventory of Factors GAMIN (6);
3. Group evaluation of the subject on ten variables;
4. Subject's predictions of the evaluation;
5. Subject's evaluation of other members of the group.

An individual's adjustment may be said to reflect how well he gets along with himself and his social environment. Adjustment defined in this way may be measured most directly by sources 2 and 3 above. The GAMIN tells us something about how well the individual gets along with himself, while the group evaluation tells us something about how well he gets along in his social environment. The group evaluation yields the most objective criterion of adjustment since it is a source external to the *S*'s self-evaluation. The GAMIN, while not immune from the bias inherent in self-evaluation, is nevertheless a standardized instrument developed to measure certain aspects of adjustment.

In contrast, sources 1, 4, and 5, dealing with *S*'s behavior in evaluating himself and others, provide what might be properly considered secondary measures of adjustment. They do not measure adjustment directly, but they do permit us to make inferences about adjustment.

GROUP EVALUATION PROCEDURES AND THE MEASURES DERIVED FROM THEM

Group members evaluated each other on the following ten variables:

1. Knowing (How well do you know him?)
2. Liking (How well do you like him?)
3. Prestige (How much prestige does he have in your eyes?)
4. Popularity (How popular do you think he is with the group?)
5. Consistency
6. Intelligence
7. Flexibility
8. Understanding of Others
9. Dependability
10. Over-all Adjustment

These variables, except for 1 and 2, are also among the items of the Self-Rating Inventory and are defined in approximately the same way.

In order that each *S* would have a common standard for evaluating others, it was decided to use a ranking procedure rather than free ratings. It was felt that if each *S* ranked 16 randomly assigned group members and was in turn evaluated by 16 group members, an adequate measure of the group consensus would be obtained. Each of the 16 rankings made on a given individual was in terms of a differently constituted sample so that, ultimately, each individual was compared and then ranked in relation to the entire house membership. To reduce the strain of making fine discriminations, and also to establish a numerical frame of reference consistent with the eight-step scale used in taking the Self-Rating Inventory afterwards, *S*s were instructed to assign two individuals to each rank from 1 to 8.

On the same forms the *S*s used to evaluate group members, they also recorded predictions of the average ranking that would be assigned to them by the entire membership of the co-op house. These predictions took three forms: most accurate estimate, highest estimate, and lowest estimate of the average ranking on each variable. It is possible to obtain from these data a measure similar to the stability index: the difference between the highest and lowest estimate, summed over all ten variables without regard to sign. The resulting index was identified as "stability-of-prediction." It constitutes a measure of the stability of another aspect of the self, the social self, the self as one believes it is perceived by others.

We were also interested in investigating the individual's ability to predict how the group saw him. The difference between an *S*'s most accurate estimate of group rankings of him and the actual mean of rankings made by the group members (summed over all ten variables without regard to sign) provides one measure of the *S*'s social insight. This measure will be referred to as "insight I."

Eight of the variables on which *S*s ranked each other were also items in the Self-Rating Inventory. On these eight variables a second measure of insight was obtained: the difference between self-ratings in the private frame of judgment and the mean of group rankings (summed over all eight variables without regard to sign). This measure is an index of the congruence between the self as it is privately seen and the self as others perceive it. This discrepancy score will be referred to as "insight II." This measure is operationally similar to the way Sears (10) defined insight in his study of projection.

As would be expected, both indices of insight tend to measure the same psychological variable, as shown by a correlation of .63 ($N = 62$; $p < .001$).

Some characteristics of the stability index

Since the stability index is a measure unique to this study, it is important to know something about some of its characteristics, particularly its reliability and its susceptibility to possible artifacts. In this section, these characteristics of the stability index will be reported in terms of the total sample. In the section dealing with the test of the hypothesis, in terms of differences between the stable and unstable groups, further light will be cast on the stability index by showing its relation to various measures of adjustment.

The odd-even reliability of the stability index, estimated by the Spearman-Brown formula, is .93 for the total sample of 62. Such a reliability coefficient indicates that, in spite of the diversity of items making up the Self-Rating Inventory, stability of the self-concept affects self-rating behavior in a general way over all the inventory.

The tests of the hypothesis will deal in some detail with the relation between the stability index and private self-ratings. For the entire sample of 62, the correlation between the two measures is —.25 ($p < .05$). Lower self-esteem is more likely to be associated with an unstable self-concept.

The question immediately arises: might not the stability index be in part an artifact of the level of self-rating? That is, as the level of private self-rating rises, there is less room to shift upward in the positive frame of judgment; hence the stability index is apt to be smaller. To test this, the mean of self-ratings was computed for each of the 25 *items* (averaging across the 62 *S*s). These means were then correlated with the means of the stability scores computed for the 25 items in a similar way. The correlation between the two is .19. Though this correlation is not significant, its positive direction provides an emphatic denial to the question of artifact. A high self-rating on a particular item does not *per se* reduce the stability score on that item; it is even possible for the reverse to occur.

Results

While the study was still in design stage, a series of specific predictions was made relative to differences between the stable and unstable groups on the various measures of adjustment. The findings are confined for the most part to tests of those specific predictions.

The statistical technique used to test significance of differences between means of the stable and unstable groups on the criteria of adjustment is Fisher's *t*, using the appropriate small sample formula. In testing the significance of *t* values for findings, one half of the probability curve was used since in such instances direction of difference between the stable and unstable groups was predicted. Probabilities which attain the .05 level will be considered significant. Degrees of freedom in *t* tests is 28 unless otherwise indicated.

Self-Ratings

Table 2 shows that the stable *S*s have both a higher level of self-rating in the private frame of judgment and a lower intertrait variability in these ratings. The stable group may be characterized, therefore, as having a greater amount of self-esteem. The stable *S*s also see themselves in a more constant way while, by contrast, the unstable *S*s see themselves in a more variable way from trait to trait, suggesting that they have an ambivalent attitude toward themselves which is expressed in a lower rating of certain attributes of the self and what might be a compensatory accentuation of other attributes of the self.

On 21 of the 25 items of the Self-Rating Inventory, stable *S*s rate themselves higher than do unstable *S*s (data not shown). Differences on five of these items attain significance ($p<.05$). These are Cheerfulness, Self-Acceptance, Over-all Adjustment, Consistency, and Trustfulness. On none of the four items on which the unstables rate themselves higher is the difference significant. Of the four items (Self-Understanding, Intelligence, General Culture, and Dependability, it is the difference on Intelligence that comes closest to being significant. Since the grade point average of the unstable *S*s approximates a B and that of the stable *S*s a C+ (difference significant at .01 level), it follows that there is some reality basis for the higher self-evaluation of the unstable *S*s on Intelligence.

The reader will recall that the difference between the way *S* sees himself (private self) and the way he believes others see him (social self) was labeled the social-conflict index. As Table 2 indicates, *S*s in the unstable group, as compared to the stable group, show an enormous incongruity between the private perception of the self and the perception of the self they attribute to other people. According to the rationale of the social conflict index, the greater this discrepancy score the larger the "breeding ground" for difficulty in interpersonal relations. Later evidence will show that the unstable *S*s are indeed less well adjusted socially than the stable *S*s.

TABLE 2

DIFFERENCES BETWEEN STABLE AND UNSTABLE GROUPS ON LEVEL AND VARIABILITY OF PRIVATE SELF-RATINGS AND ON THE SOCIAL CONFLICT INDEX

Measure	*Mean*		*Diff.*	t *Value*	p<
	Stable	*Unstable*			
Mean of self-ratings	6.09	5.64	.45	1.802*	.05
S.D. of self-ratings	1.25	1.62	—.37	3.064*	.005
Social conflict index	18.58	34.95	—16.37	4.052*	.001

*Probabilities for these *t* values are based upon one half of the probability curve since direction of difference was predicted before analysis of data.

GUILFORD-MARTIN INVENTORY OF FACTORS GAMIN

Except for the GAMIN, all measures of adjustment were derived from instruments especially developed for purposes of the study. The findings on the GAMIN are therefore particularly noteworthy. While it was felt that the stable group would in general have "healthier" GAMIN profiles, specific predictions were made in their favor only with respect to the I and N factors scores.

The evidence from the GAMIN, as Table 3 shows, altogether substantiates the fact that the stable *S*s are better adjusted than the unstable *S*s. On only one factor (G) does the difference favor the unstable *S*s and this difference is not significant.

On the other four factors, the stable *S*s have the "healthier" scores.

They score somewhat more ascendant and more masculine. They are less afflicted by inferiority feelings and by nervousness. The significant difference on the N factor is especially noteworthy since it was established that this factor is not significantly correlated with the mean of private self-ratings as are the A and I factors.

TABLE 3

DIFFERENCES BETWEEN STABLE AND UNSTABLE GROUPS ON THE INVENTORY OF FACTORS GAMIN*

	Mean				
C-scores **	*Stable*	*Unstable*	*Diff.*	t *Value*	p<
General activity	4.07	4.60	—.53	.882	.40
Ascendance	5.50	4.60	.90	1.304	.30
Masculinity	7.36	6.13	1.23	2.014	.10
Inferiority (lack)	4.93	3.47	1.46	2.028***	.05
Nervousness (lack)	5.29	3.73	1.56	2.108***	.025

*Since one member of the stable group did not complete the GAMIN, $df=27$.
**The median C-score for the 160 university students on which the Guilford-Martin norms are based is 5.
***Probabilities for these t values are based upon one half of the probability curve since direction of difference was predicted before analysis of data.

In scoring the GAMIN, a technique developed by Ernest Tupes [2] to measure the amount of "facade" (*i.e.*, the tendency of a subject to "fake" responses in order to present himself in a more favorable light) was used. The facade scores for the stable and unstable groups as well as for the entire sample are so low that, to quote Tupes (private communication) the subjects must be considered to have approached the GAMIN with "almost painful honesty." Such a finding enhances the validity of the GAMIN scores which were obtained and suggests furthermore that the *S*s were very likely optimally sincere and cooperative in completing other instruments in accordance with instructions.

THE GROUP'S EVALUATION OF EACH SUBJECT

So intimate is the relationship between self and the social environment that it may be asserted that there is no maladjustment in personality that is not somehow reflected in maladjustment in interpersonal relations. One would therefore look to the group's evaluation of each individual as a crucial criterion of his adjustment.

We shall first examine the differences between mean ranks of the stable

[2] E. C. Tupes. The detection of "faking" on the Guilford-Martin Personality Inventory GAMIN. Unpublished study.

and unstable *Ss* on the ten group evaluation variables as presented in Table 4. Nine of the ten differences favor the stable group. Some of these differences may result from the intercorrelations among these variables due to "halo." Even so, it is interesting that the three significant differences are on variables most pertinent to self-group relationships, variables measuring how well known and how well liked the individual is, and how much popularity is attributed to him.

The difference on *knowing* is especially revealing since mean length of membership for stable and unstable groups was exactly the same.[3] The

TABLE 4

DIFFERENCES BETWEEN MEAN RANKS OF STABLE AND UNSTABLE GROUPS ON THE TEN GROUP EVALUATION VARIABLES

Variables	*Mean* *Stable*	*Mean* *Unstable*	*Diff.*	t *Value*	p<
Knowing (how well known)	5.50	4.73	.77	1.944*	.05
Liking (how well liked)	4.87	4.03	.84	1.809*	.05
Prestige (how prestigeful)	4.82	4.05	.77	1.645*	.10
Popularity (attributed to group)	5.43	4.47	.96	1.844*	.05
Consistency	4.55	3.86	.69	1.647*	.10
Flexibility	4.63	4.14	.49	1.111	.30
Intelligence	4.33	4.89	—.56	1.090	.30
Understanding of Others	4.86	4.13	.73	1.460*	.10
Dependability	4.47	4.10	.37	.678	.60
Over-all Adjustment	4.81	4.05	.76	1.652*	.10
Mean of all ten ranks	4.83	4.25	.58	1.563*	.10

*Probabilities for these *t* values are based upon one half of the probability curve since direction of difference was predicted before analysis of data.

stables must be the more active socializers to be known better. It would appear that the unstables tend to withdraw from group contact. On only one out of the ten variables are the unstable *Ss* favored and that is on *intelligence*. This is understandable in view of their superior academic achievement.

SUBJECTS' PREDICTION OF THE GROUP EVALUATION

We are concerned with three aspects of the predictions made by the *Ss* of the group evaluation: their level, their stability, and their accuracy. These findings are presented in Table 5 and are limited to an analysis of

[3] Subjects were asked to report how many people they knew well or fairly well among the 40 to 45 members belonging to their co-op house. The difference between the stables and unstables in this regard is striking. The stables report knowing on the average 31 people in the co-op, the unstables 21 (t value 2.472; $p<.01$).

TABLE 5

DIFFERENCES BETWEEN STABLE AND UNSTABLE GROUPS ON LEVEL, STABILITY, AND ACCURACY OF PREDICTION OF THE GROUP EVALUATION

Measure	*Mean*		*Diff.*	t *Value**	p<
	Stable	*Unstable*			
Mean of ten predictions	5.25	4.86	.39	1.639	.10
Stability-of-prediction index (total for ten variables)	24.53	32.20	—7.74	2.847	.005
Insight I index (total discrepancy for ten variables)	10.73	12.20	—1.47	.624	.30
Insight II index (total discrepancy for each of eight variables)	12.07	14.87	—2.80	1.418	.10

*Probabilities for these *t* values are based upon one half of the probability curve since direction of difference was predicted before analysis of data.

over-all scores rather than scores on each of the ten group evaluation variables.

The stable *S*s show by way of their higher level predictions that they expect the group to evaluate them more favorably. On nine of the ten variables (the exception being *intelligence*) the stable *S*s make higher level predictions (data not shown). While it is only on *over-all adjustment* that the difference is statistically significant, the trend is nevertheless unmistakable. Of course, the stable *S*s see themselves privately in a more favorable light than do the unstable *Ss,* and they are in reality more highly regarded by the group as a whole. Their predictions undoubtedly reflect both their self-esteem and the reality picture.

The level of predictions was based upon the "most accurate estimate" made by *Ss* of the group's evaluation. The *Ss* also recorded their highest and lowest estimates of the group's evaluation. From these data was derived a measure similar to the stability index called the stability-of-predictions. On all 10 variables (not shown) the stable *S*s make more stable predictions than do the unstable *S*s. When this behavior is considered for the total of the 10 variables, the difference between the two groups becomes highly significant. The stable *S*s are more confident that they know what the group thinks about them.

We now deal with the third aspect of *S*s' predictions—their accuracy. Two indices of insight into social reality have been described. Table 5 shows for both Insight I and Insight II a slight tendency for the stable *S*s to estimate more accurately the group consensus about them.

Looking at Insight II, we see that the stable *S*s tend to see themselves privately in a way which is more congruent with the social estimate of them than is true of the unstable *S*s. Even though the difference for the small *N* fails to attain significance, it is interesting to speculate about the possible meaning of this. It appears that what the stable *S*s really think about themselves comes closer to what the group really thinks about them. When this finding is related to the fact that the stable *S*s are also more apt to see themselves in a way congruent with the way they think other people see them (as discussed in the analysis of the social conflict index), we may infer that the stable *S*s are more free to "be themselves" in interpersonal situations and that others are better able to evaluate them as they really are.

Subjects' evaluations of others

The group evaluation data not only tell us what the group thinks about the individual, but they also permit us to draw certain inferences about the way the *S* perceives the people he evaluates. The reader will recall

TABLE 6

Differences Between Stable and Unstable Groups on Rank Orders Correlations Between Pairs of Group Evaluation Rankings

Rho	*Mean* *Stable*	*Mean* *Unstable*	*Diff.*	t *Value**	p<
Liking and knowing	.62	.44	.18	1.755	.05
Liking and popularity	.62	.47	.15	1.569	.10
Liking and prestige	.72	.69	.03	.411	.35

*Probabilities for these *t* values are based upon one half of the probability curve since direction of difference was predicted before analysis of data.

that each *S* ranked 16 members of the cooperative on ten different variables. For each *S* separately a rank-order correlation (rho) may be computed between any two sets of rankings. For example, a rho may be computed between the way a given *S* ranks his 16 people on how well he knows them and the way he ranks them on how well he likes them. Rho's for all the stable *S*s and the unstable *S*s respectively may be averaged (following a transformation of rho's into normally distributed variates) to find out whether the stable and unstable groups differ in the degree to which they associate any two sets of rankings. Differences between the stable and unstable groups on three pairs of rankings treated this way are presented in Table 6.

The unstable *S*s, as shown by their lower mean rho between *liking* and *knowing,* are less likely to like the people they know well (or, conversely, to know well the people they like best) than are the stable *S*s. We may speculate that the maladjusted person is more likely to take out his conflicts upon those he knows well and becomes emotionally involved with, a state of affairs which leads to alienation. He may end up preferring individuals whom he knows less well and against whom he is protected by social distance.

The unstable *S*s are less likely to like people they consider popular in the group than is true of the stable *S*s, as shown by their lower mean rho between *liking* and *popularity*. Perhaps envy, values rooted in rationalizations (*e.g.*, popular people are superficial), or a sense of painful contrast could account for this.

The relationship between *liking* and *prestige* was investigated because it was felt that less secure people (the unstable ones) would feel threatened by or envious of prestigeful figures and would be less likely to like them than in the case of the more secure (stable) people. The difference, although in the predicted direction, is not significant.

To summarize, *S*s with the more stable self-concepts are better adjusted than those with less stable self-concepts on all of our criteria of adjustment whether these criteria are derived from self-evaluation on the Self-Rating Inventory and the Guilford-Martin Inventory of Factors GAMIN, from the group's evaluation of the *S*, or from the *S*'s evaluation of group members. Certain differences do not attain statistical significance. Yet, in spite of the small number of *S*s involved in testing the hypothesis, all the differences are in the direction of the theoretical prediction. It is this consistency of results obtained from an extensive analysis which provides the most impressive basis for accepting the hypothesis concerning differences between the stable and unstable groups in our co-op sample.

Discussion

The hypothesis was tested in terms of criteria of adjustment. Some of the main ingredients of this "adjustment" are those referring to self-esteem. Measures dealing with self-evaluation, whether the Self-Rating Inventory or the Guilford-Martin GAMIN, are more than anything else reflective of such qualities as self-adequacy, self-acceptance, self-confidence—reflective, in a word, of self-esteem. A major correlate of the stable self-concept (provided that this stability does not function in the interest of a defensive rigidity) is a high level of self-esteem. The individual with a stable self-concept is the individual who accepts himself, who values himself highly, who feels secure about himself. When he asks of himself the question "Who am I?", he is able to answer himself in a confident manner and he is generally pleased with his answer. But the individual with an unstable self-concept is deficient in self-esteem. He is uncertain about who he is and is not likely to be pleased with the answer he gives himself. It is true that such an individual may be capable of seeing himself in a highly flattering way, but this is just one pole of his ambivalence. When he thinks he's good, he thinks he's very good, but when he thinks he's bad, he thinks he's horrid.

While self-esteem may be considered a correlate of stability of the self-concept, one cannot say whether it is the cause or effect. It would be more reasonable to posit a circular-causal relationship between the two. Two speculative explanations of this circular-causal relationship are suggested.

The first type of explanation posits a compensatory reaction to low self-esteem. The individual who is deficient in self-esteem must defend himself against the insecurity which accompanies this condition so that, for good defensive reasons, he is also capable of seeing himself in a positive way. People with unstable self-concepts are unable to consolidate their various self-concepts into a stable organization because they cannot tolerate the negative elements which are inherent in low self-esteem. So long as they are casting about for an acceptable self-picture, the self-concept must remain fluid.

The relationship between self-esteem and stability of the self-concept might be examined in another way. When a person evaluates himself in the positive and negative frames of judgment, his behavior is likely to be governed by some awareness of his having been at some time or other particularly adequate or inadequate in various situations. The individual lacking in self-esteem is more likely to be "situation dominated." Uncertain about what to expect from the environment, his behavior becomes more dependent upon what he perceives as its demands. If the situation is favorable enough, his self-esteem is inordinately heightened, but if the situation is unfavorable, self-esteem is inordinately lowered. Whether he is his adequate or inadequate self seems to hinge upon the eddies in the emotional environment. On the other hand, the individual with high self-esteem is less likely to see himself as dominated by a situation. His self-concept is relatively stable because he is sufficiently the master of his environment that a radical restructuring of the self-concept need not be the consequence of changing situations.

Just as evidence from self-evaluation shows that the people who have unstable self-concepts also have lower self-esteem, the findings based on the group evaluation show that the group esteems them less too. The group is likely to share the individual's attitude toward himself. This may be, it is true, partly a function of the reality about the individual—that is, he stands low on a number of traits and both he and the group may be aware or this. But on the other hand, his own attitude toward himself may generate a similar attitude in the group toward him. To illustrate this, the unstables do not, to begin with, value themselves highly, but they see the group as valuing them far less than they do themselves. This makes them fearful of the group and this fear motivates them to withdraw from the group. As a consequence they know fewer people in the group and are less well known by the group. Of course, it is not only their withdrawal from social contact which fosters the rejection. If the individual perceives the social environment as threatening, then he may respond to it with hostility which provokes counterhostility in the group, leading to still further alienation.

The behavior of the individual with an unstable self-concept, which has as one correlate lowered self-esteem, is quite in accordance with Adlerian theory. Adler (1, p. 23) has remarked that people who feel inferior tend to withdraw from social participation until only a small group is left over for the "maneuvers aiming at the various types of superiority to expend themselves upon." There is, of course, evidence that the unstables do withdraw and that they do use the defense of compensation which Allport (3) has called the "most interesting of all the shy handmaidens of self-esteem." However, the writer does not wish to impose the Adlerian conception on the findings of this study. There are undoubtedly other correlates of the unstable self-concept which were not, within the confines of this study, brought to light as was self-esteem. It is possible that a study using clinical techniques such as the detailed case history and projective tests would reveal other correlates of instability of the self-concept, defense mechanisms other than what has been referred to so grossly as "compensatory."

Summary

The purpose of this study was to develop an operational measure of the stability of the self-concept and to demonstrate that stability of the self-concept is a dimension of personality serviceable to the work of undertanding and predicting behavior.

The primary data of this investigation consist of several series of self-ratings on 25 personality variables, obtained successively under different instructions from 62 members of two men's cooperative houses at the University of Michigan. Under one set of instructions, the *S* gave himself the benefit of any realistic doubt he had about his standing on each inventory item, thus yielding a "positive" self-concept. Under another set of instructions, the *S* denied himself the benefit of such doubt, thus yielding a "negative" self-concept. The difference between these positively and negatively slanted self-ratings on each item, summed over all the items of the inventory without regard to sign, was the operational measure of stability. The larger this discrepancy, the more unstable the self-concept is assumed to be. This measure of stability has an estimated reliability of .93.

The hypothesis was: *S*s who have the most stable self-concepts are, according to a number of criteria, better adjusted than *S*s with the least stable self-concepts.

In making this hypothesis, it was assumed that stability reflects an integrative function rather than rigidity of personality. Therefore, the 15 *S*s identified as rigid, on the basis of high scores on the F (Predisposition for Fascism) Scale developed by Frenkel-Brunswik, were eliminated from the sample before testing the hypothesis.

Adjustment was measured in terms of inferences derived from *S*'s behavior in rating himself and others, *S*'s scores on the Guilford-Martin Inventory of Factors GAMIN, and the group's evaluation of *S*. Fisher's *t* was used to test significance of differences between the means of these measures for the 15 *S*s with the most stable and the 15 with the least stable self-concepts.

All findings support the theoretical prediction that *S*s with stable self-concepts are better adjusted than those with unstable self-concepts. The following are the more salient findings which favor the *S*s with more stable self-concepts ($p < .05$):

1. They have a higher level of self-esteem as manifested by a higher mean self-rating and also by a higher self-rating on the inventory item defining self-acceptance. The intertrait variability of their self-ratings is lower, indicating that their self-esteem is generalized.
2. They are freer of inferiority feelings and nervousness as measured by the GAMIN.
3. They are better liked and considered more popular by the group.
4. They see themselves more as they believe other people see them.
5. They know more people in the group and are better known by the group, indicating more active social participation.
6. They show less evidence of compensatory behavior of a defensive kind.

References

1. Adler, A., *The Practice and Theory of Individual Psychology* (London: Routledge, 1925).
2. Adorno, T. W., Else Frenkel-Brunswik, D. J. Levinson, and R. N. Sanford, *The Authoritarian Personality* (New York: Harper, 1950).

3. Allport, G. W., *Personality, A Psychological Interpretation* (New York: Holt, Rinehart & Winston, 1937).
4. Cameron, N., *The Psychology of Behavior Disorders* (Boston: Houghton, 1947).
5. Cattell, R. B., "Confirmation and Clarification of Primary Personality Factors," *Psychometrika,* Vol. 12 (1947), pp. 197-220.
6. Guilford, J. P., and H. G. Martin, *The Guilford-Martin Inventory of Factors GAMIN: Manual of Directions and Norms* (Beverly Hills, Calif.: Sheridan Supply Company, 1945).
7. James, W., *Principles of Psychology,* Vol. I (New York: Holt, Rinehart & Winston, 1890).
8. Kelly, E. L., "Research on the Selection of Clinical Psychologists," *Journal of Clinical Psychology,* Vol. 3 (1947), pp. 39-42.
9. Rogers, C. R., "The Organization of Personality," *American Psychologist,* Vol. 2 (1947), pp. 358-368.
10. Sears, R. R., "Experimental Studies of Projection: I. Attribution of Traits," *Journal of Social Psychology,* Vol. 7 (1936), pp. 151-163.

3. Men's and women's beliefs, ideals, and self-concepts

JOHN P. MCKEE
AND ALEX C. SHERRIFFS

Reprinted from the *American Journal of Sociology,* Vol. 44 (1959), 356-363, by permission of The University of Chicago Press.

What differences are there in the belief systems, ideals, and self-concepts between men and women? Changes in traditional sex roles are noted along with discussion about why these changes are occurring. Increasingly, the authors report that there is more and more pressure brought to bear on men to incorporate "feminine" qualities into their personality organizations.

This paper is the report on the third of a series of studies of sex roles in American society. These are investigations of the status, content, developmental aspects, and implications of the stereotypes of males and females.

We have previously determined by each of three quite different methods, and for procedural variations within each, that college men and women regard the male more highly than the female sex group (4). These results are consistent with findings reported by Komarovsky based on yet another approach and on a different college population (1, 2, 3). We consider the higher evaluation of males by college students of both sexes as established beyond reasonable doubt.

We have also examined the characteristics that college men and women ascribe to themselves and to each other (7). When such subjects were asked to indicate on an adjective check list those characteristics that are true of men in general and of women in general, the resulting male "stereotype" contained many more individual favorable characteristics than did the female "stereotype." Male subjects particularly emphasized males' favorable characteristics, but female subjects emphasized females' *un*favorable characteristics. Furthermore, women's self-descriptions also emphasized their unfavorable characteristics much more than did men's. In general, these stereotypes were confirmed by means of a different method when each of one hundred subjects was asked to list ten characteristics for each sex. It was possible to sort the many individual responses into a limited number of rational categories which differentiated the sex groups.

While undertaking our investigations, we accept without hesitation two basic assumptions made by nearly every writer in this field: that the roles of the two sex groups are changing today and that the relationship between the groups is in disequilibrium. Our data themselves give confirming evidence for these assumptions.

Our aim in this, the third investigation, is to study certain aspects of the attitudinal and belief systems of our subjects which might be expected to reflect the changes in roles of, and the disequilibrium between, the sex groups. Recognizing the differential status still accorded the groups and possessing empirical evidence regarding the definitions currently given the sex roles, we believe that we can find meaning in the resulting information.

We ask these questions about beliefs: What do men and women believe the other sex wants them to be? To what degree does each sex group believe that the other *wants* it to conform to the sex-role stereotype? Our subjects certainly subscribe to stereotypes when describing men and women. This we had found earlier. And the stereotypes closely resembled those outlined by Komarovsky and Mead. In a period of cultural change for sex roles, however, we would expect to find differences between what are thought to be the characteristics of the sex groups and what is thought by members of one sex group to be desired of them by members of the other sex group. More specifically, we ask: Do women really believe that men are jealous of the characteristics that are allegedly masculine? Komarovsky and Mead (5) argue that women hold such beliefs; Wallin (8) does not go so far. And what about men? What characteristics do men believe women would like them to have? Komarovsky writes: "We place an intolerable burden upon men by re-emphasizing a model of 'masculinity' which is increasingly difficult to attain in modern society" (3, p. 299). But do men believe that women want them to demonstrate superiority and to personify virile and adequate masculinity to the extent that this writer suggests? We suspect that the situation will by now have been modified by the realities of the new social goals which have emerged for both men and women and by the very cultural contradictions which Komarovsky describes so well.

In the literature on sex differences there are statements that one sex must conform more rigidly to society's traditional mold than the other. However, in the literature there are nearly as many arguments for this sex's being male as for its being female. Belief about what the other sex wants should indicate some significant pressures for conformity—and conformity to what. How do the sex groups compare?

Questions about sex typing in the subjects' beliefs immediately raise questions about the correspondence between such sex typing and the sex typing that the two sexes actually do want in each other. Examination of this correspondence will throw light on the relative awareness by the sex groups of each other's desires. Further, examination of what each sex actually wants in the other will reveal whether the two sexes are equally insistent that the traditional roles be maintained.

Finally, it is of interest to see how these matters relate to the sex typing in what men and women say they would *like* to be. Are men and women equally able to express and exhibit the characteristics that they desire? "Equally able" in terms of what they believe the other sex wants and "equally able" in terms of what the other sex really does want?

Subjects and Procedure

One hundred unmarried men and one hundred unmarried women enrolled in introductory courses in psychology at the University of California were given four cards on which Sarbin's Adjective-Check List was printed (6). The responses to the ACL's are the basic data for this investigation. The subjects were asked to check on the first card "those adjectives which describe what you would *ideally* like to be." On the second card subjects checked "those adjectives which describe yourself as you really are." On the third card they checked "those adjectives which describe your ideal woman" ("man" for female subjects). On the fourth card men checked "those adjectives which *you think* describe the ideal man for women of your age," and women checked their beliefs about the desires of *men* of their own age.

We explained to the subjects that they were to try to predict, or guess, what members of the other sex had checked on the preceding card. For the sake of brevity we refer to card 1 as indicating the "Ideal Self," card 2 as "Real Self," card 3 as "Ideal Member of Other Sex," and card 4 as "Belief." Ideal Self was given before Real Self largely because this seemed the least threatening task. Cards 3 and 4 were placed in order to help clarify the instructions for card 4. In presenting the results, we shall follow the order of our logic rather than the order of procedure. Thus, we shall go from Belief to Ideal Member of Other Sex (or what other sex "really" wants) to Ideal Self and finally to Real Self.

Results

We have analyzed the data as follows. Each adjective received a score based on the proportion of subjects who chose it. These proportions were

TABLE 1

SUBGROUP MEANS FOR FAVORABLE WORDS

	I *Belief* Words		II *Ideal Member of Other Sex* Words	
	Male	Female	Male	Female
Men** (I) / Men (II)	78	76	63	78
Women (I) / Women*** (II)	58	86	82	80
Interaction*** (I) / Interaction** (II)				

	III *Ideal Self* Words		IV *Real Self* Words	
	Male	Female	Male	Female
Men	76	65	53	51
Women**	75	82	46	68
Interaction***				

SUBGROUP MEANS FOR UNFAVORABLE WORDS

	I *Belief* Words		II *Ideal Member of Other Sex* Words	
	Male	Female	Male	Female
Men	5	4	2	5
Women	3	9	8	4
Interaction* (I) / Interaction*** (II)				

	III *Ideal Self* Words		IV *Real Self* Words	
	Male	Female	Male	Female
Men	5	2	25	17
Women (III) / Women** (IV)	4	5	23	27
Interaction (III) / Interaction* (IV)				

*$p<.05$.
**$p<.01$.
***$p<.001$.

then transformed (arc sine transformation) and the resulting distributions subjected to a "Subjects × Words" analysis of variance. The subject categories are "men" and "women"; the word categories are "male" and "female." A "male" or "female" word is one that is agreed by *both* men and women to characterize the stereotypes of men or of women (7). With *masculine* and *feminine* eliminated, there are twenty-nine favorable "male" words and twenty favorable "female" words in the stereotypes. There are eight unfavorable "male" words and seventeen unfavorable "female" words [1] (4). The requirement that *both* men and woman agree on the stereotypic character of a word was made to facilitate the computation and interpretation of the analyses of variance. Since this requirement eliminates those adjectives that only one sex or the other includes in a stereotype, we shall present subsidiary findings to augment the analysis.

With four sets of instructions and with the favorable and unfavorable words analyzed separately, there result eight different analyses of variance. Table 1 presents the four means (given in percentages corresponding to the means of the transformed scores) for each of the eight analyses. We shall consider the favorable words first.

The table shows that for favorable words there is a significant subjects effect under each set of instructions: men select a larger number of favorable adjectives than women when indicating their Belief about what the other sex wants; for all other instructions women select a larger number of favorable adjectives than men.[2] Table 1 also shows significant words × subjects' interactions for the favorable words for each set of instructions. For the unfavorable words there is one significant main effect: to describe the Real Self, women choose a larger number of unfavorable words than men do. There are also significant interactions for the unfavorable words for all instructions except Ideal Self.

Belief

What sort of sex typing do members of one sex believe that members of the other sex want in them? Column I of Table 1 suggests that men believe that women want them to have the favorable qualities of both sexes

---

[1] Favorableness or unfavorableness was determined by the judgments of members of a different sample from the same student population. For details see McKee and Sherriffs, *op. cit.* (4).

[2] That the significant judges effect for Belief is different from the judges effect under other instructions gives us a good deal of confidence that the ACL reflects motives and attitudes and not simply verbality or *n* check adjectives. We do not assume the ultimate validity of a self-description (or any other description) given on an ACL, but to some extent the proof of the pudding is in the eating, and the qualitative aspects of previous findings seem to us to make good sense. So do the qualitative findings presented in later sections of this paper.

and about equally. But women believe that men want them to possess favorable feminine characteristics to a much greater degree [3] than favorable masculine characteristics. In fact, womens' choices of sex-*in*appropriate adjectives are so reduced that the over-all subjects effect is significant in favor of men, while in columns II, III, and IV it favors women. In short, Komarovsky's view of women's beliefs about the amount of sex typing demanded of them appears to be confirmed: women *do* think men wish to restrict them from characteristics that are thought to be masculine.

But what about men's Beliefs? For men the picture is different. Where women believe they are restricted by men, one might almost say that men believe that in the eyes of women the ideal male is one who exemplifies not only much that society alleges to be masculine *but also much that society alleges to be feminine.*

IDEAL MEMBER OF OTHER SEX

And the men are correct. At least they are correct if we take women's description of their Ideal Man as the criterion. In column II of Table 1 we find that, when women describe the ideal male, he is almost exactly what men believe women would have him be. He has the favorable characteristics of both sexes equally, and he has most of them. Significantly more is asked of him than he himself asks of women. And most of this over-all subject difference is due to women's greater choice of the sex-*in*appropriate characteristics. In fact, the median (but not the mean) discrepancy between women's choices of favorable female characteristics for the Ideal Self and for the Ideal Male is *negative.*

To some extent the women's Beliefs are also correct: men do restrict women. But women's Beliefs exaggerate the degree of this restriction. On the average, the favorable female characteristics are selected by 78 per cent of the men for the ideal woman, while the favorable male characteristics are selected by only 63 per cent. But this 15 per cent differential is not nearly so large as the 28 per cent differential that women *believe* to be the case.

There are qualitative aspects of men's "restrictions" which help to clarify the picture. In describing the ideal woman, men selected ten of the twenty-nine adjectives in the male stereotype significantly less often than other male words. These ten words are *aggressive, courageous, daring, deliberate,*

---

[3] Technically, the term "degree" is perhaps misleading. The scores are based on the percentage of the subjects who selected each adjective in the two stereotypes. Theoretically, all subjects could select an item, but none of them feels very strongly about it. Marbe's Law suggests that this possibility is not in fact likely. Consequently, we have used this simplest terminology.

dominant, dynamic, forceful, independent, rugged, and *sharp-witted.* On the average, these words were selected by only 31 per cent of the men to describe their Ideal Woman. Eight of these words, all save *deliberate,* and *sharp-witted,* are members of our (7) twelve adjective, third masculine "cluster" which appears to represent action, vigor, and a kind of almost "muscular" effectiveness. *Deliberate* and *sharp-witted* are from the twelve-item "cluster" of rational competence and effectiveness, and there are no items from the small "cluster" involving uninhibited social style. In short, if men are somehow jealous of their masculinity or feel that some characteristics are simply inappropriate in women, that feeling seems to apply primarily to those characteristics related to strength and personal force.

IDEAL SELF

The data for the Ideal Self cast more light on just which characteristics seem to be peculiarly masculine and peculiarly feminine. Women's Ideal Self is a trifle less differentiated than men's. That is, for favorable words men show an 11 per cent differential between their average choice of sex-appropriate and sex-inappropriate characteristics, while for women the differential is 7 per cent. We had expected the sex difference to be somewhat larger; that is, we had expected women to show a much greater interest in male characteristics than men showed in female characteristics. This was apparently just somewhat naive: to some extent women simply accept men's pre-emption of the cluster involving strength and personal force. Well under 50 per cent of the women choose *aggressive, daring, dominant, forceful,* and *rugged* for the Ideal Self. And each of these is in the upper half of the distribution of discrepancies between women's choices for the Ideal Self and their choices for the Ideal Man. Furthermore, three additional adjectives from the same cluster are also in the upper half of this distribution of discrepancies, even though they are chosen by over half of the women for the Ideal Self. These three are *adventurous, ambitious,* and *individualistic.* In other words, for eight of the twelve items in the strength and personal force cluster, there is evidence that women, even as men, feel them to be more appropriate in men than in themselves. But this is as far as the women go. They choose the remaining four words in the cluster (*courageous, dynamic, independent,* and *self-confident*) at least as often for the Ideal Self as for the Ideal Man, and the vast majority of women choose them. And much the same is true of the remaining favorable items in the male stereotype—most women choose them for the Ideal Self, and they choose them as frequently for the Ideal Self as for the Ideal Man.

But, while this is true for women's choices of adjectives in the male stereotype, the converse is not true for men's choices of adjectives in the female stereotype. In every case but one, men select favorable female characteristics less often for the Ideal Self than for the Ideal Woman. Since fifteen of these twenty female characteristics are chosen for the Ideal Self by over half of the men, one can hardly say that they *reject* female traits. But we do suspect that simple positive affect in themselves, or at least the thought of it, is a little unsettling to men—*affectionate, lovable, sentimental, sensitive,* and *soft-hearted* are the five words for which men's choices for Ideal Self and Ideal Woman are most discrepant, and the discrepancies are very large (mean = 31 per cent). Compelling as this is, it is not quite conclusive, for, while *gentle* and *kind* are also in the top half of the distribution of such discrepancies (speaking now only of female words), the magnitude of the discrepancy for these two words is only 12 per cent. And for *warm* and *sympathetic* the discrepancies are less than for the average female word.

In any event, and for whatever reasons, it is true that, apart from the strength and forcefulness cluster, women do desire allegedly male characteristics more than men desire allegedly female characteristics. If one's *ideals* be taken as the criterion of one's conformance to a social norm, then, rather surprisingly, it is men who conform to the norm more than women, rather than the other way around.

REAL SELF

But if one's self-description be the criterion, then women are the conformers. The data for the Real Self (col. IV of Table 1) show that for the favorable characteristics there are a significant interaction and a significant subjects effect favoring women. The key to both effects is women's choice of female words. On the average, female words are chosen by 68 per cent of the women, while male words are chosen by only 53 per cent of the men. It is this difference between men's and women's choices of the sex-appropriate items which must be responsible for the main effect, for the sex difference in choice of sex-*in*appropriate items would give a subjects difference in the other direction—one favoring men rather than women. Another way of putting it is to say that women, so far as the favorable elements of their self-descriptions are concerned, are more exclusively feminine than men are exclusively masculine. This, of course, corresponds to the subjects' Beliefs about what the other sex wants and also to what the other sex "in fact" does want. When *all* the favorable adjectives are examined (as opposed to only those which both men and women agree to be stereotypic), we find that, on the average, the sex-appropriate adjectives are selected by 55 per cent of the men and 67 per cent of the women; neutral words, by 55 per cent of the men and 61 per cent of the women;

and sex-inappropriate words, by 52 per cent of the men and 49 per cent of the women.[4] Thus, men show an average difference of only 3 per cent between their choices of sex-appropriate and sex-inappropriate items, while for women this differential is 18 per cent. For all favorable words combined the values are 55 per cent for men and 59 per cent for women, and the difference is not significant.

One other feature of the self-descriptions calls for comment. This is the fact that women choose a significantly larger number of *un*favorable characteristics than men do. The effect is present for both male and female words and somewhat more marked for the sex-inappropriate ones (6 per cent) than for the sex-appropriate (2 per cent). However, the somewhat greater effect for the sex-inappropriate adjectives turns out to be due to the fact that the analysis is based on only those characteristics which *both* men and women agree to be stereotypic. Examination of *all* the unfavorable characteristics reveals that the sex-appropriate ones are selected by 22 per cent of the men and by 29 per cent of the women, while the sex-inappropriate ones are selected by 21 per cent of the men and 23 per cent of the women. Thus the differential is greater (7 per cent) for the sex-appropriate ones than for the sex-inappropriate (2 per cent), which is in keeping with the results for favorable characteristics.

Summary and Discussion

1. For all instructions except Belief, women check more favorable stereotyped adjectives than men. For Belief instructions, men check more. This finding does not relate to questions raised earlier except, perhaps, to reflect a greater person-orientedness on the part of women—an expression of the role for which they are trained in our society (and these words *do* describe people).

2. Women believe that, from men's point of view, the Ideal Woman is markedly sex-typed. This corroborates the thinking and findings of other investigators. Here, as in the case of our other variables, we have quantitative results for the present day which we will be able to compare with responses to the same method in future years.

3. Men believe that, from women's point of view, favorable male characteristics and favorable female characteristics are equally desirable.

4. And when women describe their Ideal Man, they do select favorable female characteristics as often as they select favorable male characteristics.

[4] For this analysis "sex-appropriate" and "sex-inappropriate" refer to those adjectives which members of the *subjects' own sex* ascribe significantly more often to own sex or the other sex.

Two findings above are new to us. They suggest not only that the "model of masculinity [is] increasingly difficult to attain in modern society" (Komarovsky) but that there are now in fact strong pressures to bring about a change. We do not have evidence for a decrease in pressure on men to maintain their masculine qualities, but we find a pressure by women to have men more oriented to interpersonal relations and more expressive of human (feminine in the stereotype) feelings. If college women now exert such pressure and if they have communicated it to men, then both men and women should, as they become parents during the next few years, teach these values in rearing the new generation of sons (and daughters).

Our findings do not support that part of Komarovsky's statement which refers to boys: "If the more rigid masculine model penalizes the boys who have feminine tendencies, it also has its advantages. Once a boy can adjust himself to the masculine model, he will be spared the contradictory pressures which tend to impinge upon the growing girl no matter which model she accepts in childhood" (3, p. 76). The masculine model no longer seems so rigid.

5. Men, when they describe their Ideal Woman, include favorable male characteristics considerably less often than they include favorable female characteristics. However, when we examine the data which led to this conclusion along with our information concerning women's beliefs in this regard, we see that men are—or at least claim to be—somewhat less restrictive than women believe them to be; they allow women to have some "masculine" characteristics. The fact that there is least "give" by men on what are probably the most basically masculine variables (action, vigor, and achievement effectiveness) suggests the hypothesis that a change in the traditional female sex role stereotype may be under way, with the most crucial variables to be affected last, if at all.

6. Women's Ideal Self is a trifle, and by statistical test insignificantly, *less* sex typed than men's. Close examination of individual items of the ACL suggests that women, though often including male attributes in their Ideal Self, do not yet, by and large, desire a life of robust and vigorous masculinity. Similarly, men, though valuing for themselves such traits as "warm" and "sympathetic," and accepting the virtue of being "gentle" and "kind," balk at attributes which would require open demonstration of personalized feelings or which might suggest sentimentality. When those adjectives most related to such "essence of sex-role" traits are set aside, then, for the large remainder women's Ideal Self is, indeed, less sex linked in its content than men's.

7. Women's Real Self is more sex typed than men's. We subscribe to the interpretation made by Komarovsky that in their everyday life women still

feel that they must behave according to the traditional stereotype; and men, we would guess, though behaving less like this hypothetical norm, are probably uneasy in their failure to do so.

8. Women's Real Self is also more unfavorable than men's; this we have found before.

In summary, the findings are completely consistent with the assumptions that the roles of men and women are changing and that there is disequilibrium in the relationship between the groups. During a time of such change it is to be expected that attitudes will shift more rapidly than overt behaviors, that beliefs about the demands of others will reflect both the present facts and the traditional expectations (and therefore not perfectly predict either), that the sex with higher status in the society will be able to express overt change sooner than the sex with less security, and, finally, that those attributes which are at the core of the sex-role stereotypes will change least and last. We would interpret the discrepancy which we have found between college women's ideals for themselves and the attributes they say they actually express as reflecting in addition the dual training of American daughters: preparation to meet economic exigencies and the responsibilities of modern life (emphasized in the Ideal Self) and training to be feminine in the tradition of the female stereotype (emphasized in the Real Self).

Thus far our findings are either supportive of or consistent with the ideas of Komarovsky, who has published widely on such questions as they relate to the American scene.

However, we also present data which indicate that there is no inconsiderable pressure on men to modify their role by incorporating more of the traditionally "feminine" qualities. This pressure we assume to be present because of the wishes of our women subjects—wishes of which the men are well aware. This important fact has hitherto been understressed, but it seems to us eminently reasonable under present circumstances of social change. Also, we observe that men subjects are more perceptive of what women desire in them as attributes than are women subjects insightful about the current desires of men for characteristics in them. The often made generalization about the greater social perceptiveness of women may require modification under particular psychosociological circumstances.

References

1. Komarovsky, Mirra, "Cultural Contradictions and Sex Roles," *American Journal of Sociology,* Vol. 52 (1946), pp. 184-189.

2. ———, "Functional Analysis of Sex Roles," *American Sociological Review,* Vol. 15 (1950), pp. 508-516.
3. ———, *Women in the Modern World* (Boston: Little, 1953).
4. McKee, J. P. and A. C. Sherriffs, "The Differential Evaluation of Males and Females," *Journal of Personality,* Vol. 25 (1957), pp. 356-371.
5. Mead, Margaret, *Male and Female* (New York: Morrow, 1949).
6. Sarbin, T. R., *Personality Word Card* (Berkeley: U. of Calif., n.d.).
7. Sherriffs, A. C., and J. P. McKee, "Qualitative Aspects of Beliefs About Men and Women," *Journal of Personality,* Vol. 25 (1957), pp. 451-464.
8. Wallin, P., "Cultural Contradictions and Sex Roles: A Repeat Study," *American Sociological Review,* Vol. 15 (1950), pp. 288-293.

4. Some personality differences in children related to strict or permissive parental discipline [1]

Goodwin Watson

Reprinted from the *Journal of Psychology*, Vol. 44 (1957), 227-249, by permission of the author and The Journal Press.

Strategy for discipline is only one dimension of the total spectrum of parent-child interaction patterns, but in terms of personality development generally and self-concept formation specifically, it is crucial. Permissiveness or strictness? The author details possible consequences of each.

A. Introduction

In controversies over parental discipline of children, few of the arguments advanced for more permissiveness or for more strict adult control have yet been empirically tested. Does early indulgence "spoil" children or does it give them a foundation of "security" to meet life's stress and strain? Does firm and consistent discipline by the parents create in children inner hostilities, anxieties, and self-rejection, or does it relieve anxiety and foster more successful self-discipline? Psychologists, psychoanalysts, teachers, parents, grandparents have often spoken with strong conviction on one or the other side of these issues, but the evidence has usually come from personal experience, clinical cases, plausible theories, or unconscious bias.

A generation ago this writer made a

[1] This study was made possible by a grant from the Columbia University Council for Research in the Social Sciences.

first effort at empirical study of this problem, comparing the self-reports of 230 graduate students who rated their home discipline during childhood along a continuum from the most strict to the most lenient. Those who came from the strictest quartile of homes reported: (*a*) more hatred for and constraint in relation to parents; (*b*) more rejection of teachers; (*c*) poorer relations with classmates, more quarrels, and shyness; (*d*) more broken engagements and unsatisfactory love affairs; (*e*) more worry, anxiety, and guilt feeling; (*f*) more unhappiness and crying; (*g*) more dependence on parents; but (*h*) better school grades and stronger ambition (16).[2] Two cogent criticisms should be made of this study. First, the "strict" category included homes where there was severe punishment and quite possible rejection. The "lax" category included possible indifference and neglect along with genuine concern for freedom. Second, since all data came from the students' self-reports, a generally negative or optimistic outlook may have permeated both the reports on home discipline and the present self-evaluation.

A few years later (1938) Carpenter and Eisenberg (4) reported findings leading to similar conclusions. Among 500 college women, the 50 rated as most "dominant" reported a childhood in which their own "freedom" and "individuality" had been stressed. The more "submissive," like the shy, dependent, anxious students in our 1929 study, came almost entirely from adult-dominated homes. Those who "had to have parents' permission to do practically everything" turned out at college age to be "submissives" (21 per cent) rather than "dominants" (2 per cent).

Studies attempting to relate specific early child-rearing practices (*e.g.*, breast feeding, self-demand feeding, method of toilet training, *etc.*) to child personality seem to have been inconclusive (*Cf.* Sewell [13] and review by Orlansky [11]). Those which center upon the general social climate in the home, on the other hand, reveal marked and generally consistent differences. One exception is Myers (10) who, in 1935, reported that a pupil adjustment questionnaire and high school teacher ratings on quality of personality adjustment were unrelated to strictness of home discipline.

Hattwick (6, 7) in 1936 found that "over-attentive" homes which "favor" the child or "revolve around" the child were positively correlated (.20 to .40) with tendencies of nursery school pupils to be babyish in such matters as "cries easily," "asks unnecessary help," and "avoids risk." On

---

[2] Results reported to the 10th International Congress of Psychology in 1929 and later published in G. Watson, "A comparison of the effects of lax versus strict home training." *Journal of Social Psychology,* 5 (1934), 102-105. A popular version appeared in *Parents' Magazine,* 9 (1934), 13-20.

the other hand, these same over-indulged children were less likely to take the property of others or to mistreat animals.

Ayer and Bernreuter (2) in 1951 reported on another study of the personality traits of nursery school children in relation to their home discipline. Significant correlations appeared between physical punishment at home and a tendency of children not to face reality ($r = .35$) and between permissiveness of parents (letting children learn from the natural consequences of their acts) and a more "attractive" personality in the child ($r = .33$).

Symonds (15) matched 28 parents who "dominated" their children in an authoritative way with 28 who permitted the child much freedom and who usually acceded to child wishes. He found the children from stricter homes more courteous, obedient, and neat, but also more shy, timid, withdrawing, docile, and troubled. The more permissive parents brought up children who were more aggressive, more disobedient, and who had more eating problems, but who also were more self-confident, better at self-expression, freer, and more independent.

Anderson (1) identified a group of junior high school pupils who had been brought up with warm affection but little adult dominance. He found these children marked by a high degree of maturity, poise, cheerfulness, cooperation, obedience, and responsibility.

Lafore (9), using techniques of direct, on-the-scene observation, made two half-hour visits in the homes of 21 nursery school children, and reported that:

> Parents who presented the largest number of instances of dictating (to) and interfering with their children, received the largest number of expressions of hostility from their children. . . .
> Parents who showed large numbers of instances of blaming, hurrying, punishing, threatening and interfering had children who presented large numbers of crying. . . .
> Children who were frequently threatened scored high on fearfulness. . . .
> Children who were cautioned most often scored low on resourcefulness.

Radke's study (12) is in some ways closest to the one to be reported here. She studied 43 children of nursery school or kindergarten age, giving the parents a questionnaire and observing the children in free play and picture-interpretation test situations. Children from more restrictive and autocratic home discipline showed less aggressiveness, less rivalry, were more passive, more colorless, and less popular. They did not get along so well with other children. The children from homes with freer discipline were more active, showed more rivalry, and were more popular. Radke found that parents who were "democratic" in their disciplinary methods, giving more respect to the youngsters, fostered children who themselves showed more consideration for others.

Baldwin (3) in 1948, reported on a study of 64 four-year olds, showing that parents who were strict and undemocratic in their methods of control were likely to have children who were quiet, well-behaved, unaggressive, but restricted in curiosity, originality, and imagination.

Shoben (14) found that when parents of "problem children" (defined as: referred for clinical help, or brought into custody of juvenile authorities at least twice) were given an attitude scale they were more apt than were parents of nonproblem children to agree with statements approving strict discipline and demand for obedience. Biserial correlation was .80 on the original group and .62 on a validating group for this variable which Shoben called "Dominating."

There is considerable convergence among the findings of these studies. There seems to be reason to suppose that firm, strict adult domination will produce the conforming, obedient child but will handicap him in initiative and probably burden him with shyness and a sense of inadequacy. More permissive treatment seems, in these studies, to result in more independence and aggressiveness on the part of the child. These children are less docile but in some studies appear to be more popular and more considerate of others. Shoben's results challenge a popular belief that juvenile delinquency is associated with lack of punishment by parents.

B. Selection of Subjects

This study was conducted under the auspices of the Guidance Center, a child-guidance clinic in New Rochelle. Associated with the Guidance Center was a positive program of education in mental health and of community service, reaching hundreds of parents of "normal" children in the eastern part of Westchester County. Subjects for this study were limited to normal children in school from kindergarten through sixth grade. Only "good" homes where children were wanted, loved, and well cared for were included. Any children who had ever been referred for physchological or psychiatric treatment were excluded. Nominations were sought from parents, teachers, and social workers, to find good homes that were known to be clearly "strict" or "permissive."

During a preliminary period, social workers visited the recommended homes and talked with these parents about their practices in child-raising. On the basis of the interviews a multiple-answer questionnaire was constructed and printed under the title, *How I Am Bringing Up My Child.* The instrument asked about parental reaction to each of 35 fairly common situations, such as children's eating, sleeping, toilet training, dressing, keeping clean, caring for toys, quarreling, anger at parents, sex curiosity, attendance at school and church, choice of television programs, friends, *etc.* Each situation was followed by three kinds of possible response: (*a*) a clearly permissive reaction, (*b*) a middle-of-the-road or "sometimes this and sometimes that" answer, and (*c*) a reply characteristic of the parent who sets standards and enforces strict obedience. The responses were assigned weights of 5 for the most permissive, 3 for the neutral, and 1 for the strict reaction. There was opportunity for parents to write in a response to each situation in their own words if none of the proposed answers seemed to fit well enough. If a parent's qualified answer fell between "strict" and "middle-of-the-road," it was given 2 points; if it fell between "middle-of-the-road" and "permissive," it was given 4 points. Consistent choice of the "strict" responses would result in a score of 35; consistent "middle-of-the-road" responses would give a total of 105; consistent "permissiveness" would bring a total score of 175. The actual range was from 55 to 158.

A range of 20 points on either side of the neutral point of 105 was arbitrarily set as representing the area of common practice—strict about some things at some times and more lenient on other matters or at other times. Although we had made special efforts to reach the more extreme groups—the permissive parents with scores of 125 or over, and the strict parents with scores of 85 or less—more than half (53 per cent) of our responses fell in the 40 point middle range and were not used in this study.

The home discipline for 34 of the children was rated by fathers independently of the mother's rating. Fathers usually reported a less permissive attitude than did mothers. For these cases, fathers averaged a score of 105 and mothers 115. In only seven instances did the mother's report indicate a stricter attitude than that of the father. Correlation between mother's rating and father's was .61. For the sake of consistency, since mother's rating was available in all cases and since in suburban communities today the mother is more directly and more frequently responsible for discipline in the type of situation listed, our classification into strict or permissive is based only on the mother's report. In no instance would a child's classification have moved from one extreme category to the other if the father's questionnaire had been used instead of the mother's.

C. Procedure

Parents whose questionnaire score was extreme, falling under 86 (strict) or over 124 (permissive), were visited by a trained social worker [3] who

[3] The writer wishes to acknowledge indebtedness to Mrs. Helen Service and Mrs. Seth Solomon who contributed significantly to this study.

conducted an interview designed to check both directly and indirectly on the reported attitudes and practices, to evaluate the general climate of the home, and to obtain the parents' perception of their child's strength and weaknesses. The social workers were not informed as to whether the home to be visited had been reported as permissive or as strict but the differences were so marked that this was seldom in doubt. In the few instances in which the social worker felt that the questionnaire classification was questionable because the home really belonged in the middle-of-the-road category rather than at the extreme, the case was not included in our comparative study. Thus every case which was included met both the criteria: extreme score on the questionnaire, and confirming judgment of a social worker who had independently observed parent and child in the home.

We endeavored to get school behavior ratings for all the children, but this proved impossible in some cases. Wherever they cooperated, teachers or school guidance officers rated the children on a scale which provided intervals from 1 to 5 on: (*a*) level of activity; (*b*) initiative; (*c*) independence, spontaneity, self-reliance; (*d*) confidence, good adjustment; (*e*) friendliness and popularity; (*f*) cooperation; (*g*) self-control; and (*h*) persistence. In the case of 16 or 36 children rated by teachers a trained worker from the Guidance Center made an independent appraisal using the same scale. Agreement of the teacher and the outside observer is represented by a correlation of .77. Of 121 parallel judgments, 59 per cent agreed exactly; 31 per cent differed by only one scale step; and 10 per cent were two steps apart. Thus 90 per cent assigned the same or an adjoining category.

D. Results

1. Permissiveness is rare

The first surprise of the study was our difficulty in finding parents who were fairly consistently permissive. Perhaps this should have been anticipated.

Whiting and Child (17) have estimated the over-all indulgence or severity of child training in 47 societies studied by competent anthropological observers. The aspects of discipline which they included in their index were: (*a*) earliness and severity of weaning; (*b*) toilet training; (*c*) repression of sexual activity; (*d*) repression of aggression; and (*e*) effort toward child's independence. They found only two of the 47 cultures as severe on the younger child as is the typical American middle-class white family described by Davis and Havighurst. No culture in the records is less permissive with children than we are. The short-shrift given to "progressive education" in this country might further have warned us.

We had been led to believe, however, that in certain subcultures of the United States the ideal of respecting the child and of permitting him great freedom to mature in his own way and at his own good time had taken root. We knew that psychoanalytic concepts were commonly heard in upper-middle-class Westchester child-study groups and that "mental hygiene" was looked upon as favorably as Divine Grace once had been. Some teachers complained that children were being given too much freedom at home and writers in popular journals freely listed lack of firm parental discipline as a major cause of juvenile delinquency. It was easy to find citizens who thought that some of their neighbors were overly permissive parents.

We set the modest goal of 50 cases—25 boys and 25 girls—from child-centered, permissive homes. After strenuous search, with the cooperation of the Guidance Center, the Child Study Association, the Mental Hygiene Association, social workers, clergymen, teachers, pediatricians, and P.T.A.'s; and after extending our quest for an extra year and modifying our qualifying scores a step or two downward toward the middle; we eventually located 38 permissively brought-up children—21 boys and 17 girls. (Four of these could not be included in the later testing.) The distribution of our questionnaire returns is shown in Table 1. We emphasize

TABLE 1

DISTRIBUTION OF SCORES ON "HOW I AM BRINGING UP MY CHILD"

Score	*No. of boys*	*No. of girls*	*Both*	*Per cent of total*
"Permissive" extreme				(12%)
145 and over	3	5	8	
135–144	5	4	9	
125–134	13	8	21	
"Middle-of-the-road"				(53%)
115–124	13	14	27	
105–114	30	39	69	
95–104	31	48	79	
"Strict" extreme				(35%)
85–94	33	41	74	
75–84	20	8	28	
74 and below	9	4	13	
Total	157	171	328	(100%)

again that this is not a normal cross section. We were not interested in "middle-of-the-road" cases for this particular comparison. The point of the table is that with much less effort, we found three times as many "strict" as "permissive" homes in the most "liberal" section of an upper-middle-class suburban community. The obtained median score of 101 is below (*i.e.*, more strict than) the arbitrary neutral score of 105.

2. Age, sex, and discipline

Demands for conformity to adult standards become stronger as a child grows older. Babies are not expected, except by pathological parents, to "behave" themselves. Many cultures treat young children very indulgently, only later expecting them to exercise mature levels of self-control. Pearl Buck reports that in the China she knew, children were usually treated very permissively until about the age of seven. Their demands were gratified whenever possible. But after seven, they were expected to behave like proper adults, and they did so.

Our data from 328 children in Eastern Westchester county, reported in Table 2, show no clear and consistent age trend. The anticipated transition from infant indulgence to mature demands does not appear in this cross-sectional survey. Longitudinal studies of qualitative changes in the same child-parent relationship might reveal that tolerance for some kinds of childish misbehavior is decreasing, but that with advancing age children are treated with increased freedom which offsets these restrictions.

TABLE 2

Age and Sex of Child in Relation to Permissiveness of Home Discipline

(Higher scores are more permissive)

	Boys		*Girls*	
Age	*No.*	*Median score*	*No.*	*Median score*
5	11	102	13	101
6	32	105	27	112
7	34	98.5	32	98.5
8	19	96	23	102
9	25	97.5	31	99
10	13	87	27	103
11	17	111	13	100
12	6	104	5	110
All	157	100.3	171	101.7

3. The two groups compared

Table 3 shows that although our two groups of children, one from exceptionally "permissive" and the other from very "strict" homes, are far apart on Home Discipline score, they are not significantly different in

TABLE 3

COMPARISON OF "STRICT" GROUP AND "PERMISSIVE" GROUP ON AGE, ON SEX, AND INTELLIGENCE SCORES

Home Discipline scores

Scores	*No. of strict*	*No. of permissive*
145 and over	0	7
135–144	0	7
125–134	0	17
120–124	0	3
91–120	0	0
81– 90	19	0
71– 80	17	0
61– 70	6	0
51– 60	2	0
Total	44	34
Median	79.8	133.3

Age/Sex

Age	*No. of strict*	*No. of permissive*
11	3	3
10	3	3
9	9	2
8	10	7
7	11	7
6	8	12
Total	44	34
Mean	7.9	7.6

Sex	*Strict*	*Permissive*
Boys	25	21
Girls	19	13
Total	44	34

Intelligence scores

Vocabulary I.Q.	*Strict*	*Permissive*
150–159	1	4
140–149	2	4
130–139	8	5
120–129	5	2
110–119	3	1
Below 110	0	0
	19	16

Rorschach	*Strict*	*Permissive*
Superior	10	13
Above aver.	25	12
Average	9	9
Below aver.	0	0
	44	34

proportion of boys (57 per cent and 62 per cent), or in age. The distributions of intelligence, as estimated from Rorschach or quite independently from a vocabulary test, show relatively a few more top-level I.Q.'s from the permissive homes, but this difference is not large enough to be statistically significant. It is noteworthy that all children in this study have I.Q.'s of 110 or higher as estimated from their vocabulary.

4. PLAN OF PERSONALITY STUDY

Children who are strictly brought up will be compared with children who are treated much more permissively, on each of nine dimensions of personality as follows:

Overt Behavior

1. Independence—dependence.
2. Socialization—ego-centrism.
3. Persistence—easy discouragement.
4. Self-control—disintegration.
5. Energy—passivity.

Inner Feelings

6. Creativity—stereotyping.
7. Friendliness—hostility.
8. Security—anxiety.
9. Happiness—sadness.

In each instance the null hypothesis—that there is no significant difference between the two groups—will be statistically tested.

a. Independence—Dependence

Hypothesis 1. Is there no difference between children from strict and those from permissive homes in the personality dimension of independence versus dependence?

Five measures bearing upon this hypothesis have been combined to give an index of independence. One is a rating by the psychologist of the child's behavior as he was brought into the playroom, shown the toys, games, puzzles, craft materials, *etc.,* and told he might play with them in any way he chose. A rating of "5" is assigned to those children who promptly sized up the situation and went to work on their own responsibility with no further demands on the adult. The low extreme of the scale, a rating of "1," is assigned to those children who were unable to get going despite repeated instruction and reassurance. This rating correlates .70 with the composite index.

The second measure is a rating of the child's evident need for adult attention during the later activities of the testing period. Those children who independently judged their own performance with little reference to cues from the psychologist are at the high—5—end of the scale; those who were so dependent on adult approval that without definite reassurance their behavior was disrupted are given a rating of 1. This mcasure correlates .71 with the composite.

The third rating is based on a period of free play with doll figures representing a family. If the examiner was asked to make decisions for the child, the rating is low; high ratings represent independent, self-reliant structuring of the interpersonal play. This measure has the highest correlation (.76) with the composite index.

The fourth measure is based on the story interpretations which the child assigned to several *TAT* and *CAT* pictures. If the figures with whom the child seemed to identify most were self-reliant, acting on their own responsibility, the rating is 5. The lowest rating, 1, means that the identification figures were generally passive, helpless, or dependent. This correlates only .51 with the composite.

Our fifth rating is derived from Rorschach responses. Whether M (movement) responses were active and extensor or passive and flexor, or absent; whether the balance of C, CF, and FC tended toward or away from control, and the content of food and adult-child relationships were all taken into account. The Rorschach estimate correlates .67 with the composite.

TABLE 4

DIFFERENCES IN INDEPENDENCE—DEPENDENCE *

	Boys		*Girls*		*All*	
Rating	*Strict*	*Permissive*	*Strict*	*Permissive*	*Strict*	*Permissive*
High independence (20–23)	1	7	1	3	2	10
Above average (17–19)	9	6	6	4	15	10
Below average (13–16)	10	7	8	5	18	12
Very dependent (9–12)	5	1	4	1	9	2
Total	25	21	19	13	44	34

* $x^2 = 20.95$. P. $< .01$.

The reliability of the total index is estimated (Spearman-Brown) at .80. Theoretically, scores might range from 5 to 25; the actual range is from 9 (very dependent) to 23 (highly independent). Distributions shown in Table 4 find some children from each type of home at every level of independence but the null hypothesis—that no real difference will be found—must be rejected. Differences (based on x^2 with Yates' correction) are significant at better than the .01 level (5). The highly independent children include 29 per cent of our permissive sample, but only 5 per cent of the strictly disciplined children. The very dependent children represent 6 per cent of those from permissive homes and 21 per cent of those from strict homes. We find, therefore, a *marked tendency for greater freedom in the home to show itself in greater independence in the child's behavior outside the home.*

A study of teacher ratings on "initiative" and "independence," available for only 38 of our 78 cases, yields no significant difference. The distributions are shown in Table 5. A possible explanation for the apparent disagreement between these ratings and those based on our tests may be the teachers' preference for the kind of initiative which is in close conformity to classroom demands. This seems especially plausible when we note that very low ratings on initiative and independence have been given by the teachers to seven boys but to only one girl.

TABLE 5

TEACHER RATINGS ON INITIATIVE AND INDEPENDENCE *

	Boys		Girls		All	
Rating	*Strict*	*Permissive*	*Strict*	*Permissive*	*Strict*	*Permissive*
9–10	6	2	5	4	11	6
5– 8	5	3	3	2	8	5
1– 4	4	3	1	0	5	3
Total	15	8	9	6	24	14

* No significant difference.

b. Socialization—Ego-centrism

Hypothesis 2. Is there no difference between children from strict and those from permissive homes in the personality dimension of socialization versus ego-centrism?

Our index combines four separate ratings: (*a*) verbal negativism (or overcompliance) versus cooperative consideration of the child's own wishes and the adult requests; (*b*) behavioral negativism (or overcompliance) versus "positive but differentiated cooperation"; (*c*) stories told in response to several *TAT* and *CAT* pictures, rated for quality of parent-child relations from resistance to friendly interaction; and (*d*) responses to Card IV of Rorschach. Average intercorrelation of these ratings on socially integrative responses is .52, yielding a predicted reliability, for the four combined, of .81.

TABLE 6

DIFFERENCES IN SOCIALIZATION—EGO-CENTRISM *

	Boys		Girls		All	
Rating	*Strict*	*Permissive*	*Strict*	*Permissive*	*Strict*	*Permissive*
Well socialized, cooperative (15–18)	2	7	2	4	4	11
Above average (12–14)	7	6	2	6	9	12
Below average (10–11)	10	6	9	1	19	7
Negativistic or overcompliant (7–9)	6	2	6	2	12	4
Total	25	21	19	13	44	34

* $x^2 = 15.14$. $P. < .01$.

Differences, reported in Table 6, show markedly better cooperation by children from permissive homes. Differences are statistically significant, being large enough to have a probability of chance occurrence, less than .01. The highest level of mature cooperation is found among 32 per cent of the children from permissive homes but only 9 per cent of the children strictly disciplined. The null hypothesis must be rejected and so also must the "spoiled child" or "little monster" tradition. *Exceptionally permissive discipline seems on the whole to be associated with better socialization and more effective cooperation with others.* At the same time, it should be remembered that children from each type of home can be found at every step of the socialization scale.

This study does not demonstrate that the higher average level of independence reported earlier, or of cooperation reported here, is produced by the permissive discipline. It may be true—and the data on freedom from hostility to be reported later make this plausible—that the more relaxed home atmosphere is responsible for the observed differences in personality. Alternative explanations cannot, however, be excluded. Perhaps the kind of parents who choose the permissive role transmit, via heredity or via associated cultural influences, a different temperament or pattern of living. It should not be assumed that if parents who have heretofore practiced strict discipline were simply to change over to great permissiveness, their children would thereby become more independent or cooperative. They might, or might not. A correlational study cannot satisfactorily answer questions of causation.

TABLE 7

DIFFERENCES IN SOCIALIZATION AS RATED BY TEACHER ($N = 38$) *

	Boys		*Girls*		*All*	
Rating	*Strict*	*Permissive*	*Strict*	*Permissive*	*Strict*	*Permissive*
	A. Cooperation in classroom					
Cooperative (4–5)	8	4	6	5	14	9
Average (3)	5	2	3	0	8	2
Uncooperative (1–2)	2	2	0	1	2	3
Total	15	8	9	6	24	14
	B. Popularity with other children					
Popular (4–5)	8	3	7	5	15	8
Average (3)	4	5	1	1	5	6
Less well liked (1–2)	3	0	1	0	4	0
Total	15	8	9	6	24	14

* Differences not statistically significant.

Table 7 reports teacher ratings for 38 of our children on cooperation and popularity in the classroom. The number of cases is small and differences are without statistical significance. The most impressive fact in this little sample is that no child from a permissive home was rated below average in friendliness or popularity with other children.

c. Persistence—Easy Discouragement

Hypothesis 3. Is there no difference between children from strict and those from permissive homes in the personality dimension of persistence versus being easily discouraged?

All subjects were given the Alexander Passalong test which begins with easy problems in block movement and arrangement but proceeds to those which, although they seem workable, are impossibly difficult. The psychologist noted how long the child persisted at the task and also the effect of increasing difficulty and frustration upon personality organization and ability to make intelligent use of experience.

Table 8 is in accord with the null hypothesis, since the two groups cannot confidently be regarded as from different statistical distributions. The null hypothesis is likewise supported by teacher ratings (for 38 cases) on persistence at school tasks which showed similar distributions for children from strict and from permissive homes.

If our hypothesis were revised to state that permissive discipline is associated with a moderate degree of persistence, while strict discipline is associated with either unusually persistent or easily discouraged behavior, this *post hoc* revised hypothesis would be supported by the psychological test data of Table 8 at better than the .01 level of significance. The revised hypothesis makes good psychological sense. Since we already know that the

TABLE 8

DIFFERENCES IN PERSISTENCE—EASY DISCOURAGEMENT *

	Boys		*Girls*		*All*	
Rating	*Strict*	*Permissive*	*Strict*	*Permissive*	*Strict*	*Permissive*
4 Very persistent	13	6	8	3	21	9
3 Moderate	3	7	4	9	7	16
1–2 Evade, give up	9	7	7	1	16	8
Total	25	20	19	13	44	33

* Distributions not statistically significant, but association of permissive discipline with moderate rather than high or low persistence is significant ($x^2 = 12.49$) at better than the .01 level of confidence.

children from permissive homes are more inclined to act independently and on their own initiative, we might expect them to make a try at a very difficult problem, but to use their own judgment in giving it up when no progress is made. In contrast, the children accustomed to firm adult control might more readily feel helpless, or, if instructed to keep on trying, persist in their vain efforts. The data on intellectual quality of the continued effort will be helpful in assessing this expectation.

TABLE 9

DIFFERENCES IN EFFECT OF FRUSTRATION ON LEARNING *

	Boys		*Girls*		*All*	
Rating	*Strict*	*Permissive*	*Strict*	*Permissive*	*Strict*	*Permissive*
3 = Improves despite frustration	8	11	6	9	14	20
2 = No marked effect	7	8	7	3	14	11
1 = Deterioration from frustration	7	1	6	1	13	2
Total	22	20	19	13	41	33

* $x^2 = 6.73$. Differences significant at .02 to .05 level.

As the task grew more difficult, some children became frustrated and deteriorated in their learning process. Others continued to study the problem, did not repeat errors, and evidenced growing insight into the difficulty. Type of home discipline does seem to be related to quality of behavior under difficulties, as reported in Table 9. Serious deterioration in intellectual quality of response was found in 13 (32 per cent) of the children with strict up-bringing, but in only 2 (6 per cent) of the children given greater freedom.

The hypothesis that home discipline is unrelated to persistence-discouragement should probably be rejected. The observed differences certainly do not sustain the popular fear that children who are allowed their own way much of the time at home will collapse when faced by difficult tasks. Apparently—with due allowance, again, for the fact that some children from each type of home can be found at every level—there is some tendency for *permissive discipline to foster the type of personality which makes a reasonable effort, continues effective intellectual attack upon problems, but is unlikely to persist indefinitely against odds.* Differences in school work are not significant.

d. Self-Control—Emotional Disintegration

Hypothesis 4. Is there no difference between children from strict and those from permissive homes in the personality dimension of self-control versus emotional disintegration?

Closely related to the quality of intellectual attack upon a difficult problem is the emotional response during frustration. The data in Table 10

TABLE 10

DIFFERENCES IN SELF-CONTROL DURING FRUSTRATION TEST *

	Boys		*Girls*		*All*	
Rating	*Strict*	*Permissive*	*Strict*	*Permissive*	*Strict*	*Permissive*
Undisturbed	10	12	8	6	18	18
Moderate impatience	10	7	9	5	19	12
Extremely upset	4	1	2	2	6	3
Total	24	20	19	13	43	33

* Differences not statistically significant.

come from the psychologist's rating of the child's emotional reactions as the Passalong test became too difficult for him. The null hypothesis is acceptable; observed differences are not statistically significant. A further test of the hypothesis may be made, using the teacher's rating for 37 of the children. Again, as shown in Table 11, differences fall within what might well be expected by chance.

TABLE 11

TEACHER RATING ON SELF-CONTROL *

	Boys		*Girls*		*All*	
Rating	*Strict*	*Permissive*	*Strict*	*Permissive*	*Strict*	*Permissive*
Well balanced; not easily upset	5	2	6	6	11	8
About average	3	2	2	0	5	2
Loses temper, cries, easily upset	7	3	1	0	8	3
Total	15	7	9	6	24	13

* Differences not statistically significant.

Our data do not support the view that children given firm control at home are better able to withstand frustration; neither do they support those who argue that strict parental control interferes with the development of the child's self-control.

e. Energy—Passivity

Hypothesis 5. Is there no difference between children from strict and those from permissive homes in the dimension of energetic versus passive personality?

Three ratings are applicable to testing of this hypothesis. One is a rating by the psychologist of the apparent energy level of the child. Scores range from 1 for "inert, uninvolved" manner during play and testing, through 2 for subdued activity, to 5 for very lively participation. This variable refers to focused personality energy, not to merely physical, muscular activity.

The second rating is derived wholly from the Rorschach performance, taking account of total number of responses, number of content categories, number of wholes, and amount of movement.

The third estimate is based on an exercise in which the child drew a man, a woman, and himself.

Average intercorrelation of the three ratings is .46; predicted reliability for the three combined is .72.

As shown in Table 12, the differences between groups are not significant and the null hypothesis is acceptable.

TABLE 12

DIFFERENCES IN ENERGY—PASSIVITY *

	Boys		*Girls*		*All*	
Rating	*Strict*	*Permissive*	*Strict*	*Permissive*	*Strict*	*Permissive*
Energetic, active productive (13–15)	3	4	3	4	6	8
Above average (11–12)	10	4	8	5	18	9
Average (9–10)	10	3	3	4	13	7
Inert, passive (5–8)	2	9	5	0	7	9
Total	25	20	19	13	44	33

* Differences not statistically significant.

"Activity level" has also been rated by the teachers of 38 of our children. Results are reported in Table 13. High (4 or 5) ratings are given to 15 (63 per cent) of 24 children from strict homes as compared

TABLE 13

DIFFERENCES IN ACTIVITY LEVEL AS RATED BY TEACHERS *

	Boys		*Girls*		*All*	
Rating	*Strict*	*Permis-sive*	*Strict*	*Permis-sive*	*Strict*	*Permis-sive*
Active, energetic 4–5	8	2	7	3	15	5
Average 3	6	3	1	2	7	5
Quiet, inert 1–2	1	3	1	1	2	4
Total	15	8	9	6	24	14

* $x^2 = 4.20$. P between .02 and .05.

with only 5 of 14 children (36 per cent) from permissive homes. Differences between the two distributions are significant at a probability level between $P = .02$ and $P = .05$; with higher ratings for the children from stricter homes. That pupils from strictly disciplined homes are seen by teachers as more energetic and active may be related to their more ready acceptance of teacher direction. This point came out earlier in connection with teacher ratings on "independence." The sex difference again raises a question about what the typical teacher means by "energetic." High ratings on activity and energy were assigned to 67 per cent of the girls but to only 43 per cent of the boys.

Neither the data from the psychological tests nor those from the classroom would support the view that strict home discipline typically represses impulses to such an extent as to make children inactive. In the test situation no difference is apparent; at school the well-disciplined children appear, on the whole, more active along approved lines.

f. Creativity—Conformity

Hypothesis 6. Is there no difference between children from strict and those from permissive homes in the personality dimension of creativity versus conformity?

Five measures of this variable are available. One is based on the child's behavior, ranging from free and imaginative to stereotyped and monotonous, during a free-play period. A second has been similarly observed during a period of play with a full family of dolls. The third estimates originality and imagination in stories composed as responses to *CAT* and *TAT* pictures. The fourth comes from Rorschach responses and the fifth from human figure-drawing. The average intercorrelation of these measures is .53 and the predicted reliability for the combined rating is .85.

TABLE 14

DIFFERENCES IN CREATIVITY—CONFORMITY *

	Boys		*Girls*		*All*	
Rating	*Strict*	*Permissive*	*Strict*	*Permissive*	*Strict*	*Permissive*
Highly creative, imaginative, spontaneous, original	1	6	1	5	2	11
Above average	12	5	6	1	18	6
Below average	8	4	8	7	16	11
Stereotyped, conventional, restricted	4	6	4	0	8	6
Total	25	21	19	13	44	34

* $x^2 = 29.35$. $P < .01$.

The differences shown in Table 14 are the most impressive of any in our comparisons, and compel rejection of the null hypothesis. *High creativity characterizes* 11 (33 per cent) *of the children brought up with unusual freedom, but only* 2 (5 per cent) *of those from strict homes.* The more firmly disciplined children are most apt to be found near the middle of the range in this variable.

g. Friendliness—Hostility

Hypothesis 7. Is there no difference between children from strict and those from permissive homes along the dimension of friendly versus hostile feelings toward others?

Our psychological testing yields four projective indications of inner hostility. One is based on observation of free play with dolls. Hostile contacts or avoidance of contacts is rated 1; friendly interaction is rated 5.

The second is based on the *TAT* and *CAT* stories. The low end of the scale (rating 1) is assigned to stories of violent conflict, death, and destruction. High scores represent stories of friendly interaction.

The third rating is based on such Rorschach signs as content items interpreted as aggressive weapons, mutilated human or animal bodies, and aggressive or hostile M or FM.

The fourth has been drawn from analysis of the figure-drawing test and responses during the drawing.

Intercorrelations among these tests range from .50 to .74, averaging .60; the predicted reliability for the four combined is .87—the highest of any of our measures.

Hostility versus friendliness scores of the two groups are compared in Table 15. The null hypothesis should be rejected. *More hostility is evident*

TABLE 15

DIFFERENCES IN FRIENDLINESS—HOSTILITY *

	Boys		*Girls*		*All*	
Rating	*Strict*	*Permissive*	*Strict*	*Permissive*	*Strict*	*Permissive*
High friendliness, little hostility (16 and over)	1	2	0	4	1	6
Above average friendliness; below average hostility (Scores 13–15)	5	8	8	6	13	14
Above average hostility (Scores 10–12)	12	8	10	1	22	9
High degree of aggressive hostility (Scores 9 and lower)	7	4	1	1	8	5
Total	25	22	19	12	44	34

* $x^2 = 10.64$ (Yates correction). $P < .02$.

in those children who have been strictly disciplined; more positive feelings toward others are expressed by children whose parents have been permissive; these differences are consistent through the distribution and are statistically significant. At the same time, it should be remembered that neither group has a complete monopoly on positive, friendly feelings toward others or on inner hostility.

Reactions to frustration on the Passalong test make possible another rating which has in it a high component of hostility for some children. Half of the *TAT* story-completion test was administered before the frustrating experience of failure on the too-difficult block test. The other half was given immediately after the somewhat annoying defeat. For a few children, the consequence was that the stories in the latter part of the test were briefer, the child was less cooperative and gave more evidence of hostility. This behavior characterized 6 (15 per cent) of the 41 children from strict homes; but only 1 (3 per cent) of the 32 children from permissive homes. This difference is not statistically significant, but its direction is in accord with the evidence from Table 15 indicating that strict discipline does leave a residue of inner hostility.

h. Security—Anxiety

Hypothesis 8. Is there no difference between children from strict and those from permissive homes in the personality dimension of security versus anxiety?

Five different ratings compose our measure of anxiety. One is the psychologist's impression of the overtly confident or insecure behavior of the child. Three are based on projective tests: one on Card 9 of the *CAT*, one on the Rorschach, and one on the figure-drawing test. The fifth measure is the anxiety evident during failure on the Passalong test. These five measures have an average intercorrelation of .33; the combined index would have a predicted reliability of .71 which is not high but would suffice if the groups turn out to be markedly different.

TABLE 16

DIFFERENCES IN SECURITY—ANXIETY *

	Boys		*Girls*		*All*	
Rating	*Strict*	*Permissive*	*Strict*	*Permissive*	*Strict*	*Permissive*
Secure, relaxed (16–19)	1	4	4	3	5	7
Less than average anxiety (14–15)	10	6	5	7	15	13
More than average anxiety (12–13)	8	7	7	1	15	8
Anxious, tense (7–11)	6	4	3	2	9	6
Total	25	21	19	13	44	34

* $x^2 = 1.81$. Differences not significant.

As shown in Table 16 the two groups are not clearly distinguished. The null hypothesis is acceptable. Half a dozen children from each type of discipline show marked evidence of anxiety—another half-dozen from each category behave in an easy, secure manner. What makes for anxiety in a child must be something other than unusually strict or unusually lax parental control.

i. Happiness—Sadness

Hypothesis 9. Is there no difference between children from strict and those from permissive homes in the personality dimension of happiness versus sadness?

Three measures are related to general level of happiness. One is a rating of the overt manner and apparent mood of the child during his play and testing periods. Scores range from 5 for the most euphoric to 1 for the most depressed. A second measure is derived by analysis of the imaginative stories given in response to *CAT* and *TAT* pictures. Predominantly optimistic and enjoyable events result in high ratings; stories in which distress, sadness, and unhappiness come to the leading figures result in a low score. The third measure is based upon Rorschach test responses. Predominant use of black, and perception of figures as torn and broken, are used as indicators of depression.

Intercorrelations among the several indices (except for overt behavior and the Rorschach which correlate .54) are low, averaging .28 and giving a combined predictive reliability of .54.[4]

TABLE 17

DIFFERENCES IN HAPPINESS—SADNESS *

	Boys		Girls		All	
Rating	*Strict*	*Permissive*	*Strict*	*Permissive*	*Strict*	*Permissive*
Unusually happy, optimistic, cheerful, buoyant	2	6	4	3	6	9
Average or above	18	7	11	8	29	15
Below average; sad, depressed, melancholy	5	8	4	2	9	10
Total	25	21	19	13	44	34

* Differences not statistically significant.

Results, shown in Table 17, conform to the null hypothesis. While our data show a slightly larger proportion of permissive discipline subjects in both the "happy" and the "unhappy" categories, the differences are unreliable.

E. Summary

Forty-four children brought up in good, loving, but strictly disciplined homes are compared with 34 children from the same community and also brought up in good, loving homes but with an extraordinary degree of permissiveness. Two periods of psychological testing, supplemented (in 38 cases) by teacher ratings, have yielded measures of nine dimensions of personality. On three of the nine, no statistically significant difference is found: these are the dimensions of self-control, inner security, and happiness. Factors making for anxiety, emotional disorganization, and un-

[4] This reliability might have been increased slightly by omission of the picture-story rating, but it seemed better to include all available indications of euphoria or sadness. One test might bring out a response different from the others but still pertinent to an estimate of general level of euphoria.

happiness are found about equally often under either type of home discipline. No difference in activity and energy level was observed during the psychological testing, but teacher ratings indicate higher activity level of an approved sort, at school for the children accustomed to stricter discipline.

On persistence, teachers observe no differences, but on a psychological test children from strict homes are more apt to fall in extreme categories, being either unusually persistent or very easily discouraged. A moderate persistence is more characteristic of the children from permissive homes. These children maintain a better quality of intellectual activity under difficulty than do the children from strict homes.

On the four remaining variables (which are also those most reliably measured, with predicted *r*'s from .80 to .87) significant differences in each instance are in favor of the children from permissive homes. Greater freedom for the child is clearly associated with: (*a*) more initiative and independence (except, perhaps, at school tasks); (*b*) better socialization and cooperation; (*c*) less inner hostility and more friendly feelings toward others; and (*d*) a higher level of spontaneity, originality, and creativity.

None of the personality differences applies to all cases; some children from strict and some from permissive homes may be found at every level on every characteristic tested. It is impressive, however, to find no clear personality advantage associated in general with strict discipline in a good home. Where differences do emerge, these are consistently to the credit of the more permissive upbringing. This study cannot distinguish the extent to which the advantages associated with permissiveness are due to that procedure alone and the extent to which more permissive parents may convey hereditary or cultural assets with which the permissive attitudes happen to be correlated.

References

1. Anderson, J. P., *The Relationships Between Certain Aspects of Parental Behavior and Attitudes of Junior High School Pupils* (New York: Teachers College, Columbia University, 1940).
2. Ayer, M. E., and R. Bernreuter, "A Study of the Relationship Between Discipline and Personality in Young Children," *Journal of Genetic Psychology,* Vol. 50 (1937), pp. 165-170.
3. Baldwin, A. L., "Socialization and the Parent-Child Relationship," *Child Development,* Vol. 19 (1948), pp. 127-136.
4. Carpenter, J., and P. Eisenberg, "Some Relationships Between Family Background and Personality," *Journal of Psychology,* Vol. 6 (1938), pp. 115-136.

5. Fisher, R. A., *Statistical Methods for Research Workers,* 7th ed. (Edinburgh: Oliver and Boyd, 1938).
6. Hattwick, Berta W., "Interrelations Between the Preschool Child's Behavior and Certain Factors in the Home," *Child Development,* Vol. 7 1936), pp. 200-226.
7. ———, and Margaret Stowell, "The Relation of Parental Over-Attentiveness to Children's Work Habits and Social Adjustment in Kindergarten and the First Six Grades of School," *Journal of Educational Research,* Vol. 30 (1936), pp. 162-176.
8. Heinicke, C., and B. B. Whiting, *Bibliographies on Personality and Social Development of the Child* (New York: Social Science Research Council Pamphlet No. 10, 1953).
9. Lafore, Gertrude, "Practices of Parents in Dealing with Pre-school Children," *Child Development Monographs,* Vol. 31 (1945), pp. 3-150.
10. Myers, T. R., *Intrafamily Relationships and Pupil Adjustment* (New York: Teachers College, Columbia University, 1935).
11. Orlansky, H., "Infant Care and Personality," *Psychological Bulletin,* Vol. 46 (1949), pp. 1-48.
12. Radke, Marian J., *The Relation of Parental Authority to Children's Behavior and Attitudes* (Minneapolis: U. of Minn., 1946).
13. Sewell, W. H., "Infant Training and the Personality of the Child," *American Journal of Sociology,* Vol. 58 (1952), pp. 150-157.
14. Shoben, E. J., Jr., "The Assessment of Parental Attitudes in Relation to Child Adjustment," *Genetic Psychology Monographs,* Vol. 39 (1949), pp. 101-148.
15. Symonds, P. M., *Psychology of Parent-Child Relationships* (New York: Appleton, 1939).
16. Watson, G., "A Comparison of the Effects of Law Versus Strict Home Discipline," *Journal of Social Psychology,* Vol. 5 (1934), pp. 102-105.
17. Whiting, J. W. M., and I. L. Child, *Child Training and Personality* (New Haven: Yale, 1953).
18. Wolfenstein, Martha, "Trends in Infant Care," *American Journal of Orthopsychiatry,* Vol. 33 (1953), pp. 120-130.
19. Wright, G. O., "Projection and Displacement: A Cross-Cultural Study of Folktale Aggression," *Journal of Abnormal and Social Psychology,* Vol. 49 (1954), pp. 523-528.

QUESTIONS FOR DISCUSSION

Maslow Article

1. Examine carefully the need hierarchy suggested by Maslow. Do you agree with the "order" of his five identified needs? Why or why not?
2. What role does gratification play in Maslow's theory?
3. How can one *know* he has reached the self-actualization stage?
4. What implications does this theory have for teachers? What practical value does the theory have for you as a person?

Brownfain Article

1. In what ways is self-esteem related to stability or instability of the self-concept?
2. Why would a person who lacks self-esteem be more likely to be "situation dominated" than one with higher self-esteem?

McKee and Sherriffs Article

1. To what extent do men and women react favorably to what they believe the opposite sex wants them to be?
2. Do you suppose the results would have been different if the subjects were married rather than unmarried? Why?
3. How would you explain the discrepancy between college women's ideals for themselves and the attributes they say they actually express? Would you say that this is unique only to college women? Why or why not?

Watson Article

1. What are the essential differences between children from strict versus permissive homes?
2. Although the author points out clear advantages of permissive over strict child-rearing practices, there are nonetheless risks to being a permissive parent. What are some of these risks? Would you be willing to take them? Why or why not?
3. In terms of initiative and creativity, what brand of child-rearing is better? Why?
4. From the standpoint of one's total development and future well-being, would you advocate more strictness or less permissiveness? Why?

Part VI
growth processes and the self

1. Youth and the life cycle

ERIK H. ERIKSON

Reprinted from *Children,* Vol. 7, No. 2 (Mar.-Apr., 1960), by permission of the author and the Children's Bureau, Department of Health, Education, and Welfare.

The self is formed as one progresses through successive stages of the life cycle. In the following interview article, Erikson expands on his eight "stages of psychosocial development," which are actually eight individual crisis periods, each of which must be successfully resolved before one can effectively meet the subsequent psychosocial stage. Erikson's eight stages have proved to be an extremely helpful framework for understanding the dynamics of growth and self-development.

Question: *Are there any points about your concepts of psychosocial development which you would now like to stress in the light of what you have heard about how they have been interpreted during the past decade in the training of professional persons and through them of parents and future parents?*

Yes, I am grateful for the opportunity of making a few observations on the reception of these concepts. You emphasize their influence on teaching in various fields; let me pick out a few misunderstandings.

I should confess to you here how it all started. It was on a drive in the countryside with Mrs. Erikson that I became a bit expansive, telling her about a kind of ground plan in the human life cycle, which I seemed to discern in life histories. After a while she began to write, urging me just to go on; she had found my "plan" immediately convincing. Afterward, a number of audiences of different professional backgrounds had that same sense of conviction—so much so that I (and others) became somewhat uneasy: after all, these psychosocial signposts are hardly *concepts* yet, even if the whole plan represents a valid *conception,* one which suggests a great deal of work.

What Mrs. Erikson and I subsequently offered to the White House Conference of 1950 was a kind of worksheet, which has, indeed, been used by others as well as myself in scientific investigation, and well integrated in a few textbooks. But its "convincingness" has also led to oversimplifications. Let me tell you about a few.

There has been a tendency here and there to turn the eight stages into a sort of rosary of achievement, a device for counting the fruits of each stage—trust, autonomy, initiative, and so forth—as though each were achieved as a permanent trait. People of this bent are apt to leave out the negative counterparts of each stage, as if the healthy personality had permanently conquered these hazards. The fact is that the healthy personality must reconquer them continuously in the same way that the body's metabolism resists decay. All that we learn are certain fundamental means and mechanisms for retaining and regaining mastery. Life is a sequence not only of developmental but also of accidental crises. It is hardest to take when both types of crisis coincide.

The Eight Stages in the Life Cycle of Man

"Personality," Erikson has written, "can be said to develop according to steps predetermined in the human organism's readiness to be driven toward, to be aware of, and to interact with a widening social radius, beginning with a dim image of a mother and ending with an image of mankind. . . ." Following are the steps he has identified in man's psychosocial development, and the special crises they bring. In presenting them, he has emphasized that while the struggle between the negatives and positives in each crisis must be fought through successfully if the next developmental stage is to be reached, no victory is completely or forever won.

I. Infancy: TRUST VERSUS MISTRUST

The first "task" of the infant is to develop "the cornerstone of a healthy personality," a basic sense of trust—in himself and in his environment. This comes from a feeling of inner goodness derived from "the mutual regulation of his receptive capacities with the maternal techniques of provision" [1]—a quality of care that transmits a sense of trustworthiness and meaning. The danger, most acute in the second half of the first year, is that discontinuities in care may increase a natural sense of loss, as the child gradually recognizes his separateness from his mother, to a basic sense of mistrust that may last through life.

II. Early childhood: autonomy versus shame and doubt

With muscular maturation the child experiments with holding on and letting go and begins to attach enormous value to his autonomous will. The danger here is the development of a deep sense of shame and doubt if he is deprived of the opportunity to learn to develop his will as he learns his "duty," and therefore learns to expect defeat in any battle of wills with those who are bigger and stronger.

III. Play age: initiative versus guilt

In this stage the child's imagination is greatly expanded because of his increased ability to move around freely and to communicate. It is an age of intrusive activity, avid curiosity, and consuming fantasies which lead to feelings of guilt and anxiety. It is also the stage of the establishment of conscience. If this tendency to feel guilty is "overburdened by all-too-eager adults" the child may develop a deep-seated conviction that he is essentially bad, with a resultant stifling of initiative or a conversion of his moralism to vindictiveness.

IV. School age: industry versus inferiority

The long period of sexual latency before puberty is the age when the child wants to learn how to do and make things with others. In learning to accept instruction and to win recognition by producing "things" he opens the way for the capacity of work enjoyment. The danger in this period is the development of a sense of inadequacy and inferiority in a child who does not receive recognition for his efforts.

V. Adolescence: identity versus identity diffusion

The physiological revolution that comes with puberty—rapid body growth and sexual maturity—forces the young person to question "all sameness and continuities relied on earlier" and to "refight many of the earlier battles." The developmental task is to integrate childhood identifications "with the basic biological drives, native endowment, and the opportunities offered in social roles." The danger is that identity diffusion, temporarily unavoidable in this period of physical and psychological upheaval, may result in a permanent inability to "take hold" or, because of youth's tendency to total commitment, in the fixation in the young person of a negative identity, a devoted attempt to become what parents, class, or community do not want him to be.

VI. YOUNG ADULTHOOD:
INTIMACY VERSUS ISOLATION

Only as a young person begins to feel more secure in his identity is he able to establish intimacy with himself (with his inner life) and with others, both in friendships and eventually in a love-based mutually satisfying sexual relationship with a member of the opposite sex. A person who cannot enter wholly into an intimate relationship because of the fear of losing his identity may develop a deep sense of isolation.

VII. ADULTHOOD:
GENERATIVITY VERSUS SELF-ABSORPTION

Out of the intimacies of adulthood grows generativity—the mature person's interest in establishing and guiding the next generation. The lack of this results in self-absorption and frequently in a "pervading sense of stagnation and interpersonal impoverishment."

VIII. SENESCENCE:
INTEGRITY VERSUS DISGUST

The person who has achieved a satisfying intimacy with other human beings and who has adapted to the triumphs and disappointments of his generative activities as parent and coworker reaches the end of life with a certain ego integrity—an acceptance of his own responsibility for what his life is and was and of its place in the flow of history. . . .

In each crisis, under favorable conditions, the positive is likely to outbalance the negative, and each reintegration builds strength for the next crisis. But the negative is always with us to some degree in the form of a measure of infantile anxiety, fear of abandonment—a residue of immaturity carried throughout life, which is perhaps the price man has to pay for a childhood long enough to permit him to be the learning and the teaching animal, and thus to achieve his particular mastery of reality.

You may be interested to know that further clinical research has indi-

[1] Erik H. Erikson, "Growth and Crises of the 'Healthy Personality,'" Symposium on the Healthy Personality (New York: Josiah Macy, Jr., Foundation, 1950).

cated that our dream life often depicts a recovery of mastery along the lines of these stages. Moreover, nurses have observed that any adult who undergoes serious surgery has to repeat the battle with these nemeses in the process of recovery. A person moves up and down the scale of maturity, but if his ego has gained a positive balance during his developmental crises, the downward movements will be less devastating than if the balance, at one stage or another, was in the negative.

Of all the positive aspects mentioned, trust seems to have been the most convincing—so convincing, in fact, that some discussions never reach a consideration of the other stages. I don't mean to detract from the obvious importance of trust as the foundation of the development of a healthy personality. A basic sense of trust in living as such, developed in infancy through the reciprocal relationship of child and mother, is essential to winning the positive fruits of all the succeeding crises in the life cycle: maybe this is what Christmas, with its Madonna images, conveys to us. Yet, it is the nature of human life that each succeeding crisis takes place within a widened social radius where an ever-larger number of significant persons have a bearing on the outcome. There is in childhood, first, the maternal person, then the parental combination, then the basic family and other instructing adults. Youth demands "confirmation" from strangers who hold to a design of life; and later, the adult needs challenges from mates and partners, and even from his growing children and expanding works, in order to continue to grow himself, And all of these relationships must be imbedded in an "ethos," a cultural order, to guide the individual's course.

In our one-family culture (supported by pediatricians and psychiatrists who exclusively emphasize the mother-child relationship) we tend to lose sight of the fact that other people besides parents are important to youth. Too often we ask only where a given youth came from and what he once was, and not also where he was going, and who was ready to receive him and his intentions and his specific gifts. Thus we have movements to punish parents for the transgressions of their children, ignoring all the other persons and environmental factors that entered into the production of a young person's unacceptable behavior and failed to offer support to his positive search.

Another way in which the life cycle theory has been oversimplified is in the omission of stages which do not fit into the preconceived ideas of the person who is adopting or adapting the theory. Thus a large organization devoted to parenthood distributed a list of the stages but omitted *integrity versus despair*—the problem of senescence. This is too easy a way to dispose of grandparents; it robs life of an inescapable final step; and, of course, it defeats this whole conception of an intrinsic order in the life cycle.

This kind of omission ignores the "cogwheeling" of infantile and adult stages—the fact that each further stage of growth in a given individual is not only dependent upon the relatively successful completion of his own previous stages, but also on the completion of the subsequent stages in those other individuals with whom he interacts and whom he accepts as models.

Finally, I should point to the fact that what my psychoanalytic colleagues warned me of most energetically has, on occasion, come to pass: even sincere workers have chosen to ignore my emphasis on the intrinsic relation of the psychosocial to the psychosexual stages which form the basis of much of Freud's work.

All of these misuses, however, may be to a large extent the fault of my choice of words. The use of simple, familiar words like "trust" and "mistrust" apparently leads people to assume that they know "by feel" what the theory is all about. Perhaps this semantic problem would have been avoided if I had used Latin terms, which call for definitions.

I may point out, however, that I originally suggested my terms as a basis for discussions—discussions led by people who have an idea of the interrelatedness of all aspects of human development. For the eight stages of psychosocial development are, in fact, inextricably entwined in and derived from the various stages of psychosexual development that were described by Freud, as well as from the child's stages of physical, motor, and cognitive development. Each type of development affects the other and is affected by it. Thus, I feel that discussants would do well to study each key word in its origins, in its usages in various periods and regions, and in other languages. Simple words that touch upon universal human values have their counterpart in every living language, and can become vehicles of understanding at international conferences.

Incidentally, I made up one new word because I thought it was needed. To me, "generativity" described the chief characteristic of the mature adult. It was turned into a comfortable, if inaccurate, homespun word before it ever left the Fact-Finding Committee of 1950. I had deliberately chosen "generativity" rather than "parenthood," or "creativity," because these narrowed the matter down to a biological and an artistic issue instead of describing the deep absorption in guiding the young or in helping to create a new world for the young, which is a mark of maturity in parents and nonparents, working people and "creative" people alike.

Enough of this faultfinding! But it *is* interesting to see what can happen to new ideas; and you *did* ask me.

Question: *During the past 10 years you have been treating and studying mentally ill young people at a public clinic in a low-income area in Pitts-*

burgh and at a private, comparatively expensive, mental hospital in the Berkshires. Have you found any common denominator in the disturbances of these patients—from such opposite walks of life—that would seem to point to any special difficulty harassing the young people of our land today?

Since 1950, I have concentrated on the life histories of sick young people in late adolescence and early adulthood primarily in order to study one of the crises magnified, as it were, with the clinical microscope. I think that our initial formulations of the identity crisis have been clinically validated and much refined.

Many of these sick young people in their late teens and early twenties had failed during their adolescence to win out in the struggle against identity confusion. They were suffering so seriously from a feeling of being (or, indeed, wanting to be) "nobody" that they were withdrawing from reality, and in some cases even attempting to withdraw from life itself: in other words, they were regressing to a position where trust had to be reinstated. Their malaise proved to be related to the same sense of diffuseness which drives other young adults to incessant and sometimes delinquent activity—an effort to show the world, including themselves, that they are "somebody" even if deep down they do not believe it.

In the meantime, of course, the identity issue has been taken up by many writers and by some magazines, almost in the form of a slogan. We are prone to think that we have cornered an issue when we have found a name for it, and to have resolved it when we have found something to blame. So now we blame "the changing world."

Actually, there is no reason why youth should not participate with enthusiasm in radical change; young people are freer for change than we are. The bewildering thing for them must be that we now complain about change, having eagerly caused it ourselves with inventions and discoveries; that we seem to have played at change rather than to have planned it. If we had the courage of our inventions, if we would grow into the world we have helped to create, and would give youth coresponsibility in it, I think that all the potential power of the identity crisis would serve a better world than we can now envisage.

Let me say a word about identity, or rather about what it is not. The young person seeking an identity does not go around saying, even to himself, "Who am I?" as an editorial in a national magazine suggested last year's college graduates were doing on their way home. Nor does the person with a secure sense of identity usually stop to think or to brag about the fact that he has this priceless possession, and of what it consists. He simply feels and acts predominantly in tune with himself, his capacities, and his opportunities; and he has the inner means and finds the outer ways to recover from experiences which impair this feeling. He knows where he fits (or knowingly prefers not to fit) into present conditions. . . .

This sense of a coincidence between inner resources, traditional values, and opportunities of action is derived from a fusion of slowly grown, unconscious personality processes—and contemporary social forces. It has its earliest beginnings in the infant's first feelings of affirmation by maternal recognition and is nurtured on the quality and consistency of the parental style of upbringing. Thus identity is in a sense an outgrowth of all the earlier stages; but the crucial period for its development to maturity comes with the adolescent crisis.

Every adolescent is apt to go through some serious struggle at one time or another. The crises of earlier stages may return in some form as he seeks to free himself from the alignments of childhood because of both his own eagerness for adulthood and the pressures of society. For a while he may distrust what he once trusted implicity; may be ashamed of his body, and doubtful of his future. He experiments, looking for affirmation and recognition from his friends and from the adults who mean most to him. Unconsciously, he revamps his repertory of childhood identifications, reviving some and repudiating others. He goes in for extremes—total commitments and total repudiation. His struggle is to make sense out of what has gone before in relation to what he now perceives the world to be, in an effort to find a persistent sameness in himself and a persistent sharing of some kind of essential character with others.

Far from considering this process to be a kind of maturational malaise, a morbid egocentricity of which adolescents must be "cured," we must recognize in it the search for new values, the willingness to serve loyalties which prove to be "true" (in any number of spiritual, scientific, technical, political, philosophical, and personal meanings of "truth") and thus a prime force in cultural rejuvenation.

The strengths a young person finds in adults at this time—their willingness to let him experiment, their eagerness to confirm him at his best, their consistency in correcting his excesses, and the guidance they give him—will codetermine whether or not he eventually makes order out of necessary inner confusion and applies himself to the correction of disordered conditions. He needs freedom to choose, but not so much freedom that he cannot, in fact, make a choice.

In some adolescents, in some cultures, in some historical epochs this crisis is minimal; in others it holds real perils for both the individual and society. Some individuals, particularly those with a weak preparation in their preceding developmental crises, succumb to it with the formation of neuroses and psychoses. Others try to resolve it through adherence—

often temporary—to radical kinds of religious, political, artistic, or criminal ideologies.

A few fight the battle alone and, after a prolonged period of agony characterized by erratic mood swings and unpredictable and apparently dangerous behavior, become the spokesmen of new directions. Their sense of impending danger forces them to mobilize their capacities to new ways of thinking and doing which have meaning, at the same time, for themselves and their times. In my book *Young Man Luther* I have tried to show how identity is related to ideology and how the identity struggle of one intense young genius produced a new person, a new faith, a new kind of man, and a new era.

I think I chose to write about Luther and his time because there are many analogies between our time and his, although today the problems which beset all historical crises are global and, as it were, semifinal in character. Today, throughout the world, the increasing pace of technological change has encroached upon traditional group solidarities and on their ability to transmit a sense of cosmic wholeness and technological planfulness to the young.

To me one of the most disturbing aspects of our technological culture is the imbalance between passive stimulation and active outlet in the pleasures that are sanctioned for young people. With the passing of the western frontier and the accelerated appearance of automatic gadgets, young people have become increasingly occupied with passive pursuits which require little participation of mind or body—being conveyed rapidly through space by machines and watching violent fantasies at the movies or on television—without the possibility of matching the passive experience with active pursuits. When an adolescent substitutes passivity for the adventure and activity which his muscular development and sexual drives require, there is always the danger of explosion—and I think that this accounts for much of the explosive, unexpected, and delinquent acts on the part of even our "nice" young people.

This is probably why "Westerns," always on the borderline of the criminal and the lawful, capture the passive imagination of a youth which has traditionally substituted identification with the rugged individualist—the pioneer who ventures into the unknown—for commitment to a political ideology; and which now finds itself confronted with increasing demands for standardization, uniformity, and conformity to the rituals of a status-convention. While the national prototype has historically been based on readiness for change, the range of possibilities of what one might choose to be and of opportunities to make a change [has] narrowed. To this has been added most recently the rude shaking of the once "eternal" image of our Nation's superiority in productivity and technical ingenuity through the appearance of Sputnik and its successors.

Thus one might say the complexity of the adolescent state and the confusion of the times meet head on.

However, I believe that the "confusion" derives from a hypocritical denial of our true position, both in regard to obvious dangers and true resources. When youth is permitted to see its place in a crisis, it will, out of its very inner dangers, gain the strength to meet the demands of the time.

Clinical experience with young people has, it is true, verified that combination of inner and outer dangers which explains aggravated identity crises. On the other hand, it has convinced me and my colleagues, even in hospital work, of the surprising resources which young people can muster if their social responsibilities are called upon in a total environment of psychological understanding.

Question: *Does this kind of confusion have anything to do with juvenile delinquency?*

I would not want to add here to the many claims concerning distinct and isolated causes of juvenile delinquency. But I would like to stress one contributing factor: the confused attitudes of adults—both laymen and professionals—toward the young people whom we, with a mixture of condescension and fear, call teenagers.

Except perhaps in some rare instances of congenital defects resulting in a low capacity to comprehend values, juvenile delinquents are made, not born; and we adults make them. Here, I am not referring to their parents exclusively. True, many parents, because of their own personalities and backgrounds, are not able to give their children a chance for a favorable resolution of the identity crisis. Nor am I referring to the failure of society at large to correct those blights on the social scene—such as overcrowded slums and inequality of opportunities for minority groups—which make it impossible for tens of thousands of young people to envisage an identity in line with the prevailing success-and-status ideology.

Rather I am referring to the attitudes of adults—in the press, in court, and in some professional and social institutions—which push the delinquent young person into a "negative identity," a prideful and stubborn acceptance of himself as a juvenile delinquent—and this at a time when his experimentation with available roles will make him exquisitely vulnerable (although he may not admit or even know it) to the opinions of the representatives of society. When a young person is adjudicated as a potential criminal because he has taken a girl for a ride in somebody else's car (which he intended to abandon, not to appropriate), he may well decide, half consciously, of course, but none the less with finality, that to have any real identity at all he must be what he obviously *can* be—a delinquent. The scolding of young people in public for the indiscretions they have committed, with the expectation that they show remorse, often ignores all the factors in their histories that force them into a delinquent kind of experimentation. It is certainly no help toward a positive identity formation.

In his insistence on holding on to an active identity, even if it is temporarily a "negative" one from the point of view of society, the delinquent is sometimes potentially healthier than the young person who withdraws into a neurotic or a psychotic state. Some delinquents, perhaps, in their determination to be themselves at all costs and under terrible conditions have more strength and a greater potential for contributing to the richness of the national life than do many excessively conforming or neurotically defeatist members of their generation, who have given up youth's prerogatives to dream and to dare. We must study this problem until we can overcome the kind of outraged bewilderment which makes the adult world seem untrustworthy to youth and hence may seem to justify the choice of a delinquent identity.

Actually, transitory delinquency, as well as other forms of antisocial or asocial behavior, often may be what I have called a *psychosocial moratorium*—a period of delay in the assumption of adult commitment. Some youths need a period of relaxed expectations, of guidance to the various possibilities for positive identification through opportunities to participate in adult work, or even of introspection and experimentation—none of which can be replaced by either moralistic punishment or condescending forgiveness.

Question: *The theme of the 1960 White House Conference on Children and Youth charges the Conference with studying and understanding "the values and ideals of our society" in its efforts "to promote opportunties for children and youth to realize their full potential for a creative life in freedom and dignity." On the basis of the scheme which you presented to us in 1950, couuld you add a word about how these values, once identified, can be transmitted in a way that will insure their incorporation into the value systems of the young?*

Like every other aspect of maturity the virtues which we expect in a civilized human being grow in stages as the child develops from an infant to an adult. What is expected of a child at any time must be related to his total maturation and level of egostrength, which are related to his motor, cognitive, psychosexual, and psychosocial stages. You can't expect total obedience from a two-year-old who must test a growing sense of autonomy, nor total truth from a four-year-old involved in the creative but often guilt-ridden fantasies of the oedipal stage.

It would be in line with the course of other historical crises if in our nation today a certain sense of moral weakness were producing a kind of frantic wish to enforce moral strength in our youth with punitive or purely exhortative measures.

Today, a sense of crisis has been aggravated by the long cold war and the sudden revelation of the technical strength of a supposedly "backward" rival. We are wondering whether we have made our children strong enough for living in such an unpredictably dangerous world. Some people, who suddenly realize that they have not been responsible guardians of all the nation's young, now wonder whether they should have beaten moral strength into them or preached certain absolute values more adamantly.

No period, however, can afford to go back on its advances in values and in knowledge, and I trust that the 1960 White House Conference will find a way to integrate our knowledge of personality development with our national values, necessities, and resources. What we need is not a plan whereby relatively irresponsible adults can enforce morality in their children, but rather national insistence on a more *responsible* morality on the part of adults, paired with an *informal* attitude toward the *development* of moral values in children. Values can only be fostered gradually by adults who have a clear conception of what to expect and what not to expect of the child as, at each stage, he comes to understand new segments of reality and of himself, and who are firm about what they are sure they *may* expect.

It must be admitted that psychiatry has added relatively little to the understanding of morality, except perhaps by delineating the great dangers of moralistic attitudes and measures which convince the child only of the adult's greater executive power, not of his actual moral power or true superiority. To this whole question, I can, on the basis of my own work, only indicate that the psychosocial stages discussed in 1950 seem to open up the possibility of studying the way in which in each stage of growth the healthy child's developmental drives dispose him toward a certain set of qualities which are the necessary fundaments of a responsible character: in *infancy,* hope and drive; in *early childhood,* will and control; in the *play age* purpose and direction; in the *school age,* skill and method; and in *adolescence,* devotion and fidelity. The development of these basic qualities in children, however, depends on the corresponding development in adults of qualities related to: in *young adulthood,* love, work, and affiliation; in *adulthood,* care, parenthood, and production; and in *old age,* "wisdom" and responsible renunciation.

Now I have given you another set of nice words, throwing to the winds my own warning regarding the way they can be misunderstood and misused. Let me point out, therefore, that I consider these basic virtues in line with our advancing psychoanalytic ego-psychology, on the one hand, and without advancing knowledge of psychosocial evolution, on the other, and that the conception behind this list can only be studied in the context of advancing science. I will discuss this further in a forthcoming publication, but I mention it now because I thought I owed you a reference to the way in which my contribution of 1950 has gradually led me in the direction of the great problem of the anchoring of virtue in human nature as it has evolved in our universe.

We ought to regard the breaking of a child's spirit—by cruel punishment, by senseless spoiling, by persistent hypocrisy—as a sin against humanity. Yet today we have back-to-the-woodshed movements. Last year in the legislature of one of our greatest states a bill was introduced to allow corporal punishment in the public schools and was lauded by part of the press. This gave the Soviets a chance to declare publicly against corporal punishment, implying that they are not sufficiently scared by their own youth to go back on certain considered principles in the rearing of the young. Actually, I think that we stand with the rest of the civilized world on the principle that if adult man reconsiders his moral position in the light of historical fact, and in the light of his most advanced knowledge of human nature, he can afford, in relation to his children, to rely on a forbearance which step by step will bring the best *out* of them. . . .

2. The stability of the self-concept in adolescence [1]

Mary Engel [2]

Reprinted from the *Journal of Abnormal and Social Psychology,* Vol. 58 (1959), 211-215, by permission of the author and the American Psychological Association.

How stable is self-concept in adolescence? What relationships are there between stability and quality of self-concept? How is a high or low self-concept related to stability of self-concept over a two-year period? You will want to compare this study with Brownfain's article in Part V.

Recent theory and research point to the importance of the self-concept in understanding and predicting constancies as well as changes in behavior (3, 10, 12). It is generally believed that an individual's concept of himself achieves a rather high degree of organization during the course of development and comes to resist change once self-differentiation and self-definition have taken place (9). As yet it is not known by what age the process of self-definition reaches stability. While we know that the concept of self remains relatively stable, even over extended periods of time, in young adults (12), and while there are a number of theoretical and partially

---

[1] Based upon a dissertation submitted in partial fulfillment of the requirements for the Ph.D. degree, George Peabody College. The writer wishes to express her gratitude to Nicholas Hobbs and Julius Seeman for their guidance. She is also indebted to the Vanderbilt-Peabody Self Concept Research Group for helpful suggestions and comments.

[2] Written while USPHS postdoctoral, clinical research fellow at the Menninger Foundation (MF–6502–C).

supported statements in the literature about the storms and stresses of certain aspects of adolescent development (6, 8), the fate of the self-concept in adolescence is still a matter for speculation. The studies that examine individual differences in the self-concepts of adolescents from a number of vantage points and in several settings (1, 2, 4) represent an inroad into the area of self-concept development. However, it is the longitudinal approach that is most appropriate when seeking answers to questions of development.

The primary purpose of the present study was to investigate the stability of the self-concept in adolescence over a two-year period. It was also its purpose to examine the relationship between whatever stability is found and the quality of the self-concept. The interrelationship between self-concept stability, quality of the self-concept, and several indices of adjustment was also examined.

Method

The data were obtained by testing and retesting 172 public school students, 104 of whom were in the eighth grade and 68 of whom were in the tenth grade at the time of the first testing. The same students served as subjects in 1954 and in 1956.[3] Table 1 presents the grade and sex distribution of *S*s in the two-year study. An analysis of the fathers' occupations revealed that the *S*s were mostly of lower-middle and middle-class background.

TABLE 1

SEX DISTRIBUTION OF SUBJECTS

Subjects	*8th–10th grade*	*10th–12th grade*
Boys	48	28
Girls	56	40
Total	104	68
Grand Total	172	

The hypotheses were formulated in 1954. Their testing required the use of the following measures:

[3] There were 243 *S*s in 1954; the discrepancy between the 1954 and 1956 *N* can be accounted for by attrition during the two-year period. Detailed analysis of data from the attrition group will be presented elsewhere. Whereas the over-all *N* of the longitudinal sample was 172, an *N* of approximately 149 was available for the testing of certain hypotheses, due to the absence of some *S*s on some of the testing days in 1956.

1. Self-concept *Q* sort, paper and pencil form, consisting of items relevant to adolescent concerns.[4]
2. Verbal Subscale of the Differential Aptitude Test, as an estimate of intelligence.
3. Scales *D, Pd,* and *K* of the Minnesota Multiphasic Personality Inventory (MMPI), as measures of adjustment and "defensiveness."
4. Peer Rating Scale, as a sociometric assessment of adjustment, based on the model provided by Tuddenham (13).
5. Teachers' Forced Choice Test as another independent measure of adjustment, developed by Ullman (14).

The set of *Q*-sort items for the assessment of the self-concept in adolescents was developed along lines largely in conformity with the principles put forth by Stephenson (11). Briefly, a large pool of items was gathered covering areas of adolescent self-concern as empirically defined by Jersild (7). The pooled judgments as psychologists, nonprofessional adults, and adolescents were used to reduce and refine the original set, 100 *Q*-sort items being retained. Judges could agree with demonstrable certainty that these items represent either positively or negatively toned self-referent attitudes. Examples are: "I can take criticism without resentment." "I see little about myself that's outstanding."

In responding, *S*s had to distribute the 50 positively and 50 negatively toned items into 11 categories, ranging from "most like me" to "least like me." The frequency distribution of items was as follows:

Number of items	4	7	9	11	12	14	12	11	9	7	4
Category	1	2	3	4	5	6	7	8	9	10	11

Paper and pencil administration incurs some errors of measurement, probably not pertaining to item sampling, that are not involved when the usual card sorting procedure is used. The test-retest reliability of the instrument was .68 over a ten-day period with an *N* of 23 (tenth-grade students). This reliability figure was obtained by correlating the values assigned to each item, by each *S*, on two occasions and represents the mean of 23 correlations (z transformations were used in computing the mean *r*). It is slightly lower than similar statistics obtained by others, using the card sort (12).

The maximum positiveness score that can be obtained on the *Q* sort used in this study is 600. A score of this magnitude would result from

[4] Copyright applied for. A complete list of *Q*-sort items is included in University Microfilms Publication: Mic 57-2914. Send $2.25 to University Microfilms, 313 No. First Street, Ann Arbor, Michigan.

placing every one of the 50 positive items in the "most like me" end of the continuum. Placing an equal number of positive and negative items on the upper and the lower end of the continuum would give rise to a score of 300, the point of ambivalence. Customarily, the negative self-concept is defined as a positiveness score falling below the point of ambivalence, whereas the positive self-concept is usually defined as a positiveness score above the point of ambivalence.

In responding to the Peer Rating Scale, each member of a class writes down one to three names of others who seem to suit some brief behavioral description, for example: "Who is the good sport, the person who always plays fair?" "Who gets mad easily and loses his or her temper often?" These descriptions can be roughly ordered along an adjustment-maladjustment continuum. Each *S* receives a score that reflects the extent to which his peers see him as well functioning in the school situation. The reliability of the Peer Rating Scale was established by test-retest of 2 *S*s (ninth graders) over a one-week interval. The resulting value of .96 indicates that the adjustment scores derived from ratings of any one subject by the group as a whole are highly reliable.

Results and Discussion

Stability of self-concept

Analysis of the data obtained in 1954 from *S*s who subsequently dropped out of school indicates that certain important personality differences may have existed between those who left and those who remained in the school.[5] Because of the strong possibility of selective attrition, caution is indicated when generalizing from the results of the present study.

It was expected that the *S*s would form three groups with regard to the self-concept: those maintaining positive self-regarding attitudes, those with negative self-regarding attitudes, and those with defensively positive self-concepts. Hypotheses were formulated on the basis of this expectation. All predictions were made in 1954 and were tested in 1956.

It was hypothesized that the self-concept of adolescents would be relatively stable over the two-year period. This hypothesis implies that the stability, internal organization, and crystallization of the self-concept is achieved earlier in development. Stability was defined by relatively high correlations between self-concept *Q* sorts in 1954 and 1956. Relevant data are presented in Table 2. The over-all mean correlation of .53, for all *S*s,

---

[5] Analysis of personality differences between *S*s in the longitudinal sample and the attrition group will be presented elsewhere.

TABLE 2

THE STABILITY OF THE SELF-CONCEPT OVER A TWO-YEAR PERIOD
ITEM-BY-ITEM CORRELATIONS OF Q SORTS IN 1954 AND 1956

Group	*N*	*Mean z*	*Ss*	*r corresponding to mean z scores*
Girls				
8th–10th grade	45	.6107	.2059	.54
10th–12th grade	37	.6794	.2204	.59
Boys				
8th–10th grade	44	.4775	.2636	.45
10th–12th grade	23	.6004	.2222	.54
Mean		.5919		.53

indicates the extent of stability of the self-concept of adolescents over a two-year period, between grades eight and ten, and ten and twelve. Corrected for attenuation, the over-all mean correlation between the self-concept in 1954 and 1956 is .78.

It was also predicted that the self-concept of *S*s with a positive attitude toward themselves in 1954 would be significantly more stable over the two-year period than the self-concept of *S*s with a negative or defensive-positive self-concept. Results bearing on this prediction are presented in Table 3, in which the negative self-concept is defined by scores falling in the lower 20 per cent of the distribution of self-concept scores, and posi-

TABLE 3

COMPARISON OF SELF-CONCEPT STABILITY BETWEEN POSITIVE, NEGATIVE, AND DEFENSIVE-POSITIVE SELF-CONCEPT GROUPS OVER THE TWO-YEAR PERIOD

Group	*N*[a]	*Per cent of total N (172)*	*Mean stability*[b]	*s*	*t*
Positive self-concept	106	62	.6928	.2060	7.61*
Negative self-concept	34	20	.3383	.1977	6.99*
Defensive-positive self-concept	32	18	.6379	.2138	
Defensive-positive self-concept and positive self-concept	—	—	—		1.30

*Significant beyond the .05 level.
[a] Classification on basis of 1954 data.
[b] Based on 1954 and 1956 data, total *N* for this column 149.

tive self-concept by scores in the upper 80 per cent. Where the self-concept was positive, and *S* also obtained a *K* score greater than 17 (measure of "defensiveness" derived from the MMPI), *S* was classified as manifesting a defensive-positive self-concept.

To test the hypotheses, correlations between *Q* sorts were converted into z scores as measures of stability. An over-all *F* test of differences in stability between self-concept groups resulted in an *F* ratio of 28.12, greatly exceeding the ratio of 5.30 needed for significance at $p = .05$. Individual *t* tests between groups support the conclusions that (*a*) *S*s whose self-concept was positive in 1954 were significantly more stable over the two-year period than *S*s who had negative self-concepts in 1954; (*b*) *S*s whose self-concept was defensive-positive in 1954 were significantly more stable than those who had negative self-concepts; (*c*) *S*s whose self-concept was positive in 1954 did not differ significantly in stability from those whose self-concept was defensive-positive in 1954.

The prediction that older and younger *S*s would not differ significantly in stability of self-concept over the two-year period was supported. Age group differences in magnitude of *Q*-sort correlations (self-concept stability) resulted in a *t* ratio of .60.

It was also expected that stability of the self-concept would be statistically unrelated in intelligence. Testing this prediction required correlating verbal intelligence scores (DAT) with self-concept stability scores. Correlations were nonsignificant, lending support to the hypothesis, except in the case of the tenth-twelfth-grade girls, where an *r* of .36 was found between these two variables, which, with an *N* of 35, was significant beyond the .05 level.

On the assumption that cultural ambiguities concerning sex roles should be more likely to affect girls than boys, it was hypothesized that the self-concept of boys would be significantly more stable over the two-year period than that of girls. This hypothesis was not upheld. The comparison of the mean stability between boys and girls resulted in a *t* ratio of .76.

TABLE 4

POSITIVENESS OF THE SELF-CONCEPT IN 1954 AND IN 1956

	1954			*1956*		
Group	*N*	*M*	*s*	*N*	*M*	*s*
Girls						
8th–10th grade	56	359.98	32.01	45	362.76	29.41
10th–12th grade	40	358.40	36.82	37	365.59	38.44
Boys						
8th–10th grade	48	351.29	34.68	45	352.25	37.15
10th–12th grade	27	360.81	23.03	24	369.75	25.72

In comparing the mean positiveness scores of the *S*s in 1954 and in 1956 (Table 4) we found an unpredicted increase in mean positiveness. With the sexes combined, both grades shifted in a positive direction, the mean shift being significant beyond the .05 level in case of the older group ($t = -2.44$).

STABILITY OF SELF-CONCEPT AND ADJUSTMENT

The relationship between the stability of the self-concept and three measures of adjustment (teacher ratings, peer ratings, and MMPI measures) was explored through the following prediction: *S*s who persist in a positive self-regarding attitude should be better adjusted, in terms of the MMPI, teacher ratings, and peer ratings, than those who persist in negative or defensive-positive self-concepts. Table 5 summarizes the "fate" of

TABLE 5

THE DISTRIBUTION OF ALL SUBJECTS IN THE LONGITUDINAL SAMPLE WITH REGARD TO THE CHANGES AND CONSTANCIES OF THE SELF-CONCEPT AS SEEN IN 1956

Changes and constancies of the self-concept between 1954 and 1956	*Number*	*Per cent of number subjects*
Maintained positive self-concept	76	44
Maintained negative self-concept	14	8
Maintained defensive-positive self-concept	11	6
Was defensive-positive in 1954 but did not maintain either defensiveness or positiveness of self-concept	16	9
Was positive but shifted to negative self-concept by more than 20 points	15	9
Was negative but shifted to positive by more than 20 points	17	10
Absent on more than one testing session in 1956 (unclassified)	23	13
Total	172	99

the quality of the self-concept for all *S*s over the two-year period.[6] More detailed analysis revealed that most of the shift in self-concept quality occurred in the negative self-concept group. *S*s who were classified as having negative self-concepts in 1954 more closely approached the mean by 1956. Such shift could be attributed to regression, except that no such shifting toward the mean took place in the case of *S*s originally giving evidence of a positive self-concept.

[6] The method of categorization used is too detailed for presentation here but is described in detail elsewhere (5).

In applying analyses of variance to adjustment indices between groups, 1956 adjustment measures were used. Table 6 shows that *F* ratios on MMPI scores were significant, whereas *F* ratios based on other adjustment measures were not.

TABLE 6

COLUMN MEANS AND F RATIOS FOR THREE SELF-CONCEPT GROUPS ON MEASURES OF ADJUSTMENT (1956 MEASURES USED)

	Maintaining positive self-concept		*Maintaining negative self-concept*		*Maintaining positive-defensive self-concept*		
Measures	*N*	*M*	*N*	*M*	*N*	*M*	*F*
Pd	73	13.51	12	20.17	11	13.64	15.27*
D	73	14.90	12	22.25	11	15.18	21.20*
Peer rating	71	232.62	12	175.17	10	268.70	2.77
Teacher rating	72	22.00	14	18.86	10	23.00	2.18

*Significant beyond the .05 level.

Differences in MMPI measures were further examined by individual *t* tests applied to the column means. MMPI adjustment measures showed the group maintaining negative self-concepts to be significantly less well adjusted (scoring higher on *D* and *Pd*) in 1956 than others, partially upholding the hypothesis.

CONCOMITANCE OF CHANGE IN SELF-CONCEPT AND IN ADJUSTMENT

It was predicted that a change in self-concept in the positive direction would be related to improved adjustment, and a change in self-concept in the negative direction would be related to impaired adjustment. For the purpose of testing this hypothesis *S*s were regrouped and considered either "positive shifters" or "negative shifters" depending on a change of 20 points away from their original positive self-concept score either in the positive or negative direction. Only *S*s on whom full sets of adjustment scores were available were included in this analysis. Adjustment scores for 1956 were subtracted from 1954 adjustment scores, and *t* tests were applied to the mean difference scores. Table 7 presents the results bearing on this hypothesis and supports the conclusion that "negative shifters" obtained significantly higher *Pd* and *D* scores in 1956 as predicted; however, "positive shifters" became more "defensive" in that they obtained significantly higher *K* scores in 1956 than in 1954; "positive shifters"

TABLE 7

CHANGES IN ADJUSTMENT MEASURES CONCOMITANT WITH SHIFTS IN SELF-CONCEPT (BASED ON DIFFERENCE SCORES; 1956 SCORES SUBTRACTED FROM 1954 MEASURES)

Adjustment measures	"*Positive shifters*"				"*Negative shifters*"			
	N	*M*	*s*	*t*	*N*	*M*	*s*	*t*
Pd (MMPI)	30	—.47	3.83	.67	13	—3.15	3.53	—3.22**
D (MMPI)	35	—.60	4.89	.73	15	—3.80	4.75	—3.10**
K (MMPI)	35	—2.94	4.41	—3.95*	22	.23	4.85	.22
Teacher rating	40	.83	7.33	.02	22	.23	4.85	.23
Peer rating	37	—25.97	66.55	—2.37**	17	15.53	93.24	—.69

*Significant beyond the .05 level and in the direction opposite from the predicted one.
**Significant beyond the .05 level and in the predicted direction.

were seen as significantly more well adjusted by their peers in 1956 than in 1954. Changes in teacher ratings did not differentiate between groups. Thus, this final hypothesis was only partially confirmed.

It should be borne in mind that this study explored mainly one aspect of the self-concept, the conscious self-concept. It may well be that in spite of the consistencies found in adolescents over a two-year period, considerable changes took place in aspects of the concept of self that are less readily admissible into awareness. The exploration of self-concept consistency and its concomitants on a deeper level of personality would require a clinical approach which was precluded by the use of a fairly large number of *S*s in the present study.

Summary

A study of the stability of the self-concept over two years in adolescence resulted in the following conclusions:

1. Relative stability of the self-concept was demonstrated by an over-all item-by-item correlation of .53 between *Q* sorts obtained in 1954 and in 1956, with an instrument of which the ten-day test-retest reliability was .68.

2. Subjects whose self-concept was negative at the first testing were significantly less stable in self-concept than subjects whose self-concept was positive.

3. Subjects who persisted in a negative self-concept over the two-year period gave evidence of significantly more maladjustment than subjects who persisted in a positive self-concept, when maladjustment is measured by high scores of scales *Pd* and *D* of the MMPI.

4. Subjects who showed less regard for themselves on the *Q* sort on

retest, also shifted toward significantly more maladjustment on scales *Pd* and *D* of the MMPI.

5. Subjects who showed more regard for themselves on the *Q* sort on retest, also shifted toward significantly more adjustment on peer ratings.

6. The positive self-concept scores increased significantly between the two testings for the tenth-twelfth-grade subjects, an increase which could not be attributed entirely to the effect of regression.

References

1. Balester, R. S., *The Self-Concept and Juvenile Delinquency,* Unpublished doctoral dissertation, Vanderbilt University, 1955.
2. Blodgett, N. E., *An Experimental Approach to the Measurement of Self-Evaluation Among Adolescent Girls,* Unpublished doctoral dissertation, University of Minnesota, 1953.
3. Brownfain, J. J., "Stability of Self-Concept as a Dimension of Personality," *Journal of Abnormal Psychology,* Vol. 47 (1952), pp. 597-606.
4. DeLisle, F. H., *A Study of the Relationship of the Self-Concept to Adjustment in a Selected Group of College Women,* Unpublished doctoral dissertation, Michigan State University, 1953.
5. Engel, M., *The Stability of the Self-Concept in Adolescence,* Unpublished doctoral dissertation, George Peabody College, 1956.
6. Hall, G. S., *Adolescence,* Vol. I (New York: Appleton, 1904).
7. Jersild, A. T., *In Search of Self* (New York: Teachers College, Columbia University, 1952).
8. Kuhlen, R. G., "Age Trends in Adjustment During Adult Years as Reflected in Happiness Ratings," *American Psychologist,* Vol. 3 (1948), p. 307.
9. Lecky, P., *Self-Consistence: A Theory of Personality* (Fort Myers Beach, Fla.: Island, 1945).
10. Rogers, C. R., and R. F. Dymond, eds., *Psychotherapy and Personality Change* (Chicago: U. of Chicago, 1954).
11. Stephenson, W., "Correlating Persons Instead of Tests," *Character Personality,* Vol. 6 (1935), pp. 17-24.
12. Taylor, D. M., "Changes in the Self-Concept Without Psychotherapy," *Journal of Consulting Psychology,* Vol. 19 (1955), pp. 205-209.
13. Tuddenham, R. D., "Studies in Reputation," *Psychological Monographs,* Vol. 66, No. 1 (1952).
14. Ullman, C. A., "Identification of Maladjusted School Children," *U. S. Public Health Monographs,* Vol. 11 (1952), pp. 255-264.

3. Self-conceptions, motivations, and interpersonal attitudes of late- and early-maturing boys[1]

PAUL H. MUSSEN
AND MARY C. JONES

Reprinted from *Child Development,* Vol. 28 (1957), 243-256, by permission of the senior author and the Society for Research in Child Development.

Does rate of physical maturing influence personality? We know that some youngsters grow up "faster" than others, but can we identify the residue of fast or slow maturation? Mussen and Jones carefully analyze data from late- and early-maturing boys and make it abundantly clear that a boy's maturational pace can have a striking impact on his over-all personality development.

While many intensive case studies show that personal and social adjustment during adolescence may be profoundly influenced by rate of physical maturation, there is a scarcity of systematic data on the relationship between the adolescent's physical status and his underlying motivations, self-conceptions and interpersonal attitudes. There is, however, a small body of evidence which demonstrates that greater physical maturity is associated with greater maturity of interest among girls (10) and that early-maturing boys differ from their late-maturing peers in both overt behavior and reputational status. In one study (8) in which a staff of trained observers assessed a large group of adolescents on a number of personality variables, boys who were consistently retarded in physical development were rated lower than those who

[1] The TAT data for this study were obtained by Harold E. Jones in connection with a test program at the Institute of Child Welfare.

were consistently accelerated, in physical attractiveness, grooming and matter-of-factness; and higher in sociability, social initiative (often of a childish, attention-getting sort), and eagerness. Reputation Test (11) data indicated that classmates regarded the late-maturing boys as more attention-getting, more restless, more bossy, less grown-up, and less good-looking than those who were physically accelerated.

On the basis of these findings, it may be inferred that adult and peer attitudes toward the adolescent, as well as their treatment and acceptance of him, are related to his physical status. This means that the sociopsychological environment to which late-maturers are subjected—and consequently the social learning situations they encounter—may be significantly different from that of their early-maturing peers. As a consequence, according to the ratings summarized above, they acquire different patterns of overt social behavior. It seems reasonable to hypothesize that groups differing in physical status will also differ in more covert aspects of behavior and personality.

Indirect evidence relevant to this hypothesis comes from an investigation of the long-term consequences of physical acceleration or retardation during adolescence. Jones (6) found that group differences in physique had practically disappeared by the time her early- and late-maturing subjects reached their early thirties. Nevertheless young adults who had been physically retarded adolescents differed from those who had been accelerated in several important psychological characteristics. In general, it appeared that the adult subjects could be described much as they had been during adolescence. Thus, those who had been early-maturers scored higher on the good impression, socialization, dominance, self-control (low score on impulsivity), and responsibility scales of the California Personality Inventory, while those who had been slow in maturing scored higher on the flexibility scale. On the Edwards Personal Preference Schedule, early-maturers scored significantly higher on the dominance scale, while the late-maturing were high in succorance. Jones concludes that the early-maturing "present a consistently favorable personality picture with regard to . . . important social variables" (6). Moreover, there was some evidence that these men had attained more stable vocational adjustments than those who had been late in maturing. These group differences in later adjustment suggest that the sociopsychological atmosphere in which the adolescent lives may have profound immediate and enduring effects on his personality structure as well as on his overt behavior.

The present study was designed to investigate the relationship between maturational status and certain important, covert aspects of personality during late adolescence. Personality structure was assessed by means of the Thematic Apperception Test (TAT) which seems to be the most appropriate and sensitive instrument for this purpose. More specifically, on the basis of the literature reviewed above and other general works on the psychology of adolescence (1, 4, 5), we formulated and tested a series of propositions relating to differences between the physically retarded and the accelerated in self-conceptions, underlying motivations, and basic interpersonal attitudes. These variables were translated into TAT categories—needs (*n*), press (*p*), and descriptions (defined briefly in Table 1)—and the scores of early- and late-maturers in each of these categories were compared. The propositions and the rationale underlying them, together with the TAT variables involved, follow.

1. In view of their obvious physical retardation, relatively unfavorable reputations and disadvantageous competitive position in many activities, the late-maturing boys are more likely to have feelings of inadequacy. Hence, more boys in this group than in the early-maturing group are likely to have negative self-conceptions (TAT category: *negative characteristics*).

2. The adolescent in our culture generally desires more independence and adult status. This may be the source of a major problem for the late-maturer, however, since he is often regarded and treated as a small boy by adults and peers and is not likely to be granted independence as early as physically accelerated boys. Therefore, it may be anticipated that more late- than early-maturers regard adults, particularly their parents, as dominating, forcing them to do things they don't want to or preventing them from doing things they want to do (high scores in *p Dominance*). Moreover, the parental treatment these boys experience and parental refusal to grant them independent status may be interpreted as personal rejection. Hence, we predicted that more late-maturing boys would score high in *p Rejection.*

3. These feelings of being dominated and rejected may result in attitudes of rebellion against the family and in feelings of hostility. We therefore expected that more of the late-maturing group would reveal strong aggressive needs (high scores in *n Aggression*) and desires to escape from (*n Autonomy—leaving parents*), or to defy, the family (*n Autonomy—defying parents*).

4. On the basis of the data indicating that slow-maturers showed a great deal of social interest (although often of an immature kind), we hypothesized that more members of this, than of the early-maturing group would reveal strong interests in friendly, intimate interpersonal relationships (*high scores* in *n Affiliation*).

5. Assuming that, as Jones and Bayley (8) suggest, the social initiative and attention-getting devices of the late-maturers are of a compensatory nature, we would expect this group to be basically dependent and to have

strong needs for support from others. These should be manifest by higher scores in TAT *n Succorance* and *p Nurturance*. The latter may be considered a most indirect measure of dependence, a kind of wish-fulfilling view of the world as helpful and friendly.

6. The early-maturer, being regarded and treated as more adult, is more likely to become self-confident, and to acquire high status goals. For these reasons, we predicted that more of the physically accelerated would give evidence of high achievement goals (high scores in *n Achievement*) and concern with personal recognition (high scores in *n Recognition*).

7. Late-maturing boys in our culture probably face more problems of personal adjustment than do their early-maturing peers. As a result of this, they may become more aware of their problems, and, as the high degree of flexibility of young adults who had been retarded in maturing suggests, more insightful. Hence, we predicted that they would be more willing and able than early-maturers to face their own feelings and emotions (low scores in the TAT variable *denial of feeling*).

In summary, we attempted to test seven propositions related to differences in the personalities of early- and late-maturing boys. It was hypothesized that more late-maturers would score high in variables relating to negative self-conceptions, dependence, aggression, affiliation, rebelliousness, and feelings of being dominated and rejected. More early-maturers, on the other hand, were expected to reveal strong achievement and recognition needs, feelings of personal success, and tendencies toward denial of feelings.

Procedure

The 33 seventeen-year-old male subjects of this investigation were members of the Adolescent Growth Study which included a normal sample of boys in an urban public school system (3). The subjects of the present investigation represented two contrasting groups, selected on the basis of their physical maturity status: 16 of them had been among the most consistently accelerated throughout the adolescent period; the other 17 had been among the most consistently retarded.[2] All of them took the Thematic Apperception Test, which provides the basic data of this study, at age 17.

The TAT consisted of 18 pictures: nine from the Murray set which is

[2] The present sample includes 27 of Jones and Bayley's (8) 32 subjects (the 16 most consistently retarded and 16 most consistently accelerated boys in the study). The other five boys had not taken the TAT at age 17. The six subjects who were in the present study but not in Jones and Bayley's study are the three "runners-up" from each end of the physical maturity distribution, *i.e.*, the three who were closest to the 16 most accelerated cases and the three cases next to the 16 most retarded.

now standard (cards 1, 5, 6, 7BM, 10, 11, 14, 15, 17); five pictures from the set generally used in 1938 when these data were collected (a man and woman seated on a park bench; a bearded old man writing in an open book; a thin, sullen, young man standing behind a well-dressed older man; a tea table and two chairs; an abstract drawing of two bearded men); and four designed especially for this investigation (the nave of a large church; a madonna and child; a dramatic view of mountains; a boy gazing at a cross which is wreathed in clouds).

The tests were administered individually. Each card was projected on a screen while the subject told a story which was recorded verbatim. Standard instructions were given for the Murray cards, and subjects were asked to describe the feelings elicited by the other four pictures. Most of the stories were brief, consisting of only one or two sentences.

As we noted earlier, each of the personality variables involved in the seven propositions was translated into a TAT scoring category. The scoring scheme involved counting the relevant needs, press, and description of the heroes of the stories, the assumption being that the storyteller has identified with the hero: the hero's needs are the same as the boy's; the press that impinge upon the hero are the ones that affect the boy telling the story. A total of 20 needs, press, and descriptive categories, each defined as specifically as possible, was developed in the analysis of the protocols. A score for each subject for each TAT category was derived by counting the number of stories in which it appeared. A list of the categories used, together with brief descriptions of them, is found in Table 1.

To test the reliability of this analysis, one of the authors (PM) and another psychologist [3] independently scored 15 complete protocols (300 stories). The percentage of interrater agreement was .90, computed by the usual formula (number of agreements divided by number of agreements plus number of disagreements).

In order to eliminate bias, the scoring used in the present study was done "blind," that is, independently of knowledge of the subject's maturational status.

Results

Frequency distributions of the scores of all subjects were made for all the TAT variables. Each distribution was then dichotomized at the point which most nearly enabled the placing of half of the 33 subjects above, and half of them below, the dividing point. Subjects having scores above

[3] We are indebted to Dr. Virginia B. Ware for her participation in this aspect of the study.

this point were considered high in this particular variable; those with scores below that point were considered low in this variable. Chi square tests were used to test the seven propositions, *i.e.,* to ascertain whether or not high scores in certain TAT variables were in fact more characteristic of one group (late- or early-maturers) than of the other.

Table 1 lists the TAT variables, the number of late- and early-maturers with high scores in the variable, the chi square value obtained and the level of significance. It should be noted that the hypotheses tested were one-sided hypotheses, while the chi square value is in terms of a two-sided hypothesis. When chi square has only one degree of freedom, the square root of chi square has a distribution which is the right hand half of a normal distribution. In order to test a one-sided hypothesis, the chi square test must be converted into the equivalent value in terms of a unit normal deviate (2). The levels of significance reported in Table 1 were evaluated in these terms.

Table 1 shows that, as had been predicted, more late-maturing than early-maturing boys revealed feelings of inadequacy and negative self-concepts, *i.e.,* scored high in the TAT variable negative characteristics. Hence, proposition 1 was confirmed. This finding is consistent with the frequently made clinical observation that retardation in physical maturation may be an important source of personal maladjustments and attitudes of inferiority.

Proposition 2 stated that more late-maturers regard their parents as highly dominating and rejecting. The evidence summarized in Table 1 substantially supported this proposition. While the difference was not statistically significant, more late- than early-maturers scored high in *p Dominance by parents* (total). There was a marked difference between the groups in the variable which involves parental domination by forcing the child to do something he does not want to do (*p Dominance by parents, forcing*). However, examination of the data with respect to the variable *p Dominance by parents* (*prevention*) makes it necessary to reject that part of the proposition which maintains that late-maturers are more likely to view their parents as highly restrictive of their activities.

That aspect of proposition 2 which deals with feelings of rejection was confirmed by our data. Compared with the early-maturing group, a significantly greater proportion of the late-maturers told stories in which the hero was rejected by parents or authority figures. These feelings of rejection may stem from different sources. In some cases, the parents' behavior may make it clear that they are disappointed in their physically retarded son whom they regard as immature. The boy, perceiving this attitude, may interpret it as rejection. In other cases, parental reluctance to allow the late-maturing boy to establish his independence may lead to considerable

TABLE 1

NUMBER OF EARLY- AND LATE-MATURERS SCORING HIGH IN TAT VARIABLES

TAT variable	*Definition of variable*	*High early-maturers*	*High late-maturers*	*Chi square value*	p
Proposition 1					
Negative characteristics	H* is described in negative terms (*e.g.*, imbecile, weakling, fanatic)	5	13	6.80	<.01
Proposition 2					
p Dominance 1	H forced by parents to do something he doesn't want to	4	8	1.73	.09
p Dominance 2	If prevented by parents from doing something he wants to	6	8	.31	>.30
p Dominance 3	Total instances of H's being forced by parents to do something and/or prevented from doing something	7	11	1.46	.11
p Rejection	H rejected, scorned, or disapproved of by parents or authorities	5	11	3.69	.03
Proposition 3					
n Aggression 1	H is aggressive in physical, asocial way	8	3	3.88	.02
n Aggression 2	H is mad at someone, argues	7	4	1.52	.10
n Aggression 3	Total of all H's aggressive actions	11	8	1.26	.10
n Autonomy 1	H leaves home	7	10	.75	.20
n Autonomy 2	H disobeys or defies parents	7	11	1.46	.11
n Autonomy 3	Total of instances in which hero leaves and/or defies his parents	3	9	4.16	.02

tension in the family and the boy's feelings of rejection may simply reflect the ongoing parent-child conflict.

It is possible that earlier in their teens, soon after the physical changes of adolescence became apparent, many of the early-maturing boys also experienced conflicts with their parents, arising from difficulties in establishing their independence or in handling emerging heterosexual interests. At that time they too may have felt dominated or rejected. However, by the age of 17, when these data were collected, these boys were ordinarily treated as adults and granted more freedom. Hence, they were more likely to have resolved many of their conflicts with their parents and to feel accepted and independent.

The hypothesis (part of proposition 3) that more late-maturers would be highly aggressive was rejected on the basis of the evidence given in Table 1. In fact, the differences between the two groups on all the TAT

TABLE 1 (CONT.)

NUMBER OF EARLY- AND LATE-MATURERS SCORING HIGH IN TAT VARIABLES

TAT variable	*Definition of variable*	*High early-maturers*	*High late-maturers*	*Chi square value*	p
Proposition 4					
n Affiliation 1	H establishes good relations with his parents	8	8	.00	>.50
n Affiliation 2	H falls in love, has a romance, marries	9	14	2.66	.05
n Affiliation 3	Total instances in which H establishes and/or maintains friendly relations	8	12	1.46	.11
Proposition 5					
n Succorance	H feels helpless, seeks aid or sympathy	7	12	2.43	.06
p Nurturance 1	H is helped, encouraged, or given something by parents	5	8	.93	.18
p Nurturance 2	H is helped, encouraged, or given something by someone else (not parents)	8	14	3.88	.02
Proposition 6					
n Achievement	H attempts to attain a high goal or to do something creditable	9	10	.02	>.50
n Recognition	H seeks fame and/or high prestige status	9	8	.28	>.30
Proposition 7					
Denial of feeling	S states that picture elicits no thoughts or feelings	9	5	2.43	.06

*H stands for hero.

aggression variables were in the opposite direction from the prediction. High scores in the variables relating to aggression of the most overt and violent type were significantly more frequent among the early-maturers, and more members of this group also scored high in measures of milder (verbal) aggression and of total aggression. While late-maturers may experience more problems of adjustment and greater frustrations than their early-maturing peers, they apparently do not manifest greater aggressive motivation. It may be that their own feelings of inadequacy or fears of retaliation and punishment for aggression inhibit their expression of hostile feelings, even in fantasy. On the other hand, the early-maturers who feel more secure personally, and recognize their own relatively advantageous physical and social status, may feel freer to express their aggressive needs. Since aggression is a culturally stereotyped masculine trait, it seems possible that the physically accelerated, being accepted as mature and identifying readily with adult males, are more likely to acquire this characteristic. In any case, the finding that early-maturers express higher aggressive motivation during late adolescence seems consistent with Jones' finding that, as young adults, they score high on the dominance scale of the Edwards Personal Preference test (6). Perhaps the relatively strong aggressive motivation of the early-maturer, or the mature sex-role identification it may imply, serves as a basis for the development of later qualities of leadership and persuasiveness (7).

As Table 1 indicates, the other aspect of proposition 3 was confirmed: a significantly greater proportion of late- than of early-maturers displayed strong motivations to escape from, or defy, their parents. These may be essentially aggressive reactions, stemming from feelings of parental domination and rejection, or they may reflect the late-maturers' awareness of their strife with their parents whom they perceive as blocking their drives for independence. These strong needs for escape and defiance may also be considered evidence of a generally immature way of handling parent-child conflicts. Perhaps, by the age of 17, the early-maturers have already resolved many of their conflicts with their families and/or have learned to handle these in less rebellious and in more direct and mature ways.

Proposition 4 stated that, compared with their early-maturing peers, more late-maturers would manifest strong needs for establishing close social contacts with others. While there was some confirmatory evidence, the results were not clear-cut. When all affiliative needs were considered together (score for *n Affiliation—total*), the group differences were in the predicted direction, but not statistically significant. Examination of the protocols revealed that almost all instances of affiliation concerned either parents or the opposite sex; there were very few stories involving close, friendly associations between like-sexed peers. The two major types of affiliation were scored separately. As Table 1 shows, late-maturers did not differ from early-maturers with respect to need for affiliation with parents, but a significantly greater proportion of the former group displayed strong motivation for heterosexual affiliation.

In view of the late-maturers' strong feelings of inadequacy and dependent needs (see below), it is surprising that a greater proportion of this group did not exhibit strong needs to establish and maintain close bonds with their parents. This may be due to the late-maturers' more intense conflicts with their parents at this age (17 years), their fears of being rejected and dominated by them, and their generally defiant attitudes which prevent them from admitting, even in fantasy, their strong underlying needs to form close contacts with them.

The significant difference between the groups in *n Affiliation* (*love, romance, marriage*) is subject to several possible interpretations. For one thing, this category may refer to general needs to establish close relations with others (with peers or adults other than parents) and not merely to desire for contact with the opposite sex. The set of stimulus cards may not have been adequate to elicit responses indicative of more general affiliative needs; hence, these were expressed through responses in the heterosexual affiliation category. If this is true, proposition 4 was confirmed, and the late-maturers' high scores in this variable indicate their greater general interest in establishing and maintaining friendly relationships.

It is also possible that the late-maturers' strong affiliative needs are actually directed only toward members of the opposite sex, *i.e.,* that *n Affiliation* (*love, romance, marriage*) measures specifically heterosexual interest. Assuming that this is true, there is another plausible explanation for the discovered difference. As we saw earlier, the late-maturer may be afraid to admit that he desires close association with his parents. He may also feel that his immaturity and poor reputational status prevent him from establishing successful social relationships with like-sexed peers. Hence, he may "displace" his affiliative needs to members of the opposite sex, who, in his fantasies, may seem more responsive.

A third possible explanation of the difference is based on Jones and Bayley's findings that the late-maturers show less overt interest in girls and are regarded as less good-looking (8). From these data, it may be inferred that the physically retarded probably do not have successful and rewarding experiences with girls. Hence, their heightened need for affiliation with the opposite sex, expressed in the TAT, may reflect their attempts to satisfy in fantasy needs which they cannot satisfy adequately in reality.

The data were generally supportive of proposition 5 which stated that late-maturers are likely to have strong underlying dependent needs. A higher proportion of this group than of their early-maturing peers scored high in *n Succorance,* the difference between the two groups approaching statistical significance ($p = .06$). Furthermore, high scores in the category involving receiving help and support from others (not including parents) (*p Nurturance—nonparents*)—an indirect measure of dependent needs—were significantly more characteristic of the physically retarded than of the physically accelerated. In view of the late-maturers' attitudes toward their parents, discussed above, it is not surprising to find that perceptions of parents as kindly and supportive (high scores in *p Nurturance—parents*) were not significantly more common in this group than in the early-maturing group.

On the basis of the data involving the TAT variables *n Achievement* and *n Recognition,* we rejected proposition 6 which stated that more early-maturers would be self-confident and have high needs for achievement and personal recognition. In our culture there is strong pressure to develop needs for achievement and personal recognition, and, according to our results, these needs and feelings may become intense regardless of—or perhaps in spite of—the child's maturational status, feelings of personal adequacy, dependency, and adjustment to parents.

Two interesting incidental findings from the TAT data seem to be consistent with the proposition that more early- than late-maturers are likely to be self-confident. Seven boys in this sample of 33 adolescents told stories in which the hero was helpful or kind to someone else (*n Nurturance*). Of this group, six were early-maturers, while only one was a late-maturer ($x^2 = 2.09$, $p = .07$). Insofar as *n Nurturance* may be a measure of the storyteller's own feelings that he can accept an active, mature role, more of the accelerated group feel self-assured with respect to having attained mature status.

The other incidental finding which seems to support proposition 6 is based on responses only to card 1 of the Murray series which depicts a young boy contemplating a violin which rests on a table in front of him. Eight of the subjects spoke of the boy (the hero) as a prodigy or a genius. Of these, seven were early-maturers; only one was physically retarded ($x^2 = 5.25$, $p = .01$). If the attribution of this prestige status and accomplishment to the hero reflects the subject's own feeling that he has been an achiever, it follows that more of the physically accelerated have positive self-concepts. In view of the small number of cases involved, both of these findings must be considered tentative, but they do offer some evidence in support of proposition 6.

Proposition 7, which stated that relatively few of the physically retarded boys are unwilling or unable to face their own feelings and emotions, received some support from the TAT data summarized in Table 1. A smaller proportion of the members of this group than of the physically accelerated group specifically denied that the pictures evoked any feelings or emotions (*e.g.*, "It doesn't make me think of anything"). While this variable may not adequately measure *denial of feeling* as a major defense mechanism, this result seems to indicate that late-maturers are more sensitive to their own feelings and more ready to admit and face them openly. Since these qualities are basic to the development of psychological insight, it may be inferred that late-maturers, as a group, are more likely to become insightful individuals.

Discussion

The results of the study support the general hypothesis that, in our culture, the boy whose physical development is retarded is exposed to a socio-psychological environment which may have adverse effects on his personality development. Apparently, being in a disadvantageous competitive position in athletic activities, as well as being regarded and treated as immature by others, may lead to negative self-conceptions, heightened feelings of rejection by others, prolonged dependent needs, and rebellious attitudes toward parents. Hence, the physically retarded boy is more likely than his early-maturing peer to be personally and socially maladjusted during late adolescence. Moreover, some of his attitudes are likely to interfere with the process of identification with his parents, which is generally based on perceptions of them as warm and accepting (9). This, in turn, may inhibit or delay the acquisition of mature characteristics and attitudes which are ordinarily established through identification with parents. Fortunately for the late-maturers' subsequent adjustments, they seem more willing and able to face their feelings and emotions. This may be a result of their awareness of others' attitudes toward their immaturity or their feelings of personal inadequacy and dependency.

The physically accelerated boys, on the other hand, are likely to experience environmental circumstances which are much more conducive to good psychological adjustment. Hence, their psychological picture, as reflected in their TAT stories, is much more favorable. By the time they were 17, relatively few early-maturers harbored strong feelings of inadequacy, perceived themselves as rejected or dominated by parents or authorities, or felt rebellious toward their families. As a group, they appeared to have acquired more self-confidence and had probably made stronger identifications with mature adults. Hence, they perceived themselves as more mature individuals, less dependent and in need of help, and more capable of playing an adult male role in interpersonal relationships.

These findings assume additional, probably greater, importance when they are considered in the light of Jones' findings on the early adult (age 33) adjustments of boys who had been retarded or accelerated in physical maturing (6). It should be recalled that by this age physical differences between the two groups had practically disappeared. Certain important psychological differences were noted, however, and these were consistent with the differences at age 17, reported in the present study. For example, the responses of the early-maturing group to two paper-and-pencil tests, revealed that, as young adults, they were more dominant, more able to make a good impression and more likely to be turned to for advice and reassurance; more self-controlled; and more willing and able to carry social responsibility. In short, they present a general picture of psychological maturity. Moreover, more of the early-maturers seemed to have made successful vocational adjustments. In contrast to this, when the late-maturers became adults, they tended to be highly dependent individuals who could be described, on the basis of their test responses, as tending to be rebellious, touchy, impulsive, self-indulgent, and insightful. Most of these characteristics are indicative of poor adjustment and psychological immaturity. Fewer members of this group had made good vocational adjustments.

The striking correspondence between the two descriptions of the groups, derived from different kinds of tests and collected at widely separated periods of time, lends further support to Jones' conclusion that "the adolescent handicaps and advantages associated with late- or early-maturing appear to carry over into adulthood to some extent" (6). It seems clear that many attitudes of adolescent personality (patterns of motivation, self-conceptions, and attitudes toward others) characteristic of late- and early-maturing boys are relatively stable and durable rather than situational and transitory. This may be attributable to the fact that in our culture adolescence is generally a critical and difficult period of adjustment. Within a relatively brief interval of time, the child must work out numerous complex and vitally important personal problems—*e.g.,* adaptation to his changed biological and social status, establishment of independence, vocational adjustment. In dealing with these problems, he may acquire new behaviors and personality attributes which have broad ramifications, not only on his current adjustment, but also on his subsequent development. If the adolescent can cope with his problems without too much inner stress and turmoil, his self-esteem, feelings of adequacy, and consequently his subsequent adjustment, are likely to be enhanced. On the other hand, if his problems induce great tension and anxiety, he is likely to feel frustrated and inadequate, and, if these feelings are maintained, to adjust less satisfactorily as an adult.

Obviously, the adolescent's success or failure, as well as ease or tension, in handling his problems will be determined to a large degree by the socio-psychological forces to which he is subjected during this time and these, as we have seen, may be significantly related to his rate of maturation. Thus, physical status during adolescence—mediated through the socio-psychological environment—may exert profound and lasting influences on personality. For this reason, many aspects of the adult's behavior and personality seem consistent with his adolescent adjustments, attitudes and motivations.

Insofar as our results permit generalization, they suggest that some important aspects of motivation, such as needs for achievement and personal recognition, are not significantly affected by maturational status. It may be that among subjects whose achievements are strongly encouraged and rewarded from very early childhood, the need to achieve becomes powerful and resistant to change even in the face of feelings of helplessness and inadequacy. The latter may inhibit the achievement-oriented overt behavior of some late-maturers, but the underlying motivation to achieve seems as strong in this group as it is among the physically accelerated.

In conclusion, it should be noted that, although rate of maturing and associated factors may affect personality development, the relationship between physical status and psychological characteristics is by no means simple. A vast number of complex, interacting factors, including rate of maturation, determine each adolescent's unique personality structure. Hence, in any specific instance, the group findings of the present study may not be directly applicable, for other physical, psychological, or social factors may attenuate the effects of late- or early-maturing. For example, an adolescent boy who is fundamentally secure and has warm, accepting parents and generally rewarding social relationships may not develop strong feelings of inadequacy even if he matures slowly. Analogously, the early-maturing boy who has deep feelings of insecurity, for whatever reasons, will probably not gain self-confidence simply because he matures early. In summary, in understanding any individual case, generalizations based on the data of the present study must be particularized in the light of the individual's past history and present circumstances.

Summary

The present investigation was designed to test seven propositions concerning the relationship between rate of physical maturation and important aspects of personality structure, specifically self-conceptions, underlying motivations, and basic interpersonal attitudes. The TAT protocols of 33 seventeen-year-old boys—16 who had been consistently physically accelerated throughout adolescence and 17 who had been consistently retarded—were analyzed according to a scoring schema involving 20 needs, press, and descriptive categories. The scores of early- and late-maturers in each of the categories were compared.

An earlier study (8) demonstrated that late-maturing boys are more likely than their early-maturing peers to encounter a generally unfavorable sociopsychological environment. Analysis of the data of the present study indicates that this situation may have adverse effects on the personalities of the physically retarded. These boys are more likely to have negative self-conceptions, feelings of inadequacy, strong feelings of being rejected and dominated, prolonged dependency needs, and rebellious attitudes toward parents. In contrast, the early-maturing boys present a much more favorable psychological picture during adolescence. Relatively few of them felt inadequate, rejected, dominated, or rebellious toward their families. More of them appeared to be self-confident, independent, and capable of playing an adult role in interpersonal relationships. Early- and late-maturing groups did not differ significantly from each other in needs for achievement or personal recognition.

These findings make it clear that rate of physical maturing may affect personality development in crucially important ways. However, it is important to note that in any particular case the effects of early- or late-maturing may be significantly modified by the individual's psychological history and present circumstances.

References

1. Farnam, M. L., *The Adolescent* (New York: Harper, 1951).
2. Fisher, R. A., *Statistical Methods for Research Workers,* 7th ed. (Edinburgh: Oliver & Boyd, 1938).
3. Jones, H. E., "Observational Methods in the Study of Individual Development," *Journal of Consulting Psychology,* Vol. 4 (1940), pp. 234-238.
4. ———, *Development in Adolescence* (New York: Appleton, 1943.)
5. ———, "Adolescence in Our Society," in *The Family in a Democratic Society,* Anniversary Papers of the Community Service Society of New York (New York: Columbia, 1949), pp. 70-82.
6. Jones, Mary C., "The Later Careers of Boys Who Were Early- or Late-Maturing," *Child Development,* Vol. 28 (1957), pp. 113-128.
7. ———, "A Study of Socialization at the High School Level" (In preparation).
8. ———, and Nancy Bayley, "Physical Maturing Among Boys as Related to Behavior," *Journal of Educational Psychology,* Vol. 41 (1950), pp. 129-148.
9. Payne, D. E., and P. H. Mussen, "Parent-Child Relations and Father Identification Among Adolescent Boys," *Journal of Abnormal Social Psychology,* Vol. 52 (1956), pp. 358-362.
10. Stone, C. P., and R. G. Baker, "The Attitudes and Interests of Premenarcheal and Postmenarcheal Girls," *Journal of Genetic Psychology,* Vol. 54 (1939), pp. 27-71.
11. Tyron, Caroline M., "Evaluation of Adolescent Personality by Adolescents," *Monographs of the Society for Research in Child Development,* Vol. 4, No. 4 (1939).

4. The later careers of boys who were early- or late-maturing

MARY C. JONES

Reprinted from *Child Development*, Vol. 28 (1957), 113-128, by permission of the author and the Society for Research in Child Development.

Do late-maturing boys eventually "catch up" to the early-maturers? What psychological differences exist in adulthood between boys who were early- or late-maturing adolescents? In the preceding article Mussen and Jones examined differences that can exist in adolescence between early- and late-maturers, while in this selection Jones conducts an inquiry into the longer-term effects in adult life.

A previous study (7) compared two groups of boys who had been classified as physically accelerated or retarded, in terms of skeletal age. These groups represented approximately the 20 per cent at each extreme of a normal public school sample. The comparison showed differences in physical growth, sexual maturing, and in a number of psychological measures, and led to the conclusion that ". . . those who are physically accelerated are usually accepted and treated by adults and other children as more mature. They appear to have relatively little need to strive for status. From their ranks come the outstanding student body leaders in senior high school. In contrast, the physically retarded boys exhibit many forms of relatively immature behavior: this may be in part because others tend to treat them as the little boys they appear to be. Furthermore, a fair proportion of these give evidence of needing to counteract their physical disadvantages in some way—usually by greater activity and striving for attention, although in some cases by withdrawal" (7, p. 146).

It is clear that early- or late-maturing may have a considerable bearing upon the social life and personal adjustment of some individuals during the middle years of their adolescence. Perhaps of greater importance, however, is the inquiry as to longer-term effects or relationships in adult life, and on this point no evidence has previously been offered.

The subjects who participated in the original study are now in their early thirties. Contacts have been maintained with many of the group during the intervening years; in a systematic follow-up study [1] beginning in 1954 current data have been obtained for 20 of the early- and late-maturing boys, out of an original sample of 32.

Adolescent Differences

Figures 1 to 7 present data from the adolescent period for the original groups, and for the subsamples available in the present study. Figure 1

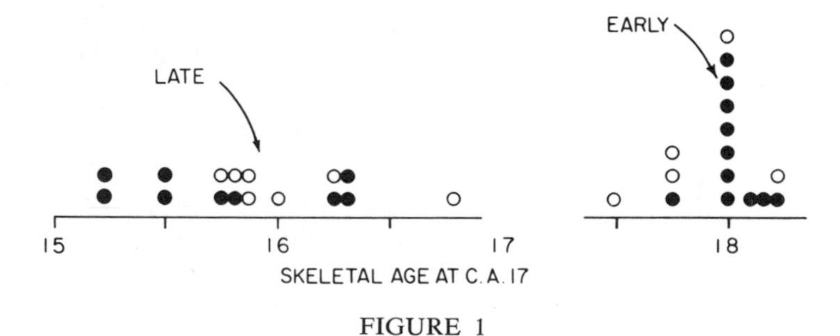

FIGURE 1

SKELETAL AGES AT 17 YEARS, OF THE LATE- AND EARLY-MATURING

shows the distribution of skeletal ages (at around chronological age 17) for the early- and late-maturing. Each circle represents an individual case: the black circles those included in the follow-up and the open circles those who have dropped out.[2] It can be seen that the new selection has not substantially altered the maturity differential of the two groups.

[1] Acknowledgments are due to the U.S. Public Health Service for a grant in support of this study. The follow-up study was a joint project of the Institute of Child Welfare and the Donner Laboratory.

[2] Skeletal age was assessed from X rays of the hand and knee, using Todd standards. Of the 12 cases lost from the original sample, three have died, one has not been located, one is noncooperative, three have been scheduled but not yet seen in the follow-up and the remaining four have moved away and are for the time being unavailable because of residence abroad, or in other states.

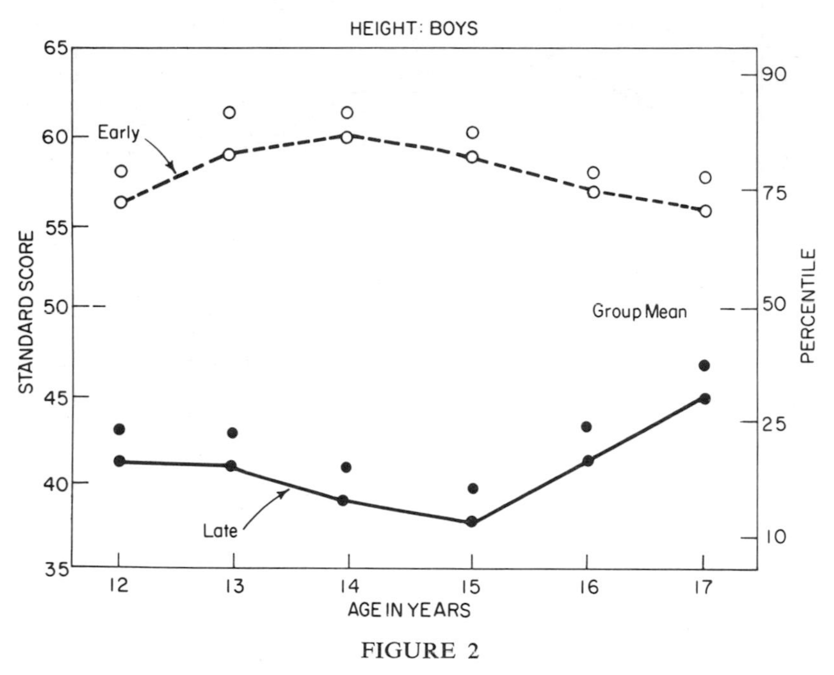

FIGURE 2

HEIGHT COMPARISONS FOR TWO CONTRASTING GROUPS

Figures 2 and 3 present cumulative records for height and weight in terms of standard scores at ages 12 to 17. Standard scores (in which 50 is taken as the mean and 10 as the SD) are indicated on the left vertical axis, and percentiles on the right. In these and the following figures, the points on connecting lines represent averages for the follow-up group, consisting of 11 early- and 9 late-maturing individuals. The adjacent points denote averages for the original 16 early- and 16 late-maturing.

The early-maturing tend to fall at the 75 percentile or above, and the late-maturing at the 25 percentile or below, with differences which are at a maximum at around 14 years, when the early-maturing are on the average approximately 8 inches taller and 34 pounds heavier.

In these physical measures the adolescent data for the follow-up sample are similar to those of the original sample, and this is also shown in Figure 4, based on a measure of static dynamometer strength (right grip).

Other physical comparisons included Greulich's (6) 5-point standards of maturity (rated by physicians from pubic hair and external genitalia) and Bayley's ratings of androgeny (1). On the Greulich scale the late-maturing boys at age 14 averaged only 2.0, well below the norm; while the early-maturing averaged 4.5, or close to the scale maximum. In the androgeny assessments, the early-maturing were nearly all in the "masculine"

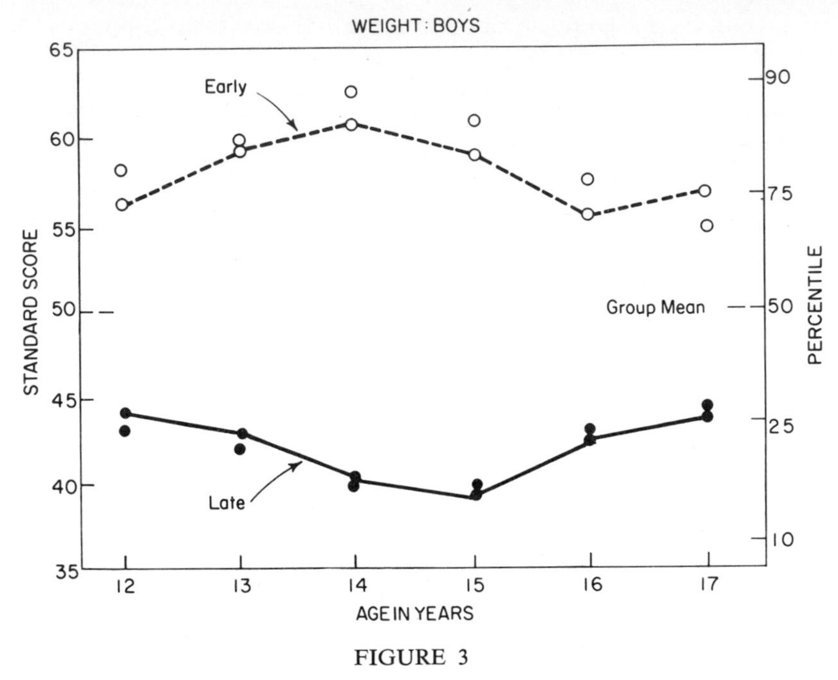

FIGURE 3

WEIGHT COMPARISONS FOR TWO CONTRASTING GROUPS

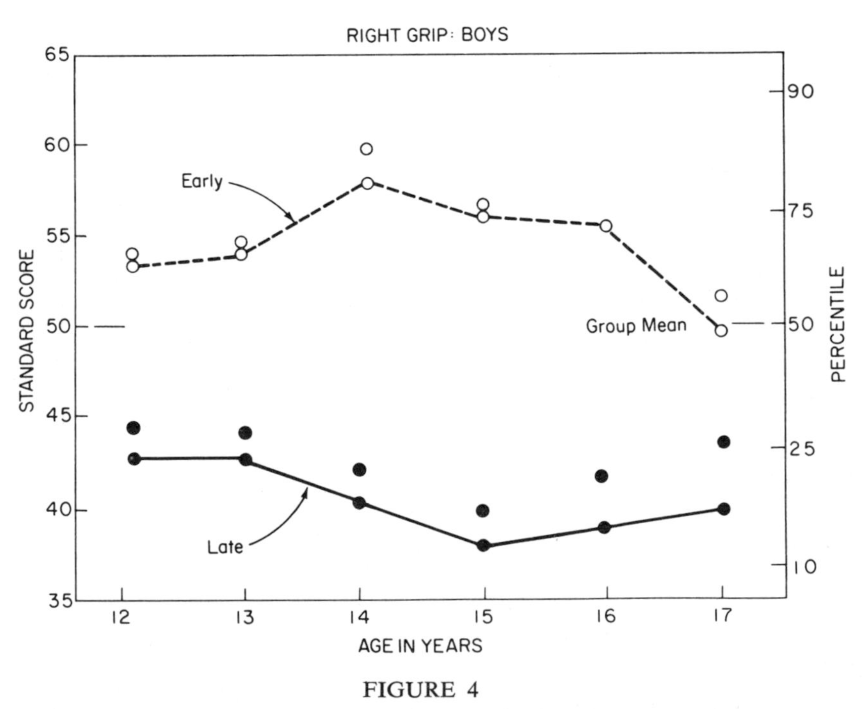

FIGURE 4

STRENGTH COMPARISONS FOR TWO CONTRASTING GROUPS

or "hypermasculine" zone, while approximately half of the late-maturing were classified as "asexual," "bisexual," "hypobisexual," or physically "disharmonious." In these as in other respects the follow-up samples yielded distributions similar to those of the original study.

With such marked adolescent differences in size, strength, masculine conformation, and associated athletic abilities, we might also predict, in our culture, average differences in reputational status and in some aspects of self-acceptance. In the original study comparisons were presented, at an average age of 16, for a series of ratings made in "free-play" situations. The early-maturing were judged to be more attractive in physique and as showing more attention to grooming. They tended to be more relaxed, more matter-of-fact and less affected in their behavior. Differences were significant at the .05 level for each of these traits; for a number of other characteristics, such as interest in the opposite sex, and "good-naturedness," quite consistent differences were obtained over nine semesters of observation. The late-maturing were significantly more expressive, but their small-boy eagerness was also associated with greater tenseness and more affected attention-seeking mannerisms.

Figure 5 represents average measures for attractiveness of physique,

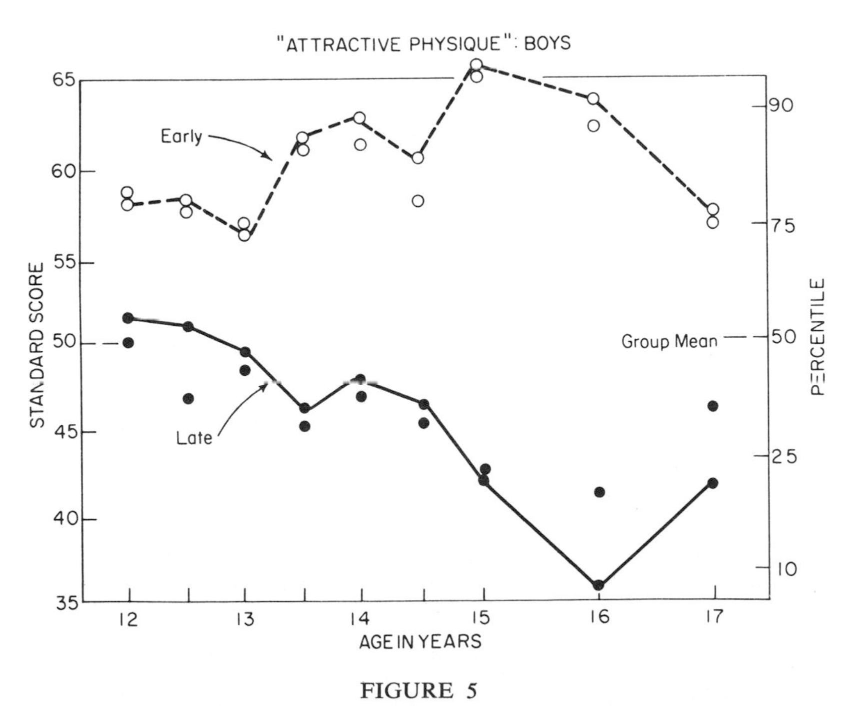

FIGURE 5

COMPARATIVE RATINGS OF "ATTRACTIVE PHYSIQUES"

based on independent ratings by three staff members. Figure 6 gives similar cumulative records for an illustrative aspect of expressive behavior (eagerness). The early-maturing are centered close to the average in this characteristic while the late-maturing are judged to be more juvenile and

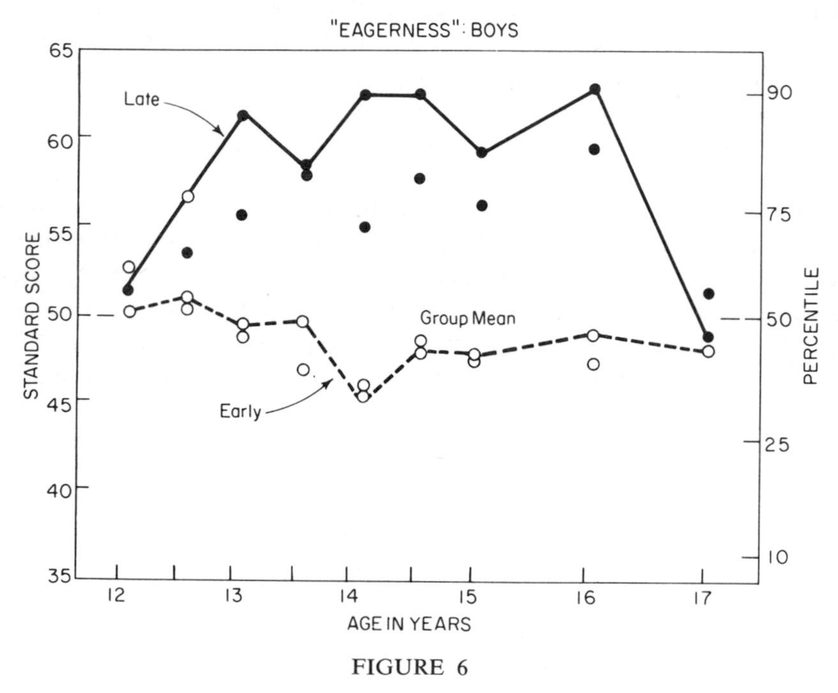

FIGURE 6

Comparative Ratings of "Eagerness"

less poised in their expressiveness, especially in the middle years of adolescence. Similar results were found for such characteristics as "animated," "talkative," and "uninhibited."

On behavior items suggesting a large component of self-acceptance (being relaxed, unaffected, and matter-of-fact) the early-maturing were rated higher at the end of the study, with the late-maturing becoming increasingly "tense" and "affected" in the high school years.[3] Figure 7 illustrates this for the characteristic which we have called "matter-of-fact." Both groups fluctuate around the average in this trait until age 16 when they separate noticeably, the early-maturing falling on the favorable or

[3] A study of the Thematic Apperception Test responses at age 17 suggests that early-maturing boys tend to be more self-accepting and to feel less threatened than late-maturing. These data will be presented in a forthcoming article by Paul H. Mussen and Mary C. Jones.

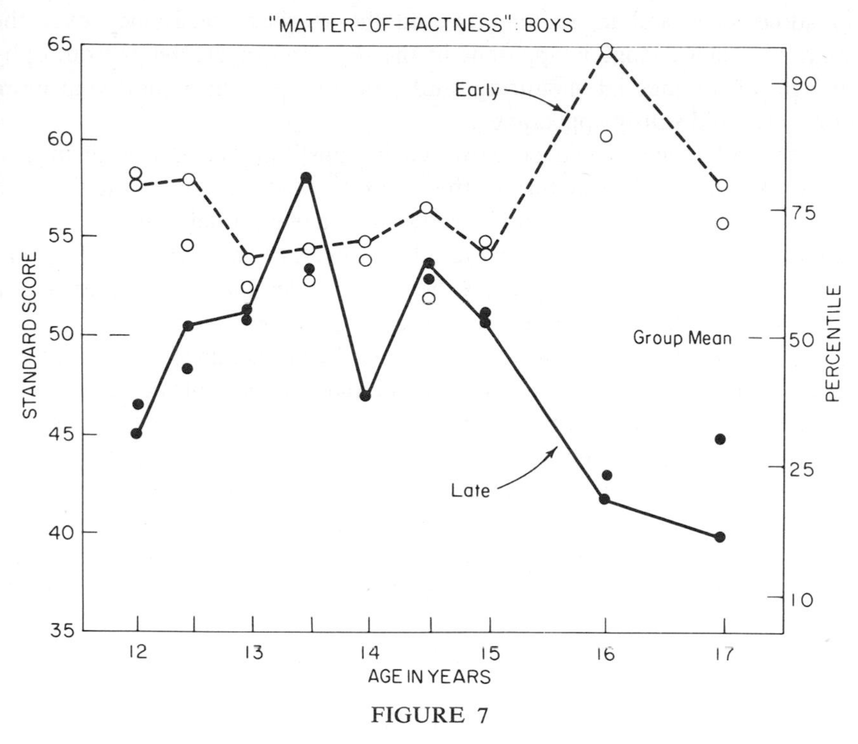

FIGURE 7

COMPARATIVE RATINGS OF "MATTER-OF-FACTNESS"

well-adjusted side, and the late-maturing on the attention-seeking or show-off side of the scale. Similar wide separation at ages 16 and 17 has been found for the trait "unaffected-affected" and for "relaxed-tense." In these, as in other relevant psychological measures, the follow-up groups had adolescent records similar to those of the original study; the loss of cases has not substantially changed the selection.

Adult Differences

We may now consider the adult characteristics of the early- and late-maturing, as observed at an average age of 33 years. As was predicted at age 17, the differences in gross size tend to disappear. The early-maturing average only half an inch taller, at 5 feet 10 inches; and 7 pounds heavier, at 172 pounds. These differences are not significant. In body build, the prediction is that the early-maturing would be more mesomorphic. The tendency is in this direction, but the differences are not significant. The chief thing to note is the wide range of physiques within each group (both in adolescence and in adulthood) and the marked consistency over the years. A slight change is apparent in the direction of greater mesomorphy in eight of the nine late-maturing, and they now present a somewhat more developed and sturdy appearance.

Some differences would be expected in constitutional indices of masculinity. Among the late-maturing, the majority of the original study and of those included in the follow-up were rated as having a deficiency in masculine development, at age 17. At age 33, however, Sheldon ratings of gynandromorphy (8) in the two groups showed considerable overlap and only a small and nonsignificant difference in favor of the early-maturing.

Personality differences in adult life have been examined with reference to a number of criteria. Two sources of data to be considered here are Gough's California Psychological Inventory and the Edwards Personal Preference Schedule. The first of these, the CPI, attempts to appraise aspects of character and temperament which are significant for social living and interpersonal behavior and which are related to personal maturity and creative achievement. Eighteen scales are available which describe individuals in terms of social responsibility, tolerance, flexibility, academic motivation, self-control,[4] and the like (3).

Most of the above scales did not show significant differences between the groups. One outstanding exception is the scale entitled "good impression" (interest in, and capacity for, creating a "good impression" on others) (4). Differences here favored the early-maturing with a significance at the .006 level.

Some of the interpretative phrases associated with high scores on this scale include: "is turned to for advance and reassurance; fatherly; is concerned with making a good impression; is persistent in working toward his goal." High scorers on this "Gi" scale are also designated as responsible, cooperative, enterprising, sociable, and warm.

In our groups the early-maturing tend in addition to obtain higher scores on the CPI scales for socialization, dominance, self-control, and responsibility. Although none of these shows differences at a significance level better than .07, it is true that the early-maturing have high average scores and present a consistently favorable personality picture with regard to these important social variables.

The phrases and adjectives associated with high scores on these five scales (good impression, socialization, dominance, self-control, and responsibility) remind us strikingly of the social behavior and personal traits attributed, by their peers and by adults, to the early-maturing boys in adolescence. For the total group of 43 boys thus far included in the follow-up,

[4] "Self-control" is indicated by a low score on the impulsivity scale.

a correlation of .50 (significant at the .01 level) was found between the "good impression" score on the CPI, and their level of skeletal maturity 18 years earlier. The corresponding Pearson *r* for the socialization [5] score at age 33, and skeletal maturity at age 15, was .40, significant at the .01 level. For these correlations skeletal quotients were computed (skeletal age over chronological age), to make allowance for slight differences in the age at which the skeletal X-rays were obtained.

One other scale yields an interesting difference, significant at the .05 level. This is the scale for what has been termed "flexibility." Those who score high on this scale are described by Gough as tending to be rebellious, touchy, impulsive, self-indulgent, assertive, and also insightful. Low scorers are described as deliberate, methodical, industrious, rigid, mannerly, overly-controlling of impulses, compliant. In these terms, the late-maturers tend to be more "flexible" than the early-maturers.

We might hazard the guess that some of the little-boy behavior—the impulsiveness, playfulness, and also the "touchiness" repeatedly noted in late-maturing adolescents—is mirrored in the description of high scorers on this scale. We might speculate further that in the course of having to adapt to difficult status problems, the late-maturers have gained some insights and are indeed more flexible, while the early-maturing, capitalizing on their ability to make a good impression, may have clung to their earlier success pattern to the extent of becoming somewhat rigid or overcontrolled.

The Edwards Personal Preference test shows relatively few significant differences between the two groups. This is a self-report device which measures 15 variables named from Murray's list of needs (2).

On the Edwards test, two of the scales are discriminating for our groups at the 4 and 5 per cent levels respectively. The early-maturing group scores high on the *dominance* scale: "to be a leader, persuade, argue for a point of view," while the late-maturing score high in *succorance:* "to seek encouragement, to be helped by others, to have a fuss made over one when hurt." For the total group of 40 who took the Edwards test at around age 33, skeletal maturing at age 17 correlated .40 with dominance, and —.48 with succorance (both significant at the .01 level). Table 1 summarizes the statistical findings for the follow-up comparisons.[6]

To those of us who have known these young men for over 20 years, some of the most interesting questions remain to be answered. What have

[5] This "socialization" scale was first presented by Gough (5) and described as a scale for "delinquency." It is now scored in the opposite direction so as to emphasize the "socialization" side of a socialization-asocialization continuum. In a validation study lowest scores were obtained by those nominated as high school "best citizens"; highest scores by delinquents.

[6] Statistical analysis of the data was completed under a research grant from the Department of Education, University of California.

TABLE 1

SUMMARY OF STATISTICAL FINDINGS FOR THE FOLLOW-UP COMPARISONS

PHYSICAL MEASURES: MEANS

	Early		*Late*	
Measures	*Age 14*	*Age 33*	*Age 14*	*Age 33*
Height	5 ft. 8 in.	5 ft. 10 in.	5 ft.	5 ft. 9½ in.
Weight	126.9 lb.	172 lb.	93.2 lb.	165 lb.
Endomorphy*	2.6	3.1	3.1	3.3
Mesomorphy*	4.5	4.6	3.9	4.3
Ectomorphy*	3.4	3.4	3.7	3.7

PSYCHOLOGICAL SCALES

	Means				
Scales	*Early*	*Late*	*Signif. of difference*†	*r*‡	*Signif. level*
California Psychological Inventory					
Good Impression	25.6	15.7	.006	.50	<.01
Flexibility	9.7	13.8	.05	—.23	
Delinquency§	13.9	20.3	.07	—.40	<.01
Impulsivity	17.1	23.4	.13	—.31	<.05
Dominance	31.7	27.4	.17	.26	
Responsibility	32.9	30.0	.19	.35	<.05
Edwards Personal Preference Schedule					
Dominance	19.4	12.6	.04	.40	<.01
Succorance	7.1	12.4	.05	—.48	<.01

*Rating on 7-point scale; 7 is high.
†Significance level, Wilcoxon Rank Test.
‡Pearson product-moment correlation with skeletal age / chronological age, at 15 years.
§A low score indicates "socialization."

been their successes and failures in achieving occupational and personal goals? All are married, and in each group the present number of children averages 2.3. Socioeconomic ratings, based on homes and neighborhoods, show no differences for the two groups. There are no significant differences in average educational level, although a slightly higher proportion of the later-maturing have college degrees and the only college teacher is in this group.[7]

[7] The writer is indebted to Mr. Read Tuddenham who secured much of the interview material through a grant from the Office of Naval Research.

There is some indication that more of the early-maturing have attained vocational goals which are satisfying and status-conferring. Among this group five are in professional careers; four are executives; one is a skilled mechanic, and one is in a clerical position. Of the executives, three are in positions of somewhat impressive status.

Among the late-maturing, four are in professions, two are still university students, two are salesmen, and one is a carpenter. None has attained an important managerial position and several, by their own account and the nature of their work, seem somewhat precariously unsettled.

In the former study descriptive pictures were given of late-maturing boys who illustrated contrasting behavior patterns of attention-seeking activity and of withdrawal. It may be appropriate here to summarize individual records for several of those at the early- and late-maturing extremes.

Tom, a late-maturing boy as described in a previous article (7), was at the age of 13 a chubby small boy, very rosy of cheek, sparkling-eyed, laughing and dimpled. He was gay, active, good-humored, emotionally volatile. Even as a senior in high school he was still a "little boy." His voice had not changed. At a time when most of his classmates were paying careful attention to cleanliness and grooming, he often came to school with dirty hands and in misfit clothes. He was likely to get into childish scuffles; physically, however, he was not able to cope with his classmates, and would sometimes break down and cry when things went badly.

Unlike most of the physiologically retarded group, he seemed not to be anxious about his immaturity. Growth continued during his college years, when he added four inches to his height, and 20 pounds to his weight. As a graduate student Tom began to play baseball on an intramural team and for the first time, according to his own report, was able to hold up his end of the game. So impressed was he with his own physical gains (there had never been any doubt about his mental abilities) that he raised his sights in regard to vocational goals, achieved a graduate degree and joined the academic ranks as a college teacher.

The interviewer who saw him most recently at the age of 33 described him as: "A genial smiling young man, well integrated, mature, observant, well satisfied with his life situation." He is making excellent progress professionally, and achieving recognition among his colleagues. We now feel that we were justified in the impression gained during his high school years, that Tom was able to cope with the problems of late-maturing without permitting these to create a basic feeling of handicap.

Lonnie, on the other hand, was a late-maturing boy whose physical deficiencies in size and athletic prowess were a persistent source of tension and anxiety. His activity pattern was expressed in excessive verbalizations which became more aggressive and compulsive as he progressed through adolescence.

Excerpts from a staff group conference after a camping trip illustrate this point:

> (W.J.C.) Lonnie was by far the most talkative in this very talkative crowd. . . . Saturday night after most of the boys had gone to sleep Lonnie turned to a question which had to do with the history of religion. He pursued the subject with vehemence.
>
> (M.C.J.) On Sunday morning when we were just finishing breakfast, Mr. G. mentioned a friend who had been working with a growth-promoting hormone. He had hardly uttered a sentence when Lonnie, who had been at the next table, suddenly appeared by his side.
>
> (J.C.) This led to further discussion throughout the day and on Monday, at school. . . . He was again on the subject of the hormone. He wanted to offer himself as a subject because he had always been small and underweight, "skinny." . . .
>
> (T.C.) Lonnie talks with ceaseless energy, with a good deal of ego at stake . . . "I know a fellow who is a grandson of a Senator. But when we argue I can beat him everytime with cold facts—statistics."

In a current interview many of the same characteristics of restless energy emerged. The interviewer commented that he was hard to rate because of tendencies which were superficially in contradiction to each other. He seemed self-centered, self-sufficient, and with a strong drive for autonomy, but was also dependent on his wife and "socially minded" in the sense of having abstract interests in groups, social issues, *etc.* "He seems to have achieved a fairly stabilized adjustment—if not a conventional one. Seems able to work toward long-term goals because he has considerable personal freedom. He is tense, rebellious, intellectual, too bent on satisfying his own needs in relationships to relate well to groups either as a member or a leader."

When asked what he would do differently if he had the last 15 years to live over again, Lonnie replied that he would have gone ahead as fast as possible with academic work. "As it was, I was out for Adventure with a capital A and Experience with a capital E—a hollow sort of goal which doesn't satisfy. I traveled a lot but could have done as much living just around the corner."

Late-maturing was merely one of Lonnie's problems, but it led to an impaired status which was an immediate source of frustration, and of rebellious compensatory strivings. These patterns are still apparent in his adult life, although he now seems to take a more realistic view of the roles which are possible for him.

A third late-maturing boy, with a very different set of behavior patterns, was *Charles*—one of the two brothers described in the earlier publication as socially inconspicuous, extremely quiet and self-contained. Although not especially noticed or approved by his peer group, he had a variety of substantial individual interests, and congenial family ties.

Charles is described as "Frank and open in expression, individualistic, and outspoken, primarily an introvert. Though somewhat odd, he is probably fairly well liked by his associates. He seems relatively insecure, requiring support and reassurance. He expresses both hostility and dependence in relation to authority figures. . . . He is mildly self-centered, somewhat imperceptive of others' feelings."

In his own description of current activities, he observed, "My job requires relatively little contact with people. I like it this way. . . . My wife is not overly fond of people. . . . My wife and I are very congenial, we talk over everything together."

Charles, who used to be so shy about girls, so retiring and quietly accepting of his own physical deficiencies, now seems to have established a way of life similar to that of his parents, and one which meets his needs with reasonable adequacy.

Howard was early-maturing. In the eyes of adult observers and classmates, he was advantaged in this respect as well as in family background and personal endowment. He was the younger of two boys from a home well above average in financial security, community status, and interpersonal compatibility.

He was well-liked by both boys and girls but although Howard had the same best friend for many years he seemed less dependent upon social ties than was the case with most youngsters of his age. "The girls would like him to take more interest in them," wrote one observer in the ninth grade. He learned to dance in the eighth grade but was a little shy at first with girls.

By the ninth grade he had lost his shyness, but led too busy a life with his own individual projects and his family's activities to be more than casually interested in girls or to accept more than a few of the many party invitations which he received. "He is a grand-looking boy and the girls feel it a great loss that he is not more interested in them."

Even in his senior year at high school when one girl seemed to be steadfastly claiming his attention, he was described as follows at a staff conference after a party which involved both swimming and dancing: "In his customary manner, Howard left Clare to her own devices and went to join the boys in the pool. He enjoys athletic activities even more than devotion to his lady love. . . . I have a feeling that any girl who goes with Howard will have to stand for that arrangement. . . ."

Referring to his social development 15 years later he said, "My interest in girls was not any problem in high school."

Throughout the years of the study, descriptions of Howard stressed his maturity in relation to the group: "Has always been one of the largest and best looking. . . . His prestige among boys is quite marked, with no striving on his part (age 14.4). . . . Howard, like several of his friends this semester, seemed to have reached the stage of 'putting away the childish.' They sat and talked after lunch while the other boys played ball. He has unquestioned prestige, though he seems unaware of it . . ." (14.9).

"Howard is large, seems much more mature than almost any of our group (15.9). . . . Considerable maturity of manner, talked at length to H. E. J., and as an equal, about cameras and photographic equipment" (16.0). A student assistant in the physiology laboratory, impressed with Howard as a 16-year-old said: "He doesn't attempt to make a show of himself or his accomplishments although he now holds the record for vital capacity of 6.40 liters and of 3 minutes 37 seconds for holding his breath."

In spite of the fact that others recognized his accelerated maturity from the time he was in elementary school, Howard, in retrospect, described his own development as physically retarded.

A possible clue to this erroneous belief comes from his position in the family, as the younger boy. His father was past middle age when Howard was born and according to his own analysis of the situation, it was the older brother who had received the understanding and attention of a young, vigorous, active father. Howard missed this when he was growing up. It was his older brother who, in turn, furnished the active interested companionship in which Howard may have felt a fatherly, as well as a brotherly quality. He certainly compared himself to this older brother and may have, growing up in the shadow of this comparison, thought of himself as inadequate in many ways, including rate of maturing. An interpretation of his response to the Murray pictures suggests that this is so:

> Age 17: Howard's conflict seems to lie in his inability to reconcile his position as an individual with his position as a member of his family. . . . He tells of his fear that he is inadequate as a family member. His relationship to his older brother is basic to his difficulty. He is impressed with his older brother's superiority. Howard is far from the inadequate person he imagines himself to be in comparison with his brother. It seems likely that he does not feel inadequate except when measuring himself against his exaggerated notion of his brother's accomplishment.
>
> In other circumstances, while his demands on himself are high, he appears to be able to meet them. In his struggle to emulate his brother he has developed qualities basic to superior performance. He shows determination and persistence, a high level

> of energy, and the capacity to direct and maintain effort toward the goal he sets for himself. In the stories, he exaggerates his weakness but he indicates, as well, his strength.

As an adult in his early thirties, Howard seems to have come to realize his potentialities. "I've developed a good deal more self-confidence. . . . I feel I have had enough education and experience to tackle a job that I have some feel for, so I'm optimistic. In my work, I'm in a dominant position and you build up self-confidence. In college, fraternity life and athletics helped, too."

The interviewer summarizes: "Mr. F. has strong needs for acquisition and mastery. He is dominant, active, a leader, and autonomous. It would be hard to keep him down."

Bob provides another example of the socially advantaged early-maturing boy. An only son in a prosperous upper-middle-class family, Bob had a pattern cut out for him to follow. He was expected to enter his father's business. His mother knew exactly how she wanted him to grow toward manhood and what course to pursue in fulfilling this goal. "I will not have a dirty boy," she said on one occasion. But this meant that he had to wash up after strenuous play, not that activity was prohibited. She understood that boys like to ride bicycles, build boats, and later, drive cars; that they are happy when playing with neighborhood boys in the backyard as preadolescents, and that as adolescents their social interests include girls, dancing, parties. Creditable scholarship and practice in leadership were encouraged in school.

All of these goals were easily attained. Bob was slightly above the average of our group in intelligence and achievement tests. He was rated consistently on the favorable side, in a wide range of social and personal characteristics. Classmates placed him very high in leadership and popularity. In self-report, he was consistently on the well-adjusted side—above the eightieth percentile for the group in all categories, which implied family, social, school, and personal satisfactions.

After 15 years, Bob has achieved the realization of his own and his family's goals: "I enjoy my work very much . . . it's a business of my father's that I've always been interested in going into." To the question about how he might live his last 15 years over again he responded: "I'd do them about the same."

Two interviewers, a man and a woman, reveal their own somewhat different biases when summing up their impressions of Bob: The male psychologist wrote: "Mr. A is a tanned, dark-haired, immaculately dressed businessman, self-assertive, confident in general bearing but not quite at ease during the interview. He is satisfied with himself and the mores of his business milieu . . . a rigid personality with little insight, little ability to relax and enjoy himself. He puts business first. He has no conflict since he faces no difficult external problems."

The woman who interviewed Bob reacted as follows: "Mr. A fits happily into the 'ideal' stereotype of a successful upper-middle-class business man with no strain and with none of the unfavorable connotations. Although he has social ambitions not yet attained and lets work invade leisure time to a minor extent, he does not seem under pressure about his work. His range of interests are not wide or differentiated . . . he accepts the stereotype of upper-middle-class without much thought . . . his interests are social (in the sense of personal enjoyment) rather than directed along power lines . . . he exhibits more freedom from anxiety than any subject I have seen so far."

Unlike the two preceding cases, *Rod* was an early-maturing boy with persistent difficulties in social adjustment. These stemmed in part from a family background which was a handicap in a school where acceptable behavior followed upper-middle-class standards.

In our first records (at 10.5 years) he was described as tall and thin, talkative and outgoing with adults, friendly with strange boys whom he was meeting for the first time. These characteristics were continued during the period of the study.

But from the classroom and the playground came reports of difficulties. While some of the attributes ascribed to him by classmates were socially desirable—"a leader, daring, active in games, happy and enthusiastic," he was also said to be a fighter, lacking in a sense of humor about himself, inclined to be extremely bossy, and attention-seeking. His friendship relations must have been unsatisfactory also, in the early adolescent years, since he mentioned five boys as best friends but was mentioned by none of them in return. He was quarrelsome in games.

During a period of exceptionally rapid growth, in the seventh and eighth grades, this rough and quarrelsome behavior seemed to increase. Rod's superior size and strength provided an easy means of dominating others. "Rod seems driven by an urge to tease; the other boys do not like him very well but cannot dispute his attacks since none of the group approaches his size." Although recognized as a stormy adolescent, often using physical aggression as a defense against his feelings of social inadequacy, he gradually learned to channel his energies in more acceptable directions. He was active in games, and gained some prestige as an athlete. As the other boys caught up with him in size and strength, he was less tempted to draw them into situations involving bullying or fighting. He became more popular, and although still considered "bossy," he was less of a show-off and more considerate of others.

Usually the physical build and stature of early-maturing boys is attractive. During the middle years of adolescence this was not the case with Rod, whose growth in weight did not keep up with his growth in height. He was embarrassed rather than pleased by his height; he worried about it, and seemed to slump as he sat and to stoop as he walked.

In the later years of high school he gained better proportions and began to be rated as "good-looking." He became an expert dancer, and although still preferring athletics he was now frequently included in mixed parties. His classmates rated him as a leader, and as having a good sense of humor.

Thus we see that a boy from "across the tracks" at first used the physical competence accompanying early-maturing as a means of asserting himself in an environment in which he felt ill at ease. He was disliked for his undisciplined behavior, and his physical power was a liability rather than an asset.

By the end of adolescence, however, he had learned more effective social techniques. His size and strength were not to be disregarded, and his classmates began to perceive him in a more favorable light.

After high school Rod saw service in the Pacific—a handsome, swashbuckling soldier who wrote of his adventures to various members of the study staff. He is now settled down as a businessman. Interviewers describe him as devoted to his wife and three children, hard-working, ambitious. He impressed an interviewer as not being very perceptive about or concerned with other people's opinions, except as having a general wish to make a good impression. "Interests in others' motivations and his own are relatively superficial. He expresses his feelings impulsively without much anxiety; seems to be able to disregard the needs of others but is probably warm to those close to him. Perhaps he is too self-centered to care much about group activity and does not seem to care for the kind of prestige which he would get from exploiting a group."

Though friendly he was thought to be a little defensive about having no recreational or cultural interests to report. He said, "I have three main interests: the family, the business, and sports." But an account of his daily living revealed that the business got most of his attention. He was able to report fair financial success as the result of his devotion to work. He described with some pride the house which he owns: "It is supposed to be elite. I lived on the wrong side of the tracks too long. But now where I live each house has its own patio and there are lots of swimming pools in the subdivision."

Summary and Conclusion

Boys who had been classified as physically accelerated or retarded in terms of skeletal age during adolescence were compared as young adults at age 33, to determine the long-term effects of rate of maturing upon personality.

Although some cases were lost from the original sample, the data for the follow-up group as reconstituted showed no substantial alteration in the adolescent differentials of the early- and late-maturing.

For the original sample and for the subsample available in the present study, analysis of ratings by adults and classmates indicated that the early-maturing boys were significantly more attractive in physique, more relaxed, poised, and matter-of-fact. Consistent differences in other characteristics, such as interest in the opposite sex and "good-naturedness," were obtained over nine semesters of observation. Late-maturing boys were described as more expressive, active, talkative, eager, attention-getting.

The physical differences noted for these boys at adolescence have tended to disappear in adulthood. Personality characteristics as appraised by the California Psychological Inventory and the Edwards Personal Preference Schedule have shown a number of significant differences on the various scales for which the tests are scored (*e.g.*, higher scores for the early-maturing on measures of "good impression" and "socialization.") Where such differences were found, they tended to describe the young adults much as they had been described in adolescence.

No differences were found between the early- and late-maturing in present marital status, family size, or educational level. A few of the early-maturing have made exceptionally rapid progress as junior executives and a few of the late-maturing are still somewhat unsettled, vocationally.

The foregoing presentation of data and the case summaries remind us again of the conclusions to the original study which stressed individual differences within each group, resulting from the complex interplay of factors. During the adolescent period late-maturing is a handicap for many boys and can rarely be found to offer special advantages. Early-maturing carries both advantages and disadvantages. In our culture it frequently gives competitive status, but sometimes also involves handicaps in the necessity for rapid readjustments and in requiring the adolescent to meet adult expectations which are more appropriate to size and appearance than to other aspects of maturing. The adolescent handicaps and advantages associated with late- or early-maturing appear to carry over into adulthood to some extent, and perhaps to a greater extent in psychological than in physical characteristics.

References

1. Bayley, Nancy, and Leona M. Bayer, "The Assessment of Somatic Andogyny," *American Journal of Physical Anthropology,* Vol. 4 (1946), pp. 433-462.
2. Edwards, A. L., *Edwards Personal Preference Schedule* (New York: Psychological Corporation, 1954).
3. Gough, H. G., *The California Psychological Inventory* (Stanford, Calif.: Consulting Psychologists' Press, 1951).

4. ———, "On Making A Good Impression," *Journal of Educational Research,* Vol. 46 (1952), pp. 33-42.
5. ———, "Systematic Validation of a Test For Delinquency," *American Psychologist,* Vol. 9 (1954), p. 380 (abstract).
6. Greulech, W. W., *et al.,* "Somatic and Endocrine Studies of Puberal and Adolescent Boys," *Monographs of the Society for Research in Child Development,* Vol. 7, No. 3 (1942).
7. Jones, Mary C., and Nancy Bayley, "Physical Maturing Among Boys as Related to Behavior," *Journal of Educational Psychology,* Vol. 41 (1950), pp. 129-148.
8. Sheldon, W. H., S. S. Stevens, and W. B. Tucker, *The Varieties of Human Physique* (New York: Harper, 1940).

5. Self-conceptions, motivations, and interpersonal attitudes of early- and late-maturing girls [1]

MARY C. JONES
AND PAUL H. MUSSEN

Reprinted from *Child Development,* Vol. 29 (1958), 491-501, by permission of the authors and the Society for Research in Child Development.

As demonstrated in the two previous selections, a youngster's concept of self is influenced to some extent by his physical maturation. Early-maturing boys apparently have the edge over their late-maturing male counterparts as far as a positive concept of self is concerned. What is the case for girls? Do the early-maturers have the advantage over late-maturing girls? Or would you expect to find the reverse true? Compare this article closely with the prior selection by Mussen and Jones.

"The changing body and the changing self" is a phrase associated with adolescent development (18). It suggests that the shaping into mature form of the childhood body pattern is accompanied by new self-concepts. These altered attitudes toward the self reflect at least in part the youth's response to his physical metamorphosis.

What "growing-up" connotes for the individual adolescent depends upon a complex of psychobiological factors. One of the most important of these is rate of physical maturation. Adolescent growth may be relatively regular and even, or it may be uneven or abrupt. The timing of puberty, in relation to social norms of the peer group, may present problems of special importance for some adolescents.

Previous reports of systematic com-

[1] The TAT data for this study were obtained by Harold E. Jones in connection with a test program at the Institute of Child Welfare.

parisons between the behavior and personality characteristics of early- and late-maturing adolescents have indicated that acceleration in growth tends to carry social advantages for boys (9, pp. 243-256) but disadvantages for girls (5, pp. 70-82). At their peak of growth, early-maturing girls are not only taller than their girl classmates but are actually taller than most of the boys in their class (14). They are conspicuously large at a time when physical size is not an asset for girls in our culture. Many girls consider tallness to be a physical stigma (15, pp. 80-89). At the end of adolescence the early-maturing are no longer taller than their age-mates, but in body proportion they tend to have a broad and stocky build (13), less attractive (in terms of current feminine standards) than the more slender physique of the late-maturing.

Among boys, ascendance in size and musculature is an asset because of our cultural values and the functional advantages of such a build for athletic prowess. This more favorable status is indicated in observational records for early-maturing boys. Staff members rated them as physically more attractive and better-groomed than the late-maturing, and in social situations they were more poised and matter-of-fact, and less attention-seeking (5).

In contrast, both classmates (16) and adult observers (12) saw the early-maturing girls as relatively submissive, listless, or indifferent in social situations and lacking in poise (5). Such girls have little influence upon the group and seldom attain a high degree of popularity, prestige, or leadership (8, pp. 87-111).

The girls in the slower-maturing classification were seen as relatively more outgoing and more assured. They were eager, animated, peppy, and talkative. This behavior seems to be acceptable among girls since those who exhibit it are also described as confident and having leadership abilities (5). While the same characteristics of expressiveness are attributed to slow-growing boys, it is associated in their case more specifically (and especially in later adolescence) with show-off behavior, affection, and tenseness (5, 9).

In accounting for these sex differences in the response to early or late puberty, we may note that although early-maturing boys have physical advantages over other boys and are socially in step with girls, the girl who develops earlier than her classmates may be temporarily isolated. H. E. Jones has expressed this as follows:

> The early-maturing girl quite naturally has interests in boys and in social usages and activities more mature than those of her chronological age group. But the males of her own age are unreceptive, for while she is physiologically a year or two out of step with the girls

> in her class, she is three or four years out of step with the boys—a vast and terrifying degree of developmental distance (5).

A study of responses to the Thematic Apperception Test, given to members of the Adolescent Growth Study when they were seniors in high school, yielded a somewhat unfavorable psychological picture for the late-maturing boys. Compared with their early-maturing peers, they showed greater evidence of negative self-concepts, prolonged dependency needs, feelings of rejection by others, rebellious attitudes toward parents, and strong affiliative needs. These findings were in agreement with evidence from other sources (11).

A similar TAT comparison of early- and late-maturing girls should be expected to show results different from those obtained for boys. Thus, it might be expected that early-maturing girls would reveal negative self-feeling and less satisfactory interpersonal attitudes.

Procedure

The present study, paralleling that for boys, was designed to investigate the relationship between maturational status and self-conceptions, motivations, and interpersonal attitudes in a normal public school sample of girls (7, pp. 234-238). Personality assessment was made on the basis of their responses to the Thematic Apperception Test (TAT).

The 34 17-year-old girls of this investigation constitute approximately the 20 per cent at each extreme of the total sample of the Adolescent Growth Study, selected on the basis of their physical maturity status as determined by X-rays of the wrists and hands (1, pp. 51-89). Sixteen had been among the most consistently accelerated over a four-year period during adolescence; the other 18 were among the most consistently retarded. All of the subjects took the TAT at around age 17 when they were seniors in high school.

The TAT consisted of 18 pictures: nine from the Murray set which is now standard (cards 1, 5, 6, 7BM, 10, 11, 14, 15, 17); five pictures from the set generally used in 1938 when these data were collected (a man and woman seated on a park bench; a bearded old man writing in an open book; a thin, sullen, young man standing behind a well-dressed older man; a tea table and two chairs; an abstract drawing of two bearded men); and four cards not in the Murray series (a madonna and child, the nave of a large church, a dramatic view of mountains, a boy gazing at a cross which is wreathed in clouds).

The tests were administered individually. Each card was projected on a screen while the subject told a story which was recorded verbatim. Standard instructions were given for the Murray cards, and subjects were asked to describe the feelings elicited by the other four pictures. Most of the stories were brief.

The scoring scheme involved counting the relevant needs, press, and descriptions of the heroes of the stories, the assumption being that the storyteller has identified with the hero; the hero's needs are the same as the girl's; the press that impinge upon the hero are the ones that affect the girl telling the story. A total of 20 needs, press, and descriptive categories, each defined as specifically as possible, was developed in the analysis of the protocols. A score for each subject for each TAT catogery was derived by counting the number of stories in which it appeared. Table 1 presents a list of the categories used, together with definitions of these categories.

To test the reliability of this analysis, one of the authors (PM) and another psychologist [2] independently scored 15 complete protocols (300 stories). The percentage of interrater agreement was .90, computed by the usual formula (number of agreements divided by number of agreements plus number of disagreements).

In order to eliminate bias, the scoring used in the present study was done "blind," that is, independently of knowledge of the subject's maturational status.

Results

Frequency distributions of the scores of all subjects were made for all the TAT variables. Each distribution was then dichotomized at the point which most nearly enabled the placing of half of the 34 subjects above, and half of them below, the dividing point. Subjects having scores above this point were considered high in this particular variable; those with scores below this point were considered low in this variable.

Table 1 lists the TAT variables together with the number of late- and early-maturers with high scores in each variable. The exact probabilities of obtaining these distributions of high and low scores in the two groups (or all other possible more extreme sets), calculated in accordance with Fisher's method (3), are given in the fourth column. The last column gives the levels of significance of the differences between early- and late-maturing boys on these same variables, previously reported by the authors (11).

---

[2] We are indebted to Dr. Virginia B. Ware for her participation in this aspect of the study.

As may be seen from Table 1, early- and late-maturing boys differed from each other on many more characteristics than the two groups of girls did. The boys' groups were significantly different from each other, at the 5 per cent level or better, in six of the 20 variables scored, while the early- and late-maturing girls differ significantly in only two of the variables (negative characteristics and *n* Recognition). It should be noted, however, that the direction of the differences tended to be the same, rather than reversed, in the two sets of data. For example, the following similarities may be noted:

1. In this list of characteristics a significantly greater proportion of late-maturing girls than of early-maturing girls have high scores on negative characteristics. This finding is similar to that found in the comparison of early- and late-maturing boys. For girls, it is contrary to expectation.
2. The differences between early- and late-maturing girls in respect to *p* Dominance and *p* Rejection are similar to those for early- and late-maturing boys in these variables. These may be interpreted to indicate slightly poorer parent-child relationships among the late-maturing.
3. The early- and late-maturing boys differ significantly on *n* Autonomy 1, suggesting a greater tendency for the late-maturing to avoid or defy authority. The differences are in the same direction for girls, but are not significant.
4. Similar results for boys and girls in *n* Succorance may be interpreted as showing some tendency for stronger dependency needs in the late-maturing.
5. Similar results for boys and girls in *p* Nurturance (significant in one variable for boys) may also be interpreted as indirect indications of stronger dependency needs in the late-maturing.

The chief differences between the sexes are as follows:

1. With respect to *n* Aggression, more early- than late-maturing girls show "argumentative aggression," but the two groups of girls do not differ in physical aggression. On the other hand, more early-maturing than late-maturing boys show high degrees of both kinds of aggression.
2. On one category of *n* Affiliation (involving romantic love) higher proportions of high scores are shown for early-maturing girls as contrasted with their late-maturing peers. The differences between the early-maturing and the late-maturing boys are in the opposite direction for this category.
3. The variables *n* Achievement and *n* Recognition do not differentiate the two groups of boys. Among girls scores are higher for the late-maturing, very significantly so in the case of *n* Recognition.
4. Denial of feeling does not differentiate early- and late-maturing girls but tends to yield higher scores for early-maturing boys.

TABLE 1

NUMBER OF EARLY- AND LATE-MATURERS SCORING HIGH IN TAT VARIABLES

TAT variable (with definition)	*High early-maturers*	*High late-maturers*	p	p (*boys*)
Negative Characteristics—H is described in negative terms (*e.g.*, imbecile, weakling, fanatic)	3	13	.002	.01
p Dominance 1—H forced by parents to do something he doesn't want to	2	7	.08	.09
p Dominance 2—H prevented by parents from doing something he wants to	3	6	—	—
p Dominance 3—Total instances of H's being forced by parents to do something and/or prevented from doing something	4	10	.07	.11
p Rejection—H rejected, scorned, or disapproved by parents or authorities	3	7	.21	.03
n Aggression 1—H is aggressive in physical, asocial way	8	9	—	.02*
n Aggression 2—H is mad at someone, argues	12	14	—	.10*
n Aggression 3—Total of all H's aggressive actions	5	8	—	.10*
n Autonomy 1—H leaves home	8	10	—	.20
n Autonomy 2—H disobeys or defies parents	4	5	—	.11
n Autonomy 3—Total of instances in which hero leaves and/or defies his parents	5	7	—	.02
n Affiliation 1—H establishes good relations with his parents	9	8	—	—
n Affiliation 2—H falls in love, has a romance, marries	11	7	.08	.05*
n Affiliation 3—Total instances in which H establishes and/or maintains friendly relations	7	6	—	.11*
n Succorance—H feels helpless, seeks aid or sympathy	5	10	.16	.06
p Nurturancc 1—H is helped, encouraged, or given something by parents	5	7	—	.18
p Nurturance 2—H is helped, encouraged, or given something by someone else (not parents)	5	10	.16	.02
n Achievement—H attempts to attain a high goal or do something creditable	7	13	.09	—
n Recognition—H seeks fame and/or high prestige status	3	12	.01	—
Denial of Feelings—S states that picture elicits no thoughts or feelings	10	9	—	.06

* Differences are in the opposite direction for boys as compared with girls.

Discussion

The failure of the TAT data to support observational findings, especially with reference to the variable, negative characteristics, might be accounted for in a number of ways. Some writers report that in many cases thematic fantasies and manifest behavior operate independently and are even negatively related (10, pp. 235-240). If we assume this to be the case for our subjects, no further explanation would be needed. But there is also evidence from the literature that, for some groups, TAT findings and overt behavior may be congruent (4, pp. 60-88). Our data on boys are in line with this assumption, since, according to observational ratings, late-maturing boys tend to be socially disadvantaged, and, according to the TAT, personally more maladjusted.

The findings for girls are quite different, however. The early-maturing received more unfavorable ratings from both peers and adult observers on many characteristics. But in the TAT they appear to be somewhat better adjusted than their late-maturing peers. This discrepancy between observers' ratings and the picture derived from the personality tests may stem partly from the fact that the reported observational records represented an average of repeated ratings taken over a period of time (from 11 to 17 years), while the TAT stories were collected at the end of this period.

Girls who enter puberty early would be expected to have more difficulties in personal-social relations when they are out of phase with their group. However, after the peer group "catches up," these difficulties would be reduced. By the end of senior high school maturational discrepancies, and social distance due to this factor, would be less marked. It is also possible that even a slight improvement in status would bolster morale and be reflected in a projective technique designed to register attitudes and self-concepts.

There is some slight evidence of a trend toward improved social status for the early-maturing in observational ratings over the seven-year period. Twenty-five items concerned with appearance, emotional tone, social participation, responsiveness, and assurance were used in the comparison. Three of these reflected an improved status at the twelfth-grade level for early-maturing girls (2). In two of these, "laughing" versus "sober" and "sociable" versus "unsociable," the accelerated girls, while still rated lower than the late-maturing, had improved sufficiently so that the differences betwen the two groups were no longer significant. But for one important characteristic, "popular" versus "unpopular," the average ratings for the accelerated girls were now actually slightly higher than for the late-maturing, though the differences were not significant. This last year at high school was the only period when the early-maturing girls were rated by observers as above average in popularity.

It is conceivable that other improvements in social relationships were undetected because of the "halo effect" which, in spite of precautions, may have influenced observers who had rated these same adolescents in earlier years. It is not unlikely that if these girls of more mature status had been observed in social groups of their own choosing (presumably outside of school) the behavior picture might have been more favorable.

It may be noted that over the seven-year period the observational records received little corroboration from a self-report inventory (17). Although differences were not consistent in all categories, the early-maturing girls tended to score more favorably than the slow-maturing on "total adjustment," and also on family adjustment and feelings of personal adequacy. These data from the self-report inventory seem to be generally consistent with the findings from the TAT.

However, we may note that in both the inventory and the TAT the early-maturing girls appear in a somewhat better light than in their reputation scores or in ratings by adult observers. In some individual cases a favorable self-report score should not be taken at face value, in view of the tendency for some individuals to cover up or deny their deficiencies.

The only other variable which yields a significant difference between the maturity groups is in the category *n* Recognition, late-maturing girls manifesting a greater desire for personal recognition. The results for *n* Achievement, though not showing significant differences, tend to support these findings. Other data for this group of girls would lead us to expect this relationship between maturity status and desire for recognition. Late-maturing girls were rated by adult observers as attaining higher prestige, showing more leadership, and having greater stimulus value than their early-maturing peers (5). They were also mentioned more frequently in the high school daily paper over a three-year period and were elected to more offices in extracurricular activities (8). The late-maturing girls' leadership abilities, their greater social participation, and their apparent social success may have been more closely related to desires for recognition and achievement in the social sphere than to a need for affiliation (8).

It should be noted that, among boys, *n* Achievement and *n* Recognition were not significantly associated with rate of physical maturation. Perhaps this is due to the fact that for boys in our culture the pressures to strive for achievement and personal recognition are powerful and pervasive; hence, the boy's physical status may have little influence on his acquisition of strong achievement and recognition needs. Since these cultural pressures are undoubtedly less severe for girls, the strength of these personal needs may be more influenced by such factors as rate of physical maturation.

As we have pointed out in an earlier article (11), the relationship between physical status and psychological characteristics in boys is by no means simple. The evidence of the present study indicates that this relationship is even more complex in the case of girls. While the TAT analysis reported in this study suggests that early-maturing girls have fewer negative self-concepts and fewer needs for personal recognition, the results must be interpreted very cautiously. Since only two variables were found to be significantly related to physical status, it is obvious that many psychological and social factors are more important than rate of maturing in determining girls' self-concepts and personality characteristics. Furthermore, these data, considered together with the data from earlier studies on girls (5, 8), suggest that the rate of maturation may affect overt behavior and covert characteristics in different—sometimes seemingly contradictory—ways.

It is also possible that, at least for girls, early- or late-maturing means different things at different stages of adolescent development. It has been proposed that since girls who enter puberty early are out of step physically with both the boys and girls in their classrooms, they tend to be socially handicapped during early adolescence. We have assumed that this would carry emotional hazards, and evidence is available from observational data and reputation measures to indicate that this is the case (5).

However, the accelerated girl may gain assurance from knowing that she is on the way toward a goal which is a common task for all adolescents, that of being an adult. By the end of high school, many girls in this group were beginning to feel that they had made satisfactory progress toward this goal. If, in addition to this, she can cope with the problems of this period without too much stress, her self-esteem and feelings of adequacy may be enhanced. A resulting improvement in self-concepts may be reflected in the relative infrequency of negative characteristics in TAT stories.

In conclusion, it is evident that each individual's unique personality structure is determined by a complex of interacting variables, including rate of maturation. Comments made by these subjects as young adults indicate that they were aware of a variety of surface phenomena which affected their adolescent adjustment:

> "High school is not a pleasant memory. I felt remote from my mother. If I could have talked to her, it would have helped" (a slow-maturer).
>
> "I wasn't very happy in adolescence. My father was out of work. I

felt inferior outside my own circle of friends—I always aimed to please" (a very popular late-maturing girl).

"I was slightly rattle-brained" (a popular late-maturing girl).

"I didn't have much fun in high school. I look forward to more happiness now than I did when I was in high school. I was an ugly duckling" (a slow-maturer who ascribed many negative characteristics to the hero).

"I seemed to be separated from friends in high school. I'm more outgoing now, less cautious and fearful" (accelerated girl).

"I was overweight and sensitive about it—now I take things more for granted" (accelerated girl).

"I had a feeling of being different when growing up" (accelerated girl).

"I felt stupid in school" (accelerated girl).

"I was very lacking in self-confidence in high school" (accelerated girl).

"I'm more optimistic now. I didn't know many people in high school. I would make an effort to get on with people if I had it to do over again" (accelerated girl).

Feelings of inadequacy and isolation are expressed by these girls and they are attributed to lack of mental ability, financial difficulties, separation from parents, poor social status, overweight, and unattractiveness. They are about equally common among those whose maturational status was at one extreme or the other.

It is obvious that the findings for this specific group of girls need to be particularized for each individual. These results might be modified also for girls in another geographical area or social level or in another generation. It is possible that school and community programs may be able to de-emphasize maturational status by providing an easier access to mixed social groups through classroom, extracurricular, and recreational activities which cut across age classifications.

Summary

The present study was designed to investigate the relationship between maturational status and TAT scores for a group of physically-accelerated as contrasted with a group of slow-developing girls from a normal classroom sample. The TAT protocols of 34 17-year-old girls—16 who had been consistently accelerated and 18 who had been consistently retarded—were analyzed according to a scoring scheme involving 20 needs, press, and descriptive categories.

The scores of early- and late-maturing in each of the categories were compared. Earlier reports (8) had indicated that girls who reach puberty early are likely to be socially disadvantaged, at least until the rest of their age group "catch up" with them. It was assumed that this social disadvantage would be reflected in the TAT protocols and that differences between the two maturity groups in self-concepts, attitudes, and motivations would be found. Analysis of the data of the present study found few striking differences between the two groups of girls. However, early-maturing girls had significantly lower scores on the category of negative characteristics, indicating more favorable self-concepts. This finding is contrary to what might have been expected on the basis of observational ratings by adults and reputational ratings by classmates. On the other hand, the TAT results are in line with scores (total adjustment, self-adequacy, family adjustment) on a self-report inventory.

Late-maturing girls have significantly higher scores on *n* Recognition, which is corroborated by data from other sources.

When the differences between early- and late-maturing girls are compared with the differences between early- and late-maturing boys (11), they are found to be in the same direction more often than in the opposite. These findings are interpreted to indicate that late-maturing adolescents of both sexes are characterized by less adequate self-concepts, slightly poorer parent-child relationships, and some tendency for stronger dependency needs.

It has been emphasized that complex psychological and cultural factors as well as maturational status contribute to personality development and that the pattern of these influences varies for each individual.

References

1. Bayley, N., "Size and Body Build of Adolescents in Relation to Rate of Skeletal Maturing," *Child Development,* Vol. 14 (1943), pp. 51-89.
2. Everett, E. G., *Behavioral Characteristics of Early- and Late-Maturing Girls,* Unpublished Master's thesis, University of California, 1943.
3. Fisher, R. A., *Statistical Methods for Research Workers,* 7th ed. (Edinburgh: Oliver & Boyd, 1938).
4. Harrison, R., "The Thematic Apperception Test," in "Personality Development in Adolescent Girls," L. K. Frank, *et al., Monographs of the Society for Research in Child Development,* Vol. 16 (1951), pp. 60-88.
5. Jones, H. E., "Adolescence in Our Society," Anniversary Papers of the Community Service Society of New York in *The Family in a Democratic Society* (New York: Columbia, 1949), pp. 70-82.
6. ———, *Development in Adolescence* (New York: Appleton, 1943).
7. ———, "Observational Methods in the Study of Individual Development," *Journal of Consulting Psychology,* Vol. 4 (1940), pp. 234-238.

8. Jones, M. C., "A Study of Socialization at the High School Level," *Journal of Genetic Psychology,* Vol. 93 (1958), pp. 87-111.
9. ———, and N. Bayley, "Physical Maturing Among Boys As Related to Behavior," *Journal of Educational Psychology,* Vol. 41 (1950), pp. 129-148.
10. Mussen, P. H., and H. K. Naylor, "The Relationship Between Overt and Fantasy Aggression," *Journal of Abnormal Social Psychology,* Vol. 49 (1954), pp. 235-240.
11. ———, and M. C. Jones, "Self-Conceptions, Motivations, and Interpersonal Attitudes of Late- and Early-Maturing Boys," *Child Development,* Vol. 28 (1957), pp. 243-256.
12. Newman, F. B., "The Adolescent in Social Groups," *Applied Psychological Monographs,* Vol. 9 (1946).
13. Shuttleworth, F. K., "Sexual Maturation and the Physical Growth of Girls Age 6 to 19," *Monographs of the Society for Research in Child Development,* Vol. 2 (1937).
14. ———, "The Physical and Mental Growth of Girls and Boys Age 6 to 19 in Relation to Age at Maximum Growth," *Monographs of the Society for Research in Child Development,* Vol. 4 (1939).
15. Stolz, H. R., and L. M. Stolz, "Adolescent Problems Related to Somatic Variations," *Yearbook of the National Society for the Study of Education,* Vol. 43, Part I (1944), pp. 80-99.
16. Tryon, C. M., "Evaluations of Adolescent Personality By Adolescents," *Monographs of the Society for Research in Child Development,* Vol. 4 (1939).
17. ———, *U. C. Adjustment Inventory I: Social and Emotional Adjustment* (Berkeley: U. of Calif., 1939).
18. Zachry, C. B., *Emotion and Conduct in Adolescence* (New York: Appleton, 1940).

6. The appraisal of body-cathexis: body-cathexis and the self

PAUL F. SECORD
AND SIDNEY M. JOURARD

Reprinted from the *Journal of Consulting Psychology,* Vol. 17 (1953), 343-347, by permission of the senior author and the American Psychological Association.

Is there a relationship between one's feelings about his body and his feelings about "self"? You will recall from the selections by Mussen and Jones in this section that the rate *at which one matures can have a very significant impact on "self" development. Secord and Jourard assert that one's* attitude *about his body is also related to self-concept and offer interesting evidence to substantiate their thesis.*

A substantial amount of current research in personality is devoted to the study of the individual's personal world. One object which is ever present in this personal world is the body. It is the thesis of the present writers that the individual's attitudes toward his body are of crucial importance to any comprehensive theory of personality; yet little attention has been given to this subject by psychologists. The present paper is concerned with one variety of attitude, namely, *body-cathexis.* By *body-cathexis* is meant the degree of feeling of satisfaction or dissatisfaction with the various parts or processes of the body.

If the variable body-cathexis is to be deemed important for personality theory, it is necessary to demonstrate that it is related to other personality variables which are recognized as significant. For reasons which need not be discussed here, body-cathexis is believed to be integrally related to the self-concept, although identifiable as a separate aspect thereof. From this notion of relatedness of body and self, the following more specific hypotheses were formulated and tested:

1. Feelings about the body are commensurate with feelings about the self, when both are appraised by similar scales.
2. Negative feelings about the body are associated with anxiety, in the form of undue autistic concern with pain, disease, or bodily injury.
3. Negative feelings about the body are associated with feelings of insecurity involving the self.

> One of the few empirical studies relevant to the present focus is that of Schilder (4), who used a set of questionnaires which probed the feelings, associations, and memories of his patients toward various aspects of their bodies. These semiobjective questionnaires suggested the more objective scale employed in the present study. Another relevant paper, that of Secord (6), describes the use of a homonym word-association technique for the appraisal of body-cathexis in a disguised "projective" fashion. This technique was used here for purposes of comparison with the more direct *BC-SC Scale*.

The BC-SC Scale

The writers approached the problem of appraising body-cathexis (BC) by asking the person to indicate on a scale the strength and direction of feeling which he has about each of the various parts or functions of his body. Such a direct approach, of course, has certain of the theoretical disadvantages which the more typical self-inventories also possess, but it was believed that the technique might have some usefulness in spite of these limitations. The first part of this scale consisted of a listing of 46 body parts and functions. Each item was followed by the numbers 1 through 5. The following instructions appeared on the cover page of the scale:

> On the following pages are listed a number of things characteristic of yourself or related to you. You are asked to indicate which things you are satisfied with exactly as they are, which things you worry about and would like to change if it were possible, and which things you have no feelings about one way or the other.
>
> Consider each item listed below and encircle the number which best represents your feelings according to the following scale:
>
> 1. Have strong feelings and wish change could somehow be made.
> 2. Don't like, but can put up with.
> 3. Have no particular feelings one way or the other.
> 4. Am satisfied.
> 5. Consider myself fortunate.

The second part of the scale concerned self-cathexis (SC), and listed 55 items believed to represent a sampling of the various conceptual aspects of the self, which were rated by the respondents according to the same instructions used for the body scale. The self-traits included were phrased in nontechnical, popular terms, such as *morals, conscience,* and *personality,* so that they might approximate the terms in which the individual actually thinks of himself. Tables 1 and 2 list the items included in both parts.

TABLE 1

BODY-CATHEXIS ITEMS USED IN BC SCALE

hair	exercise	legs
facial complexion	ankles	teeth
appetite	neck	forehead
hands	shape of head	feet
distribution of hair over body	body build	sleep
	profile	voice
nose	height	health
fingers	age	sex activities
elimination	width of shoulders	knees
wrists	arms	posture
breathing	chest	face
waist	eyes	weight
energy level	digestion	sex (male or female)
back	hips	back view of head
ears	skin texture	trunk
chin	lips	

TABLE 2

SELF-CATHEXIS ITEMS USED IN SC SCALE

first name	impulses	memory
morals	manners	thriftiness
ability to express self	handwriting	personality
taste in clothes	intelligence level	self-respect
sense of duty	athletic skills	ability to concentrate
sophistication	happiness	ability to take orders
self-understanding	creativeness	fears
life goals	love life	capacity for work
artistic talents	strength of conviction	conscientiousness
tolerance	conscience	ability to meet people
moods	skill with hands	self-discipline
general knowledge	ability to express sympathy	suggestibility
imagination		neatness
popularity	emotional control	vocabulary
self-confidence	self-consciousness	procrastination
sensitivity to opinions of others	generosity	will power
	ability to accept criticism	self-assertiveness
ability to lead	thoughts	ability to make decisions
last name	artistic & literary taste	dreams

The form of the scale presented in Tables 1 and 2 is the result of considerable preliminary work in which previous forms were tried out on college students. Items which were difficult to understand, difficult for the subject to assign a meaningful rating, or which resulted in little variability from subject to subject were generally eliminated, provided that they did not leave an important part of the body or self unrepresented. One exception to the latter qualification was allowed: organs pertaining to sexual and excretory functions were deliberately omitted from the body list because it was feared that their presence in thc scale might give rise to an evasive attitude which would transfer to other items, resulting in an avoidance of the two answer categories representing negative feelings towards the body.

The Homonym Test of Body-Cathexis (H Test)

The H test consisted of a list of 75 homonyms, each of which has meanings pertaining to the body and meanings not related to the body. A substantial proportion of the words have meanings pertaining to pain, disease, or bodily injury. Twenty-five neutral or nonbody words were interspersed with the homonyms for purposes of disguise. This list was presented to the testees orally, the homonyms being read at the rate of one every five seconds, with instruction to the subjects to respond by writing down the first word that occurred to them. A score for each individual was obtained by totaling responses to bodily meanings. It was employed here to provide an independent measure of anxiety-related BC. This test has been fully described elsewhere, and some tentative evidence that it is related to anxiety has been offered (5, 6).

Procedure

The H test and the BC-SC Scale were administered in a group situation to 70 college males and 56 college females. The BC-SC Scale and the Maslow Test of Psychological Security-Insecurity (3) were subsequently administered to an additional group of 47 college men and women.

A study of the patterns of responses of individuals to the BC-SC Scale suggested that response sets were operating for some individuals (1, 2). In order that split-half reliability coefficients for the BC and SC scores, as well as intercorrelations between these scores, might not be inflated by the artifact of response sets, subjects falling in any of the following arbitrary classes were not included in computations: (*a*) a frequency $\geqq$ 32 in category 4; (*b*) a frequency $\geqq$ 28 in category 5; and (*c*) a frequency $\geqq$ 24 in category 5, when accompanied by less than 2 responses in categories 1 and 2 combined. As a result, the 70 male subjects were reduced to 45, and the 56 females to 43. It should be emphasized that this selection of subjects *lowers* the correlation coefficients obtained between parts of the BC-SC Scale, and *reduces* the split-half reliabilities of the various subscores.

Results

Statistics pertaining to the BC-SC Scale and the Homonym Test

A single score for each individual was obtained on the H test, consisting of the total number of body responses to the 75 homonyms. Three types of scores were obtained on the BC-SC Scale. These were:

1. Total BC, obtained by summing the ratings for each individual on the 46 body items and dividing by 46.
2. Total SC, obtained by summing the ratings for each individual on the 55 self items and dividing by 55.
3. An *anxiety-indicator* score, obtained by summing the ratings for each male individual on the 11 BC-Scale items most negatively cathected by the group of males: facial complexion, nose, energy level, body build, profile, height, chest, teeth, sex activities, posture, and weight. These sums were divided by 11. A similar score, based on the 11 items most negatively cathected by females, was also obtained.

TABLE 3

Means, Standard Deviations, and Reliabilities of BC-SC Scale and the Homonym Test
(N = 45 males; 43 females.)

Test	*Mean*	SD	*Reliability**
Homonym test			
Males	22.00	6.04	.63
Females	21.14	5.70	.66
Body-cathexis			
Males	3.43	.337	.78
Females	3.46	.401	.83
Self-cathexis			
Males	3.43	.393	.88
Females	3.35	.510	.92
Anxiety indicator			
Males	3.09	.524	.72
Females	3.05	.625	.73

*Corrected by the Spearman-Brown formula.

Split-half reliability coefficients were obtained for all of the above scores. These are given in Table 3. Reliability coefficients for the homonym test are about .15 lower than those obtained in previous studies, but are still satisfactory. Reliabilities for the various BC-SC scores are moderately high; they may be regarded as more impressive when it is recalled that subjects displaying the most consistency were removed from the sample.

No important differences between means of the various scores for the two sexes were obtained.

Relationship between body-cathexis and self-cathexis

Intercorrelations between total BC scores and total SC scores are shown in Table 4. The r for men is .58, and for women .66, suggesting that individuals have a moderate tendency to cathect their body to the same degree and in the same direction that they cathect their self; that is, the two kinds of cathexis covary.

TABLE 4

Intercorrelations Between BC-SC Scores, the Homonym Test, and the Maslow Test
(N = 45 males; 43 females; except for the Maslow test, for which N = 46 males and females.)

Test	*Body-cathexis*	*Self-cathexis*	*Anxiety indicator*
Homonym test			
Males	—.18	—.15	—.37*
Females	—.41**	—.23	—.40**
Maslow test	—.37**	—.52**	—.41**
Self-cathexis			
Males	.58**		
Females	.66**		

*Significant at the .05 level.
**Significant at the .01 level.

Relationships between body-cathexis and the homonym test

An examination of Table 4 reveals no significant correlations between the H test and BC, for the 45 males, or between the H test and SC. There was, however, an r of —.37 between the H test and the anxiety-indicator score which, although low, was significant at the .02 level. For the 43 females, on the other hand, correlations significant beyond the .01 level were obtained between H-test scores and BC ($r = —.41$), and H-test scores and the anxiety-indicator score ($r = —.40$). Correlations between homonym scores and SC were not significant. In general, then, there is a low but significant relationship between BC as measured by the scale and anxiety-related BC as measured by the H test.

A concrete case may perhaps serve to indicate more specifically the manner in which the BC Scale and the H test concern anxiety.

> A woman with an extremely high H-test score and an extremely low BC score responded to the test items in the following way:
>
> 1. Items on the BC Scale rated in category 1 (*Have strong feelings and wish change could somehow be made*) were: facial complexion, appetite, hands, distribution of body hair, nose, fingers, waist, energy level, ears, body build, skin texture, knees, and weight. Items rated category 2 (*Don't like, but can put up with*) were: hips, sleep, sex activities and posture. None of the 46 body items was rated in category 5 (*Consider myself fortunate*).
>
> 2. On the homonym test, responses to meanings pertaining to the body, body processes, or pain and disease are shown below, preceded by the homonym stimulus word in italics: *acid*-sour, *arch*-bend, *back*-broken, *bare*-ugly, *condition*-sick, *crisis*-sick, *enlarged*-grown, *extract*-tooth, *function*-stomach, *gag*-whiskey, *gall*-bile sac, *gas*-dying, *glassy*-dead, *patient*-doctor, *rash*-heat, *red*-hands, *scarlet*-disease, *side*-hurt, *sling*-broken arm, *stain*-blood, *stiff*-corpse, *strip*-New Orleans, *system*-biology, *tablet*-sleeping pill, *tan*-Daytona Beach, *tape*-sprained ankle, *tender*-skin, *trunk*-body, and *waist*-starve.
>
> These item responses give some idea of the importance of the body to this woman and reveal her anxiety concerning it. A consideration of the diverse nature of the processes involved in the BC Scale and the H test as revealed by these items lends significance to the correlation obtained between these two tests.

Sex differences in degree of cathexis

It was found that females cathect their bodies, irrespective of direction, more highly than do males, in that they do not assign as many *3*'s to body items (3—*Have no particular feelings one way or the other*). The mean number of *3*'s for all of the 46 body items was 10.76 for men, and 7.86 for women. This difference of 2.90 yielded a critical ratio of 1.92, which approached significance at the .05 level. Consistent with this datum is the greater variability of BC scores among women, as previously shown in Table 3, although this difference in sigmas is not significant.

Relationships between the Maslow Test and the BC-SC Scale

The Maslow test was found to correlate —.37 with BC, —.41 with the anxiety-indicator score, and —.52 with SC. These *r*'s are significant at the .01 level. It may be concluded that low cathexis is associated with insecurity to some degree.

Discussion

One of the most significant results is the demonstration that the body and the self tend to be cathected to the same degree. This supports the hypothesis that valuation of the body and the self tend to be commensurate.

Since the persons who obtain a high score on the H test are regarded as being more anxious concerning their bodies than those obtaining a low score, a moderate negative correlation would be anticipated between BC and the H test. This is consistent with the negative *r* actually obtained for women.

In the case of men, the relative lack of significant relationships between the homonym test and the BC-SC Scale cannot be clearly explained on the basis of available data. A likely but unproved hypothesis is that women are more likely than men to develop anxiety concerning their bodies, because of the social importance of the female body. This hypothesis is consistent with the datum that women cathect their bodies more highly than men, irrespective of the direction of cathexis, and with the fact that when a BC score based only on those body items most frequently arousing negative feelings in men was employed, a significant *r* of —.37 was obtained for men between this "anxiety-indicator" score and H-test scores.

A final support for the interpretation of BC as a self-related variable is found in the significant correlation between BC and insecurity, as measured by the Maslow test.

Summary and Conclusions

The purpose of the present study was to develop a method for appraising the feelings af an individual towards his body and to ascertain whether or not variables derived from these appraised feelings are significant for personality theory. The latter was determined by testing the hypotheses stated under 2, 3, and 4 below.

A scale for the determination of the degree of cathexis towards various aspects of the body was designed and administered to groups of college males and females, along with a similar scale for aspects of the self, a homonym test of anxiety-related body-cathexis, and the Maslow Test of Psychological Security-Insecurity.

The following conclusions may be drawn:

1. The split-half reliabilities of the two parts of the scale were found to be satisfactory: .81 for body-cathexis, and .90 for self-cathexis.

2. The hypothesis that feelings about the body are commensurate with feelings about the self was supported by significant correlations between the two parts of the scale.

3. The hypothesis that low body-cathexis is associated with anxiety in the form of undue autistic concern with pain, disease, or bodily injury was upheld by the demonstration of significant relationships between low body-cathexis as determined by the scale and by the homonym test.

4. The hypothesis that low body-cathexis is associated with insecurity was sustained by the demonstration of correlation between the former and the Maslow test.

References

1. Cronbach, L. J., "Response Sets and Test Validity," *Educational and Psychological Measurement,* Vol. 6 (1946), pp. 475-494.
2. ———, "Further Evidence on Response Sets and Test Design," *Educational and Psychological Measurement,* Vol. 10 (1950), pp. 3-31.
3. Maslow, A. H., E. Hirsh, M. Stein, and I. Honigmann, "A Clinically Derived Test for Measuring Psychological Security-Insecurity," *Journal of Genetic Psychology,* Vol. 33 (1945), pp. 21-41.
4. Schilder, P., *Psychotherapy* (New York: Norton, 1938).
5. Secord, P. F., *The Homonym Word Association Test,* Unpublished Doctoral Dissertation, Stanford University, 1950.
6. ———, "Objectification of Word Association Procedures by the Use of Homonyms: A Measure of Body-Cathexis," *Journal of Personality,* Vol. 21 (1953), pp. 479-495.

QUESTIONS FOR DISCUSSION

Erikson Article

1. Why is it necessary, as Erikson maintains, to successfully complete one stage of development prior to going to the next one?
2. In what ways does Erikson support the position offered by Haimowitz, whose selection appears in Part IV?
3. Which one or two of Erikson's eight stages would you champion as being, perhaps, more important or more crucial than the rest? Why?

Engel Article

1. Is a stable self-concept likely to indicate a positive self-concept? Why or why not?
2. How consistent were these adolescent self-concepts over a two-year period? Would you say that this finding is surprising? Explain your answer.

Mussen and Jones Article

1. Why do early-maturing boys find a more favorable social environment than late-maturing boys?
2. Why do you suppose that parents, teachers, and adults generally respond more favorably to the fast-growing boy than to his slower-growing peer?
3. What implications grow out of this study for physical education teachers in particular?

Jones Article

1. What differences between early- and late-maturing boys persisted into adulthood? How would you explain the persistence of these differences?
2. What is the author really saying when she reminds the reader of the profound individual differences in each group of early- and late-maturers? What are the implications of this reminder?

Jones and Mussen

1. Compare the results of this study with the one reported on early- and late-maturing boys. Are the results the same?
2. In relation to both this and the two previous selections, what can you conclude about the relationship between self-concept and physical maturation?

Secord and Jourard Article

1. Why do you suppose that low body-cathexis is associated with high anxiety in the form of undue concern about pain, or bodily injury?
2. What relationships were found between feelings about the body and feelings about the self? Were there any differences noted for men and women? What psychological explanation can you give your answer?
3. Do you think the findings would have been the same if a sample of high school students had been used? Explain.

Part VII

teaching and the self

1. The self-picture as a factor in the classroom

J. W. STAINES

Reprinted from the *British Journal of Educational Psychology,* Vol. 28 (1958), 97-111, by permission.

If the self develops in response to environmental stimuli, what part do teachers play in the development of the self-picture? Is it possible for a teacher to consciously and deliberately change a student's concept of self? What methods are available for changing self-concept? In a fascinating study, the author explores these and related questions and draws conclusions important for all persons concerned about the healthy development of young people.

SUMMARY

1. A theoretical analysis of the concept of the self shows it to be a learned structure, growing mainly from comments made by other people and from inferences drawn by children out of their experience in home, school, and other social groups. Amongst the people likely to be most influential in determining the self-picture are teachers. Two hypotheses were formulated: that it is possible to distinguish reliably between teachers in normal classrooms in respect to the frequency and kind of comments they make with reference to the self; and that it is possible to teach so that, while aiming at the normal results of teaching, specific changes can be made in the self-picture.

2. The results of the investigation indicated that:

(*a*) The first hypothesis was supported. Marked differences occurred between teachers in the frequency of self-reference in their comments, particularly in their positive or negative comments on the child's performance, status, and self-confidence or potency.

(*b*) The second hypothesis was also supported. One teacher studied the self-ratings of his class and tried to teach so that certain self-ratings were changed. A small number of changes occurred in self-traits, but statistically significant changes were found in two dimensions of the self, certainty and differentiation. Both changes were interpreted as indicating greater psychological security.

(*c*) A control class taught by a teacher regarded as typically "sound" and having no awareness of the self-picture as an outcome of education showed significant decreases in certainty about the self and in differentiation. The uncertainty spread throughout the self and was significantly greater than that of the experimental group. Both changes were interpreted as leading to a marked psychological insecurity. These changes, usually indicative of poor adjustment, were the unsought and unnoticed concomitant outcomes of normal methods aimed at securing the usual academic results.

(*d*) Standardized tests showed that both classes made about the same gains in some aspects of English and arithmetic over the experimental period.

(*e*) The analysis of the self into categories and dimensions and the use of a self-rating scale appear to provide a useful method of discriminating between teachers according to the self-reference of their words and of their methods of managing situations in the classroom.

I. Introduction: The Empirical and Theoretical Importance of the Self-Picture

The importance of the self in psychological thinking has both empirical and theoretical foundations. Self-reference is frequent in the conversation of adults, and classroom data show that this is also true of children. Clinical records stress the importance of the self-picture and of self-acceptance and rejection. From such evidence it appears that the self is empirically a matter of prime importance in that a great deal of behavior is concerned with maintaining and enhancing the established pattern of the self as it appears to the person, as he thinks it ought to be, and as he thinks other people believe it to be. Most psychological theorists introduce the self or a related concept in considering motivation, and writers on personality postulate the self as the integrating factor in personality. Cattell (5) calls it the fourth factor in the economy of the personality, "the keystone of personality" integrating id, ego, and superego into "one dynamic structure or unified sentiment." Lewin (9) sees the self as an inner, relatively permanent structure, giving consistency to the personality. Stagner (15) believes that the self image contributes stability to the personality, while Murphy (11) has claimed that no part of behavior is free of the self.

If the self is so closely related to the empirical data of behavior and to the theoretical aspects of personality, it is important for education and for the teacher. This is particularly so since the self is both an outcome of education and, once it has developed, a condition of subsequent learning. Such educational relevance should lead to an investigation of the conditions under which the self develops, the methods by which it is changed, the limitations upon change once it has developed, and the effect of a particular kind of self-picture upon learning.

II. Theoretical Considerations

The notion of the self is highly complex. It is primarily perceptual, "a learned perceptual system which functions as an object in the perceptual field." (12) It is built from many perceptual experiences. The child learns about his self from his own experiences and from the behavior of others. From the teacher who says: "John, go to the back. You're one of the big ones," the boy learns about himself and about himself-in-relation-to-others, as well as something of the social expectations centered on that aspect of his physique. He learns that he can run faster than some others, that he can read well, or that he cannot sing. Gradually, the raw perceptual materials of the self are transformed by the manufacturing processes of the mind, so that the self also becomes conceptual. Memory images and other kinds of mental structures, notably concepts, are developed. The self, as known to the individual, is thus both perceptual and conceptual.

> One method of analysis of this complex self-structure is to see the self in three levels or phases, each level having a number of sectors or categories. The first level is the Cognized or Known Self which comprises all those characteristics of the individual that he recognizes as part of the "Me." Whether or not these correspond to objective reality or to what others think about him does not matter. The cognized self is what the individual perceives and conceives himself to be. The second level of the self, called the Other Self, is what the person believes others think of him: "The teacher thinks I'm no good at English." The third level is the Ideal Self, part wish, part "ought," the standard to be reached: "I ought to be more careful of detail." These elements of the self are of supreme importance for behavior since many of the individual's actions are ordered by his

constant efforts to maintain and enhance these various aspects of the self-picture.

The categories are those aspects of the self which individuals commonly report on. The most obvious are physical characteristics and skills of various kinds. Others appearing in conversations and in such clinical records as Roger's (13) include traits, attitudes and interests, values, wants and goals, status and role, in-groups, and philosophy of life. Each of these categories appears in all three levels of the self-picture. The individual has, for example, a picture of his physique as part of the cognized self, a belief that others see his physique in a certain way and a wish that it were something else.

In addition to the levels and categories, the data require the postulation of dimensions. A dimension is a direction in which people may vary, and at least nine major dimensions may be distinguished. Individuals may be placed along a continuum of self-awareness, from the person who, through momentary preoccupation with a task, is little aware of himself to the person who is continually and painfully self-conscious. This is the dimension of salience: Differentiation means the degree to which the person distinguishes the various levels and categories within the self. He may have his concept of his status differentiated in great detail but his values category may be relatively undifferentiated. Potency is the sense of confidence a person develops in his own adequacy. The dimension of integration concerns the development of a hierarchy in the levels and categories so that the person can predict his behavior, knowing that he will not be the victim of rash impulses and that he can trust himself in conflict situations. Insight is the degree to which the self-picture corresponds to reality. Stability refers to Stagner's contention that the self must be stable in order to give a consistent basis for personality and action. People will vary in their resistance to change and in their willingness to accommodate the self-picture to new data. Self-acceptance is the name given to a continuum whose limiting points are an unreal overvaluation of the self and self-rejection. Between them lies the optimal region of self-acceptance which occurs when the cognized and ideal self are close together: "I am like this and happy to be this way." Concomitance of cognized and other self is also a sign of self-acceptance: "I am like this and others think so too." When this occurs, the ideal self loses the tyrannical quality that Horney (6) finds in neurotics. The real dimension refers to the number of identifications which a person makes with ideas, groups, institutions, and objects. Finally, people differ in the degree of certainty with which they can report on what they are like. Position on the dimension of certainty should change with age and development of the self-picture.[1]

---

[1] For a full description of categories and dimensions, see J. W. Staines, *A Sociological and Psychological Study of the Self-Picture and Its Importance in Education*. Unpublished Ph.D. Thesis, University of London, 1954.

III. The First Hypothesis and Empirical Procedures

The self-structure develops in response to environmental stimuli. Since teachers are an important aspect of the child's environment, it is likely that they have some effect on the child's self-picture. A number of questions arise. What part do teachers play in the development of the self-picture? Can teachers change the child's self-picture if they try to do so? If they can, what methods of teaching produce what kinds of self-picture? Is it possible to distinguish between teachers in the frequency and kind of comment which they make about the child's self? An investigation was planned to answer this last question, and to show what effects, if any, followed deliberate teaching for change in the self-picture.

The research followed the tradition established by Lewin (10), more fully developed by Anderson and his colleagues (2), and followed with modifications by Bales (3) and Whithall (16), of seeing a class as a group and attempting to record and analyze data from teacher-child and child-child interaction. Their data on the educational outcomes of the interaction between personalities in the atmosphere of the classroom were sufficiently reliable to show that classroom situations are much more complex than was suspected and are producing other than orthodox lesson outcomes.

Observation of a number of teachers showed that the data of self-reference were likely to provide a tentative answer to the investigation. Teachers made frequent comments on the child's self: "You're better at sums than you are at spelling," "Let Rosemary come to the front—she's only small," "We expect more from you because you're older," and so on. Some teachers make such remarks more frequently than others. An hypothesis was formulated: that teachers may be reliably distinguished by the frequency of their use of words and kinds of situational management which, in the opinion of competent judges, are likely to mold the self.

To test this hypothesis, two problems had to be solved, how to gather and how to order the data. Two pairs of teachers, one pair in the junior and one in the infants' school, agreed to participate in the investigation although they did not know its purpose until all the data had been collected. They permitted the investigator to copy down and classify all that was said and to interview the children at any time. The pairs of teachers were comparable in experience and were rated by their respective head teachers as similar in proficiency. The classes were similar in numbers of boys and girls, in age, in intelligence, and in social class as judged from fathers' occupations. The children were mainly working class.

TABLE 1

CLASSES USED IN OBSERVATION PERIOD

	Numbers		*Age in months*		*I.Q.*	
Classes	*Boys*	*Girls*	*Mean*	*Range*	*Mean*	*S.D.*
Junior A	15	14	129	122–134	114.4	10.4
Junior B	16	15	128	123–134	112.8	10.1
Infants C	20	24	89	84–96	No tests used in this department.	
Infants D	26	17	87	84–100		

The times spent in observation of lessons are recorded in Table 2.

TABLE 2

MINUTES OF OBSERVATION FOR VARIOUS LESSONS

Class	*Arithmetic*	*English*	*Social Studies*	*Nature Study*	*Music*	*Handwork*
A	100	105	30	—	—	15
B	97	87	51	—	—	15
C	86	100	30	—	20	15
D	105	100	—	30	—	15

The preponderance of arithmetic and English in the lessons observed reflects the importance attached to these subjects in the junior school, and the infants' school periods were chosen to match. The children became accustomed to the presence of the observer in a preliminary period and quickly accepted him as part of the classroom set-up.

The data were classified in terms of the categories and dimensions of the self, using a method of scoring with symbols, supplemented by the indicators, "+," "—," "n," and "ambi"; "+" meant that the effect of the comment or situation was thought to be positive, "—" implied a probable negative effect, and "n" stood for neutral. "Ambi" indicated that the effect was likely to be positive for some and negative for other children. The following are examples of the scoring in two of the categories:

1. PHYSIQUE.

(*a*) "Jack, you're tall. Help me with this." Score Ph. + since the teacher values tallness and Jack sees his height as a valued possession.

(*b*) "Marie has the best complexion for Cinderella. We'll have her." Score Ph. ambi. since Marie is chosen from a group of volunteers and the comment is positive for Marie, negative for the others.

(*c*) "You won't do for the queen—you're not tall enough." Score Ph. — because the child feels her physique is not valued.

(*d*)"You're taller than the others. You're just right for this part." Score Ph. O. since a marked comparison with others is made, and positive, negative and ambivalent judgments are included. Interview evidence showed the importance of this kind of situation.

2. PERFORMANCE.

Comments on performance may be positive, negative, or ambivalent. They may build up the child's self-picture as able to do things, break it down, or be ambivalent in their effects. Skills may bring the correct answer or performance with no comment from the teacher. The child sees himself as able by his success, or incompetent because of failure. A correct answer is scored Sk. +. Failure by silence, slowness, or the wrong answer is scored Sk. —. In comments other than the routine "Yes," "You're good at . . . ," "Wrong," "You don't know your . . . ," one score is given for the achievement or the failure and a second for status (St. + or St. —). That the teacher's comments are related by the child to his status in the eyes of the class was revealed by such comments as these made in interviews: "They think I can't do it." "Everyone thinks how good you are."

A comment by the teacher is sometimes followed by a class reaction: "Good boy! Look at this everyone!" (Class approves). "Wrong. Just look what Jack's done!" (Class laughs). Each element in the situation is scored, skill, status for the teacher's comment, and status for the reaction of the class. Sk. ambi. is scored when a comment makes possible a positive as well as a negative self-picture and it is impossible to determine which occurs: "Who's right? Hands up those right." Some children are right, some wrong. Hierarchy in skills is used when the teacher's comments tend to make the child see himself as better in one skill than another, so leading to greater differentiation: "You're better at English than Arithmetic."

Similar methods of scoring were used for other dimensions and categories. The potency is the score total of all scores relating to the child's confidence in any aspect of himself. It is got by subtracting the negative from the positive self-reference comments. The salience score is the total of all self-ratings together with the self-orientation total. The latter comments refer to the person as a whole rather than to any category; "You're a fine one, you are." Incisions are interruptions by the teacher in the child's own sequences of purpose and achievements, usually by way of unnecessary directions. The self-direction category includes those comments which give the child an opportunity to see himself as a purposing, planning individual. A classification for classroom management distinguishes two modes, direct and indirect. Direct management is any routine command by the teacher. The indirect method is illustrated by cooperative relationships between the teacher and the class. It will help to form the child's concept of himself as causal. Level of aspiration is related to the ideal self. Task-oriented comments are those with no salience nor self-reference.

Treatment of Data

The material was rated by the writer (Judge X) and two school counsellors with three years' training in psychology at Sydney University. When the data were divided into units by each judge, agreement on the units between Judges X and Y and Z was above 90 per cent, and this was held to indicate sufficient accuracy. Units where agreement was not finally reached after discussion were eliminated. The remaining units were rated for categories and dimensions. After two months, a page was taken at random from the records and remarked by Judges X and Y with a retest reliability for X of 94 per cent, and for Y of 92 per cent.

A survey was made of the ratings for the various teachers, a total found for each teacher, and the score in each category and dimension represented

TABLE 3

Categories Showing Most Marked Differences Between Teachers

Categories	*A*	*B*
Performance		
Skill+	107	73
Skill−	19	50
Total	141	129
Status		
Positive (+)	70	30
Negative (−)	14	48
Total	84	78
Values		
Responsibility	5	0
General	5	0
Total	11	2
Wants		
Level of aspiration	11	7
Self-direction	85	14
Incisions	1	14
Classroom management		
Direct	11	33

Categories	*C*	*D*
Performance		
Skill+	64	76
Skill−	15	37
Total	79	113
Status		
Positive (+)	71	67
Negative (−)	24	63
Total	95	130
Values		
General	8	1
Total	12	5
Physique		
Total	16	1
Wants		
Level of aspiration	15	22
Self-direction	24	20
Incisions	8	36
Classroom management		
Direct	34	40
Traits		
Negative (−)	7	25
Self-orientation		
Total	9	35

as a percentage of the total. Many of the differences between the scores of the teachers were very small and are not reported here because of lack of space.[2] Table 3 gives the categories where the differences are greatest or of most interest. Table 4 shows an analysis of the data for the dimensions. Many of the differences between the teachers were found by chi-squared to be significant at the 1 per cent or 5 per cent level,[3] but because of the small numbers in many categories comparisons were made simply on the basis of observed scores.

In general the infants' teachers used more self-references than the junior teachers. B differs considerably from A, and very widely from C and D in the categories of the self. In the dimensions, salience scores will, by definition, closely parallel the total scores, and with this sample of teachers, differentiation does also. Wide individual differences between teachers are

TABLE 4

SCORES ON DIMENSIONS OF SELF AND ON FREQUENCY OF EACH DIVISION AS A PERCENTAGE OF TOTAL UNITS

	Teachers							
	Junior A		*Junior B*		*Infants' C*		*Infants' D*	
Dimensions	*Raw score*	*% of total*	*Raw score*	*% of total*	*Raw score*	*% of total*	*Raw score*	*% of total*
Salience	372	96.7	317	98.3	383	91.9	481	96.2
Differentiation	371	96.5	313	97.0	380	90.2	475	95.0
Potency +	290	75.4	130	40.3	223	53.5	217	43.4
—	54	14.0	160	49.6	93	22.3	205	41.0
Integrity	1	.3	—	—	—	—	—	—
Insight	5	1.3	2	.6	3	.7	1	.2
Acceptance	1	.3	—	—	3	.7	1	.2
Rejection	—	—	5	1.6	4	1.0	2	.4

evident in the totals for both salience and differentiation, but not in the percentages. It is in the potency dimension, however, that the most striking difference occurs. Scores in the other three dimensions show small differences, largely because of the method of scoring the data. If all positive scores are regarded as acceptance scores, and all negative scores as rejection, then the characteristics of the teachers and the classroom atmospheres are very different indeed.

[2] For full details of methods of scoring and of results, see J. W. Staines, *loc. cit.*

[3] Between A and B: 1 per cent level, Sk. —, Status +, Status —, Self-direction, Incisions, direct Classroom Management. 5 per cent level, Skill +, Values.

Between C and D: 1 per cent level, Performance Total, Status —, Incisions, Self-orientation, Traits. 5 per cent level, Skills —, Status Total.

IV. Discussion of Results

The junior teachers are most alike where scores are small. In categories and dimensions where scores are large, these teachers differ widely, particularly in the performance and status categories, in the four major dimensions—areal, salience, differentiation and potency—in self-direction and in direct classroom management, that is, in the giving of orders rather than opportunities for seeing oneself as purposing, choosing and causal.

TEACHER A. The pattern is clear-cut. Teacher A is particularly strong in positive emphasis on skills and makes few negative comments. The status category shows the same pattern. He is outstanding in the opportunity he offers children for self-determination—an important feature if, as Murphy (11) suggests, the self develops best where there is opportunity for self-direction. He puts more stress on values than do two of the others. In the dimensions of salience, potency, and differentiation, Teacher A's scores suggest that he is likely to make the child self-aware—to teach him, as Kilpatrick (7) suggests, that "It is I who am doing it." It will be a positive, self-accepting salience. His emphasis is strongly on differentiation so that children may see their strengths and weaknesses more accurately and in greater detail, making for more adequate adjustment. A's score on the potency dimension is significant. Teachers B and D give confidence with one hand and take it away with the other. Teacher A gives most (score 290) and takes least (score 54).

TEACHER B. The pattern here is also clear-cut but very different. In the performance category, B makes fewer positive and many more negative comments than A. In the status category, although the totals are approximately the same as A's (A 84, B 78), the constituents are strikingly different. The pattern of the performance category is repeated in having a smaller number of positive and a greater number of negative comments. The pattern occurs again when B makes less effort than A to hold up a level of aspiration, although the difference in scores is not great. He gives very few opportunities for self-direction. The effect of this on the self-picture must be magnified by the repetition of incisions. The absence of self-choice and the interference with the child's goal-directed or purposive sequences are complementary.

In the dimensions, B is widely different from the other teachers. The amount of salience is less. There is less differentiation and a tendency to use the wholistic approach with children ("You're no good . . ."). Totals for the potency dimension are widely different from those of the other teachers, as are the positive (score 130) and negative (score 160) constituents. This teacher shows less positive development of confidence or self-potency than the others and, at the same time, more negative effects. He gives least and takes most.

The infants' teachers are slightly more alike than are the junior teachers, particularly in In-group comments, values, attitudes and interests, and in the salience and differentiation dimensions.

TEACHER C. This teacher comments on the physique of children more often than the other teachers, and is the only one to draw comparisons at this point. Her comments on skills are more positive than negative. She prefers positive to negative comment on status and places more emphasis on traits than the junior teachers, but not so much as Teacher D. She gives little opportunity for self-direction and as might be expected, her classroom management is largely direct. In dimensions, her outstanding score is in potency, where there is a tendency to build up the child's confidence (score 223), with only a small score for negative comments (93).

TEACHER D. Teacher D stresses performance on the positive side and negative comments are less frequent than Teacher B's, and more than A's and C's. Status comments are greater than for the other three teachers, but are chiefly negative. This is also true for traits. The opportunity that she gives for self-direction is slight, and her scores for incisions and salience are highest of all. The differentiation score is high. The potency score, got by algebraically totaling the high positive score (217) and the high negative score (205), is very low. If her effect on the self-picture were predicted from this evidence, it would seem that Teacher D tends to make children highly self-aware in many categories, but not particularly confident in any aspect of themselves.

In summary, the teachers' comments overwhelmingly stress performance and status. It is inevitable that where the stress is on performance, it should also be on status; but the latter category is also evident independently in the verbal material, although not distinguished in the scores. The psychological significance of such emphasis on status may be argued from its numerical preponderance, but the writer feels from his experience with teachers and students that it is largely overlooked by teachers. They are, indeed, careful to avoid most of the obvious status aspects where the child's feelings are involved and are usually considerate of them. But material taken in a number of interviews with the children suggests that, much more frequently than teachers believe, the ordinary run-of-the-day comments on success and failure, and incidents where a child is casually preferred to another for what seems to the teacher an unimportant task or role, may be fraught with status possibilities and intense emotional content. While no claim is made that these unnoticed situations are always significant for all children, it is reasonable to conclude that the teachers who most frequently invoke status situations and make relevant comments are most likely to modify the child's self-picture in this direction.

How effective is this method of distinguishing teachers? It would seem to separate them on what competent judges believe are likely to be the effects of their words and situational management on a number of categories and dimensions. These categories and dimensions are held to be central aspects of the self, and it is useful to know that teachers differ so widely in relation to them. A second obvious conclusion from the scores is that teachers do not develop to any significant degree many of the other important educational outcomes to which subject matter and teaching methods may be closely geared, and which might be drawn into the self in order to be most effectively related to behavior.

The point at which this method of investigation is least effective is in gauging the effect upon the child of the various verbal and situational interactions. Categorization of what a teacher says, while indicating a prevailing classroom atmosphere, gives no clue as to how effective it really is in forming the self-picture. Teacher D, for instance, uses reproof much more frequently than any other teacher, and each reproof is rated St. —. Yet the observer could not say what effects her words had. Interviews showed that some children had a "water-off-a-duck's-back" attitude toward her but that others were much more sensitive to her flow of personal comment. In an attempt to discover whether the different teaching styles and aims would lead to changes in the self-picture, the second part of the investigation was carried out.

V. The Second Hypothesis and Empirical Procedures

The hypothesis was formulated that teachers who differ in the frequency of their self-referential comments would produce significantly different self-pictures. If this were so, it would follow that classroom situations would produce educational outcomes other than the traditional skills, knowledges, and appreciations.

To test this hypothesis it was decided to use the two junior teachers previously observed, since they differed widely in certain known aspects, particularly in the opportunities they gave children for self-direction, in their attitudes toward children's skills, and their care for preserving status. Teacher A was more likely than Teacher B to produce socially desirable changes in the self-picture as he was interested in children and their problems. Accordingly, class A was chosen as the experimental group, class B as the control. Such a design would show whether Teacher A's methods would support the hypothesis, while the results from Teacher B's class could supply additional confirmatory evidence.

The subjects

Though the two classes were matched for age, intelligence and socio-economic class, they were not equal in attainments. The experimental group had a greater number of children whose achievement scores on standardized tests were low, although eight of them were the most intelligent children in either class. Both classes were tested with a self-rating card test [4] to measure the phases and categories of the self-picture before and after the experimental teaching period.

The experimental teaching methods

The teaching period for the experiment was twelve weeks. Teacher A rated his class on the categories in the card test for each phase of the self, and compared his ratings with the children's self-ratings in order to decide what treatment might be given to each child. In doing so he became familiar with the general concepts used in the analysis of the self and accepted the idea that these could be used as ends of the teaching process. He planned his methods so that situations could be arranged in which the child would be led by the teaching methods to see himself in various ways. These would include seeing himself as a planning, purposing, choosing individual, responsible, and accountable, for these are basic aspects of the healthy socialized self. The child should test his purposes by carrying them through, see himself as adequate and causal, and, at the same time, differentiate his relative strengths and weaknesses. Particular attention was to be paid to preserving his status. At the same time the syllabus for entrance to grammar school was to be covered without interfering with the prospects of the candidates. For the ideal self, the teacher planned to hold up a suitable level of aspiration, either directly and by commendation or indirectly by allusion and suggestion. The teacher also planned to convey his judgments which make up the child's other self in such a way that the child would be unlikely to reject them as incongruous with the self-picture he already had.

Provision was made for teaching methods relevant to the child's place on the dimensions of the self. The areal self for each child could be increased by indentification with more objects, values, ideas, and people. For the over-self-conscious child (high in salience), treatment was to include

[4] See J. W. Staines, *loc. cit.*, for details of construction and validation.

a reduction in comments referring specifically to the self, an increase in Alper's task-involved (1) comments and in Ruger's (14) technique of the "scientific attitude," and care with the use of such simple situations as the public display of work. Differentiation was related to the avoidance of "whole" comments such as "Good" and "You're hopeless," and to an emphasis on seeing various characteristics more accurately. Adequacy or potency was to be built up by success and appreciation and by the teacher's care for the child's status. Accepting behavior by the teacher was thought to be the best way of teaching self-acceptance.

The experimental period began at the end of the first month of the school term when the card test was administered for the first time. After twelve weeks, the test was readministered and the data analyzed for significant differences between the classes. To understand the results, it is necessary to make brief explanatory comments on the instructions given for the card test. In a pilot study, children were given the self-ratings in the form of 66 cards and asked to place them in heaps or columns labeled Not True, Neither True nor Untrue, True, and Not Sure. The children asked for finer gradings. For instance, of two cards that could be placed in the "True" column, one might be "more true than the other." Accordingly, ratings were made in Columns 1, 2, 3 for Untrue items, 4, 5, 6 for Neither True nor Untrue, 7, 8, 9 for True and 10 for Not Sure. Columns 1 (Most Untrue of Me), 5, and 9 (Most True of Me) contained items about which the children were most certain.

VI. Results

The first of two ways of considering results is to ask what differences there were between the two groups at the end of the period.

> The percentage frequencies of children's rankings of various items as "Most true of me" served as the basis of the calculation. Six items of the card test showed differences between the classes at the 1 per cent level and 5 per cent level. At the 1 per cent level were "I try to see fair play," "Good at games," "Willing to have a try at things no matter how hard they are," and "Like hobbies." At the 5 per cent level were a greater willingness to admit cheating and an item testing self-direction. All the differences were in favor of the experimental class. Teacher A believed of the item relating to cheating that the greater freedom in his class, and the rational approach led children to admit it more freely. In the item testing self-direction ("Make up my own mind"), little change had taken place in the experimental class, but a major one had occurred in the control class. Teacher B's methods were characterized by incisions and a great deal of direction

in classroom management and were likely to produce widespread uncertainty and insecurity. The effects of his methods appear in significant differences between the classes in the responses to this item. The hypothesis is thus supported in relation to a limited number of characteristics.

The second method of estimating the results of the experiment is concerned with the dimensions.

Highly significant differences were found between the initial and final scores of the experimental class and also between the final scores of the two classes in the dimensions of certainty and differentiation. For the certainty dimension, the evidence is found in the movement toward or away from the rating "Not sure" and is presented in Table 5 as the total numbers of cards placed by each class in the "Not sure" category (column 10), for each level of the self. That is, the 29 children in the experimental class had placed a total of 123 cards in this category in the first test and 72 in the second test. This change is interpreted as an increase in the certainty as to what the self really was.

TABLE 5

UNCERTAINTY SCORES (COLUMN 10) AT THE BEGINNING AND END OF THE EXPERIMENTAL PERIOD

	Test 1			*Test 2*		
Group	*Self*	*Ideal self*	*Other self*	*Self*	*Ideal self*	*Other self*
Experimental	123	159	385	72	34	149
Control	370	89	582	448	300	932

When the significance of the figures for the various levels of the self is tested by chi-squared technique, Teacher A shows a significant decrease in "Not sure" scores for the self, ideal self and the other self. The class gained significantly in certainty about the boundaries of the self. Equally significant statistically, and numerically much greater, is the increase in scores in the "Not sure" rating in the control group. Starting with a significantly greater degree (1 per cent level) of uncertainty than the experimental group in the self and other self, after the "settling-down" period of one month, this group increased its uncertainty over its own initial score and over the experimental group in all three levels of the self. Particularly striking are the figures for the ideal self and the other self.

DIFFERENTIATION. The figures for differentiation are found by taking the scores for "Least true" and "Most true" ratings (Table 6). A movement toward the middle ranges and away from the extreme points on the scale is differentiation. A movement toward the extremes, Columns 1 and 9, indicates a tendency to see oneself as black or white, and an inability to make moderate adjustments of the various aspects of the self.

TABLE 6

DIFFERENTIATION OF THE SELF AT THE BEGINNING AND END OF THE EXPERIMENTAL PERIOD

Group	*Test 1*		*Test 2*	
	Most true	*Least true*	*Most true*	*Least true*
Experimental	621	299	522	288
Control	340	191	357	209

There is a significant decrease (1 per cent level) for the experimental group for "Most true," and a small nonsignificant decrease in "Least true." The control group shows a slight nonsignificant increase for both columns. It is clear that the experimental group has moved significantly away from "Most true" and, to a lesser degree, from "Least true." Since the numbers in "Not sure" have also decreased significantly, the movement from all three must be in the direction of the middle ranges toward greater differentiation. The control group not only failed to move away from "Most true" and "Least true," but actually increased these numbers slightly. When these two totals are added to the flight to the "Not sure" column, it can be seen to what degree the middle ranges are depleted. It indicates how little these children, compared with the experimental group, can see themselves with either certainty or moderation. If it is true that insecurity is marked by rigidity, then the scores on the differentiation dimension reinforce the conclusion drawn from the uncertainty scores. The hypothesis is thus very strongly supported.

One further line of evidence must be considered. Both classes used for the investigation were scholarship classes. Teacher A believed that, while working on the lines of the experiment, he could still secure the necessary academic results. No check was kept on scholarship results, but standardized tests for word recognition and mechanical arithmetic were given at the beginning and end of the experimental period. The results appear in Table 7.

The experimental teaching can be seen to have improved attainments while achieving those changes in the self-picture detailed above. The methods used with the control group, while securing slightly less improvement, produced the very maladjustment changes in certainty and differentiation indicated earlier. This is further support for the second hypothesis in the investigation.

TABLE 7

MEAN SCORES ON STANDARDIZED TESTS BEFORE AND AFTER THE EXPERIMENTAL PERIOD

	Test 1		*Test 2*	
Group	*Vernon word recognition*	*Mechanical arithmetic*	*Vernon word recognition*	*Mechanical arithmetic*
Experimental	108.4	119.8	111.8	141.1
Control	127.0	130.1	129.5	145.0

VII. Discussion

These results have implications related to both teaching goals and methods, and a number of points may be briefly discussed: new light has been thrown on the variables operating in the learning situation; these are now seen to be related inevitably to adjustment; they occur in every classroom but can be controlled by appropriate teaching methods; they are the product of group situations as well as of individual attention and they can be controlled within the present examination framework.

The experiment has shown the existence of additional variables in the learning situation other than the skills, knowledges, attitudes and appreciations commonly expected as the outcomes of teaching. The measuring instrument evolved shows that changes have occurred in the self-picture, in the ideal self, in the other self, and in the attitudes to each of these aspects. Awareness of such variables is important for learning theory and for practical teaching. Learning experiments, as well as practical teaching situations, show many conflicting results, some of which are undoubtedly due to the presence of unrecognized factors in the learning set-up. The next step in the investigation of the problems of learning is the isolation of other variables that contribute to the unpredictability of learning situations. This experiment has shown that the self-picture is probably one such variable. Changes occur in this as an outcome of learning situations, and the self-picture must be recognized as a hitherto unnoticed factor occurring in every learning situation. Furthermore, since any learning becomes a condition of subsequent learning, the kind of self-picture that is learned becomes a factor to be controlled in both experimental and practical teaching situations.

The experiment has shown that good and poor adjustment are linked with the goals and teaching methods of the typical classroom. The changes that occurred in the self-picture are usually accepted as symptoms of good and poor adjustment. Teacher A, using the free methods indicated, and stressing the aspects of the self-picture discussed above, is able to make his pupils more sure of what they are like and more accepting of what they are, more able to differentiate themselves and to see themselves with moderation as well as with certainty, more certain of what they want to be like, and more aware of what judgments they think others make of them. Such changes are accepted as the marks of good adjustment, and Teacher A clearly produces these characteristics in his children. Teacher B's data shows that typical high-pressure teaching, with vigorous personal emphasis, with great stress on correctness and on the serious consequences of failure, and with constant emphasis on the passing of examinations, can lead to significantly greater signs of insecurity. It is shown further that this insecurity spreads, not only through the items of the self, but through the ideal and other self, that is, through all the aspects of one major integrational factor of personality. Clinical evidence, of course, shows that this does happen, but the appearance and spread of insecurity in the self have not hitherto been recorded in the ordinary classroom situation. In the light of this information, the educational significance of the self becomes clearer and both teaching goals and teaching methods should be modified.

The educational significance of the self is reaffirmed when it is realized that changes in the self-picture are an inevitable part of both outcomes and conditions of learning in every classroom, whether or not the teacher is aware of them or aiming for them. They occur, as in A's class, where the teacher deliberately included them in his teaching goals and adapted his methods accordingly, and they occur in B's class where the teacher aimed at orthodox goals and was ignorant of these correlative factors. Since both classes were reasonably typical and both teachers recognized by their headmasters as competent teachers, it is reasonable to generalize and expect such factors to operate in all classrooms.

It is also clear from the experiment that teaching methods can be adapted so that definite changes of the kind sought for will occur in the self. The self can be deliberately produced by suitable teaching methods. In this experiment a start has been made in the task of relating aspects of teaching methods to categories, levels, and dimensions of the self.

One of the conditions for producing the self-picture as an outcome of education is that it is, and always will be produced in group situations. It can, of course, be produced in the special group situation of two, the teacher giving individual attention to the child, but in this experiment the normal group situation was always present. This makes the problem of obtaining the self-picture relevant to normal classroom conditions where group situations must always hold.

Finally, the self is relevant to classroom situations in another very important way. It was produced in this experiment in the normal conditions of teaching for examination results. Both classes were scholarship classes and it was agreed that any experimental conditions under which class A worked should not endanger the scholarship prospects of the children. On standardized tests in reading and number, Teacher A produced slightly greater mean improvement in his class. If it is objected that a teacher cannot spend his time teaching for an improved self-picture and better adjustment because of examination pressure, here is some evidence that at least equally good academic results may be got while improving adjustment. In other words, it is possible for a teacher to conceive his educational goals in the wider terms of the self-picture and to secure these while attaining the necessary academic standards. On the negative side, it is likely that Teacher B, conceiving his goals in academic terms and ignorant of the concomitant outcomes, laid the child open to failure in the future because he failed to strengthen the child's self-picture. A changed emphasis thus became feasible, from subject-matter goals to goals expressed in terms of the self, for in this way both academic and adjustment goals become attainable.

These points suggest that, because the self is an ubiquitous factor in all learning experiences, its presence should be recognized and its importance stressed by all teachers, and its controlled development made a major teaching aim. But since the psychology of the self has been little emphasized in courses on educational psychology and not at all by traditional practice in schools, it is certain that few teachers are aware of its importance. The implications for pre-service and in-service training are clear, but much more research must be done in the field. Two lines of investigation are likely to be fruitful. The first concerns the persistence of the pattern of the self-picture emerging from each class. How long do such self-pictures persist under similar conditions? What is the effect upon later learning of a child spending a second year with either A or B? Could A reverse B's pattern of self-picture or would B, in the child's most formative years, undo A's constructive work? Do the answers differ for different "types" of personalities? Should care be taken to prevent a child experiencing two successive teachers like B? The second line of investigation concerns the range of the curve of teachers on which A and B would be placed if the experiment were extended to include more teachers. Would B be an extreme type and A be near the norm? Or is B near the norm and A atypical? Only a wider investigation can answer such questions.

Acknowledgments

I wish to acknowledge with gratitude the grant in 1952 of a Fellowship from the Imperial Relations Trust Fund which made this investigation possible, and to express my appreciation of the help and guidance of Dr.

C. M. Fleming, Reader in Education at the University of London Institute of Education. I am grateful also to the New South Wales Department of Education which granted me leave for the period of study, and to the Education Officers, heads and teachers of public and private schools in England who allowed me to gather the data.

References

1. Alper, T. G., "Task-Orientation vs. Ego-Orientation in Learning and Retention," *American Journal of Psychology,* Vol. 59 (1946), pp. 236-248.
2. Anderson, H. H., and J. E. Brewer, "Studies of Teachers' Classroom Personalities, II," *Applied Psychological Monographs,* 8, Stanford University Press.
3. Bales, R. F., *Interaction Process Analysis: A Method for the Study of Small Groups* (Cambridge: Addison-Wesley, 1951).
4. Bruner, J. F., "Personality, Dynamics, and Perceiving," in J. S. Blake and G. V. Ramsay, eds., *Perception, an Approach to Personality* (New York: Ronald, 1951).
5. Cattell, R. B., *Personality, A Systematic, Theoretical and Factual Study* (New York: McGraw, 1950).
6. Horney, K., *Self Analysis* (New York: Norton, 1942).
7. Kilpatrick, W. H., *Selfhood and Civilization, A Study of the Self-Other Process* (New York: Bureau of Publications, Teachers College, Columbia University, 1941).
8. Kluckhohn, F. R., "Dominant and Variant Value Orientations," in C. Kluckhohn and H. A. Murray, eds., *Personality* (London: Jonathon, 1949, rev. ed., 1953).
9. Lewin, K., *Dynamic Theory of Personality* (New York: McGraw, 1935).
10. ———, R. Lippitt, and R. K. White, "Patterns of Aggressive Behavior in Experimentally Created Social Climates," *Journal of Social Psychology,* Vol. 10 (1939), pp. 271-300.
11. Murphy, G., *Personality, A Biosocial Approach to Origins and Structure* (New York: Harper, 1947).
12. Raimy, V. C., "Self-reference in Counseling Interviews," *Journal of Consulting Psychology,* Vol. 12 (1948), p. 3.
13. Rogers, C. R., *Client-Centered Therapy: Its Current Practice, Implications and Theory* (Boston: Houghton, 1951).
14. Ruger, H. A., "The Psychology of Efficiency," *Archives of Psychology,* Vol. 15 (1910).
15. Stagner, R., "Homeostasis as a Unifying Concept in Personality Theory," *Psychological Review,* Vol. 58 (1951), pp. 2-17.
16. Withall, J., "The Development of a Technique for the Measurement of Social-Emotional Climates in Classrooms," *Journal of Experimental Education,* Vol. 18 (1948).
17. Woolf, W., *The Personality of the Pre-School Child* (New York: Grune, 1946).

2. Children's perceptions of their teachers' feelings toward them related to self-perception, school achievement, and behavior [1]

HELEN H. DAVIDSON
AND GERHARD LANG

Reprinted from the *Journal of Experimental Education,* Vol. 29 (1960), 107-118, by permission of the senior author and Dembar Publications.

In the previous article by Staines, it was demonstrated that it is well within the power of a teacher to change a student's concept of himself. Is there a relation between children's perception of their teachers' feelings and academic achievement? What relationships exist between self-perception, behavior, and the way a youngster perceives the way his teacher feels about him? The authors closely examine how the self is influenced in classroom settings.

Introduction

The child's self-concept arises and develops in an interpersonal setting (30). Feelings about the self are established early in life and are modified by subsequent experiences. Among the significant people believed to affect the child's feelings about himself are first, his parents, and, later his teachers. Ausubel (2) and Jourard and Remy (16) are among the few investigators who have reported results which support these theoretical contentions.

Rogers (24), Snygg and Combs (27), among others, assign the self-concept a central place in their personality theories and suggest that the individual's self-concept is a major factor influencing his behavior. Vigorous research in this area by Martire

[1] This study was supported by a grant from the James McKeen Cattell Fund.

(17) and Steiner (28) has produced corroborative evidence for these views.

Only recently has the concept of the self been introduced into the school setting. Typical studies are those by Jersild (15), Reeder (23), and Stevens (29). Jersild demonstrated the value of the self-concept theory in making the educative process more valuable. Reeder, using grade school children, and Stevens, working with college students, explored the relation between self-concept and school achievement. Both of these investigators found that positive feelings about the self are associated with good academic achievement.

A series of studies dealing with teacher-pupil relations have sought to determine (a) how children see and feel about their teachers (11); (b) how teachers see and feel about their pupils (5, 20); and (c) how teachers think their pupils see themselves (22).

It has been widely recognized that teachers influence the personality development of their pupils (21). Perkins, for example, found that teachers who had completed several years of child study were able to promote healthier personality growth in children, defined in terms of congruency between the self and the ideal self. For this reason, many researchers, among them Barr and Jones (3) and Symonds (31), are engaged in the study of personality development of the teacher herself.

Despite the abundance of research on these aspects of the school setting, an important dimension, not previously investigated, is how the child perceives his teacher's feelings toward him. In an investigation of this interaction, we not only may gain insight into the question of what qualities make for an effective teacher, but also an understanding of how the child's perception of his teacher's feelings, irrespective of its accuracy, relates to his self-concept, school achievement, and classroom behavior.

It is the purpose of this investigation to determine what the relation is between children's perception of their teachers' feelings toward them and the variables: self-perception, academic achievement, and classroom behavior.

Specifically, three hypotheses were tested:

1. There exists a positive correlation between children's perception of their teachers' feelings toward them and children's perception of themselves. In behavioral terms it is predicted that the more favorable the child's perception of himself, the more positive will be his perception of teachers' feelings toward him.

2. There exists a positive relationship between favorable perception of teachers' feelings and good academic achievement.

3. There exists a positive relationship between favorable perception of teachers' feelings and desirable classroom behavior.

The Instrument

To test the hypotheses proposed, it was necessary to develop an instrument to measure self-perception and the perception of the feelings of others. It was decided to use an adjective checking method, since it is direct and simple. Adjective check lists have been used to measure adjustment (18), self-acceptance (4), empathy (9), character traits (13), and to distinguish the self-perceptions of persons classified according to some social and psychological variables (26). In the main, these lists have been used with adults.

In developing the check list with children, words and phrases to be included were selected on the basis of the following three criteria:

1. The words should be those commonly used to describe how people feel toward and how people think of others, especially how teachers feel toward and think of children. An attempt was made to cover varied aspects of behavior and personality. For this purpose, lists already developed, like those of Allport (1), Gough (12), and Hartshorne and May (13), were scanned for appropriate words.
2. The words should be easy enough for children in approximately the 10–16 year age range to read and comprehend. The Thorndike-Lorge Frequency Count (33) was used to eliminate words which would be too difficult.
3. The list should contain about an equal number of words connoting positive and negative feelings.

From an initial pool of 200 trait names, 135 remained after the application of criteria 1 and 2. The next step was to determine the feeling tone of the 135 words. Each of the words was then rated by 35 teachers and 50 junior high school pupils as *favorable, unfavorable,* or *neutral.* Only those words were retained which were judged by more than 80 per cent of the teachers and 80 per cent of the pupils as being favorable or unfavorable. The words judged neutral were eliminated.

Fifty words remained after the teachers and students judged them as favorable or unfavorable. The 35 words finally used are listed below along with the F or U rating received. Fifteen words were dropped either because of the level of difficulty or because of some duplication in meaning.

Fair	(F)	A hard worker	(F)
A nuisance	(U)	Bad	(U)
Afraid	(U)	A good sport	(F)
Cheerful	(F)	Considerate	(F)
A time waster	(U)	Not eager to study	(U)

Neat	(F)	Helpful	(F)
Not eager to learn	(U)	Careless	(U)
A leader	(F)	Sociable	(F)
Unhappy	(U)	Clever	(F)
Loving	(F)	Not alert	(U)
Outstanding	(F)	Smart	(F)
Loud	(U)	Silly	(U)
Generous	(F)	Kind	(F)
Nervous	(U)	Shy	(U)
Sensible	(F)	A sloppy worker	(U)
Polite	(F)	Dependable	(F)
Lazy	(U)	A day dreamer	(U)
Forgetful	(U)		

Administration and scoring of the check list

The children are instructed to decide how the teacher feels toward them with respect to each trait name, and then to rate it on a three-point rating scale: *most of the time, half of the time, seldom or almost never.* A favorable word is assigned a score of 3 when it is checked in the most-of-the-time column, a score of 2 for half of the time, and 1 for seldom or almost never. For an unfavorable word the scoring is reversed.

The total score, the Index of Favorability, is obtained by adding the scores of all the words and dividing the total by the number of words checked. The higher the index, the more favorable is the child's perception of the teacher's feelings toward him. Theoretically, the index can range from 1.00 to 3.00.

Reliability and validity

The Check List of Trait Names was administered twice to four classes comprising 105 junior high school children. The interval between the two administrations was from four to six weeks. A correlation of .85 was obtained (rank difference, $p < .001$).

The check list may be considered to have logical validity. However, it was desired to obtain a measure of empirical and concurrent validity. This was done by correlating the child's own perception of his teacher's appraisal of him with his classmates' perceptions of the teachers' feelings toward him. For this purpose, a modified version of the de Groat and Thompson *Teacher Approval and Disapproval Scale* (7) was administered along with check list to 93 children (3 classes). The de Groat and Thompson scale, as modified, consisted of 8 positive statements, such as, "Here is someone whom the teacher praises for trying hard," and 8 negative statements, such as, "Here is someone whom the teacher often points out as wasting too much time." For each statement, pupils were asked to name one to four of their classmates to whom these characteristics applied. They could also name themselves, if they so desired. Of the 93 children, 56 received 5 or more votes on one of the teacher approval and disapproval statements. For these 56 children, a teacher-approval score was determined by subtracting the number of unfavorable statements on which five or more votes were received from the number of favorable statements on which five or more votes were received. A correlation of .51 was obtained (rank difference, $p < .001$) between the Index of Favorability and the teacher-approval score.

The check list developed to assess children's perception of their teachers' feelings toward them appears to have satisfactory reliability and validity. Although the estimate of reliability and validity was based on a sample of junior high school students, the list was considered appropriate also for the upper grades of the elementary school because of the way the words were chosen.

Experimental Design

SUBJECTS

The subjects of this study were 89 boys and 114 girls, attending fourth, fifth, and sixth grades of a New York City public school. These children were distributed in 10 different classrooms. In terms of reading ability, the classes selected were in the upper half of their respective grade level. Originally, it was planned to test all fourth-, fifth-, and sixth-grade children, but after preliminary experimentation, it was found that several words were two difficult for children of limited language ability. It was therefore decided to test children in those classes which were known to have the better readers.

The children represented a wide range in socioeconomic status. It was possible to divide them into three distinct groups on the basis of their fathers' and mothers' occupation. The upper group, consisting of 63 children, came from families of professional people, white-collar workers and businessmen; the middle social class group of 57 children had parents who were skilled workers, policemen, and firemen; the low group contained 83 children of semiskilled and unskilled workers and a number of unemployed.

Table 1 presents the background information for the 203 children involved in the study.

TABLE 1

DISTRIBUTION OF SUBJECTS IN THE TEN CLASSROOMS BY SEX AND SOCIAL CLASS STATUS

	Socioeconomic Status							
	Upper		*Middle*		*Lower*		*Total*	
Classroom	*Boys*	*Girls*	*Boys*	*Girls*	*Boys*	*Girls*	*Boys*	*Girls*
4–1	8	5	3	8	–	2	11	15
5–1	1	–	–	2	7	8	8	10
5–2	–	–	–	–	3	5	3	5
5–3	7	10	7	2	–	1	14	13
5–4	–	2	3	1	9	8	12	11
5–5	2	4	6	3	3	7	11	14
6–1	5	5	4	3	–	–	9	8
6–2	2	5	4	2	1	6	7	13
6–3	3	3	5	3	–	9	8	15
6–4	–	1	–	1	6	8	6	10
Total	28	35	32	25	29	54	89	114

PROCEDURE

The Check List of Trait Names was administered twice to the children. At the first administration, the children were instructed to respond to the 35 adjectives comprising the list in terms of "My teacher thinks I am," and at the second testing, in terms of "I think I am." The first testing was done in the morning, the second in the afternoon. The "My teacher thinks I am" scale yields a measure of perceived teacher feelings, referred to henceforth as the Index of Favorability; the "I think I am" scale yields a measure of self-perception.

The teachers, nine women and one man, rated their pupils on academic achievement, on a four-point scale: Very Well, Adequately, Below Average, and Very Poorly. In the analysis of data, the last two categories were combined due to the paucity of cases in the category Very Poorly. At the same time, the teacher also rated each child on 10 behavioral or personality characteristics. A weight of +1 was assigned to each of the traits judged to be desirable. The four desirable traits were: eager, obedient, cooperative, assertive. A weight of —1 was given to the characteristics judged to be undesirable: disorderly, destructive, hostile, defiant, unfriendly, and troublesome. The sum of the weights yielded a behavior rating score ranging theoretically, from +4 (very desirable) to —6 (very undesirable). Subjects who received the 0 and minus behavioral ratings were combined into one group due to the small number of cases in these categories.

Results and Discussion

HYPOTHESIS 1

There exists a positive correlation between children's perception of their teachers' feelings toward them and children's perception of themselves.

The two perceptual favorability indexes correlated .82 (product-moment, $p < .001$). The children who had a more favorable or a more adequate self-concept, that is, those who achieved a higher self-perception score also perceived their teachers' feelings toward them more favorably.

The finding of a significant correlation between the two kinds of perception lends support to the view that a child's assessment of himself is related to the assessment "significant people" make of him (30). In two previous research investigations, a close relationship was found between self-appraisal and children's perception of their parents' feelings toward them (2, 16). The present study for the first time has shown that a child's self-appraisal is significantly related to his perception of his teacher's feelings as well. Such a finding was anticipated in view of the fact that one role of the teacher, at least at the elementary level, is that of a "parent substitute." Several interesting questions may be raised: To what extent does a child's perception of his teacher's feelings resemble his perception of his mother's or father's feelings toward him? Does the child's perception of his present teacher differ from his perception of his previous teacher? Does favorability or perception decrease or increase with years in school?

HYPOTHESIS 2

There exists a positive relationship between favorable perception of teachers' feelings and academic achievement. Table 2 presents the mean favorability scores and their standard deviations for the three levels of estimated achievement. The *F* ratio of 15.61 was significant at less than the .001 level. The three *t* tests were also significant at better than the .01 level.

TABLE 2

INDEX OF FAVORABILITY AS RELATED TO THREE LEVELS OF ESTIMATED ACHIEVEMENT

	Achievement category		
Measure	*Very well*	*Adequately*	*Below average*
Mean favorability score	2.68* N = 53	2.57 N = 111	2.40 N = 39
S. D.	.22	.24	.25

*The higher the score, the more favorable the child's perception of his teacher's feelings toward him.

HYPOTHESIS 3

There exists a positive relationship between favorable perception of teachers' feelings and desirable classroom behavior. The findings pertaining to the relationship between children's perception and their classroom behavior are shown in Table 3.

TABLE 3

INDEX OF FAVORABILITY AS RELATED TO FIVE LEVELS OF RATED BEHAVIOR

	Behavior rating category				
	Very desirable		*Desirable*		*Undesirable (0 and*
Measure	*(+4*	*+3)*	*(+2*	*+1)*	*minus scores)*
Mean favorability score	2.62* N = 40	2.65 N = 54	2.58 N = 46	2.53 N = 23	2.39 N = 40
S. D.	.26	.19	.27	.27	.28

*The higher the score, the more favorable the child's perception of his teacher's feelings toward him.

The over-all *F* ratio of 7.38 was significant at less than the .001 level. The only significant *t* tests were those between the lowest category (0 and less) and all the other categories. In other words, the children who were rated as being disorderly, defiant, unfriendly, or troublesome, perceived their teachers' feelings toward them as being less favorable than the children who were rated as being eager, cooperative, assertive, and the like.

One of the axioms of educational psychology is the statement that a child learns only when he is motivated to learn. Furthermore, the basic incentives which a teacher can furnish are her acceptance of the child on the one hand, and approval on the other. The findings of the present study furnish supporting evidence. The teacher's feelings of acceptance and approval are communicated to the child and perceived by him as positive appraisals. It is likely that these appraisals encourage the child to seek further teacher approval by achieving well and behaving in a manner acceptable to his teacher. We may also begin this cycle with the child's behavior. The child who achieves well and behaves satisfactorily is bound to please his teacher. She, in turn, communicates positive feelings toward the child, thus reinforcing his desire to be a good pupil. Which of these variables serves as the primary determiner is a fact difficult to ascertain. It seems rather that they reinforce each other. The implication is clear. It is essential that teachers communicate positive feelings to their children and thus not only strengthen their positive self-appraisals but stimulate their growth, academically as well as interpersonally.

It should be emphasized that these findings do not imply causality but rather suggest that certain pupil characteristics, such as self-perception, perceived teacher feelings, achievement, and behavior in school are interrelated.

In addition to the results relevant to the tested hypotheses, other findings will now be reported.

Sex differences

Sex differences were observed with regard to the three variables studied: Index of Favorability,[2] achievement, and behavior in school. Girls perceived their teachers' feelings toward them more favorably than did the boys (girls' mean = 2.60; boys' mean = 2.52; $t = 2.41$, $p < .02$). The behavior ratings of the girls were more favorable than those of the boys ($x^2 = 10.72$, $df = 4$, $p < .05$); the girls were likewise rated more favorably in achievement, although this difference was not significant ($x^2 = 3.41$, $df = 2$, $.10 < p < .20$).

Past research has consistently shown that teachers report more problem behavior among boys (32). One explanation, though not widely accepted, is that boys are naturally more aggressive. Another view, more plausible, holds that our society encourages aggressive behavior in men (and men to be) and submissive behavior in women. Teachers, most of whom are women, especially in the primary grades, therefore regard boys' classroom behavior as disturbingly different from the norms of behavior appropriate to their own female sex. The temptation is great to reward children of one's own sex. Meyer and Thompson's study (19) is pertinent here. Teacher-pupil interaction of sixth-grade pupils was studied over a one-year period and analyzed in terms of "approval" and "disapproval" contacts. In addition, children were asked to nominate by the "Guess Who" technique which of their classmates receive their teacher's approval and disapproval. Both approaches yielded the same finding. Classroom observers, as well as the children themselves, noted that teachers expressed greater approval of girls and greater disapproval of boys. The findings of the present investigation, which ascertained directly children's perceptions of their teachers' feelings, are in accord with the results of prior research. The suggestion has been frequently made that more men should be urged to teach at the primary level. Findings such as those discussed above suggest the urgency to establish a sexual balance in the teaching staff at the primary grades.

---

[2] The index used in this and subsequent analyses is based on the check list score of the child's perception of his teacher's feelings toward him.

Not only is it desirable for boys to have a male model with whom to identify, but conditions may then be created which may assure greater teacher approval for boys and reduce teacher disapproval for behavior which is, to a large extent, culturally instigated.

SOCIAL CLASS DIFFERENCES

Because of the distinct differences found in social class status in this group of children, it was decided to investigate the relation of social class to the Index of Favorability, achievement, and behavior in school. All three variables are related to social class in the direction one would predict. These data are shown in Table 4.

TABLE 4

SOCIAL CLASS STATUS RELATED TO FAVORABILITY INDEX, ACHIEVEMENT, AND BEHAVIOR

Variable	*Upper social class N = 63*	*Middle social class N = 57*	*Lower social class N = 83*
Mean favorability index	2.63	2.60	2.49
S. D.	.26	.22	.26
Achievement rating category:			
Very well N = 53	43%*	34%	23%
Adequately N = 111	31%	22%	47%
Below average N = 39	15%	36%	49%
Behavioral rating category:			
Very desirable N = 94	41%	29%	30%
Desirable N = 69	23%	30%	46%
Undesirable N = 40	20%	22%	58%

*These percentages are based on the N's of the achievement and behavior categories.

It may be observed from Table 4 that there is a decline in mean favorability index from the upper to the lower social class. Two of the three *t* tests were significant at better than the .01 level; *t* was not significant between the upper and middle social class groups. Children in the two advantaged social class groups perceive their teachers' feelings toward them more favorably than do the children in the lower class group.

Social class and achievement in school are significantly related ($x^2 =$

18.38, 4df, $p < .01$). The differences in the percentage of children in the several categories may be pointed out, especially the difference between the two extremes; in the upper social class 43 per cent of the children were rated by their teachers as doing very well in school while only 15 per cent were rated as doing below average work.

Social class and behavior in school as rated by the teachers were not significantly related ($x^2 = 14.97$, 8df, $.05 < p < .10$). However, the distribution of children in the several categories reveal interesting differences. While the great majority of the children in the group were rated favorably by their teachers, there were 58 per cent of the children in the lower class whose behavior was rated as undesirable while only 20 per cent of the upper class children were so rated.

It has been suggested that teachers, as surrogates of middle class values, tend to give preferential treatment to the middle and upper socioeconomic class pupils, and to withhold rewards from pupils who belong to the lower socioeconomic class (6, 8). Furthermore, previous research has shown that lower class children do not achieve as well as middle and upper class children (10, 14), in part due to lower motivation (25). The data obtained in the present study corroborate these observations.

The interrelations found between children's perception of teachers' feelings, school achievement, behavior, and socioeconomic status are particularly significant since the majority of children in the public schools throughout the country come from families of low social class status. It is therefore likely that a lower class child, especially if he is not doing well in school, will have a negative perception of his teachers' feelings toward him. These negative perceptions will in turn tend to lower his efforts to achieve in school and/or increase the probability that he will misbehave. His poor school achievement will aggravate the negative attitudes of his teachers toward him, which in turn will affect his self-confidence, and so on. This vicious entanglement must be interrupted at some point. The point of attack may well be the teacher whose capacity to reflect feelings conducive to the child's growth should be of concern to educators.

Analysis of variance of favorability scores

It was found that the Index of Favorability was positively related to achievement in school as well as to social class position. It is also evident from this and other studies that achievement in school is correlated with social class position. In order to study the influence of each of these factors on Index of Favorability, the favorability scores were reanalyzed first, for the three achievement levels within each social class and second, for the three social class groups within each achievement category. The mean favorability indexes for these separate groups are presented in Table 5.

TABLE 5

MEAN INDEXES OF FAVORABILITY FOR THE THREE ACHIEVEMENT CATEGORIES AND FOR THE THREE SOCIAL CLASS GROUPS

	Achievement category		
Social class groups	*Very well*	*Adequately*	*Below average*
Upper social class	2.71* N = 23	2.61 N = 34	2.51 N = 6
Middle social class	2.71 N = 18	2.60 N = 25	2.44 N = 14
Lower social class	2.59 N = 12	2.52 N = 52	2.34 N = 19

*The higher the score, the more favorable the child's perception of his teacher's feelings toward him.

Reading Table 5 vertically, it may be observed that the mean favorability score declines from the upper social class to the lowest social class for each of the achievement categories; this decline is most noticeable between the two highest social class groups and the lowest social class group. It is apparent that the social class variable plays a part in the way a child perceives his teacher's feelings toward him regardless of his achievement in school. Similarly, reading Table 5 horizontally, the mean favorability score is observed to decrease from the highest achievement level to the lowest within each social class group. The evidence here suggests that achievement in school colors the child's perception of his teacher's feelings, regardless of his social class position. Analysis of variance of the data yielded two significant F ratios. These results indicate that both the factors of social class position and achievement are operating independently in affecting the way a child will perceive his teacher's feelings toward him.

These findings should arouse the educator for they imply that a teacher's reaction to a child is not solely influenced by the individuality of the child but also by his social class and achievement characteristics.

DIFFERENCES AMONG TEACHERS

It may be assumed that teachers reflect a variety of feelings toward children, either because of their own personality needs, or because of the way they use punishment or praise or for any other reason. These differences from teacher to teacher should be observable in the perceptions of the children affected by them. Table 6 presents the mean favorability indexes for the 10 teachers in this study.

TABLE 6

THE INDEX OF FAVORABILITY FOR THE TEN CLASSROOMS

Class	*N*	*Mean*	*S. D.*
4–1	26	2.61*	.26
5–1	18	2.25	.21
5–2	8	2.45	.29
5–3	27	2.62	.17
5–4	23	2.45	.23
5–5	25	2.62	.22
6–1	17	2.57	.08
6–2	20	2.64	.23
6–3	23	2.64	.19
6–4	16	2.70	.10

*The higher the score, the more favorable the child's perception of his teacher's feelings toward him.

It may be observed that the range in mean favorability score is from 2.25 to 2.70. Although the children generally perceived their teachers' feelings more favorably than otherwise, and the actual differences among the classrooms were not large, there were 3 or 4 classrooms with markedly low mean scores. The over-all F ratio of 2.95 is significant at less than the .01 level. It should be remembered, at this point, that the classes were selected for better than average ability in reading, which makes the finding of significant differences even more compelling. Teachers do seem to vary in their inclination and/or their capacity to communicate favorable feelings. It seems urgent that teachers be helped to recognize the significance of the feelings which they express toward children, consciously or unconsciously. Some teachers, in addition, may need the help which can only come through a process of self-understanding, in order to avoid or to minimize the expression of negatively toned feelings toward children, because of their sex, their socioeconomic status, their behavior or achievement in school.

POSSIBLE USES OF THE CHECK LIST

The Check List of Trait Names, in addition to its use as a research tool, may be adapted to practical school situations. Conceivably, it can be employed for the purpose of teacher selection and guidance. For instance, a principal might wish to select a teacher for a class comprised of underprivileged or troublesome children who are very much in need of acceptance and approval. A good candidate for such a class would be a teacher who can easily project positive feelings. Supervisors of student teachers may find the check list useful in evaluating the quality of teacher-student relations.

Teachers who are found to communicate largely negative feelings may be advised to participate in some kind of counseling or therapy. Similarly, children whose perceptions are primarily negative and/or distorted can be identified for personality diagnosis and thus be helped in self-understanding or in obtaining a more accurate perception of reality.

Summary

The purpose of the study was to relate children's perception of their teachers' feelings toward them to self-perception, academic achievement, and classroom behavior. A Check List of Trait Names, consisting of 35 descriptive terms, was administered to 89 boys and 114 girls in grades 4, 5, and 6 in a New York City public school. The children were rated by their teachers for achievement and on a number of behavioral characteristics.

The major findings were:

1. The children's perception of their teachers' feelings toward them correlated positively and significantly with self-perception. The child with the more favorable self image was the one who more likely than not perceived his teacher's feelings toward him more favorably.

2. The more positive the children's perception of their teachers' feelings, the better was their academic achievement, and the more desirable their classroom behavior as rated by the teachers.

3. Further, children in the upper and middle social class groups perceived their teachers' feelings toward them more favorably than did the children in the lower social class group.

4. Social class position was also found to be positively related with achievement in school.

5. However, even when the favorability index data were reanalyzed separately for each social class and for each achievement category, the mean favorability index declined with decline in achievement level, regardless of social class position and, similarly, the mean favorability index declined with social class regardless of achievement level.

6. Girls generally perceived their teachers' feelings more favorably than did the boys.

7. Finally, there were some significant classroom differences in the favorability of the children's perception of their teachers' feelings. These findings must be considered in light of the nonrandom selection of the sample. Nevertheless, it is reasonable to assume that these subjects are representative of the population of New York City elementary school children at these grades levels. . . .

References

1. Allport, G., and H. Odbert, "Trait Names: A Psycho-Lexical Study," *Psychological Monographs,* Vol. 47 (1936).
2. Ausubel, D. P., *et al.,* "Perceived Parental Attitudes as Determinants of Children's Ego Structure," *Child Development,* Vol. 25 (1954), pp. 173-183.
3. Barr, A. S., and R. E. Jones, "The Measurement and Prediction of Teacher Efficiency," *Review of Educational Research,* Vol. 28 (1958), pp. 256-264.
4. Bills, R. E., *et al.,* "An Index of Adjustment and Values," *Journal of Consulting Psychology,* Vol. 15 (1951), pp. 257-261.
5. Cook, W. W., "Significant Factors in Teachers' Classroom Attitudes," *Journal of Education,* Vol. 7 (1956), pp. 274-279.
6. Davis, A., *Social Class Influences Upon Learning* (Cambridge: Harvard, 1952).
7. de Groat, A. F., and G. G. Thompson, "A Study of the Distribution of Teacher Approval and Disapproval Among Sixth-Grade Pupils," *Journal of Experimental Education,* Vol. 18 (1949), pp. 57-75.
8. Dixon, N. R., "Social Class and Education," *Harvard Educational Review,* Vol. 23 (1953), pp. 330-338.
9. Dymod, Rosalind F., "A Scale for Measurement of Empathic Ability," *Journal of Consulting Psychology,* Vol. 13 (1949), pp. 127-133.
10. Friedhoff, W. H., "Relationship Among Various Measures of Socio-Economic Status, Social Class Identification, Intelligence, and School Achievement," *Dissertation Abstract,* Vol. 15 (1955), p. 2098.
11. Gage, N. L., *et al.,* "Teachers' Understanding of Their Pupils and Pupils' Ratings of Their Teachers," *Psychological Monographs,* Vol. 69 (1955).
12. Gough, H. G., *Reference Handbook for the Gough Adjective Check List,* Mimeographed (Berkeley: U. of Calif., Institute of Personality Assessment and Research, 1955).
13. Hartshorne, H., and H. A. May, *Studies in the Nature of Character, III: Studies in the Organization of Character* (New York: Macmillan, 1930).
14. Heimann, R. A., and A. F. Schenk, "Relations of Social Class and Sex Differences to High School Achievement," *School Review,* Vol. 62 (1954), pp. 213-221.
15. Jersild, A. T., *In Search of Self* (New York: Bureau of Publications, Teachers College, Columbia University, 1952).
16. Jourard, S. M., and R. M. Remy, "Perceived Parental Attitudes, the Self, and Security," *Journal of Consulting Psychology,* Vol. 19 (1955), pp. 364-366.
17. Martire, J. G., "Relationship Between the Self Concept and Differences in the Strength and Generality of Achievement Motivation," *Journal of Personality,* Vol. 24 (1956), pp. 364-375.
18. Merrill, R. M., and L. B. Heathers, "The Use of an Adjective Check List as a Measure of Adjustment," *Journal of Consulting Psychology,* Vol. 1 (1954), pp. 137-143.

19. Meyer, W. J., and G. G. Thompson, "Sex Differences in the Distribution of Teacher Approval and Disapproval Among Sixth-Grade Children," *Journal of Educational Psychology,* Vol. 47 (1956), pp. 285-296.
20. National Education Association, Research Division, "Teacher Opinion on Pupil Behavior," *Research Bulletin,* Vol. 34 (1956), pp. 51-107.
21. Perkins, H. V., "Factors Influencing Change in Children's Self-Concepts," *Child Development,* Vol. 29 (1958), pp. 221-230.
22. ———, "Teachers' and Peers' Perceptions of Children's Self-Concepts," *Child Development,* Vol. 29 (1958), pp. 203-220.
23. Reeder, T. A., "A Study of Some Relationships Between Level of Self-Concept, Academic Achievement, and Classroom Adjustment," *Dissertation Abstract,* Vol. 15 (1955), p. 2472.
24. Rogers, C. R., *Client-Centered Therapy* (Boston: Houghton, 1951).
25. Rosen, B. C., "The Achievement Syndrome: A Psychocultural Dimension of Social Stratification," *American Sociological Review,* Vol. 21 (1956), pp. 203-211.
26. Sarbin, T. R., and B. C. Rosenberg, "Contributions to Role-Taking Theory: IV. A Method for Obtaining a Qualitative Estimate of the Self," *Journal of Social Psychology,* Vol. 42 (1955), pp. 71-81.
27. Snygg, D., and A. W. Combs, *Individual Behavior* (New York: Harper, 1949).
28. Steiner, I. D., "Self-Perception and Goal-Setting Behavior," *Journal of Personality,* Vo. 25 (1957), pp. 344-355.
29. Stevens, P. H., "An Investigation of the Relationship Between Certain Aspects of Self-Concept Behavior and Students' Academic Achievement," *Dissertation Abstract,* Vol. 16 (1956), pp. 2531-2532.
30. Sullivan, H. S., *Conceptions of Modern Psychiatry* (Washington, D.C.: W. A. White Psychiatric Foundation, 1947).
31. Symonds, P. M., "Characteristics of the Effective Teacher Based on Pupil Evaluation," *Journal of Experimental Education,* Vol. 23 (1955), pp. 289-310.
32. Terman, L. M., and L. E. Tyler, "Psychological Sex Differences," in L. Carmichael, ed., *Manual of Child Psychology,* 2d ed. (New York: Wiley, 1954).
33. Thorndike, E. L., and I. Lorge, *The Teacher's Word Book of 30,000 Words* (New York: Bureau of Publications, Teachers College, Columbia University, 1944).

3. The effect of repeated praise or blame on the work achievement of "introverts" and "extroverts"

George G. Thompson
and Clarence W. Hunnicutt

Reprinted from the *Journal of Educational Psychology,* Vol. 35 (1944), 257-266, by permission of the senior author and the publisher.

The two previous articles in this section point dramatically to how teachers can influence the self and the impact of this influence on subsequent self-perception and achievement. Do the findings so far indicate that teachers interact in the same way with all youngsters? If interaction patterns are successful with one student in enhancing his self-concept and achievement, will these same interaction patterns be successful with all students? Take the use of praise or blame, for example. Do they have the same or differential effects on children with dissimilar personality characteristics? The authors draw some interesting conclusions about this.

An investigation by Forlano and Axelrod (1) has indicated that repeated applications of praise or blame have differential effects on the work performance of "introverts" and "extroverts." In the investigation conducted by them, praise or blame was repeated only two times. The present study was conducted to determine the effects of more extended applications of praise or blame on the work achievement of "introverts" and "extroverts." The methods employed, however, are quite similar to those used by Forlano and Axelrod.

If praise or blame has differential effects on children with different personality characteristics, teachers should be cognizant of the fact. It seems altogether possible that indiscriminate praise may be as detrimental to a pupil's school achievement and personality development as indiscriminate blame. It also seems possible that the skillful teacher could at times employ blame, as well as praise, to foster the child's general adjustment.

Method

Subjects

Fifth-grade pupils from five classes in the Syracuse Public Schools [1] were selected as subjects for this study. One class of twenty-seven pupils was used for the control group. The remaining four classes (comprising ninety-seven pupils) were subdivided into the various experimental groups in the manner described below.

Several days before the experiment proper was conducted the introversion-extroversion section of a personality test by Pintner and others was administered to all of the one hundred twenty-four subjects employed in this study. On the basis of total scores obtained on this thirty-five-item test the children in each class were divided into two groups. Pupils with scores above the median were considered "extroverts," while those pupils with scores below the median were considered "introverts."

In the first class of fifth-grade pupils the "extroverts" were praised after each task, and the "introverts" were blamed. In the second class of pupils this procedure was reversed, and the "extroverts" were blamed while the "introverts" were praised. By alternating this procedure in the remaining two classes it was possible to obtain approximately the same number of pupils in each of the four experimental combinations.

Introversion-extroversion scores

The forty-seven subjects who were praised after each task (including both "introverts" and "extroverts") obtained a mean score on the introversion-extroversion test of 21.2. The fifty subjects who were blamed after each task (including both "introverts" and "extroverts") obtained a mean score of 21.9. The control group of twenty-seven pupils obtained a mean score of 21.5. A statistical analysis of the introversion-extroversion scores obtained by these three groups resulted in an F of 0.317, which is not significant at any acceptable level of confidence. Hence, these three groups may be accepted as unbiased samples from the same population with respect to introversion-extroversion.

The mean introversion-extroversion scores obtained by the pupils in each of the four experimental combinations are shown in Table 1.

[1] The experimenters wish to express thanks to Mr. C. Spencer Chambers, Principal of Lincoln School, and to Mr. Horace Roberts, Principal of Seymour School in Syracuse, New York, and to the teachers of these schools for their enthusiastic cooperation.

TABLE 1

Experimental groups	*Number of subjects*	*Mean score on introversion-extroversion test*
Extroverts—Praised	23	24.4
Extroverts—Blamed	28	23.8
Introverts—Praised	24	18.2
Introverts—Blamed	22	19.5

The results of a statistical analysis of the mean introversion-extroversion scores obtained by the subjects of the four experimental combinations are presented in Table 2. It may be concluded from these results that the

TABLE 2

Experimental groups	t	*Level of confidence*
E-P and E-B	0.47	—
I-P and I-B	0.46	—
E-P and I-P	7.95	1%
E-P and I-B	3.23	1%
E-B and I-P	4.20	1%
E-B and I-B	3.17	1%

extrovert-praised and the extrovert-blamed groups are not significantly different in mean introversion-extroversion scores; and that the mean introversion-extroversion scores obtained by the introvert-praised and the introvert-blamed groups are also not significantly different. All of the other combinations within the four experimental groups are significantly different with respect to mean introversion-extroversion scores. The results of this analysis satisfy the requisite conditions for this experiment: (1) that the two extrovert groups be unbiased samples from a population of "extroverts," and (2) that the two introvert groups be unbiased samples from a population of "introverts." [2]

[2] The control group was not included in the comparisons because of its obvious overlap in introversion-extroversion scores with the two extrovert and the two introvert groups. A control group is not necessary to test the differential effect of praise or blame on "introverts" and "extroverts," if the pupils in different experimental combinations do not differ significantly in their performance on the first assigned task. It will be shown later in this report that the subjects in the four experimental groups obtained essentially the same scores not only on the first task, but also on the second task (after the first differential incentives had been given).

Tasks and procedure

Six alternate forms of a cancellation test were constructed in order to measure each pupil's work achievement under the various experimental conditions. The different forms of this test were made sufficiently long so that no subject would be able to complete the task during any testing session. Each of these cancellation tests consisted of Arabic numerals from zero to nine presented in random sequences within each row. The pupils were instructed to draw a line through each of the 7's on the test sheet. Previous research has indicated that a cancellation test of this type has a low correlation with either intelligence or chronological age and has a substantially high reliability coefficient. In the present experiment employing one hundred twenty-four pupils a positive correlation of 0.87 was obtained between the combined scores of the three odd-tests and the combined scores of the three even-tests.

Before copies of the first test were distributed to any group of subjects, an example of several numerals was placed on the blackboard and the experimenter demonstrated the manner in which a line was to be drawn through each of the 7's. The usual precautions were taken to insure each subject's readiness to start work on the "begin" signal and to cease work immediately after the "stop" signal.

The duration of each test period for both the control and the experimental groups was thirty seconds. A work period of such short duration seemed advisable because of the intrinsic dullness of the task. In thirty seconds it seemed unlikely that the subjects would become satiated with the task or that they would reach in six test periods a level of performance that would preclude any further improvement in work output. Analysis of the results has shown that test periods of thirty-seconds duration provide reliable scores; however, there is some indication in the data that the experimental groups showing the greatest improvement in work achievement may have reached a level of performance that tended to make further improvement increasingly difficult.

In the control group no comments were made between any of the testing sessions. After the sixth and last task had been completed, the experimenter announced that all of the pupils had done satisfactory work.

In order to provide individual incentives to the subjects in the experimental groups, the teacher passed around the room after each testing period, studied each pupil's paper for a few seconds, and placed a "P" or a "G" on it. The pupils were asked to keep their marks secret. The teacher had been previously instructed as to which subjects were to receive marks of "P" (poor) and which subjects were to receive marks of "G" (good). After marking the first set of test papers, the teacher wrote a large "P" and a large "G" on the blackboard, and informed the pupils that those who had received "P's" had done very poorly and those who had received "G's" had done exceedingly well. After marking the papers for each of the subsequent tests the teacher reminded the subjects that "P" stood for poor work and "G" for good work.

It is assumed in this study that a mark of "G" represented to the subjects a form of teacher praise; and that a mark of "P" represented a form of teacher blame. The fact that the pupils had no assurance that their "good" or "poor" marks would not be made known to the entire class may also have been functioning as a form of motivation. The experimenters observed that some of the children who were blamed after each test became increasingly disturbed when they failed to obtain a "G" on their test papers. It was observed that some of the "blamed" pupils increased their efforts after receiving a poor mark, while other pupils who were blamed became distracted or sullen when the next test was given. One pupil who was continuously blamed became so resentful that he refused to try on the last test; his teacher reported that this was his typical reaction when he was reprimanded for poor school work.

At the end of the final test all children were marked "G." This could have no experimental effect and might leave the children with a pleasanter emotion. Most of the students who had been receiving "P" now showed marked signs of elation, indicating that the motivation had been functioning. This was particularly true of those "blamed" students who were normally accustomed to receiving good grades.

The "unfairness" of the experimental situation could not have been unusually disturbing. It was of short duration. More important, the customary pattern of assigning marks in school continues over a period of years to "blame" individuals for inadequacies beyond their control.

Results

Comparison of blamed, praised, and control groups

To compare the work achievement of the blamed (both introverts and extroverts), the praised (both introverts and extroverts), and the control groups, the cancellation scores obtained by each subject on the first test were subtracted from the scores obtained on each of the succeeding five tests. This procedure was followed because the control group obtained somewhat higher scores on the first test than did the blamed or the praised groups. The derived data are shown in Table 3. It should be recalled that no extrinsic incentives were applied before the first test.

TABLE 3

	Mean gains in cancellation scores				
Experimental groups	*Test* 2	*Test* 3	*Test* 4	*Test* 5	*Test* 6
Total blamed group	18.1	16.3	17.9	20.3	21.1
Total praised group	18.3	16.2	16.6	19.6	19.9
Control group	11.6	11.4	11.2	12.5	14.9

An analysis of variance was made of the gains shown by these three groups on tests 2, 3, 4, 5, and 6. F was found to be significant at the one per cent level of confidence for each of the five gains. Since F was found to be significant for each of the five gains, it was permissible to compare the mean gains of the three groups for each of the last five tests. The results of this analysis are presented in Table 4.

The values presented in Table 4 show that there are no significant differences between any of the mean gains obtained by the blamed and the praised groups on the last five tests. These values further show that all five of the mean gains obtained by the control group are significantly smaller than those obtained by either the praised or the blamed group.

It may be concluded: (1) that either praise or blame was more effective than no external incentive in increasing the work output of these fifth-grade pupils; and (2) that praise and blame were equally effective in motivating fifth-grade pupils when "introverts" and "extroverts" were not differentiated.

However, it should be pointed out that the increased work output shown by the praised and the blamed groups is almost entirely the result of the first incentive applied. The succeeding applications of praise or blame did

TABLE 4

	*t's for differences between mean gains**				
Experimental groups	*Test* 2	*Test* 3	*Test* 4	*Test* 5	*Test* 6
Total praised group vs. total blamed group	0.23	0.10	1.07	0.50	0.69
Total praised group vs. control group	6.45	4.14	3.72	4.55	2.86
Total blamed group vs. control group	6.30	4.26	4.68	5.06	3.62

**t*'s with the number of degrees of freedom available for these comparisons must be 2.75 or greater to be significant at the one per cent level of confidence and at least 2.42 to be significant at the five per cent level of confidence.

not materially alter the pupils' mean scores, although the initial superiority attained by the praised and the blamed groups after the application of the first incentives was maintained consistently during the later tests.

COMPARISON OF E-B, E-P, I-B, AND I-P GROUPS

The mean cancellation scores obtained on each of the six tests by the extrovert-blamed, the extrovert-praised, the introvert-blamed, and the introvert-praised groups are presented graphically in Figure 1.

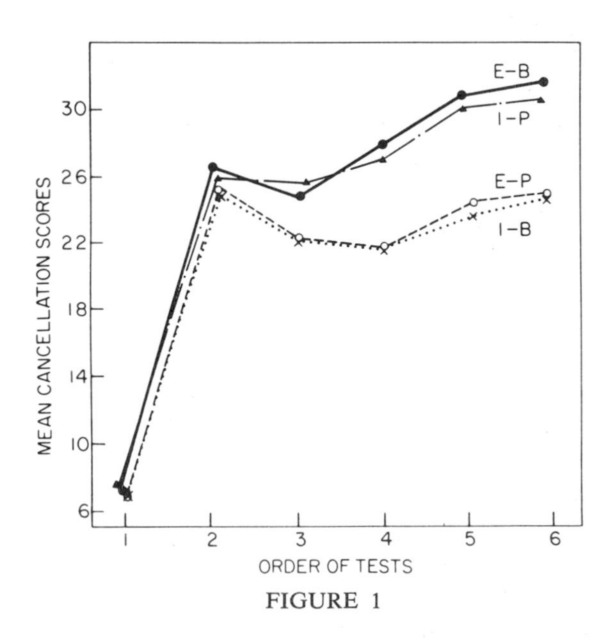

FIGURE 1

An analysis of variance of the cancellation scores obtained by these four experimental groups on each of the six tests shows that F was not significant for tests 1, 2, and 3 but was significant at the one per cent level of confidence for tests 4, 5, and 6. It may be concluded that there were no significant differences in work output between any of the four experimental groups on tests 1, 2, and 3, although the differences on test 3 showed a consistent trend toward the significant differences found for tests 4, 5, and 6. The results of this analysis permit a comparison of the mean cancellation scores obtained by these four experimental groups on tests 4, 5, and 6. The *t*'s for differences between mean scores are presented in Table 5.

These comparisons of mean scores substantiate what one could reasonably predict by examining Figure 1.

1. On tests 4, 5, and 6 the extroverts who were blamed (E-B) obtained significantly higher cancellation scores than either the E-P or the I-B groups.
2. On tests 4, 5, and 6 the introverts who were praised (I-P) obtained significantly higher cancellation scores than either the E-P or the I-B groups.
3. On tests 4, 5, and 6, as well as on tests 1, 2, and 3, the E-P and the I-B groups did not differ significantly in mean scores. There were also no significant differences between the mean cancellation scores obtained by the E-B and the I-P groups on any of the six tests.

TABLE 5

	t's for differences between mean scores								
	Test 4			*Test 5*			*Test 6*		
Experimental groups	*Diff.*	t	*Level of confidence*	*Diff.*	t	*Level of confidence*	*Diff.*	t	*Level of confidence*
E-B minus E-P	5.9	2.80	1%	6.3	3.01	1%	6.4	2.83	1%
E-B minus I-B	5.9	2.76	1%	7.1	3.31	1%	6.6	2.87	1%
I-P minus E-P	4.8	2.21	5%	5.8	2.71	1%	5.4	2.32	5%
I-P minus I-B	4.8	2.18	5%	6.6	3.05	1%	5.6	2.35	5%
E-P minus I-B	0.0	——	—	0.8	0.37	—	0.2	0.01	—
E-B minus I-P	1.1	0.53	—	0.5	0.25	—	1.0	0.45	—

In more general terms, it may be concluded from these results that applications of praise or blame, when repeated often enough in the form of school marks, have differential effects on the cancellation scores of introverted and extroverted fifth-grade pupils. Introverts achieve a higher level of performance when praised, and extroverts respond most favorably when blamed. The increasing divergence of the curves (Figure 1) further indicates that there is a cumulative effect of repeated praise or blame on "introverts" and "extroverts."

SUMMARY AND CONCLUSIONS

The purpose of the present study was to determine the effects of repeated applications of praise or blame on introverted and extroverted fifth-grade pupils. One hundred and twenty-four fifth-grade pupils were selected as subjects. The introversion-extroversion section of a personality test by Pintner and others was used to classify the pupils into two groups with regard to introversion-extroversion. Cancellation tests were employed to measure the effects of repeated praise or blame on the experimental groups. Praise or blame was administered by the teacher's placing a mark of "G" (good) or "P" (poor) on the subject's test paper. A control group was employed to test the effects of repeated applications of praise or blame on an unclassified population of fifth-grade pupils (introverts and extroverts grouped together).

The analysis of the data collected indicate that:

1. When introverts and extroverts are grouped together, praise and blame are equally effective in motivating the work achievement of fifth-grade pupils. Either praise or blame is more effective in increasing the work output of fifth-grade pupils than no external incentives.
2. If repeated often enough, praise increases the work output of introverts until it is significantly higher than that of introverts who are blamed or extroverts who are praised.
3. If repeated often enough, blame increases the work output of extroverts until it is significantly higher than that of extroverts who are praised or introverts who are blamed.

The results of this study indicate that praise, as well as blame, can be used unwisely by the elementary school teacher if he does not fully appreciate and understand the different personalities present in his classroom. Praise and blame should not be judged on an either-or basis, but should be used to fit the case.

Reference

1. Forlano, George, and H. C. Axelrod, "The Effect of Repeated Praise or Blame on the Performance of Introverts and Extroverts," *Journal of Educational Psychology,* Vol. 28 (1937), pp. 92-100.

4. Changing perceptions of self

HUGH V. PERKINS

Reprinted by permission of the Association for Childhood Education International, 3615 Wisconsin Avenue, N. W., Washington, D. C. 20016, "Changing Perceptions of Self," by Hugh V. Perkins. From *Childhood Education,* October 1957, Vol. 34, No. 2.

What relationships exist between changes in children's school achievement and peer group acceptance and changes in their self-ideal self congruency? Do children differ by grade and sex in their self-concepts? What happens to students taught by teachers who participate in in-service child study programs? In a clear, uncluttered fashion, Perkins examines these and related issues.

Children change in so many ways as they grow up! Taking the first toddling steps, entering the world of reading experiences, earning the first dollar, finishing the dress or model airplane, going out on the first date—all are milestones in the steady march toward maturity. Witnessing these and other landmarks in children's development gives teachers and parents their proudest moments. Less apparent changes, but nevertheless real and crucial to learning and development, are changes in ways children see and feel about themselves. How a child sees and feels about himself is revealed by his behavior, actions, words, gestures, and facial expressions. Perceiving how another person sees himself is not a simple task, since most people tend to conceal many of their real feelings behind a mask of conventional behavior.

Behavior Changes with Self-Concept

A knowledge of how the child sees himself in various situations is helpful to parents and teachers because it enables them to understand more clearly the child's past behavior and to anticipate how he will react in similar future situations. Since the child behaves in terms of the way he sees himself, it is evident that change in behavior cannot take place unless there is modification in his self-concept. A child can succeed in gaining love and acceptance, learning to read, making the team, and being honest and responsible only as he has incorporated these qualities and roles into his self-concept.

The individual's self-concept consists not of a single perception of self; it consists of the persisting ways he sees himself in the many life situations that he faces or might face. It includes not only his bodily features and characteristics, but also his identifications with people, cultures, ideas, and values. His perceptions of himself in many situations together with the objects, people, ideas, and values which he views as part or characteristic of himself constitute his self-concept. This self-concept emerged through the process of taking over the responses of others toward himself and incorporating these into his perceptions of himself. People with whom the child interacts—parents, siblings, teachers, and peers—exert a pervasive influence on formation and change of the self-concept. A child looked upon and treated as tall but awkward, intelligent but lazy, talented but careless, alert but mischievous, will in the absence of conflicting evidence also see himself as possessing these qualities and he will act accordingly.

Many self-descriptive qualities and traits of self-concept will become generalized, while others will be differentiated in relation to specific roles or situations. Since these qualities are organized in a hierarchy, there are some that the child values highly and others that he would prefer to disown or to forget. Although wanting to disown these qualities, the individual reveals through his behavior an awareness of them as part of self. Failure to accept them as a part of self results in conflict.

Not only does a person have a perception of himself, but he also has an image of the kind of person he would like to become. This latter is referred to as the self-ideal and is described in a similar manner as self-concept. Parents and teachers are interested in knowing something of the extent of discrepancy between the child's self-concept and self-ideal because it is an indication of development and learning that has taken place. It also reveals the degree of inner harmony and self-adjustment.

A Study of Children's Self-Concepts

The seeming importance of the degree of congruency and change in congruency between children's perceptions of themselves and of the kinds of persons they wish to become prompted the writer to make a study of this aspect of development. The study investigated the influences of selected factors on the changes in self-ideal self congruency which fourth- and sixth-grade children revealed during a six-month period. A further purpose of the study was to discover the relationships between changes in children's school achievement and peer group acceptance and changes in their self-ideal self congruency.

Two hundred fifty-one children in four fourth-grade and four sixth-grade classrooms reported their self-concepts by a procedure in which each child ranked a series of fifty self-referrent statements as each was judged to describe "me" or "not me." On the succeeding day the children revealed their ideal self-concepts by ranking the same fifty statements as they judged each to describe the person "I would like to be" or the person "I would not like to be." Correlating these two measures for each child provided evidences of self-ideal self congruency.

The fifty self-referrent statements which the children ranked were a random sample of a much larger group of self-descriptive statements relating to physical characteristics, social relationships, abilities and talents, school work, sports, and personality traits. Although the major purpose of the ranking procedure was to obtain a measure of each child's self-concept and ideal-self, the highest rankings of self-referrent statements by all the children reveal the ways these fourth- and sixth-grade boys and girls in general tend to see themselves.

It is interesting to note that these children, regardless of age and sex, attributed to themselves most frequently this self-percept: "I like my parents." The self-percepts most frequently as not being descriptive of self were: (1) "I do not like animals." (2) "I have a brother or sister that I don't like." (3) "I have poor health." (4) "I am weak." (5) "I am unpopular."

Fourth graders tended to see themselves most frequently as being fast runners, liking to read, and being good in their school work. The self-concepts of sixth graders, especially the boys, revealed a confidence in their own abilities. Children in this grade did not see themselves as unhappy but as persons who look on the bright side of things.

Boys as a group saw themselves most frequently as being or wishing to be tall and to be fast runners. They also saw themselves as persons who felt that money was very important. Girls, on the other hand, saw themselves generally as liking reading, being good in their school work, and watching and listening to TV and radio. An attribute belonging to the person these girls wished to become was that of being good looking. The self-ideal of fourth-grade girls included the habit of getting places on time.

It is clearly evident from these results that children in general reveal in their self-concepts many of the sex, age and cultural differences which substantiate and enlarge our knowledge of child development.

Changes in Self-Concepts with Maturity

Not only do children differ by grade and sex in the percepts or traits which they generally incorporate into or exclude from their self-concepts, but they also tend to differ in the stability and consistency of their self-concepts. Sixth graders and girls generally tended to reveal greater stability of self-concept than did, respectively, fourth graders and boys. Little relationship, however, was found between stability of children's self-concepts and their levels of reading achievement and mental ages.

The self-concepts and ideal self-concepts of children generally become increasingly and significantly more congruent through time. The tendency for children to see themselves more nearly like the persons they would like to become seems to be influenced by and to be a consequence of their growth and development and school experience.

Schools are not uniformly successful in facilitating greater self-ideal self congruency in all children. It was found that boys in general achieve significantly less congruency of self-concept and ideal-self than do girls. The greater physical maturity of girls when compared with boys generally may be a partial explanation of this. Since girls generally are ahead of boys in physical maturity until the end of pubescence, it may be that the greater self-ideal self congruency registered by girls is an interrelated aspect and concomitant of their increased physical maturity.

It seems likely too that boys in elementary school classrooms may have fewer opportunities for experiences which would enable them to achieve self-ideal self congruencies comparable to those achieved by girls. If patterns of behavior and activities in school are largely governed by feminine mores and codes, it seems likely that boys would be less able to behave in ways which would permit their achieving self-ideal congruencies comparable to those of girls.

Sixth-grade children achieved significantly greater self-ideal self congruency than did fourth-grade children. This would seem to be due to their greater maturity and experience. The greater self-ideal self congruency of children taught by teachers who had participated in an in-service child study program may well be a consequence of these teachers having a greater sensitivity to and providing for children's needs. The changes in children's self-ideal self congruencies are unrelated to changes in their school achievement and acceptance by peers. This seems to suggest children who may not achieve well in academic skills can and do achieve in other areas of self-development.

A Challenge

The educational implications of our growing knowledge of children's self-concepts seem to be clearly evident. Schools must provide opportunities for experiences which enable people to develop self-concepts for effective living. The plea is for education to focus on facilitating changes in ways the learner sees and feels about himself in relation to his life experiences rather than upon producing stereotyped and identical behavioral responses of conformity with standardized norms. Everyday experiences and results of research amply demonstrate that it is not merely what a person knows which determines his behavior—it is the way the individual feels and perceives himself in that situation.

Children need opportunities for increasing their sensitivity to and perceptions of other self-concepts. Their progress in narrowing the gap between what they are and what they want to become is a major aspect of their self-development and a measure of their increased self-adjustment. Such an educational program will enable schools to implement further their efforts in providing for individual differences. Need for developing this program constitutes a significant challenge for education in the years ahead.

5. Personal thoughts on teaching and learning

CARL R. ROGERS

From *On Becoming a Person* (Boston: Houghton Mifflin Co., 1961), Chapter 13, pp. 275-278.

Is it true that one cannot teach another person how to teach? Are all things that can be taught inconsequential? Is the only "real" learning that which is self-discovered? As you read, compare your beliefs with those of Rogers. What is your stand?

I wish to present some very brief remarks, in the hope that if they bring forth any reaction from you, I may get some new light on my own ideas.

I find it a very troubling thing to *think,* particularly when I think about my own experiences and try to extract from those experiences the meaning that seems genuinely inherent in them. At first such thinking is very satisfying because it seems to discover sense and pattern in a whole host of discrete events. But then it very often becomes dismaying because I realize how ridiculous these thoughts, which have much value to me, would seem to most people. My impression is that if I try to find the meaning of my own experience it leads me, nearly always, in directions regarded as absurd.

So in the next three or four minutes, I will try to digest some of the meanings which have come to me from my classroom experience and the experience I have had in individual and group therapy. They are in no way intended as conclusions for someone else, or a guide to what others should do or be. They are the very tentative meanings, as of April 1952, which my experience has had for me, and some of the bothersome questions which their absurdity raises. I will put each idea or meaning in a separate lettered paragraph, not because they are in any particular logical order, but because each meaning is separately important to me.

(a) I may as well start with this one in view of the purposes of this conference. My experience has been that I cannot teach another person how to teach. To attempt it is for me, in the long run, futile.

(b) It seems to me that anything that can be taught to another is relatively inconsequential, and has little or no significant influence on behavior. That sounds so ridiculous I can't help but question it at the same time that I present it.

(c) I realize increasingly that I am only interested in learnings which significantly influence behavior. Quite possibly this is simply a personal idiosyncrasy.

(d) I have come to feel that the only learning which significantly influences behavior is self-discovered, self-appropriated learning.

(e) Such self-discovered learning, truth that has been personally appropriated and assimilated in experience, cannot be directly communicated to another. As soon as an individual tries to communicate such experience directly, often with a quite natural enthusiasm, it becomes teaching, and its results are inconsequential. It was some relief recently to discover that Soren Kierkegaard, the Danish philosopher, had found this too, in his own experience, and stated it very clearly a century ago. It made it seem less absurd.

(f) As a consequence of the above, I realize that I have lost interest in being a teacher.

(g) When I try to teach, as I do sometimes, I am appalled by the results, which seem a little more than inconsequential, because sometimes the teaching appears to succeed. When this happens, I find that the results are damaging. It seems to cause the individual to distrust his own experience and to stifle significant learning. Hence, I have come to feel that the outcomes of teaching are either unimportant or hurtful.

(h) When I look back at the results of my past teaching, the real results seem the same—either damage was done or nothing significant occurred. This is frankly troubling.

(i) As a consequence, I realize that I am only interested in being a learner, preferably learning things that matter, that have some significant influence on my own behavior.

(j) I find it very rewarding to learn, in groups, in relationships with one person as in therapy, or by myself.

(k) I find that one of the best, but most difficult ways for me to learn, is to drop my own defensiveness, at least temporarily, and to try to understand the way in which his experience seems and feels to the other person.

(l) I find that another way of learning for me is to state my own uncertainties, to try to clarify my puzzlements, and thus get closer to the meaning that my experience actually seems to have.

(m) This whole train of experiencing, and the meanings that I have thus far discovered in it, seem to have launched me on a process which is both fascinating and at times a little frightening. It seems to mean letting my experience carry me on, in a direction which appears to be forward, toward goals that I can but dimly define, as I try to understand at least the current meaning of that experience. The sensation is that of floating with a complex stream of experience, with the fascinating possibility of trying to comprehend its ever changing complexity.

I am almost afraid I may seem to have gotten away from any discussion of learning, as well as teaching. Let me again introduce a practical note by saying that by themselves these interpretations of my own experience may sound queer and aberrant, but not particularly shocking. It is when I realize the implications that I shudder a bit at the distance I have come from the common-sense world that everyone knows is right. I can best illustrate that by saying that if the experiences of others had been the same as mine, and if they had discovered similar meanings in it, many consequences would be implied.

6. Teachers too are individuals

Arthur W. Combs

Unpublished address delivered at the Association for Supervision and Curriculum Development Conference (1962). Reproduced by permission of the author.

A good deal has been written about "good" students and how to teach in such a way as to turn out even better and more self-accepting students. But what about "good" teachers? What is it that makes "good" teachers "individuals" in the fullest sense of the word? How does the "self" of a good teacher differ from that of all other persons? Combs offers some fascinating speculations.

We have been talking much at this conference about the individuality of children. We need to remind ourselves, however, that teachers, too, are human. For some people this is a fact easy to overlook, but in recent years we have begun to have a new appreciation of its significance.

For many years we have been trying to define the nature of the good teacher. Tremendous amounts of time, effort, and money have gone into researches aimed at defining what they are like. But, now, millions of man-hours and dollars later we are forced to conclude that our efforts are fruitless; you simply cannot tell the difference between good teachers and poor ones on the basis of what they know, on the basis of what they do, or on the basis of the methods they use. There seems to be no objective measure which can be relied upon with any degree of certainty that will distinguish the good teachers from the bad ones!

In spite of the failure of this research, however, *you* and *I* know who the good teachers are. In a very short time in a new school or a faculty we are able to state with a high degree of confidence who are the best teachers in the group. We can do this even when we have never entered a teacher's classroom. Somehow we pick up the information we need to make such judgments by a kind of osmosis. Why, then, can't we *measure* good teaching? The answer is simple; because teachers are unique human beings. Like the children they teach, teachers, too, are individuals. No good teacher is like any other. The good teacher is no carbon copy. He is an individual who has learned to use his particular self in effective and efficient ways. Since every self is different, what is more, every good teacher will necessarily behave in ways that are individual and unique. No wonder our research is unable to find any common criteria!

Just as we have had to shift our understanding of the learning process from the process to the learner, so we are now discovering the understanding of teaching is not to be found in methods but in the teacher. The teacher is first and foremost a person, a self. He is not a library, not a machine, not a disseminator of knowledge. He is a human being interacting with other human beings in a very human process. Learning to teach is not a question of learning to *do* something; it is a matter of learning to be *something*.

In recent years we have come to understand that there is simply no such thing as "right" methods or "wrong" methods of teaching. Whatever methods a teacher uses can never be considered separate and apart from the personality of the teacher himself or from the situations he is involved in. Methods, we now know, like the clothes we wear, must fit the people we are. It is folly to talk about methods separate and apart from the people who use them. Let us take the question of the argument over heterogeneous or homogeneous grouping as an example. It is easy to find people who argue for one or the other of these methods of dealing with children as though one or the other were good or bad in itself. But this is not so. For my part, I suspect that if I had a very, very good teacher who was able to do it, I would like to have my child taught in a heterogeneous class. However, if I must make the choice, I would much prefer to have him taught in a homogeneous class by a teacher who felt comfortable doing what he was doing, than in a heterogeneous class where the teacher was going mad trying to deal with a problem that he did not understand and could not adapt himself to. *No* method is any good unless the teacher can use it! The question of methods can never be considered separate and apart from the particular teacher and the particular situation in which he finds himself.

This new understanding about methods, it seems to me, is tremendously good news. It means that it is all right for me to be different. Indeed, it means more than that. It means the very fact of difference is itself a thing of value. The only way in which I can help a child to be an individual is through being intensely individual myself. It means I can teach *my* way and the teacher next door to me can teach his way, and each of us can be good teachers even if the methods we use and the techniques we follow are as widely divergent as A and Z. Years ago leaving Ohio State's College of Education I had an illustration of this principle, but at the time I did not know what it meant. When I graduated in 1935, Ohio State was in the midst of its farthest out experiment with the progressive movement. I left there, so help me, convinced that I must be a "pal" to all my students. I began teaching in the middle of the year in an industrial community, in a strictly authoritarian school with a group of the liveliest ninth graders you ever saw. One of my assignments was a study hall with 250 students the last period of the day! I will never forget that year! I still have nightmares about it. I know now that the reason why I failed was my attempt to be a "pal" to my students when I am simply not the "pally" type. This is not my way of relating to people, and the attempt to make myself something I was not, almost drove me out of the profession altogether.

Good teachers are not like other people. They are not even like each other. They are intensely themselves and have learned to use those selves effectively and efficiently in tune with the situations and purposes within which they operate. If good teachers are highly unique, then a good school must be a place where unique and different people work together. Since good teaching is a highly unique and personal thing, the school which seeks to make its teachers all alike will only succeed in producing the most banal mediocrity. A good school is a place where difference is valued, not rejected. Just as it seeks increasing uniqueness for its students, so also will it encourage and respect individuality in its teachers. It will recognize that from just such differences in teachers the most significant values for children come about.

What does this understanding of the unique character of good teaching mean for us? For me, it means at least the following:

1. If we are to meet the great challenges of our time, then it is necessary that we recognize this unique character of good teaching and give up trying to make teachers over in our own or someone else's prescribed image. This is not easy, however. It calls for a high degree of self-discipline from each of us. Permitting people to see and be different is hard because the way things seem to us always seem to us so right and so absolutely so. Thus, when other people do not see things as we do, we are likely to jump to one of two conclusions: Either he is frightfully stupid—or he is just being

stubborn and perverse! We need a great deal more recognition of the ideas that my way is the right way for *me* but may be a very wrong way for anyone else.

2. If we are to meet the challenges of our time, it is necessary that we value and encourage difference. We talk much of creativity these days and heaven knows we need creative people as never before. But creativity calls for change. And there will be no change unless someone sticks his neck out. In our yearbook John Greene has described the Louisiana terrapin who cannot go anywhere until he sticks his neck out. "If you frighten him," says John, "he stays inside his shell. If you frighten him a great deal he just stays inside and dies there." Somehow, all of us, but especially those of us who are in teacher training, supervision, and administration must become far more skillful in creating atmospheres that help teachers to feel that difference is desirable. Strange as it seems, despite the fact that the one thing we know about people above all else is that they are different, nevertheless, we need to reassure teachers that it is all right to be different! Unless our leaders value difference, there will be but little progress.

3. We need to overcome the terrible fear of making mistakes that dogs our profession. You know, this is a strange business we are involved in: It is built entirely on right answers. We pay off on right answers and punish wrong ones. We are scared to death that children may make mistakes, and so we often protect them from the very experiences which might have taught them the most. Even worse, we have absorbed this fear into ourselves, so that many teachers, too, have become overly fearful of making mistakes. Yet, people learn from their mistakes, and mistakes can be good for people.

Indeed, it has been said that the outstanding characteristic of a genius is his delight in getting into trouble for the sheer joy of getting out of it again! For many of us, however, the making of a mistake is almost synonymous with sinning. It is a kind of heinous crime. But if people are too fearful of making mistakes, then they also will not try. We need to encourage experimentation on every hand, but we cannot do this if we make people afraid to make mistakes. We need to remind ourselves of President Roosevelt's advice during the war years, "The only thing we have to fear is fear itself." Let us not be afraid to try. Perhaps we need even to encourage people to make mistakes.

4. Teaching, it now appears, is primarily a relationship. This means to me—a teacher must *be* somebody. There can be no relationship with a nonentity! The frantic search for commonality and objective measurement, I am afraid, has often undermined our faith in human judgment. It has depersonalized us so that we are often fearful of our own judgment unless

this can be backed up with a test score or reams of objective evidence. In my own classes I have broken with this forever. I tell my classes forthwith, "Your grade will depend in part on the written material you hand in, but it will also depend upon what I think of you." I believe that if I cannot make a valid judgment about a student after thirty years of teaching, I had better give up.

A good teacher is first and foremost a person. To be a good teacher does not mean I must give up who I am. Rather, it means I must find ways of being me, even more than ever. The 1962 Yearbook emphasizes the importance of becoming, and this is true of teachers as well as students. A teacher must stand for something. His personness must be evident. As a matter of fact, a profession that can be pushed around, that is uncertain of its beliefs only serves to frighten the public. The public wants to feel its institutions are secure and manned by people who know what they are about. To accomplish this, each of us needs to stand four square as a person of professional dignity and integrity.

5. The uniqueness of good teaching means one more thing to me. It means that whatever changes we make in education must be made by individual teachers—and that means you and me. Institutions are made up of people and only change as people change. If, therefore, we are to meet the great challenges of our generation, each of us must seek to become the very best self he can be. It is only as each of us is encouraged to experiment and to try, each in his own place and his own way, that the things we seek for children and for our profession will be brought to fruition.

Some of us, I am afraid, have been frightened into immobility by the criticism to which we have been subjected. Not long ago I was in Washington visiting the United States Office of Education. Three times as I walked through that rabbit warren I lost my way. I was in a huge building surrounded by thousands of people involved in all aspects of education, and behind each of those offices were many more thousands of people all over the country equally involved in our profession. Like many of you I had been feeling very distressed at the kind of criticism we have been having lately. As I walked down the hall, however, it suddenly struck me very funny because it came to me that—you *can't* sink this! It's just too big! And indeed that is true! In the final analysis the only changes that are going to be made in education are going to be made by teachers in the classroom. Changes are not going to be made by patterns, surveys, budgets, buildings, policies until these somehow reach the individual teacher in the individual classroom, working out his daily problems where he is. Despite the detailed job descriptions administrators are so fond of making, jobs are made by people and become what the people in them make them.

Whatever changes are made in education are going to be made in the final analysis by professional educators for the very good reason that no one else is prepared to do the job.

It is characteristic of the kind of society we live in that our nation expects its public servants to carry out their duties. It is in the nature of our way of life, however, that the public always reserves the right to kick like the dickens if they don't think its being done well. I believe that some of us need to understand that more clearly. Sometimes we are deeply hurt because the public does not seem to appreciate us in the way we would like to be appreciated. Next time you get to feeling rejected and unappreciated, however, try asking yourself, when was the last time you were down to the sewage disposal works to tell them what a good job they were doing? Or when have you dropped in at the police station to tell the policemen how much you appreciated their work? Or for that matter, when was the last time you attended a city council meeting or even wrote your congressman with anything more than a complaint?

Though the responsibility for changing education is essentially ours, this does not mean that we can sit idly by and go back to business as usual at the same old stands. The world we live in has new needs of us and has given us vast new responsibilities. These must be met by each of us as best he can through a process of individual experimentation and trying in his local situation. Oh, you may say, "That's all very well in your situation, but you ought to be in mine. Nobody can do anything new in our school." But this is not true. Lance Hunnicutt once said, "No matter what situation you are in, there is always room to wriggle. If you would like to find how free you are, try wriggling!" I think that is good advice for all of us.

QUESTIONS FOR DISCUSSION

Staines Article

1. What does this study suggest about the possibility of improving a student's academic performance, while at the same time working to improve his self-picture?
2. What evidence is here to support or refute the notion that teachers are perceived as "significant others" by their students?
3. Identify the essential differences in the teaching methods of teachers A and B.
4. How would you account for the fact that some children had a "water-off-the-duck's-back" attitude toward a particular teacher, while others were much more sensitive to her flow of personal comment?

Davidson and Lang Article

1. Identify the essential differences between the procedures used in this study and those used in the study of Staines.
2. Why do girls generally perceive their teachers' feelings toward them more favorably than do boys?
3. Why do you suppose that more lower-class children were rated by their teachers as having undesirable behavior than was the case for upper-class children? What implications does this have for self-concept development?

Thompson and Hunnicutt Article

1. If students respond differentially to praise and blame, how would this relate to question 4 of the Staines article?
2. Why is the use of indiscriminate praise or blame ineffective as a means for motivation?
3. Explain the dynamics behind why an extroverted youngster who is "blamed" would work harder than extroverts who are praised and introverts who are blamed. Under which conditions do *you* work hardest?

Perkins Article

1. Why are schools *not* uniformally successful in encouraging greater self-ideal self in all children?
2. The author states, "The self-concepts of sixth graders, especially the boys, revealed a confidence in their own abilities." As a group, do you think these boys will get more, or less, self-confident as they move through high school? Explain your reasoning.

Rogers Article

1. What is your reaction to the idea that one cannot teach another person how to teach? Why would you agree or disagree?
2. How would one manage a classroom if he accepted the thesis offered by Rogers? Would you like to teach or be taught according to Rogers' ideas?

Combs Article

1. Would you agree with Combs that we cannot *measure* good teaching? Why or why not?
2. At least one message in this article is that teachers are reluctant to assert a "self" that might be "different." Do you agree that this is generally true of teachers? If so, why? Why, for that matter, should any person be reluctant to assert a "different" self? Explain your position.

Part VIII
learning and the self

1. Self-evaluation and academic achievement [1]

Bernard Borislow

Reprinted from the *Journal of Counseling Psychology,* Vol. 9 (1962), 246-254, by permission of the author and the publisher.

The author is specifically concerned with the importance of self-evaluation as a nonintellectual factor in academic achievement. Does one's "student" self-evaluation go up or down according to the academic success he experiences? Do underachievers have unrealistically optimistic conceptions of themselves prior to their academic efforts, or do they have pessimistic conceptions of themselves? The author contends that his findings have important implications for a more specific self-evaluation theory.

Despite continuing efforts to improve scholastic aptitude tests as predictors of early college grades, the obtained validity coefficients appear to have reached an asymptote in the area of about .50. A review of past research (22) and recent findings (5) indicates that one of our best predictors, the Scholastic Aptitude Test (SAT), can account for about 25 per cent of those variables that constitute early college grades. This fact has prompted researchers to explore the variance remaining to be identified. Of course, a portion of this undefined area is probably "chance" variation (test unreliability, criterion unreliability, subject variability, *etc.*), but, as McQuarry (16) has demonstrated, a major portion may also be said to include nonintellectual, nonaptitude, or personality factors.

[1] This paper is based upon the author's Ph.D. dissertation (University of Pennsylvania, 1961). Grateful acknowledgment is made to James C. Diggory, Miles Murphy (now deceased), and Julius Wishner who served as dissertation committee members. Morris S. Viteles, dissertation supervisor, is due special thanks for his counsel, encouragement, and patience.

Much work has been done in attempting to identify some of these personality determinants of early college achievement (7, 9, 12, 13, 15, 17, 21). For the most part, the work has been devoid of any theoretical orientation and the results only descriptive.

The Problem

This research was designed to investigate the importance of self-evaluation as a nonintellectual factor in scholastic achievement. Theoretically, self-evaluation is defined in terms of the discrepancy between a self-perception and a concept of the ideal. Rogers and his group (23) have firmly established the notion of general self-evaluation (self-ideal self-discrepancy) in the area of self-concept theory. It appears that the larger the discrepancy, the greater will be the degree of personality maladjustment. Research supporting this view can be found in Block and Thomas (1), Butler and Haigh (3), Chodorkoff (4), Hanlon, Hofstaetter and O'Connor (14), Smith (26), and Turner and Vanderlippe (27).

If we accept the view that scholastic underachievement is a form of maladjustment, then we would expect potential underachievers to start their academic program in college with lower general self-evaluation than would potential achievers.

On the other hand, self-evaluation may be specific in nature; that is, subjects produce different self-descriptions when asked to view themselves in a general way than they do when asked to view themselves within a specific context (2, 24). Thus, the subject's perception of himself as a student was of concern in this research and was based upon a student self-ideal student discrepancy. It was assumed that students would begin their college career with uniform student self-evaluation (regardless of eventual achievement level) but, after a semester's work, that this would be higher for the achievers and lower for the underachievers.

Further, Diggory (8) has added certain theoretical refinements to self-concept theory. He believes that it is imperative, especially for general self-evaluation change, for the subject to value highly a specific goal and to perceive himself to possess the specific "capacity" to reach the goal. Therefore, general self-evaluation should change only where student self-evaluation is high and academic achievement is a prime goal. Where these conditions are absent, no general self-evaluation changes are predicted. An additional consideration is suggested: self-evaluation change is dependent upon an accurate perception of the outcomes of behavior, *i.e.,* a correct perception of success or failure. As will be seen, a check was made to determine whether actual achievement level corresponded with perceived level of success.

In summary, it was hypothesized that: (1) achieving students will show higher general self-evaluation than underachieving students prior to academic performance, where scholastic achievement is a prime goal; (2) achieving students will increase and underachieving students will decrease their general self-evaluation from pre- to postsemester assessments, where scholastic achievement is a prime goal and student self-evaluation is high; (3) no difference will be found between achievers and underachievers in terms of student self-evaluation prior to academic performance, where scholastic achievement is a prime goal; (4) achieving students will show higher student self-evaluation than underachieving students after academic performance, where scholastic achievement is a prime goal.

The differences predicted above were not predicted in comparing achievers and underachievers who did not indicate that scholastic achievement was a prime goal.

Method

MEASURING INSTRUMENTS

In order to obtain indices of general and student self-evaluation for each student, a modification of Fielder's 24-item adjective scale was used (10, pp. 64-65). Each subject completed the same 24-item scale four times (at one sitting) under different sets of instructions: general self, student self, ideal self, and ideal student. The semantic differential format of the scale (19) with its scaling feature of unit equivalence (18) lends itself to easy computation of the two self-evaluation indices. Using the *D* statistic [2] described by Cronbach and Gleser (7) and Osgood and Suci (20), a measure of general self-evaluation was derived from the discrepancy between general-self and ideal-self responses. Similarly, a measure of student self-evaluation was derived from the discrepancy between student-self and ideal-student responses.[3]

A second instrument used was the Student Behavior Description (11). This inventory appears able to identify which of five "goal areas" a student will be more inclined toward while in college. The areas are: A. Organizational leadership; B. Scholastic achievement; C. Ethical conformity; D. Social acceptance; and E. Self-adjustment. For the purpose of this study, it is assumed that if a student obtains a rank of one or two (of the five goal areas) for scale B (Scholastic achievement), he is predisposed to strive for scholastic achievement as a prime goal (SA-High). If a student

[2] $D = \sqrt{\Sigma d^2}$

[3] Based on 10 of the 24 items selected by each student as being "important for student success."

obtains a rank of 3, 4, or 5 for scale B, it is assumed that he is not predisposed to strive for scholastic achievement as a prime goal (SA-Low).

PROCEDURE AND SUBJECTS

A questionnaire consisting of the Student Behavior Description, four adjective scales (self, student self, ideal, ideal student, in this order) and a personal history page was distributed to the entire September 1958 freshman class of the College, University of Pennsylvania, immediately prior to their first semester. Just after the semester, the scales were redistributed to the presemester respondents.

The experimental population was the freshman class that entered the College of Arts and Science in September of 1958. Out of 361 students, 197 completed both a presemester and a postsemester questionnaire and became the sample used in this study. The sample was divided into two groups, Achievers and Underachievers. This classification was based upon the extent to which the student achieved or failed to achieve a first-semester grade-point average (GPA) concordant with his aptitude test score (SAT total score). Specifically, the correlation between SAT total score and GPA was computed for the entire freshman class. This proved to be .39 ($P < .01$). By regression analysis, estimates of GPA were calculated for each level of scholastic aptitude (SAT total score).[4] All subjects in the experimental population whose actual GPA fell below one half of the standard error of estimate of GPA predicted by the regression formula were classified as Underachievers. All others were classified as Achievers.

The two groups were further refined by distinguishing between Achievers and Underachievers who indicated an intention to strive for scholastic achievement as a prime goal and those who did not (this was accomplished via the Student Behavior Description). Four groups were then composed, for data analysis purposes: Achievers ($N = 84$) and Underachievers ($N = 21$), both groups oriented toward academic achievement (SA-High); and Achievers ($N = 55$) and Underachievers ($N = 26$), these two groups not oriented toward academic achievement (SA-Low). Eleven respondents were not included in the above groups since their total SAT scores were not characteristic of the class as a whole.

The experimental sample (respondents) was found not to differ from the class as a whole on the variables of SAT, GPA, and Scale B score[5] (chi-square tests of distribution, P's $> .05$).

[4] The regression equation is: GPA = .002566 (SAT total score) + .308.

[5] Since 288 students, of 361, responded to the presemester questionnaire, this group served as the basis of comparison for the scale B score distribution.

In addition, no differences were found between the two SA-High groups and between the two SA-Low groups in terms of SAT scores (P's $> .05$, Mann-Whitney U test), various demographic factors (father's vocation, parents' education, hours of outside work, type of secondary school), future educational plans, and course load.

Results

Table 1 shows the mean General Self-Evaluation *D* scores obtained by the two groups characterized as striving for scholastic achievement as a prime goal (SA-High) and for the two groups not so characterized (SA-Low).

TABLE 1

GENERAL SELF-EVALUATION D SCORES[a] (MEANS)

SA-High[b] *groups*	*Achievers (A)* $N = 84$	*Underachievers (U)* $N = 21$	*A-U difference*
Presemester	9.20	8.69	.51 (NS)
Postsemester	8.34	8.52	.18 (NS)
Pre-Post difference	.86*	.17 (NS)	

SA-Low[b] *groups*	*Achievers (A)* $N = 55$	*Underachievers (U)* $N = 26$	*A-U difference*
Presemester	8.07	8.99	.92 (NS)
Postsemester	7.85	8.36	.51 (NS)
Pre-Post difference	.22 (NS)	.63 (NS)	

*$P < .01$.

[a] It should be noted that high *D* scores are indicative of low self-evaluation and vice versa.

[b] SA-High = scholastic achievement motivation is high.
SA-Low = scholastic achievement motivation is low.

These findings are represented graphically in Figure 1.

GENERAL SELF-EVALUATION

Contrary to prediction, there was no significant difference between achievers and underachievers in general self-evaluation, where academic achievement is a prime goal ($P > .05$, Mann-Whitney U Test). In addition, no difference was obtained between the two SA-High groups after the semester's performance; these same findings hold true for the SA-Low groups both pre- and postsemester.

Thus far, then, the findings indicate that regardless of the distinction

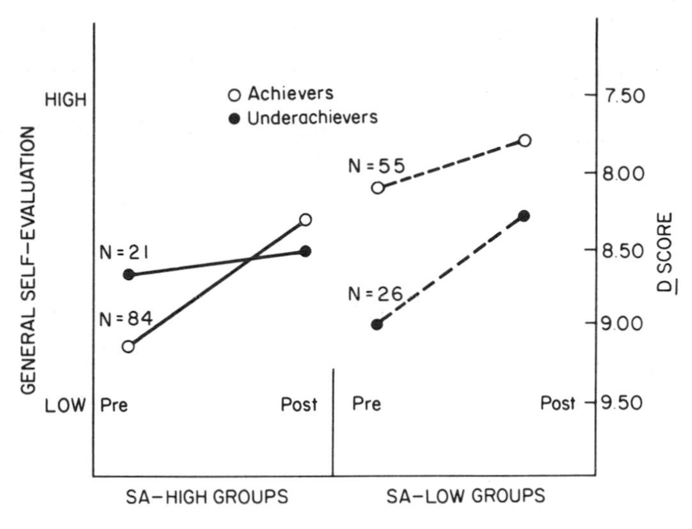

FIGURE 1

General Self-Evaluation Mean Scores
for the Achieving and Underachieving Groups
(SA-Low indicates level of scholastic achievement motivation)

between students having scholastic achievement as a prime goal and those who do not, no general self-evaluation differences can be found between groups of achieving and underachieving students either prior to or after one semester's work.

Unfortunately, it was impossible to test adequately the hypothesis that general self-evaluation should become more favorable following scholastic achievement and less favorable following scholastic underachievement (where scholastic achievement is a prime goal and the subject has high student self-evaluation). Just two underachievers materialized with these traits.

However, as will be seen below, SA-High achievers as a group are prone to evaluate themselves highly as students. Reference to Table 1 shows that they demonstrated a significant increase [6] in general self-evaluation (from pre- to postsemester assessments), while the SA-High underachievers showed no change.

Also of interest is the fact that the SA-High achievers begin the semester with a lower level of general self-evaluation ($P < .05$) than the SA-Low achievers and then increase their level to that of the SA-Low subjects on postsemester assessment (see Table 1 and Figure 1). Since the achievers do not differ from the underachievers in terms of general self-evaluation,

[6] $P < .01$, Wilcoxon Match-Pairs Signed-Ranks Test.

the above finding seems not to imply that the SA-High achievers have low general self-evaluation prior to performance; rather it appears that achievers who are motivated to strive for scholastic achievement as a prime goal (SA-High) are so motivated because they may see scholastic achievement as a means to enhance their general self-evaluation.

Student self-evaluation

Contrary to prediction, the SA-High achievers demonstrated significantly higher student self-evaluation than the SA-High underachievers prior to the semester ($P < .01$, Mann-Whitney U Test; see Table 2 and Figure 2). No such difference was found between the two SA-Low groups.

TABLE 2

Student Self-Evaluation D Scores (Means)

SA-High groups	*Achievers (A)* *N = 84*	*Underachievers (U)* *N = 21*	*A-U difference*
Presemester	5.75	7.89	2.14*
Postsemester	5.98	8.44	2.46**
Pre-Post difference	.23 (NS)	.55 (NS)	

SA-Low groups	*Achievers (A)* *N = 55*	*Underachievers (U)* *N = 26*	*A-U difference*
Presemester	5.94	6.79	.85 (NS)
Postsemester	6.17	7.89	1.72*
Pre-Post difference	.23 (NS)	1.10 (NS)	

*$P < .01$.
**$P < .001$.
(NS) = Not significant.

As predicted, the SA-High achievers had significantly higher student self-evaluation than the SA-High underachievers after the semester ($P < .001$). Similarly for the SA-Low groups, the achievers demonstrated significantly higher student self-evaluation than the underachievers on the postsemester assessment ($P < .01$).

Inspection of the results reported above on student self-evaluation, clearly indicates that the variables of (a) level of academic achievement and (b) scholastic achievement as a goal are important concomitants of the level of student self-evaluation. In all cases where a significant difference was found between the groups of achievers and underachievers, the achieving

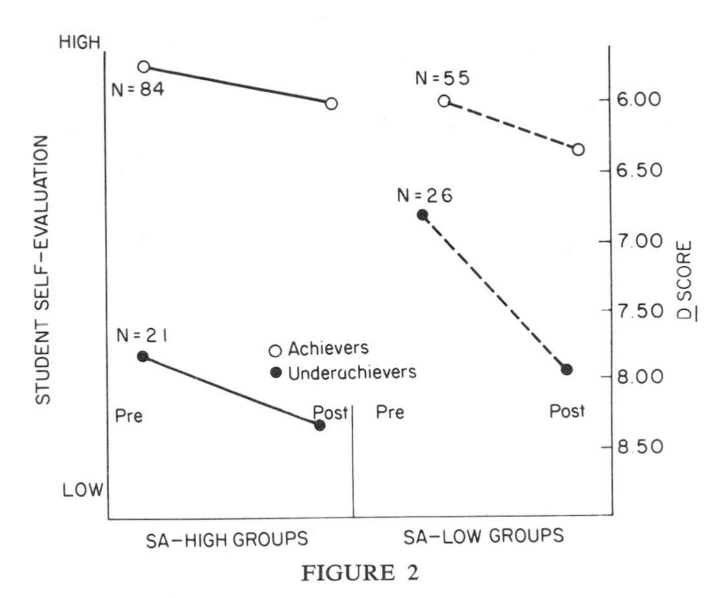

FIGURE 2

STUDENT SELF-EVALUATION MEAN SCORES
FOR THE ACHIEVING AND UNDERACHIEVING GROUPS
(SA-High and SA-Low indicate level of scholastic achievement motivation)

group was characterized by higher student self-evaluation than the underachieving group. In addition, whereas the achieving group (of the "scholastic achievement high goal" subjects) had higher student self-evaluation than the underachiever group both presemester and postsemester, only a postsemester difference occurred for the same comparison of the "scholastic achievement not a high goal" groups. That is, students who stated an intention to strive for scholastic achievement as a goal seem to indicate their level of achievement by reflecting it in their level of preperformance student self-evaluation. Such a situation is absent for those students who do not indicate an intention to strive for scholastic achievement as a goal.

SELF-PERCEPTIONS OF SUCCESS

It was stated earlier that "appropriate feelings of success or failure" on the part of achieving or underachieving students is a necessary condition for self-evaluation between-group differences and pre- to postsemester changes. In order to evaluate the degree to which such "appropriate feelings" were present in this research, the following question was asked on the postsemester Personal Data Sheet: "How would you rate your success as a student thus far?" The subject was asked to place a check mark in one of eight spaces rated from "Extremely Successful" to "Extremely

Unsuccessful" (four spaces for degrees of "successful" and four for degrees of "unsuccessful"). The responses were tabulated by two response categories: Successful and Unsuccessful. Table 3 shows the results of the tabulation for the SA-High and the SA-Low groups separately.

TABLE 3

JUDGMENTS OF DEGREE OF STUDENT SUCCESS

	SA-High groups		*SA-Low groups*	
Response categories	*A**	*U**	*A*	*U*
"Successful"	66	3	37	4
"Unsuccessful"	18	18	18	22
	($P_x^2 < .001$)		($P_x^2 < .001$)	

**A* and *U* denote Achievers and Underachievers, respectively.

Without a doubt, the perceived level of scholastic success corresponds with the statistically defined achievement level. This appears to be an obvious finding. However, due to the nature of the statistical definition of achievement level (grades relative to aptitude), the student's perception of success or failure seems to involve not only a reaction to his grades, but also takes into account his feelings about his scholastic aptitude or capacity.

Thus, the two conditions whose presence seems desirable for self-evaluation assessment were evident in the research. The first, acceptance of scholastic achievement as a goal, has been controlled by treating separately students who received a high rank on the "scholastic achievement as a goal" scale of the Student Behavior Description, from those who received a low rank; and second, the correspondence of perceived success level to actual achievement level (as reported above).

Discussion

The results of this research do not support the contention that students who turn out to be underachievers exhibit lower general self-evaluation either prior to or subsequent to academic performance than do achievers.

However, where students indicate an intention to strive for good grades, it is clear that those who turn out to be underachievers possess a more pessimistic picture of themselves as students than do achievers both prior to and subsequent to academic performance.

Where the intent to strive for good grades is not dominant, underachievers can be distinguished from achievers in terms of lower student self-evaluation only after scholastic performance. No such pessimistic student self-perception exists prior to academic behavior for these underachieving students.

Theoretically, it was expected that students who indicate an intention to strive for scholastic achievement (SA-High) and who rate their student "capacity" high should demonstrate significant general self-evaluation change in the direction of their level of academic achievement. It was impossible to test the above view completely since there were very few SA-High underachievers who placed high in student self-evaluation; and, in addition, SA-High underachievers devalue themselves as students when compared to SA-High achievers. Therefore, a comparison of general self-evaluation changes between goal-striving achievers and underachievers, who think highly of themselves in terms of student self-evaluation ("capacity"), was impossible because goal-striving underachievers devalue their "capacity" as students.

The achieving group (SA-High), however, increased their general self-evaluation subsequent to successful student performance while the underachieving group did not change. That is, failure in the exercise of a specific "capacity" believed to be weak had no effect upon the students' feelings of general worth. Success in the exercise of a specific "capacity" believed to be strong positively influenced the subjects' feeling of general worth.

Questions which prompt consideration for further research are apparent. Why does the underachiever, who has the ability and intent to achieve, along with favorable feelings of general worth, begin his first semester in college with a negative student self-image? Is it the end effect of borderline experience in the way of educational achievement at the secondary school level? Or, if we assume that negative general self-evaluation is indicative of general personality maladjustment, does this mean that the presence of negative student self-evaluation, in a sense, represents some type of specific personality maladjustment? If so, then future research dealing with personality concomitants of scholastic underachievement might best concern itself with the integrity of the "student role" rather than with the "whole person."

This research is based upon hypotheses derived from two different approaches to self-evaluation theory. One approach, proposed by Diggory (8), emphasizes the contribution of many self "roles" or "capacity" evaluations to the more global or general self-percept. The other approach, exemplified by the Rogerian group (23), emphasizes the relevance of a global or general self-percept to the efficiency of the person with no apparent attention to unique sub-"roles." The former theoretical view has proven more fruitful for this investigation into the nonintellectual factors of academic achievement.

Summary and Conclusions

This study represents an attempt to determine the importance of self-evaluation as a nonintellectual factor in scholastic achievement. A distinction was made between general self-evaluation and student self-evaluation.

A representative sample of 197 students, of a college freshman class of 361, replied to both a presemester and a postsemester questionnaire designed to yield indices of general and student self-evaluation. Four experimental groups were extracted which did not differ in terms of scholastic aptitude, certain demographic factors, and educational-vocational plans: achievers (N = 84) and underachievers (N = 21), both oriented toward academic attainment; and achievers (N = 55) and underachievers (N = 26), not so oriented.

The following conclusions seem warranted:

1. Regardless of an intention to strive for scholastic achievement as a prime goal, students who underachieve scholastically cannot be distinguished from those who achieve scholastically on the basis of general self-evaluation prior to or subsequent to their first semester in college.

2. Students who underachieve scholastically have a poorer conception of themselves as students than do achievers subsequent to their scholastic performance, regardless of initial intention to strive for scholastic achievement as a goal.

3. Where students exhibit an intention to strive for scholastic achievement as a prime goal, underachievers have a more pessimistic conception of themselves as students than do achievers prior to their actual scholastic performance. This does not hold true where scholastic achievement is not a prime goal.

4. Where scholastic achievement is a prime goal, where the student has a good conception of himself as a student, and where he does achieve scholastically, his general self-evaluation becomes more favorable from pre- to postsemester assessments. This does not hold true where scholastic achievement is not a prime goal.

The above findings were interpreted as lending support to the usefulness of a more specific ("role" or "capacity") self-evaluation theory which takes into consideration relevant motivation. They do not support general self-evaluation, based on the global concept of personality adjustment, as a factor in investigating nonintellectual factors in academic achievement.

References

1. Block, J., and H. Thomas, "Is Satisfaction with Self a Measure of Adjustment?" *Journal of Abnormal Social Psychology,* Vol. 51 (1955), pp. 254-259.
2. Borislow, B., "The Edwards Personal Preference Schedule (EPPS) and Fakability," *Journal of Applied Psychology,* Vol. 42 (1958), pp. 22-27.
3. Butler, J. M., and G. V. Haigh, "Changes in the Relation Between Self-Concepts and Ideal Concepts Consequent Upon Client-Centered Counseling," in C. R. Rogers and Rosalind F. Dymond (eds.), *Psychotherapy and Personality Change* (Chicago: U. of Chicago, 1955).
4. Chodorkoff, B., "Adjustment and the Discrepancy Between the Perceived and Ideal Self," *Journal of Clinical Psychology,* Vol. 10 (1954), pp. 266-268.
5. College Entrance Examination Board, *1957 Supplement to College Board Scores No. 2* (New York: College Entrance Examination Board, 1957).
6. Cronbach, L. J., "Studies of the Group Rorschach in Relation to Success in the College of the University of Chicago," *Journal of Educational Psychology,* Vol. 41 (1950), pp. 65-82.
7. ———, and G. C. Gleser, "Assessing Similarity Between Profiles," *Psychological Bulletin,* Vol. 50 (1953), pp. 456-473.
8. Diggory, J. C., and D. E. Magaziner, "Self-Evaluation as a Function of Instrumentally Relevant Capacities," *Bulletin of the International Association of Applied Psychology,* Vol. 8, No. 1 (1959).
9. Dowd, R. J., "Underachieving Students of High Capacity," *Journal of Higher Education,* Vol. 23 (1952), pp. 327-330.
10. Fiedler, F. E., *Leader Attitudes and Group Effectiveness* (Urbana: U. of Ill., 1958).
11. Florence, E. de C., *Motivational Factors in Individual and Group Productivity. II. Validation and Standardization of the Student Behavior Description* (Columbus: The Ohio State University Research Foundation, 1956).
12. Gough, H. G., "The Construction of a Personality Scale to Predict Scholastic Achievement," *Journal of Applied Psychology,* Vol. 37 (1953), pp. 361-366.
13. Griffiths, G. R., "The Relationship Between Scholastic Achievement and Personality Adjustment of Men College Students," *Journal of Applied Psychology,* Vol. 29 (1945), pp. 360-367.
14. Hanlon, T. E., P. R. Hofstaetter, and J. P. O'Connor, "Congruence of Self and Ideal Self in Relation to Personality Adjustment," *Journal of Consulting Psychology,* Vol. 18 (1954), pp. 215-218.
15. Hoyt, D. P., and W. T. Norman, "Adjustment and Academic Predictability," *Journal of Counseling Psychology,* Vol. 1 (1954), pp. 96-99.
16. McQuarry, J. P., "Some Relationships Between Non-Intellectual Characteristics and Academic Achievement," *Journal of Educational Psychology,* Vol. 44 (1953), pp. 215-228.
17. ———, "An Under-Achievement Scale," *Journal of Educational Research,* Vol. 48 (1954-1955), pp. 393-399.

18. Messick, S. J., "Metric Properties of the Semantic Differential," *Educational and Psychological Measurement,* Vol. 17 (1957), pp. 200-206.
19. Osgood, C. E., "The Nature and Measurement of Meaning," *Psychological Bulletin,* Vol. 49 (1952), pp. 197-237.
20. ———, and G. J. Suci, "A Measure of Relation Determined by Both Mean Difference and Profile Information," *Psychological Bulletin,* Vol. 49 (1952), pp. 251-262.
21. Owens, W. A., and W. C. Johnson, "Some Measured Personality Traits of Collegiate Underachievers," *Journal of Educational Psychology,* Vol. 40 (1949), pp. 41-46.
22. Parres, J. G., *Prediction of Academic Success in the Undergraduate Schools of the University of Pennsylvania,* Unpublished Ed.D. Dissertation, University of Pennsylvania, 1955.
23. Rogers, C. R., and Rosalind F. Dymond, eds., *Psychotherapy and Personality Change* (Chicago: U. of Chicago, 1955).
24. Rosen, E., "Self-Appraisal, Personal Desirability, and Perceived Social Desirability of Personality Traits," *Journal of Abnormal Social Psychology,* Vol. 52 (1956), pp. 151-158.
25. Siegel, S., *Nonparametric Statistics for the Behavioral Sciences* (New York: McGraw, 1956).
26. Smith, G. M., "Six Measures of Self-Concept Discrepancy and Instability: Their Interrelations, Reliability and Relations to Other Personality Measures," *Journal of Consulting Psychology,* Vol. 22 (1958), pp. 101-112.
27. Turner, R. H., and R. H. Vanderlippe, "Q-Sort Methodology as an Index of Adjustment," Paper read at the 1957 Convention of the American Psychological Association, New York.
28. Walker, H. M., and J. Lev., *Statistical Inference* (New York: Holt, Rinehart & Winston, 1953).

2. Self-concept of ability and school achievement [1]

Wilbur B. Brookover,
Shailor Thomas,
and Ann Paterson

Reprinted from *Sociology of Education,* Vol. 37 (Spring, 1964), 271-278, by permission of the senior author and the American Sociological Association.

Does one have a general self-concept of ability or does he have more specific self-concepts of ability related to specific areas of scholastic performance? What is the relationship between self-concept and performance in an academic role? Are the perceived expectations of significant others related to one's self-concept of ability? These and related questions are attended to in this important study. You will note, again, the influence of significant others on personality development.

The Interactionist Theories of self and role performance based on the work of G. H. Mead and C. H. Cooley have been increasingly accepted in social psychology but have seldom been considered relevant to learning in a school situation. A formalized statement of the relevant theory has been made by Kinch (8), and postulates concerned with classroom learning have been developed by Brookover (3, 4). Briefly, the general theory states that self-concept is developed through interaction with significant others which in turn influences one's behavior. When applied to the specific school learning situation, a relevant aspect of self-concept is the person's conception of his own ability to learn the accepted types of academic behavior; per-

[1] A revised version of a paper presented at the annual meeting of the Ohio Valley Sociological Society, May 4-5, 1962, at East Lansing, Michigan. The data reported in this paper are part of research performed pursuant to contract 845 with the United States Office of Education, Department of Health, Education, and Welfare, Wilbur B. Brookover, Project Director.

formance in terms of school achievement is the relevant behavior influenced. The student role is composed of several subroles, including one involving academic achievement; the student self-concept similarly is a complex of several segments, including self-concept of ability. This study focuses on these particular aspects: self-concept of ability in school and academic achievement.

The study tests three major hypotheses: (1) Self-concept of ability in school is significantly and positively related to the academic performance of students even with an ability dimension controlled. (2) Self-concept of ability in school is differentiated into specific self-concepts which correspond to specific subject areas in the school program, and these specific self-concepts are better predictors of academic performance in the relevant area than is the general self-concept of ability. (3) Self-concept of ability is significantly and positively correlated with the evaluation that one perceives significant others to hold of one's ability.

A number of studies have demonstrated that various types of behavior are related to self-assessment as determined by instruments designed to give a gross or total measure of self (1, 9, 12, 15). There is some evidence that school achievement is related to such criteria of self (1, 2, 7, 13, 14), but previous studies have not attempted to measure the academic ability segment of self-concept and test its relationship to achievement and to the perception of others' evaluation.

Method of Research

SAMPLE

The sample consisted of 1,050 seventh-grade students (513 males and 537 females) in an urban school system. Negro students were excluded from this analysis on the assumption that their self-concept of ability and its relation to achievement would differ from those of the white population. Subsequent analysis verified this assumption (11).

INSTRUMENTS

In order to measure self-concept of ability or how the subjects perceived their ability to perform in the academic setting, an eight-item multiple-choice questionnaire was utilized. These items formed a Guttman scale with a reproducibility coefficient of .95 for males and .96 for females. The scale has an internal reliability of .82 for males and .77 for females (6). This "Self-Concept of Ability Scale" was administered in two parallel forms: the first was designed to measure the student's self-concept of ability in general; the second, to measure self-concept of ability in each of four specific school subject areas—Arithmetic, English, Social Studies, and Science. Though the references were changed, the substance of the questions remained the same in both forms.

Since it has often been said, particularly in the school situation, that "innate ability" determines performance, I.Q. was controlled, even though it may also be affected by self-concept of ability. Intelligence scores were obtained from the "California Test of Mental Maturity" administered in the 4th and 6th grades. Since an average of I.Q. scores for two test administrations would tend to be more stable than a single assessment, an average of two total scores on the CTMM was used in this study. Grade-point average (GPA) in the four subjects, Arithmetic, English, Social Studies, and Science, was used as an index of academic performance.

Analysis and Results

The product-moment correlations between variables of this study and the correlations of pairs of these variables with the effect of the third variable partialed out are presented in Table 1. Even with the effect of I.Q. partialed out, self-concept and GPA (the index of performance) remain significantly and positively correlated. The correlation between self-concept and I.Q. is low (though significantly different from zero) when the effect of achievement is statistically controlled. If the I.Q.—GPA correlation (with the effect of self-concept partialed out)—is compared to the multiple correlation of I.Q. plus self-concept to predict GPA, the correlation increases from .48 to .69 for males, and from .53 to .72 for females. Such increases approximately double the variance accounted for.

TABLE 1

CORRELATIONS BETWEEN SEVENTH-GRADE GPA, INTELLIGENCE, AND SELF-CONCEPT OF ABILITY *

	Correlation coefficients				
	No variables controlled		*Third variable controlled*		
Variables correlated	*Males N = 513*	*Females N = 537*	*Variable controlled*	*Male N = 513*	*Female N = 537*
7th GPA—I.Q.	.61	.65	S-C	.48	.53
7th GPA—S-C	.57	.57	I.Q.	.42	.39
Self-Concept—I.Q.	.46	.48	GPA	.17	.17

*The Multiple Correlation (R 1.23) of Self-Concept and I.Q. with GPA is .69 for males and .72 for females.

These multiple correlations have, for the males, beta weights of .44 for I.Q. and .37 for self-concept; for females, beta weights are .49 for I.Q. and .34 for self-concept. Although I.Q. is weighted slightly higher than self-concept for both sexes, this is more evident for females than for males. It is concluded that there is a significant relationship between self-concept and GPA even with the "ability" factor controlled.

The second hypothesis stated that the self-concepts which relate to specific areas of performance in school would be differentiated from the general self-concept of ability and would be better predictors of specific subject achievement than would the general self-concept of ability. The means of general self-concept of ability scores and specific subject self-concept of ability scores, and the corresponding GPA's are presented in

TABLE 2

MEAN SELF-CONCEPT OF ABILITY SCORES AND MEAN GRADE-POINT AVERAGES IN ALL SUBJECTS AND FOR EACH OF FOUR SCHOOL SUBJECTS (THE HIGHER THE SELF-CONCEPT SCORE THE MORE POSITIVE THE SELF-CONCEPT. RANGE POSSIBLE, 8-40)

	Males (N = 513) Mean self-concept	Mean GPA	*Females (N = 537)* Mean self-concept	Mean GPA
General S-C	27.35*	2.07*	28.25*	2.43
Mathematics	26.97	2.10	27.47**	2.36**
English	25.45**	2.00**	28.17	2.61**
Social Studies	25.63**	1.99**	26.58**	2.29**
Science	27.18	2.21**	27.73	2.49**

*Means of general self-concept of ability scores, not means of specific subject self-concept of ability scores.

**Significantly different ($p < .05$) from the mean score for all subjects using a two-tailed "t" test for correlated data.

Table 2. The general self-concept score is higher than any of the specific subject scores. This may indicate that the student's general self-concept is closer to his areas of successful academic performance than to his areas of failure. (The general self-concept of ability score is not an average of the other scores but was obtained from a separate assessment of self-concept.)

To test the hypothesis that the specific subject-matter self-concept is a better predictor of achievement in that subject than is general self-concept, the correlation of general self-concept of ability and achievement in a specific subject was compared with the correlation of specific subject self-concept of ability and specific subject achievement. These correlations are shown in Table 3. The specific self-concept of ability correlations are significantly higher for males in Mathematics, Social Studies, and Science; for the females the correlation is significantly higher in Social Studies. On the other hand, the correlation between specific self-concept and achievement in English is lower (although not significantly so) than the correlation between general self-concept of ability and achievement in English.

While the findings indicate that specific self-concept is a significantly better predictor of GPA in Mathematics, Social Studies, and Science for males, the same does not hold for females except in Social Studies. Although these sex differences may be a reflection of factors in this particular community and school system, it is interesting that Math and Science are

TABLE 3

CORRELATION AMONG GENERAL SELF-CONCEPT OF ABILITY, SELF-CONCEPT OF ABILITY IN SPECIFIC SUBJECTS, AND SEVENTH-YEAR GRADES IN FOUR SUBJECTS FOR 513 MALES AND 537 FEMALES

	Correlation coefficients							
Variables correlated	*Math*		*English*		*Social Studies*		*Science*	
	M	*F*	*M*	*F*	*M*	*F*	*M*	*F*
General S-C and grade	.50	.52	.44	.52	.51	.50	.52	.48
Specific S-C and grade	.59*	.54	.43	.47	.56*	.58*	.61*	.51
General S-C, Specific S-C and grade (R 1.23)	.60	.59	.48	.55	.60	.61	.63	.57

*Significantly greater than correlation between general S-C and grade on one-tailed "t" test.

subjects usually defined as important areas of achievement for males. By the same argument it might have been expected that self-concept in English would have been a better predictor among females. Why Social Studies alone is so distinguished among females is not clear. Since this is the subject in which females have the lowest achievement (see Table 2), it may be that Social Studies is important only because it is an area of concern—perhaps girls cannot tolerate a nonuniform achievement pattern.

The last row of Table 3 contains the multiple correlation of general self-concept and specific self-concept with grades. All of the multiple correlations account for significantly more variance than the correlations in row one.

The third hypothesis stated that an individual's self-concept of ability is significantly correlated with the images that he perceives significant others to have of his ability. This hypothesis has been tested on data from interviews with 110 over- and underachievers, and the test, therefore, does not reflect all achievement and ability levels (6). It is expected, however, that the same relationships would hold in a sample of normal achievers.[2]

The "significant others" in this research were: mother, father, favorite teacher, and best friend. A list of significant others was obtained by administering two open-ended questions: "List the people who you feel are important in your life" and "List the people who you feel are concerned about how well you do in school." All students mentioned at least one parent as a significant other and approximately 90 per cent mentioned a teacher as someone who was concerned about their achievement. Peers were mentioned as significant others by slightly less than half of the group. These four categories of significant others (mother, father, teacher, peer) were thus the most frequently mentioned by the subjects.

TABLE 4

CORRELATIONS BETWEEN THE STUDENT'S SELF-CONCEPT OF HIS GENERAL ABILITY AND THE IMAGES THAT HE PERCEIVES EACH OF FOUR SIGNIFICANT PERSONS TO HOLD OF HIS ABILITY (MALES AND FEMALES COMBINED: N = 100)

Student's perception of:	*Correlation with self-concept*
Mother's image	.50
Father's image	.52
Teacher's image	.55
Peer's image	.47
Student's self-concept and a combination of the images of all four significant others	.58

The questions which were asked about the student's perception of significant others were directly parallel to the questions the student had answered earlier about himself. Table 4 shows the correlations between the over- and underachieving student's general self-concept of ability and the evaluations of his ability that he perceives the four significant others to hold. All correlations are moderately high and roughly comparable. The highest correlation is with a composite (a sum) of the perceived evaluations of ability of all significant others. In the last column of Table 5 are found the correlations of the composite conceptions of specific subject ability held by the significant others and the over- and underachieving student's self-concept of ability in that subject. The correlations in this column of Table 5 are much lower than the correlations between general

[2] The assumption that the hypothesis would be supported in a sample of normal achievers was tested in a replication of the study one year later. The correlations of general self-concept with perception of significant others are for males (N = 731); Parents .64, Teachers .49, Peers .50. Total .60. For females (N = 751) the eighth-grade correlations are: Parents .75, Teachers .63, Peers .58. Total .74.

TABLE 5

CORRELATIONS OF THE STUDENT'S SELF-CONCEPT OF ABILITY IN FOUR SCHOOL SUBJECTS WITH THE IMAGE HE PERCEIVES FOUR SIGNIFICANT OTHERS TO HOLD OF HIS ABILITY IN FOUR SUBJECTS (MALES AND FEMALES COMBINED: N = 110)

	Significant others				
Subject	*Mother*	*Father*	*Favorite teacher*	*Best friend*	*Composite of four significant others*
Arithmetic	.31	.22	.25	.28	.31
English	.29	.15*	.18*	.30	.27
Social Studies	.38	.16*	.34	.38	.37
Science	.29	.28	.29	.26	.32

*Correlation is not significantly different from zero.

self-concept of ability and perceived evaluations by significant others. This may indicate that significant others contribute heavily to an individual's general self-concept of ability, but that the interaction between a specific significant other and the student does not specify evaluations in specific areas of the student role. Such an interpretation gains support when we examine the remainder of Table 5. Here are presented the correlations between specific subject self-concept of ability and perception of specific significant others' evaluations; these correlations are generally lower than the correlations in the last column, and three of them are so small as to not be significantly different from zero for this sample.

Such a pattern of correlations may be an indication that self-concept is not a reflection of a specific significant other but rather it may reflect a community of opinion. If it is accepted that self-concept is not a reflection of or a result of evaluations made by an individual significant other but corresponds more closely to the evaluations made by a community of "significant others," then it may be more accurate to speak in Mead's terms of the "generalized other" rather than individual significant others. This may be taken as additional support of the findings of Miyamoto and Dornbusch that an individual's self-concept is more closely related to his estimate of general attitudes toward him than it is to the perceived responses of a particular group (10).

When the correlations of the student's self-concepts of ability in each of the four subjects with the perceived evaluations of each of the four significant others were examined, it was found that there are some differences in the correlations for each of the significant others. The student's self-concept was generally more highly correlated with the images that he perceived his mother and best friend held of him than it was with the images he felt his father and teacher held of him.

Summary

Using seventh-grade students in an urban school system, it was found that: (1) There is a significant and positive correlation between self-concept and performance in the academic role; this relationship is substantial even when measured I.Q. is controlled. (2) There are specific self-concepts of ability related to specific areas of academic role performance, which differ from the general self-concept of ability. These are, in some subjects, significantly better predictors of specific subject achievement than is the general self-concept of ability. (3) Self-concept is significantly and positively correlated with the perceived evaluations that significant others hold of the student; however, it is the composite image rather than the images of specific others that appears to be most closely correlated with the student's self-concept in specific subjects.

Further Research

The demonstrated correlation between the student's self-concept and the evaluations that the student perceives others to hold of him leads to the question as to whether it is possible to change self-concept. Furthermore, if self-concept is in fact a key factor in role performance, changes in self-concept should result in changes in performance. In an attempt to answer these questions, three experiments have been designed which will constitute the second phase of this research (5). An attempt will be made to develop more positive self-concepts.

If results turn out as hypothesized, then one of the questions concerning the development of self-concept will be answered. Such results should indicate that the evaluations of others are sufficient to lead to enhancement of self and thus to increased achievement. This is not to say that the experience of success does not operate to enhance self-concept, but only that it is not a necessary prior condition for self-concept enhancement. Changing the performance of individuals through changes in self-concept would have great practical implications for the operation of educational programs.

References

1. Bledsoe, Joseph C., and K. C. Garrison, *The Self-Concepts of Elementary School Children in Relation to Their Academic Achievement, Intelligence, Interests, and Manifest Anxiety,* U. S. Office of Education Cooperative Research Project No. 1008 (Athens, Ga.: U. of Ga., 1962).

2. Borislow, Bernard, "Self-Evaluation and Academic Achievement," *Journal of Counseling Psychology,* Vol. 9 (Fall, 1962).
3. Brookover, Wilbur B., "A Social Psychological Conception of Classroom Learning," *School and Society,* Vol. 87 (Feb. 28, 1959), pp. 84-87.
4. ———, and David Gottlieb, *A Sociology of Education* (New York: Am. Bk. Co., 1964), Chapter 16.
5. ———, Don E. Hamachek, and Jean LePere, *Improving Academic Achievement Through Students' Self-Concept Enhancement,* U. S. Office of Education, Project No. 1636 (now in process).
6. ———, Ann Paterson, and Shailer Thomas, *Self-Concept of Ability and School Achievement,* U. S. Office of Education Cooperative Research Project No. 845 (East Lansing: Bureau of Research and Publications, Michigan State University, 1962).
7. Davidson, Helen H., and Gerhard Lang, "Children's Perceptions of Their Teachers' Feelings Toward Them Related to Self-Perception, School Achievement and Behavior," *Journal of Experimental Education,* Vol. 29 (1960), pp. 107-118.
8. Kinch, John W., "A Formalized Theory of Self-Concept (Research Note)," *American Journal of Sociology,* Vol. 68 (January, 1963), pp. 481-486.
9. McPartland, Thomas S., John H. Cumming, and Wynona S. Garretson, "Self-Conception and Ward Behavior in Two Psychiatric Hospitals," *Sociometry,* Vol. 24 (June, 1961), pp. 111-124.
10. Miyamoto, Frank, and Sanford Dornbusch, "A Test of the Interactionists' Hypotheses of Self-Conception," *American Journal of Sociology,* Vol. 61 (March, 1956), pp. 399-403.
11. Morse, Richard J., *Self-Concept of Ability, Significant Others, and School Achievement of Eighth-Grade Students: A Comparative Investigation of Negro and Caucasian Students,* M. A. Thesis, Michigan State University, 1963.
12. Reckless, Walter C., Simon Dinitz, and Ellen Murray, "Self-Concept As an Insulator Against Delinquency," *American Sociological Review,* Vol. 21 (December, 1956), pp. 744-746.
13. Reeder, Thelma Adams, *A Study of Some Relationships Between Level of Self-Concept, Academic Achievement, and Classroom Adjustment,* Ph.D. Thesis, North Texas State College, 1955.
14. Renzaglia, G. A., *Some Correlates of the Self Structure as Measured by an Index of Adjustment and Value,* Ph.D. Thesis, University of Minnesota, 1952.
15. Wiley, Ruth, *The Self-Concept* (Lincoln, Neb.: U. of Neb., 1961).

3. Self-concept as it relates to academic underachievement

MARTIN B. FINK

Reprinted from the *California Journal of Educational Research,* Vol. XIII, No. 2 (1962), 57-62, by permission of the author and the California Teachers' Association.

Is there a relationship between adequacy of self-concept and level of academic achievement? Are there differences in this regard between males and females? This selection points to further speculations about the relationships between self-concept and learning.

This study was conceived as the result of a clinical impression that self-concept is related to academic achievement; that is, that an adequate self-concept is related to high achievement, and an inadequate self-concept is related to low achievement (underachievement).

Academic underachievers often obtain average or better scores on tests of intelligence. This would appear to indicate that the primary operant factor in academic underachievement is not intelligence alone.

While it is evident that intelligence per se is not the *sine qua non* of academic achievement, there is no definitive explanation. Many suggestions have been advanced. Terman (10) sees academic underachievement as the result of a lack of perseverance. For Gough (1) academic underachievement is essentially an asocial act. Green (2) sees the underachiever as a person caught in a basic conflict between submission and aggressiveness. Other authors (4, 6, 8) find hostility to be a characteristic of the underachiever. Additionally, academic underachievement has been related to emotional disturbances, organic brain damage, poor home background, low socioeconomic level, poor teaching, inadequate school facilities.

These explanations of academic underachievement often appear to be too superficial, too fragmentary, or in many cases they do not appear to apply. It is suggested, therefore, that the problem is based on a central rather than a peripheral motivating force and further that this force is essentially molar rather than molecular. The conceptualization that appears tc satisfy best the above requirements is that of the concept of self. This study postulates a relationship between concept of self and academic underachievement.

For the purpose of this study self-concept is defined as the attitudes and feelings that a person has regarding himself. It is implicit in this definition that these attitudes and feelings lead to attempts on the part of the individual through various actions to enhance or defend himself (5, 9, 3).

Method

All subjects were selected from the freshman class of a rural high school located in the Central Valley of California. For the purposes of this study, academic achievement was determined by grade-point average. The grade-point average, based on all marks in the ninth grade, was determined for all freshmen falling within the 90-110 I.Q. range on the California Test of Mental Maturity. The median grade-point average was computed. Those whose grade-point average was above the median were considered achievers, those whose grade-point average fell below the median, underachievers. Pairs of achievers and underachievers were formed, matched for sex and I.Q. The resulting study group consisted of 20 matched pairs of boys and 24 matched pairs of girls.

Self-concept was measured by instruments generally used by school psychologists in clinical situations. Data were collected for each child, using the following devices:

California Psychological Inventory
Bender Visual Motor Gestalt Test
Draw-a-Person Test
Gough Adjective Check List (completed by pupil)
Gough Adjective Check List (completed by teacher)
Personal data sheet
Brief essay describing "What I will be in 20 years."

The data were presented to three judges—two school psychologists and a clinical psychologist working with children. The judges were asked, using all the psychological data, and none of the school data, to make a determination as to adequacy or inadequacy of self-concept of each child. Each judge worked alone. No attempt was made to define an adequate self-concept for the judges. Only one judge asked for such a definition, and he was instructed to use his own concept of adequacy, bearing in mind that the subjects were ninth-grade students.

Results

The data from all three judges were placed in contingency tables using self-concept as one variable and achievement as the other. Self-concept was classified into two categories, adequate and inadequate; and achievement into two categories, high and low.

The data were treated by *chi* square, with Yates correction for continuity to test for independence. For each table there is one degree of freedom. The results are indicated in Tables 1–8.

TABLE 1

JUDGE 1
BOYS

Achievement	*Adequate self-concept*	*Inadequate self-concept*
High achievement	19	1
Low achievement	3	17
	$X^2 = 22.7$	
	P .01	

TABLE 2

JUDGE 1
GIRLS

Achievement	*Adequate self-concept*	*Inadequate self-concept*
High achievement	20	4
Low achievement	11	13
	$X^2 = 5.8$	
	P .02	

TABLE 3

JUDGE 2
BOYS

Achievement	Adequate self-concept	Inadequate self-concept
High achievement	17	3
Low achievement	10	10
	$X^2 = 4.1$	
	P .05	

TABLE 4

JUDGE 2
GIRLS

Achievement	Adequate self-concept	Inadequate self-concept
High achievement	19	5
Low achievement	16	8
	$X^2 = .42$	
	P .70	
	.50	

TABLE 5

JUDGE 3
BOYS

Achievement	Adequate self-concept	Inadequate self-concept
High achievement	17	3
Low achievement	4	16
	$X^2 = 14.4$	
	P .01	

TABLE 6

JUDGE 3
GIRLS

Achievement	Adequate self-concept	Inadequate self-concept
High achievement	14	10
Low achievement	10	14
	$X^2 = .75$	
	P .70	
	.50	

TABLE 7

COMBINED GROUPINGS
BOYS

Achievement	Adequate self-concept	Inadequate self-concept
High achievement	17	4
Low achievement	3	16
	$X^2 = 14.4$	
	P .01	

TABLE 8

COMBINED GROUPINGS
GIRLS

Achievement	Adequate self-concept	Inadequate self-concept
High achievement	15	9
Low achievement	9	15
	$X^2 = 2.1$	
	P .20	
	.10	

Conclusions

The results of this study appear to confirm the hypothesis that a relationship does in fact exist between adequacy of self-concept and level of academic achievement. This conclusion appears to be unquestionable for boys, considerably less so for girls. Similar difficulty in obtaining clear-cut findings for girls has been encountered by other researchers (7). The relationship of sex differences to academic achievement would appear to warrant further research. Of value, too, would be the investigation of the differential effect of low socioeconomic environment and emotionally disturbed homes on the male and female high school student. It appears that, for whatever reasons, the psychological burden for the male is heavier than for the female.

This study indicates that psychologists, using psychological instruments and given no specific definition of self-concept, can make a determination as to adequacy or inadequacy of self-concept and that such adequacy or inadequacy of self-concept is related to level of academic achievement. However, in order to further validate the judges' findings, objectification of the data upon which such decisions were based would appear to be warranted. Objectification of the data could also be used to investigate the relationship of sex differences to academic achievement.

Summary

Observations made in the clinical practice of school psychology led to the hypothesis that an adequate self-concept is related to high academic achievement and an inadequate self-concept is related to low academic achievement.

Based on grade-point average, pairs of achievers and underachievers were formed, matched for sex and I.Q. The study group consists of eighty-eight students from the freshman class of a rural California high school; 20 matched pairs of boys and 24 matched pairs of girls.

The psychological data collected for these students were submitted to three judges, two school psychologists and a clinical psychologist working with children. The judges were asked to make a clinical judgment as to the adequacy or inadequacy of self-concept of each student.

The results clearly bear out the hypothesis for boys. They are considerably less positive for girls.

Objectification of some of the psychological data upon which the judges' decisions were based, investigation of the relationships of sex differences to academic achievement, investigation into the development of adequate and inadequate self-concept would all appear to be fruitful areas for further research.

References

1. Gough, Harrison G., "Factors Related to Differential Achievement Among Persons," Invited paper given at 1955 meetings of the A.P.A., copies on file: The Institute of Personality Assessment and Research, University of California, Berkeley.
2. Green, Arnold W., "The Middle-Class Male Child and Neurosis," *A Modern Introduction to the Family* (New York: Free Press, 1959), pp. 562-572.
3. Hall, C., and G. Lindzey, *Theories of Personality* (New York: Wiley, 1957), p. 468.
4. Kirk, Barbara, "Test Versus Academic Performance in Malfunctioning Students," *Journal of Consulting Psychology,* Vol. 16, No. 3 (1952), pp. 213-215.
5. Lecky, Prescott, *Self-Consistency, A Theory of Personality* (Fort Myers Beach, Fla.: Island, 1945), p. 150.
6. Shaw, Merville C., and Donald J. Brown, "Scholastic Underachievement of Bright College Students," *Personnel and Guidance Journal,* Vol. 56 (1957), pp. 195-198.
7. ———, Kenneth Edson, and Hugh M. Bell, "The Self-Concept of Bright Underachieving High School Students as Revealed by an Adjective Check List," *Personnel and Guidance Journal* (in press).

8. ———, and James Grubb, "Hostility and Able High School Underachievers," *Journal of Counseling Psychology,* Vol. 5, No. 4 (1958), pp. 263-265.
9. Snygg, D., and H. Combs, *Individual Behavior* (New York: Harper, 1959), p. 258.
10. Terman, Lewis M., and Melita H. Oden, "The Development and Adult Status of Gifted Children," *Psychological Studies of Human Development, Century Psychological Series* (New York: Appleton, 1952), p. 199.

4. The use of the parent-attitude research inventory with the parents of bright academic underachievers [1]

MERVILLE C. SHAW
AND BERT E. DUTTON

Reprinted from the *Journal of Educational Psychology,* Vol. 53 (1962), 203-208, by permission of the senior author and the American Psychological Association.

The previous two selections have offered evidence to suggest that there is a relationship between level of academic achievement and self-concept. It has been suggested that level of achievement is influenced by self-concept and that self-concept is influenced by significant others, who, not infrequently, are parents. This research effort examines the parents of achievers and the parents of underachievers with respect to their attitudes toward their children.

In an earlier study of academic underachievement, Shaw and McCuen (5) demonstrated that children classified as academic underachievers on the basis of their grades in high school typically had a long history of such behavior. In males trends toward this kind of behavior were seen as early as the first grade and were generally a characteristic of the group by the third grade. Such early appearance was not a characteristic of the female groups, the trend toward underachievement not beginning until Grade 6.

The findings of this study suggested the possibility that conditions antecedent to school entrance might have at least a partial bearing on the development of underachieving behavior, and more specifically, that parent attitudes might be associated with failure to perform effectively in school. The present study represents an attempt to

[1] This research is part of a project which was supported by a grant from the National Institute of Mental Health.

determine whether or not differences exist between the parents of achievers and the parents of underachievers with respect to their attitudes toward children and an attempt to determine, in a limited way, what the nature of these differences may be.

Procedure

Tenth- and eleventh-grade students in a high school of 1,800 students constituted the pool from which subjects were drawn. The California Test of Mental Maturity (CTMM) was administered to all of the 850 students in these two grades as a part of the study. Only those who attained an IQ of 110 or over on the Language section of the test, using published norms, were considered potential subjects. Any student who performed at this minimum level or higher and who had achieved a cumulative high school grade-point average (GPA) of 2.7 or below on a 4-point scale was considered an underachiever. Only academic subjects were used in computing these averages. The selection of 2.7 as a cutting point was based on the fact that it approximated the mean cumulative GPA on the tenth- and eleventh-grade classes. A student was considered an achiever if his cumulative high school GPA was 3.0 or higher. Table 1 reports the number of children identified in each category.

TABLE 1

NUMBER OF PARTICIPATING STUDENTS AND PARENTS CLASSIFIED BY GRADE, SEX, AND ACHIEVEMENT LEVEL

Achievement level	*Students*		*Parents*	
	Grade 10	*Grade 11*	*Mothers*	*Fathers*
Male achievers	17	14	22	21
Male underachievers	23	13	28	21
Female achievers	18	15	28	19
Female underachievers	8	7	8	4

Following the identification of subjects, their parents were contacted, first by letter, then by telephone, to request their participation in the study. This participation involved coming to the school in the evening and participating in an individual interview and in the completion of several objective inventories including the Parent Attitude Research Inventory (PARI). Parents were not informed that it was a study involving academic achievement, but were told only that children in the top 25 per cent, with respect to ability, were being studied. The time that any parent was involved ranged from 2 to 4 hours. Table 1 reports the number of mothers and fathers in each of the eight categories studied who completed all project requirements.

An examination of Table 1 reveals that cooperation was generally better from mothers than from fathers and from the parents of achievers than from the parents of underachievers. The fathers of female underachievers were the most reluctant group. A total of 151 parents completed the necessary procedures. The size of the sample did not permit socioeconomic stratification. Inspection of data relative to occupational level of fathers indicated a tendency for underachievers to come from families lower on the occupational scale, but marked overlap between achiever and underachiever groups was also obvious.

The PARI was used as a measure of attitude. It was developed by Schaeffer, Bell, and Bayley (3) and has been used extensively. There are forms for both mothers and fathers. The Mother Form of the inventory consists of 23 factored scales of 5 items each with the items cyclically arranged on the question blank. The Father Form consists of 30 factored scales of 8 items each, with items also cyclically arranged. These scales have the advantage of covering, in an objective way, a wide range of parent attitudes and also of presenting data in a manner which makes statistical treatment easily possible. Four categories of answers ranging from strongly agree to strongly disagree are possible. In the present study, IBM answer sheets were provided for parents to respond on.

The PARI was administered to each parent following a lengthy individual interview. The subject of the interview was the particular underachieving child included in the sample, and instructions to parents with respect to completing the PARI were that they should complete it with this particular child in mind. Following the administration of the PARI to all parents who participated in the study, answer sheets were scored on each scale and mean scores were completed for each group included in the study. In addition, the three factors isolated by Zuckerman and Ribback (6) from the Mother Form of the inventory were scored, and comparisons were made between mothers of achievers and underachievers on each of the factors.

For purposes of comparison, the fathers of male achievers were compared with fathers of male underachievers, and the fathers of female achievers were compared with the fathers of female underachievers, although in the latter case the number of fathers involved is so small as to make the reliability of results open to question. The mothers of male achievers were compared with the mothers of male underachievers, and the mothers of female achievers were compared with the mothers of female underachievers. This kind of breakdown for comparative purposes seemed appropriate in the light of previous studies indicating differences in the dynamics of underachieving behavior between males and females. The F test to determine homogeneity of variance and the t test of significance were carried out between appropriate groups. When F was significant at the .05 level or less, t was computed by a method suggested by Cochran and Cox (1) described by Edwards (2).

Results

Table 2 reports the scales on which significant differences were found between the mothers of female achievers and female underachievers. Differences significant at the .05 level or less were found on Scale 2, Fostering Dependency; Scale 5, Martyrdom; Scale 6, Fear of Harming the Baby; Scale 11, Deification of the Parent; Scale 12, Suppression of Aggression; Scale 16, Avoidance of Communication; Scale 17, Inconsiderateness of the Husband; Scale 19, Ascendancy of the Mother; Scale 22, Acceleration of Development; and Scale 23, Dependency of the Mother. In all cases the mean scores of the mothers of female underachievers exceeded the mean of the mothers of achievers.

Table 3 summarizes scales which differentiated significantly between the mothers of male achievers and male underachievers. It will be readily seen that in this case only two scales differentiated significantly. These were Scale 3, Seclusion of the Mother; and Scale 18, Suppression of Sexuality. In both cases the means obtained by mothers of underachievers were larger.

The three factors derived by Zuckerman (6) in a previous study were used as a basis for further analysis. Factor A, an Authoritarian Control factor, seems to measure authoritarian suppression and punitive and restricting attitudes, according to Zuckerman. Factor B, a Hostility Rejection factor, is described as measuring hostility toward children and husband and

TABLE 2

PARI SCALES ON WHICH DIFFERENCES BETWEEN MOTHERS OF FEMALE SUBJECTS WERE SIGNIFICANT AT THE .05 LEVEL OR LESS

Scale number	*Achievers' mean*	*Underachievers' mean*	F	t
2	9.07	13.75	5.36***	2.50[a]*
5	7.21	12.50	7.92****	2.94[a]*
6	12.61	16.25	1.64	2.93****
11	11.04	14.38	1.54	2.23**
12	9.89	13.14	1.54	3.19****
16	8.75	11.00	1.94	2.15**
17	9.62	13.71	1.58	2.80****
19	9.57	14.88	1.21	4.09****
22	10.30	13.88	2.88	3.39****
23	9.56	12.13	1.19	2.05**

[a]When F was significant at the .05 level or less, t was obtained by an approximation suggested by Cochran and Cox (1950).

*$p = .05$.

**$.05 > p > .02$.

***$.05 > p > .01$.

****$p = .01$.

TABLE 3

PARI Scales on Which Differences Between Mothers of Male Subjects Were Significant at the .05 Level or Less

Scale number	*Achievers' mean*	*Underachievers' mean*	F	t
3	10.55	12.54	1.26	2.48**
18	7.85	9.74	1.02	2.21*

*.05 > p > .02.
**.02 > p > .01.

rejection of the maternal role. Factor C, a Democratic Attitude factor, is composed of the three positively worded scales and seems to measure democratic attitudes. The only difference was found between the mothers of female subjects, with the mothers of underachievers scoring significantly higher on Factor A. Factors B and C did not differentiate between the two groups. Table 4 summarizes these results. When similar techniques were

TABLE 4

Results Obtained on Mothers of Female Subjects from PARI Scales Analyzed According to Zuckerman's Factors

Factor	*Achievers' mean*	*Underachievers' mean*	F	t
A	9.87	13.23	1.63	4.50**
B	10.83	12.50	2.44*	.14
C	17.27	17.25	1.65	.02

*.05 > p > .02.
**.01

applied to the mothers of male subjects included in the group, no significant differences were found between the mothers of male achievers and the mothers of male underachievers on any of the three factors. Table 5 summarizes these results.

TABLE 5

Results Obtained on Mothers of Male Subjects from PARI Scales Analyzed According to Zuckerman's Factors

Factor	*Achievers' mean*	*Underachievers' mean*	F	t
A	10.12	11.24	1.21	1.24
B	10.91	11.64	1.01	.90
C	17.13	16.96	1.40	.31

Analysis of the PARI scores obtained from the fathers of female subjects was carried out in a manner similar to that used for the mothers of our subjects. Application of F and t tests to the mean scale scores obtained by the fathers of female subjects revealed significant differences on four scales. These were Scale 7, Marital Conflict; Scale 18, Suppression of Sexuality; Scale 22, Avoidance of the Expression of Affection; and Scale 28, Change Orientation. These results are summarized in Table 6.

TABLE 6

PARI SCALES ON WHICH DIFFERENCES BETWEEN FATHERS OF FEMALE SUBJECTS WERE SIGNIFICANT AT THE .05 LEVEL OR LESS

Scale number	*Achievers' mean*	*Underachievers' mean*	F	t
7	24.89	19.75	2.67	2.39*
18	13.16	19.50	3.31	3.41**
22	15.21	21.00	1.29	3.29**
28	18.65	22.75	1.36	2.13*

*$.05 > p > .02$.
**$p = .01$.

Analysis of the PARI scale for the fathers of males included in the study revealed only two scales which differentiated significantly between the two groups. These were Scale 18, Suppression of Sexuality; and Scale 12, Irresponsibility of the Father. These results are indicated in Table 7.

TABLE 7

PARI SCALES ON WHICH DIFFERENCES BETWEEN FATHERS OF MALE SUBJECTS WERE SIGNIFICANT AT THE .05 LEVEL OR LESS

Scale number	*Achievers' mean*	*Underachievers' mean*	F	t
12	14.94	17.75	2.44*	1.54[a]*
18	14.69	18.40	1.09	2.35**

[a]When F was signficant at the .05 level or less, t was obtained by an approximation suggested by Cochran and Cox (1950).
*$p = .05$.
**$.02 > p > .01$.

Discussion

Examination of the results obtained from analysis of the data on mothers of our female subjects revealed 10 scales which differentiated significantly between the mothers of achievers and underachievers. To a greater extent than the mothers of female achievers, the mothers of our female underachievers appear to be more dependent, dominant, and in need of respect and the dependency of their children. They seem to have some fear of their own hostile impulses and cannot tolerate the aggressive behavior of their children.

Results obtained from the mothers of male subjects are not nearly so definite. The only two scales which differentiated significantly between the mothers of male achievers and underachievers were the Seclusion of the Mother and Suppression of Sexuality scales. The mothers of underachieving males appear to be both more seclusive and to suppress sexuality more strongly than the mothers of male achievers.

Analysis of the data obtained from the mothers using Zuckerman's three factors tends to be in line with the findings reported above. The mothers of female subjects showed significant differences on only one of the three factors. On Factor A, the mothers of underachieving girls exceeded significantly the scores obtained by the mothers of achieving girls. This is not at all surprising in view of the fact that the 10 scales on which the mothers of underachieving females receive significantly higher scores are all included in the 16 scales which make up Factor A. No differences were found between the two groups on Factors B and C. These results would seem to indicate that the mothers of female underachievers were dependent, dominant, and felt put upon in their roles of wives and mothers. They could not tolerate the expression of aggression on the part of their children and, at the same time, feared their own hostile impulses.

No differences were found on any of the three factors between the mothers of male achievers and underachievers. Apparently, among the subjects in our sample, negative feelings were most strongly exhibited by the mothers of female underachievers.

Results obtained from the fathers of female subjects were somewhat equivocal. The fathers of female achievers expressed significantly more strongly the feeling that marital conflict existed in their family. It is interesting to note in this regard that none of the mothers of these same children expressed this feeling to a significant degree. The fathers of underachieving females exceeded the fathers of achieving females on three scales: Suppression of Sexuality, Avoidance of the Expression of Affection, and Change Orientation. Interpretation of these findings leads to the conclusion that the suppression of overt demonstrations of emotion is accompanied in these fathers by a suppression of any behavior which to them implies sexuality. There is some basis for assuming a relationship between these two variables. The high score of these fathers on change orientation may indicate the existence of a subtle dissatisfaction with the role of husband and parent.

The fathers of male subjects differed significantly on two scales, and in both cases, the fathers of underachievers exceeded the fathers of achievers. These scales were Irresponsibility of the Father and, again, the Suppression of Sexuality. The suggestion of a basic anxiety with respect to sexual matters among the parents of underachieving children is strongly borne out. Again, there is a hint of dissatisfaction with the parental role on the part of the parents of underachievers.

It would appear that parents of underachieving children have more strongly negative attitudes toward these particular children than do the parents of achieving youngsters. The present study does not reveal definitely, however, whether these attitudes are one of the results of underachievement, or one of its causes. From a logical point of view, it is easier to build a case for such attitudes as causal rather than resultant factors. The early appearance of underachievement among males lends some support to the causal interpretation. The finding of negative self-concepts among underachievers (Shaw, Edson, & Bell, [4]) also is mildly supportive of parental attitudes as causal factors since negative attitudes on the part of parents toward a child would result in the formation of negative attitudes toward self on the part of the child. The problem of why only certain children in the same family are underachievers has not been explored, although presumably it is related to the fact that parents have different attitudes toward their various children. This is a problem which should not be too difficult to explore, from a methodological point of view. In the present study an effort was made to establish a response set relative to the *specific* child under consideration.

References

1. Cochran, W. G., and G. Cox, *Experimental Designs* (New York: Wiley, 1950).
2. Edwards, A. L., *Experimental Design in Psychological Research* (New York: Holt, Rinehart & Winston, 1950).
3. Schaeffer, E. S., R. Q. Bell, and Nancy Bayley, "Development of a Parental Attitude Research Instrument," *Child Development,* Vol. 29 (1958), pp. 339-361.
4. Shaw, M. C., K. Edson, and H. M. Bell, "Self-Concept of Bright Academic Underachieving Students as Revealed by an Adjective Check List," *Personnel and Guidance Journal,* Vol. 39 (1960), pp. 193-196.
5. ———, and J. T. McCuen, "The Onset of Academic Underachievement in Bright Children," *Journal of Educational Psychology,* Vol. 51 (1960), pp. 103-108.
6. Zuckerman, M., and Beatrice Ribback, "Normative Data and Factor Analysis on the Parental Attitude Research Instrument," *Journal of Consulting Psychology,* Vol. 22 (1958), pp. 165-171.

5. When school and home focus on achievement

Mildred B. Smith
and Carl I. Brahce

Reprinted from *Educational Leadership,* Vol. 20 (1963), 314-318, by permission of the authors and the Association for Supervision and Curriculum Development.

What happens when parents and teachers work together in an all-out self-enhancement program for children? What happens when parents and teachers work to become "significant" in the most positive sense of the word? The authors investigated these and other questions and end up with a plan that could well be adopted by other communities.

The idea that parents can be enthusiastic about elementary curriculum to the extent of improving academic achievement may seem to be a misty dream. Yet, unlike the illusory apparition that plagued Hamlet, such a vision appears to have practical benefits for elementary educators.

An experimental program designed to raise the achievement level of culturally deprived elementary children has brought illuminating evidence. This program has proved that parents and teachers, with cooperative support of administrators, can kindle in children a fresh interest in learning. Statistical evaluation subsequently showed marked gains in academic achievement.

This experimental program was designated, "School and Home: Focus on Achievement." It was started following a decision by the teachers in an elementary school and a curriculum consultant to "quit talking and do something" about raising the students' levels of achievement and of interest in the classrooms.

The hypothesis of the program, though not academically new by any means, centered around an idea that many teachers long have held—that children will achieve more if they learn early to develop sound work habits and attitudes. Underlying this thought is a corollary, that to perform such an educational awakening, the cooperative support of parents is important.

The school principal, teachers, and administrative staff offered their services. This resulted in a meeting with students' parents at the school. At this discussion meeting, pertinent facts were presented. If the parents wanted their children to finish school, they had an obligation to begin now to help prepare their youngsters. The current industrial picture was studied. The fact that automation is cutting off many young, unskilled workers from many jobs was explained. Parents learned of the teachers' and administrators' concern and interest in giving their children an education that would prepare them to be useful, responsible citizens.

The cooperative program that grew out of this session stimulated much enthusiasm among parents. The program also created interest on the part of students, and a concerted effort by teachers, principals and administrators to work together on this team objective.

Setting of the Program

The experiment was undertaken in one elementary school, and later was started in a second school during the 1961-62 school year. The program involved children enrolled in kindergarten through the sixth grade. These youngsters were primarily from the low-income families living in the industrial hub of Flint, Michigan. With few exceptions, the parents had moved to the city from the rural South to seek employment in local industrial plants. A majority represented limited educational backgrounds. Approximately 1100 children were included in the program.

A control group was established in another Flint public elementary school. These children represented similar socioeconomic backgrounds.

It should be noted that the Flint Public Schools are community centers, having gained national recognition as working-action examples of the community education concept. These schools, open after regular hours for all neighborhood persons, are regularly used by thousands of youngsters and adults in a variety of educational, recreational, and cultural programs. Such a program gives the teachers and staffs a ready acceptance for new ideas from the standpoint of parental interest, since many of the parents previously had been involved in some school functions. The Charles Stewart Mott Foundation, operating in partnership with the Flint Board of Education as the Mott Program, had provided opportunities for eduational advancement and achievement for students in the study and for ther students also.

This favorable "climate" doubtless provided a short cut for gaining ublic and parental acceptance of an experimental program that would re-uire more planning and graduated involvement in other schools where such rograms are not in operation.

rame of Reference

The theoretical frame of reference for the study is based on the action heorists' postulations (1, 4) that the group in which the individual is ocialized influences his motivation to achieve in school.

It seemed that a program designed to raise the achievement of children vho lacked the necessary motivation to achieve adequately must involve vorking with these children's "significant others"[1] for the purpose of etting them to expect more of these children. The students were expected o "internalize" the expectations of these "significant others" and, therefore, o expect more of themselves. It was predicted that this change in their ttitudes and values would take place as they learned their values from 'significant others."

Role of Parents

The "significant others" for elementary school children were assumed to be parents and teachers. In the parent-teacher meetings, mothers and fathers learned that their attitudes and values greatly influenced those of their children. The parents were made to understand that without awareness and intent, they were not setting the kind of example that brings about desirable attitudes and habits toward schoolwork.

Parents were: (a) impressed that they must do more than *tell* their children that they need to achieve in school. They were frequently reminded that they must *show* the children that their schoolwork is important; (b) given suggestions of activities and behavior which would provide at home a climate conducive to academic achievement.

The interest evidenced by parents was heartwarming to the teachers and administrators. The parents not only agreed to carry out the suggestions, but for the most part were highly supportive. The reason, so the program planners believe, was that the parents realized that school officials cared enough about their children to seek help from them.

---

[1] "Significant others" is defined as those people who are important to an individual.

Another facet of parental involvement was that of getting parents themselves to call on other parents. Some of the mothers, anxious to do a little extra, took the initiative in getting all parents involved. These community leaders made numerous home calls, followed up with telephone reminders. The school communities were divided into blocks, so that every section was contacted. The stimulating result was that parents heeded the message and supported the experimental program in greater participation than imagined by the program's initiators.

Role of Teachers

It has already been shown that the teachers had a real interest and concern in the achievement of their students. This interest stimulated their own group meetings, discussions involving principals and curriculum consultants. The interest shown by parents in the open meetings whetted the teachers' appetites for upgrading instruction in the classrooms. Ideas were freely shared and explored, as were materials and teaching techniques.

The teachers at both schools placed primary emphasis on reading comprehension and vocabulary development. The students took books home frequently for individual as well as family reading. The teachers saw that each primary child was given an inexpensive metal file box and word cards to aid in improving sight vocabulary. These word cards frequently were sent home for study.

In all these activities, the teachers worked closely with parents. The teachers: (a) sent books home with students, (b) sent study assignments home, and (c) called parent conferences as needed. Parental contacts included home visits, inviting parents to the schools for discussion-information conferences and special problems. The staff developed a reading incentives program for students in second through sixth grades. Called The Bookworm Club, this special project appealed to young imaginative minds offering incentives to progress in reading skills. Parents assisted teachers in the preparation of small booklets designed to stimulate interest.

Teachers came up with creative hints for parents. Students arrived home wearing tags that read: "Please read to me," "May I read to you?" and "Please help me study my spelling." Students, too, took an active part in their own study assignments. Under direction of teachers, each class developed a check list for doing assigned work. The students did their own self-checking, adding to the fun atmosphere of learning at school and home.

Getting the support of the parents meant continuing their interest in the program. To help accomplish this over an extensive period of time, parents were given these suggestions which sum up basic objectives:

1. Read daily to your children—preschoolers included. Fathers also are encouraged to take turns reading to their youngsters.
2. Listen to your children read.
3. Provide a quiet period in the home each day for reading and study. This should be at a regular time so that it becomes a part of the family's routine. (Research indicates that low-income families lack routine and regularity in the home [2, 3].)
4. See that children have pencils, paper, a notebook, and a dictionary for home study. (Observation indicates that children of low-income families often lack proper tools for schoolwork. These same children may have an abundance of gum, candy, and gadgets, indicating the problem to be one of values rather than a problem of money.)
5. Parents were reminded that if they show that they value school achievement, their children likewise will value it.

To supplement these suggestions, teachers gave booklets to the parents, explaining techniques of reading aloud to their children, ways that parents can help their children improve their study habits, and ways to develop favorable attitudes toward school. Again, the handbooks were discussed with parents.

During the summer vacation, the program was continued through use of summer materials. Parents asked that they be provided with a list of summer activities to help them in maintaining the attitudes and habits their children had acquired during the school year. Each child also was given a summer Reading Record Booklet. The child was expected to keep a record of books read during the summer and to return this record to his teacher when fall classes resumed.

Forms 1 and 2 of the Gates Revised Reading Tests were administered in pre- and post-test situations to all children in the two experimental schools. The same test was administered simultaneously to all second- and fifth-grade students in the control school. Their reading gains were compared with gains made by second- and fifth-year children in the two experimental schools.

Evaluation of the Program

Children in the two experimental schools showed over-all gains of 5.4 months in reading during the five-month period between pre- and post-tests. Children in the control school showed an over-all gain of 2.7 months in reading during the same period.

The evaluation showed that gains made by Experimental School C generally were greater than those made by Experimental School B. One factor which may contribute to this finding is that Experimental School B entered the program somewhat later than did the Experimental School C, with some problems in getting total staff involvement in School B. Children in all schools showed greater gains in reading vocabulary than in reading comprehension. Since reading comprehension encompasses a broader base than vocabulary, equivalent progress in comprehension can be expected with time.

The second-grade children in the two experimental schools made greater mean gains in vocabulary and comprehension than did children in the control school. The mean gain differences are highly significant [2] for vocabulary for Experimental Schools B and C, compared with Control School A. The mean difference for comprehension is highly significant for Experimental School C, but is not significant for Experimental School B.

Fifth-grade children in the two experimental schools also made significantly greater gains in vocabulary than did children in the control school. Gains made in comprehension are moderately significantly greater for children in Experimental School C but not significantly greater in Experimental School B.

A questionnaire was sent to each family in the two experimental schools to determine what opinions parents held about the Focus on Achievement Program. Approximately two thirds of all questionnaires were returned. Of these, 85 per cent contained written-in comments and suggestions. The questionnaire contained three check-type questions and three open-ended questions. Parents indicated that they felt the program helped the children with schoolwork. They also said they would like to have the program continued. As a side benefit, the parents indicated that their involvement had helped them to improve their own academic skills.

The teachers conducted a home-study survey to see if parents had set aside the quiet time for study and reading. Parents indicated the daily study time, with not one reporting that the home study was not helpful. Results of this survey showed that 90 per cent of the children in the experimental schools returned their completed questionnaires, another indication of parental interest in the program.

The experimental study has definitely resulted in improved student work habits and attitudes toward schoolwork, teachers report. The experiment is continuing at the two schools. In addition, the administrators and teachers are cooperating in establishing the program in a third school following a request by parents.

The Flint Community School administrative staff and teachers have ob-

---

[2] A probability of .05 is interpreted as moderately significant. A probability of .01 is interpreted as highly significant.

ained as complete statistical evidence as possible. This corroborates find-
igs that, as good practicing educators, they believe to be true.

In summary, they believe these findings offer sound evidence to educators
a the elementary field, and perhaps higher levels as well, that education
oday is and must be a cooperative home-school project. Educators need
ot be afraid to go to parents with their educational problems. Indeed, as
hown by the Flint experimentation, parents, when approached with forth-
ight honesty, will return a thousandfold creative efforts of their own.

eferences

. Brookover, W. B., "Some Social Psychological Conceptions of Classroom Learning," *School and Society,* Vol. 87 (1959), pp. 84-87.
. Davis, Allison, and Robert J. Havighurst, *Father of the Man* (Boston: Houghton, 1947).
. Ericson, Martha, "Child Rearing and Social Status," *American Journal of Sociology,* Vol. 52 (1946), pp. 190-192.
. Mead, George H., *Mind, Self, and Society* (Chicago: U. of Chicago, 1934).

QUESTIONS FOR DISCUSSION

3orislow Article

1. Why should the "intention" to strive for good marks or not make a difference in the optimism or pessimism of achievers or underachievers?
2. If a high self-concept student gets good marks even though this was not his prime goal, his general self-evaluation does not improve. Why do you suppose this is so?
3. What does the author mean by a specific "role" self-evaluation theory as contrasted to the more general self-evaluation theory? What are the essential differences between these two frames of reference?

Brookover, Thomas, Paterson Article

1. A positive relationship between self-concept and performance is evident even when I.Q. is controlled or held constant. What are the implications of this finding? What does this suggest about the relative influences of self-concept and I.Q. on academic achievement?
2. What reasons would you advance for why specific self-concepts of ability are significantly better predictors of specific achievement in some subjects than is the general self-concept of ability? Is this conclusion consistent with those of Borislow? In what way?
3. Speculate. Is a high (low) academic self-concept the *cause* of good (poor) grades or the *result* of them? Explain your position.

Fink Article

1. In what ways is this study similar to the Brookover investigation? How does it differ, particularly in methodology?
2. Why do you suppose the results clearly bear out the hypothesis for boys but less so for girls?

Shaw and Dutton Article

1. Examine again the characteristics found to typify the mothers of underachieving girls. How would you explain the fact that mothers like this are likely to have underachieving daughters?
2. Does this study support or refute the idea mentioned throughout this book that significant others act as a strong influence on behavior? Explain your answer.

Smith and Brahce

1. Do you think the results would have been the same if high school students had been used? Explain.
2. What does "internalization of the expectations of significant others" mean? Why do you suppose that some parents have such a hard time understanding that they must do more than *tell* their children to do better in school?
3. How is the idea behind this study related to the interactionist theories mentioned in the Brookover, Thomas, Paterson article? Do you feel that interactionists theories are useful for predicting and understanding human behavior? Why or why not?

Part IX

toward understanding self

1. The role of self-understanding in the prediction of behavior

CARL R. ROGERS, BILL L. KELL, AND HELEN MCNEIL

Reprinted from the *Journal of Consulting Psychology,* Vol. 12 (1948), 174-186, by permission of the senior author and the American Psychological Association.

What is the predictive power of an individual's understanding of himself? To what extent do one's attitudes about himself operate to influence his future behavior? The two investigations cited in this selection report the results of independent ratings made on the adjustment of delinquent children two years after a diagnostic study. The authors point to some interesting reasons why we need deeper research into the way in which the individual views himself, and the manner in which his personal view of experience influences behavior.

A number of years ago a study in prediction of the behavior and adjustment of delinquent adolescents was made by Kell (3) under the supervision of the senior author. The major finding of the study was so striking and so unexpected that the completed research was laid aside until it might be confirmed or disproved by additional work. Later Miss McNeil repeated the identical method of study on a new group of cases (4) with results which confirmed, though less strikingly, the same findings. It now appears appropriate to present these two studies in somewhat condensed form, together with some of the implications which they seem to have for clinical practice and personality research.

The Hypothesis

The hypothesis was the same in both studies. It was that given sufficient information concerning the factors which presumably enter into the determination of an individual's behavior, it should be possible to make ratings of these factors which would predict with some degree of accuracy the individual's later adjustment. More specifically, given information regarding an individual's heredity, physical condition, mental status, family environment, cultural background, social experience, educational experience, and self-insight, it should be possible to rate these factors as to their favorableness for normal development, and on the basis of these ratings, predict future adjustment. If behavior is caused by factors such as those listed then an evaluation of such factors should provide a basis for estimating the type of behavioral adjustment which is likely to ensue.

The Plan of the Studies

The plan of both studies was identical and contained the following general elements.

1. To select a group of delinquent children for whom there was an adequate amount of diagnostic information, and follow-up reports of adjustment covering a period of approximately two years following the initial study.

2. To make ratings of the various factors which might determine behavior, by means of the so-called "Component Factor Method" (described below), these ratings to be entirely on the basis of information available at the time of the initial study, without any reference to the follow-up data.

3. To make independent ratings of the adjustment of the individual two years after the diagnostic study, these ratings to be made without reference to the information obtained in the diagnostic evaluation.

4. To analyze the material for possible correlations between each component factor and later adjustment, also for correlations between all the factors taken together and later adjustment. To consider whether the behavior of these delinquents might have been in any way predicted by this method, from the information available at the time of the initial study.

The way in which these steps were carried out is presented in some detail in the sections which follow.

The Selection of the Groups

The cases which were used in this study were obtained from the files of the Bureau of Juvenile Research, Columbus, Ohio, and it was due to the wholehearted cooperation of this organization that the research was possible. The procedure was as follows. Mr. Kell went over a few cases to see whether the information contained in the case histories and in the follow-up files was adequate for the type of analysis which he wished to make. It appeared that in many cases the information was adequate for his purposes. None of these preliminary cases was used in the research. He then took 155 cases which had been studied by the BJR after June 1937, and on which there was reported to be follow-up information two to three years after the diagnostic study. Cases were selected at random except that there was some perusal of the follow-up reports to make sure that both failures and successes in adjustment were being included. This was the only contact with the follow-up reports prior to the specific study of the follow-up material reported later.

When the Component Factor ratings were made on these 155 cases, it was found that the information was inadequate in 71 cases, and these were dropped. In making the ratings on follow-up adjustment, information was found to be inadequate in 9 additional cases, thus bringing the total number included in the research to 75. It does not appear that lack of information in the case record would be a selective factor related to the problems being studied in this research.

In the study made by Miss McNeil, 141 cases were initially selected, the criteria being similar, with the added item that they should all be new cases which had not been utilized in the Kell study. She found it necessary to drop out 65 cases because of inadequate information, thus leaving 76 individuals in her group. Thus in the two studies taken together there are 151 individuals on whom the reported findings are based.

Certain general facts about the two groups are listed in Table 1.

TABLE 1

CHARACTERISTICS OF THE GROUPS INCLUDED IN THE KELL AND MCNEIL STUDIES

Characteristic	*Kell's group*	*McNeil's group*
Average age at time of diagnostic study	15-2	14-6
Range in age	8-9 to 17-11	7-9 to 18-1
Number of boys	57	59
Number of girls	18	17
Whites	65	66
Negroes	10	10
Average I.Q.	94	90
Range in I.Q.	45 to 136	41 to 140
From rural homes	unknown	9
From urban homes	unknown	67

In an analysis made of Miss McNeil's group it was found that the behavior difficulties were those that we have come to regard as typical of a juvenile delinquent group—stealing, truancy from school and home, incorrigible behavior, untruthfulness, and sex misdemeanors heading the list of complaints. There were 27 of the group who had previously been in court. Broken and discordant homes were the rule, and more than half of the group had had some foster home or institutional experience away from their own home. In general it may be said that the adolescents included in the study appear to be typical of individuals coming to a juvenile court or behavior clinic.

The Rating of Component Factors

When the groups had been selected the next step was to rate those factors in the child's background and experience which might presumably be related to future behavior and adjustment. For this purpose the component factor method of case analysis, devised by Rogers and the staff of the Rochester Guidance Center, and described in an earlier publication (5, ch. 3) was used. Since the findings are in terms of the categories used in this device, some description of it is given here, though for a full account of its development or its use in other research (3, 2), the reader is referred elsewhere.

The rationale behind this method of rating and analysis, and a brief description of the method, is given by Rogers in the following statement:

> Behavior problems are due to the fact that a child of certain hereditary equipment is dealt with in a certain manner by members of his family environment and at the same time affected by certain broader cultural and social influences. If any one of these elements is altered, the behavior picture is also altered. To understand behavior we must view it as the complex result of all these component factors. Thus in the method under consideration, the forces which have operated in the child's experience are grouped under eight factors, defined so far as possible in terms which will have general understanding. Each of these factors . . . is rated in the case of the individual child on a seven-point scale, ranging from influences which are destructive to the child's welfare, to conditions and forces ideal for the child's adjustment. This rating scale is made more objective by means of sample ratings, with experimentally determined values, set up as guideposts (5, pp. 40-41).

The eight factors which are to be rated on the basis of material in the case history are defined in specific terms. For each factor there are also a series of illustrative ratings, taken from cases, and showing the average scale value which was given to the material by six clinician judges. The definitions to be kept in mind by the rater are stated below as given in the original description by Rogers, and as used by Kell and McNeil in these studies. In the interests of brevity the illustrative ratings have been omitted, except for the family factor, the factor of social experience, and the factor of self-insight. These are included to show the type of guide which was available to the rater.

Rating on hereditary factor

Consider the child's strain of inheritance, as evidenced by parents, relatives, siblings; hereditary predisposition to disease; feeble-mindedness, epilepsy, or psychoses in the ancestry; evidence of neuroses or physical or emotional instability in the ancestry; marked social inadequacy in the ancestry as shown by chronic alcoholism, repeated jail terms. On the constructive side consider freedom from disease and taints and marked social adequacy.

Rating on physical factors

Consider the child's inherited physical and neurological constitution; his physical development, size, and weight in relation to norm; physical defects, inferiorities, or abnormalities; glandular dysfunction; physical instability, nervousness, hyperactivity; disease history, with special attention to long periods of illness, or diseases such as tuberculosis, epilepsy, encephalitis, venereal disease, chorea; defects of the special senses. On the constructive side consider freedom from illness or defects, superior physique.

Rating on mentality factor

Consider the child's mental capacities as shown by his development, intelligence test ratings, school achievement, vocational achievement. Consider special abilities and disabilities which have a bearing on his mental functioning. Consider the quality of his intelligence, alertness, persistence, ability to concentrate.

Rating on family influences

Consider the family circle within which the child has developed—the attitudes which have surrounded him. Consider the emotional atmosphere within the home—marital discord or harmony, sibling rivalries, attitudes of domination, oversolicitude, rejection, or normal parental love. Frictions or conflicts in regard to illegitimacy or other family irregularity. The child's reaction to the home is also to be considered—reactions toward parents and siblings, toward family standards and discipline. Degree of community of interests with other members of the family.

Illustrative ratings—family

—3 Mother quite openly immoral; father a weak individual who plays little part at home except when drunk when there are terrific quarrels. Mother controls children by beatings. They are at least partially aware of her immorality.

—2 Parents not congenial; whole home dominated by father who is rigid, puritanical, and uses excessive discipline. He favors daughter and rejects this boy. Home atmosphere very tense. Mother furtively takes the boy's side.

—1 Father died when child in infancy. Mother centers all her attention and affection on this only child. Mother is extremely oversolicitous and overindulgent, and has few outside interests.

0 This boy is somewhat his father's favorite, and being the oldest child, tends to dominate his younger sibs. Parents are both interested in the home, seem happy together, and have a great deal of affection for their children.

+3 Parents are very congenial. Family atmosphere harmonious and pleasant. Many special interests and activities fostered by parents. Children encouraged to develop independence. This child feels very secure in the parental affection.

Rating on economic and cultural influences

Consider the family income, status of father's occupation, social standing in the community, degree of comfort and educative influences within the home; consider the community type—whether delinquency area, residential area, rural area; consider the community standards of behavior and culture; the school, libraries, and recreational resources available.

Rating on the social factor

Consider range and extent of child's social experience; isolation or group contacts; the type of companions available; the social skills the child has achieved considered in relation to his age; experience in group membership and leadership; organizing ability and social initiative; status in the schoolroom group; friendships with own and opposite sex, considered in relation to age; social relationships with adults; social adjustment to the neighborhood and community; general social maturity or lack of it.

ILLUSTRATIVE RATINGS—SOCIAL

—3 This child is the sissy of the neighborhood—picked on by other boys, unhappy when with them. At school gets on satisfactorily, is well liked by the teacher, has trouble at recess. Has no real friends, but spends most of his free time with his sister three years younger.

—2 Child has always been kept from much contact with other children; in a group is shy, backward, cannot play games; has two friends younger than self; gets on easily with adults.

—1 This girl belongs to a YW club, attends irregularly, prefers to stay by herself and read; is a passively accepted individual in the schoolroom; has some companions in the neighborhood but no close friends.

0 Boy 13, belongs to no organized club or gang. He has one chum with whom he goes to the movies, builds model planes, *etc.* Friendly with his school and neighborhood group. Plays on corner lot when urged by the group.

+1 Boy 12, enthusiastic Scout, member of his grade team at school, lives in isolated home, and has few neighborhood companions, goes to visit one of his Scout friends frequently. Is fair in baseball and swimming.

+3 This girl is president of her high school class, popular at parties, interested in boys, has a girl chum who has been her companion for years; has taken an active part in school athletics.

RATING ON EDUCATION, TRAINING, AND SUPERVISION

Consider the education, training, and supervision the child has had outside the home. Ordinarily this will mean primarily his school experience. Consider such things as the type of school which the child has attended; the changes of school; the continuity and consistency of school experience; consistency of discipline, both in school and between home and school; the degree of healthy stimulation, the extent to which tasks have been adapted to ability; the insight shown by teachers and school authorities; the behavior ideals actually inculcated; the cooperation and similarity of viewpoint betwen home and school.

RATNG ON SELF-INSIGHT

Consider in relation to the norm for his age, the degree to which the child has or lacks understanding of his own situation and problems; consider such things as defensiveness; inability to admit faults, or tendency to depreciate self and exaggerate faults. Consider not only intellectual understanding of problem but emotional acceptance of the reality situation. Consider child's planfulness and willingness to take responsibility for self; ability to be objectively self-critical. Consider stability of attitudes—whether erratic and changeable or cautious and settled.

ILLUSTRATIVE RATINGS—INSIGHT

—3 This girl blames everyone else for her trouble and readily excuses herself. She will not face the fact that her situation is serious, and has a breezy optimism entirely unrelated to reality.

—1 (or —2) This boy's sex behavior indicates real mental conflict. He can give a fair verbal account of the cause of his behavior, but his actions are little influenced.

0 This boy has a rather inadequate knowledge of his own assets and liabilities; he has thought only a very little about his own future; he realizes to some extent the fact that his parents tend to keep him childish. He shows no serious behavior problems.

+2 (or +3) Living in a most unhappy home situation, this boy makes calm judgments as to the degree to which he and his stepfather are to blame, and helps make plans for his own future, away from home, on a carefully reasoned basis (5, pp. 378-383).

In view of some of the findings to be presented later it should be pointed out that in the development of this instrument, the factor of self-insight was added rather apologetically at the end of the list. Says Rogers, in introducing a discussion of this factor, "The seven factors which have been described would seem to be the basic elements which, coming together in complex fashion, determine the behavior of the individual. For the young child an evaluation of these factors should be sufficient to gain an understanding of the child's reactions. With the older child, however, the attitudes which he holds toward himself and his behavior are decidedly significant and worthy of evaluation. That these attitudes are formed by the interaction of the other factors in the child's experience is undoubtedly true, but they also operate as an important influence to shape his future behavior" (5, pp. 48-49).

Using this component factor instrument as described, Kell and McNeil rated each of the eight factors for each of the subjects in their groups. The material on which the ratings were based was the initial diagnostic study of the child made while he was at the Bureau of Juvenile Research. This material included written case histories, psychometric examinations, interviews with the child by a psychologist or psychiatrist, or both, report of physical examination, and other similar information. The only materials which were not used in making the rating judgments were the over-all diagnostic report compiled by the Bureau, and the follow-up information. The former was excluded because it was felt the ratings should be made on the basis of the material itself, rather than on someone's interpretation of that material. The follow-up information was of course excluded because it was to be rated independently.

No measure of the reliability of the ratings in the present studies was made, but it has been shown by Rogers that the degree of reliability in the clinical use of these rating scales may be expressed by the statement that in rating specific items, the standard deviation of clinician's judgments ranges from .3 to .6 of a scale step, with heredity and mentality showing the highest reliability, and family and self-insight factors the lowest. When six clinicians rated five cases (rather than specific items from cases) on every factor, the reliability was somewhat lower, 66 per cent of the judgments being in agreement within two scale steps on the seven point scale (5, ch. 3).

The Rating of Later Adjustment

In order to provide an objective measure of the individual's later adjustment, with which the initial ratings might be correlated, Kell devised a scale for rating the behavior of the individual during the two- or three-year period following the diagnostic study. This too was a seven-point scale ranging from extremely poor adjustment to excellent adjustment. The typical characteristics which were set up for the different points on the scale are as follows.

RATING SCALE
OF FOLLOW-UP ADJUSTMENT

—3 Extremely poor adjustment. Individual in difficulties constantly. A confirmed delinquent or criminal. If institutionalized, makes an unsatisfactory adjustment there—fights continuously against regulations, disliked by other inmates, *etc.* If in own home, continually disrupts the family, a constant behavior problem at home and in school. Insane or extremely neurotic. Finds few, if any, normal satisfactions. No satisfactory adjustment in any situation.

—2 Poor adjustment. Continues in some delinquent or criminal activities, but does not seem hopeless. In court a number of times. Gains most satisfactions in an antisocial manner. If institutionalized, makes a partial adjustment to the institution's routine and regulations. If in own home, continues as a behavior problem most of the time, in conflict with school and may drop out. Cannot hold a job or function satisfactorily at one. May adjust satisfactorily in a few situations. Seems quite neurotic. Cannot adjust in foster home.

—1 Near average adjustment. Continues in a few delinquent activities. May be in court once or twice. If institutionalized, makes a satisfactory adjustment and shows evidence of adjusting outside the institution. If in own home, continues as a problem, but not as a severe one. Continues as a school problem, but makes some progress. May be able to hold a job, but does not function too well at it. May exhibit some neurotic symptoms which have a slight effect on total adjustment. May have to be placed in several foster homes, but finally makes a fairly satisfactory adjustment. Adjusts in some situations and not in others.

0 Average adjustment. In few, if any, delinquencies. May be in court once for minor delinquencies and then released. Neurotic tendencies mild and have little effect on total adjustment. Makes a satisfactory adjustment in the home—may have a few minor family difficulties. Makes average progress in school in relation to ability. Makes satisfactory adjustment in foster home. Is able to hold a job, but is not exceptional at it. Adjusts in most situations.

+1 Above average adjustment. Never in court again. Delinquent tendencies, if any, must be so mild that he is never in any serious difficulty. No evident neurotic symptoms. Very little aggressive, antisocial behavior. Makes a good adjustment to the family situation if returned home. Makes good progress in school. Does quite well on a job. Makes a good foster home adjustment. Adjusts in nearly all situations.

+2 Very good adjustment. Seems to make the best of nearly every situation. No evidence of any delinquent tendencies. No antisocial behavior. Makes a good school adjustment. Does very well on a job. Never any evident conflict with family if returned home. Makes a very satisfactory foster home adjustment.

+3 Excellent adjustment. Makes the best of every situation. Never any question of stability or antisocial trends. Seems to make best possible adjustment to family. Excellent adjustment in school, college indicated, *etc.* Makes excellent progress on a job. Foster home adjustment the best possible (3, pp. 26-27).

Using this rating scale Kell and McNeil turned to the follow-up reports of the cases in their respective groups, and, without reference to the diagnostic study, evaluated the two to three years of behavior which were described in the follow-up material. This material was made up of reports from probation officers, social workers, and institution officials.

To illustrate the range of later adjustments which were found in the group, and the use of the rating scale on adjustments, Kell's notes abstracting the follow-up reports on three cases, and the ratings assigned to these cases, are given below:

> —3 Ran away from foster home. Committed to Boys' Industrial School for stealing. Later released. Practiced sex perversion. Committed to Massillon State Hospital—ran away from there. Very poor present adjustment. Continuing sex perversion.
>
> 0 Girl made a fair adjustment in first foster home. Did not get along well in second and third foster homes. Later made a good adjustment in a fourth foster home. Now married. Apparently is doing well.
>
> +2 Boy has graduated from high school with good marks. Now employed as a blueprint reader at $40.00 per week. Adjustment very good. Says, "BJR is the best thing that ever happened to me" (3, pp. 28-29).

A word is in order in regard to the experiences of these children during the follow-up period. It is fortunate for the purposes of this study (though not for the children) that very little in the way of intensive casework or psychotherapy was utilized in the treatment of these delinquents. We say that this is fortunate for the study, because obviously the aim of all treatment is to defeat the statistical probabilities involved in prediction. That is, the caseworker or therapist in working with a person is endeavoring to alter the behavior which would objectively be predicted for this individual, and thus is hoping to make the prediction an erroneous one. The only type of treatment recommendations which were apt to be carried out in the group under study were the recommendations that the child be placed on probation, or placed in a foster home or institution. There is no way of measuring or indicating the amount of treatment effort invested in these children. It may be said, however, that the amount was relatively small, and that if one grants any efficacy to treatment effort then in so far as this study is concerned, it would only act to reduce the accuracy of behavioral prediction. In other words, whatever predictive accuracy is achieved by the method used, it is safe to say that it would have been greater had no treatment of any kind been attempted.

Findings

We are now ready to consider the analysis of the data collected. It should be clear that for each child in the two groups we have a rating on each of eight factors as to the extent to which those factors are likely to produce normal or well adjusted behavior. These ratings were made on the basis of information available at the time the child came to the BJR.

We have also independent ratings of the child's adjustment during the two-year period following the initial study. The major aspect of the analysis consists in the correlation of these predictive judgments with the evaluations of actual behavior.

The first finding of significance is that all the predictive factors which were rated showed a positive correlation with later adjustment. That is the child with good heredity, or good health, or favorable family environment, *etc.*, is more likely to display normal and well-adjusted behavior during the two-year period following the study than is the child who is less favored in any of these respects. This would tend to support the general hypothesis that behavior is the result of multiple causation, and that the factors which were selected for study are at least some of the effective elements which seem to determine adjustment or maladjustment.

TABLE 2

CORRELATION OF RATINGS ON COMPONENT FACTORS WITH RATINGS OF LATER ADJUSTMENT

	Correlations with adjustment	
Factor	*Kell study* $N = 75$	*McNeil study* $N = 76$
Self-insight	.84**	.41**
Social experience	.55**	.36**
Mentality	.39**	.15
Hereditary	.37**	.23*
Family environment	.36**	.14
Economic and cultural	.28*	.07
Physical	.25*	.13
Education and training	.11	.20
Total averaged ratings	.66**	.27*

*These correlations are significant at the 5 per cent lecel of confidence.
**These correlations are significant at the 1 per cent level of confidence.

But the unexpected finding which gives quite a different meaning to this material is the predictive importance of the individual's understanding of himself. As will be seen from Table 2, the correlation between self-insight and later adjustment was .84, an unusually high relationship for material of this sort. It was this surprising finding which lead the investigators first to check the data for possible errors and finally to lay it aside until it could be thoroughly rechecked on a new group. In the McNeil study, all the correlations are consistently lower, a puzzling fact which we have been unable to explain, but self-insight again comes out as the best predictor of behavior, correlating .41 with outcome.

In both studies the factor which was second in predictive significance was the social experience and social adequacy of the child. The respective correlations were .55 and .36, both statistically significant. The relationship between the other factors and adjustment was positive, but lower than these two, with the McNeil study finding lower significance for the factors of mentality and economic-cultural influence, and somewhat higher weight for education and training, when her results are compared with those of Kell.

As would be expected, when the various ratings on the separate factors were averaged, they correlated positively with outcome, *r*'s of .66 and .27 respectively being obtained in the two studies. This represents a questionable method of prediction, where the factors obviously have different weightings.

The material from Table 2 may be summarized by stating that in predicting the behavior of a problem adolescent, the extent to which he faces and accepts himself, and has a realistic view of himself and reality, provides, of the factors studied, the best estimate of his future adjustment. The second best predictor would be the satisfactoriness of his social contacts, the adequacy of his social relationships. These two are outstandingly better bases of prediction than any of the other factors studied, but positive correlation with later adjustments is found in ratings of the hereditary stock from which the individual has sprung; his mentality and mental functioning; the emotional climate of his family environment; his physical condition and health; and finally the economic, cultural, and educational influences to which he has been exposed. These factors would be of predictive significance roughly in the order named.

FURTHER ANALYSIS RELATED TO SELF-INSIGHT

Since the factor which had most doubtfully been included in the Component Factor method proved to correlate most highly with outcome, special attention will be given to its analysis.

In the first place, the reader may wish to know the type of material upon which the ratings were based. Here are some of the summarized notes from the two investigators' records, indicating the material relating to self-insight which was found in the cases, and the rating based upon it.

—3 Refuses to discuss his delinquencies; will not or cannot discuss problems arising out of family conflicts; denies his share of responsibility even when confronted with the facts (4, p. 34).

—2 Quite frank and open in discussing her misbehavior, but stories are unreliable. Is proud of her misbehavior—does not feel responsible. Does not recognize that family situation is the cause of much of her trouble (3, p. 20).

—1 Cautious, fairly truthful, correcting statements on own initiative. Feels some responsibility, realizing he is too easily influenced. Makes no complaints about the family but appears to understand somewhat its poor influence (4, p. 35).

+1 Understands his home situation fairly well, not clear about his relationship to it. Recognizes source of difficulties, but needs help in managing them. Admits his delinquencies truthfully with something similar to "They were not to blame. I was on the wrong track" (4, p. 35).

+2 Freely admits her delinquencies, recognizing and accepting the basis of parental antagonism and rejection. Planful and cooperative. Responsible when placed on her own. Tells facts frankly, recognizes and understands mother's instability and her own need for personal responsibility. Responsive and cooperative in behavior and in making future plans (4, p. 35).

These examples may be sufficient to indicate the rather crude character of the material available for making this as well as the other ratings. If such significant correlations are achieved on the basis of general case material, the possibility is at least suggested that more refined ways of investigating the degree of self-understanding might give even more significant results.

Since both self-insight and the social factor gave high correlations with outcome, it was thought wise to investigate the degree of relationship between these two factors. In the Kell group the correlation between the ratings on self-insight and the ratings on the social factor was .66, in the McNeil group .63. This is a high degree of interrelationship which does not seem to be explainable on the basis of similarity of definitions of the two factors, or similarity of the material being rated. For example, the notes from three cases as to the social factor, with their respective ratings, are as follows.

—3 Does not get along well with sibs or school companions. Quarrelsome. Mistreats other children, and cruel to small children and animals. Not successful in trial social adjustment opportunities.

0 Somewhat of a leader among the older delinquent boys. Has a passable manner, likes sports, likes to impress the girls.

+2 Plays on a team. Friends are not delinquents. Good mixer, liked by others in the neighborhood and school. Has a good stamp collection. Has three very close friends (4, pp. 35-36).

There would seem to be no obvious reason why ratings based on this type of data should correlate closely with ratings made on self-insight. It would seem that the relationship may be of a more underlying nature.

In another attempt to analyze the meaning of the high correlation of the self-insight factor with later adjustment, this correlation was separately computed for boys and girls, and for Negroes and whites. The differences were not striking, and some of the groups were small, but in both studies the correlation was higher for the girls than for the boys, and for the Negroes than for the whites.

Another line of investigation gave special consideration to those children who remained in their own homes during the follow-up period. It had been a surprise to the investigators that family environment had not correlated highly with outcome, and that self-understanding had correlated so highly. As the material was examined, it appeared possible that the fact that a sizable number of children from the poorest homes had been removed from their own families as a result of the diagnostic study might have influenced these results. Consequently both Kell and McNeil selected from their groups those children who had been returned to their own homes during the follow-up period. They also endeavored to determine whether the factor of self-insight was less operative when the home conditions were very unfavorable, by selecting out those with family factors rated —2 or —3, who had been returned to these very unfavorable homes.

TABLE 3

THE CORRELATION OF SELF-INSIGHT WITH ADJUSTMENT AMONG CHILDREN RETURNED TO THEIR OWN HOMES

	Kell's study		*McNeil's study*	
Group	*N*	*r*	*N*	*r*
Children whose family environment was rated −2 or −3	28	.76*	28	.31
Children whose family environment was rated −1 or 0	15	.78*	12	.49
All children returned to their own homes	43	.79*	47	.43*

*Significant at the 1 per cent level of confidence.

The results are shown in Table 3. It will be seen that the correlation between insight and later adjustment is relatively unchanged, even when the child comes from and returns to, a very unfavorable home situation. It is still true that a much better prediction of adjustment can be based upon a consideration of the degree of self-understanding, than upon any analysis of the home environment. McNeil further checked this by correlating the family environment factor with later adjustment in the group of 47 children returned to their own homes. This *r* was .20. It is higher than the similar correlation for the group as a whole (.14 in her study), but much lower than the correlation of .43 between self-insight and later adjustment.

When the child is removed from his own home and placed in a foster home, the operation of self-insight as a predictor is enhanced. There were 10 children in Kell's group thus placed and 15 in McNeil's. The correlations between self-insight and later adjustment for these two small groups were .98 (!) and .54 respectively. Both of these correlations are significant, the first at the 1 per cent level and the second at the 5 per cent level, in spite of the small numbers involved.

Limitations of the findings

Since some of the findings of these studies appear to have considerable significance if they are confirmed by other research, it should be mentioned that they were uncovered in investigations which have certain flaws and limitations. Those limitations which are evident to the investigators will be briefly stated.

It is unfortunate that there is no study of the reliability of the component-factor ratings in these two studies. Knowledge of the degree of reliability present in a previous study does not entirely compensate for this. There is no study of the reliability of the ratings on final adjustment.

A more serious flaw is the fact that the same judge rated both the initial factors and the final adjustment, even though these ratings were made independently and some time apart. The investigator made some 600 ratings of individual factors in the 75 cases, then, without reference to these or to the material upon which they were based, made the ratings on the follow-up material. It would certainly be preferable to have another judge make these judgments. It may be said, however, that if there was any unconscious bias operating in this situation, it could not account for the surprising showing of the self-insight factor, since whatever bias existed was in the direction of supposing that the emotional climate of the family was probably the most influential factor in the determination of behavior.

Another limitation of the studies as a whole is the fact that the rating scales for the eight factors and also for the later adjustment are crude instruments lacking in the degree of refinement which would be desirable in objective research. The information in the case folders was also often lacking in the specificity which would be desirable.

These limitations are real, yet their operation would for the most part tend to reduce correlations. There would seem to be nothing in the design or conduct of the study which would explain the degree of relationship which was found between self-insight and adjustment.

There is one other element in the studies which deserves critical consideration, and that is the sharp difference in the correlations found by the two investigators. It appears from an examination of the data that it is not due to any difference in the range of the ratings, or to any statistical artifact which can be discovered. Whether it is due to a difference in clinical discrimination in making the ratings, or to some other cause, is unknown. As long as it is unexplained, it would appear that it might cover some unrecognized source of error.

Summary of the Findings

To recapitulate the findings of the two investigations:

1. The ratings of the eight factors specified in the component-factor method all showed a positive correlation with ratings of the individual's later adjustment, in the group of 151 cases studied.
2. The size of these correlations as found in the two studies differed sharply in amount, but there was a high degree of correspondence in the relative significance of the factors.
3. The rating of the individual's understanding and acceptance of himself and the reality situation was, in both studies, the best predictor of what his future adjustment would be.
4. In both studies the factor which was second in predictive capacity was the social experience and social adequacy of the individual.
5. In decreasing order, these factors were also found to have some capacity for prediction of future behavior: the heredity of the individual; his intellectual functioning; the emotional atmosphere which the child has experienced in the family; the economic and cultural conditions which have surrounded him; the quality and consistency of his educational environment.
6. A high degree of relationship was found between the rating on self-insight and the rating on social experience. This correlation does not appear to be explained on the basis of simple overlapping of materials rated, but may involve some deeper relationship between the two factors.
7. In the group of children who came from, and remained in, highly undesirable atmospheres, it was still true that the degree of self-understanding was the best predictor of adjustment, much better than an evaluation of the home influence itself.
8. In children who are removed from highly undesirable home atmosphere and placed in foster homes, the degree of self-understanding is a decidedly accurate predictor of future adjustment or maladjustment.

Implications of the Findings

Only gradually, as the clinical experience of the authors has pointed in the same direction as the results of this research, has the full significance of the foregoing findings been recognized and appreciated. Only as work in psychotherapy has driven home the importance of the individual's concept of himself and his relation to reality, and the close relationship between these perceptions and his behavior, have the findings of this research been understood. (See reference 6 for an expression of this line of thought.) It is another experience to illustrate that objective facts have little meaning until they fit, in some recognizable way, into our frame of reference.

If the present studies are confirmed in their central findings by further research, then there are three broad implications which deserve consideration. The first is the socially hopeful character of the findings. Studies in prediction based upon correlating isolated background facts with later adjustment seem uniformly depressing because they add up to the total conclusion that the more adverse the factors operating in the individual's life, the more hopeless he becomes, from any social point of view. The present studies do not flatly contradict this conclusion. It is true that a poor heredity and the presence of destructive organic factors, and a culturally deprived background, all predispose, to some degree, toward a less adequate adjustment. But the significant fact is that the element which above all others should be the most subject to natural change or planned alteration, the individual's acceptance of himself and of reality, is also the most important determiner of his future behavior. Rather than feeling that a person is inevitably doomed by unalterable forces which have shaped him, this study suggests that the most potent influence in his future behavior is one which is certainly alterable to some degree without any change in his physical or social heredity or in his present environment. The most powerful determinant would appear to lie in the attitudes of the person himself.

A second implication which should be mentioned is that the results of these studies would point toward a drastic revision of the methods of dealing with or treating individuals who exhibit delinquent or problem behavior. In the groups which were studied, and in other similar groups, practically all of the investment of money and effort is directed toward altering factors which appear to be only to a small degree determinative of behavior. Vast amounts are expended on foster homes and children's institutions in order to alter the child's whole environment, considerable amounts on probationary supervision which is little more than a checking-up on the youngster, considerable sums on the alleviation of physical deficiencies, but practically nothing on any direct approach to the problem of revising the child's attitudes toward himself. Likewise only a small fraction of the total treatment effort goes to changing the child's social adjustment, which appears to be second only to self-insight in its significance.

If treatment effort was to be expended in most efficient form, in the light of the results of this study, then effective psychotherapy, either individual or group, aimed at helping the child achieve a more realistic acceptance of his impulses and abilities, and a realistic appraisal of his situation, would be the major investment. Social experiences might need to be provided concurrently, or the psychotherapy might assist him in developing more constructively the social relationships which he has. In any event, it would not be the quantity of social contact, but the degree to which the individual built mature give-and-take relationships with others, which would be regarded as important. A distinctly lesser amount of effort might be expended in endeavoring to improve the family relationships, and the economic status. Some effort to enrich the cultural stimulation of the child might also be justified. The primary aim throughout would be to provide the opportunities for emotional release, insightful acceptance of self, and positive reorientation of self, which every successful psychotherapy entails. Such opportunities might be offered through the clinic, through the classroom with a specially trained teacher, through special school counseling services, or through group therapy carried on in conjunction with a recreational group. The whole focus of effort would be almost the reverse of the accepted procedures at the present time.

The final implication carried by the results of this study is that if the individual's view of himself and reality is so important—the degree of his defensiveness, the degree of acceptance of himself, his realistic appraisal of reality, his degree of independence and planfulness, his ability to be objectively self-critical—then a great deal of research is needed in this area. Studies are needed to discover how healthy perceptions of this sort occur, and the circumstances which cause the individual to become defensive and lacking in insight. We need much deeper research into the way in which the individual views himself, and the fashion in which his internal view of experience influences his behavior. Finally we need penetrating investigations of the ways in which such views of experience may be altered in the direction of realism and self-acceptance. Such research would move us forward a great distance in our knowledge of how to deal with those with behavior disorders.

References

1. Bennett, C. C., and C. R. Rogers, "Predicting the Outcomes of Treatment," *American Journal of Orthopsychiatry,* Vol. 11 (1941), pp. 210-221.
2. ———, and ———, "The Clinical Significance of Problem Syndromes," *American Journal of Orthopsychiatry,* Vol. 11 (1941), pp. 222-229.
3. Kell, B. L., *The Predictive Possibilities of the Component-Factor Method of Diagnosis as Applied to Children with Behavior Problems,* Unpublished Master's thesis, Ohio State University, 1942.
4. McNeil, Helen, *Factors Significantly Related to the Later Adjustment of Children Presenting Problem and Delinquent Behavior,* Unpublished Master's thesis, Ohio State University, 1944.
5. Rogers, C. R., *The Clinical Treatment of the Problem Child* (Boston: Houghton, 1939).
6. ———, "Some Observations on the Organization of Personality," *American Psychologist,* Vol. 2 (1947), pp. 358-368.

2. Self-understanding in childhood and adolescence [1]

Arthur T. Jersild

Reprinted from *American Psychologist,* Vol. 6 (1951), 122-126, by permission of the author and the American Psychological Association.

What part can schools play in the enhancement of self-understanding and self-acceptance? What implications are there in this notion for the way in which we train our teachers and design our curriculums? If self-understanding is to be more than a theoretical construct to be talked about in mystical terms, then it must represent an idea for research and education. Ways for implementing its researchable aspects and educational dimensions are suggested by Jersild.

Historically the psychology of childhood and adolescence has been a science which some psychologists try to teach to other psychologists and to college students. My theme today is that we have held too restricted a conception of what child psychology is and what it might be. The proper study for all human beings from the earliest possible age is the human being himself.

Every child is actually or potentially a child psychologist. From an early age, without being deliberate about it, he acquires ideas and attitudes about himself and others. These are woven into the pattern of his life. They may be true or false, healthy or morbid. Their development is left largely to chance. This is not as it should be, in my judgment. I propose that the study of child psychology, designed to

[1] Adapted from a presidential address given before the Division on Childhood and Adolescence, American Psychological Association, State College, Pennsylvania, September 7, 1950.

promote understanding and acceptance of self and understanding of others should be a planned feature of the education children receive from nursery school onward.

Need for Understanding

There is one gloomy fact about children who now are growing up which underscores, as I see it, the need for such a program. A large proportion of children will move into adulthood troubled and unhappy about many things. Many will be afflicted by irrational fears which do not represent dangers in the external environment but unresolved problems within themselves. Many, as adults, will suffer from attitudes of hostility, vindictiveness, and defensiveness which are not a response to hostile forces in the outside world but represent attitudes carried over from unresolved childhood struggles. Many persons similarly will acquire persisting feelings of inferiority or other unhealthy attitudes regarding their personal worth which represent either an irrational estimate of themselves or a failure to accept themselves realistically as they are.

In numerous ways there is a vast carry-over of unhealthy attitudes regarding self and others from childhood and adolescence into adult life.

Is so much distress inevitable? I do not think we have to assume that it is. But I do not think the picture can be changed substantially if we simply try to extend the special services we now provide. These services are good, and need to be continued. But the answer cannot be found simply by offering more psychological counseling, psychoanalysis, or other forms of treatment of the kind now provided for severely disturbed people after they already are on the rocks. A bolder measure is needed for the benefit of the population at large. This measure, I maintain, must involve a vastly enhanced conception of the social functions of research in child psychology and of the role that child psychology might play in the education of children.

The Underlying Hypothesis

There is a general hypothesis underlying this proposal and it is this: human beings, from an early age, have more capacity for learning to face and to understand and to deal constructively with the realities of life than we have hitherto assumed in our psychological theories or in our educational practices.

Current Evasion and Neglect of Self-Understanding

It is a curious thing that the subject of self-understanding has been so neglected when we consider how eager we are to teach other things. Children learn to bound the states of the Union and they memorize the names and dates of bygone wars; they study the habits of beavers, learn about the distant stars, and the antics of Mother Goose. But the subject of human behavior, human motives, and the inner life of man has been pretty much ignored.

Much of what we do in education is an evasion rather than a way of facing problems that occur in the lives of children and adolescents. I have recently been involved in a study of children's interests in which several thousand youngsters in various parts of this country participated (7). This study emphasizes, as some other studies have emphasized, that the interests children are induced to acquire often are superficial, stereotyped, and fail to lead the child on a road toward facing his real problems. However, we also found in this study that many of the older children expressed a desire to learn more about themselves and others, even though little was done in some of the schools they attended to encourage such a desire or to suggest that it might be fulfilled. What I propose is that we encourage this desire and try to fill it by developing a program to promote wholesome understanding of self and others as a basic feature of the general education of all children.

Implications of Self-Understanding

I have used expressions such as "self-understanding" and "self-acceptance" in describing my position. These particular words are not, in my judgment, as important as the intention and purpose which I am trying to express. But the concept of the self, especially as it has developed in recent literature in psychology [2] and in some of the newer theoretical formulations in psychiatry and psychoanalysis,[3] is a fruitful one in this connection.

---

[2] There is not space to properly acknowledge these contributions, but I would mention especially William James (*5*), and the later works of Mead (*9*), Murphy (*10*), Lecky (*8*), Rogers (*11*), and Snygg and Combs (*12*).

[3] I refer especially to the works of Horney (see *e.g., 3* and *4*), Harry Stack Sullivan (*13*), Allen (*1*), and Fromm (*2*).

I believe this to be true even though in the present state of our knowledge the meaning of "the self" can be defined only in arbitrary and tentative terms.

When we speak of "the self," we mean, among other things, a system of ideas, attitudes, appraisals, and commitments pertaining to one's own person. The person experiences these as distinctly belonging to him, and all of them together constitute the person's awareness of his individual existence and his conception of who and what he is. These attitudes and ideas are, of course, influenced by learning. This is an obvious but very crucial fact.

The self has been defined as a perceiver and a thing perceived, a knower and a thing that is known. Probably the self can best be studied if viewed as a composite.

I shall not try to list all the features of the composite. But I will mention some of the things which children and adolescents themselves report when they describe themselves. Recently my colleagues and I have gathered compositions from several hundred children from the fourth grade through high school on "What I like about myself" and "What I don't like about myself" and other themes pertaining to self-description or self-evaluation (6).

When evaluating and describing themselves, many children think, in part, of specific physical characteristics, including stature, facial features, posture, and bearing. (In passing I will mention that some of our preliminary data suggest that there is a great deal of irrational overrating, often in the form of self-disparagement, of physical characteristics during childhood.)

A very large proportion of children at all ages describe or appraise themselves favorably and unfavorably in terms of social criteria—their relations with people, their feelings about them, the attitudes others have toward them, and the attitudes they have toward others. Many children also assess their worth or worthlessness in terms of their relationship with their parents. Here again, as in connection with the development of other forms of self-appraisal, it appears that there are many possibilities for misinterpretation and irrational self-disparagement.

Also in the picture, according to our data, there may be attitudes which a person has concerning his inner resources, his talents, powers, and abilities; his weaknesses, his defects, shortcomings, past misdeeds, present impulses, and temptations; his role or roles in life; and his responsibilities; and (mainly at older levels) his anticipation of the future.

Some children emphasize awareness of religious affiliation and of moral obligations, and some mention commitment to values, goals, causes, which, as recognized by them, give content or direction to their individual ways of life.

Selfhood, in the literature, is often described by using "self" as part of a compound expression with modifiers which highlight one aspect or another of what the term denotes.

In the present context there are some modifiers that are particularly meaningful. We can distinguish, for example, between self-appraisal and appraisal by others and note that a person's self-estimation may be true or false or realistic or unrealistic when judged by group standards or by objective criteria. We can roughly distinguish between self-acceptance and self-rejection, as in the case of the person who lives comfortably with himself, or, by contrast, disparages himself or is ashamed of features in his past life or of his family background or is frightened by his present habits and impulses.

And to do a thorough job we would also have to try to distinguish between the "real self" and idealized or distorted versions of the self.

Needed Research

To carry out the program I am proposing, we would need a vast amount of new research.

We especially need to study self-development from a genetic point of view, with attention to normal trends and the influence of various experiences on this development. We need to find out what is the nature of the growing child's perception of himself and others. What concepts pertaining to understanding of self or others is he able to learn to use meaningfully and to apply? By what means is it possible to communicate with him? What are early symptoms and signs of false or morbid self-evaluation? These are only a few of the questions.

By way of an illustration or two: what is the approximate phase or level of development at which a child can appreciate the fact, say, that children who bully him are not simply unpleasant persons but troubled persons whose reproaches and adverse opinions should not lower his own self-esteem? At what juncture in his development might the child have the capacity for making allowances for others (or for himself) when they are peevish or irritable, or the ability to "see through" some of the arts and dodges, masquerades, concealments, and camouflages of human motives, including his own?

Another research need is the need for finding out how children can be helped to use their capacity for self-discovery and for understanding others. In the literature there already are some promising leads.

Professional and Practical Ramifications

The subject I am dealing with raises questions that have a bearing on the definition of what our Division stands for and on our professional affiliations within the APA. There is a crisscrossing here of what we normally think of as matters belonging to several divisions.

Usually we think of something in the teaching field as belonging primarily to educational psychology. But the basic research here required is definitely in the field of genetic and developmental psychology—that is, in our Division.

Much of the information we now have concerning the kinds of problems children face and their capacity for coping with them has come from case work in the branches of psychology and psychiatry which deal with psychotherapy and psychological counseling. But the scope of what would be involved in my proposal goes far beyond the population now reached by these professional groups and involves research that goes beyond the conception which some mental hygienists have concerning the nature of their work, although we will still need to retain special psychotherapeutic services for deeply disturbed children.

The aim in clinical psychology and psychiatry has largely been to help individuals who have failed to make a comfortable adjustment to the conditions of life. The aim in the program I propose is to help the growing person while he is in the process of adjusting to these conditions, including conditions within himself. The aim in psychotherapy, according to one school of thought, is to bring conscious processes to bear upon hidden or unconscious sources of conflict. The aim in the progrem here proposed would be to try to discover and apply ways of reducing the hiatus between conscious or unconscious factors in the growing person's experience, by trying to help him to develop to the fullest whatever capacity he may have for understanding and interpreting the events of life as they befall, his ability to deal as forthrightly and knowingly as possible with his own feelings and impulses as these come into play, his capacity for discovering his potentialities, for acquiring a realistic appreciation of his assets and limitations, and his capacity for developing goals that might enable him to be true to himself rather than seeking to conform to standards that are out of harmony with what he is or ever could hope to be.

Unanswered Questions

I am sure all of you have thought of questions or misgivings regarding this proposal. Perhaps the greatest skepticism concerning the capacity of children to gain psychological understanding through everyday educational experience, as distinct from special professional treatment, will be found among psychologists themselves.

One misgiving may be phrased in the claim that the business of facing reality in a happy way is more an emotional by-product than a job that can be achieved by a studied approach. People don't make themselves happy by studying how to be happy. We might also phrase a misgiving as follows: If a child already is unhappy or anxious, would it not be impossible for him, while in such a mood, to gain in self-understanding by way of anything the school might offer? And if he is quite happy and free from anxiety, is there any reason why he should try to understand himself? Does it not follow then that the proposal in the first instance is hopeless and, in the second instance, needless? Again, someone might claim that the intellect can do little at the adult level to influence basic attitudes and it perhaps is even more powerless at the childhood level.

I agree that the learning of psychology on an academic level alone is not likely to make much difference, if any. A person can possess a vast knowledge of psychological facts and principles and still be an unhappy neurotic. Yet I do believe that a discovery about self that is first perceived on an intellectual level can sometimes initiate a chain of reactions that have profound emotional consequences in a person's life. And, besides, what I here propose is not just an intellectual or academic approach. In attempting this program wc would have to recognize that the process of developing self-understanding involves all of the growing person's faculties for feeling and thinking.

The program would probably make much use of group projects as an aid to self-discovery and self-acceptance.

It would mean a greatly enhanced conception of the psychological possibilities inherent in a calculated use of present features of the school's program such as what is offered, for example, in physical education.

It would mean that each subject that is retained in the curriculum would be used, as far as feasible, as a vehicle for increased understanding of self or others. There is a rich psychological content, for example, in history and in the study of current events. If these subjects are properly scaled to the pupil's maturity level and if they are treated in realistic terms, they give play to a wide range of human motives, hopes, conflicts, and perplexities which the pupil can relate to some of the happenings in his own life.

While the program would definitely not be confined to academic learning, intellectual processes would certainly come into the picture. It is true that there are people in psychology who take a dim view of what the intellect can accomplish. Even those who have attached great importance to intelligence have sometimes underestimated the possibilities of intellectual growth. Actually, I don't believe we have begun to fathom what the human intellect can do.

In passing, I would add that, on the basis of limited observations, I have a hunch that the ability which enables a person to be wise to himself does not necessarily show a very high correlation with the kind of ability we measure by means of our common intelligence tests. From everyday observation it appears that a person can have a very high I.Q. and still thoroughly fool himself and that people with modest I.Q.'s sometimes achieve a very canny and healthy picture of themselves.

One can overrate rational processes, it is true, but it is also absurd to belittle the role intellectual or cognitive processes may play in giving structure to experiences as they occur in life and in modifying or reconstructing the effects of experiences that have occurred. A crucial feature in many of the emotional experiences that might influence a child's self-evaluation is the child's perception of what is happening—a perception which leads him to react to an event as a form of success or failure, as a threat or an affront or a source of joy.

The question as to ways in which rational processes and emotional reactions interact in the course of self-development and in the process of self-discovery, and the question as to the interplay between a person's intellectual insights and the attitudes which govern his life, would constitute an important feature of the research demanded by the hypothesis I set forth early in this paper. Certainly at the present stage of our knowledge it would be ill-timed to settle this question by concluding in advance that understanding and insight occur only as incidental by-products.

Another question is, assuming that we could learn in theory how to do all this, where could we find parents or teachers who could put the theory into practice? That is not easily answered. But I believe that this question represents a problem of research and education rather than a theoretical obstruction that dooms the idea in advance.

To carry out the program it would, of course, be necessary to give careful attention to the selection and training of teachers. Moreover, child study would be a crucial feature of the teacher's job and a very important consideration in the school budget.

We might also ask, is it really possible for parents and teachers and children to establish the kind of relationship out of which mutual understanding and self-understanding might develop? The parent or teacher is a disciplinarian, we are told. He holds authority. He cannot permit conditions from which understanding such as here described might evolve. But this view may be questioned. This question should be raised as a problem for study, not as a problem regarded in advance as one that either can't be solved or is bound to yield a negative answer.

It might also be maintained that it is dangerous for teachers, or parents, to dabble with psychology. They might damage a child's mind just as an amateur surgeon might damage a child's body. This point certainly deserves attention. But let us be realistic. Every hour, every day, millions of parents and thousands of teachers practice psychology and, in effect, teach psychology in their dealings with children whether they know it or not. They are involved in situations in which children meet success or failure, acceptance or rejection, and countless other circumstances in which children are discovering themselves and developing attitudes regarding themselves for better or for worse.

This does not mean that we must try to get parents and teachers to take over the functions which psychiatrists and clinical psychologists are now responsible for. At best, there will always be a limit to what a parent and teacher, no matter how well trained, can do in dealing with problems that arise in their relations with children who are in their immediate care from day to day. Actually, we need to learn more concerning the overlapping and the distinctive and exclusive roles of the parent and teacher, on the one hand, and the specialist in psychology or psychiatry, on the other. Among other matters, we also need more light on the question as to how, in the *education* of children, we might achieve some of the things which the psychological specialist tries to achieve in the *re-education* of his patients.

So I say, let us as far as possible bring the forces which now operate in darkness out into the light. Let us recognize that the most important psychological facts in a child's life are his relationships with others and his relationship to himself. These relationships are constantly in the process of development and are constantly involved in the learning that goes with the business of living. Learning which pertains to anything so crucial should properly be part of the child's planned education and indeed should, in my judgment, be regarded as the most important part of the educational program.

Each child is a student of human nature within the limits of his maturity level and what he has had an opportunity to learn. The home, the classroom, the playground, and other situations are psychological laboratories in which he is now a subject and now an observer. Child psychology will fully come into its own when it discovers the capacities children have for learning from these laboratories and explores the conditions under which these capacities can best be developed.

References

1. Allen, Frederick, *Psychotherapy with Children* (New York: Norton, 1942).

2. Fromm, Eric, *Man for Himself* (New York: Holt, Rinehart & Winston, 1947).
3. Horney, Karen, *The Neurotic Personality of Our Time* (New York: Norton, 1937).
4. ———, *Our Inner Conflicts* (New York: Norton, 1945).[a]
5. James, William, *Principles of Psychology* (New York: Holt, Rinehart & Winston, 1890).
6. Jersild, Arthur T., *Self-Evaluation During Childhood and Adolescence: A Preliminary Study* (Unpublished).
7. ———, and Ruth Tasch, *Children's Interests* (New York: Bureau of Publications, Teachers College, Columbia University, 1949).
8. Lecky, Prescott, *Self-Consistency* (Fort Myers Beach, Fla.: Island, 1945).
9. Mead, George, *Mind, Self and Society* (Chicago: U. of Chicago, 1934).
10. Murphy, Gardner, *Personality* (New York: Harper, 1947).
11. Rogers, Carl, *Counseling and Psychotherapy* (Boston: Houghton, 1942).
12. Snygg, Donald, and Arthur Combs, *Individual Behavior* (New York: Harper, 1949).
13. Sullivan, Harry Stack, *Conceptions of Modern Psychiatry* (Washington, D.C.: The William Alanson White Psychiatric Foundation, 1947).

---

[a] A more comprehensive statement of Karen Horney's position was published after this address was written. See K. Horney, *Neurosis and Human Growth* (New York: Norton, 1950).

3. The search for meaning

ARTHUR T. JERSILD

In the previous article Jersild suggested that schools have a distinct responsibility for assisting students not only to know *but to* be. *If we agree that achieving greater self-understanding must ultimately involve finding greater meaning, then there are definite implications here for how teachers can enhance the "meaning" of subject matter to their students. How do teachers encourage "meaning"? Indeed, what dimensions are there to "meaningless"? Jersild examines these and related questions in this sensitive excerpt.*

The search for meaning is essentially a search for self. Meaning constitutes, in many respects, the substance of the self.

Where there is meaning, there is involvement. When something has meaning, one is committed to it. Where there is meaning, there is conviction. Such commitment and conviction is something different from conformity, or merely playing a part, or living as a cog in a machine, or losing one's individuality in what Kierkegaard has called the "featureless crowd." Where meaning is lacking in one's work as a teacher, the self is uninvolved. The substance is lacking, and teaching is just an empty formality.

The problem of meaninglessness overlaps in many ways the problems of anxiety and loneliness. It is largely by virtue of a lack of meaning—a kind of emotional emptiness that prevails when things don't matter—that the lonely person feels lonely. It is partly because of a lack of meaning or a distortion of meaning such as is found in pretenses and inner disharmonies that the anxious person is anxious.

About 60 per cent of the people responding to the Personal Issues Inventory * indicated that meaninglessness was a problem on which they would like to have help in understanding themselves. In expressing this problem, many said they were not sure what they wanted from life—what it was important to be or do or get from life; some said that what they were doing or what was happening didn't seem to mean much; some said they saw little or no meaning in many of the things they had to learn or teach. Some expressed meaninglessness by default, so to speak, indicating that they got involved in so many activities and responsibilities that they had little time for themselves.

The need for helping children and grown men and women to face and find something essentially meaningful glares at us from headlines telling of tensions in the world we live in. Man has made fabulous progress in exploring the external dimensions of his world and in controlling its physical properties, but this power has not been matched by a cultivation of his courage to draw upon other resources of his humanity. We are frightened lest he use his power to destroy himself. Modern man, for all his contrivances, is still as much in need of finding himself and facing the meaning of his existence as he was many eras ago. No invention in science or gimmick in education can obviate the necessity for this search.

The problem of meaninglessness—which Tillich has referred to as the anxiety of emptiness and the anxiety of meaninglessness—prevails not simply among teachers and their captive pupils. Meaninglessness is a common condition in college and graduate teaching. Much of what goes on in the name of learning is simply an academic enterprise. Even religion, as has been pointed out earlier, can be pursued in a meaningless way.

Education and the Search for Meaning

The crucial test in the search for meaning in education is the *personal implication* of what we learn and teach. In some educational circles this will sound strange, for it often seems to be assumed that a body of information is in itself meaningful.

If we as educators are to face the problem of meaninglessness, we must make an effort to conduct education in depth—to move toward something that is personally significant beyond the facade of facts, subject matter, logic, and reason behind which human motives and a person's real struggles and strivings are often concealed. This does not mean the rejection of

---

* The reader will find a complete breakdown of this inventory in the original source of this article, pp. 149-163 (Ed. Note).

subject matter—far from it—but it does mean helping the learner to relate himself to what he is learning and to fit what he learns into the fabric of his life in a meaningful way.

Such an endeavor means an effort to overcome the prevailing tendency in education to encourage the learner to understand everything except himself.

It means an effort to achieve a better integration of thinking and feeling on the part of both children and adults.

It means an effort to cut through the pretense of "interest" in learning, which children and adults so widely adopt in order to conform or to escape disapproval from their elders. It means also that the process of learning will not be used as a means of competing with others and gaining power over them.

Actually, each subject that is taught in elementary or high school or college could, in one way or another, for certain learners, be deeply charged with meaning. Each subject could, in one way or another, help some young person discover his skills and explore or use his resources.

The study of history, to give only one example, can be an intensely meaningful experience, for history is filled with the substance of human hopes and fears: man's struggles, his pride, his shame, his courage, his joy. Much of history—perhaps all—can be taught in such a way that there is a direct line of emotional and intellectual communication from historical characters and actions to the intimate personal lives of the learners.

The same is true with respect to literature and all other academic subjects. It is certainly true with respect to physical education and all the arts, skills, and crafts, for each of these enterprises can be undertaken in a manner that has a direct and immediate personal implication.

But instead, much of what teachers have to learn, much of what they have to teach, and much of what the millions of pupils who attend our schools are compelled to study is not meaningful but meaningless, largely because we have assumed that knowledge has value apart from its meaning for the one who acquires it. When we consider the problem of meaninglessness, it is not extreme to say that one of the basic troubles in education is that as educators we have not had the courage to face the personal implications of our calling.

Helping Others Through Facing Oneself

To help a pupil to have meaningful experiences, a teacher must know the pupil as a person. This means, as has been repeatedly emphasized in this book, that the teacher must strive to know himself.

In the school there are countless opportunities for helping the child in his search to find himself. He can be helped to discover his aptitudes and abilities, to face some of his inner difficulties, and to realize his limits. What the teacher does strongly affects the pupil's attitudes regarding his worth as a person since, as has been noted, life at school is heavily invested with praise and blame, pride and shame, acceptance and rejection, success and failure. Everything in the relation between a teacher and a student has or might have a significant effect on what a child thinks and feels about himself.

To have insight into the child's strivings and the problems he faces, the teacher must strive to face the same problems within his own life. These problems are largely emotional in nature.

To be able to understand and sympathize with a child who is hostile (and all children are, more or less), the teacher must face his own hostile tendencies and try to accept the implications of his anger as it occurs, say, in his annoyance with his pupils, in his impatience with himself, and in his feuds with other teachers.

He must seek to understand the devices he uses to avoid responsibility for himself by blaming others.

To appreciate another's fears, a person must try to examine his own fears. He must face them as they appear in his phobias, squeamishness, fear of misfortune, timidity, uncertainties, unwillingness to take a chance, worry concerning what others may think of him.

Unless a teacher can, at least to some extent, face his own anxiety, he will be uncomprehending when children helplessly express theirs. He may be harsh when children's anxieties break through in such signs as inability to learn, impertinence, inattentiveness, restlessness, irritability, and the like.

A teacher's understanding of others can be only as deep as the wisdom he possesses when he looks inward upon himself. The more genuinely he seeks to face the problems of his own life, the more he will be able to realize his kinship with others, whether they are younger or older, like him or unlike him in education, wealth, religion, or professional rank.

How does one achieve understanding of self?

One broad principle is this: *To gain in knowledge of self, one must have the courage to seek it and the humility to accept what one may find.* If one has such courage and such humility, one can seek professional help and one can draw on many resources in everyday life.

One can learn from experience of life's joys and tragedies. One can profit from trying to catch the meaning of one's anger, joy, depression, fear, desire to inflict pain, and so forth.

A valuable help in self-examination, which may be mainly intellectual but may also strike at a deep emotional level, is the reading of books written by compassionate people who have made some progress in their own painful struggle to know themselves.

The method of "participant observation" offers one means of taking a look at oneself. One records what one hears and sees and what one's feelings are as one listens in on a discussion or visits a class. Then, with the help of others, one examines this record and compares it with records kept by other observers. This comparison may show how what one notices is determined by habits of thought that are taken for granted. What one perceives "objectively" is often a projection of one's own subjective state, and thus may tell more about oneself than about the people one observes.

This broad principle also holds: *Just as it is within an interpersonal setting that one acquires most of the attitudes involved in one's view of oneself, so it is likely that only in an interpersonal setting can a person be helped to come to grips with some of the meanings of these attitudes.*

A relationship that can promote knowledge of self prevails when one seeks private therapy or joins with others in a group therapy situation.[1] It exists also, to some degree, whenever one enters into relationship with people in any walk of life who can help one gain perspective on oneself. In a group, a person may be helped to see his anger, fear, and protective devices as others see them. The way others express themselves or respond to him may help him perceive in a new and self-revealing light some of the evidences of shame, self-effacement, anxiety, vindictiveness, and other outcroppings of deep-seated attitudes of which ordinarily he is not aware. Similarly, to witness a mimicking of his conduct by a child or by a role-playing peer may throw some light on unrecognized conflicts.

Some of the richest possibilities for self-examination can be found in relationships with others from month to month and from year to year. In the teaching profession we have hardly begun to explore and to tap these resources for growth in self-knowledge, although some work is being done in this area. If people could encourage one another to come out from behind the curtain that commonly conceals their emotions from others

---

[1] In an earlier study in this series, a workshop consisting of teachers of psychology in the high school recommended that *all* high school teachers (not just psychology teachers) should be provided with such opportunities to grow in self-understanding as might be obtained through group therapy under the leadership of people professionally trained for such work. Such a proposal would involve many practical considerations that will not be discussed here, and it might not be an adequate solution for some people. It is mentioned here, however, to emphasize the point that many teachers recognize the need for help if they are to make full use of their personal and professional potentialities. As indicated in the first chapter, over 40 per cent of the people in a majority of the groups answering the questionnaire on self-understanding stated that they thought they would need personal help such as might be gotten from group therapy if they were to put the concept of self-understanding (which over 90 per cent endorsed) into practice in their professional work.

and from themselves, these emotions might be faced in an insight-producing way.

In a larger sense, particular procedures that are used for growing in self-understanding are less important than the courage to face this need. Self-knowledge can be acquired in many ways. It is not something that is attained once and for all. Those who are blind to themselves have a little of it, and a capacity to acquire more; and an outstanding mark of those who have acquired the deepest knowledge is that they still are seeking. No one procedure alone will give the answer, since the search for selfhood, when genuine, is pursued through all channels of experience as long as a person lives.

Facing the role of feeling in thinking

In the foregoing section the emphasis has been on the need for facing our own emotions if we are to make any progress in understanding the emotions of others. But there is a need for facing emotion also in dealing with what, on the surface, may seem to be the purely intellectual and academic aspects of the school's program. Much of what is called thinking is actually governed by undisclosed feelings. Logic is often ruled by desire; intellectual arguments are often the instruments of fear or anger. To the extent that this is true, the full meaning of what seems to be an intellectual discourse is not revealed or shared. To think straight, to communicate what we are thinking, and to think effectively about what someone else is trying to communicate, it is important to know how we feel, and how feeling influences our thoughts and the thoughts of others. It is necessary to take account of emotional factors in thinking if the intellect is to be given a chance to function freely.

We let our feelings govern the nature of our reasoning, without knowing that we are doing so, when we project our own bias onto a discussion of a historical issue, or a problem of discipline or scholarship, or a decision as to what courses a high school student *must* take to be allowed to go to college, *etc.,* without once asking ourselves: Is this really pure reasoning, or am I perhaps projecting my own prejudices or yielding in meek but compulsive compliance to what others have demanded?

During the presidential campaign of 1952 a forum was held whose avowed purpose was to try to inquire beneath the reasons people usually gave to others and to themselves for supporting one candidate or opposing another. The members of the forum were instructors and graduate students. It soon became apparent that it was very difficult for these people even to ask themselves: Is there *perhaps* an emotional reason, apart from the logical reasons I give, for my support of one candidate or bitter opposition to another? What, on an *emotional* level, does this campaign mean, and what do the candidates symbolize in my own emotional life? How do I *feel* toward the personalities, parties, and issues, as distinguished from what I believe I *think* about them? The venture was a failure. The hour was spent in a rehash of the hackneyed arguments used in the campaign materials of both parties.

Someone might say that to ask people in education even to consider that there might be an emotional bias in the reasoning they use to support a political candidate is simply asking too much of human nature. Maybe it is. But unless we at least try to understand the role of feeling in our thinking, we are simply going through the motions of thinking. We are not making full use of our capacity to reason.

Facing the Personal Implications of Ideas

One complaint often made by teachers in training is that they have to learn a lot of theory without being shown how to put the theory into practice. This is a problem, but it is probably not the basic problem. The problem may be that teachers are resisting the meaning of the theory as it applies to themselves. Any theory in education that has its roots in the realities of life has an immediate practical meaning to those who are willing to accept it.

Often, when teachers look for a practical application—a method, a gimmick, a prescription, a rule of thumb—they are trying not to grasp but to avoid the meaning a theory might have for them. Theory and practice are often out of gear in education because as teachers—like all other human beings—we like to externalize rather than internalize a theory. Our immediate response often is to become manipulative: to do something to someone else.

The writer has faced this problem repeatedly in his work with the concept underlying this book: that an essential function of education is to help the growing child understand himself and develop healthy attitudes of self-acceptance. In some classroom situations dealing with self-understanding which the writer has had an opportunity to observe, teachers have done almost everything except the one thing that is needful. They have gotten long check lists of children's interests. They have talked to parents about the pupils. They have gotten the young people to express by a vote what to them seemed to be their most urgent and important problems.

They have supplied movies and exhibits and have used all kinds of paraphernalia. But in doing all this, they often seemed to leave out the one essential thing: their own direct, personal involvement.

Hopelessness and Despair

Many people interviewed in connection with this study expressed themselves as rather hopeless of ever finding a solution for some problem or problems in their lives. In no instance, however, was there a consistent or pure attitude of hopelessness. The people who said or implied that they were without hope with respect to a particular difficulty also showed they still had a lot of courage left.

The concept of hopelessness was also included in the Personal Issues Inventory. Over a third of those responding indicated that one or more of the conditions of hopelessness described in the Inventory represented a problem in their own lives.

What we treated as hopelessness was expressed by statements such as the following: "I feel that there are important things in life I have missed and never will find, no matter how hard I try or how much I accomplish; I feel that there are things in life I have had to give up, and I suspect that at my age it is too late to make up for them; Although I believe life's struggle may be worth while, it often seems rather hopeless; I sometimes feel that life is so complicated and mixed up that I wonder whether it is worth while to keep up the struggle." There is a note of hopelessness in all these statements, and it is true that a person who shares the feelings expressed by them probably faces a large area of emptiness in his life. But there is a more terrible condition of emptiness—the condition of despair.

The utmost condition of meaninglessness in life is a state of despair. Where there is awareness of hopelessness, there is an awareness of what might be, and this in itself contains a ray of hope. There is still a possibility, as the Prophet has said, that the well of pain might yet be filled with joy. In a state of despair the prospect is bleaker than this. To despair is to surrender. The one who completely despairs has given up the quest for meaning. He has given up the struggle to be himself or to find himself. Despair is like death, but it is deeper than death. It is a kind of living death. It is what Kierkegaard has called "the sickness unto death."

Death is not in itself a symbol of despair. The prospect of death is a recurring theme in the history of a life in which there is still a surge of growth. Death can never be denied. But the one who is still in search of selfhood faces death and incorporates the thought of it into the larger sweep of his existence. He may go even further and accept death as something swallowed up in life. He may believe, or try to believe, that his identity lives on even after death—a belief that many hold but others deny. He may believe, as some have sought to believe, that he will live on in the memory of those who remain. He may believe that somehow he will survive even though his bones have been interred. He may believe, as some have endeavored to believe, that he can find eternal life, not through timeless existence, but through fullness of existence. According to this belief, a self that plunges deeply and fully into the possibilities of living captures and embraces the essence of immortality, whether or not the spirit survives the body. These are some of the ways of accepting or seeking to accept the threat of death and the inescapable fact that death will occur.

As was stated earlier, he who accepts himself fully accepts himself as one who will die. He who is best able to live is best prepared to die. He is one who, though facing the prospect of dying, still lives. In a state of despair, it is otherwise. For the one who despairs, if his despair is complete, has died while he is still alive. His is a living death.

Who are these despairing ones? The despairing ones, according to the view presented here, are not those who, in this study, spoke of areas of meaninglessness in their lives, or said they felt lonely or homeless or hopeless. These people are still alive in the search for selfhood. They have the courage, and the humility, to accept the fact that there is something empty in their lives. They say that there is something of deadness in their existence, but by virtue of facing this condition they are among those who are most alive. The despairing ones are not found among those who have the courage to face their anxiety, hostility, loneliness, and search for meaning, as did the people in this study who openly affirmed that they needed help and courageously asked for it. The despairing ones are more likely to be among those who pretend to be well adjusted and claim to be above ordinary human frailty. Their "adjustment" may be a form of despair: Adjustment to conformity. Adjustment by way of surrender of feeling. Adjustment to a condition of not even daring to face the issues of anxiety and meaning. Adjustment gained at the price of not daring to ask the question: Who and what and why am I?

There is doubt and fear and perhaps an element of hopelessness when one says, "I *don't* know what *really* matters." But there is something deeper than this—there is despair—when a person says, in effect, "Nothing matters." A person despairs when he renounces the most intimate possessions of humanity—feeling, passion, meaning, and choice. He expresses despair when he says that existence is simply a mechanical link in a chain of cause and effect, one event in an endless succession of antecedents and consequences, and that the search for meaning and value, or even the notion of the uniqueness of humanity itself, is just an illusion.

It is good to feel sympathy for those who weep, but more in need of sympathy are those who despairingly have surrendered the right to weep. It is good to go out in fellow-feeling to those who feel lonely, but more in need of fellow-feeling are those despairing ones who do not dare to face their loneliness or hope for anything else. One's heart goes out to those who say their lives are empty, but more deeply in need of compassion are those who say that life itself is empty.

The Paradox of Meaninglessness

When people feel that meaninglessness is a problem in their own lives—as so many in this study did—they express a kind of despondency. But there is a paradox in this despondency, for it expresses both an awareness of emptiness and an undercurrent of hope. There is hope because concern with meaninglessness in itself implies the possibility that meaning might be found. If a person did not have some hope, he would not ask for help—he would give up in despair. Where there is a desire to seek for meaning, there remains some assurance that life has, or might have, meaning. Most teachers who raise the problem of meaning probably have an unspoken faith that life has some worth, and an unvoiced conviction that their existence might have a significance richer than anything they have yet discovered.

This hope, which persists in spite of disappointment, has roots deep in the soil of life's early experiences. One outstanding characteristic of the young child is that he actively seeks to understand. In his first explorations, at first wordlessly and then through language, he seeks to examine, to probe into the what, the how, and the why. Even at an early stage of life he strives as though he had implicit faith that there *is* a how, a what, a why. Early in his strivings, likewise, he proceeds as though it were possible to get and to give an accounting of things. A remnant of this hope persists even though the child is often rebuked when, in school, he seeks to grasp the significance, for him, of the vast body of academic material he is compelled to learn. This hope persists in the teachers who took part in this study, even when, by their own testimony, they see so much that is empty and meaningless in what they are compelled to teach.

Granting that this hope persists, it remains true that many people who were interviewed and many who responded to questionnaires in this study revealed deep suffering when they testified that there were areas of emptiness and meaninglessness in their lives; that they tried helplessly to live up to impossible expectations; that they were not in touch with their real feelings. There is pain and probably often an element of tragedy when people say, as did a goodly number in this study, that they feel lonely, homeless, and hopeless.

If a limited encounter with the idea of self-discovery elicits so much awareness of lack, meaninglessness, and loneliness, and so many evidences of disquiet, would not the picture become even gloomier if these people launched into a further and deeper search into themselves? The answer is Yes. And would it not be better to avoid this, to leave untouched these longings and yearnings, to leave uncovered these undercurrents of tragedy? The answer is No.

It is true that often, as a person inquires into the meaning of his life, he is likely to feel uncomfortable. He will find that he has been pretending. He will face feelings that are disturbing and depressing. But these conditions were there before he started to inquire. To feel actively disturbed by them can be the beginning of a process of repair and growth. And as long as the conditions are there, even if hidden, they mean trouble, even if the trouble is not directly perceived and is experienced through states of restlessness or aimlessness or vague apprehension, depression, boredom, anger, or frustration, such as were discussed in the chapter on anxiety. When there are dislocations in one's life, one pays a price somehow. The problems that are faced when one looks at these are old and troublesome, even if they seem utterly new.

The search for meaning—the search for selfhood—is painful, and although it is healing, the person who undertakes it is likely to feel worse before he feels better. It is only by accepting oneself as one is—having the courage to perceive and the humility to appreciate and to savor one's loneliness and hostility and the meaninglessness of so much of what one does—that the process of healing and repair can get under way.

The position in this book is that we should face the question of meaning in education, not evade or avoid it, even if it hurts. This is a position on which not all will agree. The writer has been told by some people that education should not enter into this area. We should not touch upon issues that might arouse anxiety. We should not press into the deeper areas of meaning lest the student become distressed. We should not even discuss anxiety (so a few have said), for to do so might make people more anxious than they already are. Yet what is the alternative? Actually, there is nothing significant that we can undertake at any level in education that will not arouse anxiety in some students.

As has already been noted, in the most conventionally oriented and psychologically naive learning situations, children face failure, ridicule, and rejection on a monumental scale. They constantly face conditions that create anxiety or aggravate that which already prevails. So to center our attention only on the academic, and to avoid any emphasis on what has implications for the self, will not rule out anxiety, even though it might rule out some occasions for anxiety. We do not avoid the actuality of anxiety by ignoring it or by refusing to look at life as it is. The only way to sidestep anxiety in education completely is to stop educating children altogether.

But, even apart from this, what is the alternative?

Should we, in order to avoid the risk of stirring people up, proceed in our pedagogy as though we were dealing in a mechanical way with disembodied facts? Should the teacher of English, for example, in sharing a poem or a novel filled with hate or passion or tears, avoid these emotions because they might evoke a resonance of feeling in this or that member of the class? Should he blunt the impact, strip out the passion, dry up the tears? Should he water things down so that no one will feel anything? If the answer is Yes, then why teach poetry, drama, or fiction? If No, then why not try for the fullest impact and the deepest possible significance?

The same question can be raised concerning everything we teach—every subject, every skill, every art, every craft that is part of the curriculum.

But the question, What is the alternative? becomes even more insistent when we look at the children we teach. If we look at them realistically, we see that their lives, like the lives of teachers, are touched by anxiety, hostility, loneliness, guilt, and many other conditions of distress. If we are to face these children as they are, we must face the conditions as realistically as we can.

Religion

Many of the people interviewed in connection with this study spoke of religion. Some spoke in a mood of charity; some voiced bitterness and hostility. Some spoke with quiet assurance of their faith; some spoke of their religion as though they were trying by means of it to escape from anxiety and were not succeeding very well.

There was not enough material or enough of a common thread in the statements about religion to provide the basis for a separate chapter in this book. But one feature of the comments on religion does fit into the present context—the search for meaning.

Several people, when referring to religion, did so in what seemed to be a rather self-conscious manner, as though religion were hardly a proper thing to discuss when one teacher talks to another. In the opinion of the writer, this attitude is rather depressing, emphasizing again how people have been schooled to avoid sharing with others the things that concern them most. It is another symptom of a tendency to avoid the implications of the search for meaning.

Religion, if it means anything at all, has a profound and intimate personal meaning. The religious person, if he is sincere, seeks through his religion to find what to him is of ultimate concern. Religion is, at least for some, the utmost in the search for meaning. In the view of many people, the question of meaning a person raises when he asks "Who and what and why am I?" becomes a religious question when pursued to a final decision. For it raises other questions: What is the ground of my being? What is the foundation of my assurance that life is worth living? What is the substance on which I build my hope?

It is not just the credulous and unlearned or those seeking an easy escape who raise questions of religion. These questions face every scientist and every scholar when he has gone to the outermost reaches of his discipline, if not before. So it is anomalous that when questions of religion are raised in education, they are often raised apologetically—as though a person should apologize for seeking. or claiming to have found, the ultimate answer to the meaning of his life.

Humility

In this book humility has been mentioned as essential to the search for meaning. Why is this, and what is meant by humility?

Humility is a form of inner strength, a kind of dignity that makes it less necessary for a person to pretend.

It is something quite different from weakness. The humble one is not humble because he is spineless. To be humble is not the same as to be obsequious, or an easy mark, or a person without robust convictions.

Why is the one who seeks for meaning humble?

He cannot help but be humble when he looks beyond the appearances of things and contemplates the vast reaches of the unknown. The more he grows in understanding, the more he realizes how much there is that yet lies hidden. He realizes that he cannot see the distant scene, but he can accept this fact without bitterness.

He cannot help but be humble when he looks upon the marvel of human growth. What parent can contemplate, for example, the development of language in a child without a feeling of awe? What teacher has not had an experience of reverent wonder while watching the mental life of his pupils unfold?

When a person seeks to realize the meaning of his own emotions, he cannot help but be humble. He is baffled by the play of love and hate in his life. He cannot penetrate the clouds of anxiety that move across the horizons of his inner world. He is perplexed by the conditions that sometimes move him toward depths of longing. He is bewildered by the complexity of his feelings, which lead him at times to accept what he should reject and to reject what by rights he should accept. He is baffled by the worries that assail him and the forebodings that sometimes seize him.

He cannot help but be humble when he considers the poignancy of his grief; the weight of his melancholy on occasion; the inexpressible quality of the joy that sometimes wells up in him; the ominous waves that threaten to engulf him as he stands on the brink of despair; and the thrill that surges through him as he tastes in advance a happy fulfillment of his hopes.

He cannot help but feel humble as he absorbs all that he can know, and in so doing glimpses depths he can never fathom and heights he can never scale in the majestic peaks and valleys of his inner life.

What are the marks of one who is humble?

Above all, he is one who is able to wait and to be silent. He can wait, for he does not expect that he should immediately understand each question from within or have a response to each query from without. He can wait, for he does not expect to reach an instantaneous insight or to have an instantaneous answer or to offer an immediate competing or echoing remark when others speak. He does not feel guilty about not knowing—at least not always. Nor does he feel guilty when he is assailed by doubts concerning something he once thought he knew.

Being able to wait enables him to listen. He is a good listener when others have something to say, and he will hear them out if he thinks it is fit or timely to do so. But even more, he is a good listener to his own inner voice, which often speaks very slowly and indistinctly. If he were not a good listener, he would not give himself time to experience the impact of his feelings, to catch the meaning or at least to try to capture the meaning of a nascent mood or a vaguely pleasant or disquieting thought that crosses his mind.

This ability to wait and to listen is not just a cultivated pose. It is acquired only when a person has become able to dispense with some of his pretensions and has begun to learn not to make exorbitant demands upon himself. He is then able to appreciate, without enthusiasm but also without protest, the simple fact that so much in his life and in life about him is uncertain, untried, untested, and unknown.

There is a condition opposite to that of humility—a false kind of pride and a harsh kind of arrogance, which cannot tolerate doubt. This arrogance is a form of anxiety. It is a condition of feeling mortally threatened unless one has immediately at hand the absolute and certain answers to questions pertaining to the nature of man's existence. When such an attitude prevails, a person cannot search for meaning; and even the meaning he has found, or thinks he has found, is probably only an academic possession. It is the kind of precarious truth embraced by one whose faith is so weak that he does not have courage to doubt.

The humble person can tolerate himself not only as one whose knowledge is imperfect but also as one who himself is imperfect. Here humility interweaves with compassion and provides a person with the beginning of wisdom. It is only when he can tolerate himself as an imperfect creature, without feeling apologetic about it, that he can have the freedom to listen and to learn.

The humble person is willing to accept truth and to seek it wherever it may be found. A humble teacher, for example, will accept a child as one who, in a given situation, may give a clearer and more profound glimpse into the meaning of things than the teacher himself. And a humble scholar is one who realizes that when a less learned person is puzzled and asks why, he may be more profound than the erudite person who knows the contents of a hundred books but never wonders what his erudition means.

Reference

1. Jersild, A. T., K. Helfant, and associates, *Education for Self-Understanding* (New York: Bureau of Publications, Teachers College, Columbia University, 1953).

4. Self-understanding for teachers

William C. Menninger

Reprinted from the *National Educational Association Journal,* Vol. 42 (1953), 331-333, by permission of the author and the National Education Association.

All persons whose work places them in constant and daily interaction with other people have an obligation for self-understanding, teachers particularly. What steps can a teacher take in search of self-understanding? What can teachers (or any one else for that matter) do to enhance self-acceptance? Menninger outlines some practical suggestions for increasing self-understanding, for implementing the "search" discussed in the previous article by Jersild.

If you are like most teachers, there are many things about yourself and your relationships with children that are often difficult to understand. Why do you sometimes lose your temper for no good reason? Why do you take a dislike to a new student without being able to explain your prejudice? Why do you sometimes make excessive demands, knowing that you will regret your behavior later?

Because of the complexity of human behavior, no one can really understand himself completely. But everyone, if he tries, can understand himself better.

Teachers should have a special interest in self-understanding. Their behavior not only determines their own success or failure, happiness or unhappiness, but more importantly, it gravely affects their students.

People usually have some idea about their physical anatomy—the way their bodies are made and how the parts operate. But the how and why of their feelings, actions, and thoughts, they vaguely attribute to "personality" and let it go at that.

But let's keep in mind that personality is the *total* you. It is your physical equipment—brains, bones, skin, organs, muscles, blood vessels, winning smile, Roman nose, and jutting chin. It also is your feelings, hopes, ideas, longings, loves, hates, friendships, and interests.

What we call mind and body really are *one*. Your mind affects your body. Your physical condition affects your mental state.

Most teachers are acquainted with what psychiatrists call the three basic parts of the personality—the *conscious,* the *unconscious,* and the *conscience.* The unseen energy drives or forces generated in these parts of the "personality anatomy" make us the people we are.

Some of our automatic responses and behavior patterns are the result of attitudes formed in early childhood. Relationships with our parents, our brothers and sisters, and our *teachers* have all played a part in the development of our personality—just as, in turn, our personality and attitudes toward our students are affecting *their* development.

The Struggle

Every minute of our waking hours, our personality reacts to people and to our surroundings. Unfortunately, our environment and personality always are competing with each other. What we want to do and what our environment allows us to do are often quite different. This results in a struggle between the two.

The outcome of this struggle may be determined by several factors—the particular situation in the environment, our own individual pattern of behavior, or a personal conflict within ourselves. In the latter case, what we want to do may not coincide with what we think we *ought* to do. A conflict within yourself, conscious or unconscious, weakens your ability to cope with demands made on you.

Our physical health also affects our dealing with our environment. When we don't feel well or are merely tired, the demands of our work and environment may seem overwhelming.

Sometimes we are able to make a compromise that satisfies, in part, both our needs and those of our environment. On the other hand, we may try to avoid our problems by not meeting them or by fighting them—battling against everything and everyone in the environment.

Whether we react by fleeing or fighting, the chances are that our decision is not deliberate. The way we react is usually the result of patterns laid down in early years and ingrained further by habit as we grew up. Since your students may be affected by your patterns, it is important that you understand them.

Everybody has used some form of the *flight reaction* at times. It may have taken the form of repeatedly forgetting to make a dental appointment, despite your best intentions. Again, it might take the form of escape unconsciously resorted to by Mrs. Field, an eighth-grade teacher:

Her classroom was badly overcrowded, and she had to contend with a group of boisterous boys. After struggling with the situation for two weeks, she developed a sick headache and stayed home from school.

Mrs. Field was taking flight from a situation in her environment; the pressure of an intolerable problem had made her physically sick. Other people react by using up all their energy feeling sorry for themselves or becoming depressed.

The *fight reaction* occurs when someone or something in our environment refuses to yield to our wishes, and we feel we must damage or destroy it. We lash out at the person or situation that is opposing us. We call a child names or shake him by the shoulders. The children in our care have similar reactions. The youngster who annoys the children around him is expressing the fight reaction, too.

The inability to stand frustration leads to hostile, angry response in everyone occasionally. It is when the fight reaction becomes a customary method of dealing with problems that serious trouble develops.

Teachers must learn to recognize the fight reaction in children. A temper tantrum or destructiveness in a child is an indication that something is wrong. Teachers can help children deal constructively with frustrating circumstances.

That is where the *constructive compromise* comes in. All through life, situations arise in which the individual's wishes and those of others conflict—two little children get into a tug-of-war over a tricycle; a husband is eager to stay at home when his wife is all set to go to the movies. The support and encouragement we received as we were growing up, or the restraints and frustrations we encountered, have made it easier or more difficult for us to compromise now. Similarly, the kind of guidance you give your students will influence their ability to meet the later demands of life.

Mental Mechanisms

In the unending struggle between our personality and environment which began when we were born, we learned ways to react to our problems. We formed patterns of behavior. These patterns make it easier for the personality to adjust to the environment and act as a defense against feelings of insecurity, fear, or anxiety.

As a teacher, you are perhaps most interested in the mechanism of *introjection*. Through this process, your children gradually adopt many of your attitudes and ideas—whether they are good or bad. It's the same process that made *you* a Congregationalist, a Democrat, and afraid of snakes—if your parents were.

In the classroom the relationship of the pupil to the teacher has this important bearing on what is learned: If the pupil does not like the teacher, he'll often reject him and what he teaches. Studies show, in fact, that well-liked teachers make for well-liked subjects; that the subjects taught by well-liked high school teachers are voluntarily continued by students, while subjects taught by disliked teachers are continued only if they are required.

Working hand in hand with introjection is *identification*. Throughout life we identify with people for whom we have a strong emotional attachment. A child identifies with his favorite teacher, as well as with his parents. People also identify with groups. That is why a child wants to wear the kind of clothes "all the other kids" wear.

To live in accordance with the laws and customs of society, we must *sublimate* the primitive impulses of love and hate. Everyone must find constructive channels for thcsc two high-pressure drives which are continually pushing up from the unconscious in one way or another. The drive to love is modified into thoughts and acts that are creative, constructive, and generous. The hate urge can be modified into such qualities as initiative and ambition.

Mental health depends on ability to sublimate unconscious drives. In general, the greater this ability, the sounder one's mental health. One of the mechanisms all of us use is *compensation*—making up for the lack of some specific ability. We work hard to develop an asset to compensate for some imaginary or real handicap.

Many persons who feel insecure or inferior devise ways to compensate these feelings. Short men sometimes make themselves very conspicuous and loud to try to compensate for their lack of height, for example.

A particularly unhealthy kind of compensation is substituting gifts or special favors for time and attention. Unfortunately, parents and even teachers sometimes use this trick with children.

Compensation can be helpful, too. The boy who can't do well in athletics can get needed ego satisfaction out of becomine an outstanding student.

Unlike a lie or an excuse that is consciously devised, *rationalization* is an unconscious process—our personality's device for justifying ideas and behavior so that they seem reasonable to us. It's easier to see other people's rationalization than it is to see our own.

All of us rationalize many times every day. We use rationalization to defend ourselves when we have planned unwisely, when we put things off, when we have been unnecessarily severe with a child.

We also use rationalization to support a belief or prejudice. We defend our likes as well as our hates. We explain why we prefer one child to another, why we overslept this morning, or why we are afraid of mice—usually unaware of the real reason buried in our unconscious.

We all know people who consistently blame others for their troubles or shortcomings. Others believe they never get a square deal. These people are using the mechanism called *projection*—attributing to others wishes or faults that they will not claim as their own.

The device by which your feelings toward one person are expressed toward another is called *displacement*. We are more apt to displace our feelings of resentment and disappointment than any other emotions. We "take it out" on persons who are not to blame because we cannot express open resentment to those who have caused our angry reaction. Teachers sometimes displace on their pupils the animosity that has been aroused by the principal.

If you have ever felt anxious or disturbed for a long time, you may have developed a headache or stomach upset. This we call *conversion*. Your emotional distress has been *converted* into a physical upset.

Most of the ideas or wishes in the unconscious can't be directly expressed because the conscious part of the personality won't accept or release them. Many of them continually exert great force—like steam being stored up under pressure—and when they have no direct outlet, they pop out in some other way.

Looking at Yourself

The first step toward improving your behavior is to recognize that it *can* be improved. We must try to see our problems. How can we recognize that all is not well in our emotional lives? Here are some questions that might provide helpful clues:

Are you always unhappy and dissatisfied?

Do you frequently have vague physical complaints for which the doctor can find no physical cause?

Do you feel more or less lonesome and discouraged all the time?

Do you have a continuing feeling that people don't like you?

Are you always in friction with children or other adults—always arguing about one thing or another?

Do you complain a lot? Are most things—your work, your social life, your friends—unsatisfactory to you?

Everyone occasionally has these symptoms. That's why the questions are qualified with the words "always" or "frequently." If your answers to these questions are "yes," it would be advisable to take some steps to change the answers to "no."

After you have taken a look at yourself, look at your environment. It may be making too many demands on you. You may have real problems in the family. You may be expected to meet impossible demands by your associates or superiors.

Once you recognize your problems and really want help with them, there is a lot of hope. This is true whether your problems involve your personality or your environment.

There are three methods of working out solutions to problems: (1) you can change yourself; (2) you can change your environment; (3) you can change both. The third method is the one that usually works best.

One of your difficulties may be that because of deeply formed habits of acting and thinking, you can't see what kind of changes are needed in yourself or in your environment. Your very problems prevent you from doing anything constructive.

Many times, of course, a good hard look at a problem is all that's needed to make it disappear. By thinking it through carefully, you find a solution or get the problem down to manageable size.

It's when your problems persist, when you can no longer handle them yourself, when they adversely affect your relationships with your students and your friends, that you should seek outside help.

Staying Well Mentally

Although there is no sure-fire method for the prevention of personality maladjustment, most people can maintain good mental health. Mental health depends not on being free of problems but on facing and solving them.

The most important factor in your personal happiness and effectiveness is your ability to get along well with other people. This ability really depends on whether you *can love* and *are loved* more than you hate. And by love we mean family affection and friendship, as well as love of husband or wife. Difficulties and unhappiness almost always are related to the fact that one does not give and receive enough love to balance hate.

To be mentally healthy, and to help children attain good mental health, you must get satisfaction from life. Satisfactions come from filling your personal needs, from making wishes come true. You can get satisfaction from creating a beautiful product, from carrying out a plan, doing a worthwhile job, or working toward an important goal.

The amount of satisfaction you get from life depends largely on *your* own ingenuity and self-sufficiency. People who wait for life to supply their satisfaction usually find boredom instead. You can achieve greater satisfaction if you:

Stand aside and look at how you may be contributing to your own unhappiness. (You may be too dependent or too aggressive.)

Do something out of the ordinary now and then. Use your imagination —explore new ideas and activities.

Make a serious effort to find ways of doing your main job better.

Recreate and refresh yourself. The more fun you have in your leisure, the better it is for you. Everyone needs time to do what he wants, with full freedom of conscience to be happy in his own way.

Develop the art of friendliness. Most of the joys of life, and sorrows, too, depend on how you get along with other people. Friends can be your greatest source of satisfaction—your strong support in times of crisis.

Finally, take a look at your life goals. If you have a goal that is high enough and worthy enough, your achievement will come with your growth toward emotional maturity.

You are emotionally mature to the extent that you:

Find greater satisfaction in giving than in receiving.

Form satisfying and permanent loyalties in give-and-take relationships.

Use your leisure creatively.

Contribute to the improvement of your home, school, community, nation, and world.

Learn to profit from your mistakes and successes.

Are relatively free from fears, anxieties, and tensions.

No one needs emotional maturity more than parents and teachers. We can hardly expect our children to be more mature adults than we are ourselves. If we hope to have a healthy, happier, more effective—*more mature*—next generation, we must come closer to maturity ourselves.

5. What can man become?

Arthur W. Combs

Reprinted from the *California Journal for Instructional Improvement,* Vol. 4 (1961), 15-23, by permission of the author and the California Association for Supervision and Curriculum Development.

In Part I we began our study of the self and its multiple dimensions by introducing Anderson's conceptual framework for behavior. You have studied the self in relation to theoretical issues, perception, growth processes, personality development, teaching, and learning. We move now to this book's logical conclusion as Combs examines what must be, in the final analysis, the ultimate question. What, indeed, can *man become?*

In his inaugural address President Kennedy said to us, "Ask not what your country can do for you. Ask, rather, what you can do for your country?"

This eloquent plea was immediately met with an answering cry from millions of Americans. "Tell us what we can do," we cried. We long for a goal to live for and die for. We long for goals that will define for us where we should stand, what we should work for, what we can commit our lives and fortunes to. These are not idle questions. They are deeply serious ones, for upon our answers to these questions will rest the outcome of the great ideological struggle in which we are now engaged. In such a struggle it is the beliefs, convictions, values we hold that will determine whether we win or lose. We simply cannot sit down at the same table to bargain with adversaries who have already decided before they begin, that they are willing to die for their beliefs unless we have an equally firm commitment. A man without conviction, engaged in discussion with one whose convictions are practically a religion, is a sitting duck to be changed. This is one of the things we learned from our research on the "brain-washed" soldiers who returned from Korea.

Well, what is our commitment? What do we stand for? Freedom, we have said, is our goal. For our forefathers this was easy to define. It was freedom from the tyranny of the British kings, freedom from religious persecution, freedom from want, freedom for the slaves. Even in our own times when we have been attacked we have risen magnificently to defend ourselves against outside aggressors. But what shall be our goals in times of peace and plenty or when outside forces do not press upon us? Goals for the have-nots are self-evident. Goals for those whose basic needs are satisfied are more difficult to define and less pressing to pursue.

Redefining Freedom in Terms of Becoming

We all recognize that meaning and character come from striving. We are most alive when happily engaged in the pursuit of a goal. Freedom, we have said, is our goal—but freedom for what? What does freedom mean in a nation of incredible wealth? It is apparent we need a redefinition of freedom translatable into action, not in a time of crisis alone, but applicable as well in times of peace and security.

We have stated our fundamental belief in democracy in these terms: "When men are free, they can find their own best ways." But what is a free man? A man with a full belly? A man without problems? A man with no pressures? Free to do as he pleases? When such things are achieved, a man is still no more than a vegetable. It is not enough to be free to *be*. We need freedom to *become*.

But what can man become? What is the ultimate in human freedom? What does it mean for a man to achieve the fullest possible fulfillment of his potentialities? This is a question which a number of psychologists, sociologists, educators, and humanitarians have been asking for a generation. What does it mean to be a fully-functioning person, operating at the highest peak of his potentialities? What does it mean to be self-actualizing, self-realizing, a truly adequate person in the fullest possible sense of the word?

It would be hard to overestimate the importance of this search. For whatever we decide is a fully functioning, self-actualizing human being must, automatically, become the goal for all of us engaged in the helping relationships. These are the kinds of people we are trying to produce. It is to produce such people that our public schools exist, and the descriptions of these people provide us with the criteria in terms of which we can measure our success or failure.

As a result of the thinking and study of scholars and researchers, little by little, the picture begins to unfold. We begin to get some inkling of what the fully functioning person is like. This is no average man they are describing. Who, after all, wants to be average? This is a Free man with a capital F. This is a goal for us to shoot for, a picture of what can be and might be. Here is a concept of a free man that lifts our sights to what, perhaps, one day man may become.

What is more, a study of the characteristics emerging from the studies provides us with a blueprint for education practice. I believe the work of these people in defining the nature of self-actualization is certainly among the most exciting steps forward in our generation. For me, it has provided new meaning in life. It provides new goals and direction for me, not just in times of crisis, but in the quiet hours between, and in my professional work as well.

I cannot discuss all of the characteristics of these fully functioning, self-actualizing people which have now been described. In the time we have here together, let me describe only two or three of these characteristics and go on to discuss what these characteristics seem to me to mean for education. Each of the characteristics of these people could be spelled out in many aspects of curriculum in terms of what we need to do to produce that kind of characteristic. In fact, this is what the 1962 ASCD Yearbook attempts to do and I recommend it to your attention when it appears.

Self-Actualizing People See Themselves in Positive Ways

Highly free people, the studies seem to show, see themselves as liked, wanted, acceptable, able, dignified, and worthy. Feeling this way about themselves, moreover, they are likely to have a deep feeling of personal security which makes it much easier to confront the emergencies of life with far less fear and trembling than the rest of us. They feel about themselves that they are people of dignity and worth and they *behave* as though they were. Indeed, it is in this factor of how the individual sees himself that we are likely to find the most outstanding differences between well-adjusted and poorly adjusted people. It is not the people who feel about themselves that they are liked and wanted and acceptable and able and so on who fill our jails and mental hospitals. Rather, it is those who feel themselves deeply inadequate, unliked, unwanted, unacceptable, unable, and the like.

This characteristic of fully functioning personalities, it seems to me, has at least four distinctly important implications for us in education.

In the first place, it seems to me, it means *we must regard the individual's self as a recognized part of the curriculum.* People learn who they are and what they are from the ways in which they are treated by those who surround them in the process of their growing up. What we do in class, therefore, affects the individual's ways of seeing himself whether we are aware of our impact or not. We *teach* children who they are and what they are by the kinds of experiences we provide. Many school deficiencies we now know are the result of a child's *belief* that he cannot read, write, or do math. A child may be taught that he cannot read from the impatience and frustration among those who sought to teach him.

We cannot rule the self out of the classroom, even if we wanted to. A child does not park himself at the door. The self is the dearest thing he owns, and he cannot be induced to part with it for any reason. Even a poor, ragged, and unhappy self must be dragged along wherever he goes. It is, after all, the only one he owns. The self, we now know, determines even what we see and what we hear. Right now in this audience as you listen to me speak, you are judging, determining, deciding about what I am saying, and you will carry away from here only that which, for one reason or another, has basically affected your very personal self.

For some time now it has been a part of our education in philosophy that we need to be concerned about the learner as well as the subject. Consequently, we have emphasized the importance of the child in the process and have developed a so-called, child-centered school. Indeed, we have sometimes carried this so far that the general public has sometimes become concerned lest we get so involved in understanding the child that we forget to teach him something!

Sometimes this has been expressed in the question, "Are you educating for intellect or educating for adjustment?" Such a dichotomy is, of course, ridiculous. Surely, we are not seeking to produce either smart psychotics, on the one hand, nor well-adjusted dopes, on the other! The fact of the matter is, we simply cannot separate what an individual learns from the nature of the individual himself. Indeed, we do not have to. This is nicely demonstrated in a recent experiment by Staines in New Zealand.

As you know, at the end of the fourth year under the British system children take an examination which determines the direction of their educational program from that point on. Staines studied two groups of fourth-grade children preparing for these examinations. One group was taught by a teacher who paid no attention to the self-concepts of the children. The other class was taught by a teacher who was simply aware of and thinking about the self-concepts of the children, although he did nothing specifically planned to make changes in these matters. At the end of the year the two groups of children did about equally well on the academic aspects of the examination they took.

The adjustment level of the children in the two grades, however, was quite different. Adjustment levels in the classes taught by the teacher who was interested in the youngsters' self-concepts rose, while the adjustment level of the youngsters taught by the teacher who had ignored this factor actually decreased. Being concerned about the child's self-concept does not mean in any sense of the word that it is necessary for us to teach him any less.

Learning, itself, is a highly personal matter. Whether or not any given piece of information will be really learned by a youngster, we now know, is dependent upon whether or not he has discovered the personal meaning of that bit of information for him. It is the personal feeling I have about information, the personal commitment I have with respect to it that determines whether or not I behave differently as a result of having that information. Learning is not the cold, antiseptic examination of facts we once considered it. This is perhaps nowhere better illustrated than in the matter of dietetics. Dietitians have at their fingertips vast stores of information about what people *ought* to eat. Even you and I who are far less well informed know a good deal about what we ought to eat—but don't eat that! We go right on eating what we *want* to eat and *like* to eat, in spite of our information about the matter, until one day we cannot get into our favorite dress or a son says, "Gee, Mom, you're getting fat" or when, perhaps, like me, you visit your doctor for your annual check-up and, poking his finger in your stomach, he says, "Blubber! Sheer blubber!" Then, suddenly the information you have had all along takes on a new meaning and may even, just possibly, begin to affect your behavior.

Learning only happens to people. To ignore the presence of the person in the process simply runs the risk of failing to accomplish anything of very much importance. We cannot afford to ignore this important aspect of our problem. To do so runs the risk of making ourselves ineffective. The self is a part of the learning process and to ignore it is about as silly as saying, "I know my car needs a carburetor to run, but I think I'll run mine without one!"

Since the self is what matters to each of us, if we cast this out of school, we run the serious danger of teaching children that school is only about things that don't matter. If we are totally preoccupied with teaching subject matter, we may miss entirely the child to whom we are trying to teach it. We are all familiar with the examination time "boners." These represent the way the things we taught were seen by those whom we tried to teach.

Secondly, it seems to me, *the need for people who see themselves posi-*

tively means that whatever diminishes the child's self has no place in education. Humiliation, degradation, and failure are destructive to the self. It is commonly assumed in some places that shame and guilt are good for people, but this is rarely true, for the people who feel these things the most are the people who need them least.

Whatever makes the self smaller and meaner is not just bad for mental health. It undermines confidence and produces fear and withdrawal. It cuts down freedom of movement, the possibilities of intelligent behavior. What diminishes the self is stupefying and stultifying. Such people are a drag on the rest of us. Even worse are those who see themselves in negative terms as unliked, unwanted, unacceptable, unable, undignified, unworthy, and so on. These are the dangerous people of our society.

A positive self calls for success experience for everyone. People learn they *can* by succeeding, not by failing. There is a general feeling abroad in some places that failure is good for people, but nothing could be further from the truth. Self-actualizing people see themselves in positive ways, and you do not get this from having failures. If we teach a child he is a failure, we have no one to blame but ourselves if he comes to believe us and after that behaves so.

I do not believe it is an accident that for most children, after the third grade, there is very little variation in their grades for the rest of the time they are in school. It is as though, by the time a child reaches the third grade, he has discovered what his quota is, and after that he lives up to it. One learns he is *able* only from his successes. Even the "self-made man" who beats his chest and says, "What a fine fellow I am! I came up the hard way. Kids ought to have it hard," got this way precisely because he did *not* fail. He is a walking example of the man who did not fail.

But failure and success are feelings. They have to do with how the person to whom something happens sees the situation, not how it seems to those who look on from the outside. Success or failure does not happen unless the individual thinks it so. If a child believes he has failed, it doesn't make much difference whether other people think so or not. The important thing is what *he* believes, not what someone else does.

The provision of success for all students obviously calls for widespread curricula changes. Some sixty years ago we decided to educate everyone in this country, but we are still a long ways from discovering how to carry that out. We are still spending vast amounts of money, time, and energy trying to find ways to treat everyone alike. This, despite the fact that the most outstanding thing we know about human beings is that they are almost infinitely different. We are still providing many children with experiences of failure and self-reduction, not because we want to but because we seek to force them into a common mold which they do not fit.

We must provide for individual differences. We have talked now for a generation or more about individual differences, but we have made only a little progress in this direction. We see little in our elementary schools, practically none in our secondary schools, and in our colleges we are not even sure it is a good idea in the first place. Despite all our talk about individual differences we still continue to insist upon group goals and standards, to organize our schools around age groups with thirty students to a class. Many teachers are fearful and insecure when they leave the familiar territory of the textbook or traditional methods and the familiar lock-step of lecture, recitation, and grades. Even our beautiful new buildings are often no more than a dull series of similar boxes, light and airy and cheerful to be sure, but still designed for fixed-size groups.

What would it mean, I ask myself, if we were to organize in such a fashion as to *really* give each child an experience of success? We have talked about it, discussed it, even advocated it on occasion, but mostly we have been too timid and fearful to put it into effect.

The plain fact of the matter is we often impose failure on students by the kind of structure upon which we insist. Many a child in our large modern high school gets lost in the shuffle. What high school teacher can know all 300 students drifting through his class in the course of the day? Adolescence is lonely enough without further subjecting the child to this kind of experience.

We have decided that rich curricula require schools of large size. But people can and do get lost in large schools, and we run the risk of losing on the bananas what we made on the oranges. I recall the snow sculpture standing on the lawn of one of our dormitories at Syracuse University some years ago, a kind of cartoon in 3-D. It had a freshmen student jauntily walking into the University on one side and walking out the other side was, not a student, but an IBM card fully equipped with diploma and all his holes in the right places!

Surely it must be possible to organize our schools in such a way that somebody, somewhere in a junior or senior high school, is in contact with a child for a sufficiently long time to really get to know him. Guidance counselors who see him only an hour or two each semester are no solution. There is no substitute for the classroom teacher. The guidance function cannot be turned over to specialists. One good reason for this is the fact that adolescents simply do not take their problems to strangers. Adolescence is a deeply sensitive time of life, and the persons such children seek out for help are those with whom they have a continuing contact and that usually means a teacher, not a specialist. Some of the world's best guidance is done by coaches, advisers of the HiY, and even by the detention room keeper. The responsibility for knowing and understanding a child cannot be sloughed off. It remains the primary responsibility of the classroom teacher.

We must apply our criteria for self-actualization to every educational experience. Truly free, self-actualizing, fully-functioning people, we are told, are people who see themselves as liked, wanted, acceptable, able, dignified, worthy, and so on. Seeing oneself like this, however, is something one learns as a result of his experience during the years of his growing up. People *learn* that they are liked, wanted, acceptable, able from the things that happen to them and from the important people in their lives. In these statements we find the criteria for what we need to do in order to produce freer, more fully functioning people for our society. Let us apply these criteria to every aspect of educational experience. Let us ask about this school, this program, this policy, this method, this action, plan, or curriculum—does this help our students to feel more liked, wanted, acceptable, able, dignified, worthy, important, and so on? I have tried this with my own classes at the University with fascinating results. It has led me in some cases to reject time-honored methods and procedures. In others, it corroborated things I have known and believed for a long time. But perhaps best of all, it has led me in new directions, to new techniques, new principles. It has not always been easy, for sometimes I have had to give up cherished beliefs, to tread on unfamiliar paths with fear and trembling. Sometimes, even, I have gotten into trouble. I can only conclude, however, that despite the difficulties and tribulations the experimenting has been eminently worthwhile, and certainly never dull!

It is necessary for us to learn how things seem to our pupils. To produce the kinds of people the experts tell us we need and to do the kinds of things we have been talking about here require that we learn to understand how things look from the point of view of our students. Since students behave just as we do, according to how things seem to them, it follows that it is necessary for us to learn how things seem to our pupils. This, however, is not easy for two reasons: We have been taught for so long the importance of being objective, "of getting the facts," that for many of us it is a difficult thing to give up this scientific way of looking. On the other hand, how things seem to each of us seems so right and so *so* that it is a very difficult thing to understand that it may not be. Indeed the way things seem to us seems so certain that when other people do not see them the way we do we jump to either one of two conclusions: Either they must be very stupid or they are simply being perverse. Phyllis McGinley once expressed it very nicely when she said,

> I think we must give up the fiction
> That we can argue any view
> For what in me is pure conviction
> Is simply prejudice in you!

We need to develop a sensitivity to how things seem to the people with whom we are working. For a long time we have advocated in teacher-training institutions the idea that teachers need to understand the child. What has often happened, however, is that we have confused understanding *about* a child with understanding the child *himself*. Even when I know a great deal about human growth and development I may fail to understand a given child. When I have made a careful study of him, when I have interviewed his parents, searched his school records, looked over his health and physical records, tested and examined him fore and aft, I still may not understand him. I do not really understand him until I have learned to see how he sees himself and how he sees the world in which he lives. All this information about him will be of limited value until I have come to understand the way he sees things in his private world of meaning and feeling. There is a world of difference between understanding a *person* and understanding *about* him.

The kind of understanding we are talking about here is not a *knowledge about,* but a *sensitivity* to people. It is a kind of empathy, the ability to put oneself in another's shoes, to feel and see as he does. All of us have this ability to some extent, but good teachers have a lot of it.

In some research we have been carrying on at the University of Florida we find that we cannot tell the difference between good teachers and poor teachers on the basis of the methods they use. One of the differences that does seem to exist, however, between good and poor ones has to do with this question of sensitivity. Good teachers seem to be much more sensitive to how things seem to the people with whom they are working. In fact, this sensitivity seems so important that apparently intelligent people who have it can do pretty well at teaching without any instruction in methods whatever. With such sensitivity they find their own methods. On the other hand, equally intelligent people with much instruction in methods may do very badly because they are unable to assess the effect of their methods upon the people they are trying to teach.

Self-Actualizing People Are Open to Their Experience

Let us turn now to a second characteristic of these highly self-actualizing, fully functioning personalities. All such people seem to be characterized by a high degree of openness to their experience. That is to say, they are people who are able to look at themselves and the world about them openly and without fear. They are able to see themselves accurately and realistically. Psychologists have sometimes called this the capacity for "acceptance" by which they seem to mean the ability to confront evidence.

Highly self-actualizing people seem to have such a degree of trust in themselves that they are able to look at any and all data without the necessity for defending themselves or distorting events in ways they would like them to be. They are able to accept the facts about the world and about themselves, and because they are able to do this, they are people with a high degree of autonomy. They are free wheelers able to move off in new directions, and this of course is what is meant by creativity. Believing and trusting in themselves, they are able to move out in new directions. What is more, because they are more open to data they are much more likely to have right answers than other people and consequently are much more likely to behave intelligently and efficiently than are the rest of us.

Self-actualizers enjoy exploring; they enjoy discovering. They are not thrown by their experience or defensive against it. They are able to accept what is and to deal with it effectively. Please note that acceptance in the sense we are using it here means the willingness to confront data. It does not mean that acceptance and resignation are synonymous. Because an individual is willing to say, "Yes, it is true I am a stinker," does not mean that he is necessarily resigned to that fact!

This capacity for acceptance, trust in oneself, and openness to experience points to at least three important principles for us in educational practice.

The kind of openness to experience we have been talking about calls for rich opportunities for individuals to explore and test themselves. Such openness comes from opportunities to permit oneself to get involved in events. Like learning to swim, one needs sufficient help to be sure that he does not drown. On the other hand, one can *never* learn to swim if he never goes near the water. Such openness to experience comes about as a consequence of being sufficiently secure where one is that he is able to branch out into new events with courage and determination. This is the road to creativity, so needed in this generation.

One cannot be creative, however, without opportunities to get into difficulties. Indeed, it has been said that the characteristic of genius is the enjoyment of getting into difficulties for the sheer pleasure of getting out of them. Creativity calls for breaking with tradition, going out in the blue, trying one's wings, breaking out of the established ruts. Creativity is bound to be accompanied with a high amount of disorder. A creative class will not be a quiet one, and a rigidly ordered class will not be a creative one. An overemphasis upon order, procedure, custom, tradition, the "right" may actually destroy the kind of openness we are talking about.

This is a strange profession we are in. It is a profession built upon right answers. We pay off on right answers and discourage wrong ones at every level of the teaching profession. Now it is certainly a good thing to be right, but if we are so preoccupied with "being right" that we have no room for people to make mistakes, we may rob them of their most important learning experience. People learn from their mistakes. Some of the most important learnings that most of us have ever had probably came about as a consequence of our mistakes, much more than those instances where we were right.

The fear of making mistakes is almost a disease of our profession. However, an overemphasis on the importance of being right and insistence upon perfection may boomerang to discourage people from trying at all. We need a great deal more freedom to look, to try, to experiment, to explore, to talk about, to discuss. We need to open up our curricula to things we do not grade for. This was beautifully stated by a little boy in the fifth grade who wrote to his teacher after they had had a discussion about love in his classroom: "I was very surprised when we talked in our class about love yesterday. I learned a lot of things and I found out about how lots of others feel. But I was surely surprised because I never knew you could talk about things in school that you didn't get grades for."

The kind of openness called for by the experts requires of us that we help young people to cut loose from dependency far earlier than they do. One of the criticisms we hear most often these days about our public schools is that we are producing a generation of irresponsibles. Like many of the criticisms leveled against us, I do not believe it is by any means as serious as that. I do believe, however, there is a germ of truth to be given some real consideration. The continued extension of childhood, characteristic of every phase of our modern life, tends to keep young people dependent far longer than they need be. Most of this dependency comes about as a consequence of our fear that young people may make mistakes if we set them free. The kind of openness characteristic of self-actualization, however, does not come about as a consequence of increased dependency. Quite the contrary, it comes about as a consequence of responsibility.

There are some who feel the setting up of a separate society by our adolescents is a consequence of this fear. The word "teenager" is practically a cuss word in our society. We simply do not like teenagers. They are permitted no real worthwhile place. We have built a world where there is little or no opportunity for them to have any feeling that they belong or are part of the larger society in which they live. They have little or no voice in what happens to them. They long for a feeling of importance and meaning, something to commit themselves to.

But the usual adult approach to these young people is to build them a new playground or Teen-Town where they are told to "go and play" some more. The plain fact of the matter is they are often an embarrassment to us. Consequently, we treat them as outsiders. It should not surprise us then if they build their own society. Look around you, and you will see that that is precisely what they have done—with their own language, their own customs, traditions, codes of values, even their own music, ways of dress, and symbols of status and prestige. They have done this because we have made no real place for them in our society.

This kind of separation of young people from their culture has the potentiality for great danger. They are people who do not feel they belong, do not feel under any necessity to pay their dues or look out for the members. Membership in a society is not felt by those who are cast out from it. Feelings of belonging and responsibility come about only as a consequence of feeling a part of and being given responsibility for other people.

Responsibility and independence, we need to remind ourselves, are not learned from having these things withheld. Take the case of the teacher who believes her class, for example. The teacher leaves her class telling the group, "I am going down to the office for a few minutes. I want you to be good kids until I get back." She goes to the office and returns to find the room in bedlam. Seeing this, she enters the room and says to her youngsters, "I will never leave you alone again!" If she means this, she has thereby robbed these youngsters of their only opportunity to learn how to behave when the teacher is not there. You cannot learn how to behave when the teacher is not there if the teacher never leaves you!

We do the same thing in the high school with student government. We are so afraid the youngsters might make a wrong decision that we do not let them make any. Whenever they make a decision, we veto that, and it doesn't take long before they get the idea that student government is only a game. Having come to this conclusion, they then tend to treat it like a game, and this infuriates us. We then cry out in despair, "See there, they do not even treat their government as anything but a game!" Perhaps, if they treat it like a game, we have no one to blame but ourselves for teaching them that that is what it is. In order to try one's wings there must be freedom of movement and opportunity to look and explore. If the fears of adults prevent this exploration, we have no one but ourselves to blame.

Let us not be misled by the cries of the young people themselves in this connection. I have often had teachers say to me, "But I want to give them responsibility and they don't want to take it!" This, of course, is often true, but should not discourage us from giving youngsters responsibility. It is only another indication that they are fearful of it because they had so little successful experience with it. The youngster who has not had much responsibility is quite likely to be frightened by having a large dose given to him before he is ready to assimilate it.

The rules of readiness that apply to everything else we know in education apply to learning about responsibility as well. Opportunities have to be paced to capacities. Readiness and capacity, however, are achieved from experience. You cannot expect a child to read if you never let him try, and you cannot expect him to be responsible without some successful experience with it. This is beautifully illustrated in the two old sayings: "If you want something done, get a busy man to do it" and "The rich get richer and the poor get poorer."

When Men Are Free, They Find Their Own Ways

It is a basic principle of democracy that "when men are free, they can find their own best ways." Modern psychology tells us that in each of us there is a deep and never-ending drive to become the very most we can. Despite the assurances of the psychologists about man's basic nature and the beliefs we ourselves so glibly state about the nature of democracy, nevertheless, most of us still approach children with serious doubts and misgivings. We don't *really* believe they can find their own best ways if we provide the proper conditions.

Recently I have been reading A. S. Neill's fascinating book, *Summerhill.* This is a description of a school in England run by a headmaster who believes in giving children freedom, even to the extent of deciding for themselves whether they will go to class at all. (They do!) The lengths he has gone to in giving personal responsibility are fascinating, even shocking, to many people. Certainly he goes far beyond what I have been willing to do in my teaching. The fascinating thing is this: He has been doing this for forty years *and it works!* Here is a living demonstration that individual freedom can work, that we do not need to be afraid as we have been, that maybe, if we can really have the courage to try, it will work out all right.

In recent years I have been trying to place more responsibility and trust in my students. One thing I have done is to use a method of grading that places most of the responsibility for planning, study, and evaluation on the student. This has been much criticized by my colleagues, but the results it gets in more and better work, in individual commitment, in increased freedom for the student, in more reading and thought and effort are well worth the price. Besides, as one of my students expressed it, "Well, Dr. Combs, sure, some students take advantage of your method of grading, but then the old method took advantage of the student!"

The production of openness and responsibility in students requires courage and trust on the part of teachers. If we ourselves are afraid to try and let others try, if we are so fearful they may make mistakes, we may rob them of their most priceless opportunities to learn and will defeat ourselves as well. We need to remind ourselves of Roosevelt's "The only thing we have to fear is fear itself."

When An Individual Finds Inner Security, He Can Become Open to His Experience

The kind of openness characteristic of the truly adequate, full functioning personality the experts are describing for us comes about as a consequence of the individual's own feeling of security in himself. It is a product of his feeling that he is important, that he counts, that he is a part of the situation and the world in which he is moving. This feeling is created by the kind of atmosphere in which he lives and works. It is encouraged by atmospheres we are able to create in the classroom and the halls and laboratories that help young people to develop a feeling of trust in themselves.

What causes a person to feel outside undermines and destroys his feelings of trust. Differences must be respected and encouraged, not merely tolerated. As Earl Kelley has told us, the goal of education must be the increasing uniqueness of people, not increasing likeness. It is the flowering of individuality we seek, not the production of automatons. This means differences of all kinds must be encouraged, appreciated, valued. Segregation is not only socially undesirable; it is demoralizing and diminishing as well. We need to remind ourselves there is segregation on a thousand other bases than segregation of white and Negro that can equally as well get in our way. There is segregation, too, on the basis of age, social status, athletic prowess, dress, language, and religion, to name but a few.

The kind of openness we seek in the free personality requires a trust in self, and this means, to me, we need to change the situations we sometimes find in our teaching where the impression is given the student that all the answers worth having lie "out there." I believe it is necessary for us to recognize that the only important answers are those which the individual has within himself, for these are the only ones that will ever show up in his behavior. Consequently, the classroom must be a place where children explore "what I believe, what I think, what seems to me to be so" as well as what other people think and believe and hold to be true.

Since most human behavior is the product of beliefs, values, and convictions, it is these values that must make up a larger and larger part of our educational experience. We have been in the grip of a concept of teaching that worships objectivity for a long time now. Objectivity is of value to be sure, but objectivity requires looking at events with cold and dispassionate regard. People simply do not behave objectively. They behave in terms of their feelings, attitudes, and convictions even about the most scientific matters. I can be objective about your child; I cannot be objective about my own! The things that affect my behavior most importantly and most closely are those things in the realm of values and beliefs. An education system which does not permit me to explore these or which regards these vital aspects of life as unimportant or inadmissible to the classroom runs the risk of making itself an esthetic exercise valuable to only a few, having little to do with life, and making little impact upon the generations it hopes to affect.

QUESTIONS FOR DISCUSSION

Rogers, Kell, and McNeil Article

1. What limitations in the two studies reported in this selection are important to take into account?
2. If, as suggested in previous articles, significant others can have such a strong influence on shaping an individual's self-picture, how would you explain the finding in this investigation which indicates that an analysis of a youngster's self-understanding is a better predictor of his future behavior than an analysis of his home environment? In order to understand another person, do you feel it is more important to know about his past or his current perceptions and understanding of self? Why?

Jersild Article ("Self-Understanding in Childhood and Adolescence")

1. In addition to those mentioned by the author, what research ideas can you think of which are relevant to the theme of this article?
2. Do you think it is the teacher's business to teach for self-understanding? Why or why not?

Jersild Article ("The Search for Meaning")

1. Describe the implications of this article for teaching practices. Which ones have most meaning for you. Why?
2. Explain what the author means by "The Paradox of Meaninglessness" as it relates to self-understanding.
3. Why, as Jersild contends, is the search for meaning—for selfhood—a painful process?

Menninger Article

1. What implications are here which suggest an "unconscious" dimension of the self?
2. Why do you suppose it is important to understand psychological defense mechanisms in order to fully understand one's ownself or another person?

Combs Article

1. If, as Combs asserts, one learns he is able only from his successes, under what conditions is failure ever tolerable?
2. What relationships are there between self-actualization and freedom?
3. What does the author mean when he says, "Learning is a highly personal matter"? Can learning still be personal in a class of 35? How? Indeed, how is it possible for a teacher to *make* it personal?
4. What do you suppose, in the final analysis, will determine what *you* become? Explain why you feel as you do. Perhaps we should ask first *who* you want to become. Do you know?